RICHARD OVERY

The Morbid Age

Britain Between the Wars

ALLEN LANE
an imprint of
PENGUIN BOOKS

ALLEN LANE

Published by the Penguin Group
Penguin Books Ltd, 80 Strand, London WC2R ORL, England
Penguin Group (USA) Inc., 375 Hudson Street, New York, New York 10014, USA
Penguin Group (Canada), 90 Eglinton Avenue East, Suite 700, Toronto, Ontario, Canada M4P 2Y3
(a division of Pearson Penguin Canada Inc.)
Penguin Ireland, 25 St Stephen's Green, Dublin 2, Ireland
(a division of Penguin Books Ltd)
Penguin Group (Australia), 250 Camberwell Road, Camberwell, Victoria 3124, Australia
(a division of Pearson Australia Group Pty Ltd)
Penguin Books India Pvt Ltd, 11 Community Centre, Panchsheel Park, New Delhi – 110 017, India
Penguin Group (NZ), 67 Apollo Drive, Rosedale, North Shore 0632, New Zealand
(a division of Pearson New Zealand Ltd)
Penguin Books (South Africa) (Pty) Ltd, 24 Sturdee Avenue, Rosebank, Johannesburg 2196, South Africa

Penguin Books Ltd, Registered Offices: 80 Strand, London WC2R ORL, England

www.penguin.com

First published 2009
1

Set in 10.5/14 pt PostScript Linotype Sabon
Typeset by Rowland Phototypesetting Ltd, Bury St Edmunds, Suffolk
Printed in England by Clays Ltd, St Ives plc

ISBN: 978-0-713-99563-3

www.greenpenguin.co.uk

The Morbid Age

This is the crisis. At bottom we have no faith. We have lost our belief in capitalism and socialism, in the churches and scientific progress. Deep, deep down, we do not believe in any of these things any more. Despair of everything, at least of everything that the past has produced, has overtaken us.

And unless we take the fact of this despair into account, all we may do, or write, or think, must come to nothing.

It is a hard thought.

Tosco Fyvel, *The Malady and the Vision*, 1940, p. 12

Contents

Illustrations

p. 122: Julian Huxley, Secretary of the Royal Zoological Society, at the opening of the children's zoo in 1935, with Robert and Edward Kennedy (Getty Images)

p. 129: The Eugenics Society stand at the Exhibition of Health and Housing, 1935 (Wellcome Library)

p. 137: The psychologist Cyril Burt in 1931 (University of Liverpool Library)

p. 143: Ernest Jones at work at the British Psycho-Analytical Society in the 1930s (British Psycho-Analytical Society)

p. 155: The cover of 'What Fathers Should Tell Their Sons', published in 1933 (Wellcome Library)

p. 171: Sigmund Freud in London in 1938, with Ernest Jones and members of his family (Freud Museum)

p. 179: An anti-war cartoon from the 'Air Display Special' produced for the Duxford air show, July 1935 (Cambridge University Library)

p 189: The Labour MP Ellen Wilkinson addressing a crowd in Trafalgar Square, September 1938 (Getty Images)

p. 193: Covers from two pamphlets on British rearmament and the arms trade, 1935–6

p. 198: The anatomist Sir Arthur Keith at work in the Royal College of Surgeons, 1914 (Royal College of Surgeons Library)

p. 206: The social anthropologist Bronislaw Malinowski in 1940 (Getty Images)

p. 206: The psychoanalyst Edward Glover pictured in the 1930s (British Psycho-Analytical Society)

p. 222: The novelist Storm Jameson (Margaret Chapman) c. 1930 (Getty Images)

p. 226: Lord Robert Cecil at a rally of the Women's International League in 1932 (Getty Images)

p. 238: A delegation of the British No More War Movement in 1924 (Getty Images)

p. 242: March for peace in London organized by the Labour League of Youth, 1936 (Getty Images)

p. 380: A summer school of the Society for Cultural Relations with the USSR, 1938 (SCRSS)

p. 380: The South Place Ethical Society summer school in Ryde, Sussex in the early 1930s (South Place Ethical Society)

I am grateful to the following for generous help in locating and supplying images: Melissa Atkinson, Rachael Cross, John Cunningham, Allie Dillon, Betty Dixon, Bill Hetherington, Jennifer Jeynes, Ian Johnston, Roy Lumb, Hayley Murphy and Caroline Theakestone. I would like to thank the British Psycho-Analytical Society, the Marx Memorial Library, the Peace Pledge Union, the Royal College of Surgeons, the Society for Co-operation in Russian and Soviet Studies, and the South Place Ethical Society for permission to reproduce images. The portrait of Cyril Burt is courtesy of the University of Liverpool, the picture of Freud and Ernest Jones is courtesy of the Freud Museum, London, the picture of Walter Greenwood courtesy of Salford University Special Collections, the portrait of Gilbert Murray courtesy of the National Portrait Gallery.

Preface and Acknowledgements

In his recent memoirs, the historian Eric Hobsbawm remarked of the 1930s that 'we lived in a time of crisis'. Nothing very surprising about that. But I recall a conversation with him a few years ago, shortly before starting the research for this book, when he told me that he could remember a day in Cambridge in early 1939 when he and some friends discussed their sudden realization that very soon they might all of them be dead. This did strike me as surprising, and it runs against the drift of the memoirs, in which he argued that communists were less infected by pessimism than everyone else because of their confidence in the future. It is also very different from my own memories of life in Cambridge thirty years later in the late 1960s where, despite labouring under the shadow of the bomb and the threat of war in Europe during the second Czech crisis, students did not contemplate early extinction but preferred to listen to Leonard Cohen in rooms made mellow by too much smoke and cheap wine.

This book is an exploration of British society in the 1920s and 1930s while it wrestled sometimes fatalistically, sometimes with undisguised relish, with this idea of crisis. The result is, I hope, an unexpected and unusual window on to the social, cultural and intellectual world of inter-war Britain. In some small way it may explain why students in the secure Cambridge of the late 1930s could contemplate the death of civilization in a country whose political and social system had proved almost impervious to the savage violence and upheavals that scarred the history of the rest of Europe, and from which Hobsbawm himself was an exile. This was not just a time of crisis, but indeed a morbid age.

During the writing of the book I have amassed a large pile of intellectual and practical debts. I am very grateful to Monika Baar, Claudia Baldoli, Kate Fisher, Tim Rees, Richard Toye and Frances Wilson for reading parts of the manuscript and offering me sound advice. The following have been helpful in a variety of ways: Jeremy Black, Jane Caplan, Chris Clarke, Patricia Clavin, Claire Feehily, Lara Feigel, Eileen Gunn, Tom Hoy, Jonathan Moffatt, Martin Thomas, Andrew Thorpe, Alex Walsham. I owe a special debt of gratitude to Vyvyan and Piers Brendon, who were kind enough to put me up, often at a few days' notice, for all my archive trips to Cambridge. I am grateful to the Penguin Group for permission to use the Allen Lane archive at Bristol University and to Jean Rose for permission to quote from the files of Jonathan Cape in the Reading University Special Collections. I would also like to thank Verity Andrews and Brian Ryder for help in locating material in the Cape collection and the Allen & Unwin papers. Eva Guggemos gave me assistance with the Lawrence and Wishart papers at Yale. I am glad to be able to thank Elizabeth al-Qadhi for allowing me to use the papers of her father, John Strachey. I am also grateful to Faber and Faber for permission to quote from the work of T. S. Eliot and W. H. Auden. I would like to thank the archivists and librarians in all the many places I have visited over the past two years while researching the book, but I would like in particular to acknowledge the staff at the LSE Archive for their unfailing courtesy and helpfulness. My new academic home at the University of Exeter has been a keen supporter of this project and I would like to record my thanks for the financial assistance which has made much of this research possible and for the helpfulness and advice of my colleagues. Simon Winder has been as ever an inestimable editor, and my agent Gill Coleridge a true friend and supporter, and I am conscious of the large debt I owe them both. My new editor in New York, Wendy Wolf, has rightly asked me to make the 'English-ness' of the text more accessible and has made it a better book as a result. A final thanks to my family for their persistent interest in and enthusiasm for what I do.

Richard Overy
September 2008

Note on Currency

Throughout the text I have used the currency of the time in pounds, shillings and pence. The price of books or membership fees or the cost of running an organization is a necessary part of the narrative of communicating discourse. In the inter-war years an average worker might take home between £2 and £3 a week in wages. Journalists and writers might make £10 to £15 a week. The wealthier middle and upper-middle classes, if they also had inherited wealth, might have an annual income of anything over £1,000. To give a modern equivalent would be almost meaningless because of inflationary increases in purchasing power over the past seventy years, but these contemporary income figures give a sense of proportion. These sums should be kept in mind when considering what could be bought on the mass market or who could afford to go to congresses or summer schools or weekend conferences. A pamphlet costing 2d (2 pence) could be bought by all; a book for 25/- (25 shillings) could be bought only by wealthier customers, and would be read by a wider audience only in lending libraries, which multiplied in the inter-war years. Penguin Specials (price 6d) or Left Book Club choices (price 2/6 or 5/-) were both within the means of the working population, as was membership of most of the mass-based organizations such as the League of Nations Union, whose fees remained at 1/- per year throughout the period.

One pound = 20 shillings = 240 pence
One shilling = 12 pence

Britain 1919–1939:
A Chronological Introduction

POLITICS

British politics between 1919 and 1939 was dominated by the Conservative Party, which was in office for six years between 1922 and 1929 and was the largest element both in the post-war coalition from 1919 to 1922 organized by Lloyd George and in the National Government set up in August 1931 by Ramsay MacDonald to cope with the economic depression and which lasted until 1940. The other major pre-1914 party, the Liberal Party, declined in popular support and never formed a government again after the collapse of the Liberal administration in 1916. In its place came a new political force, the Labour Party, which held office briefly from January to November 1924 and from June 1929 until the formation of the National Government. The Labour Party was supported in the 1920s by a smaller socialist party, the Independent Labour Party.

The National Government comprised a coalition of Conservatives, Labour members who supported MacDonald (who were known as National Labour) and Liberals who supported MacDonald (known as National Liberals). The opposition to the National Government was made up of Labour members of parliament who refused to accept MacDonald's leadership, and the Independent Labour Party (and, from the 1935 general election, one Communist MP). The 1931 election returned 470 Conservatives out of 615 MPs and the 1935 election 387 out of 615. The combined opposition to the National Government won 56 seats in 1931 and 171 in 1935. The National Government ended in May 1940 when Churchill became prime minister and formed a wartime coalition including the opposition Labour Party.

GOVERNMENTS AND PRIME MINISTERS

Coalition government January 1919 to October 1922
  Prime minister: David Lloyd George
Conservative government October 1922 to January 1924
  Prime ministers: Arthur Bonar Law (October 1922 to May 1923)
              Stanley Baldwin (May 1923 to January 1924)
Labour government January 1924 to November 1924
  Prime minister: Ramsay MacDonald
Conservative government November 1924 to June 1929
  Prime minister: Stanley Baldwin
Labour government June 1929 to August 1931
  Prime minister: Ramsay MacDonald
National Government August 1931 to May 1940
  Prime ministers: Ramsay MacDonald (August 1931 to June 1935)
              Stanley Baldwin (June 1935 to May 1937)
              Neville Chamberlain (May 1937 to May 1940)

FOREIGN POLICY

From the founding of the League of Nations in 1920, which Britain played an important part in constructing, British governments were formally committed to working within its framework to ensure that international crises were resolved through negotiation. In practice Britain played a more detached role during the 1920s and 1930s, and continued to conduct a foreign policy based on collaboration among the major powers. For much of the period Britain hoped to reintegrate defeated Germany back into the international system and was not unwilling to renegotiate aspects of the Versailles Treaty. British governments tended to distrust France and French ambitions in Europe and to collaborate with the United States, which had refused to join the League in 1920. Britain's chief interests were to preserve the Empire and to maintain international peace and a stable international economy. By the 1930s none of these ambitions could be fully realized. The world economy went into crisis, the Empire became a source of growing unrest (in India and Palestine in particular) and the search for international peace was challenged by the Japanese occupation of Manchuria in northern China in 1931, the Italian conquest of Ethiopia in 1935–6 and the rearmament of Germany which Hitler declared in 1935 and made explicit with the remilitarization of the Rhineland provinces in March 1936. The rise of Soviet power following implementation of the USSR's Five-Year Plans for industrial development (and the large-scale rearmament programme that accompanied them) was also regarded by British leaders as a potentially dangerous development. British politicians continued to seek peaceful solutions to all these issues, but from 1934 onwards Britain began its own rearmament, accelerated in 1936 when Neville Chamberlain, then Chancellor of the Exchequer, introduced a four-year programme of military expansion, and again in 1938 in response to German expansion in Austria and Czechoslovakia. From 1937 Chamberlain tried to find a way to achieve what he called a 'Grand Settlement' of world affairs through co-operation, but this strategy, more generally termed 'appeasement', failed to prevent further crisis and led to the dismemberment of Czechoslovakia through the Munich Agreement of September 1938. By 1939 Britain faced the paradoxical prospect of having to use war as a means to restore a peaceable international political and economic order.

FOREIGN POLICY: KEY DATES

June 1919	Signature of the Versailles Treaty.
January 1920	League of Nations begins its operations.
February 1922	Washington Naval Treaty for naval disarmament.
December 1925	Locarno Treaty between Germany, Britain, France, Italy and Belgium confirms Versailles frontiers in western Europe.
September 1926	Britain supports German membership of League of Nations.
August 1928	Kellogg–Briand Pact of Paris outlawing war as an instrument of policy.

September 1931	Japanese Kwantung Army seizes control of Manchuria.
February 1932	Disarmament Conference convenes at Geneva.
January 1933	Hitler becomes German chancellor.
June 1933	World Economic Conference in London.
October 1933	Germany withdraws from League and from Disarmament Conference.
February 1935	Government of India Act gives Indians limited autonomy.
March 1935	Hitler announces German rearmament.
October 1935	Italy invades Ethiopia.
March 1936	Germany remilitarizes the Rhineland.
July 1936	Outbreak of Spanish Civil War.
April 1937	German and Italian planes bomb Guernica.
March 1938	Germany occupies Austria.
September 1938	Chamberlain flies three times to Germany to try to reach agreement over the Czech crisis; Munich Agreement gives Czech Sudeten areas to Germany.
February 1939	Chamberlain pledges military support for France.
March 1939	German forces occupy Czech areas; Chamberlain guarantees Polish sovereignty.
April 1939	Britain reintroduces conscription.
August 1939	Britain signs Anglo-Polish Treaty.
September 1939	Britain declares war on Germany, as does France.

ECONOMY

The British economy was the largest trading economy in the world in 1914 and the third largest manufacturing economy. Britain was also enormously wealthy and supplied a large part of world investment and credit. In the inter-war years Britain's position declined relatively as other countries expanded trade and industrial output. British trade failed to return to the pre-1914 levels and foreign investment was directed more to the Empire while in the 1920s American loans became the important engine of world economic growth. Britain's major industries (cotton, shipbuilding, coal, iron and steel) suffered heavily in the 1920s and 1930s resulting in long-term unemployment in particular regions of the country. There was a shift away from exports as the major element in economic growth towards the home market. Falling food and material prices in the 1920s and 1930s meant cheaper imports and rising living standards for those with a job. This in turn fuelled rising demand for new consumer goods such as cars and radios, which became the new industrial leaders. In 1932, in response to the collapse of the world market after the Wall Street Crash of October 1929, Britain switched from a policy of free trade to one of protection. The Imperial Preference scheme gave guaranteed markets to Empire producers of food and raw materials and gave Britain guaranteed markets for exports. The change meant that Britain suffered less than other economies during the 1930s and for those with jobs there were rising living standards for much of the decade. In the 1930s the government came to play a fuller part in sustaining economic revival, particularly through large house-building pro-grammes. From 1936 onwards the economy began to grow in response to a rearmament boom which created new jobs even in the depressed regions, though at the same time it put pressure on the balance of payments and increased state debt.

THE INTER-WAR BUSINESS CYCLE

1920–21:	post-war recession.
1922–6:	period of relative stagnation.
1926:	short economic downturn.
1927–9:	short period of boom.
1929–32:	major recession, known in Britain as the 'Great Slump'.
1932–7:	slow economic revival.
1937:	brief recession followed by armaments boom.

Introduction:
Cassandras and Jeremiahs

RECORDING ANGEL: *The picture you present of Earth is exceedingly depressing. Man's great achievement of civilisation, with its elaborate material equipment and its network of social institutions and activities, is in peril of early and complete destruction by the failure of man to overcome the ravages of war and waste which the Adversary has contrived against the purpose of the Highest. Do I present the situation correctly?*
MESSENGER: *Alas, sir, you do.*   J. A. Hobson, 1932[1]

For some years now there has existed a popular belief that the Western world faces a profound crisis. Whether the doom-mongers predict terminal decline or just a radical transformation, they have helped to generate a language of anxiety and sentiments of uncertainty. The very titles betray morbid fears: *Suicide of the West*, *The End of Order*, *Dark Age Ahead* and perhaps the best known of all, Patrick Buchanan's *The Death of the West*.[2] The fact that the Western world has never been richer, more secure or more heavily armed in its history is taken not as a sign that 'decline' is at best a misuse of the term, at worst a historical absurdity in the early years of the twenty-first century, but as evidence of a disconcerting vulnerability in the face of malign forces, both of nature and of man, for which the West actually bears a good deal of the responsibility. How often in the last few years has the 'defence of our way of life' or 'the defence of democracy' been mobilized as an argument, as if they really were endangered from within or without. This sense of crisis has been shaped and enlarged by the concepts, metaphors and language exploited to describe it, and not because of the intrinsic nature of the historical reality the West confronts. What is said develops a reality of its own.

The theme of this book deals with an earlier age in which a strong presentiment of impending disaster also touched many areas of public discourse. The subject-matter is the idea of 'civilization in crisis' in Britain in the years between the two world wars, a period famous for its population of Cassandras and Jeremiahs who helped to construct the popular image of the inter-war years as an age of anxiety, doubt or fear. It is true that the inter-war years differed from the current malaise in the sense that many of the issues confronted by the West were neither phantoms nor extrapolated fantasies but the fruit of real historical dramas. Yet here too the idea of Western civilization in peril, repeated endlessly as 'our way of life' is today, was persistent and widespread even during periods of relative stability or in the face of evidence to the contrary. The convention has been to see these fears as a product of the dark 1930s, but they were evident in the 1920s too, and their roots lay before the First World War, an event which threw the whole culture of crisis into sharp relief; they flourished long before the slump and the shadow of Hitler gave them more plausible substance. 'The Twenties were post-war,' wrote the Hull poet Hubert Nicholson in 1941, reflecting on twenty years in war's shadow, 'The Thirties were pre-war.'[3] In the inter-war years fear of decline or collapse was elaborated in Britain in ways that often defied historical reality. The arguments used to explain crisis appear with the passage of time fanciful or exotic or plain wrong – though it is interesting to be reminded that these fears date back only the span of a single life-time – but they must be understood in their context. No generation has a monopoly of certainty, ours no more than our grandparents'. The thesis of civilization in danger won a broad popular audience in inter-war Britain receptive to anxiety as one of the defining features of contemporary culture, cohabiting uneasily with the glittering promise of mass consumption and a narcotic hedonism, which for the lucky minority was real enough.

It has often been argued that the pessimists were marginal intellectuals, unwilling to adjust to the post-1918 social reality, or expressionist artists and writers obsessed with decadence or a self-conscious nihilism: people who should not be taken altogether seriously as harbingers of doom, however much they have attracted the attention of historians and literary critics. The historian Martin Pugh deliberately titled his recent social history of the inter-war years 'We Danced All Night' to counter what he sees as the prevailing pessimistic orthodoxy.[4] It is obviously true that other discourses existed, pointing to a brighter progressive future, but even they could be assailed in the inter-war years by doubts and uncertainties. Pessimism was highly contagious. One of the champions of planning as the path to an orderly economy and a rational society, the financial expert Sir Basil Blackett, writing about the 'world collapse of civilisation' in 1932, added the following caveat: 'We are apt to regard such statements as pleasantly scarifying, pardonable exaggerations in the mouths of those who are trying to spur us to action against the very real ills of the times, but not meant quite seriously. The threat is serious. Chaos will overtake us.'[5] It is striking that the language of menacing catastrophe surfaces in most areas of public debate and discussion and is not simply a literary trope. Dismay was a mainstream concern, specific to neither class nor region, and even if 'civilization in crisis' became a populist cliché of the inter-war years, the different ways in which it was explained derived from serious scientific, medical, economic and cultural descriptions of the present and were not simply rhetoric. The phenomenon was neither evidently reactionary nor exclusively avant-garde. For the generation living after the end of the First World War the prospect of imminent crisis, a new Dark Age, became a habitual way of looking at the world. It is a narrative that historians have in general neglected. Why and how these collective anxieties were constructed, and with what results for British society, is the theme of this book.

A significant aspect of the explanation, particularly in light of the conventional view that frightened anti-modernists or self-indulgent artists were to blame for the mood of gloom, is to recognize that the human and natural sciences had an important part to play in generating anxiety once scientific discoveries had filtered into a public arena with a large appetite for popular science. There existed a wide expectation that science could supply the truths that politics could not, though science was then, as today, only true for the time being. It is argued in much of what follows that science, despite its assumed role as the voice of material reason, played a key part, though not usually deliberately, in creating the morbid culture that inhabited the Western world view in the 1920s and 1930s. 'Every discovery in pure science is potentially subversive,' announces the Regional World Controller in Aldous Huxley's *Brave New World*, written in 1932. 'Even science must sometimes be treated as a possible enemy. Yes, even science.'[6]

Scientific modernity was indeed never a history of unalloyed progress; science provoked profound ambiguity and was popularly understood to do so. When Bertrand Russell wrote a short and polemical pamphlet on *Icarus: Or the Future of Science* in 1925, one reviewer described it as 'utter pessimism'.[7] There were solid reasons for this reaction. Physicists exploded the balanced Newtonian universe; biologists exposed the power of genetic inheritance and the possibility of degeneration; psychologists suggested that rational modern man was a chaos of instincts and urges within; chemists and engineers promised a new material environment, but also produced modern weapons of terrible destructive power; social science argued that the existing capitalist social system was corrupt and insupportable. These ambiguities are explored here in separate chapters on economics, race, psychoanalysis and the causes of war. The language used for much of this discourse was explicitly morbid, partly because a good deal of it was fuelled by the human sciences, through which the vocabulary of disease, physical decline or mental instability could be applied metaphorically to the wider world of politics and social development. The Western view of the world between the wars was essentially diagnostic: searching for the symptoms that indicated disease and fearful lest they should prove fatal.

The medicalization of much of the language of crisis suggested the possibility of cure. There could be no uniform remedy since there were so many different elements to the crisis. Even on the issue of war as a disease of the modern age there was no unanimity about the necessary prophylactic steps to take. Instead there developed a search for patent remedies – utopian politics of right or left, moral and religious revival, a planned economy, world government, eugenic engineering. Many of these remedies promised simply a dead end, since the cure seemed no better, and in some cases considerably worse, than the illness. 'We diagnosed the disease and its causes with microscopic exactness,' complains the purged communist in Arthur Koestler's second novel, *Darkness at Noon*, published in 1940, 'but whenever we applied the healing knife a new sore appeared.'[8] It was this manifest paradox, one of the many ambiguities thrown up by modernity, which gave these morbid discourses their pessimistic character: increasingly in the years immediately before the outbreak of the European war in 1939 it seemed that there was no escape from the dilemmas posed by the modern age. War came to be regarded simultaneously as the likely cause of the death of civilization but also a possible way to purge the old age and to start again. Three final chapters deal with the ultimately fruitless efforts of pacifism and political radicalism to confront the impending disaster of war. The argument developed in what follows suggests that the consciousness of fin-de-siècle in Britain before 1939 was more widely communicated and understood than it was before 1914; this awareness can be seen as a central element in explaining British readiness in the end to engage in a war in 1939 in which it was generally believed civilization would be either saved or lost.

It is never enough, however, simply to describe what is said. Ideas do not operate in a social vacuum. Much of what follows explores the many ways in which ideas were communicated and how extensively, socially and geographically. The discourse did not remain the preserve of an isolated cultured elite but flourished in the first real age of mass communication. Hence the emphasis here on mechanisms of dissemination – mass publishing, translation (into and out of English), public meetings, demonstrations, letters of protest, radio broadcasts, reading circles, print runs and book sales – in order to demonstrate that the core perceptions of crisis were not confined to the political fringes or the ivory tower. Most ordinary people did not, of course, spend all their time contemplating crisis, any more than today's war on terror or the threat of global warming has diverted Western populations from the more pleasurable and mundane aspects of daily life. But in each case an intrusive knowledge of crisis (though not necessarily understanding of its causes) can be shown to have existed at the level of both public debate and private fear. Indeed, the revolution in the mass media in the early part of the twentieth century, together with a marked increase in levels of literacy and educational achievement and spreading habits of self-improvement and voluntary lobbying, made it possible for the public concerns of politicians, academics, doctors, scientists, or soldiers, to become common property. The development of a special language for communicating those concerns – evident today in the ubiquitous and extravagant use of terms such as 'terror' and 'security', evident then in the repetition of terms such as 'decay', 'menace', 'disease', 'barbarism' – invaded the frontier between public and private and became embedded in a common, if temporary, culture.

The focus of this book is the British experience. There are a number of reasons for this. In the first place the archival sources for a history of contemporary mentality are too large and eclectic to be able to do justice to a pan-European or American history without distorting the very different national contexts in which these mentalities evolved. The sources used to construct a narrative of discourse and its dissemination in Britain are diverse and substantial enough. They can also be frustratingly diffuse, with few clear lines of demarcation. Dissecting mentalities is a little like cutting mist with a knife. The sources chiefly comprise private correspondence, diaries or lecture notes, the papers of public voluntary bodies, specialized institutes and mass movements, and the voluminous quantity of books, pamphlets, journals and other literature available at the time, which can still be found today lining the shelves of Oxfam bookshops. These sources have been chosen deliberately to differentiate the construction of public discourse from the more conventional narratives of political activity, social reform and diplomacy, for which there are already many excellent guides. There is little, for example, on the course of British foreign policy in the 1930s, or on the strategies for economic recovery, or on political conflict. These matter here only to the extent that they contributed to the idea-world which gave shape to the 'crisis of civilization'. I have tried wherever possible to go back to look at the original diary or correspondence or book draft, even where a published version exists. In many cases the original betrays some interesting changes of language; in draft lecture notes the lecturer often leaves behind intellectual doodles which give sometimes opaque clues to their state of mind. (What, for example, should one make of the anthropologist and pacifist Bronislaw Malinowski's scribbled 'good whores, good wars, bad whores, bad wars' on the edge of a lecture on the futility of modern conflict?)[9] I have also relied a good deal on private correspondence where again correspondents tended to talk more candidly about their fears and aspirations. What might be called 'networks of anxiety' played an important part in sustaining the belief that the Western world was doomed.

A second reason for choosing Britain in the inter-war years is the widespread contemporary belief that, together with the Empire, Britain was the hub of the Western world (the British elite certainly considered it to be so) in much the way that America is regarded, and regards itself, today. The perception of crisis in Britain reflected real concerns about a 'civilization' that Britain had done a good deal to construct in the first place. Yet this is in no sense an insular history, but a history of ideas and attitudes generated in Britain but then rapidly and widely disseminated in America and Europe. The things that mattered in Britain mattered internationally. A rich flow also went the other way. The sense of morbid decline and the longing for renewal reflected European anxieties; refugees from Bolshevism or from fascism brought a new dimension to public political debate in Britain. Most of those writers, scientists and philosophers who shaped the discourses of doom travelled regularly in Europe and across the Atlantic, where they came face-to-face with other perceptions of crisis. Thousands of British volunteers took part in the war in Spain, on both sides. Yet what makes the British case paradoxically different from the rest of Europe is the absence of serious threat or profound discontinuities. Britain was not invaded or occupied during the Great War; its economy survived far better than the other major states in the inter-war years; there was no real prospect of social revolution; no one was tortured or murdered by the state's secret police. Above all, open debate was possible where it was closed off in much of Europe by the 1930s. The idea of Western civilization in crisis was thus in many respects a second-hand experience, however powerfully expressed and deeply felt. The crisis of civilization appeared real enough because that was how the issues of the contemporary world were described and communicated to those of the public who cared to listen.

I

Decline and Fall

It is a fact so familiar that we seldom remember how very strange it is, that the commonest phrases we hear used about civilization at the present time all relate to the possibility, or even the prospect, of its being destroyed. G. N. Clark, 1932[1]

On 3 February 1922, at precisely 5.45 p.m., the distinguished missionary Albert Schweitzer began the first of a series of lectures at Mansfield College in Oxford. The Council of this recently founded non-conformist college had resolved the year before to invite Schweitzer to give the Dale lectures, named after one of the prominent founders.[2] He was by then a well-known figure in Europe, though less so in England. Having begun a career at a very young age in his native Alsace as a churchman and organist of prodigious talent, he had abandoned easy fame, trained as a doctor and set out for French Equatorial Africa in 1913 as a missionary-healer. He was incarcerated as an enemy alien by the French authorities during the war and spent a difficult year in a succession of filthy and poorly supervised prison camps. He settled in Strasbourg after the war, and divided his time between Europe and his hospital in Africa. He was, according to contemporary accounts, a man of exceptional physical presence, tough and strong. 'Brown haired, blue-eyed, with a pleasantly "rounded" voice, and a quiet sense of humour,' wrote one British admirer, 'he has none of those Germanic characteristics which we think of in their extreme form as Prussian.'[3] When Schweitzer arrived in Oxford, hot from a lecture tour in Sweden, as the guest of the principal of Mansfield College, he was so worried about his German background that he refused to speak German and translated into English all the German titles he had chosen for a series of organ recitals in Oxford and, later, in Westminster Abbey.[4] He careered dangerously around Oxford on a borrowed bicycle, and rumour had it that a whole fish sent to his room for supper was consumed entire down to the last bone. He charmed his college hosts, though he told a German friend a few weeks later that for a trip like this 'one needs iron nerves'.[5]

Schweitzer's chosen subject was a large one. The title of his lecture course, published in the *Oxford University Gazette* in French, was 'The Struggle for the Ethical View of the World and of Life in European Philosophy'.[6] He wrote the lectures out in German and then delivered them, without notes, in an audible and slow Alsatian French. By 1923 Schweitzer had turned them into book form and they appeared first in Munich. The two volumes were translated, with the help of one of the college fellows and a grant of £25 from the Dale Fund, and published at the end of the same year with the less long-winded title 'The Decay and Restoration of Civilization'.[7] On the opening page Schweitzer warned his readers: 'We are living to-day under the sign of the collapse of civilization'; and two pages on: 'It is clear now to everyone that the suicide of civilization is in progress.' The crisis was the crisis of all civilizations, Schweitzer thought. Western civilization had not yet been swept aside by the 'destructive pressure' that had destroyed its predecessors, but it tottered on rubble: 'the next landslide will very likely carry it away'. The crisis, he claimed, had begun before the war and had its root cause in a failure of spirit. These reflections, he explained in his preface, had matured far away from the degenerate world they described, 'ripened in the stillness of the primeval forest of Equatorial Africa'.[8]

Schweitzer was certainly right to argue that a sense of impending crisis was not just a reaction to the events of the Great War, for voices prophesying doom could be found long before 1914. But he failed perhaps to grasp just how profound the impact of the war had been on the European society he addressed from his lectern in Oxford. For a great many educated Europeans the war represented a clear fracture with pre-war expectations of relentless advance. The publication in London of Schweitzer's book with its tendentious title coincided with a wave of post-war anxiety in Britain about the apparent impossibility of reconciling a barbarous and senseless conflict with the conviction that Europe before the war had represented a high point in the development of human history. The novelist H. G. Wells, for example, often regarded as a prophet of doom before 1914 on account of the apocalyptic nature of his popular science fiction – *The War in the Air* and *The War of the Worlds* were the best known – insisted after the war was ended that it was something he had neither expected nor wanted. 'I was taken by surprise by it,' wrote Wells in 1927 in an introduction to one of the many books of its kind, J. M. Kenworthy's *Will Civilisation Crash?*.[9] In his own survey of civilization's prospects, published six years earlier under the title *The Salvaging of Civilisation*, Wells painted a picture that became familiar in the inter-war years of a rosy belle époque before the war when the 'easy general forward movement of human affairs' suggested 'a necessary and invincible progress'. The 'spectacular catastrophe' of the war ended that comfortable illusion. 'Has the cycle of prosperity and progress closed?' asked Wells, who wondered whether the crash of the ancient world would not now be repeated in the modern.[10]

The juxtaposition of illusions of pre-war progress with post-war disaster requires little historical explanation, even if it bore scant reality for those who benefited least from the pre-war social and political order. The contrast became a literary trope which survived even the experience of a second war. Reflecting in the 1960s on the world he had grown up in before 1914, the historian Arnold Toynbee explained a cast of mind that was rudely shattered by the reality of the war:

It was taken for granted by almost all Westerners – and by many non-Westerners too, including some who did not like the apparent prospect – that the Western civilization had come to stay. Pre-1914 Westerners, and pre-1914 British Westerners above all, felt that they were not as other men were or ever had been . . . Other civilizations had risen and fallen, had come and gone, but Westerners did not doubt that their own civilization was invulnerable.[11]

Even critics of European imperialism and class divisions could be seduced into believing that there was more promise in the pre-war world than in the new. The writer Leonard Woolf, who had been employed in the imperial civil service in Ceylon (Sri Lanka) before the war, observed in 1939, on the eve of a new conflict, that no one who had regularly read a newspaper in the years 1900 to 1914 could fail to be struck by the contrast with the barbarities that daily populated every newsreel and radio report about the 1930s. 'In those days,' Woolf wrote, 'there *was* an ordered way of life, a law, a temple and a city – a civilization of sorts.' It was, he continued, a system based on class privilege (a minority of fortunate 'gentlefolk', recalled Toynbee) and colonial exploitation, but it was nonetheless 'a progressing and expanding civilization'.[12] Then came the war and the end of civilized life. By the end of the war, Woolf argued, 'hatred, fear and self-preservation' were the dominant elements of social psychology.[13]

The rupture with the past was evident with the return of peace and the homecoming of millions of survivors scarred physically and psychologically by the conflict. On the day of the Armistice the poet Siegfried Sassoon jotted in his diary: 'It is a loathsome ending to the loathsome tragedy of the last four years.'[14] Sassoon remained a psychiatric casualty for years after the end of the war. In a letter to the art critic Geoffrey Keynes in 1938 he described catching a butterfly, a Camberwell Beauty, before the war: 'What a peaceful world it was! And what a bullying, barbarian world it is now!'[15] The futurist artist and writer Wyndham Lewis later recalled his sense on returning from the Western Front that 'a state of emergency came to mean for me, as for most soldiers, a permanent thing'. In such circumstances, Lewis continued, 'values change'; 'Everything now, almost, since the war seems a matter of life or death.'[16] In official circles there were fears that the returning soldiers would bring back with them the brutality and heartlessness of the trenches, though much of the social violence of the early post-war years seems to have been provoked by civilians not ex-soldiers, who displayed no great desire to continue doing the atrocious things they had been ordered to do in battle.[17] The generation that experienced and fought the war was described often enough as a 'lost generation' to encourage a self-conscious sense of differentness. The author Henry Williamson, for example, wrote searingly realistic portraits of life at the front, which he experienced for four years, but he was not certain that anyone who had not been there could understand what he wrote or the deep mood of 'melancholy and sadness' which he felt dominated his 'psychic makeup'.[18] After the war was over, Williamson wrote in 1928, 'the mental war became acute, the war against the righteous and bellicose attitudes of elderly men and women who had remained at home ... The years 1919 and 1920 ... were lived in a No-Man's-Land more bitter than that patrolled and crossed during the preceding years.'[19] After an argument in 1929 with his father, who called him a traitor for suggesting that a sense of duty to fellow man should not stop at the Straits of Dover, Williamson wrote the following passage: 'so I returned to my comrades in the scarred and rotting country of the Somme, for I am dead with them, and they live with me again'.[20]

The nihilism and pathos of those of the war generation who articulated their sense of loss or arrested hopes is well known. During the 1920s alongside Williamson there was the French writer Henri Barbusse, whose undisguised account of trench life *Le Feu*, written during the war, was translated into English in 1917 and published in the popular Everyman's Library in 1926 as *Under Fire: The Story of a Squad* ('It is said to be one long cry of pain,' wrote Williamson).[21] There was also Erich Maria Remarque's *All Quiet on the Western Front*, published in 1928 in English (Williamson thought the battle scenes this time 'read as fakes'). It was reviewed in the *Cambridge Review* by the Cambridge scholar G. Lowes Dickinson, who noted Remarque's haunting complaint in the mouth of his story's anti-hero, 'Our knowledge of life is limited to death.' This was, Lowes Dickinson thought, a book that told the truth about those who had gone through it.[22] But the generation that grew into manhood after the war also came to see itself as separated by a gulf from the pre-war world, 'a bewildered generation' in the words of the philosopher Cyril Joad. In a review of John Beevers's *World Without Faith*, published in 1935 when Beevers was in his early twenties, Joad summarized the argument in the book that 'the contemporary generation has confidence neither in the universe nor in itself, there is no purpose it seems at the heart of things', neither sanity nor freedom.[23] In 1929 the Oxford scholar Gilbert Murray published *The Ordeal of this Generation*, based on a series of lectures given the previous year, which sought to acknowledge that those growing up in the Britain of the 1920s, overshadowed by the war and the breakdown of civilized life, were faced not with the pre-war 'Cosmos' but with 'Chaos'.[24]

The role of artists and intellectuals in embedding the idea of rupture can certainly be exaggerated (not least because in artistic terms some of the rupture with conventional culture had already become manifest before 1914). Williamson was aware that he spoke to and for the soldiers of the war, but he also found that among veterans whom he knew a book like *Under Fire* was considered 'overburdened and morbid'; they were, he complained, 'like the man who told me he enjoyed every moment of the War'.[25] A more striking example is the fate of T. S. Eliot's *The Waste Land*, written in 1920, whose memorable lines 'What are the roots that clutch, what branches grow/ Out of this stony rubbish?' and the reply 'You cannot say, or guess, for you know only/ A heap of broken images', has often been taken to symbolize barren disillusionment with the post-war world and the terrible sense of loss. Yet no one at the time was willing to publish it until Leonard and Virginia Woolf (who set the type herself) brought out a private edition of 460 in 1923, which sold 360 that year and was out of print by the spring of 1925. 'The Literary Establishment', wrote Leonard Woolf many years later, 'continued to think *The Waste Land* absurd', although he recalled that it had had 'an immediate success with the young'.[26] Woolf, too, was not immune from popular criticism of the exclusive world the literary set inhabited. After reading the new edition of Woolf's *After the Deluge*, written in 1931, in which he wrestled with the problem of explaining the deeper causes of the world war, a reader from Tynemouth sent him the following complaint: 'What a conglomeration of muddled thinking you have inflicted on an unsuspecting public ... How the "matrix" of Bloomsbury thinking has moulded your judgement and warped your outlook.'[27]

There is a rich vein of historical writing that has already explored the many issues of memory and mourning after the Great War and the contours of the artistic and intellectual response that marked the culture of the 1920s, and it is not the purpose of this book to repeat it.[28] The subject here is the specific case of the crisis of civilization described by Schweitzer to his Oxford audience, or more properly the wide belief that such a state of crisis existed. The fear that civilization was under threat was a promiscuous and enduring hallmark of the two decades that separated the first great war from the second, but its causes, dynamic development and significance have seldom been given the historical weight they deserve. The degree or intensity of popular belief in crisis altered with changing historical circumstances – more marked, for example, in the early 1920s and during the economic slump and in the years immediately before the outbreak of war in 1939 – but the ideas and arguments that contributed to the construction of 'crisis' and gave it its wide explanatory power and social impact are to be found across the whole inter-war period and not just in the 1930s. Indeed, it is the contention of this book that there were few areas of intellectual endeavour, artistic, literary, scientific, philosophical, that were not affected in some form or other by the prevailing paradigms of impending decline and collapse. The sense of crisis was not specific to any one generation, though more pronounced perhaps among the young, nor was it confined to one political or social outlook, a point that is too easily overlooked. No doubt the idea of a civilization in dissolution was happily sustained by some artists and intellectuals as a trademark of the new age of disconcerting cultural production which they provoked and nourished, but it was not only the prerogative of the intellectual and artistic networks of inter-war Britain, or of the more exclusive Bloomsbury set. The idea of crisis, wrote the Oxford historian George Clark, whose epigraph prefaces this chapter, was also the property of the 'ordinary man' thanks to a popular press that promoted remorselessly, in his view, the 'most universal and comprehensive menace' of all, 'a collapse, an extinction of our civilization'.[29]

The preoccupation with civilization can be demonstrated a number of ways. That it was a private fear and not just a shared public discourse is evident from the many diary entries or letters that invoked it. The novelist E. M. Forster, writing to Leonard Woolf in March 1936 after a dangerous illness, thought how odd it was to be nursed 'with so much kindness and sense', only to return recuperated to 'a civilisation which has neither kindness nor sense'. The following year, in a letter to Elizabeth Trevelyan, he remarked how little he felt his death would matter: 'yet instead,' he continued, 'one gets this terrific general fear about the death of civilisation'.[30] His close friend at King's College, Cambridge, Goldsworthy Lowes Dickinson, observed in his private journal in 1922 that as civilization crumbled he felt 'puzzled, broken, shut out ... a strange, fatuous end of meaningless life'. In almost his last entry before the prostate operation that cost him his life in 1932, he worried that 'a breakdown in the existing order' might mean for him and his dependants 'actual starvation'.[31] William Inge, Dean of St Paul's and a public figure with a reputation for speaking his mind, confided to his diary in September 1931: 'I cannot help wishing that my life had ended before seeing these terrible misfortunes'; and, in 1937: 'Civilisation was being overloaded, too complicated, too artificial'; and finally, in his summary for 1939: 'I shall be really glad when my call comes to leave this mad world.'[32] What is striking about all these entries – and there are many more – is the morbid connection made between the death or debilitation of civilization and the death or psychological decline of the observer. The crisis of civilization was also something experienced as the crisis of individual mortality.

In the public sphere the sense of crisis can be conveyed most easily by tracing its path through the lecture series of voluntary societies and public bodies, or, like Schweitzer's guest lectures in Oxford, through the subjects that prominent public figures chose to talk about. Again, there are many examples. The lecture programmes of the Hampstead Ethical Institute, which advertised regular weekly public lectures on contemporary issues and thinkers, show clearly the break between the pre-war and post-war worlds. Pre-war there were travel talks, talks on literature and philosophy ('Nietzsche's Superman' in 1911, 'Bergson's View of Life' in 1913) and occasional reflections on civilization – 'Civilisation and Self-Control' in 1911, and two years later 'A Perfect World – Could We Endure It?'. But from 1919 the topics were remorselessly anxious: 'The Moral Interregnum'; 'The Dying Creeds'; 'The Revolt of Youth'; 'The Smoke of our Burning'; 'Ideals in Conflict' (all in 1919). In 1920 'The Policy of Violence and Terrorism', 'Class War and Social Peace' and in 1921 and 1922 a conspicuous sense of crisis: 'Can Civilisation be Saved?'; 'The Tragedy of Human Existence'; 'Light Against Death'; 'Short Cuts to the Millennium'; and 'The Decay of Moral Culture'.[33] A second case is the Fabian Society, the socialist think-tank and research group set up in the 1880s, which ran annual series of lectures and summer schools throughout the inter-war years, many of which addressed the issue of civilization in crisis. In 1923 the society ran lectures at the Kingsway Hall in central London under the title 'Is Civilisation Decaying?', in 1928 'Western Civilisation: Whither Is It Going?' (changed from the initial title 'The Alleged

Decline in Western Civilisation') which had record attendances. In 1930 a series with the ambiguous title 'The Endless Quest', which included the philosopher Bertrand Russell on 'Democracy and Civilisation'; in 1931 'Capitalism in Dissolution. What Next?'. In 1934 the lectures were moved to the Friends' Meeting House in London's Euston Road. The first series, under the title 'Liberty or Tyranny?', included suggested topics on 'The Revolt Against Reason' and 'The Nightmare of the Future' (though the last of these was not approved). In 1937 discussion in the Executive Committee produced three suggestions for lecture series from one of the founders of the society, Sidney Webb: 'Whither Britain?', 'Is Britain Drifting Towards Catastrophe?',

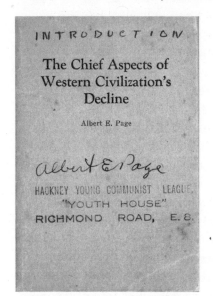 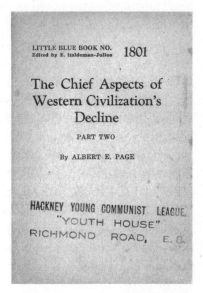

Two pamphlets on the crisis of Western civilization written and privately published by Albert E. Page in 1935 and 1937. Fears for the future became embedded in the culture of the 1930s. Page blamed the crisis on the decline of religion.

and 'What Can Britain Do to Be Saved?'. In the discussions the following year, when the international crisis certainly compelled a more pessimistic outlook, the suggested topics reflected the current mood – 'This Revolting (or Restless) World', 'Collapse of Western Democracy' and 'The New Dark Age'.[34]

The commonest form of discourse was the printed word. Hundreds of books and articles, published lectures, magazine entries and pamphlets addressed the survival of civilization either directly or more obliquely through fragments of the perceived crisis. A simple list would scarcely suffice. Books and articles began as the war ended and ran on to the outbreak of the second war and beyond. H. G. Wells's *The Salvaging of Civilisation*, published in 1921, has already been mentioned, but he continued to write jeremiads down to the Second World War, when his *The Fate of Homo Sapiens* saw Wells despair of a species sailing stupidly along the 'stream of fate to degradation, suffering and death'.[35] In 1922 the American journalist Lothrop Stoddard, obsessed with the crisis of the white races, published *The Revolt against Civilization*, which went through four impressions in London in a year. The sub-title, *The Menace of the Under-Man* – a parody on the Nietzschean concept of the 'over-man' (*Übermensch*) – revealed Stoddard's principal thesis that civilization ('a recent and a fragile thing') was in mortal danger from the rise of a biologically inferior and barbarous underclass. The more sophisticated the civilization, Stoddard continued, 'the graver the liability to irreparable disaster'.[36] This was also the central argument of a short book by the Oxford philosopher Ferdinand Schiller published two years later under the title *Tantalus or The Future of Man*. It appeared in a new series of popular pocket books on contemporary issues produced by the publisher Kegan Paul under the general title 'Today and Tomorrow'. Priced at 2/6d, the books were designed, according to the publishers, to revive a traditional form of literature, 'the Pamphlet', which they claimed had been in disuse for 200 years; they were aimed at a popular market for material on 'the future trend of Civilization'.[37] Schiller's book was a pessimistic survey of human folly. History demonstrated, according to Schiller, that human beings had never learned to be happy. Like Tantalus, doomed according to classical legend never to satisfy his appetites for having presumed to dine with the gods, modern mankind was fated to pursue the fruits of modern civilization only to find instead of satisfaction a putrefying decadence. The Great War and the Russian Revolution showed, Schiller thought, that modern civilization was not even skin-deep: 'it does not go deeper than the clothes'.[38] Schiller blamed the current crisis on biological decline and the 'flood of feeble-mindedness' created by modern social institutions, which pressed mankind back towards primitivism. 'Civilization', Schiller warned, 'carries within it the seeds of its own decay.'[39]

The idea that civilization was at the point of a possibly terminal crisis was certainly not universally accepted, but it became a reference point against which the aspirations and anxieties of the age could be measured, sometimes optimistically, more often pessimistically. In a broadcast in 1933 on 'Man and Civilisation' the Christian philosopher Christopher Dawson framed his talk around a theme which he took for granted was thoroughly familiar to the wider public: 'whether our civilisation is going to recover its stability or whether it will collapse in ruins'.[40] So embedded did the trope become that George Clark concluded that 'optimism in any form must hide her head'. The Chalcot Discussion Society, founded in London in 1899 as a forum for women to discuss issues of the day, debated the proposition in 1928 'Is it better to have as a constant companion an optimist or a pessimist?' – a subject which made sense only in the context of an increasingly institutionalized pessimism.[41] An article written in 1934 in the Oxford-based *Hibbert Journal* claimed that what made theories of decline so pessimistic was that they were almost certainly true.[42] Another article a year later in the same journal under the title 'Will Our Civilisation Survive?' quoted a speech by the Irish playwright George Bernard Shaw given in 1933 to the American Academy of Political Science in which Shaw remarked that the 'mental attitude' of the post-war world was different from that of 'our fathers and grandfathers'; once confident and uncomplicated, the mental land-scape was now a bleak and dangerous realism. After the war, Shaw suggested, mankind had reached 'the edge of the precipice' over which all previous civilizations had fallen and been 'dashed to pieces'.[43] The end of optimism was the theme of another reflection on 'The Twilight of Civilization' published in 1940 by the zoologist P. Chalmers Mitchell. Up to the war of 1914 optimistic philosophy dominated expectations for the future. If an occasional philosopher 'proclaimed pessimism', he was, Mitchell suggested, 'usually a foreigner or addicted to drink, or a victim of some kind of mental or physical derangement'.[44] But the modern world, he concluded, writing just before the outbreak of the Second World War, was faced with irrefutable evidence, both scientific and social, that the easy upward ascent of man was an illusion: 'it seems as if our Western civilization is doomed'.[45]

The widespread culture of decline or crisis evidently did not operate in a vacuum, since it was regularly replenished by evidence of social conflict, economic crisis, international disputes and occasional war. Yet much of the discourse seems to have developed independent of specific periods of post-war crisis and to have been a ready-made answer to an undifferentiated sense of malaise prompted by the reality of the war and its aftermath. It was sustained through public expressions of uncertainty, irrational anxiety and loss for which a language was sought capable of expressing these fears in the form of a persuasive and morbid myth. Its endurance and wide currency relied on public appropriation and repetitive endorsement. In time, the discourse developed its own momentum, each element feeding on the others. In his *The Shape of Things to Come*, published in 1933, H. G. Wells imagines a future looking back at his age. 'As we turn over the periodicals and literature of the time,' he wrote, 'the notes of apprehension and distress increase and deepen'; a putative collection of historical documents compiled from contemporary press cuttings is titled 'The Sense of Catastrophe in the Nineteen Thirties'. Yet in *The Shape of Things to Come*, Wells contributed a powerful stimulus to those very anxieties that he sought to parody ('a very sad mess' was the judgement of one reviewer on the contemporary world of the 1930s depicted in the book).[46] Reviewing three books on the same theme in 1933, Geoffrey West remarked that 'The Collapse of Civilization', which had been until recently 'a mere turnip-head bogey-phrase', had now become the respectable province of intellectuals who endlessly debated not 'whether' but 'when'.[47] The editor of the *Hibbert Journal*, the Oxford clergyman Lawrence Jacks, writing in 1931, found the fashion for catastrophism rooted in the 1920s; since the war, he wrote, 'the cry of "civilisation in danger" has become a text for an immense output of gloomy writing'. Jeremiah, he continued, 'has become a best seller'. Jacks himself did not consider that the danger was any greater than it had been in the past or would be in the future, but was just one of the many struggles between what he called 'the Best and Worst' which had patterned world history.

'Inwardly', he continued, 'I feel convinced that the Best will win through', though he felt 'unable to give proof of it'.[48] Even organizations such as the South Place Ethical Society in London, a Unitarian and rationalist group that held regular weekly public discourses on uplifting humanist themes to counter the modern mood of 'lassitude', capitulated in the 1930s to the prevailing orthodoxy by staging talks on 'The Future of Civilisation' (twice), 'Religion and the Decay of Civilisation' and Cyril Joad on 'What has happened to Progress in the 1930s?'. A discourse in 1936 on 'Pessimism, Optimism or Meliorism' suggested that the sensible position in the 1930s was to hope for the best but be prepared for the worst.[49]

An invitation to the opening in 1929 of the Conway Hall in Red Lion Square, London, home to the South Place Ethical Society. The hall became a central venue in the 1930s for lectures and discussions on the problems of the contemporary world.

The tireless search for crisis had limits even for publishers in search of a best-seller. When in 1934 Leonard Woolf tried to get his American publisher Donald Brace to accept his latest book *Quack Quack* (a study of the social inadequacy of contemporary capitalist society), the American city-planner and amateur philosopher Lewis Mumford recommended finding a different title that would properly reflect the manuscript's gloomy contents. Brace rejected this suggestion on grounds that there had been 'too many books with titles of this general sort'. In his view the public no longer wanted to be 'worried, warned or exhorted with any more' and *Quack-Quack*, with a hyphen inserted, remained the title.[50] This diffidence proved short lived. In October 1938 the British publisher Victor Gollancz told Woolf that it was no time any longer for optimistic books and asked him to submit a manuscript on the lines of 'The Defence of Western Civilization'. Woolf agreed and sent in a draft manuscript the following May. He called it *Barbarians at the Gate* and it was finally published in November 1939.[51] Woolf also sent the manuscript to Brace who gladly accepted it, but this time he insisted that Woolf alter the title to reflect more closely the doom-laden thesis of the book, that civilization could be destroyed not only by the external forces of war but by a rising tide of barbarism in the heart of civilized society itself. Woolf suggested *Barbarians Within and Without* and Brace accepted. The book appeared in the United States under this title in 1940.[52]

The popular assumption of a 'crisis of civilization' was reflexive as much as reflective; the phenomenon 'civilization' was all too often taken for granted rather than defined. It begged two important questions that much of the literature on crisis tried to grapple with: What was meant by civilization? And why in the post-war years was it threatened with eclipse? On neither of these issues was there any consistent agreement. The definition of civilization was seldom explored when the word was used in popular discussion, partly because there were agreed conventions in the early part of the century that civilization must represent a qualitatively superior level of political, economic, cultural and technical achievement subsumed under the term 'progress', which was widely taken for granted even if its fruits were unevenly distributed. In Britain the commitment to parliamentary rule and an impartial judicial system were generally regarded as hallmarks of a particularly British version of the broader Western experience. But in reality the definition of civilization, and the description of those who could qualify as civilized, was shaped by the social position and moral assumptions of those who chose to write about it. Since the majority of those who did so were drawn from the well-to-do intelligentsia and the political elite, it was their world view that predominated. In general this meant a version of civilization that was based on the model of recent Western development; it meant a view of civilization that reflected the prejudices and expectations of the educated classes; it meant a definition that relied on high culture and polite social behaviour as criteria for inclusion among the civilized; and it was one intimately bound up with the conception of empire as it had evolved during the course of the previous century.

All of these elements were present in one of the few serious attempts to define what was meant by civilization in the post-war period. The art critic Clive Bell, brother-in-law of Virginia Woolf, published a book titled *Civilization: An Essay* in 1928, which he dedicated to her. In his preface Bell confessed that the book had germinated in the rosy pre-war era as an account of the 'manifestations of civility' in art, thought and social life. The war altered his perspective and in 1918 he dusted down the manuscript and began to draft an essay 'modified by the war' which might explain what ideal of civilization could possibly have justified its 'front place amongst British war aims' and the 'millions of human lives' lost in its defence.[53] Bell found it easier to define what civilization was not – 'something to which savages have not attained' and therefore devoid of 'primitive virtues' – but his final definition of the necessary elements of civilization described a reality that his Bloomsbury colleagues would have found entirely familiar:

A taste for truth and beauty, tolerance, intellectual honesty, fastidiousness, a sense of humour, good manners, curiosity, a dislike of vulgarity, brutality and over-emphasis, freedom from superstition and prudery, a fearless acceptance of the good things of life, a desire for complete self-expression and for a liberal education, a contempt for utilitarianism and philistinism, in two words – sweetness and light.[54]

Civilization, Bell thought, was in the mind of man or woman, which was why 'savage communities' could not create it. But he added the rider that 'a man or woman entirely insensitive to all the arts can hardly be deemed civilized'.[55] A similar conclusion was reached by the historian A. L. Rowse as a young don at Oxford 'talking over tea in the evening sun' with Geoffrey Hudson about 'the meaning of Civilization'. After agreeing that there was no precise way of defining it, except that it was not 'savage society', Rowse put down in his diary that 'The essence of civilisation seems to consist in a <u>self-conscious</u> cultural tradition, created by the dominant class . . .'.[56]

The British intelligentsia also relied heavily on classical models of civilization, a perception encouraged by their widespread familiarity with Graeco-Roman politics, philosophy, high culture, law-making and imperialism. Ferdinand Schiller in his *Future of Man* mocked an Oxford system that produced classical graduates 'imbued with the conviction that in matters of morals and politics nothing of importance has been discovered or said since Plato or Aristotle'.[57] Arnold Toynbee observed in his memoirs that the classical education in Britain, which his whole generation of students experienced, had focused only on the period of high culture in the Greek and Roman worlds, ignoring the subsequent period of decline in order, so he thought, to promote the illusion that the British Empire was part of an unbroken succession of civilized life from the great empires of the past to the great Empire of the present. This perception was reinforced by the reading of Edward Gibbon's *The History of the Decline and Fall of the Roman Empire*, in which Gibbon, reflecting on the possible fate of his own civilization in the eighteenth century, concluded that it could not possibly suffer the disaster of the late Roman period.[58] The implicit, often explicit, identification of British civilization with those of the ancient world was rooted in the nineteenth-century elevation of the idea of the *Pax Britannica* and the separation made between 'civilized' modernity and the apparently archaic societies that peopled the colonial territories under British domination. The concept of the savage 'other', evident in the words of Bell or Rowse, mirrored the confrontation between Rome, Greece and the barbarian. This marriage of modern and ancient empire was the theme of a lengthy lecture given by the Earl of Cromer, the former ruler of British Egypt, to the Classical Association in London, of which he was president during the 1909–10 session. Under the title 'Ancient and Modern Imperialism' he argued that a 'somewhat close analogy' could be established between the 'motive power that impelled both ancient and modern Imperialists onwards'. That motive power was to be found in the spread of 'progress and civilization', whose benefits, he thought, were enjoyed rather than practised by the fortunate peoples of the Empire.[59]

One of the leading spokesmen for this view was the Oxford classicist Gilbert Murray. In the first half of the twentieth century he was perhaps Britain's most distinguished and best-known scholar, though his reputation has faded since. For his ninetieth birthday in 1956 the *Observer* published a sympathetic profile of a gentle intellectual giant, a teetotaller, vegetarian and non-smoker who, despite his Irish-Australian background, was the complete Englishman. The son of Sir Terence Murray, president of the Legislative Council of New South Wales, he attended public school in London before going on to St John's College, Oxford. At the young age of 23 he was appointed professor of Greek at Glasgow University, and in 1908 he became Regius professor of Greek at Oxford. He was a keen tennis player, and began riding a motorcycle in his fifties. His grandson, Philip Toynbee, later claimed that Murray had an abiding dislike of Shakespeare and of music. His public reputation was based on his translations of the playwrights of ancient Greece, to whose work he dedicated his whole scholarly life; by the time of his death in 1957 his translations had sold 396,000 copies. His values were liberal and his preferences were those of his class and age, though he was not a snob.[60] His wide interests and voluminous correspondence will be found in every chapter of this book.

Murray defined civilization in terms of stability, justice, a strong normative morality and respect for the highest intellectual, artistic and spiritual values. 'In antiquity', he wrote in an article reflecting on the crisis of the modern Christian age, 'the world got them from Rome, in modern times from Western Europe.'[61] In an address to a Conference of European Universities after the Second World War he argued that the great cultural traditions of European civilization, Christian and Hellenic, which had seemed up to the Great War 'not only secure but securely progressive' had to be preserved. 'Europe', he continued, 'created all that the world calls civilisation', and without claiming 'that we alone are Hellenes and all outsiders Barbaroi' he concluded that the fate of 'true civilisation' depended on reviving and sustaining the ancient lineage that united Greece, Rome and the modern age.[62]

Murray was well aware that the failure of civilization as he defined it might result in a new 'Dark Age'. He had helped to popularize that

Gilbert Murray at work in Oxford in 1931. Robert Cecil described him as 'a really angelic person'.

very term, which assumed a wide currency in Britain only in the early twentieth century, at the same time as anxieties began to surface about the durability of civilization. It supplied a ready-made metaphor for the bleak period that might follow the collapse of civilized existence and it was repeated again and again in the inter-war years as something that followed the fall of civilization as night followed day. The concept of a Dark Age was usually applied to the period following the fall of the Roman Empire of the west in the fifth century AD, though it was also used, as Murray sometimes used it, to describe the period of cultural decline in classical Greece. The understanding that the civilized life of the Roman world was followed by centuries of barbarous darkness went back to at least early Renaissance Italy; Gibbon talked about 'the darkest ages' following the fall of Rome.[63] But only in English did the term 'Dark Ages' emerge as a shorthand description of the late classical and early medieval world following the barbarian invasions. In English the term seems to have been used for the first time in 1837 in Henry Hallam's *History of England*, but it became commonplace only following the publication of *The Dark Ages* in 1893 by the future Oxford professor of modern history Sir Charles

Oman, in a series of textbooks on periods of European history.[64] The book went into six editions and twelve impressions and was still in print and regularly used sixty years later. In 1904 the philologist William Ker published a cultural history of *The Dark Ages* (in a series on periods of European literature) which also helped to lodge the term firmly in the popular historical language of the time. By the 1920s the concept was instantly recognizable and easily appropriated as a metaphor for an age anxiously observing the current prospects for civilization. Despite the efforts of modern historians to consign the Dark Ages to the historical waste-paper basket, it has a resonance still.[65]

These definitions of civilization did not go unchallenged by those who perceived its darker side. For socialists, civilization represented not a grand historical tradition but a bankrupt social order. The young Marxist Christopher Caudwell (pseudonym of Christopher St John Sprigg), who died fighting in the Spanish Civil War in 1937, wrote that 'all civilisation up to the present' was nothing more than the 'prehistoric stage of society'. For Caudwell only the world proletariat could 'inaugurate an *historic* civilisation'.[66] Leonard Woolf in *Imperialism and Civilization*, published in 1928, took a very different view of European expansion from Lord Cromer's: 'It was a belligerent, crusading, conquering, exploiting, proselytizing civilization,' wrote Woolf. 'Imperialism hitherto, by imposing it on subject peoples at the point of a gun,' he continued, 'has heavily overweighted the blessings with a load of war, barbarities, cruelties, tyrannies and exploitations.'[67] In Europe itself civilization represented for Woolf the advantage of one class over another, though this did not prevent him from arguing in a later book that the standards of civilized life as he defined them – 'liberty, equality, education, justice, knowledge, truth, humanity' – somehow transcended merely accidental differences of social position and opportunity and could be enjoyed by all.[68] Some communist writers deplored the tendency even among Marxists to share with 'bourgeois' authors an exaggerated 'respect for civilisation' on the assumption that the alternative must be barbarism.[69] John Strachey, the socialist politician and a future minister in the post-war Labour cabinet, was invited to comment on Woolf's manuscript *Barbarians at the Gate* in 1939, and he strongly criticized Woolf's acceptance of the idea that the concept of a liberal civilization had deep historical roots and that the ideals of civilization were independent of the particular social milieu in which they happened to function. Strachey, like Caudwell, could only see true civilization emerging out of the triumphant class struggle and the destruction of the old order.[70] Nevertheless, the idea of civilization as the endpoint of a progressive history and the export of 'civilization' to the non-European world as in itself likely to be progressive was, for all its paradoxes, the sense in which the term was popularly used even by those whose prospects of benefiting from its fruits were limited. During the inter-war years both those who deplored the threat to civilization and those who deplored its injustices were united by the belief that in its existing form civilization faced a potentially terminal crisis.

Why civilizations decline was also a question to which there were a great many different answers. For those who reflected on the fate of civilization the Great War was a proximate but not a sufficient explanation, a symptom as much as a cause. Leonard Woolf in *After the Deluge* argued that historians had a moral obligation to explain where the war fitted in the greater scheme of human history, 'the organic machinery of civilisation'.[71] However, wider explanations for crisis had to take account of the fact that most of the major historical narratives generated in the nineteenth century, and particularly those of the German philosophers Georg Hegel and Karl Marx, were positive in outlook. Liberal and socialist narratives alike were inherently progressive, one social or political form giving rise to another that was by definition more advanced, closer to the ultimate ideal than the one on whose foundations it was built. Charles Darwin's evolutionary theory also posited the idea of progress as something that was in the nature of things and many of those who took up his arguments as metaphors for the development of human societies assumed that they were describing the progressive movement of mankind. These Victorian narratives were based on the idea of continuous improvement, which seemed fundamentally incompatible with the war and the post-war malaise. The aftermath of war prompted a profound change in the way in which history was regarded, no longer an unbroken chain from primitive to modern but a story capable of violent interruption or termination. This changing view of the relationship between past and present gave historians a central place in explaining the current crisis of civilization as a profound historical phenomenon rather than a mere consequence of the war.

The thinker most responsible for challenging these progressive narratives was another German philosopher, Friedrich Nietzsche. Written in the 1870s and 1880s, his works were taken up across Europe. In Britain most of the key texts were translated and published before the Great War by Anthony Ludovici, who also introduced a wider audience to Nietzsche in his *Life and Works*, published in 1912. In the inter-war years Nietzsche's *Thus Spake Zarathustra* was published by at least three British publishers.[72] Nietzsche's insistence that all moral systems were relative and that progress was an illusion laid the basis in the years before 1914 for a widespread critical assault on nineteenth-century certainties. Nietzsche regarded history as cyclical and civilization as merely the current expression of man's futile efforts to fight the reality of decay with the weapons of illusory order. After Nietzsche it was possible to see that human history had many possible outcomes, not one. Nietzsche was also a scholar of the classical world, which helps to explain his immediate appeal to the pre-war intellectual elite brought up on Greece and Rome. After Nietzsche those who constructed grand historical narratives had to confront the reality that all civilizations come and go, rise and fall, are born and die. Just as those of the ancient world perished, so too the modern age, and it was this intuition that paved the way for new historical narratives that helped to give a more intellectually plausible explanation for the apparent crisis of civilization after 1919. Nietzsche asserted the uncomfortable truth that the more order was imposed and progress proclaimed, the closer civilization was to the point of dissolution. In *Ecce Homo*, his last work before his permanent state of insanity set in from 1890, published in Britain in 1927, Nietzsche suggested that Europe's 'highly cultured and weary humanity' needed 'not only wars but the greatest and most terrible of wars – temporary lapses into barbarism', which echoed the final death throes of the Roman Empire familiar to most of his readers.[73]

Many of Nietzsche's insights became central elements in the construction of the most well-known of the new grand historical narratives both inside and outside Germany, Oswald Spengler's *The Decline of the West*, published in Germany in two volumes at the end of the war and in Britain a few years later. Spengler was an unlikely prophet. At a Nietzsche Congress in 1927 in Germany an unkind critic described him as 'a fat parson with a flabby chin and a brutal mouth . . . uniformly shallow, dull, insipid and tedious'.[74] On most accounts, Spengler was an awkward and isolated figure. He was born in 1880, the son of a minor post-office official. He was an autodidact, fascinated by all aspects of culture and by mathematics and philosophy. He failed his doctoral examination in 1903, abandoned an academic career and devoted his time to constructing a major thesis on the rise and fall of civilizations. He lived from modest teaching jobs and a small inheritance, a reclusive and increasingly impoverished figure. In 1911 he settled permanently in Munich where, by 1914, the first volume of his study was ready for publication. The war intervened and it was not published until July 1918 in Vienna. The title chosen, *Der Untergang des Abendlandes*, reflected Spengler's personal desire to explain in fundamental terms what was happening in contemporary Europe, and particularly his native Germany, in the age of world war. But the content of this and the subsequent volume published in 1922 was relayed better by the sub-title, *Outline of a Morphology of World History*, for Spengler's aim was to show that all human civilizations had developed and died according to a predetermined pattern of historical development.[75]

Spengler's title and theme appealed to an extraordinary degree in post-war Germany, where the educated public sought ways to explain the defeat and post-war upheavals they experienced. The books, almost 1,200 pages in length, sold 100,000 copies in a period of acute economic crisis, making it one of the most successful publishing ventures of the decade.[76] Public reaction was divided. Academic criticism was generally hostile since Spengler had no scholarly legitimacy while his historical claims did a good deal of violence to established conceptions of the past. But there was also a popular response which saw in Spengler a writer whose apparently pessimistic conclusions matched the mood of anxiety about the future of Western civilization. Spengler's argument was deliberately determinist. He saw all civilizations, or 'cultures' (the German term *Kultur* covers much more than the English term) as destined to follow the same pattern as everything organic; 'the notions of birth, death, youth, age, lifetime', he wrote in the introduction, 'are fundamentals'. Human history, he suggested, was based upon 'general biographic archetypes', which meant that any specific culture followed predetermined patterns. Their value was also relative and each distinct culture was self-contained, rising and falling in its own terms – 'independent, plant-like, individual' – which made the thesis entirely distant from the progressive Hegelian view of a 'uniform purpose' to history and a linear progression of civiliz-ation.[77] He identified eight 'ripe' cultures from the Chinese through to the modern 'Western-American' and four chief cycles in history: the Indian, antique, Arabian and Western. Each cycle lasted around 1,000 years and went through the same stages of historical develop-ment. As the early creative, primitive and spontaneous culture ripened so it always tended to produce a mechanical, formalistic, desiccated 'civilization' that heralded the approaching winter of culture and its final eclipse. Each decaying 'civilization' would end with a brief flourish of violent universal 'Caesarism' and the emergence of new primitive religions before disappearing, to be replaced by a new and vital culture. The West, Spengler observed, had reached its winter.[78]

Spengler denied that his thesis was pessimistic. For him the rise and fall of civilization was, like individual death, simply a fact to be accepted. His attitude towards modernity was not to condemn it but to recognize its historical limitations. 'I see no progress, no goal, no path for humanity,' he wrote in a short pamphlet titled *Pessimism?*, published in 1922.[79] His work was never stridently apocalyptic but it did give a solid intellectual foundation to the idea, as one American critic put it in 1929, that Western civilization was 'on the threshold of an inevitable and all-embracing decline'.[80] It was evident that readers would apply Spengler's argument to the current post-war age. After reading a prediction from H. G. Wells in 1931 about a coming world war, Edwin Payr wrote enthusiastically to Spengler: 'Your prophecies in *The Decline of the West* are being fulfilled uncannily soon.'[81] The reception of the book in Britain, though a more modest seller than in Germany, nonetheless revealed an appetite for metahistorical expla-nation of a phenomenon that otherwise seemed difficult to explain in conventional terms. Reviewing what he called the 'now famous book' in the *Sociological Review* in 1922, Christopher Dawson reflected on the faltering western European belief that the values of its civilization were absolute and its history a history of 'progress' rather than a finite episode in world history, like any other civilization of the past. Though Dawson thought the English mind was 'ever suspicious of the theorist', he applauded Spengler's attempt to break the mould of conventional historical narrative by recognizing the cyclical nature of historical development, though like most critics he rejected Spengler's contention that each culture developed in isolation from the others.[82]

Volume I of Spengler's *Decline* appeared in English in 1926, the second volume in 1928, both published by George Allen & Unwin. Stanley Unwin was keen to publish the book following its phenomenal success in Germany, but Spengler insisted on choosing his own translator. The first translated chapter, Unwin later wrote, was 'hopeless' and Spengler was compelled to agree to Unwin's choice of Charles Atkinson.[83] In the translator's preface Atkinson reminded English readers that Spengler had already acquired a 'large following amongst thoughtful laymen', but that he had also 'forced the attention and taxed the scholarship of every branch of the learned world'.[84] The distinguished British historian George Gooch considered it 'the most important and influential book' to appear in Germany in a decade; another reviewer described reading it as 'an unforgettable experience'.[85] *The Decline of the West* sold slowly if steadily (2,856 copies of volume I, 1,473 of volume II) and the translation was also used by the American publisher Alfred Knopf, with greater success: 21,000 copies were sold in the United States by 1940.[86] The choice of title, although it did not quite convey the idea of 'downfall' in the German original, gave the book a popular impact in spite of a dense and at times obscure text. 'The title', wrote Lewis Mumford, 'had an even more immediate appeal than its contents', for the title 'whispered the soothing words, *downfall, doom, death*'.[87] Spengler and 'Spenglerian' thinking became popular shorthand for any form of pessimistic determinism applied to the decay or collapse of civilization. In 1926 an English commentary on Spengler's thesis was published under the title *Civilisation or Civilisations*, prefaced with a long introduction by Ferdinand Schiller, whose own pessimistic prognosis of the human future had been published two years before. Schiller was sceptical that anything like a fixed law of civilizations could be clearly demonstrated, but he understood the contemporary appeal of Spengler's thesis that Western civilization had entered on its final stage of decay with its 'downfall impending'.[88] The book argued that the idea of progress had been a Victorian article of faith now fatally challenged by the emergence of archaeological and anthropological evidence that there was not, and had never been, a 'continuity of progressive development'. History was a series of civilizations 'springing up sporadically' before passing away; modern civilization was no more immune to this process than any other. Spengler's law of civilization, their argument continued, bestowed the 'power of prophecy' that Western civilization in its turn must disappear.[89]

In Britain the idea that past civilizations had perished, and had done so for identifiably similar reasons, relied less on Spengler than it did in Germany or in the United States. The British grand historical narrative was based on a remarkable flowering of archaeological research, particularly in the Middle East, in the two or three decades before 1914, reflecting a popular fascination with past civilizations that continued unabated through the inter-war years. The result was a growing scientific understanding that the rise and fall of a wide range of civilizations could be effectively charted and some possible pattern detected applicable as much to the modern world as it was to the Roman Empire. The most influential professional account was by the Egyptologist Flinders Petrie, whose brief text *The Revolutions of Civilisation*, first published in a pocket-book format in 1911, argued that civilization was not a continuous thread from antiquity to the Western world but was intermittent, discontinuous but recurrent.[90] He defined each civilization of the past, in terms also employed by Spengler, of a spring and summer of birth and growth and an autumn and winter of decline and fall. Like Spengler, Petrie arrived at the view that a civilization began to decay at just the point when it seemed wealthiest and its values democratic; both elements were evidence of internal stagnation and decay – 'the easier life is rendered, the more easy is decay and degradation'.[91] New civilizations arose from the injection of fresh blood, usually in the form of barbarian invasions. The vitality and ambition of the invader mingled with the residue of a previous civilization to promote the development of a different though not necessarily superior one. Though Petrie hesitated to suggest that Western civilization was doomed to go the same way as all its predecessors, the implication was clear. In the 1920s and 1930s Petrie's conclusions were just as likely to be cited as Spengler's. The address by George Bernard Shaw on the pessimism of the present cited Flinders Petrie, not Spengler, as the source for the view that the process of democratization, urbanization and the worship of wealth invariably led to the internal degeneration and death of all civilizations.[92] Shaw exploited Petrie's 'new history' again in a radio broadcast in 1937 to support the argument that 'no civilisation, however splendid, illustrious and like our own' could survive the conflicts over wealth and democracy characteristic of the modern age.[93]

One figure stood out from all the rest in the attempt to establish a proper science of civilization. With the publication in 1934 of the first three volumes of *A Study of History*, the Oxford historian Arnold Toynbee became in the course of the 1930s the British Spengler. This is not a description he would have approved. Toynbee considered Spengler a narrow determinist and he found the 'organic' metaphor of the birth and death of cultures to be a clumsy attempt to make all history fit a prescribed template. In a list of further reading added to the published version of his radio talks on 'World Order or Downfall' in 1930, Toynbee included Spengler's *Decline* with the cautionary note 'philosophical and controversial; not suitable for beginners'.[94] But critics of Toynbee thought he owed a good deal to Spengler. In a radio debate with the Dutch historian Peter Geyl in 1948 Toynbee defended himself against Geyl's accusation that his gloomy view of civilization merely echoed the *Decline* by insisting, wrongly, that Spengler was a fatalist who had nothing to suggest other than to await 'the inevitable blow of the axe'. The doom of civilization, Toynbee continued, was a 'call to action' not 'a death sentence'.[95] Toynbee had read Spengler in German early in the 1920s – a gift from the historian Lewis Namier – and later confessed that the experience almost persuaded him that there was nothing more for him to write, but he decided that Spengler was too speculative and persisted with his own version of the grand narrative. What distinguished Toynbee from Spengler was his insistence on what he called 'English empiricism', a mountain of factual evidence to underpin a set of theoretical assumptions on the history of civilizations that differed from Spengler not in overall design, but in historical breadth and apparent plausibility.[96]

Arnold Joseph Toynbee was born in 1889 into a middle-class English family in London. His father worked for the Charity Organization Society with a modest but sufficient salary to employ two servants and to send Arnold to the best private schools. His mother had been an undergraduate at the recently founded Newnham College in Cambridge, where she earned a first in history, and it was her love for the subject, Toynbee later recalled, that drew him to his future profession. After school at Winchester he went to Balliol College, Oxford, where he was offered a fellowship to teach ancient history before he had even completed his final exam. He was a serious-minded and precocious pupil and student. In his memoirs he explained that his family's puritan background laid upon him the conscientious necessity to work as strenuously as possible (his famous uncle, the economic historian Arnold Toynbee, who coined the term 'the Industrial Revolution', died at the age of 30 from sheer overwork, it was alleged). 'To be always working, and this at full stretch,' Toynbee wrote, was a permanent duty, and there can be no other explanation for the exceptional quantity of written material that he produced over the course of a long career. He wrote day in, day out, always between breakfast and lunch 'when my mind is the most active'. 'Don't wait until you feel you are in the mood,' he wrote. 'Write whether you feel inclined to write or not!'.[97] Throughout his life Toynbee was an indefatigable scholar, broadcaster and lecturer, and a keen traveller. His early academic career at Balliol was interrupted by the war, when he took up work in the Foreign Office Intelligence division, with a special interest in the Middle East. He attended the Versailles Conference as a delegate, and in 1921 was appointed the first holder of the Koraes Chair of Modern Greek and Byzantine History at King's College, London. The appointment proved a disappointment and in 1925 he became the Stevenson Research Professor and Director of Studies at the Royal Institute of International Affairs, a post that he held with only a brief wartime interruption down to 1955. In 1913 he married Gilbert Murray's daughter, Rosalind. When the couple divorced in 1946, he married the same year Veronica Boulter, who for years had helped him to prepare the annual *Survey of International Affairs* produced by the Institute.

A portrait of the young Arnold Toynbee c. 1920. This was the period in his life, he later claimed, when he first formed in his mind the analysis of civilisation that he was to use in his later work.

Toynbee, on his own account, began to speculate on his future grand narrative just after the Great War. The conflict and post-war crisis encouraged him to question the pre-war assumption that civilization was permanent and progressive. With these ideas, Toynbee later wrote, 'already simmering in my mind', he had undertaken a train journey across western Bulgaria in 1921, returning on the Orient Express from observing the Graeco-Turkish war, during which he jotted down 'a dozen headings' on half a sheet of paper for a history of world civilizations that were to form the basic structure of the mature work written between the 1930s and the 1950s.[98] He began writing detailed notes in 1927–8 and by 1930 was ready to embark on the first of what eventually became the ten-volume *A Study of History*.[99] He claimed to have been inspired in part by an urge to reject Edward Gibbon's confident assertion that Western civilization would not go the way of Rome. This was a view, he told an audience in 1939, which had been all very well up to 1914, when it 'seemed inconceivable' that civilization should collapse like the ancient world. Gibbon he considered too optimistic. He dated the onset of the popular realization that Gibbon was wrong from the period 1929 to 1933, and it must be certain that Toynbee included himself among this number for in the early 1930s his lectures and radio broadcasts were peppered with the observation that the crisis in the West was manifestly comparable to the final crisis of the Roman Empire.[100] Western civilization, he told a radio audience in 1931, was nothing more than one of many bubbles in the stream of world history, as Rome had been: 'Isn't it most probable that our bubble will burst like the rest?'[101]

This was a view difficult to reconcile with Toynbee's insistence that he was, as he wrote to the author Arnold Wilson in 1931, 'a convinced non-determinist'. His reply to Wilson, who had sent him a draft manuscript of his book *The Epic and Tragedies of Civilisations*, provides an important insight into the way Toynbee's mind was working in the early stages of writing the *Study*. Toynbee was the product of a very individualist tradition in which personal endeavour, of which his own success was an example, was supposed to overcome the barriers imposed by circumstances. 'The issue', he told Wilson, was between 'determinism and spontaneity'. He thought that environment or ethnicity explained little about human development, a point which he elaborated later in the *Study*. For Toynbee the key lay in the spiritual power of the individual when confronted with a challenge. 'The plot of Goethe's *Faust* or of the Book of Job seems to me to be the real plot of the tragedy of civilizations,' he wrote, and he continued:

Things happen through ordeals. When somebody is subjected to an ordeal things cannot stand still. Either one or other of two things must happen. Either the person subjected to the challenge fails to meet it and goes under, or else he reacts victoriously and produces some sort of creation. I believe that there is some spark of divinity in every living creature which makes any of us capable of any one of these creative acts at any time, and I think this is the most illuminating of the many possible approaches to the history of civilisations.[102]

The idea of 'challenge and response', banal enough in itself, became one of the cornerstones of Toynbee's theory of historical development.

More than that, Toynbee came to see his own personal experience and that of his generation as a model. Challenged by the war ('the great watershed of 1914' as he later called it), he felt impelled by 'one of the great turning points' in the history of Western civilization to respond to the challenge in ways both original and creative.[103]

His work at the Royal Institute of International Affairs also stimulated his appetite for the grand narrative. In the annual *Survey* for 1931 he observed for the first time that all over the world people were beginning to realize 'that the Western system of society might break down and cease to work'.[104] In 1932 his draft outline of a future research programme for the Institute included 'A study of the history of civilisations in the light of our knowledge and experience in this generation'. Toynbee explained that recent developments in archaeology now made it possible to study and compare distant and current civilizations. In his view the contemporary world cried out for just such an enterprise. Taking civilizations rather than nations or states as the building-blocks, he not only proposed a study of 'the "highest common factors" in the histories of civilisations (e.g. their births, growths, breakdowns, disintegrations and contacts)' but also indicated his own willingness to undertake the project on the ground that he had already used his private study of history as the 'mental background' in compiling the Institute's annual *Survey* year after year.[105] Some years later he told Joseph Willetts, Director of Social Sciences at the Rockefeller Foundation, that ever since 1927 'I have always run the Survey and the Study in double harness'. Toynbee claimed that working on both side-by-side gave him 'relief and stimulus' as he switched between his two grim occupations; his employers at the Institute tolerated his workload and, for the first volumes, subsidized their preparation and publication.[106] In 1934 the first three volumes were published by Oxford University Press on the genesis and growth of civilizations; the next three volumes, detailing the breakdown and disintegration of civilizations, were published at what the historian A. J. P. Taylor described as the 'unbearably appropriate' moment a few weeks before the outbreak of the Second World War, late in July 1939.[107]

The central framework of Toynbee's argument in the first six volumes rested on a number of assumptions: first, that the unit of historical study is properly a civilization (used in the English rather than German sense of the term to embrace both 'culture' and 'civilization'); second, that there is no single continuous civilization but at least twenty-six distinct civilizations, of which sixteen are dead and nine of the remainder moribund (Western civilization or Western Christendom, as Toynbee preferred to call it, was the only one still in the process of development); third, that there are clear links between many of the major civilizations (one of the few obvious divergences from Spengler's argument); and finally, that all civilizations are not only capable of historically useful comparison, but are philosophically equivalent. On this basis Toynbee thought it possible to elucidate through 'scientific technique' the historical laws governing the development of all civilizations. Each of the major civilizations identified by Toynbee came into being through spiritual endeavour, meeting challenges through the activities of a minority of creative individuals. These challenges could be environmental, military, or social but the important point for Toynbee was their 'adversity'. If conditions were easy, no response could be stimulated (here he used the example of the people of Nyasaland (present-day Malawi), whose easy life, Toynbee thought, had left them 'primitive savages' until the arrival of the white man).[108] Each challenge provokes other challenges and as long as there is a sufficient fund of creative individuals willing to push forward, civilizations continue to grow.

Breakdown and disintegration come into play only when the fund of creativity grows weak and the responses become merely mechanical. The creative minority becomes a dominant minority of tyrants or demagogues or the wealthy while the rest of society becomes a disaffected 'internal proletariat' (in the Roman rather than the Marxist sense). Stagnation then provokes the barbarians on the frontiers, or the 'external proletariat', to become more violent. Internal degeneration is the primary cause, but external defeat the likely consequence. Breakdown provokes what Toynbee called 'a time of troubles', of social crisis and internecine warfare. This occurs in his conspectus (as it does in Spengler's) hundreds of years before the final crisis – in Western Christendom it dated from the sixteenth-century wars of religion, in Roman times from the Punic Wars of the third century BC. This stage is followed by the establishment of a universal state based on military power, but the universal state is spiritually bankrupt, an illusory revival predating the final 'rout' of civilization itself, not at once but perhaps centuries later.[109] Across the whole long period of breakdown and disintegration Toynbee claimed to have uncovered an internal pattern of 'rout–rally–rout', brief periods of revival before the next blow. He detected a precise pattern of four routs and three rallies, which always ended with a rout, an interregnum and the emergence of another civilization. Underlying it all was a loss of spiritual certainty, a 'schism in the soul', which could ultimately be healed only by a transfiguring religion. As he rediscovered his Christianity in the 1930s, Toynbee came to believe that, among the major religions, 'Jesus of Nazareth alone conquers death'.[110] Unlike Spengler, Toynbee did not put a precise length of time on all civilizations, but like Spengler he assumed that the story of every civilization was the same – creative expansion, mechanistic consolidation, internal decay prompted by cultural stagnation, social division, and a final universal Caesarism.

The publication of the first three of Toynbee's volumes was an immediate success. Many of the reviews welcomed the attempt at last to give a solid scientific foundation to the wider discussion of what was wrong with civilization. 'The greatest intellectual need of our age', wrote the reviewer in the *Times Literary Supplement*, 'is a new interpretation of history.' The economic historian R. H. Tawney hailed it as one of those rare histories 'that change men's outlook on society and human life', full of 'fertility, vitality, energy, inexhaustible *élan*'.[111] Leonard Woolf described it as a work 'of the highest and greatest importance', though he chided Toynbee for the excessive use of metaphor and analogy for which he was notorious.[112] At Oxford University Press there was a sense that something momentous had occurred. A few weeks after the publication of the first three volumes George Clark came bustling into the Press offices to urge them to publish 'Toynbee's great work . . . an epoch-making formative work' in a single volume. Clark thought the central ideas 'will be wanted by a great many people', but he considered that the multiple volumes, with their endless examples and many Greek quotations, were outside the pocket and the grasp of most potential readers, as they almost certainly were.[113] The Press finally began to explore the possibility in 1939, shortly after the publication of the second set of volumes, though his editors were clear that Toynbee was not the man to undertake the abridgement, given his unfaltering capacity for writing at great length. The general view was that the *Study* would do for the current generation what Sir James Frazer's *Golden Bough* (a vast anthropological survey of religious practices and mythology published in twelve volumes between 1906 and 1915) had done for the generation before 1914; but only if Toynbee would agree to allow someone to cut it down to two volumes 'intelligently pruned and compressed'.[114]

By chance an assistant schoolmaster and historian at Tonbridge School, D. C. Somervell, had prepared an abridgement during the early years of the war without Toynbee's knowledge. Compressing the six volumes into a single span of just 589 pages, Somervell succeeded in turning Toynbee into a best-seller. The three volumes in 1939 had sold 1,290 sets in the first four months of wartime, in itself no mean achievement; the abridgement eventually sold 300,000 copies, testament to the survival of the pre-war appetite for accounts of the pathology of civilization.[115] In 1942 Somervell sent his manuscript to Toynbee and the corrected book, delayed by Toynbee's wartime service, was ready by 1945. Oxford University Press alerted their sister organization in New York to a book which already enjoyed 'immense prestige and reputation' worldwide, and, against all expectations, it became a Book-of-the-Month selection.[116] The same year Toynbee agitated for its publication in Germany, perhaps with an eye to Spengler's impact in Britain. The Political Intelligence division of the Foreign Office hoped to publish 5,000 copies for distribution in the British zone of occupation, but a more lucrative German contract was secured in 1946. A few years later Toynbee received a copy of a German review which found his *Study* 'something better, more fundamental, and more correct than Spengler'.[117]

Although the overwhelming bulk of Toynbee's *Study* was devoted to civilizations long dead, the popular interest in what Toynbee had to say rested on the present. He was reluctant to be drawn on predicting the future, but the whole thrust of his public life in the 1930s was devoted to applying his more general theory to the crisis of the contemporary world. Long before his three volumes on breakdown and disintegration were published in 1939, his views on the prospects

for the current age were well known. Indeed, the nature of the historical enterprise on which he had embarked implied that modern civilization was as vulnerable as any other. In this Toynbee both reacted to
the current anxieties and helped to shape them. It is difficult to think
of any intellectual of comparable public standing who did more to
undermine confidence in the survivability of Western civilization. In
a 1930 radio broadcast, for example, he warned listeners that war if
it came might be civilization's death blow, leaving mankind 'at the
bottom of the ladder of civilization once again'.[118] A lecture in 1932
compared the crisis of the world economy to the 'confusion that
followed the break-down of the Roman Empire'; in the absence of
international co-operation, Toynbee continued, the West would be
caught up in 'one social upheaval after another, in war after war and
in revolution after revolution' until a final knockout blow that would
leave, 'in the Roman manner', a peace of exhaustion.[119] In the 1937
Survey he lamented the prospect that war would produce the 'self-
annihilation' of civilization. The logic of his own description of the
past forced him to the conclusion that the modern world might well
'go smash' whether Britain liked it or not.[120]

Toynbee was caught in a web of his own making. Having defined
the laws that operated throughout history to explain the death of
civilizations, he realized that the world he saw around him very closely
resembled the process he had described of a 'time of troubles', which
heralded the final 'universal state' and the eclipse of the last of the
twenty-six definable civilizations. There is a shrill note of alarm in
much of what Toynbee wrote and said in the 1930s. His one real
fear was the universal state which had always heralded the end of a
civilization; the pretensions of European fascism, particularly of its
German variety, Toynbee came to regard as a very real threat. In a
letter to the military thinker Basil Liddell Hart in May 1938 he blamed
the current crisis on 400 years of moral and intellectual error in
supporting the idea of national sovereignty and Great Power politics.
He thought Mussolini probably right that dictatorship was here to
stay and he thought the most likely outcome the conquest of the world
by a single Great Power as Rome had done in the past: 'my conclusions
are gloomy,' he continued, 'but I have no belief at all in the possibility
of "getting by", as the Americans say, in the next act of the tragedy'

– a view that Liddell Hart wholeheartedly endorsed.[121] In May 1939 Toynbee delivered the annual Hobhouse lecture at the London School of Economics on the theme 'The Downfall of Civilisations'. He had been invited to give it two years before but had postponed acceptance because he was too busy completing the next volumes of his history. The change in timing allowed him to reflect on a subject that was, he claimed, 'unmistakably topical'. He explored the many ways in which an answer could be given to the question he set himself – is civilization 'predestined to collapse?' – and although he added the caveat that there was no inexorable law that it should, all the evidence suggested that sooner or later 'the modern Western Civilisation, in its turn is likely, on the showing of all the precedents . . . to break down and disintegrate and finally dissolve'.[122]

Between 1934, when the first volumes were published, and 1939, with the appearance of three more volumes on the collapse of civilization, Toynbee wrestled with the consequences of opening his Pandora's box. His solution to the terrible dangers inherent in the current crisis of civilization, whose destructive capabilities his theories endorsed, was to embrace Christianity as the key to humanity's survival. There was from the start a mystical or metaphysical element in Toynbee's approach to history. He told Arnold Wilson in 1931 that the story of civilization could be illuminated most clearly in Manichean terms – the idea of a conflict between 'the Church Militant and an opposition force'.[123] After Leonard Woolf accused him of 'mysticism' in his review of the first three volumes, Toynbee wrote to him to explain that his 'mystical attitude' was real enough: 'this has been growing on me rather – I think, through a gradual realisation of the contrariness of the world'. He told Woolf that in his own research he found himself 'coming up rather abruptly against something beyond which I can't probe'.[124] By the time the next three volumes were published he had worked out his own position more clearly. Religions featured a good deal in his grand narrative because they were institutions that transcended time and place. They were also the fount of all spiritual value without which, Toynbee came to believe, no civilization could survive and no new one emerge. For Western Christianity – which he always distinguished from the Orthodox Christian churches – he preserved a particular place, as the highest of the world's five great religious movements. To make bearable the possible collapse of Western civilization, Toynbee argued that a universal Christian society might succeed it.

This was an argument that he began to develop publicly during the 1930s, although it was never entirely clear where his denominational sympathies lay. In a pamphlet on 'Religion and Race' published by the Universal Christian Council in July 1935 he elaborated the dualistic struggle between good and evil as the struggle between fascist tribalism and transcendental Christianity. 'We may well believe', he wrote, 'that the outcome of this battle is going to be decisive for the earthly destinies of Mankind.' He painted a lurid picture of a contest that bridged time itself back to the struggles of the Christian Church to overcome the state religion of Rome and he called on Christians to hold fast to the ground won 'by prophets, saints and martyrs' in generations past.[125] In a sermon in the University Church in Oxford in 1940, after the outbreak of war, he told the congregation that the enemy were all idolaters who had abandoned the one true God. The war, he continued, was a total war not just in military terms but a fundamental 'war of the spirit' fought out 'inside every country, in every class, in every soul'. His knowledge of history, he concluded, persuaded him that the true God would in the end prevail.[126] The same year Toynbee gave the annual Burge memorial lecture in Oxford in which he assured the audience that even if Western civilization were to perish, Christianity would not only endure 'but would grow in wisdom and stature'.[127] When the Oxford University Press publicity department decided to release a 10-inch gramophone record of Toynbee talking about the genesis of the *Study* he ended it with the declaration that history 'is the unfolding of the purpose of God'.[128]

There is no doubt that Toynbee's anxieties about the survival of Christianity were the fruit of a personal crisis about the possibility that the real world might in an excess of folly and hubris extinguish the source of the spiritual fulfilment he was trying to find. In the mid-1930s he engaged in a correspondence with his fellow-historian at Oxford, George Clark, who was going through a deep spiritual crisis at the same time (in the end unexcitingly resolved by baptism into the Church of England). Toynbee told Clark how he, too, wrestled with his spiritual future, a process he described as slow,

Arnold Toynbee lecturing in Hamburg in 1947. His life's work on the history of civilizations was finally completed in 1954 by which time he had decided that only spiritual renewal could save the Western world.

laborious and painful. He sought solace in seeking what he called 'a larger spiritual world' in which could be found a satisfactory 'meaning and purpose' for existence, but he had little time for Anglicanism.[129] In the late 1930s he undertook occasional retreats to the Catholic abbey at Ampleforth in Yorkshire, where he had sent his son to school. In a letter written to the Benedictine community in January 1937 Toynbee confessed that he sought refuge because he was 'oppressed by a view of the world that one gets from studying international affairs' and hoped his sojourn would leave him refreshed and hopeful.[130] Lord Robert Cecil, president of the League of Nations Union, listening to Toynbee in a radio broadcast the same year thought he sounded 'like a Roman Cardinal'.[131]

The alteration in Toynbee's argument did not render the threat to civilization any less, but rather placed it in a different perspective. Gilbert Murray, after hearing the Burge lecture, thought his son-in-law had indulged in 'an amazing collapse of common sense'.[132] Reviewers and critics were in general puzzled by the shift from an implicit historical relativism to a renewed idealism in which Toynbee now claimed that history had a progressive design after all in 'the generation and development of one true religion'.[133] Roger Lloyd, reviewing volumes IV to VI of the *Study* for the *Quarterly Review* in 1940, thought that Toynbee was the St Augustine of the modern age and that his history would be found on the same shelf in the world's library as *The City of God*, a book that Toynbee much admired. Lloyd thought that any Christian fighting despair, as Toynbee, according to his introduction, had fought despair, should be heartened by Toynbee's triumph over the devils of temptation and his discovery of 'assurance and hope' in history.[134] Toynbee went on after the war to a career preaching the need for a Christian universalism as the only hope in a world in which mankind faced the awesome reality that annihilation now lay in its own hands in the shape of nuclear weapons. By the time the final volumes of the *Study* were published in 1954 Toynbee had abandoned the original classification of civilizations and assumed that the so-called higher religions, now twelve in number, were central to understanding human development and the search for a spiritual universality. He later began to explore Hinduism and Buddhism as pathways to spiritual peace. In a volume of *Reconsiderations* published in 1961 Toynbee wrote that it was still impossible to be clear about whether Western civilization would perish, but it was certain that Western society had to rediscover 'the essence of religion' without which human beings cannot exist.[135] This was, in bare outline, the central message of Albert Schweitzer's Dale lectures forty years before.

The great narratives of history are a phenomenon of the inter-war years. For all the criticisms they generated then and since they represented an attempt to apply historical science to an understanding of the present age and were popularly understood to be so. Although neither Spengler nor Toynbee claimed to be a pessimist in pursuing their universal histories, no one reading either narrative or the discussions surrounding them could be left in any doubt that by analogy the current civilization of the Western world would observe the same rules of historical development and eventual degeneration as all previous civilizations. The effort to construct a science of historical development from Hegel through Marx to Toynbee only made sense as a commentary upon the present. The relativist and cyclical character of the new forms of historical explanation differed from the nineteenth century's only because they gave the modern Western civilization no special dispensation as the triumphant apogee of world historical development but instead suggested that the current crises could be understood as the final manifestation of a process of stagnation and decay that went back hundreds of years. The chief characteristic of this form of historical argument was to suggest that modern society was doomed *a priori* to collapse, whatever might take its place. Although Toynbee refused to accept that this was the logic of his argument, it is an obvious explanation for why he was given so extensive a public hearing in the 1930s. Moreover, the greater the degree of historical elaboration and sophistication, the more the decline of civilization assumed in the wider public mind a scientific certainty. Spengler's *Decline*, wrote Lawrence Jacks in 1940, presented man as 'a *fated* being'.[136]

This approach to human destiny had its counterpart in the world of the natural sciences. The popularization in the 1920s of the notion of entropy, for example, undermined any sense of certainty or durability about the wider universe. Derived from the second law of thermodynamics, entropy could be used to describe any physical state which tended towards stasis, degeneration and extinction. Applied to the universe, it suggested that whatever human beings did, their world was doomed to disappear in the cosmic future. In 1920 Joseph McCabe, a former monk turned popular author, published a book with the timely title *The End of the World* which gave a simplified account of recent developments in astronomy to show that, despite unresolved arguments about the origins and sustainability of the universe as a whole, there was no doubt that eventually the sun would end its life as a star. 'The law of the individual globe is death,' concluded McCabe.[137] The idea of entropy was easily taken over as a scientific metaphor for the apparent decay of modern civilization. In 1929 Ernest Guest published *At the End of the World: A Vision*, a self-conscious parable of the final geological end of the earth. It had strong echoes of H. G. Wells, whose own vision of possible extinction became more marked in his writings of the 1930s. Guest imagined a world in which 'the minds of even the most thoughtless were turned towards thoughts of ultimate things' as the earth cooled down and the strength of the sun waned. The earth was doomed to live 'continuously dying' until, in the ultimate night, seas froze, the land became barren and 'the last warmth quivered slowly from the entrails of the earth', all in the view of a pitiless God.[138] In 1931 Dean Inge explored 'the religious and philosophical implications of the Law of Entropy' in the first of his Warburton lectures given at Aberystwyth University in Wales. He explained that the astronomical certainty of the death of the solar system had echoes in the collapse of confidence in progress in all areas of the human sciences, a paradigm for the current 'century of disillusionment', but he puzzled over the divine plan that might now condemn the world to 'universal doom'. Perhaps God, he concluded, had had other purposes all along.[139]

In explaining the regular and extensive mobilization of general metaphors of decline and fall that characterized the inter-war years it is evident that more than the anxieties generated by the Great War and the slump were at work. Looking back at the 1920s and 1930s it might be asked what function the mythic portrayal of crisis performed in a country where the horrors of war, revolution, civil war and crude authoritarianism were always perceived at a distance rather than directly experienced. There were certainly other ways beyond regular invocations of the end of civilization through which these issues could have been addressed. These collective anxieties were shaped to some extent by the seductive power of other myths propagated in the post-war world about the nineteenth century, the 'rosy predictions' of the 'Century of Hope', as Inge called them in his lecture, which were used as a reference point against which to measure the imperfect present.[140] But there is also an argument to be made that the generation that experienced the war and survived it needed a special language and conceptual approach to describe what seemed to them the unique nature of their suffering and their profound insecurity about the nature of the contemporary world. Arnold Toynbee described this exaggerated sense of self-importance, which he readily acknowledged applied as much to himself as to his peers, in a radio broadcast in 1931: 'In our generation, we are conscious of being swept along on a stream of dizzily rapid change ... and if, instead, the current is going to carry us over a precipice, then we are convinced that our precipice is anyhow going to be the greatest fall of man there has ever been – a very Niagara . . . The crash of Modern Civilisation! Why, that will lick creation!'[141] Just as a crowd gathers dismayed but fascinated to watch a disastrous fire, so the inter-war intelligentsia wanted to be at the front of the throng of onlookers if civilization crashed, even if few wanted the disaster to happen to them.

Some contemporary writers saw in this exalted sense of doom a shifting attitude towards the idea of death itself which was approached with a degree of morbid contemplation less characteristic of the pre-war era, 'a society with an orientation towards death', as one scientist put it.[142] The theme of death also ran through the lecture series and journal literature of the inter-war years. 'Why Not Commit Suicide?' asked C. DeLisle Burns in 1924 at the South Place Ethical Society, as he analysed the current mood of 'disgust' with life.[143] Two articles in the *Hibbert Journal*, one on 'The Meaning of Death' in 1934 and one simply entitled 'Death' three years later, explored the fashionable obsession with death as end or renewal, metaphor for an age.[144] The reasons for this enhanced morbidity may perhaps be found in the experience of the war, but there is also a sense in which it became simply an overriding intellectual fashion, easily communicated through the growing media networks, powerfully attractive and not necessarily superficial, as one writer after another competed to explain the nature of the current malaise and publishers and the public indulged and colluded with them. These explanations were not generally expressed as universal narratives like those of Spengler or Toynbee, but focused on fragments of the crisis – the death of capitalism, or race suicide, or the decline of rationalism, or annihilation in war, or the triumph of political extremism. Each of these elements is explored in detail in the chapters that follow. They are sub-texts of the larger text made intellectually fashionable in inter-war Britain on the decline and probable fall of a particular conception of modern civilization at a moment in history of unstable transition and widespread social anxiety.

2

The Death of Capitalism

Get there if you can and see the land you once were proud to
own,
Though the roads have almost vanished and the expresses
never run:
Smokeless chimneys, damaged bridges, rotting wharves and
choked canals,
Tramlines buckled, smashed trucks lying on their side across
the rails;
Power-stations locked, deserted, since they drew the boiler
fires;
Pylons fallen or subsiding, trailing dead high-tension
wires . . .

W. H. Auden, 1930[1]

For anyone on the left in British politics in the two decades after the end of the Great War the crisis of civilization was handcuffed to the long-expected death of the capitalist system. The obituaries were, as it turned out, written in indecent haste but at the time a great deal of British opinion, across the class divides, believed on the basis of the evidence all around them that capitalism's days were numbered. In 1922 Beatrice and Sidney Webb, doyens of the British intellectual left, wrote a short book on the spectacular rise and eventual collapse of British capitalism. The provisional title was to be 'The Reign of Capitalism', which may have been meant to convey the idea that here was a system ripe for abdication, but its evident ambiguity perhaps persuaded Sidney Webb a few weeks before publication to alter it to

'The Decay of Capitalist Civilisation', which conveyed its central message directly.[2] The book was to be published jointly by the Fabian Society and the commercial publisher George Allen & Unwin. There were arguments with the Scottish printers over the quality and thickness of the paper; Beatrice fussed about the colour of the cover, which she wanted in the same shade of dark blue as her other books (though as long as it was blue, she was prepared to compromise on a lighter variety). She got her way with the hardback, but the paperback emerged coated in a dull grey.[3] The first printing numbered 3,750 copies, but by the end of the year sales had reached over 15,000; the book remained in print down to the mid-1930s, when British capitalism had passed through the ordeal of the crash.[4]

The Webbs invited their fellow Fabian and playwright George Bernard Shaw to go over the introduction to make it a livelier read. In a choleric postcard to Beatrice, he protested that the book hardly needed a prologue and told Beatrice bluntly that what they had written for him to correct read like the words of 'a rather bored chairman opening a meeting'. He also disliked the new title for the book, and thought the change 'the d—dest nonsense'. As an afterthought he scribbled at the foot of the card that 'The decay is pretentious enough to suggest Gibbonesque pondorosity'.[5] Nevertheless, he obliged Beatrice by removing some of the platitudes and padding of their original version, and injected into the introduction a more arresting sense of the terminal crisis faced by the modern age. He sensibly cut out 'we must at least admit the possibility, and even, as some might say, the practical certainty' and replaced it with the categorical assertion that capitalist civilization 'is dissolving before our eyes'. The Webbs' conclusion, which by any standard was limp and verbose, he deleted in full, replacing it with a second prediction that capitalism, which had 'begun to decay before it reached maturity', would be viewed by historians of the future as little more than an episode, 'a Dark Age' between two greater historical epochs.[6] This conclusion clearly did not satisfy the Webbs and they added a further three pages, burdened this time with the temporizing clauses and dull phrasing that Shaw had removed from the remainder.

Shaw much later in his long life insisted that he had neither seen nor discussed the book before it was published, perhaps because his judgement on it was a sour one: 'I thought the book should have gone much further,' he wrote to Eric Bentley, a Shaw biographer, in 1948, 'and ranked it their least thought out book.'[7] It was certainly a book written for the moment, a response to the chaotic economic conditions of the first post-war years of mass unemployment, inflation, trade crisis and revolutionary violence. The week it came out Beatrice noted in her diary that the book 'ought certainly to be timely'; she found crisis infectious, the morbid contemplation of decay affecting her own never very robust disposition. 'I become every day more pessimistic: more fearful that present generations of men are agents of destruction, not construction,' she continued, 'through their inevitable ignorance and bad will they are heading for a long period of disorder.'[8] A month later, in February 1923, 'haunted by the nearness of death' she observed how Sidney's revised title had helped to boost sales: 'who can dispute that civilisation is decaying, and who can deny that it is Capitalist?'[9] Metaphors of the organic collapse of capitalism carried over into the book itself. The Webbs summed up the components of capitalist crisis as a fatal combination of 'morbid growths and insidious diseases'. When Beatrice was invited to talk about the future of capitalism on the radio a few years later, in 1932, she took as her theme 'The Diseases of the capitalist system' with all the 'defects' and 'perversions' that the disease-riddled body of modern civilization struggled to alleviate.[10]

The central thesis of The Decay was a sustained indictment not only of the irrational character of a system based on naked profit-seeking, which pushed the worker into penury or unemployment and left the capitalist forced to seek other outlets for goods in imperial adventures or war, but above all of the moral bankruptcy of capitalism. It was this, the Webbs believed, that constituted Marx's most important contribution to the debate on the nature of capitalism. His economics (full of 'pretentious blunders') had done little to serve the socialist cause; but Marx 'called the moral bluff of capitalism' and it was this ethical enlightenment, argued the Webbs, that capitalism could never extinguish. The danger that this moral crisis provoked was the anger of the saboteur – the curiously archaic term used to define the modern anti-capitalist revolutionary – which the Webbs feared might sweep away everything: 'capitalism need not hope to die quietly in its bed; it will die by violence, and civilisation will perish with it.'[11] They preferred the path they had mapped out as good social democrats, where municipal ownership and regulation, an effective co-operative movement and trade union organization, and the 'systematic prevention of destitution' would slowly transform capitalism into something institutionally and morally distinct. From the decrepit, diseased form of capital would sprout a reinvigorated and healed community of rational and virtuous collaborators. If both sides chose instead to sabotage the path to social health, the result would threaten 'the existence of civilisation'. It was this stark choice, the Webbs concluded, that had prompted them after thirty years of work to finally frame 'an indictment of the capitalist system'.[12]

Beatrice Webb at her desk in 1926. She became increasingly convinced in the inter-war years that civilization was in decline. Present generations, she wrote in her diary in 1923, 'are heading for a long period of disorder'.

The notion that capitalism was in a state of physical, possibly fatal decay became embedded in popular perception of the economic system. How much of that perception was due to the Webbs is difficult to gauge. They were by all accounts an unusual talent. In a generous profile of his lifelong friends Shaw declared them to be 'a superextra-ordinary pair'. He thought that 'only England could have produced them', and they were English to the core. They were an oddly matched couple. Martha Beatrice Potter was tall, slender and conventionally beautiful, the daughter of a wealthy industrialist who came to her socialism, as Shaw described it, 'self-made'.[13] As a young woman she fell in love with the politician Joseph Chamberlain but could not tolerate his attitude towards a woman's household duties. She hesi-tated to marry Sidney after he had asked her and there remains speculation to this day that their marriage in 1892 was never consum-mated. In the second volume of her autobiography she gave a glaringly candid assessment of the man she shared her life with for fifty years. Beatrice was characteristically snobbish, 'full of hatreds and class prejudices', as Shaw put it; Sidney Webb was a shopkeeper's son whose wide intelligence must have been, Beatrice reflected, 'a physio-logical freak' and whose background she regarded as thoroughly lower-middle class. She considered Sidney cursed with 'ill-looks': 'his big head, bulgy eyes, bushy moustaches and square-cut short beard, small but rotund body, tapering arms and legs, and diminutive hands and feet' made, she concluded, a ridiculous impression.[14] They were united by their joint dedication to ameliorating the lot of the poor and disadvantaged by encouraging scientific administration and co-operative endeavour, loyal partners in fighting injustice and incompet-ence. They took to this task with unyielding severity; self-disciplined, remorselessly industrious, overflowing with certainty, they were a formidable research team. They ended their honeymoon at the Trades Union Congress in Glasgow and would not have found this odd. 'Why', asked Arnold Toynbee in a book of memoirs, 'did the Webbs acquire a reputation for not being human?'[15]

They were more human than their reputation. Sidney was affable but a poor speaker who could not tolerate small-talk; he was, Beatrice re-called, 'always happy'. His unselfconscious, almost childlike optimism was the counterpoint to Beatrice's poor health and what she described as her 'morbid ways'. He was an emotional simpleton; she was, re-called Kingsley Martin, editor of the *New Statesman*, the journal founded by the Webbs in 1913, 'a complex mixture of class superi-ority, intellectual impatience and puritanical morals'.[16] Sidney became an MP and a Labour minister in the 1920s, but Beatrice, for all her scarcely concealed 'love of power', as Martin put it, remained out of the public limelight, uncertain that politics, rather than sound scientific administration, ever achieved anything. In the 1930s the pair retired to their country house at Passfield Corner in Hampshire, where a stream of distinguished visitors made their way to be regaled by Beatrice and Sidney on the serious issues of the day from breakfast until midnight. All opinions were prefaced by 'we think' rather than 'I', testament to the extent to which the two minds had over the years grown to work as one. When Sidney was absent, Beatrice confessed, she was haunted 'by the dread of life without him'.[17]

This remarkable partnership was already ripe by the time *The Decay of Capitalist Civilisation* was published. Its wide currency reflected their intellectual stature. The book, wrote Kingsley Martin, expressed much of what came to be believed by British socialists 'in the next twenty years'.[18] Henry Massingham, editor of the *Nation* until 1923 when it merged with the *New Statesman*, wrote to tell Beatrice that the book expressed such an extraordinary 'concentrated power' in its assault on capitalism that it would become the classical indictment of the system.[19] The Webbs continued to argue the case that the decay of civilization was in progress through to their deaths in the 1940s. This was the theme of Beatrice's BBC talk in July 1930 on the crisis of democratic capitalism in which she surveyed the grim choice between 'catastrophic upheaval' and 'a slow decay' of living standards, health, culture and 'general civilisation'.[20] In 1931, at the height of the slump, the Fabian Society debated its choice of a lecture course for that year. Beatrice wanted something along the lines of 'The Decline of Capitalist Civilisation' so as to include a lecture on the Soviet experiment as a complete instance of the decline and fall of capitalism (though she also hoped a lecture course with that title would finally clear the remaining 600 copies of *The Decay* held by the Society).[21] The final title of the lecture series was 'Capitalism in Dissolution. What Next?', which seemed in the context of 1931 a not unreasonable premise. By 1938 the Society had just six copies of the book left.[22] In 1937, when the publisher Allen Lane asked Sidney Webb to consider reissuing some of the Webbs' out-of-print titles, Sidney suggested *The Decay of Capitalist Civilisation* because it had a more 'taking title' than the history of the Consumers' Co-operative Movement. Lane resisted the opportunity in favour of issuing Beatrice Webb's autobiography in two volumes.[23] Two years later, shortly after the outbreak of war, Beatrice wrote to a friend that she and Sidney had devoted their lives to studying the 'Christian capitalist political democracies' that defined Western civilization: 'I am sure', she continued, 'that civilisation is on the down grade, and I think it will gradually, and violently, disappear . . .' Sidney for once did not share these gloomy views. Beatrice added in a letter a week later that Sidney was 'very well and happy' and 'believes that all will be well eventually . . .'[24]

The Webbs were part, and an important part, of the intellectual quest in the 1920s and 1930s to explain why capitalism in its existing free-market form was a doomed system. The motif of decay, of something rotting like an unfilled tooth or a gangrenous limb, became the stock-in-trade of capitalism's detractors. The Oxford economist G. D. H. Cole echoed the Webbs' argument about the 'inherent rottenness' of the capitalist order, but like them he also feared that the gradual process of decay might produce, instead of socialism, simply a ruined civilization.[25] J. A. Hobson, one of the best-known popularizers of economic issues, spent much of his career analysing what he called in a pamphlet in 1932 'The seeds of decay in Capitalism'.[26] But it was also a view that infected the outlook of those whose credentials were anything but politically radical or revolutionary. The fear that the capitalist order might decline or perish entirely unless some cure could be found for its evident failings was nourished on the difficulties faced by the developed world in adjusting to the changed post-war economic realities of uneven patterns of growth, an underlying residue of high levels of unemployment and poor trade performance. In a lecture given in 1920, the economist Sir George Paish warned his audience that the selfish motives that had been the motor force of the pre-war capitalist order could not be allowed to continue unchecked: 'I ask: Upon what am I as an Economist to base my calculations? If you tell me that I am to continue to base them on selfishness, then I would reply that the selfishness of the world will increase; it will be no new world, but one relapsed into anarchy and barbarism.'[27]

The wide belief that the capitalist order was no longer capable of functioning as it had done before 1914 derived from the great confidence hitherto placed in the self-regulating character of all markets, large and small. The classical view that the principle of *laissez faire* would, on balance, always tend to the wider benefit of any community was possible only because of the special conditions that shaped the emergence of developed commercial and industrial states in Europe, and the special place played by the British economy in stabilizing the international trading and financial markets around the popular rallying cry of Free Trade. After 1919, following the wartime experience of large-scale state mobilization of resources, there emerged a less favourable economic climate in which the state was required to play a larger role in order to try to maintain stability or to encourage growth. There nevertheless survived from the pre-war age a strong aversion among politicians and businessmen to challenging market principles in any direct way. The consequence of this attitude, according to John Maynard Keynes, the Cambridge economist who rose to sudden fame after condemning the economic demands enshrined in the Versailles settlement, was to produce a period of unstable change or 'disequilibrium'. Reflecting on a visit to the Soviet Union in 1925, Keynes argued that his generation 'used to think that modern capitalism was capable, not merely of maintaining the existing standards of life, but of leading us gradually into an economic paradise . . .' He gave his Soviet audience what perhaps they wanted to hear when he told them, 'I direct all my mind and attention to the development of new methods and new ideas for effecting the transition from the economic anarchy of the individualistic capitalism which rules today in Western Europe.'[28] In the 1920s, according to another Cambridge economist, A. C. Pigou, Britain's economy arrived in 'the Doldrums', becalmed and stagnant, unable to sail back to old-fashioned capitalism, but unable to move forward to a healthier economic climate.[29]

The wider public attitude to the economy reflected these uncertainties. Popular approval of *laissez faire* was the fruit of decades of economic and political practice from the mid-nineteenth century, when Free Trade came to symbolize the emergence not only of modern consumerism but also of a progressive civil society.[30] Although the economic reality of government intervention and corporate pressure was a fact of post-war life, the idea of the free market as the measure of economic health survived fitfully into the 1920s. There was nevertheless a wide expectation that new economic mechanisms were necessary and wide interest in economic arguments. By the 1930s capitalist crisis was debated in a range of educational and institutional contexts. For workers there was the network of Labour Colleges, united in 1921 into a National Council of Labour Colleges, which by 1930 had 1.7 million members affiliated from the trade union movement. The movement made no attempt to disguise the view that capitalism was decaying. The president of the council in 1931, in the annual address, told his audience that the current crisis exposed a system whose business leaders behaved 'like lunatics' or 'Gadarene swine' rushing to perdition: 'The malady of capitalism', he continued, 'is mortal.'[31] The Workers' Educational Association, founded in 1903 by Albert Mansbridge, was another forum for the discussion of the crisis of capitalism. Its journal *Highway* sold 20,000 copies by the end of the 1930s, substantially more than *The Plebs*, published by the Labour Colleges, which sold a healthy 8,000. University lecturers and teachers took time in the evenings and at weekends to explain the nature of current issues, and to encourage critical debate.[32] Economic issues in particular, as one economist complained in the 1930s, were precisely the ones which the wider public felt able to address because they did not regard economics as a science like physics or biology, but something which 'everyone thinks he has a right to understand'.[33] In reality by the 1920s and 1930s economic science was every bit as sophisticated and intellectually complex as the natural sciences; it was also a science that had no clear answers, 'a festering mass of assumptions', as H. G. Wells unkindly put it.[34] The economy, Keynes admitted during the economic downturn of the early 1930s, was not well understood even by professional economists, 'a frightful muddle, a transitory and *unnecessary* muddle'.[35] One consequence was a growing divorce between what many academic economists were writing for each other and the popular public discourse on the future of capitalism. The debate over the decay or otherwise of capitalism came to rely much more on a generation of economic thinkers who were capable of presenting in comprehensible or practical terms the more abstruse scholarship produced by their peers.

For the wider public a key concern was to discover the reason, or reasons, for the apparent crisis of capitalism and, by implication, the prospects for its survival or transformation. It might be assumed that most people in the early part of the twentieth century who sought answers to these questions found them in the writing of the German economist Karl Marx, who spent much of his working life in London until his death in 1883. An English edition of the first volume of his major work *Capital* was prepared by his collaborator Friedrich Engels in 1886, with the help of Marx's daughter Eleanor and her partner Edward Aveling, and was regularly republished.[36] It finally appeared in a new translation in 1930 by Eden and Cedar Paul, with an introduction by G. D. H. Cole. The new version, the publishers claimed, finally removed 'all obstacles between Marx's theories and the general public'.[37] But *Capital* was, as Cole remarked, a difficult book for the general reader, its technical language and style of argument made worse by the original translation which made it 'at all points difficult to read', and in some 'almost unintelligible'.[38] Marx was more familiar as the author of pamphlets sold in cheap editions for a few pence, including the *Communist Manifesto*, *Wage-Labour and Capital* and *Value, Price and Profit*, which relayed more straightforwardly two central ideas: that the state represented the interests of the dominant economic elite and that capitalism survived only by creaming off 'surplus value' from a workforce always paid less for its work than the value of the goods it produced. Neither of these ideas was particularly original or difficult to grasp, but the stature that Marx gained in his lifetime made his description of capitalism seem sufficiently compelling. Nonetheless, *Capital* was almost certainly a book more often bought than read; nor was Marx's economic theory regarded kindly by most academic economists. In Britain economic theory critical of the existing system was largely home grown, and it relied not only on explaining why capitalism was inherently flawed but also on why it was ethically unacceptable.

Among the best known of Britain's original economic thinkers was John A. Hobson. He arrived at his views on the essential contradictions in the capitalist system that doomed it to decay, so he claimed, before he was aware of Marx's *Capital*, which he read for the first time in 1887. He later acknowledged that Marx had indeed preceded him, but he was never, he told an audience in 1932, 'a full-blooded Marxist', disliking what he regarded as the narrow egalitarianism of Marx's socialism.[39] Many of Hobson's views coincided with Marx's critical understanding of what Hobson described as 'the vices in the profiteering system', but the mature economic and social arguments promoted by Hobson also differed substantially from Marx's historical-philosophical understanding of the transition from one mode of production to the next. Marx's dialectical reasoning he dismissed, according to his friend Henry Brailsford, as 'frivolous pedantry'.[40]

Hobson was born in Derby in 1858, the son of the Liberal owner of a local newspaper. He began to study what was then known as 'political economy' before he went up to Oxford, where he read classics, a subject he went on to teach at a number of public schools. He soon returned to his interest in economics and in 1889 published *The Physiology of Industry* jointly with the eccentric mountaineer Arthur Mummery, whom he had met while teaching in Exeter and whose amateur views on economics shaped Hobson's own theory. Keynes later described the book as 'an epoch in economic thought', though he privately believed Mummery to have been the real inspiration behind it.[41] Hobson became a well-known journalist and an active speaker, particularly for the South Place Ethical Society, originally founded in 1793 by the politician Charles Fox but re-founded as a forum for ethical rationalism in 1888, where he lectured for more than thirty years. Over his long life he authored thirty-seven books, but thanks to the early hostility of the profession he never held an academic post or received academic honours for his contributions to theory. He was by all accounts a man of high moral principle who displayed an intense rationalism and humanism. In 1914 he helped to found the Union of Democratic Control, which campaigned for a just negotiated peace and a people's foreign policy, and became its chairman until his death in 1940. Kingsley Martin, who succeeded him, remembered a 'rare person' never embittered by his lack of public success, intellectually honest, and possessed of a 'rare staccato wit'. In a memorial to Hobson written just after his death, the philosopher and radio personality Cyril Joad recalled one of Hobson's best-known aphorisms: 'The Englishman always finds it easy to forgive those he has wronged.'[42]

Hobson's economic theories are best remembered for the concept of 'under-consumption' which he championed from the 1890s

The economist and political thinker J. A. Hobson, pictured in 1910. He pioneered the ideas of the mixed economy and the welfare state and deplored the irrationality and waste of the existing capitalist system.

through to the 1930s as the centrepiece of what was in effect a more wide-ranging and radical analysis of the capitalist system. Hobson argued that there existed a perpetual imbalance in capitalism between the capacity to produce goods and the capacity of ordinary people to consume them. This imbalance was due to the maldistribution of income: the rich saved too much and used their wealth either to invest in yet more capital goods (machines, factories etc.), or spent it on luxuries, or unproductive speculation; the rest of the population had too little money to consume all that the system could produce so that periodically the rich stopped investing and created the conditions for mass unemployment and economic recession. The phenomena of over-saving and under-consumption explained, according to Hobson, 'a fatal flaw in the capitalist system'.[43] Capitalism in its unregulated, *laissez-faire* complexion could not from its very nature produce either maximum productivity or full employment but laboured instead under the paradox of 'poverty in the midst of plenty'. Hobson did not accept the socialist argument that the excess income should simply be taken from the rich and given to the poor but insisted that the issue was 'want of proportion', that a larger share of the national income should go to consumption and a smaller share to the generation of new forms of production.[44]

Hobson's argument was not generally accepted by academic econ-omists as it stood, but it enjoyed, as Cole admitted in his *Guide Through World Chaos*, written in 1932, 'the largest following' among the wider public eager for comprehensible accounts of capitalist crisis (and has been taken more seriously in recent years by historians of economic thought).[45] One of the reasons for its popularity was the emphasis Hobson placed on the moral implications of his economics. A more rational proportion between consumption and saving was the key for millions to the enjoyment of greater welfare and leisure. He called this 'the vital income' element in economics, the possibility of leading a desirable life in all its aspects.[46] A free existence, he wrote in *Wealth and Life* in 1929, means liberating human energies for 'love and friendship, knowledge and thought, joy and beauty', all goods, he concluded, that are neither marketable nor consumed.[47] Although he left the Liberal Party during the Great War and later joined the Labour Party (but 'never felt quite at home in it'), Hobson's broader social philosophy owed much more to the nineteenth-century writing of J. S. Mill and John Ruskin, who placed emphasis on creating conditions for the enjoyment of the good life. Hobson thought indi-vidual liberty an essential element in creating 'the art of life', but believed that only the social control of production could ensure that every individual had the opportunities for leisure and liberty that they deserved. The combination of his commitment to welfare, freedom and economic reform made him by the 1920s, according to Brailsford, 'the most respected intellectual influence in the Labour Movement'.[48] His approach to transcending market capitalism by a form of demo-cratic socialism was evolutionary, 'a more gradual and discriminative socialism', which involved limited nationalization of socially impor-tant industries and utilities, reform of the tax system, the regulation of monopoly and the provision of adequate welfare to meet the needs of the disadvantaged, but which allowed market mechanisms to survive.[49] The costs of welfare and limited state control were to be met from part of the large surplus that accrued to the rich and which so distorted the conditions of capitalist society. 'The primary object of all social-economic reform', Hobson argued, 'should be to dissipate this surplus.'[50]

Hobson's views on the inevitability of capitalist crisis were neither strident nor politically charged but appealed because of their common-sense simplicity and firm moral commitment. By the 1930s, however, Hobson came to doubt the capacity of the system to reform itself, and grew more pessimistic. The lack of will to confront the root cause of capitalism's incapacity provoked, Hobson thought, 'a sense of impotence and apathy', a belief that 'irresistible natural forces' were responsible for economic misery when they were the product in his view of the abuse of nature by groups of 'economic and political potentates'. The widespread realization that governments were hopelessly incompetent to manage decaying capitalism provoked, he thought, 'a spirit of bewilderment and despair'.[51] In 1932 he wrote a sharp satire on the current impasse in the form of a report back to Heaven delivered by a messenger who had returned to Earth after a century's absence. In *The Recording Angel*, Hobson has the messenger explain the crisis in simple under-consumption terms, to which the angel responds, 'But this is sheer lunacy.' When he asks the messenger whether the prophets, 'men called economists', cannot save the Earth, the messenger replies: 'Unfortunately the Adversary has displayed his cunning by putting a lying spirit into the mouth of most of the prophets, so that they still prophesy smooth things for Capitalism.'[52] Hobson did not live long enough to witness the Labour victory of 1945 and the adoption of the sort of mixed economy and welfare economics that he had so long advocated.

G. D. H. Cole thought that Hobson paid too little attention to the question of how economies recovered from periodic slumps, although he accepted that Hobson's central thesis on under-consumption was 'undeniable'.[53] Cole was an original thinker in his own right, and like Hobson a clever popularizer. He was best known for pioneering the idea of 'Guild Socialism' before the Great War, which advocated the self-government of industry by associations of workers and managers.

The National Guilds League which Cole helped to inspire split up after the war over issues of revolutionary practice, but Cole remained a champion of a more democratic industrial system.[54] Like Hobson, Cole was a prodigious worker, who became in the inter-war years one of the country's best-known economists thanks to his regular journalism, broadcasting and lecturing and the publication of two widely read volumes, *The Intelligent Man's Guide Through World Chaos* written in 1932, which sold 50,000 copies, and in 1935 *The Intelligent Man's Review of Europe Today*. Like Hobson too, Cole was a socialist critical of important aspects of the body of Marx's writing, particularly the tendency to see not individuals but abstract 'class' entities operating as units of social power. Marx's theory of value was again an abstraction, 'a useless theory in the air'. Cole thought that the core of Marx's thinking was the idea of 'surplus value', which differed little in principle from Hobson's argument that the rich get too much and the poor too little.[55]

Cole was an academic economist at Oxford where he preached a socialism influenced by Marx but derived from the special conditions that existed in British economic development. He also addressed the paradox of 'poverty in the midst of plenty' as the most perplexing of capitalist contradictions, and he too did not differ greatly in his view of how this contradiction arose and how it might be resolved from the model suggested by Hobson. He dated the malfunctioning of the capitalist economy to the early 1900s, when the rapid growth of living standards came abruptly to a halt to be followed by long years of stagnant or declining real income. This decline occurred, Cole argued in an essay on 'The Changing Economic Order', despite the increased capacity of industry to turn out more and more goods and services with ever increasing efficiency: 'this potential increment of wealth', he wrote, 'was failing to pour itself out over the people in the good old way.'[56] This contradiction between the expanding powers of production and the reality of unemployment and penury was due chiefly to the urgent safeguarding of profit. 'We cannot consume what we could produce,' Cole continued, 'not because our mouths or bellies are too small, but because we cannot afford the prices.' Capitalism, Cole concluded, was now 'unprogressive, stationary', faced with the 'negation of its expanding powers', though capable nonetheless of living in its senile state for some time. Cole believed with Hobson and the Webbs that a large change was needed if the survival of civilization were to be secured, but he also shared their pessimism that the world might be laid in ruins by political violence or war before social democracy could triumph. If this happened, he warned, the 'waters of annihilation' would close over 'the very civilisation of which we are the products, the heirs, and the responsible trustees'.[57]

Even those who championed an unadorned Marxism in the 1920s owed something to Hobson. One of the earliest academic recruits to communism was the precocious young Cambridge economist Maurice Dobb. In an undergraduate essay written during the 1919/20 academic year for his tutor in Pembroke College, Dobb wrote portentously: 'The signposts of economic and social evolution point inevitably from Capitalism to Socialism and Communism.'[58] This was a belief from which he never wavered, and it simplified his own answers as to why capitalism was doomed to collapse. Dobb was the son of a successful north London draper who, like so many recruits to communism, attended public school and then Cambridge. In between the two he spent a year in London, where he became involved with the labour movement and read both Marx and Hobson. He founded the Cambridge University Labour Club in 1920, but in 1922, while working at the London School of Economics, he joined the Camden branch of the Communist Party. He became a university lecturer in economics in Cambridge in 1924, and despite his political reputation was appointed a fellow of Trinity in 1948, where he worked until his death in 1976; the college tolerated his Marxism and he, evidently, tolerated its opulence.[59] Like Cole he wrote popular economic and political journalism and spoke often, but his theoretical output was small, confined largely to one book on *Political Economy and Capitalism* which he published in 1937.

Dobb was hostile to both Cole and Hobson for assuming that if wages could be raised and the proportion of consumption increased, crises would end. Hobson's 'under-consumption theory' he regarded as a 'crude misinterpretation of Marxism', although his own rough notes on the 'Decline of Capitalism' drafted around 1923 included the idea of 'under-productivity' and over-production alongside unemployment and poverty.[60] Dobb was convinced that British capitalism in the early 1920s had reached its final stage, but he based his analysis less on the economic contradictions of the economic process and more on the political implications of crisis – a view that he derived more readily from Lenin than from Marx. He saw capitalism weakened by monopoly practices, imperial rivalry and the collapse of the international monetary system. Faced with declining wealth, the capitalist class acted defensively, attacking labour, reducing wages and creating unemployment; the endpoint of capitalist crisis was revolutionary agitation followed by fascist repression, dictatorship and state centralization.[61] The only cure, Dobb thought, in another lecture drafted in the early 1920s, was to replace capitalist control with working-class control: 'Decline of capitalism is forcing organisation on class lines. Only hope is in power of working class to control industry.'[62] He was prepared to wait some time for this eventuality. In a lecture on British capitalism in 1934 he deprecated those communists who saw the final collapse of capitalism around every corner, and like most of the critics of capitalism, he assumed that the system might well limp on, decrepit though it had become. 'When one says Cap[italis]m in decline,' he wrote in his notes, 'one does not mean it in med[ical] sense – that there must be a regular unbroken downward curve.' The factors making for disequilibrium may be stronger and crises more 'acute, frequent and prolonged' but, citing Lenin, Dobb concluded that 'there is never no way out for capitalism – it all depends on workers'.[63]

Dobb's communism was unusual in the 1920s, more commonly shared in the 1930s after the slump gave visible encouragement to the idea that this was the final crisis. What all the critical theories of the 1920s had in common was the belief that capitalism had reached the limit of what it could usefully do and was now in some form of decay or decline, and that this crisis was a necessary and inevitable consequence of the way in which capitalism operated. The conditions of the British economic crisis in the 1920s, brought briefly to a head with the General Strike of 1926 and the short downturn in the business cycle that year, made the argument for decadence plausible, and it is significant that the idea of decline was widely embedded in public discussion of the economy well before the onset of the economic crash of 1929–32 lent overwhelming historical weight to the argument. The different strands of argument were also united by the pessimistic

A lecture poster for the Society for Cultural Relations with the Soviet Union, founded in 1924 to promote friendship between Britain and the new communist state. Maurice Dobb was among the foremost economists arguing the case for comprehensive planning even before the coming of the Soviet Five-Year Plans.

expectation that capitalism might either collapse before it could be usefully exploited by any system that succeeded it, or that the system in its death throes might provoke a terrible political backlash of fascistic dictatorship. In 'Thoughts on Our Present Discontents', Hobson defined fascism as the escape route for a bankrupt capitalist system, and although he hoped that democracy was sufficiently embedded to prevent dictatorship, he thought there was no necessary reason why capitalist civilization would be transformed into social democracy without violence.[64]

Nevertheless, the majority of economists in the decade which ended with the crash still favoured the self-regulating models of economic theory and believed they were confronting not the terminal crisis of capitalism but a period of post-war transition until normal trading and financial conditions could be restored, 'in one form or another a maladjustment', as it was put by an official at the Geneva Economic Conference of 1927.[65] Keynes, who was less convinced than his orthodox colleagues that the old order would ever return, looked back in May 1929 on a decade characterized in his view by a long period of stalemate 'when the general impulse has been to get back as far as possible to Pre-War situations', and a consequent 'reluctance to take risks or make experiments'.[66] Yet even Keynes, who developed a reputation in the 1920s for predicting short-term economic disaster, did not believe that capitalism was necessarily doomed, for all its conservatism. A few weeks after the Wall Street Crash which began on 29 October 1929 Keynes wrote an article on the 'British View' in which for once his prophetic sense deserted him entirely: 'There will be no serious direct consequences in London resulting from the Wall Street Slump,' he wrote. 'We find the look ahead decidedly encouraging.'[67]

The economic crisis that set in with the Wall Street Crash was in truth a worldwide economic and social catastrophe. Though Britain was less severely affected than the German and American economies, trade nevertheless fell by 50 per cent between 1929 and 1933, the output of heavy industry fell by one-third and at its peak in 1932 there were almost 3.5 million registered unemployed and millions more working short-time. The number of people out of work was still around 2 million in 1938. Knowledge of what had happened in other countries was widespread so that the recession was viewed not just as a national disaster but as a possibly terminal crisis of world capitalism. The economic crisis was the greatest single issue facing British society during the inter-war years, and became the reference point in the 1930s not just in discussions about the economic viability of capitalism but in all assessments of the future course of civilization. Keynes soon recovered his sense of judgement. In 1930, drafting notes for an article on 'The Great Slump', he observed that if the crisis went any deeper or lasted any longer, 'gold-standard capitalism will be shaken to its foundations'.[68] The mood of despair about the economic future was endemic, though not universal. In Cambridge, G. Lowes Dickinson, one of Keynes's colleagues at King's College, in one of the last entries in his journal before his death in 1932 observed that everyone was waiting for the crisis to develop into 'universal anarchy and war'. 'The capitalistic order', he continued, 'has broken down [so] completely and hopelessly . . .'[69]

Hostile critics derided this middle-class discourse of disaster. 'The worst cases', wrote the American psychologist Cavendish Moxon, 'cannot stop short of suicide. Some retreat to a private world of insanity. Others, more vigorous, merely relapse into some form of mysticism, spiritualism, or Christian Science.'[70] G. D. H. Cole observed around him the frantic efforts of 'common men and women', psychologically unhinged by the world crisis, to indulge in 'jazz, cabaret, night club and ineffectual philandering' to provide some ephemeral anchorage 'in a world where doubt is torment'.[71] The more credulous, Cole added, followed the teachings of the American Lutheran pastor Frank Buchman, whose worldwide association of devotees became known as the Oxford Group Movement in 1928 after a group of Oxford followers had toured South Africa. (Later still it became the Movement for Moral Rearmament.) The Buchman cult was based on the idea of 'life change' and confession of sin, which took place in large open sessions at 'house parties' (one in Oxford in 1936 had 10,000 disciples). Critics uncharitably imagined them to be home to unbridled decadence and sexual extravagance.[72] The Oxford theologian, B. H. Streeter, an early convert to Buchmanism, confessed that he was drawn to it 'by my despair of the world situation' and his hope that moral revivalism would create a new mental attitude 'in economic and political conflicts'.[73] Buchman offered the distracted middle classes in the 1930s some spiritual solace, what Moxon called 'a soothing sense of security to sick souls'. The Oxford Group was cruelly satirized in W. H. Auden's play-poem *The Dance of Death*, published in 1933: 'Europe's in a hole/ Millions on the dole/ But come out into the sun ... No more tearful days, fearful days ... Some of you think he loves you. He is leading you on.'[74]

The world depression confirmed the pessimists of the 1920s in the argument that the capitalist system was doomed from its own nature and that some other way of organizing the economic life of the country was in the long run unavoidable. In a series of articles on 'The Present Confusion' written in 1933 Cole expressed a view widely current that the intellectual case against capitalism had become 'overwhelmingly strong', strengthened daily, he thought, 'by the spectacle of economic and political futility which the capitalist world represents'. Cole was, of course, unabashedly partisan in his view. In the last articles in the series he argued that socialism was the only serious alternative in an age of 'sheer economic disaster' and 'the dissolution of European civilization'.[75] As the depression intensified during 1931 and 1932 the level of alarmism grew. Even the liberal Keynes, who insisted throughout the crisis that he remained optimistic about the long-term capacity of the system to survive, thought probably only communism could cure unemployment, though he did not like the prospect of building on what he called 'the vapours of misery and discontent'.[76] In an article for publication in the United States early in 1932, Keynes stated the case for an end to *laissez faire*: 'there will be no means of escape from prolonged and perhaps interminable depression except by direct State intervention'.[77] The idea that free-market capitalism no longer worked became a commonplace of the 1930s, in Europe and the United States as well as in Britain. In an article titled 'Has the Capitalist System Failed?', written in 1932, Beatrice Webb condemned the 'moral miasma' that choked the inhabitants of the country's industrial cities and doomed them to a life of vice: 'Breathing, from infancy up, an atmosphere of morbid alcoholism and sexuality, furtive larceny and unashamed mendacity, though here and there a moral genius may survive, saddened but unscathed – the average man is, mentally as well as physically, poisoned.'[78]

One of those rare 'moral geniuses' was the author Walter Greenwood, whose novel *Love on the Dole*, published in 1933, became an immediate best-seller. Few other cultural products of the slump reached so wide an audience or relayed the reality of capitalism's failure so successfully. For the progressive intelligentsia Greenwood's novel symbolized the idiocy of a system that condemned millions to the mundane reality of closed horizons and persistent poverty. Greenwood was a clerk in a textile firm in Salford in Lancashire, centre of the declining British cotton industry. Forced into unemployment, the 29-year-old Greenwood spent nine months supported by his mother and sister while he wrote a novel about the reality of life in the decaying heart of British commerce. The book was to be called 'The Lovers' but the title was changed to *Love on the Dole: A Tale of the Two Cities*, an alteration that surely transformed the book's prospects.[79] Greenwood sent the manuscript, written out in a clear, copperplate hand, to Jonathan Cape, who published the novel in June 1933. It had an immediate success, reprinted twice in July 1933 and again in December, with two reprints in April and October 1934. In 1935 a cheap edition was issued priced at 2/- instead of 7/6d so that it could reach a real mass market; this was reprinted four times that year, and again in 1936, 1938 and 1940.[80] Between 1933 and 1940 the book sold 46,290 copies, a best-seller by the standards of the 1930s.[81] In an interview in 1933 Greenwood explained that he wrote the book to expose 'the tragedy of a lost generation', but the quotation on the title page from the poet James Russell Lowell betrayed a wider purpose: 'The Time is ripe, and rotten ripe, for change;/ Then let it come . . .' Inside, in lieu of a preface, Greenwood added a medley of further quotations all with the same message of necessary redemption, including an extract from a D. H. Lawrence letter: 'you've got to smash money and this beastly possessive spirit. I get more revolutionary every minute, but for *life's* sake.'[82]

The novel's extraordinary success can be explained by its evident timeliness, but in the chorus of critical approval which followed its publication its literary merit was regarded as equally important. The poet Edith Sitwell wrote to Greenwood that in her view he was not only a born writer but a 'great writer'; Graham Greene wrote to congratulate him; the political scientist Harold Laski thanked him for producing not only 'a notable public service' but for making 'a distinguished contribution to letters'.[83] One reviewer applauded the absence of the 'chronic melancholy' of the fashionable literary set: 'These Lancashire folk wear a rue with a difference of which your Bloomsbury novelist knows nothing.'[84] The novel was a piece of unselfconscious realism, whose impact was magnified by the absence of propaganda or self-pity. The story was a simple morality tale set in a district of Salford, one of the two cities of the title. It centres on a family of ordinary workers where the men are rendered unemployed and rely on the earnings of the daughter of the household. Harry, the son, is sacked soon after he has made his girlfriend pregnant; Sally, the daughter, falls for a local Labour Party activist, Larry, who can't face the idea of marriage with no money. He dies after a vicious police attack on a crowd of protesting workers and Sally, the tragic heroine trapped in a moral dead end, abandons all hope by selling her chastity to a local businessman to get jobs for her father and brother. The characters all speak in a strong Lancashire dialect, faithfully repro-duced in the novel; the fine observation of working-class life in a derelict system was possible only because Greenwood had intimately shared the experience. The tone throughout reflects a bewildered and involuntary stoicism in the face of an unyielding fate; 'dismay', intones the narrator after Harry is denied the dole, 'was made all the more complete by the knowledge of their impotence. What could they do about it? What?'[85] A sympathetic reviewer remarked that the novel had a quality 'curiously like Dostoevsky', with the difference that in Dostoevsky it is human failings that doom the characters where in *Love on the Dole* it is the faceless 'economic set-up', more devastating and terrifying: 'here, from the first, we have no hope'.[86]

Greenwood became a celebrity overnight. The novel was published in the United States where, despite its grim subject and opaque dialect, it won renewed success – 'one of the most moving proletarian novels of our time', remarked a New York reviewer, 'a picture of real people living in conditions that are a disgrace to the human race'.[87] In an article for the *Spectator* on 'Poverty and Freedom' Greenwood wrote how he had spent hours in the local library dreaming he was part of humanity's 'epic struggle for its emancipation', until brought down to earth by the thought that a clerk on £2 a week could never make people see justice.[88] In fact his book brought readers face-to-face with the truth about social deprivation. The reviews, in papers and journals of widely differing political allegiance, reflected the horror of the educated classes as they confronted reality – 'the tragic sense of help-lessness', 'a fierce, brutal novel', 'deeply moving and distressing', 'a terrible novel of people caught in a trap, hopeless and helpless'. Even the conservative *Daily Telegraph* thought it the best book of its kind, written 'to stir the public conscience'.[89] In 1934 the book was turned into a stage play, co-authored with the playwright Ronald Gow. Over one million people attended the various provincial runs before it moved to London, where it opened at the Garrick Theatre on the night of 30 January 1935 to an ecstatic reception. The audience included the Labour politician Herbert Morrison and the Labour Party general-secretary James Middleton, the pacifists Arthur Ponsonby and Dick Sheppard, the Trades Union Congress general-secretary Walter Citrine and a host of other celebrities. There was violent applause between each scene and at the end of the evening there were twenty curtain calls; the play ran for a total of 400 nights and netted Greenwood £5,000.[90] But efforts to turn the book into a film in 1936 foundered on official disapproval from the British Board of Film Censors, which disliked its implicit political radicalism and sexual immorality, although in 1940 the ban was relaxed and a sani-tized version of the story produced as a piece of home-front propa-ganda, even if its central message remained for government purposes intriguingly ambiguous.[91]

The wide and approving reception of *Love on the Dole*, both as novel and as play, owed something to the romantic appeal of a work-ing-class writer made good. Greenwood had all the necessary creden-tials: he left school at the age of 13, never earned more than £2 a week, spoke with a Lancashire accent, and when asked if fame had changed him responded that he only wanted to get back to Salford rather than 'live soft' in London (although he later did just that).[92] His boyish good looks and his romance and marriage to an American actress attracted the gossip magazines, which turned him briefly into a star. But above all *Love on the Dole* expressed in clear and simple terms apparent truths about the modern age that no number of econ-omic experts could match. The review in the *New Clarion* described it as one of the starkest condemnations of the government ever written:

'in 347 pages of most enthralling reading Capitalism is utterly condemned . . . a terrible indictment of modern civilisation'.[93] The economic depression needed some form of cultural symbolism (like the
photograph of the dust-bowl Madonna in depression America) which
it had hitherto lacked. As the novelist Phyllis Bentley observed shortly
after its appearance, 'the very title of Mr Greenwood's book seems
to compress the whole of the post-war era into a single significant
phrase'.[94]

The novelist Walter Greenwood (left) presenting a copy of Love on the Dole
*to an admirer. The book, published in 1933, became an instant best-seller
and turned Greenwood from unemployed clerk to literary celebrity.*

There was nevertheless a widespread sense that economists had an
obligation not only to explain, however inadequately, what had
caused the slump but also to indicate how the British economy was
to move on beyond what was widely perceived to be the end of an
economic age. Economists felt this responsibility keenly but they were
divided on academic as well as political grounds in their response to
the slump. In a review of A. C. Pigou's *Theory of Unemployment*,

published at the height of the slump, the reviewer challenged the argument that the public had any right to expect economists to supply easy answers: 'A professional book which looks to the plain man as if it were comprehensible is a menace.' Although the reviewer thought it natural that some economists would want to help 'in the present deplorable state of the world', it did not reflect the principal function of the academic economist: 'They are physiologists, not clinical practitioners; engineers, not engine drivers.'[95] G. D. H. Cole, whose own books on an intelligent man's guide to world affairs were designed to provide answers of a kind, confessed in an essay later in the 1930s that economists were too enveloped by 'the clouds of "pure theory"' to listen, even to him. 'There are so many questions to which I need answers,' he continued, 'but simply do not know where or how to find them.'[96] Keynes thought the effort scarcely worthwhile:

It is a matter that ought to be left to the experts. They ought to understand the machine. And they ought to be able to mend it when it goes wrong . . . Unhappily the machine is not well understood by anyone. In a sense there are no experts. Some of these representing themselves as such seem to me to talk much greater rubbish than an ordinary man could ever be capable of . . . We shall muddle along, just as we used to when there was something wrong with our own insides, until time or nature and, perhaps, some happy accident work a cure by themselves.[97]

Writing on the depression in 1931 Keynes could see no certainty of an end to the state of crisis. 'To assert this', he put in his notes, 'implies that we know something about its causation,' to which he simply added, 'Do we?'[98]

In the context of the economic crisis these views were at best disingenuous, for economists, businessmen and politicians all had ideas on what they believed had caused the depression and what needed to be done not only to overcome it but to prevent it from being any worse. The problem in Britain, and in other major industrial states, was the fear that any radical departure from economic orthodoxy would be a mere panacea, not a cure, and might indeed lead to more economic crisis rather than less. Economists could be found to defend every intellectual position from rigid monetary orthodoxy through to experimental Soviet-style planning. The result was to create a debilitating immobility. The crisis eventually provoked a political upheaval which made the prospects of economic reform even less likely. One of the rising stars of the Labour Party, the wealthy maverick Oswald 'Tom' Mosley, had broken away some months before to found the New Party, partly funded by the wealthy Oxford car manufacturer William Morris, who was briefly attracted by the idea that industrialists should have a greater say in policy.[99] Mosley – according to Kingsley Martin, 'clever, arrogant, handsome, impatient, rich, endlessly ambitious and, above all, wilful' – took with him briefly an array of young talent which included the MPs Harold Nicolson and John Strachey as well as Cyril Joad, who was for a short time director of propaganda.[100] In January 1931 Mosley circulated a set of proposals for a new direction in economic policy, drafted by Strachey and Aneurin Bevan, which included public works and the corporate organization of industry. Keynes was invited to comment on it and, although critical, assured Mosley that he agreed with a great deal.[101] By July the alliance had broken up when it became clear that Mosley was flirting with fascism. Strachey moved rapidly the opposite way, towards communism.[102] On 24 August Ramsay MacDonald formed a coalition National Government, bringing together the Conservatives with elements of the Labour and Liberal parties, leaving most of the more radical voices outside. The new government rejected unorthodox economics in favour of traditional retrenchment and the depression intensified for a further year.

For the broad intellectual constituency that deplored the failures of capitalism the decade that followed the crash remained a perpetual affront to the demand for a radical restructuring of the economy and a revolution in economic thinking as the only means to secure the survival of civilization. The most popular solution suggested for the crisis, which was capable of uniting individuals across the political divide, was planning. The belief that a planned economy was the necessary successor to the free market was widespread across Europe, from Stalin's Soviet Union to Mussolini's Italy. For the British left, planning was something which would make the transition from capitalism to socialism possible and secure a measure of social justice without the need for a violent revolutionary politics.[103] In her reflections on the diseases of the capitalist system broadcast by the BBC in

1932 Beatrice Webb pointed out that 'planlessness' was in her view 'the most intractable disease' suffered by contemporary capitalism, but also the one illness that capitalism could do nothing to cure. She cited with qualified approval the argument of the Oxford economist Arthur Salter that since capitalism could not save itself, the state would have to intervene, though not dictate; by so doing, she continued, the acquisitive instinct would finally be set aside and replaced by the Webbs' own ideal of 'relying on the motive of public service to plan the life of the community'.[104] The idea of a sense of collective duty underlay the arguments in the popular book by the socialist economist Barbara Wootton, *Plan or No Plan*, written in 1934, in which she rejected the violent revolutionary path in favour of the democratic transition to a planned economy run by virtuous bureaucrats: 'when plans are made', she wrote, 'the distribution and use of plant and materials appropriate for carrying them out falls as a duty upon persons who are in the position of public servants.' Private initiative would be replaced under planning by socialized industry because planning would mean nothing 'unless the planners have full control of the main instruments of production'.[105]

In the 1930s socialist ideas on planning drew heavily on the Soviet model which was eagerly examined for evidence that the death of capitalism need not mean the end of civilization. Enthusiasm for all things Soviet is discussed in greater detail in a later chapter; here it is worth observing that throughout the 1930s those progressive economists who advocated a planned system to replace a decaying capitalist order needed to argue that, for all its difficulties, the Soviet Union could demonstrate that planning worked. One of the chief advocates of the communist alternative to capitalism was the former Mosley supporter John Strachey. The son of a distinguished editor of the *Spectator*, Strachey became a Labour MP for the Birmingham constituency of Aston in the 1929 general election, and then lost the seat two years later. After his brief flirtation with the New Party, he abandoned Mosley and lived off his journalism and book-writing. From 1931 onwards he remorselessly attacked the dangerous failures of capitalism and publicized his own conversion to communism.[106] When he was invited in 1934 by the Moscow-based journal *International Literature* to answer the question 'What has [sic] the existence and achievements of the Soviet Union meant to you?' he replied that he was influenced, as all intellectuals in Britain were influenced, by the contrast between 'the successful emergence of the Soviet Union from its difficulties, and the ever-growing chaos, despair and ruin in the capitalist world'.[107] In 1935 he published *The Nature of Capitalist Crisis*, an eloquent Marxist interpretation of the terminal character of the contradictions of the capitalist order (which sold only a modest 5,735 copies), but in 1938 a new volume on the socialist alternative, *What Are We to Do* (the title, Strachey thought, should be modelled on Lenin's 'What is to be Done?'), chosen as a book of the month by Victor Gollancz's Left Book Club – for which Strachey was also one of two editorial consultants – sold 50,302 copies, bringing Strachey a genuine mass audience.[108] His views were not economically sophisticated and despite his hostility to Hobson's moderate socialism did not differ a great deal from the theory that the potential output of goods could not be absorbed by impoverished consumers or bought up as luxuries by the rich. 'There is literally no way', he announced in a lecture given in 1937, 'to use our means of production under capitalist ownership.' Strachey favoured public ownership and planned production. Capitalism had to be abolished before there set in 'a new collapse of civilisation like that of the Roman Empire'.[109]

Strachey was among the most successful of the young generation of intellectuals in reaching a wide public on the alternative of Marxist planned economy and social ownership, but the appetite for books on Marx in the 1930s was a large one. A *Handbook of Marxism* published by Gollancz in 1935 sold 33,000 copies.[110] During the 1930s Maurice Dobb found himself in demand regularly for lectures and discussions on the future of communist economics. Dobb, like Strachey, was convinced that after the slump he was witnessing the final and general crisis of capitalism. In a lecture to the British Association in 1932 he welcomed the opportunity provided by the Soviet Five-Year Plan to test Western theories about planning – 'a veritable "busman's holiday" for the economist' – and argued that the age of bourgeois 'Political Economy' was now to give way to an age of 'Planned Economy'.[111] In another lecture on 'Britain without Capitalists', given in Leeds in 1937, he contrasted the feeble efforts of capitalism to use 'fascist' planning to escape from crisis (by oppressing the labour force) with communist planning, which would oppress capital instead by expropriating without compensation all large-scale capitalist business, followed by the planned expropriation of small farms and shops, which Dobb thought would be compensated in some form. Communist planning carried risks, Dobb continued, but it was better than 'the slow stagnation and spiritual and material decay' of contemporary 'gangster' capitalism.[112] Even if it were planned, Dobb wrote in a workers' educational pamphlet, capitalism could still only produce more capitalism.[113]

Dobb may well have been the 'well-known economist' responsible for editing the anonymously published volume with the same title as his lecture, *Britain Without Capitalists*, which appeared in July 1936 with the sub-title 'What Industry in a Soviet Britain Could Achieve'.[114] In the preface the authors distinguished their argument from the conventional literature on economic planning by insisting that Soviet-style planning was only possible with working-class control of the state and workers' economic institutions. The case for Sovietization in the context of capitalist crisis was, it was argued, 'unanswerable and true'. British Soviets were the 'pre-requisite of any social planning'.[115] There followed detailed analysis of all the major industries, including building and agriculture, with recommendations on how they might be planned for social use. The Lancashire cotton industry, for example, would under workers' control plan to produce 'the most wealth with the least toil' by modernizing and rationalizing the tangled web of small producers and the financial anarchy prevailing in the trade.[116] The book was a logical if fanciful expression of the wide belief that capitalistic anarchy should make way for socialist order. The same year G. D. H. Cole, who was not a communist, told an audience that when it came to planning, the Soviet Union had supplied the only successful model.[117] He had published his own 'Plan for Britain' in 1933, in which he called for 'complete control' over the economy, planned imports and exports, and a balance between what could be produced and what could be consumed.[118] In a lecture in 1935 Cole deplored attempts at capitalist planning as a plan for enforced scarcity, worse than the 'chaotic Laissez-faire' of the previous century, and embellished his original planning proposals by advocating sweeping nationalization of heavy industry, commerce, land and banks, together with state control of trade, new investment and the supply of credit.[119]

Among progressive opinion in Britain after the slump there was an unspoken assumption, not necessarily Marxist, that capitalism meant chaos while planning equalled progress. Planning in this sense was not confined to the economy. In 1934 the Federation of Progressive Societies and Individuals, centred on the fashionably progressive London suburb of Hampstead, began publication of a monthly journal under the title *Plan*. The Federation was set up in 1932 by Cyril Joad, after he had abandoned Mosley, and consisted of the Hampstead Ethical Institute and a number of smaller associations, with Joad as its president. In its stated aims the group deplored the 'drift to catastrophe' heralded by the failure of an obsolete economic system 'totally unable to distribute for the good of all the potential wealth that science has made available'. The programme of action called for the rapid 'socialisation of the collective economic affairs of mankind' and a scientifically planned economic environment, but also the planning of education, law, landscape and population.[120] In the first issue of *Plan* Joad announced that 'Economic breakdown and international anarchy threaten to destroy civilisation' and called on all progressive intellectuals to rally round the rational planning of the future. The vice-presidents of the organization represented a roll call of progressive opinion – among them Vera Brittain, Leonard Woolf, Cyril Burt, Aldous and Julian Huxley, Kingsley Martin, Bertrand Russell, H. G. Wells and Rebecca West. Joad was succeeded by the journalist and writer Gerald Heard, and then by Barbara Wootton.[121] The journal and the Federation had a limited appeal, with never more than 600 members, but the corps of leading intellectuals and writers who participated had an influence well beyond the confines of a Hampstead discussion group. The central conviction, stated in an editorial in 1935, of the 'bankruptcy of Capitalism' was something to which most progressive opinion-formers subscribed.[122]

Planning was also far from a monopoly of the left. As a result of the slump, elements among the academic, political and business community still favourable to the idea of economic individualism came to the conclusion that reliance on market forces or economic orthodoxy alone would not save capitalism from the consequences of

Jarrow marchers passing through the Bedfordshire village of Lavendon on 26 October 1936. The unemployed protestors, led by a harmonica band, marched from north-east England to London where they presented a petition to Parliament. The marchers' plight symbolized for many people the unworkable nature of capitalism.

its own deficiencies. In contrast with the noisy demonstrations in favour of socialist planning, liberal views on planning tended to be less public and less strident. Liberal planners had to distance themselves from socialism while reassuring a largely conservative business community that planning was not as dangerous as many of them feared. Some of those interested in planning as a rational response to economic disaster came to be grouped loosely in an organization which called itself Political and Economic Planning. The organization had its roots in the decision of a group of journalists, who had resigned from the *Saturday Review* in 1930 in protest at its support for Lord Beaverbrook's crusade for 'Empire Free Trade' in order to set up a new journal critical of government policy which they christened the *Week-End Review*. They included the novelist J. B. Priestley, the political commentator Vernon Bartlett, the future Conservative minister Duff Cooper and the deputy editor of the review, Max Nicholson. Spurred on, as one of them later recalled, by the 'dire events' of the slump, they drew up in the autumn of 1930 a 'National Plan for Great Britain', which was published as a special supplement on 14 February 1931.[123] Later that month a dinner was organized to draw together three separate constituencies: the first was known as 'The 1950 Society', a small group of young intellectuals who hoped to play a role in public life by the year 1950; a dining club and discussion group led by a former financial adviser to the Indian government and now a director of the Bank of England, Sir Basil Blackett; and a third group linked to the Labour politician Kenneth Lindsay. Efforts were made to recruit as widely as possible in order to avoid appearing partisan. Among those invited were John Strachey and Oswald Mosley, the director of the London School of Economics, William Beveridge, and his successor Alexander Carr-Saunders, the trade unionists Ernest Bevin and Walter Citrine and the economists G. D. H. Cole, Lionel Robbins and Josiah Stamp. None of them in the end joined what officially became, following a second dinner at the Ivy in central London on 15 March, Political and Economic Planning or PEP.[124] With the help of an annual grant of £1,000 from Leonard and Dorothy Elmhirst (who had established in 1926 at Dartington Hall in Devon a centre for progressive education) the organization was fully launched at University College, London on 22 March with Blackett as the first chairman and Lindsay as its secretary.[125]

The broad aims of the organization were worked out by the time of the first general meeting in June and were enshrined in two resolutions, one calling for the reorganization on a national basis of the country's economic, social and political organizations in ways consistent with its liberal traditions, the second asserting that the failure to adopt a National Plan would amount to 'a major national danger'.[126] All of those who took part were committed to the idea that planning could and should be successfully reconciled with individual freedom, although there were sharp differences over the preference for micro-planning of sectors and industries and macro-planning of the whole economy, which some members regarded as too close to communism.[127] Planning was nevertheless essential to rescue the existing order from disaster. 'The anarchy and squalor of Western civilis-ation', wrote Max Nicholson in 1932 in 'A View of Planning', 'has come to a head.' The purpose of planning, he continued, is 'to rec-oncile personal freedom with an orderly community'.[128] This was the motif of a discussion document circulated in the spring of the same year by the chairman Sir Basil Blackett under the title 'Freedom and Planning, Collapsing Civilisation', which began with conventional enough expressions of profound pessimism – 'This generation is faced with the threat of a World collapse of modern civilisation and a period comparable with the Dark Ages' – but ended with a still gloomier vision of 'world disorganisation, famine, pestilence and the submerg-ence of civilisation' which sat awkwardly with his subsequent argu-ment that mankind might be saved from such horrors with a little constructive conservative planning.[129] Blackett's successor in 1932, Israel Sieff, vice-chairman of the retail chain Marks & Spencer, was less apocalyptic, but also saw planning as the only way to avoid 'chaos' and the trail to economic slavery.[130] The National Plan itself, drawn up in 1930, was an exceptionally ambitious document, pref-aced with a complex organogram with the King at the top, independ-ent shops at the foot, and functional sectors in between of a distinctly corporatist character. The plan called for controls over trade, the self-government of industry, the functional reorganization of the state, and a national planning commission.[131]

The organization gathered together 50 members by the autumn of 1931, around 100 members by early 1934, and approximately 150 by the outbreak of war. It was run by a small directorate including the zoologist Julian Huxley, who directed the research division. Prem-ises were found at 16 Queen Anne's Gate in central London, close to the Houses of Parliament, and a club established where members could meet for lunch or a glass of sherry, though it attracted at its pre-war peak only 160 members. PEP published a regular broadsheet and a journal titled *Planning* which appeared fortnightly from April 1933.[132] The hard core of its activity rested on the organization of eighteen working groups (an additional one on the planning of physi-cal resources was added in 1940) to which members were assigned to match their expertise. The groups covered all forms of economic activity, but the so-called Tec Plan (Technique of Planning) group was regarded by some of the members as the pacemaker for the whole organization until it was dissolved in 1932 following disagreements over the group's commitment to the centralized planning of physical output.[133] The purpose of the groups was to study in great depth the precise nature and problems of each sector and to produce a detailed report, with suitable statistical and technical data and recommendations for planned improvement. The high ambitions soon turned sour. Some groups took time to get going while others prospered energetically. When a concerted programme was presented in July 1932 by the organization's secretary, Blackett condemned it as 'frankly communist' and Nicholson resigned because he thought the organization too vague and woolly given that it was supposed to reflect the ethos of planning.[134] Eventually he was persuaded to return, and became secretary in succession to Lindsay, who was elected to parliament in 1935, but Blackett disappeared for a long trip to South Africa making no arrangements for his absence. The confusion was resolved by the appointment of Sieff as his successor, and three years later Blackett died, having made no further contribution. In 1935 the unwieldy nature of the organization and absence of clear lines of demarcation led to the creation of an executive, with powers to act, and a larger council, but the problem of effective planning for a planning organization gave the project an unwelcome degree of ambiguity.[135]

The extent of its influence relied not on the small number of experts recruited to prepare the group reports but on the promotion of planning ideals to a wider interested public. Early on in the life of PEP a potential circle of recipients for information and reports was drawn up with the object of creating a culture of planning among those with responsibilities. The broadsheets were circulated to the Cabinet Secretary, and to planning moles in nine other ministries.[136] *Planning* had 1,600 subscribers by the mid-1930s, and in all 100,000 documents were printed and distributed in the first five years of its existence. The first few reports sold modestly at around 1,000 copies each.[137] A central feature of PEP was regular dinners to which potential recruits were invited; lists of dinner guests were held by the central office together with notes jotted down by the members present on what the guests had said during the evening. At a dinner in March

1933, for example, Sir Arthur Salter was overheard to remark that Lionel Robbins 'was the last relic of Victorianism' while Beveridge 'does not know where he is'. The eavesdropping that night also showed that among the invited guests was a general sense that reliance on the natural working of economic laws 'was a thing of the past'.[138] Such covert intelligence gathering reflected the spirit of PEP, which shunned the limelight and did little to promote its cause publicly. This was deliberate, policy from the outset being that PEP would be non-partisan, but it generated a good deal of internal ill-will. Some members wanted a higher public profile. 'What is the terror of coming out into the open?' scribbled one member on an agenda paper in 1933. 'Why must we continue to work in the dark?'.[139] In 1935 Max Nicholson drew up redefined aims to explain that PEP's reticence was necessary in order to avoid becoming the tool of sectional party interests or a mere propaganda front.[140] The whiff of conspiracy was nevertheless sufficiently strong to occasion unkind attacks from right and left. The *Free Press*, mouthpiece of the right-wing Liberty Restoration League, accused PEP in 1935 of secretly planning to control the individual more ruthlessly than National Socialism or fascism; but the Labour newspaper the *Daily Herald*, under the headline in 1933 'Certainly Not Socialism', also described it as quasi-fascist. The liberal *English Review*, however, described it as a 'communist conspiracy', while the authors of *Britain Without Capitalists* approved the PEP Report on the cotton industry for arguing that nothing 'but a revolution' would bring useful change.[141]

The work of the PEP groups continued unevenly over the course of the 1930s, but a central problem was the absence of any integrated National Plan beyond the document originally drawn up in 1931. A special meeting of the Executive convened on 2/3 March 1935 engaged in an inquest on the failure to produce a coherent overall programme. Sieff, who presided, deplored the absence of any grand design and thought there was 'so much more gap than picture that it is difficult to see any picture', but no new National Plan was ever drawn up.[142] A few weeks later one prominent member wrote to Nicholson that in his view any positive assessment of the achievement of PEP was wildly optimistic: 'while it is perfectly true that "planning" is fashionable, yet the PEP idea of it does not seem to have been grasped by anyone'.[143] By that time some of the early supporters of PEP had drifted away to a new loosely formed Next Five Years Group promoted by a number of reformist Conservatives, Liberals and National Labour supporters which succeeded in publicizing the advantages of moderate planning while exploiting the research work already carried out and published by PEP.[144] The limits of the organization's activity were demonstrated with the executive decision to establish a new working group in mid-1937 on ways to control economic recession. A memorandum assessed the meagre possibilities open to PEP given the 'rather disillusioning character' of other attempts to understand how the business cycle worked. It was concluded that as long as the prevailing view, from the prime minister downwards, was to deflate in times of crisis and inflate during a boom there was nothing to be done: 'even if slump control is in theory possible the prevention of the next slump may be peculiarly difficult . . .'[145] For all the careful work done in describing the conditions of individual economic and social sectors, PEP was no nearer the elusive goal of avoiding further economic catastrophe, which had been its rationale in the first place.

The burden of understanding how future economic crisis might be averted rested in the end not in practical planning but in economic theory. Among the many professional economists who tried to find the key to unlock the mystery of capitalist crisis, the most important was Keynes. He had not been one of those invited to participate in PEP. Indeed, Keynes remained detached from all the lobby groups and discussion circles on planning and economic crisis, preferring to pursue his goal of supplying a better theoretical understanding of what made capitalism go wrong. Maynard Keynes was widely regarded by the 1930s as a national genius, 'the ablest man I ever knew', wrote Kingsley Martin.[146] His intellect, wrote his friend Arthur Salter, in an affectionate post-war portrait, 'was of the rarest kind, with precision, penetrating force, and the cutting edge of a razor'.[147] Salter's description of him as the 'Artist-Economist' captured the mixture of conventional scholar and maverick critic which gave him such formidable influence. The son of the registrar of Cambridge University, he went to Eton, then King's College, Cambridge, which became his academic home for the rest of his life. His rise was meteoric and by the end of the Great War he was, aged 35, the principal Treasury representative at the Versailles Conference, a position from which he famously resigned in protest at the proposed reparations schedule to be imposed on the defeated nations. Keynes was a man of many parts. A Liberal by conviction, he never became a political creature, though he offered disarmingly frank advice to governments throughout the inter-war years, including service as chair of a committee of the Economic Advisory Council set up in 1930 to find economic solutions to the crisis. Lionel Robbins, who served on the Council, but disagreed with Keynes, noted privately what he called Keynes's 'Puckish Element'; Robbins found him a difficult man to dislike, but wished that 'such a noble brain' had been combined with 'a temperament less mer- curial'.[148] Keynes was a patron of the arts, particularly ballet, founder of the Cambridge Arts Theatre, and was expert enough as a practical economist to make himself rich during the long economic malaise. If he had a fault, Martin recalled, it was that 'his judgement was not as good as his brain'. Keynes was instinctively optimistic, but also a rational and caustic pessimist, a 'Cassandra' as he styled himself, in a world of dissolving certainties.[149]

In the 1920s Keynes was a notable critic of public policy, but offered little that was genuinely constructive. In a letter to John Strachey, written in 1926, he contested the conclusions of Strachey's recent book, Revolution by Reason, on the ground that they relied too heavily on Hobson's arguments about effective demand, but went on to explain that no one had yet written clearly about the issues. 'I am still too confused in my own mind', he continued, 'to know exactly what I want to do.'[150] Keynes's own debt to Hobson, which he acknowledged belatedly in 1936 with the publication of his General Theory, has been obscured by the extraordinary historical attention devoted to what became in the 1940s 'Keynesianism', but the argu- ments about why capitalism malfunctions which Keynes developed in the first part of the 1930s clearly drew more inspiration from Hobson than from Marx.[151] Indeed, Cole wrote later in the 1950s that in his opinion what was commonly attributed to Keynes was in fact 'the Hobsonian revolution in economic and social thought'.[152] The draft of a lecture by Keynes on the causes of the crisis for the American company CBS in 1931 certainly owed a good deal to Hobson's thesis: 'we are withholding from consumption a larger part of our income that [sic] is able to find an outlet in new constructive enterprises, or in anything that will serve to increase our accumulated capital'. The result, Keynes argued, was 'an unbalanced position' between the inability to consume and the unwillingness to invest.[153] Where he felt Hobson had misunderstood the process was on the question of levels of investment, which he did not think would always tend to over-production, but ought on balance to encourage higher employment levels. He did not believe that socialism held the answer to this crisis because it was a body with 'two heads and two hearts' – the one 'ardent to do things because they are economically sound', and the other 'ardent to do things in spite of their being economically unsound'. Mac-Donald's National Government he regarded as too rigidly orthodox; radical socialism he regarded as dangerously revolutionary.[154]

During the years of slow recovery from the crash Keynes set out to produce a major piece of theoretical writing that could reconcile economic reform with economic individualism and perhaps overcome the dilemmas of contemporary capitalism, above all the persistent tendency to the underutilization of human resources. The result was the *General Theory of Employment, Interest and Money*, published in January 1936 at the modest price of 5/-. The book, as Keynes observed in his preface, was 'chiefly addressed to my fellow econom-ists', but he hoped it would find a wider non-professional audience. The central purpose, he continued, was not only to propose a new way of looking at economic stabilization, but to shed the overwhelm-ing powers of economic orthodoxy 'which ramify . . . into every corner of our minds'.[155] The economic revolution that Keynes's work eventu-ally promoted was not immediately evident. There was a mixed academic response while the popular reception reflected the very real intellectual difficulty of grappling with complex economic theory. Nevertheless, the central thesis, that the idea of a self-regulating econ-omy, guided by a 'hidden hand', was simply untrue and that the state ought to play a greater part in stimulating employment by positive intervention on interest rates, tax levels and investment, was well enough understood if not generally approved.[156] The liberal press disliked a theory which the *British Weekly* described as 'a new apology for etatism'; the radical left-wing press deplored a book of bourgeois economics which the communist *Daily Worker* regarded as an apology for monopoly capitalism with a 'decided Fascist flavour'.[157] Keynes did not expect immediate results from the book. 'I am trying to prevent my mind from crystallizing too much on the precise lines of the General Theory,' he wrote late in 1936 to the young Cambridge economist Joan Robinson. 'There is a considerable difference', he continued, 'between more or less formal theory ... and something which is meant to be applied to current events without too much qualification by people who do not fully comprehend the theory ... I am against hurry and in favour of gestation.'[158] In the late 1930s the argument that full employment could be created by a dynamic fiscal and investment strategy attracted support from those who wanted an end to unemployment but had little effect on government in a period when rearmament was beginning to absorb many of the underutilized resources. But to many of those who thought that capitalism would be transformed by planning or perhaps replaced altogether, Keynes was not necessarily seen as an ally; he favoured economic management rather than comprehensive planned economy and he favoured it in order to ensure the survival of capitalism in some form or other.[159] Moreover, Keynes's general conclusions did not favour the view that rational planning would cure crisis because in his model the natural state of any economy was inherently unstable, potentially responsive to dynamic management but always capable of a dangerous disequilibrium. If he saw himself as a representative for what he called 'rational change', he was also acutely aware of the irrational elements in the behaviour of the economy, planned or otherwise.[160]

The attempt to find radical ways to make the economy work better before 1939 made little progress. Keynesianism and economic planning were phenomena of the 1940s and 1950s, after the war had confirmed how effectively macroeconomic planning could work. The many different groups of planners were too divided between idealists and empiricists, socialists and individualists, to produce an effective planning consensus, even if in the public mind planning was an evident necessity. Keynes, for all the later power of his thesis, was just one economist among many searching for instruments to allay further crisis. As the war approached, economists who had argued that capitalism was in the final stage of crisis adjusted their arguments to take account of the armaments boom as a device to allow capitalism to linger on to yet another, perhaps more debilitating crash in the 1940s. Frederick Allen, in *Can Capitalism Last?*, published in 1937, argued that capitalism could survive only by intensifying the paradox of poverty and plenty or driving on into imperialist war. It would none-theless not 'collapse' like a bridge or a house, but needed to be abolished by radical political action.[161] G. D. H. Cole, writing late in the same year a chapter for a set of essays on *Europe into the Abyss*, acknowledged that capitalism had indeed survived the depression with levels of employment and output higher than in 1929, but concluded that the revival was still 'precarious', over-dependent on arms. Britain, he continued, still possessed an air of stability in 1929, but in 1937 was a country of 'short-run expedients and doubtful outlook'.[162] In a lecture in October 1936 to the Fabian Society, of which he was a member, on 'Can Capitalism Survive?', Cole again highlighted the unnatural character of the brief revival and its promise of further crisis:

even if we avoid war, still the capitalist system will more and more run down, more and more be faced by the inherent contradictions that Marx predicted long ago, plunged from one crisis into another, recovering, but always recovering on a lower plane of activity ... getting more and more inef-ficient.[163]

At the end of his notes for a lecture in August 1938 Maurice Dobb added the laconic conclusion 'Recovery since 1933 built on Rearm[amen]t'.[164]

Kingsley Martin coined the term 'pessimistic radicalism' to describe the outlook of that cohort of intellectuals who thought capitalism should be changed but were uncertain about whether change was possible and, if it came, entirely safe.[165] This was the ambiguity at the heart of the Webbs' analysis – belief that capitalism was in decay and anxiety about the consequences for civilization if decay prompted something even worse. In the 1930s these ambiguities sharpened as the final crisis of capitalism appeared near with no agreement on what might take its place and a profound pessimism that capitalism would linger on in a stagnant and demoralized state until it was too late to construct a viable new order. Economic individualism and class privilege, argued Julian Huxley in an essay published in 1942, had combined in the pre-war years to 'deadlock progress'.[166] The sense that capitalism was on trial in the 1920s and 1930s provoked a growing frustration for both defence and prosecution. Keynes, in an essay on 'Economic Possibilities for our Grandchildren', written early in 1930 before the slump had really bitten, thought no one would look so foolish in the future as the two opposed camps of pessimists: 'the pessimism of the revolutionaries who think that things are so bad that nothing can save us but violent change, and the pessimism of the reactionaries who consider the balance of our economic and social life so precarious that we must risk no experiments'.[167] Yet Keynes too had a popular reputation for ambiguity as both pessimist and optimist, hoping that economic reason would prevail, but uncertain that capitalists were not bent on 'committing suicide'.[168] In 1938 he suggested that the reformers 'have completely failed, indeed, to provide a substitute for these economic bogus-faiths'.[169]

The sense of frustration owed something to the fact that despite the recovery in the 1930s there were still large pockets of regional deprivation in areas of traditional heavy industry and in textiles where unemployment and social misery remained endemic throughout the decade. Capitalism otherwise showed a remarkable resilience in the 1930s. The government gradually developed a set of instruments for controlling the market, including the radical shift to protection in 1932, which are now subsumed under the term 'managed economy' to describe the interim state between *laissez faire* and the mixed-welfare economy adopted after 1945. For the employed householder in the new suburban housing of the 1930s, able to buy a small car and a radio and go on holiday each year, the discourse on capitalism in crisis made little sense. Yet in so much of the public discussion of capitalism in the 1930s the underlying assumptions and the language used suggested a system that would have to change or die, even among businessmen who were its chief beneficiaries. The ethos was one of capitalism in crisis, the prevailing reality one of consumer revival. Part of the explanation for this paradox lies in the gap between economic reality and social expectations. The intellectual rejection of capitalism was based perhaps instinctively on recognition of its social injustices rather than its inherent economic flaws, which much of the public could not understand except in simple, reductive terms. The criticism of capitalism was based largely on moral terms, which explains the extraordinary success of *Love on the Dole*, which by 1940 had been seen on stage by 3 million people.[170] The argument was not so much that capitalism did not work, but that it should not work the way it did. Perhaps the greatest moral affront in the 1930s was the knowledge that during the world crisis food stocks were destroyed to help keep up prices while everywhere in the industrial world existed hunger. George Bernard Shaw, writing in 1933 about the failed World Economic Conference held at the Natural History Museum in London in June that year, savagely attacked an economics which advocated 'the destruction by natural calamity or deliberate sabotage of the existing supply of food' when 30 million unemployed worldwide 'perished by inches'. The conference delegates, economists and politicians, he regarded as incurable lunatics, whose mad injustice would in the end smash the system they sought to salvage.[171]

3

A Sickness in the Racial Body

What are we going to do? Every defective man, woman and child is a burden. Every defective is an extra body for the nation to feed and clothe, but produces little or nothing in return. Every defective needs care, and immobilises a certain quantum of energy and goodwill which could otherwise be put to constructive ends. Every defective is an emotional burden – a sorrow to someone, and in himself, a creature doomed, when unassisted, to live an incomplete and sub-human existence. Not only that, but if their numbers continue to increase, the burden . . . will gradually drag us down.   Julian Huxley, 1930[1]

The Dorchester Hotel on London's Park Lane was the setting for one of the most remarkable events of the 1933 social round, the Malthusian Ball. It was organized under the auspices of the International Birth Control Movement based in Westminster to raise money for propagating information on modern methods of birth control. The Labour politician Dame Edith Summerskill was the honorary organizer, and the Ball was announced under the patronage of Princess Alice, Countess of Athlone.[2] It was sponsored by an array of establishment figures, including Julian Huxley. The gossip magazines highlighted the preparations. On the evening of 22 March those able to afford the £1 5s tickets were entertained with dancing, a cabaret and an auction of books kindly presented by authors and publishers, which included Bertrand Russell's *Outline of Philosophy* and a recent biography of Lenin. The Ball Programme reproduced a *Punch* cartoon with a Malthusian twist (two plump babies in prams: 'I'm told we're scarcer than we used to be'; 'Yes, but look at our condition') and a short exposition of the current crisis of population. Birth control, it was reported, would be one of the 'few unmixed blessings' for humankind were it not for the uncongenial fact that it was practised chiefly by those who could afford to raise children in a civilized setting, while the rate of population increase 'was greatest among the social classes and communities' unable to supply their offspring 'with the necessaries of civilized life'.[3] The 'disadvantageous differential birth-rate', it was argued, could be recalibrated not by advocating celibacy or abstinence but through vigorous propaganda to get the least advantaged to produce fewer children. The Ball raised £450 to help in furthering the cause of Malthusian restriction.[4]

Although not everyone who danced the polka that night on Park Lane could have been expected to know who the eighteenth-century English cleric Thomas Malthus was, or the significance of his gloomy prognosis that population will always run ahead of food supply until periodically readjusted through war, dearth and disease, those who organized it certainly did. The secretary of the International Birth Control Movement, Margaret Sanger, was a pioneer of the neo-Malthusian idea that the modern age could be saved only by the limitation of unwanted births. An American maternity nurse and Malthusian activist, she coined the term 'birth control' before the war. She had been forced to flee from New York in October 1914 or face possible imprisonment for distributing what the city authorities regarded as immoral literature. She returned from London a year later and continued her work constantly pestered by the police, but she was a regular visitor to England, which she found more receptive to her message. She was a strong supporter of the Malthusian League, founded in London in 1877 as a protest against the (unsuccessful) prosecution of Annie Besant and Charles Bradlaugh on charges of distributing an obscene book advocating family limitation. By the 1930s the League had become a forceful lobby-group for the restriction of births among the least advantaged. Its motto 'Non Quantitas sed Qualitas' said everything about its objectives.[5] The rules of the League set out this principle unequivocally: 'it is of great importance that those afflicted with hereditary diseases, or who are otherwise plainly incapable of producing or rearing physically, intellectually, and morally satisfactory children, should not become parents'.[6]

Margaret Sanger played a major part in launching the American birth control movement in the 1920s. Her work was shadowed by a powerful rival, the Englishwoman Marie Carmichael Stopes. An academic botanist, famous for a standard textbook on plant-based fossil fuels, she was one of an early generation of academic women forced to compete in a predominantly male world. In June 1915 she met Margaret Sanger and was within days converted to the idea of birth control; she understood that here was the means to liberate women from the straitjacket of repeated births and so allow married couples to enjoy the sexual act for its own sake. On its own this might well have been a subversive notion but it soon became subsumed into a single-minded, some claimed fanatical, commitment to birth control as the key to a healthier race and happier families. The two women grew to become unfriendly rivals. Marie Stopes later complained that 'the Control of human conception' was 'deplorably but irrevocably called "birth control"', the term invented by Sanger.[7] She joined the Malthusian League in 1917 but left it soon afterwards to found her own movement, the Society for Constructive Birth Control and Racial Progress. She disliked the fact that the League campaigned publicly for birth control 'in the street'.[8] The two women held many common views about the necessity for restricting the birth of the unwanted child, but were sharply divided on the merits of particular contraceptive devices. Marie Stopes pioneered with the zeal of a crusader what she christened the 'Pro-Race Cap' (sizes large or small), a thick-rimmed cervical device made of rubber shallow enough to allow the male and female secretions to be united in order to achieve, in her view, complete physical well-being. Other birth control pioneers favoured the diaphragm and spermicidal gels as demonstrably more effective, and Sanger scoffed at Stopes's claim that there was anything novel or even safe about the 'Race Cap'.[9] Stopes deployed her formidable capacity for self-promotion to insist that she had also founded the first fully functioning birth control clinic in the English-speaking world. Margaret Sanger had opened the first birth control advisory centre in New York in 1916, but it had been immediately closed down by the police, an outcome that Stopes was uncharitable enough to publicize. The first clinic that was allowed to dispense advice and contraceptive products without legal restriction was set up by Marie Stopes and her second husband, the aviation pioneer Humphrey Verdon Roe, on 17 March 1921 in the north London district of Holloway.[10]

The clinic was a milestone in the long struggle to make birth control socially acceptable. In May 1921 Marie Stopes organized a public meeting on constructive birth control at the Queen's Hall in London to publicize the new clinic. She had been advised that she might find the hall almost empty, but on the night, according to a sceptical eye-witness, there was no 'trickle of ill-dressed fanatics' but a packed crowd of 'quite normal-looking people'.[11] After a lengthy organ recital, Marie Stopes, resplendent in a shining white dress, took the stage to berate the audience about the perils and expense of allowing 'wastrels' to breed. The record of the meeting indicates applause at every opportunity. The only people who should become parents, she insisted, were those who could 'add individuals of value to the race'. In her final remarks of the evening she told the audience that if race selection were successful they would look at their grandchildren and 'think almost that the gods had descended to walk upon the earth'. Amid the hubbub that followed her speech a man stood up and called out, 'As a Roman Catholic priest I protest,' but his remonstration went unheeded, perhaps unheard by Stopes. Marie Stopes, another spectator recalled, seemed 'a fire blazing up amongst the morbid facts'.[12]

The arguments in favour of birth control were many, but they were linked in the post-war world with the widespread public fear that the quality of the population was declining to a point that threatened the continued existence of a vigorous imperial race and imperilled civilization itself. This was certainly not a new fear, since its roots went back to the energetic arguments over national efficiency and degeneration in the decades before the Great War. What gave the discourse a fresh urgency was the apparent confirmation during the war and post-war years of just how debilitated the race was at a time when national rivalry and imperial responsibilities exposed the population to exceptional challenges. The problem was famously encapsulated by David Lloyd George, the first post-war prime minis-

A birth control poster promoting the Constructive Birth Control movement founded by Marie Stopes in 1921. She deplored the fact that 'animal carelessness' rather than forethought governed the reproduction of the species.

97

ter, when he warned an audience that it was not possible to run an A1 empire with a C3 population. These alphabetic categories were used by the army to label the physical qualities of recruits. In the 1920 report of the National Service Medical Board it was demonstrated that out of almost two and a half million men examined between November 1917 and the end of the war a year later only three in every nine were fit; two were infirm, three incapable of anything more than light work and one 'a chronic invalid'.[13] In a foreword to Marie Stopes's *Contraception*, published in 1928, Sir James Barr, onetime president of the British Medical Association, testily observed that 'while the virility of the nation was carrying on the war the derelicts were carrying on the race'.[14] A survey of 2.4 million children carried out by the Chief Medical Officer of the national Board of Education in 1921 showed the same picture: 47.9 per cent, or more than 1.1 million, 'were found to be suffering from defects'.[15] It was among these apparently debilitated sections of the population that the advocates of birth control hoped to spread the gospel of contraception.

The improvement of the race was the foundation on which birth-control propaganda was built. It was the central message of Margaret Sanger's book *The Pivot of Civilisation*, published in Britain in 1923. In 'Points for Propagandists', written by Bertram Talbot in May 1925 for the Malthusian League, the crisis of race was reiterated again and again. 'Reckless breeding' – encouraged, it was claimed, by misguided welfare schemes – had only compounded the problems of poverty, disease and unemployment while abandoning 'the vital question of the number and quality of the race'. Talbot argued that birth control would, properly practised, protect the genetic future: 'A few well-born, well-bred children are worth to the nation more than hordes of rickety, under-fed, ill-cared-for little ones.'[16] Marie Stopes throughout her career believed that only birth control could allow the ideal man and woman to develop and save the racial stock from decay. At a meeting in Cambridge in April 1930 she confessed that she had 'a standard for humanity at least as high as the old Greek standard of physical beauty', but it was attainable only when the population was no longer bred by mere chance ('by indiscreet enjoyable evenings, by lust, by ignorance, by accident'). To let nature take its course was not, she argued, 'the way to rear an imperial race'.[17] When her own son later chose to marry a woman with glasses, she cut him out of her will and refused to go to the wedding on the ground that he had wilfully ruined a fine genetic inheritance. Stopes saw 'race suicide' as the chief danger faced by the genetically favoured as a result of 'excessive breeding from the inferior stock'.[18]

Marie Stopes and her son in August 1938, attending a conference on birth control in Cambridge. She was proud of what she saw as his solid genetic inheritance and was dismayed when he chose to marry the daughter of the aeronautical engineer, Barnes Wallis, because she wore spectacles.

The preoccupation with race improvement did not preclude a genuine desire to ameliorate the conditions of pauperization and chronic ill-health faced by the great majority of Britain's female population. Even though Marie Stopes used the rhetoric of race, her clinics, and the more than ninety other birth control centres operating under the auspices of local health authorities by the late 1930s, did give therapeutic help and counselling to thousands of women from impoverished backgrounds, as well as the idealized middle-class mother. But the prevailing view of birth control for those who favoured it was to be found in an article in *Nature* published by the biologist Ernest McBride in 1931 in which he claimed that 'preventing undesirable births' was the principal purpose of the movement. McBride was not alone in assuming that unlimited births among the 'less fit' would produce a profound historical crisis. He thought Britain faced little immediate danger of invasion by more 'virile races' but he was prepared to suggest that uncontrolled population growth would produce a crisis 'almost as formidable as the Tartar invasions'.[19] Earlier in the 1920s he had linked the absence of birth restriction with the bleak prospect of future 'wars of extermination and devastating famines'. Lack of a proper understanding of contraception was, according to another of McBride's scientific contemporaries, 'the greatest menace to civilisation'.[20]

It might well be argued that the use of this language of catastrophe was rhetorical, spoken to shock rather than persuade. It was clearly nourished by broader contemporary anxieties about the survival of civilization which pre-war race science had done something to encourage in the first place. But there are no grounds for assuming that it was not believed. Potential biological crisis was a central element in the morbid culture of the post-war years. The concept appealed because it gave to the popular malaise a clear scientific foundation. Scientists and non-scientists alike could be found to argue that the most plausible explanation for the rise and fall of past civilizations was biological – a cycle of racial health, impoverishment and eclipse. This assertion was made almost ad nauseam in the inter-war years. The annual Galton lecture in 1928 on the subject 'Some Causes of Racial Decay', given at University College, London, to honour the memory of the British pioneer of modern population science, Francis Galton, began by framing the biological analysis in historical terms: 'The real factors which determine the rise and fall of nations and civilizations are the racial qualities and innate capacities of the citizens themselves.' The lecturer, Charles Bond, went on to argue that all civilizations experienced a process of enervating senescence derived from the fact that '*social* outruns *biological* growth'. As civilizations become more complex, the wealthier elites decay while the masses proliferate 'like the parasitic cancer cells in the individual organism'. Medical language (the lecturer was himself a doctor) reinforced the conclusion that

biological factors were 'the chief source of the decline of past civilizations and of earlier races'.[21]

The anthropomorphic analogy was not accidental. Life scientists
and doctors played an important part in the application of biological
metaphor to the debate on the survival of past and contemporary
cultures. The Italian biologist Corrado Gini developed after the Great
War a popular model for the cyclical rise and fall of races which
replicated the development of the human individual through adoles-
cence, maturity and senescence.[22] In the 1928 Galton lecture, which
drew on Gini's work, it was assumed that the problem of 'racial
decline' in history could best be illuminated by studying the 'life
history of the individual organism'.[23] At the 1932 Congress of
Eugenics in New York, attended by an international constellation of
biologists, geneticists and doctors, one of the delegates reminded his
audience that 'races are born, sicken and die'. He continued: 'Cities,
states, and nations of high organization have reached manhood, old
age and death.'[24] At the same conference a message was read out from
Leonard Darwin, fourth son of the more famous Charles, founder
of modern evolutionary theory, warning the assembly that without
biological correction Western civilization was destined to suffer the
same slow decay that had been the lot 'of every great ancient civilization'.[25] He had developed these views more fully in his book on
Eugenic Reform published in 1925, in which he claimed that it was
the iron rule of nature, expressed through biological deterioration,
that doomed even a civilization as brilliant as ancient Greece 'to
disappear or to decline into obscurity'. The problem lay in the inherited quality of the race which, Darwin argued, had a natural tendency to decline as long as the 'less efficient strata' reproduced faster
than the biologically efficient. To stem this deterioration, 'to apply
the brake in time', as he expressed it, was the aim of the new science
of eugenics.[26]

Eugenists, as they styled themselves, were seldom modest about
their science. One of the founders of the British eugenic movement,
Caleb Saleeby, wrote in 1909 that 'eugenics is going to save the world'.
Ronald Fisher, a leading Cambridge geneticist, posed the question at
an international eugenics conference in Paris in 1926 whether the new
science might 'solve the problem of decay of civilizations'. Properly

applied, he thought, the answer was certainly yes; no less a prospect beckoned than the human ideal 'of a truly imperishable civilization'.[27] The ambitions of eugenic enthusiasts expanded with the growth of the science itself. The term was coined by Darwin's cousin, Sir Francis Galton, in a book on human inheritance published in 1883. Intrigued by the idea of natural selection, Galton speculated on the possibility of man controlling the blind forces of Nature by applying reason to the process of replicating the race. Galton borrowed freely from the language of animal breeding; better stocks would be promoted and the weaker stocks suppressed. Though the theoretical basis was supposed to be founded in scientific observation of the facts of human heredity, eugenics was as much a social as a biological phenomenon. For its success in improving human stock eugenics relied, according to the definition finally agreed on by Galton and his followers, 'on agencies under social control'; these would supply the necessary information and, when advisable, apply the requisite social policy to maximize the biological efficiency of the population. When Galton first pioneered eugenics the science of heredity was still in groping infancy. He relied on the development of 'biometrics', the statistical measurement of frequency of genius (or imbecility) in family pedigrees. Perhaps the most famous pedigree was his own, which obligingly demonstrated just how gifted the Darwins and their cousins were.[28]

The science Galton founded soon ran away from him. In the decade before the outbreak of war in 1914 Galton's biometrics was challenged by developments in human biology which focused more on identifying the internal mechanism of human heredity. The work of the German zoologist August Weissmann was a critical step in this direction. In 1883, the same year that Galton first wrote of eugenics, Weissmann developed the idea that the human body contained a quantum of germ cells which governed reproduction and inheritance alone; this 'germ plasm', as he called it, was unaffected by what happened to the rest of the body's cells, and so could not register acquired characteristics. The 'germ plasm' was the means for transferring all congenital qualities and could not be modified by environmental changes. His theory was widely accepted, though hotly debated, for the next forty years. The importance of 'germ plasm' as an explanation for the apparently unyielding transfer of inherited diseases, mental illness and

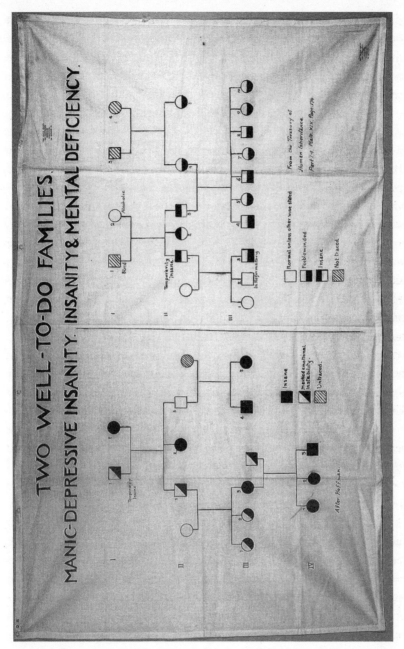

Two genealogies drawn up by the Eugenics Society as part of their campaign to demonstrate that mental deficiency was inherited, even among the more advantaged sections of the community.

deformity became a key argument in the eugenic insistence that the debilitated sections of the population could not, from the very nature of their biological endowment, be improved and should be allowed to decay and die out through operation of the harsh laws of natural selection.[29]

In the late 1890s a second major breakthrough occurred when a paper on plant hybrids first published in 1866 by Gregor Mendel, a Moravian monk and later abbot of the St Thomas Abbey in Brünn (Brno), was rediscovered by a number of European scientists working on plant cultivation. Mendel, who died in 1884, had stumbled across the key factors explaining genetic inheritance, though he lacked the language and scientific understanding to develop his theory more fully. In 1900 the first papers were published referring to Mendel's work and the foundations laid for the modern science of inheritance. A Cambridge zoologist, William Bateson, read Mendel's paper, travelled to Austria to investigate his work and returned to Cambridge to spell out in modern scientific language the laws that now bear Mendel's name. Bateson applied a new term to the study of inheritance – genetics – and in 1908 became the first professor of genetics in his university. Mendelism was at first applied to the study of plants and farmyard animals, but the implication of the new science was that key traits in human development were inherited in not dissimilar ways, and opened the possibility that defective traits could in some as yet unspecified way be bred out of human populations as they could be bred out of crops or chickens.[30]

The new science made huge strides in only a dozen years, but there remained many unanswered questions. Eugenists were attracted to it because genetics confirmed their view that the problems of race improvement were biological, not social. In Europe and America eugenic organizations were set up with the express purpose of applying the new science to the biological future. The founding meeting of the British eugenics movement took place at Caxton Hall in Westminster in November 1907. The name Eugenics Education Society was adopted in order to highlight its propagandistic ambitions, and it soon became an effective, if small, lobby-group. In 1911 Leonard Darwin agreed to become the Society's president and became the dominant figure in the movement down to the 1930s. In 1912 the first International Eugenics Congress was held in London with representatives from more than a dozen countries. By the outbreak of war the Society boasted more than 600 members, and the support of a broad circle of scientists, sociologists, economists and aspiring politicians, including the young Neville Chamberlain who joined the Birmingham branch of the Society, one of five provincial organizations founded before 1914.[31] Galton was the Society's first honorary president, though he and his followers distrusted the new association. When Galton died in 1911, his chief disciple, Karl Pearson, director of the Galton Eugenic Laboratory and London University's first professor of eugenics, would have nothing to do with the Society because of its preference for Mendelism over 'biometrics'. The eugenic establishment, small though it was, remained unusually cantankerous and argumentative, a reflection of the immature nature of the science and the divided nature of its constituency.

Eugenics has often been identified as characteristically a phenomenon of the pre-war world, a peculiarity of the Edwardian obsession with social improvement and national efficiency, but the high point of the British eugenics movement, and of eugenics internationally, came in the years between the two world wars. Before 1914 it was a marginal movement. After 1919 it grew in importance and self-confidence. The president of the Third Congress of Eugenics, held in New York in the American Museum of Natural History in late August 1932, told the assembled delegates that the two decades since the first congress in London had seen eugenics rise 'from a mire of ridicule' to become an important and established social reality; in the future he thought it would become '*the most* important influence on human advancement'.[32] In Britain the Eugenics Education Society changed its name in 1926 to simply the Eugenics Society and had by the 1930s around 800 members drawn largely from the scientific, cultural and political elite. These numbers scarcely did justice to the real size and influence of the wider eugenic establishment. There were other organizations which accepted much of the eugenic argument for race improvement – the followers of Marie Stopes, the Malthusian League, the British Social Hygiene Council and a number of national women's organizations, including the National Women's Council, which saw eugenics as a way to make women's lives less subject to the tyranny of inherited disability or enfeeblement. The ranks of self-confessed eugenists were swollen in the 1920s with a panoply of distinguished public figures in every field: the economist J. M. Keynes, who helped set up the Cambridge Eugenics Society before 1914 and remained a life-long supporter; the sexologist Havelock Ellis, who wrote pioneering books on sex before 1914; the zoologist Julian Huxley, grandson of Darwin's chief disciple Thomas Huxley and an early science celebrity; the psychologist Cyril Burt, pioneer of intelligence testing of schoolchildren and, as a result, a convinced hereditarian; the Irish playwright George Bernard Shaw, whose *Man and Superman* played on eugenic themes; William Inge, Dean of St Paul's, almost certainly the best-known churchman of his generation, who wanted an ideal British population of only 20 million, all with 'certificates of bodily and mental fitness'; and so on.[33] Eugenic concern in the inter-war years was no longer the province of people the public might have regarded as enthusiastic cranks.

The eugenic movement was a broad church whose congregation sang loudly if discordantly and declared their faith with resolution, but the conditions were particularly propitious for the eugenic message. Of all the natural sciences biology was the one most easily adapted to social and political reality and most readily understood by the wider public. The power of popular biological argument was evident in its most extreme form in Hitler's Germany, but the phenomenon was international. Biology was generally regarded as potentially benign – providing more food, better health and an improved environment. But it also had important social and ethical implications which brought it into the central arena of public debate. The distinguished biologist J. Arthur Thomson claimed that the post-war generation was witnessing the dawn of a new 'biological age' in which biology, understood as the control of life itself, would become the dominant science.[34] There was no shortage of popular publications on key biological issues. In 1926 the demographer Alexander Carr-Saunders published a short popular introduction to eugenics in the Home University Library series; a volume on *Biology and the Future*, published by Kegan Paul in 1925 in the Today and Tomorrow series of pocket books, sold more than any of the other titles, bar one, Ferdinand Schiller's book on the future of man. In the late 1920s England's most famous novelist, H. G. Wells, and his biologist son George collaborated with Julian Huxley to produce over 1,600 pages on *The Science of Life*. The book was published in 1931, then in serial form in the 1930s, and finally in a cheap popular edition in 1938, price 10/6. Its purpose, wrote Wells in the introduction, was to reduce the mass of current biological information to a form readily digested by 'ordinary busy people'.[35] It covered everything that the biologist knew by the 1930s. No other science was capable of communicating the corpus of its knowledge in ways as comprehensible and comprehensive as biology.

Eugenic arguments also reflected important shifts in public and political outlook, as the growing interest in birth control demonstrated. The government sponsored commissions of enquiry before and after the war on a wide variety of issues that were biological in nature – population policy, the 'feeble-minded', syphilis, alcoholism. Growing public concern over racial degeneration, both physical and moral, owed something to the growth of eugenic understanding but was also fuelled by the publicity given to hereditarian science by alarmist reports on crime levels, prostitution and delinquency, all of which were attributed in some degree to inherited predisposition. Indeed, the eugenic movement shifted ground in the post-war period to take account of the popularization of the breakthroughs in hereditarian biology by presenting eugenics as the science uniquely placed to understand and correct the problems facing the social body. Mendel's laws (like Weissmann's 'germ plasm') combined promise and threat in unequal measure; while a proper understanding of the laws of inheritance might make possible the distant perfection of the species (an objective, Bertrand Russell remarked facetiously, that would mean sterilizing 95 per cent of the male population), the immediate issue of inheritance was much more menacing, because the genetic material that was supposed to produce the biologically and psychologically debilitated elements of the population was already embedded in the gene pool and could not be easily eradicated nor its effects confidently predicted.[36] The image of the social body assailed by disease and psychological disorder, under attack from within in ways not sufficiently understood and of uncertain provenance, offered an image of biological catastrophe that remained the stock-in-trade of popular biological discourse down to the outbreak of the second war, and a central element in explaining the current crisis of civilization.

The divided nature of the eugenic endeavour was well understood. The aims and objectives of the Eugenics Society drew a distinction between 'positive' and 'negative' eugenics, the first designed to promote the fertility of 'superior, healthy and useful stocks', the latter to restrict or diminish 'the fertility of all persons below the average'.[37] The positive consisted of a wish-list of pro-natalist policies: family allowances and tax concessions for healthy child-rich families, health examinations before marriage. 'No War' was added in the mid-1930s to reflect the widespread fear that a second war, like the first, would promote only dysgenic effects by killing off the best males first. The negative proposals were, by contrast, far more drastic: sterilization or segregation for those 'below average'; legal prohibition of marriage; and, less commonly, abortion.[38] Birth control also appeared on both lists, a paradox enshrined in the terms used to describe it – 'value and danger'. As a positive factor it was to be promoted only for 'spacing births' to ensure that families could be planned with foresight. It was not to be encouraged among those with 'superior biological endowment'. As a negative factor the purpose was to restrict the birth rate of the less valuable sectors of the population. Although eugenists accepted that birth control could in principle help in the fight to limit the births of those regarded as hereditarily unfit, they doubted the capacity of 'the mentally backward and feckless' to practise birth control responsibly while they deplored the fact that limitation was mainly practised by those very classes whose fertility they were most anxious to promote. The birth control movement, for all its good eugenic intentions, was regarded as essentially dysgenic in its effects.[39]

Ambivalence was characteristic of much of the eugenic debate. Though there was no hesitation in accepting that the 'unfit' existed as a social reality, defining who was and who was not socially useful had no agreed basis scientifically. Yet fears of dysgenic disaster required hard facts in order to be plausible and while a great deal of experimental research was undertaken in the decades following the war, a consensus on who was unfit and how 'unfitness' was transferred from generation to generation could not be established. There was little dispute about those categories that appeared self-evident. This included the certifiably insane and the larger fraction of the population deemed to be 'feeble-minded' or 'defective', whether through some physical abnormality or observable mental disability. The Mental Deficiency Act of 1927 attempted to define this fraction of the population more carefully than earlier legislation had done. There were thought to be four clear categories: idiots (unable to look after themselves); imbeciles (unable to manage their affairs unaided); feeble-minded (requiring care and supervision); and moral defectives (deficient but also vicious).[40] For eugenists, however, there existed more contentious areas of definition. Galton had insisted that personality and behaviour, or character, also defined the unfit. These were elements with little 'civic worth' and degenerate credentials and included not only those with alleged mental defects, but epileptics, consumptives, alcoholics, drug addicts, neurotics, eccentrics and the sexually promiscuous.[41] This much larger constituency might certainly contain some deemed to be mentally deficient, but it was not necessarily so; nor could it be demonstrated, without more precise genetic science, that all those regarded as socially or physically debilitated had inherited their taint.

The problem of defining the unfit was made more acute by the division between the Galton school and the Mendelians. The possibility of eugenic improvement relied entirely on the extent to which debilitation – civic, physical or mental – could be shown to be the product of heredity. Galton and the biometricians relied on the evidence of extensive pedigrees to show the statistical likelihood of inherited traits. Numerous examples were brought forward to illustrate the links. A well-known case was the pedigree of a rural family made famous by the legend of 'Boil-Watch' Gallows, who was found one day by villagers boiling his watch in a saucepan while holding an egg to time it with. He was treated as the village idiot, and died in the workhouse. The records revealed that he had a 'feeble-minded' son, whose progeny included two feeble-minded children, three others in a home designated 'not bright' and 'thought to be feeble-minded', and a daughter who was 'simple', who in turn gave birth to an illegitimate 'feeble-minded' child.[42] These observations gave, at best, prima facie grounds for inferring a chain of heredity, but numerous other pedigrees which observed persistent alcoholism, criminality or illegitimacy were based largely on the speculative assumption that environment counted for little and that social evils were capable of genetic transmission.

Mendelian genetics challenged the view that characteristics regarded as vicious or anti-social were inherited rather than acquired, but the degree of proof was patchy at best. A list drawn up in the 1930s of what was and what was not capable of genetic transfer on Mendelian principles was a mixed bag of certain, pending and unproven. Out of 101 physical and mental conditions, which included everything from freckles to Jewish noses, nomadism to suicide, only eleven physical and nine mental traits were established with 'reasonable certainty'.[43] In the case of physical disability or malformation the role of heredity was much clearer, even if the precise mechanism of transfer was less well understood. But little of the eugenic case rested on physical inheritance. The one area in which it was thought essential to prove inheritance was the transfer of mental quality and mental deficiency. The whole case for eugenic reform relied on being able to demonstrate with reasonable certainty that genes or 'germ plasm' contained the seeds of later debility. Experimental psychology rather than genetics provided the answer. The early development of intelligence testing, chiefly associated with Cyril Burt, educational psychologist to London County Council and later professor of education at the University of London, allowed psychologists to pronounce with apparent scientific certainty that mental characteristics were inherited. In a lecture to schoolteachers in March 1916 Burt stated the case he insisted on for the rest of his long professional career, that mental capacities were inherited and immutable:

However much we educated the ignorant, trained the imbecile, cured the lunatic, and reformed the criminal, their offspring would inherit, not the results of education, but the original ignorance; not the acquired training, but the original imbecility; not the acquired sanity, but the original predisposition to lunacy; not the moral reform, but the original tendency to crime.[44]

Burt later became notorious for his insistence that the 'backward' or 'defective' child was doomed for life, but in the inter-war years the argument that genetic endowment determined mental capacity had few critics.

If mental capacity was inherited on genetic principles, it did not follow that inheritance was straightforward. Mendelian genetics suggested that not all progeny would be affected in the same way; mental deficiency did not pass from parent to child in a straight line, nor could all forms of mental defect be explained solely by inheritance. Throughout the 1920s and 1930s eugenists and psychologists wrestled with the problem of estimating the degree to which mental disabilities were inherited. They distinguished between primary 'amentia' (literally, absence of mind), which was inherited, and secondary 'amentia', which was the result of disease, accident or traumatic birth. Burt's own calculations suggested that in 82 per cent of the children with mental disabilities that he observed 'hereditary defect' was present, but only 6 per cent of his sample had a parent certified as defective. The large bulk of his control group had only a traceable family pedigree with evidence of 'subnormality', which left Burt in much the same position as Galton.[45] The figures for inherited mental disabilities were hotly contested because much rested on the outcome. By the late 1920s the popularly accepted figure for inherited mental disability hovered between two-thirds and three-fourths, and the latter figure was eventually adopted by a government committee set up in 1932 to study the possibility of sterilizing those with mental defects. However, a lecture to the Eugenics Society in 1936 based on experimental work carried out in Europe suggested that the percentage varied widely from one condition to another – a 35 per cent chance of passing on Huntington's chorea to a child; 37 per cent of the parents of psychopaths showing 'marked abnormality'; between 53 and 63 per cent of children with two schizophrenic parents developing the condition; and so on.[46]

For most of those engaged in eugenic argument these were issues that could not be easily resolved. The temptation was to make deliberately little distinction between conditions thought to be inherited and delinquent forms of social behaviour, or to assume that one in some sense caused the other. The eugenist Austin Freeman, writing in 1921, summed up 'The Unfit' without discrimination: 'lunatics, idiots, imbeciles, the feeble-minded and "backward", epileptics, deaf-mutes, the congenitally blind, and the large class of degenerates', which comprised, in his view, 'habitual criminals, the inmates of reformatories and industrial homes, tramps, vagrants, chronic inebriates, prostitutes, the subjects of drug-habits, sexual perverts and the sufferers from various congenital neuroses'.[47] The conflation of inherited disability and anti-social behaviour solved the question of where racial decay was located. Few eugenists would have argued with this list. Throughout the life of the movement the notion of the 'unfit' carried with it an evident moral stigma. The idea that mental disability and moral laxity cohabited was largely taken for granted, and the connections between them were routinely and uncritically asserted.

Masturbation, for example, was regarded by some as a principal cause of insanity. The habit was said to undermine the 'nervous organisation' of all those who fell prey to its debilitating attractions, but particularly those whose minds were already enfeebled. 'Sexual excess' and 'inebriety', hallmarks of degeneracy, were coupled in much eugenic debate with feeble-mindedness.[48] Women were singled out, as they were in much of inter-war Europe, as the culprits. 'I am disposed to believe', wrote Freeman in his account of social decay, 'that the principal agent of racial deterioration is the inferior woman.'[49] Cyril Burt had much to say on the concept of what he termed 'the over-sexed girl'. He was invited in 1932 to give his opinion on the links between prostitution and mental disability and though he found only 12 per cent of the cross-section of London prostitutes were certifiable under the 1927 Mental Deficiency Act, he pronounced that at least four-fifths of them were subnormal to some degree. A further survey of 101 'feeble-minded' women purported to show that twenty-seven had a history of promiscuity, seven had been professional prostitutes, twenty-one had given birth to illegitimate children and two were incestuous. Somehow Burt managed to elicit information to show that two-thirds of those who could recall when their 'sexual misconduct' began had been less than 21 years of age at the time.[50] The assumption that those unable to suppress the sexual instinct must be in some degree mentally subnormal condemned hundreds of young women to life imprisonment in psychiatric institutions.

To cope with the evidence that vice and deficiency clustered together in the wider community the eugenic movement searched for new forms of social definition. The report of the Board of Control on Mental Deficiency published in 1929 coined the term 'social problem group' to describe those individuals and families who were not certifiable under the Mental Deficiency Act but whose social behaviour, habits and promiscuity set them apart from the rest of society as 'subnormal', and who between them were responsible, it was claimed, for a high proportion of all those who were already certified.[51] The Eugenics Society took up the concept with a will and in July 1932 established a series of sub-committees to investigate one category each of the 'social problem group' – those on welfare, those with psychiatric diseases, epileptics, criminals, slum dwellers, the unemployed, prostitutes, inebriates and 'casuals'. Through the 1920s prominent eugenists had hinted at an even larger grey zone populated by those clearly below the average physically and mentally, prone to vice though not irredeemably vicious, and capable of contributing little to sustaining the race. The evidence for the social problem group confirmed these fears. Leonard Darwin, who had retired as president of the Society in 1929, wrote to the secretary in 1933 that it was the multiplication of the types described as 'somewhat inferior' that posed as much of a threat to the social body as those whose inferiority could be deemed 'gross'. He suggested, not surprisingly, that the population could be divided almost exactly in half, those above the average and those below.[52] Cyril Burt regarded the mentally deficient as no more than 'the tail end' of a much larger proportion of 'borderline persons' whom he defined as the 'mentally dull' and hence subnormal.[53] For eugenists brought up on morbid fears of degeneration it was difficult to know where to draw the line. The problem with genetic transference was its invisibility. Because recessive genes which carried abnormalities appeared unevenly and unpredictably in succeeding generations it was impossible to tell how far genetic damage might spread. In a pamphlet on the social problem group written for the Eugenics Society by a Liverpool University social scientist, David Caradog Jones, the most urgent task appeared to be to unmask those who seemed 'outwardly normal' but who 'inwardly carry defective genes'.[54] These were the enemy within, the 'carriers', as Julian Huxley called them, who bore with them 'grave disasters of an unknown kind', capable of permanent subterranean damage to the social fabric.[55]

The question was how much damage? The answer was destined to determine just what scale of biological threat confronted the future of civilization. There was reasonably precise knowledge about the institutionalized population certified under the law. According to the 1928 report of the Board of Control, the body whose job it was to supervise those in public care, there were 138,000 certified insane. The number of 'mentally deficient' was harder to estimate but the Mental Deficiency Committee report of 1929 suggested a total of 284,000, which was close to the figure of 300–350,000 suggested by scientific researchers.[56] This gave a figure of 8.56 per 1,000 of the population, roughly double the official figure of 140,000 or 4.6 per 1,000 recorded in 1909 by the Royal Commission on the Feeble-minded. But this figure did not include those regarded as 'carriers', which the Eugenics Society reckoned at an approximate ratio of 2:1, nor epileptics (who always appeared on lists of the biologically degenerate), nor the vast grey zone of the population with some degree of physical deformity or mental debility. This gave wide opportunity for extrapolations of the most lurid kind. The lowest figure was a little over one million of those officially certified or thought likely to be carrying defective genes; the Mental Deficiency Committee report of 1929 suggested that with the addition of the 'social problem group' the figure was four million, or one-tenth of the population; the largest figure was published in the *British Medical Journal* in 1929, suggesting a grand total of 9.5 million insane, defective or subnormal, or almost one-quarter of the entire population of the United Kingdom.[57]

These figures were estimates, but they were used by eugenists to show that the hidden dangers which genetic transfer entailed might corrupt a population in a matter of decades. Like the birth control movement, the eugenic establishment deplored the fact that those sections of the population that they regarded as least worthy were the ones in which fertility was highest or, as one biologist bluntly put it: 'We are getting larger and larger dregs at the bottom of our national vats.'[58] Cyril Burt, giving the annual Heath Clark lectures to the London School of Hygiene and Tropical Medicine in 1934, speculated from existing statistics on fertility that in two centuries 60 per cent of the British population would be certifiable as 'mentally deficient'. The evidence that the defective proportion of the population was reproducing itself faster than the rest he took for granted: 'You might almost put it as an arithmetic law: – the smaller the brains, the bigger the family.'[59] Caradog Jones, in a detailed social survey of the population of Merseyside produced in 1934, showed with apparent certainty that the 'normal' family averaged only 2.97 children, while the 'defective' family averaged 4.69, the blind 4.88, the deaf 4.59 and epileptics 4.50. If the figures included those who died in infancy, Jones found that the mean family size of the 'most subnormal' was 7.16.[60] These statistics confirmed the eugenic nightmare that unless the 'unfit' could somehow be induced or forced to have few or no offspring, the biological future of the race was doomed to a process of gradual, but irreversible, degeneration.

Eugenists were in no doubt that the crisis of morbid inheritance had to be confronted immediately and in the most radical way. The pre-war evidence had been patchy and unsystematic. The accumulating scientific knowledge in the 1920s, though not all of it confirmed earlier prognoses of disaster unambiguously, was regarded as sufficiently robust to justify government intervention before the diseased social body was past medical help. The language routinely used to describe biological intervention was uncompromising – 'elimination' of the unfit, 'festering sores' to be cut out, a 'diseased constitution' to be medically repaired.[61] This was the language of German 'race-hygiene' first developed by Alfred Ploetz in the 1890s, whose prophecies of race degeneration played an important part in the evolution of 'biological politics' in Germany in the 1930s and were generally applauded by British eugenists.[62] Cleansing the race left few options that did not involve severe levels of medical or social intervention. Segregation of the 'unfit' in institutions or colonies was considered inadequate to tackle the scale of the problem, all the more so with the expanding definition of who the 'unfit' were. Compulsory restriction on marriage was also mooted, though it was pointed out that this would do little to prevent procreation since the unfit were notoriously promiscuous inside or outside marriage. This left two possibilities. The first was 'the lethal chamber', the second sterilization.

The lethal chamber was first suggested, though not widely advocated, in the years before 1914. The chamber would use some form of gas to exterminate undesirable elements of the population in a painless and permanent way. It is mentioned in a book by the nautical engineer Arnold White, published in 1901, in which he complained that people of 'lazy mind' talked about a lethal chamber as the easy solution to ridding the country of what he later described as a 'tyrannical troop of deteriorated humanity', though he went on to favour the next best thing: 'Extirpate them by immuring them from life.'[63] Most eugenists distanced themselves from the idea, though not always on simple humanitarian grounds. George Whitehead, writing in 1925 on the necessity for medical intervention, rejected the lethal chamber on the grounds that the nation 'would not tolerate such forcible methods', but not on the ground that it was wrong.[64] One director of a colony for the mentally disabled thought that of the medical options available, the 'more kindly' was extinction in the chamber; this view was quoted with approval by General J. F. C. Fuller, a self-styled expert on war and a keen supporter of British fascism in the 1930s, who thought that sterilization and the lethal chamber would stem 'the physical dry rot' of Western civilization.[65]

One notoriously maverick eugenist, Nietzsche's English translator Anthony Ludovici, thought British opinion too soft on race regeneration and wanted elimination of the unfit to mean just that. He published a book in 1928 with the obscure title *The Night Hoers*, based on the idea that contraception was like weeding in the dark, randomly destructive of the best human stock, and unable to prevent the birth of the worst. He advocated killing all babies with clear abnormalities and exterminating ('put painlessly away', as he put it) all 'incurable lunatics'.[66] The book resulted in a frank exchange of letters between Leonard Darwin, now retired, and Charles Blacker, the secretary of the Eugenics Society appointed in 1931. Blacker thought the proposals for what Ludovici described as 'euthanasia' were misplaced because they would have little eugenic effect, but he reported the support of at least one superintendent of a psychiatric hospital who strongly favoured the lethal chamber. Darwin, who had described the chamber in 1925 as 'unhesitatingly condemned' because 'it would tend to associate the idea of murder with progress' and as a result 'increase the number of murders', privately thought that euthanasia should not be rejected out of hand but assessed on its merits. 'How much racial benefit could be gained?' he asked. Darwin thought mothers might well agree to put an end to babies with severe congenital conditions, but did not believe the Society would gain much by openly advocating euthanasia. When Blacker had asked him a few weeks earlier if mothers could ever be persuaded to agree to the killing of a child with congenital blindness, Darwin scribbled in the margin of the letter, 'My wife and I certainly would.'[67]

Most of the eugenic establishment rejected state murder as the answer (it is worth recalling that when both euthanasia and the lethal chamber were introduced in Hitler's Germany a few years later the whole programme was kept veiled from the public), but there were plenty who saw dysgenic breeding as something to be penalized and stigmatized. An article in the progressive magazine *Plan* in 1936 ('A Eugenist Runs Amok') called for compulsory sterilization 'as a *punishment*' for parents who had children in pauperized circumstances. Caradog Jones looked forward to the time when giving birth to an 'afflicted' child 'will be considered and treated as a crime'.[68] There were few, if any, eugenists who did not accept that sterilization, whether compulsory or voluntary, was the one remaining panacea capable of addressing the seriousness of their case for racial decline and they worked throughout the inter-war years to persuade the government to set in place firm procedures for a national programme of sterilization targeted at the biologically and socially undesirable.

The campaign for sterilization began in Britain before 1914, directed chiefly at the incurably insane and criminals. In a paper presented to the Medico-Psychological Association in October 1910 a senior medical officer at Bexley Asylum advocated not only the compulsory sterilization of those with severe mental illnesses but also the castration of sex offenders, particularly those in which he claimed masturbation was the chief symptom and probable cause of insanity because they were, in his view, especially 'harmful and dangerous'. Another senior medical officer, at Hanwell Asylum, wrote that though the degenerate could now be kept alive by medical science and social welfare, they and probably their entire families should be sterilized since sterilizing only the worst cases 'would be as rational as to amputate the toe when the whole leg is gangrenous'.[69] The most notorious advocate was Robert Reid Rentoul, whose book *Proposed Sterilization*, published in 1903, called for the 'extermination' of the unfit by means short of killing and launched him on a decade of strident publicity for views that most of the pre-war eugenics movement deplored as too radical an infringement of individual liberty and too great a challenge to conventional ethical standards.[70] Yet by the 1920s these objections had been substantially modified. The greater sense of biological panic and the wider degree of scientific and statistical knowledge made sterilization a more attractive option. The operations – vasectomy for a man, salpingectomy (an operation on the Fallopian tubes) for a woman – were generally regarded as less dangerous than they had once been. The example of sterilization elsewhere in Europe and America also played a part in breaking down instinctive resistance to the practice in Britain. Sterilization was first legalized in Indiana in 1907; by 1914 a further fifteen American states had approved it; by the Second World War it was being carried out in thirty states and a total of 42,000 people had been sterilized, all but 1,559 on grounds of 'feeblemindedness' or 'madness', in most cases compulsorily.[71] The ethical argument also shifted ground, from the absolute integrity of the individual to the idea that sacrificing parenthood was a moral obligation to the racial collective.

Once an important element of the eugenic movement itself came to embrace the idea of sterilization the burden shifted to educating the wider public. That the British public was 'unripe' for the idea of sterilization had been a key argument against proselytizing its cause before 1914. Propaganda to persuade public opinion to accept some measure of legislation became one of the most important of the Society's tasks in the 1920s. Leonard Darwin, whose inclinations were towards the positive eugenics of breeding better stocks, adjusted late in his eugenic career to the efficiency of sterilization as a cheap and permanent way to block off damaged hereditary streams and became a keen advocate. He was well aware of the prejudice against the idea of compulsory sterilization and pushed the Society behind support for the voluntary principle, though his private view was that, properly educated, the public might eventually come round to compulsion. In 1938 he wrote to Blacker in confidence that even if voluntary methods were 'the only ones *now* acceptable', German methods of compulsory sterilization 'may be right if *practicable*'. Democracy placed barriers that autocracies could ignore. 'We cannot imitate Germany,' he continued, 'but we may agree that German methods have merits.'[72]

There were a number of ways in which sterilization could be presented to the public. The cost involved in maintaining an ever-growing cohort of the 'unfit' and their proliferating progeny properly segregated was presented as a compelling argument for sterilization. Lord George Riddell read a paper before the Medico-Legal Society in April 1929 in which he accounted the cost of institutional and educational provision for the escalating 'unfit' at an estimated £16 million per year, or around £70 for every 'lunatic or mental defective' against £12 for every normal child. 'Can the community afford to spend so much?' asked Riddell. 'Are you going to penalise the fit for the unfit?'[73] The idea that in a time of declining economic opportunity, the good citizen should be permanently burdened with the rising cost of degeneracy became a central plank in the British case as it did in Germany and the United States. The more radical argument that there was no automatic right to parenthood was also dressed up to look respectable. The issue was expressed not in terms of everyone's right to have children, but in terms of the moral claims of children to a decent and civilized environment to grow up in and the claims of the community to a healthy racial posterity. When Blacker drafted new aims and objectives of the Eugenics Society in 1930 he included the moral assertion that 'no couple [is] to be regarded as having an absolute right to parenthood'.[74] By the 1930s the view was a commonplace. In November 1935 the BBC broadcast a light-hearted, if polemical, debate between Bertrand Russell and the writer G. K. Chesterton on the theme 'That Parents are Unfitted by Nature to Bring up their own Children'. The chair was taken by Cyril Burt, one of the stalwarts of early documentary radio, who took advantage of his position to announce that in his opinion there were parents not only unfit to raise their offspring but 'equally unfit to *have* any'.[75]

The sterilization campaign also benefited from the support of a growing number of prominent public figures who helped to open the question up for public scrutiny. Havelock Ellis had advocated the solution before 1914 and became an outspoken supporter in the 1920s, constantly berating the Society for not doing more to educate the public to accept compulsory sterilization even of those where hereditary transfer of defects was by no means certain: 'better to err on the side of care than on the side of carelessness'.[76] Ellis was by now an old man, reclusive and notoriously irascible but a powerful voice nonetheless, who felt so strongly about sterilization that he threatened in 1931 to found an alternative eugenic society to prosecute this single solution. Another supporter was Marie Stopes, who viewed birth control and sterilization as two sides of the same coin. Stopes had little time for the eugenics movement, which she thought gave insufficient support to her own ideas on birth restriction, but on this issue there was common ground. She favoured sterilization for all those regarded as 'too low grade to consider the community' by eschewing procreation. When she was asked at a meeting on birth control in Cambridge in 1930 her views on making sterilization compulsory, she had no hesitation in recommending that compulsion should be applied at the least to all those assessed with a mental age of less than 12.[77]

Two names stand out among the array of scientists, politicians and writers who flirted with sterilization in the inter-war years: Julian Huxley and his onetime pupil Charles Paton Blacker. Huxley was brought up in the shadow of his famous grandfather Thomas, whose support for evolutionary theory in the 1860s and 1870s had earned him the sobriquet 'Darwin's Bulldog'. The eldest of three brothers, one of whom was the novelist Aldous, Julian inherited the family mantle of the biological sciences. A professional zoologist who made his name with a thesis on the courtship habits of the great-crested grebe, he served in Italy during the Great War then taught briefly at New College, Oxford before taking up the chair in zoology at King's College, London in 1925 at the young age of 38. He retired from his chair two years later to concentrate on writing the book on biology with H. G. Wells, and developing his role as the media's favourite scientist. In 1935 he was appointed secretary of the Royal Zoological Society in Regent's Park. A tall, almost unnaturally slender figure, with owl-like spectacles and a limp chin, Huxley looked the epitome of the inter-war intellectual. His correspondence reveals a man almost obsessively concerned with his health, prey to endless attacks of sinusitis and bronchitis. He felt keenly all the anxieties of his age. When the BBC invited him to engage in an imaginary conversation with his famous grandfather, Huxley explained that the most striking difference between the post-war world and the late-Victorian age was the 'widespread pessimism' all about him.[78] Like so many of his peers he

deplored war, approved of Freud and worried about pending biological disaster. He was a fellow of the Eugenics Society.

Huxley was introduced to the debate on sterilization in early 1930,
after Blacker became the Society's secretary. He saw at once that this
was the answer to his own concerns about the impact of mental
deficiency on the future of the race. He threw himself into the campaign, writing articles and letters to *The Times* and lecturing countrywide. His argument was simple: mental deficiency was a social burden,
was increasing rapidly and should be curtailed as a blessing to humankind. In his 1936 Galton lecture, Huxley observed that the success of
modern medicine and welfare in keeping alive those whom natural
selection would have allowed to wither away had potentially catastrophic consequences: 'Humanity will gradually destroy itself from
within, will decay in its very core and essence . . .'[79] He placed excessive confidence in the healing powers of eugenics ('capable of becoming
one of the sacred ideals of the human race'), and looked forward to
the time when society itself had been transformed along progressive
eugenic lines. In the meantime he favoured the immediate introduction
of voluntary sterilization, organized by some form of impartial
'eugenic board' in each locality; he could see that compulsion was
more difficult to insist on, but hoped that 'a later generation may
perhaps come to it'.[80] He believed the sterile should see themselves as
honourable warriors of the race, not stigmatized failures. Sterilization,
he told an audience in Glasgow in 1934, 'should be regarded as a
privilege and a badge of good conduct'.[81]

Charles Blacker was, like Huxley, part of a younger generation of
doctors and biologists for whom eugenics had a powerful appeal as
an engine of social progress. Blacker studied zoology at Oxford, where
he met Huxley, and later qualified as a psychiatrist at Guy's Hospital
in London. He was descended on his father's side from the Peruvian
aristocracy, and he had been christened Carlos. He preferred to be
known by his nickname, 'Pip'. He shared Huxley's catastrophic view
of human prospects. In a book in 1926 he warned that humanity was
passing through 'a biological crisis unprecedented in the history of
life'.[82] He also shared Huxley's pessimism. When he was invited to
talk on 'The Modern Conception of the World' in Prague in October
1928, he devoted much of his paper to the spiritual anxieties and

Julian Huxley in 1935 at the opening of the children's zoo in Regent's Park pictured with the young Robert and Edward Kennedy, sons of the American ambassador to Britain, Joseph Kennedy. Huxley was Secretary of the Zoological Society which ran the Regent's Park Zoo.

the 'state of profound uncertainty' that had overtaken Europe. He appreciated Freud, disliked communism and deplored the effects of the war, in which he had served in the Coldstream Guards.[83] He was tall, bearded and fit, a man of great energy and a tough temperament. He was appointed secretary of the Eugenics Society in 1931 and set out to make it into a more modern, scientific and socially acceptable organization. He was patient with the many Colonel Blimps who still peopled the Society, but he was keen to modernize its image and dress up its language. He preferred to talk about 'social hygiene' in describing the eugenic programme and strongly supported the concept of the 'social problem group', the term pioneered by the Society in the 1920s, as a more useful and less pejorative description than 'the unfit'. He arrived at the Society just at the point when the campaign for sterilization was in full flow and he played a central part in efforts to present the policy as a rational and socially progressive addition to existing provision rather than a racial punishment.[84]

Blacker understood that there was no prospect of legalizing sterilization without a vigorous campaign of propaganda on its behalf. Public opinion was already inclined to listen more closely to the eugenic message but the issue of sterilization stirred strong emotions. In 1931 Blacker drafted a pamphlet titled 'Better Unborn', the purpose of which was to encourage the development of a popular 'eugenic conscience'. A second pamphlet on 'Eugenic Sterilization' was distributed to public authorities and organizations; over 10,000 were sold.[85] Lectures were held all over the country to a broad social range, including working-class audiences who were discovered to be as enthusiastic about sterilization as any other. In a Cambridge Union debate, sterilization won an overwhelming endorsement; the Cambridge Eugenics Society programme for 1930 included a lecture on 'Eugenic Sterilization' and in 1931 on 'The Sterilization Bill'. When a Eugenics Society spokesman visited Cambridge in March 1930 to talk on 'Human Heredity', the 120 undergraduates present pressed him on sterilization but showed little interest in positive eugenic solutions.[86] During the course of 1930 and 1931 a range of national organizations passed resolutions supporting sterilization – the National Council for Mental Hygiene, the National Association for the Feeble-Minded, the Conservative Women's Reform Association, and the Women's Co-Operative Guilds Congress, which, unlike the others, pressed for compulsory sterilization.[87] The National Women's Council encouraged debate on sterilization and petitioned the government early in 1931 to investigate its use as a means of reducing 'mental deficiency'.[88] After a year of countrywide debate, 'public sentiment', in the opinion of one senior doctor, 'generally expected' some official proposal for legalization.[89]

The Eugenics Society took full advantage of the rising tide of public concern. During the course of 1930 the Council of the Society agreed to set up a Committee for Legalizing Eugenic Sterilization. Its report was careful to emphasize that sterilization was intended to be voluntary, except in circumstances where the defective was unable to register an opinion. Three groups were identified as targets: mental defectives, the recovered insane and those with serious hereditary diseases. A draft sterilization bill was prepared in November 1930 which set out what were regarded as proper safeguards to ensure that someone, either the individual to be sterilized, or a spouse, or parent or guardian and agents from the Board of Control, had given their consent.[90] Sir Bernard Mallett, Leonard Darwin's successor as president of the Society, planned a campaign of lobbying members of both houses of parliament, trade union leaders, legal experts and doctors. The bill was presented to the Scientific Committee of the House of Commons, but the Committee refused to accept it unless it could be made to apply only to 'mental defectives'. A bill in that form was resubmitted and the chairman of the Scientific Committee, Major Archibald Church, the Labour MP for Central Wandsworth and a member of the Eugenics Society, agreed to present it to the House as a private member's bill in July 1931.[91] Support gathered from senior church-men, academics and doctors was published in a special pamphlet of 'Opinions upon Major Church's Sterilization Bill', though the bill was clearly the inspiration of the Society.

On the afternoon of 21 July Blacker went down to the House of Commons to sit in the gallery to watch the progress of the bill. Major Church was given only the customary few minutes in which to introduce the emasculated provisions of the original draft. He outlined the single provision to enable mental defectives or their guardians to apply for sterilization. The House, he added, might regard the provision as something 'in advance of public opinion' but it was, in his view, only a prelude to introducing a bill 'for the compulsory sterilization of the unfit'. He reported that fifty-three borough councils had expressed themselves in favour of a measure which all could see was designed only to prevent 'the progressive deterioration of our stock'. With that he sat down. He was opposed by a Catholic party colleague, Dr Hyacinth Morgan, MP for Camberwell North West, who evidently relished the opportunity to assault not just the bill, but the whole eugenic endeavour. 'Some when inebriated see beetles,' he began, 'the eugenist, intoxicated, sees defectives.' The account of racial crisis was, he urged, 'mainly moonshine', the notion of a 'degenerate civilisation' simply a eugenic nightmare. To loud jeers he asked the House to accept that segregation covered all that was required; he conjured up a vision of 'sterilised defectives' free to roam the streets 'living depraved lives, spreading disease, mainly venereal, still impulsive sexually and a dangerous menace to innocent women and children' like the damned, he concluded triumphantly, in Dante's *Inferno*.[92] The vote was taken and despite the heckling Morgan carried the day: the Ayes numbered 89 (and included the future prime minister, Anthony Eden), the Noes 167. Most of the Labour Party had voted against a measure widely regarded as a product of sheer class prejudice. The following day a disappointed Havelock Ellis wrote to Blacker that the idea of introducing the bill had been madness in the first place. Blacker replied that, given the nature of the House, they had known beforehand there was not 'the smallest chance of the bill passing'. But it had been, he concluded, good propaganda.[93]

This was not the end of the sterilization campaign. Two weeks before the defeat of the bill, the British Medical Association representing the country's medical profession inaugurated a Mental Deficiency Committee whose terms of reference were to investigate proposals for sterilization of defectives. It was a high-level committee, which sat for a year hearing evidence from across the scientific and medical fields involved. Its final report recommended that voluntary sterilization, properly administered, might well be a way forward. The Committee's chairman wrote a flowery conclusion about degeneracy 'imperilling the safety of the nation' in defiance of natural selection, but the president of the BMA overruled him and substituted a bland epilogue on the virtues of camps and colonies for the defective population, reassured, perhaps, by the evidence from one expert witness that life in a colony for mental defectives 'is very similar to that in a public school'.[94] By the time the report was circulated, the government had already responded. In February 1932 the Ministry of Health agreed to a study of sterilization, and in November that year set up a committee of the Board of Control to study mental deficiency and sterilization. The Brock Committee, as it was known, produced its report in January 1934 unanimously recommending voluntary sterilization for cases of inherited mental disease or 'grave disability, physical or mental', the operation to be performed under the supervision of two doctors, with the written consent of the patient or a guardian and, in doubtful cases, reference to a ministry committee of doctors and geneticists for advice.[95] The Eugenics Society regarded this as a real breakthrough. Blacker's own book recommending voluntary sterilization appeared shortly afterwards and there was wide evidence of public approval. Yet despite continued pressure from medical, scientific and welfare organizations right up to the outbreak of war, the recommendations were never implemented.

Why did sterilization fail in Britain? To eugenists who thought they had human destiny in their hands the failure was a pact with disaster. Yet there were many reasons negative eugenics failed to produce the kind of legislation that permitted sterilization in Germany or the United States. Though there was strong local support from councils, mental hospitals and medical practitioners, any legislation had to be channelled nationally through parliament, where a convincing case had to be made in the face of strong opposition from Catholic and Labour opinion. The Labour Party refused to endorse medical intervention, and when a National Workers' Committee for Voluntary Sterilization was set up early in 1935 the party secretary rejected any connection with it.[96] As Blacker recognized, much left-wing opinion assumed that eugenics was based on 'a consciousness of class superiority' and preferred environmental explanations for debility.[97] Catholic hostility needs little explanation and eugenists in general took it for granted. The Catholic position condemning sterilization was made clear by Pope Pius XI in his encyclical 'On Christian Marriage', published in 1930.

There were formidable opponents too from within the scientific community who believed that the case for medical intervention had simply not been proved (or not been proved with sufficient certainty) or separated enough from political bias and social snobbery. One of the most outspoken opponents of eugenic science was the biologist Lancelot Hogben, a committed Marxist, who suggested that the real problem was not the threat of a defective underclass but the parasitism of the contemporary intelligentsia whose 'selfishness, apathy and prejudice' were a far greater menace to civilization than any mental defect.[98] He was appointed professor of social biology at the London School of Economics in 1930 and used his inaugural address, chaired by H. G. Wells, as an opportunity to pour derision on the whole eugenic project. Blacker was in the audience. In a private letter to the

Cambridge molecular biologist John Bernal, a fellow Marxist, Hogben deplored 'the peculiarly English brand of Fascism which the Eugenics movement stands for'.[99] Yet even Hogben had no argument with the original aim of eugenics to improve the racial stock of future generations. The same held true for two other prominent communist biologists, the Cambridge scientists Joseph Needham and J. B. S. Haldane, both of whom disliked the political abuse of biology and the misrepresentation of its findings by the eugenic community, but neither of whom objected in principle to the idea that some form of medical intervention to prevent the hereditary transfer of genetic defect was desirable. 'Biologists', Haldane concluded in his Norman Lockyer memorial lecture, given in London in 1934, 'may legitimately demand that a proportion of mental defectives should be prevented from breeding.'[100] Disagreements surfaced just as readily between members of the Eugenics Society over the efficacy of sterilization as against segregation, or the extent to which sterility, enforced or otherwise, would really reduce the incidence of inherited defect. The government decision not to proceed with sterilization legislation seems to have rested in the end largely on the absence of unambiguous evidence of genetic transfer and not on any ethical objection to trying to improve the overall health of the community.

The collapse of the sterilization project forced the eugenic community to rethink its strategy. Shortly after the publication of the Brock report in January 1934, Leonard Darwin wrote to Blacker suggesting that it might be better to hold back on sterilization for the present and to emphasize positive eugenics once again. He recommended issuing 50,000 copies of a patriotic pamphlet for clergy, teachers and doctors to use as propaganda to get healthy parents to have large families. Those who refused to do so were, in Darwin's view, 'immoral and unpatriotic'.[101] Blacker took some time to respond but by 1937 he decided that the aims and objectives of the movement should expand the list of positive as against negative eugenic proposals. The annual report of the Society's Committee on Voluntary Sterilization for 1936–7 indicated continuing difficulty in sustaining public interest despite organizing more than sixty meetings in forty different towns and cities.[102] Slowly the moral obligation of the 'best stocks' to bear as many children as possible supplanted in importance the moral obligation of the less valuable to have no children at all. The activity of the Society changed perceptibly from the mid-1930s, away from identifying and isolating the sections of the population that were supposed to menace the race and towards finding every means to encourage large families and sensible marriage choice. The growing emphasis on maternal and child welfare, which Blacker welcomed, pushed the eugenic movement in the direction of recognizing publicly that environment also counted alongside heredity.

The search for positive strategies produced a fresh crop of more or less bizarre ideas. Blacker pursued the recommendation of compulsory 'pedigree schedules' for the population which would carry an individual's genetic information and physical description, like the 'family history' cards and the register of able families first developed by Galton forty years before.[103] Early proposals for artificial insemination, then known as entelegenesis, were debated in the Society but rejected as ethically unacceptable, though Blacker explored the idea of setting up a Society sperm bank. Leonard Darwin labelled its proponents 'cranks and rebels' and warned Blacker that public opinion would not stand for a process in which an unwary or ignorant host might find that 'a little nigger appears on the scene' at the end of nine months.[104] The Oxford philosopher Ferdinand Schiller suggested organizing eugenical baby shows each year so that the population would get used to the idea that genetic excellence won rewards: 'A eugenical first prize would soon be recognised as the greatest prize to be won in the lottery of life.'[105]

One of the few ideas that lasted was the prenuptial marriage certificate. The Society set up a sub-committee late in 1934 to draw up draft guidelines for certificates of health that would be secured before marriage and divulged to the future partner. When the proposal was added to the draft of the Society's aims Blacker included the idea that failure to disclose genetic defect might become a criminal offence.[106] However, the Council of the Society rejected the idea of advocating either compulsory health checks before marriage or a voluntary certificate of health. Instead a more modest proposal was incorporated in a Society pamphlet on 'Health Examinations Before Marriage' which advised potential spouses to volunteer for a comprehensive check of their suitability for marriage using a health schedule devised

The stand of the Eugenics Society at the Exhibition of Health and Housing in London in 1935. The poster on the side reads 'Heredity is the Basis of Freedom'.

by the Society. The form had three parts, the first for details of heredity and family illnesses, the second for the personal health of the applicant, the third a section for a doctor to complete after the medical examination. Potential users were encouraged to ask the doctor the most candid questions. Women 'who may be vaguely frightened of the sex act' and men worried about whether they could 'properly perform the sex act' were invited to chat about their fears with the family doctor. The ideal was a clean bill of health and sensible attitudes towards sex.[107]

The selection of a suitable mate was the first step in encouraging a large and healthy family. The public awareness of eugenic priorities in selecting a marriage partner went well beyond the doors of the Eugenics Society. The Advisory Council on Marriage sponsored by the National Women's Council issued a pamphlet 'To Those Thinking of Marriage' which had a strong eugenic message. Aside from conventional advice – 'Good housekeeping and good cooking help to make happy husbands' – the Council emphasized the importance of genetic health in choosing a partner. 'Certain weaknesses and inherited diseases', it was asserted, 'are definite reasons against marriage', and the prospective couple were strongly urged to have a full medical examination. The real object of marriage was to have children, the strongest bond between man and wife and the key to their 'natural fulfilment'. Those who decided against a family for selfish reasons were, in the view of the Council, making a profound mistake.[108] Sex before marriage was strongly discouraged, injurious to health as well as morals. The same stricture featured in the helpful advice on birth control issued by The Hygienic Stores on London's Strand (one of the few places in England where it was possible openly to buy contraceptives in the 1930s). The booklet included a chapter on selecting a partner 'on Right Principles' which warned both men and women that early sex would produce less healthy offspring and cause men, unless cold and phlegmatic by nature, to become 'partially bald, dim of sight, and lose elasticity of limb' in a matter of years. Couples were advised to hold themselves back from premarital 'amative indulgence' or risk severe debilitation. It was suggested that the optimum age for a man to marry was between 20 and 25; for a woman between 18 and 20.[109]

For eugenists accustomed to programmes of negative selection the switch to positive programmes of worthy advice on marriage, childbearing and sex must have been anything but congenial. The failure of the campaigns to tackle the pessimistic vision of a diseased social body perhaps explains the enthusiasm with which the eugenics community responded when in the mid-1930s a new biological disaster was suddenly unearthed that threatened not merely the biological degeneration of the race but its rapid disappearance. The root of the new panic was innocuous enough – a number of articles published in 1934 and 1935 projecting the statistical development of the British population. An article by Grace Leybourne in the *Sociological Review* in 1934 predicted on current trends a decline of the British population from 44 to 33 millions by 1976 with a sharp rise in the over-65s and a halving of the school population.[110] The novelist Aldous Huxley read the article, prompted perhaps by his zoologist brother, whose pessimism he in general shared, and was so shocked that he wrote a piece for the magazine *Everyman* headlined 'Turning Point' which predicted that the British were about to endure one of the most 'critical epochs' in the whole of their history. 'Will the depopulation of Western Europe and North America proceed to the point of extinction or military annihilation?' he asked. 'Unanswerable questions', he suggested.[111] The second article, by a social biologist at the London School of Economics, Enid Charles, presented a picture even more alarming. She set down extrapolations of the future size of the population of England and Wales up to 2035 based on current rates of fertility and mortality. She suggested two versions, one based on the assumption that these rates would stay the same, one based on a continuing decline of fertility at the same rate established over the preceding decade (1923–33). The first suggested a slow decline, but the second looked on paper to have devastating consequences, for it suggested that by 1990 the population would have almost halved to 23 million and by 2035 would arrive at a residue of just 4.4 millions. As population fell the senescent proportion grew larger, so that 57.7 per cent of the 4.4 million would be over 60 – a situation which could neither support a modern economy nor avoid the final eclipse of the race.[112]

The result of these conjectures was a fresh wave of biological panic. Two articles in *The Times* in September 1936 on 'The Dwindling Family' brought the issue into the open. The subsequent publicity forced a Commons debate in February 1937 to encourage the government to set up a new enquiry on population policy. 'I feel the nation has got to the edge of an abyss,' observed one MP who conjured up fanciful images of an England a century hence with 'derelict and deserted villages, the factories silent and the mills not turning, the schools without any children'.[113] The director of the London School of Economics, Sir William Beveridge, who had a long academic interest in the study of population, told an audience in Sheffield the same month that low fertility and excessive birth control could mean that 'the peoples of these islands were heading for disappearance'.[114] A distinguished fellow economist, Roy Harrod, saw an apocalyptic future in the 'extinction of the race'. In a letter to the Cambridge economist Joan Robinson, Harrod assured her that the consequences would be too horrible to contemplate: 'a return of a dark age, the persecution of women, purdah rigidly enforced, violent intolerance and recrudescence of crude religious superstition . . .'[115] In 1939 Guy Chapman, husband of the novelist and pacifist Storm Jameson and a researcher in the same department as Enid Charles, wrote a full study of the implications of population collapse. The title, *Culture and Survival*, showed how large were the stakes involved. Chapman tried to show that if population fell as predicted it would mean the collapse of the existing way of life within a generation: 'To attempt to sketch the disintegration and dissolution of the structure of such a society baffles all reasonable conjecture.' The psychological effect would be, he thought, 'infinitely depressing'.[116]

The dismal image of possible extinction called forth a flurry of activity. Early in 1936 the Eugenics Society set up a Population Investigation Committee under the chairmanship of the demographer Alexander Carr-Saunders, a member of the Eugenics Society Council and Beveridge's successor in 1938 as director of the London School of Economics, to try to establish why fertility was falling and to alert the public to the true state of affairs. Blacker acted as secretary and spokesman for the committee. He, like other alarmists, including Keynes as well as Harrod, adopted the more pessimistic of Enid Charles's extrapolations in his own discussions on population. The decline in fertility he found 'ominous and sinister'. If the trends continued, he, for one, could not see how the Western states 'could maintain their present state of civilization'.[117] In 1938 the Society joined forces with Political and Economic Planning (PEP) to form a Population Policies Committee to explore the social and economic factors limiting births and the political options for raising fertility rates in the short term. Blacker acted as secretary, Carr-Saunders as chair. The committees lobbied parliament to prompt government action; they discussed with the registrar general the possibility of including questions on fertility in the 1941 national census; they set up their own programmes of research so that they would be armed with the statistics necessary to be able to find palliatives or suggest amelioration.[118]

It was quickly realized that the new crisis placed the eugenics movement on the horns of an awkward dilemma. It was scarcely possible to argue for unlimited births after a quarter of a century of dire warnings about the dysgenic effects of breeding from those regarded as 'unfit'. This paradox was self-evident. At a meeting of the Joint Committee on Voluntary Sterilization in late 1937 the Bishop of Birmingham, a keen supporter of sterilization, observed that while the birth rate appeared to be falling 'ominously', there was no case for allowing more births of the 'stupid, vicious, insane or epileptic', who already tainted the race, but a strong case for breeding more from 'better stocks'.[119] Dean Inge was so horrified by the prospect of a reversal of policy that he considered resigning from the Society.[120] The two biological disasters became enmeshed in an uneasy embrace. The terms of reference for the Population Policies Committee spelt out the need to arrest population decline only by 'increasing the proportion of healthy and well-endowed persons'. In May 1939 the Committee announced its 'General Principles of Population Policy', which stated that nothing was to be gained by encouraging more births for the sake of it, whose effect was likely only 'to accentuate the dysgenic tendency' of poor heredity. Increased fertility, it was spelt out, should apply only to families where the children were free of hereditary defects, reared in a healthy fashion and utilized to best advantage for the genetic future.[121]

The reasons for the fall in fertility were identified as largely social or economic and the classes most affected were the more prosperous segments of the population. In simple terms, wrote Blacker in the *Journal of Contraception* in 1938, better-off families preferred cars to children, or as he put it, 'Baby Austins to babies'.[122] A report on fertility produced by the Cambridge University Democratic Front in response to the depopulation scare singled out the changing situation of women as a central explanation. The social effects of female emancipation, it was claimed, reduced the need to rely on a husband's earnings and hence the choice of early marriage and parenthood. The attractions of modern life provided an alternative source of distraction, while better living standards discouraged large families in favour of higher levels of consumption. The growing understanding of contraception made it possible to limit births and make a choice between relative economic deprivation and economic well-being. The report concluded that the only answer was to make parents 'Population

Conscious'.[123] The 'selfish' middle-class housewife had been the butt of eugenic disapproval ever since the observation of a differential birth rate in the 1920s; depopulation was deemed to owe a great deal to the greed, snobbishness or fastidiousness of the modern woman.

A characteristic of much of the biological discourse between the wars was to allocate blame – the tainted family, the promiscuous girl, the status-conscious wife, the feckless man. Biological crisis from its very nature involved a search for human causes and the modification or elimination of human subjects. The final disaster of depopulation brought together the three central issues of birth control, eugenic selection and differential fertility in an untidy unity, fraught with contradiction and barren of unambiguous solution. From the vantage point of history it is difficult to understand why the final crisis was given the publicity and serious attention it got before the war. There is a real sense in which the persistent search for crisis matched the age; biologists and social scientists engaged in a great deal of positive and constructive activity between the wars, much of which laid the foundation for post-war health and welfare services, but to engage in the wider diagnosis of an apparently diseased civilization was to march with the times. It is perhaps no accident that the crisis of declining fertility was also blamed on the modern 'neurasthenic age' whose anxieties and neuroses were supposed to inhibit the sex drive; or that pacifists were alleged to refuse the procreation of future 'cannon fodder'; or, as the Cambridge Democratic Front explained it: 'Increase of nervous instability due to the rush of modern life, fear of war under modern conditions, and general uncertainty as to the future'.[124]

A great many biologists wanted to believe that they could explain crisis in convincing ways, and their science seemed self-evidently appropriate to the morbid contemplation of decay and regeneration. Biological explanations had about them the unmistakable stamp of progress, rooted as they were in programmes of scientific research and statistical assessment that were demonstrably at the cutting edge of their subjects. Identifying crisis and cure gave scientists a sense of social purpose and a high public profile even if it meant presenting complex and uncertain elements of their science in vulgar form in order to be understood. Similar imperatives took German biologists and social scientists along the path to the murderous biological policies of the Third Reich and they were not entirely absent in the British case. Leonard Darwin complained to Blacker in June 1938 that the Germans were far ahead in the field of eugenic practice: 'we are losing a great deal', he thought, 'by refusing to take lessons from the totalitarian states'.[125] Blacker blamed anti-Nazi sentiment in Britain for the failure to move rapidly in the 1930s towards more radical eugenic solutions.[126] As war loomed in 1939 the arguments over the biological future sharpened and the language of disaster became more insistent. At the end of his analysis of depopulation, completed just as war broke out, Guy Chapman reflected on the terminal crisis of the modern age. It was not war that would bring about the end, he argued, but ignorance of biological necessity. Modern man was about to go down into the abyss produced by his own greed, lack of imagination and apathy about the future of the race. Nature, he claimed, in language he clearly felt appropriate to its apocalyptic subject, would turn 'the material aspirations of millions into the dust of vanished hopes'.[127]

4

Medicine and Poison: Psychoanalysis and Social Dismay

We encounter here a remarkable paradox. Civilization, our weapon and our shelter, which we have devised against pain, instead has become a house of suffering. It is at once medicine and poison.

Theodor Reik, 1942[1]

In the spring of 1946 the BBC chose to air a series of three thirty-minute features on 'The Human Mind'. One was written and presented by the educational psychologist Cyril Burt, who decided to script a small drama to introduce his topic. The play opens with a husband and wife preparing a dinner party while they debate whether their low-achieving child should seek psychotherapy. Just as the first guests arrive the husband insists that no spiritualist is going near his son. The play continues:

DAPHNE [*first guest*]: No, dear. That's psychical research. Psychology is something quite different. Isn't that the study of sex? You know, invented by that Austrian Jew – Freud wasn't it?

HUSBAND: Both equally unpleasant if you ask me. [*voices off*]

WIFE: Oh, let's ask them. James what <u>is</u> psychology? Charles says it's the study of spooks, Daphne says it's the study of sex, and Harry says it's just a pack of nonsense.

MALE VOICE: Sex? Oh, that's psycho-analysis. Psychology is just a study of consciousness; the psycho-analysts study your Unconscious.

HUSBAND: All sounds horribly morbid to me . . . !²

Burt used the play to discuss the issue of mental inheritance (one of the dinner guests is a professor who pronounces Burt's own favourite dictum: 'once a defective, always a defective') but the unconcealed sideswipe at Freud revealed not only Burt's own prejudice against psychoanalysis but also the popular image in the wider public mind that with the arrival of Freudianism in Britain after the Great War came the unwholesome odour of moral decline and social anxiety.

The psychologist Cyril Burt pictured in 1931. Burt was hostile to psychoanalysis and believed that the task of psychological science was to deal with the conscious mind in all its manifestations.

Psychoanalysis was a new branch of psychological science in the 1920s. The term was first coined by its founding father, Sigmund Freud, in 1896, but the mature theoretical underpinnings were constructed bit by bit over the following thirty years, ending with the publication of Freud's *The Ego and the Id* in 1923. There is an unavoidable impression that psychoanalysis was precisely attuned to the age in which it emerged. Barbara Low, author in 1920 of the first popular introduction to psychoanalysis in Britain, recalled Freud's own observation that 'increasingly manifest in modern civilised life are the Neurotic and the Hysteric'.[3] Low reflected that the pressure of civilization had been 'too extreme, too rapid in its action' for many people to adapt to its demands. Psychoanalysis was the therapeutic instrument for dealing with the dysfunctional nature of modern society by liberating mankind from the paralysing fear of the primitive instincts that lay concealed in the unconscious portion of the mind.[4] A few years later Freud's principal British disciple, Ernest Jones, in an essay on 'What Is Psycho-Analysis?', suggested that the crisis of civilization was particular to the post-war generation which bore within 'a much heavier burden of guilt' than its predecessor on account of the war and its aftermath. The consequences of trying to fly from 'this intolerable burden', Jones later wrote in an addendum to his original essay, assumed in the inter-war years 'desperate, panicky, and always irrational forms'.[5]

Like the eugenists, the early pioneers of psychoanalysis promised to save civilization from a menace of their own imagining; like eugenist argument, the promise of redemption was a distant one, the threat to the modern age immediate. Barbara Low acknowledged that the unchaining of the unconscious, primitive impulses with 'their own validity and splendour' might appear 'disastrous' to the civilized world but in the long run these impulses could be sublimated into socially useful action.[6] The truths about the human condition exposed by psychoanalytic theory were dangerous truths, Jones thought, 'unwelcome, wounding and repugnant', a violent threat to the edifice of 'personal responsibility [and] social ethics' painfully constructed through the civilizing process. Yet at the same time psychoanalysis promised to 'apprehend order in apparent chaos' by restoring to the individual real power to shape his own life.[7] Jones quoted approvingly, in his review of a book by the art critic J. P. Hodi on *The Dilemma of Being Modern*, the following statement on the impact of Freud's thought: 'There grows up before us a new man who, freed from the shapes of his own world of imagination, dares to take the step out of bloody chaos into a better future.'[8] The transition to greater self-expression implied by the release from fear and guilt was nonetheless a difficult passage. In another essay, drafted in 1930, Jones thought that with most modern Europeans 'one reaches a limit of their capacity to tolerate anxieties'; freeing them from the unconscious complexes that allegedly fuelled anxiety 'in the madhouse called Europe' was a process likely to be long and painful, perhaps even self-destructive.[9] If psychoanalysis was an effect of crisis, it might also be its cause, or as Freud's disciple Theodor Reik put it, both 'medicine and poison'.

The roots of psychoanalysis lay in the pre-war years when a number of psychologists and doctors began to explore the idea that neurotic behaviour could be explained and, in some cases, ameliorated by exposing unconscious residues of past trauma which the conscious mind had repressed. Most of the pioneering clinical observation was undertaken in Austria and Germany. With the publication late in 1899 of *The Interpretation of Dreams* (first published in Britain in 1913) Freud became the leading theoretical voice of a branch of psychotherapy which stressed the dynamic role of the unconscious (*Unbewusste*) in generating symptoms of neurosis, hysteria and phobia as well as the symbolic and fantastic imagery that the affected patients expressed in their dream-world. The shape of what is now conventionally regarded as 'Freudian' psychological theory only slowly emerged as Freud became more confident of his ability to explain the origin and function of the unconscious. The central element of his argument was the role of infantile sexuality, and it was this preoccupation that distinguished Freudian psychotherapy from other varieties. Freud argued that every child goes through a number of distinct stages of 'sexual' development, first oral-erotic, then anal-erotic, then phallic and finally the mature genital stage. To each of these stages is related a form of erotic impulse – first auto-erotic, then narcissistic, then homosexual and finally heterosexual. These love impulses are the principal drives of what Freud called the libido. In its early stages of unmediated impulse the libido is also the source of what came to be called the Oedipus complex, the idea that each infant loves the parent of the opposite sex and hates the other intruding parent. As the child grows, these sexual impulses or drives have to be repressed; acting in the real world means accepting restriction and inhibition and constructing a rational, self-controlled, personality, the 'ego'. The unconscious becomes the depository for all those emotions that cannot be safely exposed without punishment, and to ensure that they are not expressed the unconscious mind, according to Freud, develops a powerful internal censor or 'superego', which generates feelings of fear or guilt sufficiently powerful to ensure that in most adults the basic or primitive libidinal drives can be 'sublimated', their energy diverted to more socially acceptable or normative activities.[10]

Freud insisted that the process of mastering libido and functioning in the modern world was not automatic. There is a constant conflict between the libido and the ego which in most adults could be adapted more or less satisfactorily. But in some cases the libido finds ways of circumventing the censor and these indirect effects were expressed either in the benign form of small errors of language or behaviour ('Freudian slips'), or through dreams and fantasies, or, in more dangerous cases, in obsessive neuroses, fixations, or physical symptoms of pain or paralysis. The origin of all these manifestations of imperfect repression, Freud insisted, was to be found in sexual impulses (in the broadest sense of the term) constructed in the early stages of infancy and not in any inherited predisposition. For Freud, every human has to replicate these processes of adaptation anew. It was this argument that provoked the famous split between Freud and his most distinguished disciples in the years just before the outbreak of war. In 1911 the Viennese doctor Alfred Adler, an early and enthusiastic supporter, finally broke with Freud, insisting that neuroses were caused mainly by problems of 'organ inferiority' and the compensating 'striving for power' provoked by feelings of inadequacy. He termed his system of therapy 'individual psychology' and blamed neurotic behaviour on the failure of individuals to adapt to their environment and secure the egoistic goals which every individual must strive towards.[11] In 1914 the Swiss psychologist Carl Jung, who had been regarded by Freud as his probable successor after they first met in 1907, abandoned his mentor over what he regarded as excessive emphasis on the sex drive. Jung became a remarkably original theorist in his own right, responsible for the terms 'complex', 'introvert' and 'extravert', all of which have become absorbed into contemporary vocabulary. He termed his therapeutic method 'analytical psychology' to distinguish it from psychoanalysis. The principal divergences from Freudianism lay in Jung's insistence that neurosis could be explained more fully by current sources of frustration and anxiety, rather than regression to infantile experience, and his argument that the unconscious is filled with the residues of human development, individual fragments of a collective unconscious that reproduce the inherited 'archetypes' of human experience and give rise to a 'soul'. The soul has to be understood as the expression of a divided self; the realization of psychic harmony comes at the point where the individual persona is finally reconciled to the inner spiritual life of the collective. Jones later dismissed Jung's theories as 'occultism'; Jung referred to Freud's obsession with sex as 'filth'.[12]

The most important of Freud's remaining disciples was the British doctor Ernest Jones, who played a central part in securing a monopoly for Freudianism as the only legitimate form of psychoanalysis and in bringing the infant practice to Britain. Jones was the son of a self-made Welshman who rose from clerk to colliery manager in the village of Gowerton in South Wales. His son, born in 1879, became an outstanding medical student at University College, London. He became familiar with Freud's work in the early 1900s, including a discussion in Havelock Ellis's *Studies in the Psychology of Sex*, a pioneering exploration of a subject still difficult to discuss in pre-war Britain. In 1907 he met Jung and a year later, at a congress in Salzburg, he at last met Freud. Jones was an enthusiast from the start, so much so that Freud distrusted his fanaticism. Forthright, self-confident and clever, the young Jones also invited respect. The early correspondence between the two men makes clear Jones's eagerness to please and Freud's self-centred insecurity and defensiveness.[13] When, following allegations of misconduct, Jones felt compelled to move to Canada, where he played an intermediary role in establishing a formal psychoanalytic movement in the United States, Freud tried to keep him on a tight leash. 'You have a particular need for complicated plans,' complained Freud in 1909 about Jones's predilection for academic politics, 'instead of taking a direct route.'[14] Jones, however, remained embroiled in controversy for the rest of his career. Amid further allegations of sexual misbehaviour in Toronto, where he had settled, Jones returned to London in the autumn of 1913. Freud insisted that he should undergo psychoanalysis if he wanted to remain in the inner circle. After it was over Jones confessed to Freud that it had been extremely successful 'in making me face more clearly various character traits and dangerous tendencies'.[15] Freud finally accepted Jones without further reservation. In August, following an International

Congress of Medicine in London, in which Jones had, on his own account, defeated in public debate the opponents of psychoanalysis, Freud wrote to encourage Jones to set up the movement in Britain: 'The interest of ψα [psycho-analysis], and of your person in England is identical, now I trust you will "strike while the iron is hot".'[16]

Two months later, on 30 October 1913, Jones founded the London Psycho-Analytical Society under his presidency. Disagreements on theory divided the small group throughout the ensuing war and on 20 February 1919 Jones called a meeting which formally dissolved the original society and replaced it with a new British Psycho-Analytical Society composed at first of just twelve members. Jones played a key part in approving each applicant. In a circular letter in 1920 he stated that the main hope for a pure psychoanalysis 'lies in the steadfast binding together of our little group of paladins'. By 1923 the society still had only twenty-three members and twenty-four associate members.[17] The same year the society was founded Jones inaugurated an International Psycho-Analytical Press, which played a key role in disseminating the fruits of Freudian research in the post-war decades, and in 1920 he launched the *International Journal of Psycho-Analysis*. The two were fused into the Institute of Psycho-Analysis in 1924 and two years later, on 6 May 1926, the London Clinic of Psycho-Analysis was opened in Gloucester Place in London. Over the following decade 738 patients were examined, but the small number of staff – nine doctors in 1926, thirteen doctors and twelve psychologists by 1936 – meant long waiting lists, in some cases more than four years. Psycho-analysis was a slow process; the recommended length of treatment was four years with five or six sessions a week. Four of the patients had more than 900 treatments, the majority somewhere between 225 and 450. In 1936 nineteen new analysts were in active training to cope with the backlog. That year only thirty-nine new patients were taken on, with diagnosed conditions ranging from 'anxiety hysteria' (fifteen cases) to 'character inhibition', 'sexual inhibition', 'fetishism', 'crime' and 'homosexuality' (one each).[18]

The small scale of the organization and the closed circle of its members belied the rapid impact that psychoanalysis had in Britain in the 1920s, not all of it favourable. In 1935, on the occasion of the silver jubilee of the International Psycho-Analytical Association, an

The psychoanalyst Ernest Jones at work in the British Psycho-Analytical Society in the 1930s. Jones was convinced that psychoanalysis would become one of the foremost human sciences over the course of the century.

editorial in the BBC journal *The Listener* reminded readers that Freud had been met initially 'with bitter opposition on all sides'. It was only in the 1920s that 'complexes and repressions, transference and sublimation invaded the drawing-rooms of the English-speaking world'.[19] This achievement was not solely due to Freud. In the early 1920s public interest in psychology was sustained by debates over the nature of shell-shock and its treatment. One of the pioneers of psychotherapy for war-damaged soldiers was David Eder, Britain's first psychoanalyst and secretary of the London Psycho-Analytical Society until he broke with Jones over doctrinal issues. The other was William Rivers, a Cambridge anthropologist and psychologist, who famously analysed the poet Siegfried Sassoon in 1917. Rivers rejected the sexual basis of Freudian thinking, but popularized the idea of the unconscious and the notion of repression, both key Freudian concepts.[20] In the aftermath of war 120,000 veterans won pensions for psychiatric disability; 6,000 remained permanently insane. The psychological damage inflicted by the conflict was evident, even among those not eligible or too proud to ask for compensation.[21]

The response to shell-shock helped to fuel a growing public appetite for information on psychology of all kinds. The wider reading audience did not discriminate and the boundaries between the psychic and the psychological were often blurred. There were in the years after the war a number of different schools of psychiatry and differing approaches to psychopathology, all of them clamouring for attention. The ledgers of publishing data kept by the publishers Routledge & Kegan Paul, who specialized in books on psychological subjects, reveal a remarkable rising market in the 1920s. The books ranged from *The Technique of Psycho-Analysis*, published in 1921, to the popular *Outwitting Our Nerves*, first published in 1922 and reprinted in a seventh edition in 1947. The International Library of Psychology was launched in 1922 and Routledge not only published Freud's *Totem and Taboo*, but became the British publisher for both Jung and Adler. Jung's theory of the introvert/extravert personality was published in 1922 and reached a fifth edition in 1938, with sales of 6,500. Between 1922 and 1940 more than 22,000 copies of Jung's works were printed.[22] From the early 1920s Freud was published under the auspices of Jones's International Psycho-Analytical Press by Allen & Unwin, but following endless disputes over translation deadlines and Stanley Unwin's decision to publish a book by a psychologist hostile to Freud which carried a statement on the cover to the effect that its conclusions abolished 'the right of the science to exist', the relationship abruptly ended. In 1924 agreement was reached with Leonard and Virginia Woolf for Freud to be published exclusively by their Hogarth Press.[23] There was intense competition to publish Freud in English. James Strachey, brother of the writer Lytton and a founder member of the Psycho-Analytical Society, translated much of Freud's later work. He recalled in a letter to Jones written in 1945 how remarkable it was that the basic discoveries of psychoanalysis were usually available for English readers six months after they appeared in German.[24] The Hogarth Press nevertheless took a risk, for much of Freud's work was highly technical. The early sales were uneven, but still in the thousands. Four volumes of Freud's collected papers published in

1925 had sold 6,500 sets by 1930 and were reissued in 1934. The books sold steadily enough in the 1930s (and better than any other books in the psychoanalytic library) for Leonard Woolf to insist that Freud's last book *Moses and Monotheism*, published late in 1938, should be a trade book, not one published by the Institute. In the first year, the year of Freud's death, it sold 2,450 copies.[25]

Interest in psychoanalysis in the 1920s reflected a break with conventional psychology, much of which was positivist in outlook, interested predominantly, as Burt suggested, in the conscious mind. The division was also a generational one. 'I'm told', complained a psychologist addressing the medical section of the British Psychological Society in 1920, 'young people think psychology is a "back number" and that psycho-analysis is up-to-date!'[26] The young psychologist John Bowlby wrote to Jones in 1943 that his institute had perhaps never appreciated just how much support there was for psychoanalysis among 'the younger generation of the University men'. He recalled that among historians, economists and doctors, psychoanalysis was regarded 'as one of the outstandingly important modern movements'.[27] When Charles Blacker, as a young psychiatrist in the 1920s, was invited to lecture on 'The Modern Conception of the World', he devoted a long portion of his talk to the effect the discovery of the unconscious would have on the now old-fashioned belief that reason guided human action. In the mid-1920s the young Kingsley Martin, future editor of the *New Statesman*, contributed an essay on 'The War Generation' to a French journal. Like Blacker, Martin saw Freud as key. Though he thought the theory 'little understood', Martin argued that the influence of the Freudian argument that reason was governed by unconscious urges was very great even in the minds of 'unthoughtful persons'. The fear that reason could no longer be relied upon to sort out the problems of the modern world was, Martin continued, 'the most devastating of all'.[28]

It was difficult to be neutral about psychoanalysis in the 1920s. Although it was ostensibly a science dedicated to providing therapy for specified neurotic conditions, it was evident that the implications of Freud's theory went well beyond the consulting room. The conclusions were disconcerting for anyone not converted to the cause, and the ambiguous nature of the psychoanalytic project, which posited cure

while simultaneously undermining the ground of psychological certainty in those who had no need of it, provoked a mixed response.
From much of the medical world the reaction was deeply hostile.
Nevertheless in October 1926 at the annual meeting in Nottingham,
the British Medical Association, representing the entire medical profession, adopted a resolution to establish a committee to report on
psychoanalysis and its implications for medical practice. The resulting
investigation, which was completed with the publication of a final
report in June 1929, offers a unique window onto the many debates
surrounding psychoanalysis and the key issues that divided believers
from non-believers. The very origin of the decision reveals something
of the popular reaction. The BMA Ethical Committee set up the
investigation following allegations that a school in Hove, exploiting
'psycho-analytic' methods, had allowed boys and girls to bathe
together naked.[29] The new committee consisted of nineteen members,
drawn from hospital doctors, general practitioners and doctors
employed in clinics for nervous disorder. Following a protest from
Ernest Jones in 1927 that no psychoanalyst was on the committee, he
was added along with a representative Jungian.[30] Only Jones and one
other committee member attended every session to which they were
entitled to go.

The investigation was based on a long series of professional papers
produced by medical and psychological experts on all aspects of
psychotherapy, including Adler and Jung, though the main focus was
on Freud and psychoanalysis. The committee itself was deeply divided
between a partisan element and a caucus of irreconcilables who saw
the investigation as an opportunity to strangle psychoanalysis in its
cradle. Before the first meeting a questionnaire was devised for doctors
who practised psychotherapy to see whether they thought it worked.
It was sent out to 157 general practitioners who were members of the
Medico-Psychological Society, and seventy-eight replies were received
back six months later, sixty-nine from doctors who had recommended
therapy. Of these nineteen claimed to be Freudians, one of whom
turned out to be Ernest Jones, by now a member of the committee.
Only four were Jungians and one used the Adler method. Freudian
analysis, it was reported, took from one to three years, with five or
six sessions a week; Jungian cures took only two to three months,

with two to four sessions weekly. Most claimed that they 'cured' their patients, but relapse rates of up to 33 per cent were also recorded. To the question whether analysis did harm to patients most replied in the negative; one doctor complained that the sedentary nature of psychotherapeutic treatment had made him fat.[31]

Alongside the questionnaire were the nineteen expert opinions which formed the basis of discussion and cross-examination in the committee's sessions. Some of the criticism from other psychologists challenged the claim that psychoanalysis was remotely scientific or its conclusions capable of scientific testing. The most comprehensive rejection came from a sworn enemy of Freudianism, the psychologist Adolf Wohlgemuth, author of the book for Allen & Unwin, *A Critical Examination of Psycho-Analysis*, that had caused the rift over Freud's publications. In his memorandum he pointed out that Freud arrived at his conclusions by crude analogy. Instead of the scientific approach ('If a man swallows hydrocyanic acid, he dies'), Freud reasoned backwards ('this man is dead, hence he has swallowed hydrocyanic acid'). Wohlgemuth argued the case that all psychological phenomena could be traced back to the behaviour of the cortex; the 'Unconscious' was, he claimed, 'a facile "refuge for ignorance"', and the symptoms displayed by patients simply planted there by the analyst.[32] This opinion was shared by other critics, including William Brown, the consultant psychologist at the Bethlem Hospital in London (better known as the original Bedlam), who argued that in his view all patients under analysis become 'very suggestible' because they enter therapy in a state of mind marked by 'passivity, receptivity and lack of criticism'.[33] Wohlgemuth drew a vivid picture of the seductive milieu in which the analysed patient is set – 'the half-darkened room, the stillness ... the recumbent position on a sofa or comfortable couch, the soft modulated voice of the analyst ...'[34]

General practitioners who found psychoanalysis, as one put it, 'like a foreign language', had their own ideas about treating their neurotic patients. Three were invited to give expert opinions. The first was only interested in flesh-and-blood patients and could see no need to treat mild neurosis with anything save a 'cheerful prognosis' and 'a bottle of valerian'.[35] Another thought that most GPs solved neurosis successfully by recommending 'holidays, rest in bed, tonics, mild sedatives' and an encouraging chat.[36] The third dismissed Freudianism as the product of a 'too vivid imagination' and the unconscious as 'wild conjecture'. He was invited to attend a session of the committee to defend what the chairman described as his 'great onslaught' on psychoanalysis. There followed, according to the minutes, an ill-tempered exchange in which it emerged that the doctor had been retired since 1910, had never read Freud's theory of the unconscious, and was greatly exercised by Ernest Jones's contention that Napoleon had been an anal-erotic. He ended his cross-examination with the demand for physical scientific proof of any element of Freudian theory, for 'he had seen none'.[37] Throughout the committee's deliberations the psychoanalysts gave a robust defence of their science. When Jones's colleague Edward Glover was called to give evidence he suggested that the lack of understanding among those who were questioning him indicated a 'psychological blind-spot'; on their refusal to admit a sexual basis for neurosis, Glover suggested the operation of 'unconscious self-defences' against the idea of sex.[38] A draft appendix for the final report of the committee, almost certainly penned by Jones, concluded that the strong resistance against the 'sexual sphere' evident throughout the investigation was due to 'the unconscious difficulties of all unanalysed persons' in confronting sex. The appendix was not included in the published report. Instead, as paragraph 47 of the final version, the committee allowed the statement that psychoanalysis as 'the expression of a perverted sexuality' was 'fraught with very real danger'.[39]

The link between sex and psychoanalysis was a critical issue in the popular reception of Freud. The philosopher Bertrand Russell, writing in 1931 about Freud's theory of 'the pervasiveness of sex', recalled that he was regarded at first with 'the kind of horror that is inspired by a dangerous lunatic'. All Freud did, wrote one hostile reviewer, was talk 'sex, sex, sex'.[40] Attitudes towards sex, however, were changing rapidly in the 1920s. It was possible to talk more openly about sexual issues, and the public discussion of sex, though usually confined to the idea of sex between married couples, was as vigorous as the discussion of psychology. In September 1929 the Third Congress of the League for Sexual Reform convened in London. The chairman of the Congress, the British sexologist Norman Haire, observed in his opening address that organizing the event in London had been embarked upon with some hesitation: 'We English', he continued, 'are so backward in respect of the free discussion of sexual problems, so notorious for sexual prudery and hypocrisy.'[41] Dora Russell, Bertrand's wife, in her welcome address to colleagues, deplored the public mind in Britain that saw sex as 'nasty, or comic, or salacious'. Aldous Huxley called for an end to sex censorship in the arts, Marie Stopes for more birth control and Bertrand Russell for greater honesty in confronting sex. A note of warning came from Julian Huxley, who told the audience that the imminent collapse of traditional theological and moral standards over issues of sex, unless it were closely controlled on scientific grounds, would lead to 'a time of chaos'.[42]

Fear that the uninhibited sexuality implicit in Freudian thinking would provoke a moral crisis that might threaten social order and civilized behaviour was not confined to Britain. Freudian psychoanalysis was rejected in Stalin's Soviet Union and Hitler's Germany in the 1930s. In France Freud made little headway, but the freer sexual mores of the 1920s provoked the same mixed response from the French public, part approval, part fear of moral decay.[43] In Britain greater sexual freedom was welcomed by progressive opinion and absorbed into modernist literature, but the remorseless exploitation of sexuality by psychoanalysis was widely perceived to be socially dangerous rather than psychologically liberating. Psychoanalysts did little to help their cause, for they were intellectually committed to seeing sex in everything. At the second meeting of the newly founded British Psycho-Analytical Society Jones briefly reported a patient of his who constantly imagined a greenish snake. Her drawing of the snake was, Jones continued, 'undoubtedly a phallic symbol' and the patient clearly homosexual. At a meeting in 1922 the Society membership solemnly discussed the proposition that the flea was a 'penis symbol'. A paper on photography by the young psychologist John Rickman suggested that the hobby was a 'pseudo-perversion', a substitute for the sexual act in which 'instant exposure' provided 'libidinal gratification'.[44] When Jones was cross-examined by the BMA committee in June 1928 the discussion centred almost entirely on sex. Jones insisted that unconscious sexual impulses operated in all kinds of acts which were not conventionally regarded as 'anything to do with sex at all'. When asked to name one he suggested 'thumb-sucking'. He reminded the committee that individuals were unaware of the unconscious sexual impulse in their actions. 'This could happen', he added somewhat implausibly 'even with ordinary masturbation.'[45]

Sex was the chief source of concern and criticism throughout the committee's deliberations. Freud, one expert reported, was so 'engrossed with the cruder side of sexual life' that psychoanalysis was more of a 'contribution to pornography' than medicine.[46] The expert witness whose conclusions on the danger of sexual expression were included in the final report mocked the psychoanalytical obsession with symbols: 'Anything hollow and concave represents a woman, anything long and rigid represents the penis. Going up or down stairs or any rhythmical movement is a symbol of coitus.' The dangers of such an obsession were, he concluded, 'great and obvious'.[47] There was some discussion during the investigation of the question of homosexuality, which was generally regarded as one of a number of 'moral disorders'. Even psychoanalysts assumed that homosexuality was in some sense an abnormal condition, a manifestation of a failure to adapt to Freud's final 'heterosexual' stage of sexual development. On this issue the medical profession was unyielding. Early in 1929, for example, John Rickman asked the editor of the medical journal *The Lancet* if he could write a piece on the 'invert', those individuals who developed a sexual attraction to the same sex, and how they might be treated. The editor agreed, though not until he had given Rickman the gratuitous advice that a young man or a young woman inclined to 'inversion' could with the help of cold baths and hard exercise be turned into 'quite a cheerful citizen'.[48] Rickman duly submitted the article, which suggested that homosexuality was a result of hormone imbalance and infantile trauma. The editor responded a few weeks later, asking Rickman to rewrite it as the subject was 'too advanced' for most doctors, who found the idea of homosexuality 'disgusting'. Though Rickman promised to revise his piece the editor finally declined it on the ground that explaining inversion to doctors was impossible under current conditions because they refused to see it as anything other than 'a piece of horrible perversion' which no decent practitioner should have to deal with.[49] Rickman may have discovered from Jones that a recent court case concerning homosexuality had been discussed in the BMA investigation in December 1928. When one doctor was asked if therapy might not have been better than jail, he responded that nothing could help a homosexual, 'he could not be more perverted'.[50]

Anxieties about changing attitudes to sex evoked a widespread and disparate response in inter-war Britain, to which psychoanalysis contributed but did not entirely cause. Other psychologists distanced themselves from a branch of their discipline which they regarded as damaging to the expanding role of conventional psychology. Cyril Burt, whose prejudices against Freud have already been noted, was a serious opponent whose views on sex and normative morality were conventional responses to what he perceived to be a troubling decline in values. In 1925 he wrote an essay on psychology and social hygiene in which he argued that the uninhibited sex instinct inherited from animal and primitive ancestors disturbed 'the health and efficiency of society'. Unlike Freud, Burt assumed that with the advance of civilization the sexual instinct would become sublimated 'into wholesome social activities'.[51] In an essay on prostitution he observed that the emancipation of women materially and sexually rendered the prostitute redundant (replaced by what Burt coyly described as 'the unpaid person'). Although Burt recognized that the changing nature of moral sanction was to an extent welcome, he recoiled from the probable dangers, not simply of vice, but of frivolity. Civilization, he continued, had tamed most instincts and would meet the challenge of sexual licence. In the end the sexual drive had to be repressed or society would suffer the consequences. The drive was not, as Freud suggested, the strongest, but was on the contrary in Burt's view the easiest to control, 'apart from a few oversexed creatures'.[52] In a lecture to the Newcastle Literary and Philosophical Society in 1934 on the theme 'What's Wrong with the New Psychology?', Burt argued that psychology, properly understood, was destined to solve the problems of civilization. Freud had muddied the waters with his self-promoting 'preoccupation with sex'.[53] When Burt was invited by the BBC in 1938 to broadcast to school sixth-formers on Freud in a series on 'Forceful Thinkers', he failed to mention sex once. This was such a surprising omission that the producer asked him to reconsider 'the question of reference to sex' in case schools thought that the BBC was deliberately avoiding the issue.[54]

This was not Burt's only concern. In the early 1920s he was part of a nationwide enquiry inaugurated by the National Council of Public Morals under the presidency of the Bishop of Birmingham into the effect of the cinema on schoolchildren. A group of eight academic psychologists made up the Psychological Research Sub-Committee. In Burt's draft report on the cinema he regretted that adult life was displayed as an endless round of 'flirtation, jealousy, robbery, unscrupulous intrigue and reckless assault, incessant excitement and wild emotionalism'. Cinematic role models encouraged fantasy, daydreams and yearning to a degree that Burt regarded as 'unwholesome and morbid'. The presentation of relations between the sexes he found stimulated 'the sexual instincts and interest . . . prematurely and precociously'. He recommended that children be sent only to see films of a healthy, artistic and educational character.[55] To reinforce this idea the sub-committee undertook a two-year programme of research on the reaction (attention span, interest, retained knowledge etc.) of a group of seventy-three boys and seventy-five girls to films of a manifestly uplifting character. The seven passionless films included *The Stickleback, Solving Canada's Fuel Problem: The Peat Industry* and *Salmon Fishing*. The response was generally regarded as positive.[56] The idea that films were likely to promote sexual licence remained a persistent concern of the respectable middle classes. In Birmingham, for example, the local branch of the National Women's Council organized a committee of enquiry under the auspices of their Social and Moral Welfare Committee which undertook to send one or two representatives to sit in the cinema at times usually frequented by children to ensure that the films were wholesome enough. In May 1930 there was a mass meeting in the University of Birmingham's Medical Theatre on 'The Cinema in Relation to Young People' which resolved to petition the Home Secretary for tougher censorship laws against films deemed suitable for children which on inspection turned out to be 'sensational', 'frightening', 'vulgar' or 'indecent'.[57] In 1931 the Public Morality Council, presided over by the Bishop of London and a host of distinguished vice-presidents, undertook a review of the moral content of current cinema films in the capital as well.[58]

Burt was also involved in the work of the British Social Hygiene Council set up in 1926 to combat the spread of venereal disease and to encourage a healthy outlook on sex and marriage. The propaganda against venereal disease was extensive and countrywide. In 1930 it was estimated that there were 2.6 million patients seeking treatment for syphilis or gonorrhoea; though capable of amelioration through regular treatment, both forms of venereal disease could affect the offspring of the infected parent. The Social Hygiene Council organized regular mass meetings complete with lurid illustrations to convey to the public the necessity of observing tight moral restraint 'towards questions of sex'.[59] Films with titles such as *The Shadow*, *Deferred Payment* and *Third Party Risks* were used to try to educate the public into accepting the need to focus on marriage and to reject casual premarital relationships. In the year 1931/2 alone 182 meetings were organized in London and 188 in the rest of the country, reaching a gross audience of 96,800.[60] The teaching of sexual morality was a delicate issue. When the Council sub-committee on 'Preparations for Marriage' sat to consider the outcome of a series of lectures on the subject given in 1931 they debated how to react to a demand from one member of the audience for more information on 'how to conduct intercourse in the best possible way' and concluded that more elaboration on 'the hygiene of marriage' was undesirable.[61] They were not blind to the impact of psychology, though Freudians were described in the first draft of a booklet on marriage as 'psychoanalytical fanatics' (the phrase was changed to 'extremists').[62] At the 1932 Social Hygiene Council summer school lectures were given on 'Foundations of Psychology' and 'Psychology of Marriage'. Burt gave one of the first lectures to the Council in 1926 in which he explained that Freud's ideas on the impact of early childhood experiences in shaping later behaviour were in a general sense correct, but he saw the consequences not as neuroses in need of therapy but expressions of delinquency that required reform.[63] One way to avoid future problems was to teach young children the facts of life.

The growth of sex education in the inter-war years was regarded as a positive step in combating any tendency to a morbid or depraved sexuality. The emphasis was on turning out young adults who would be worthwhile and civilized citizens. Marie Stopes, another keen campaigner against venereal disease, called on parents to combat 'the secret enemy' by teaching their children 'cleanliness, disinfection and chastity' in the home.[64] During the 1920s and 1930s books of advice for parents indicated a shift in outlook away from punishment and crude repression towards Burt's ideas of sublimating activity and character reformation. By the late 1930s sex education in schools was widely discussed, even for children of kindergarten age. The prevailing assumption, nevertheless, was that much sexual activity consisted of 'bad moral habits' and that the sex drive should be sublimated and subordinated.[65] A booklet by 'A Workaday Mother' issued by the *Lady's Companion* tackled the thorny problem of masturbation by suggesting that children have a hard mattress and a cool bed, with plenty of cold baths from an early age. Rather than suggesting that the practice was wicked, parents were counselled to say it was silly: 'Children who are taught something of the workings of their bodies readily understand that if the various parts of this delicate and wonderful machine are tampered with, they may be unable to do their work as well as they should, just as the toy train or engine be spoilt by rough handling.'[66]

One of the best-known guides on sex education, Dr Beatrice Webb's 'The Teaching of Young Children and Girls as to Reproduction', first published in 1917 and in its twelfth edition twenty years later, stressed the need for hard physical exercise, team games and 'happy comradeship' to calm down the sexually aware teenage girl. Plenty of 'homemade bread, cake, porridge, puddings' (but fish or meat only once a week, and tea and coffee as little as possible), a hard bed pulled up next to an open window, summer and winter, and cold water splashed regularly onto 'the parts' would all divert the sexual energy away from 'morbid excitement'. Under no circumstances were they to sit on the seat of a public lavatory.[67] The Social Hygiene Council also published 'What Fathers Should Tell Their Sons'. Again, fear of masturbation was uppermost. Loners or secretive boys were the most likely suspects, and fresh air, tough exercise and adventure books the usual regime to cure them. Fathers had a responsibility to explain the facts of life and could do this most easily, the booklet continued, by analogy with the fertilization of plants. Boys should also be taught 'chivalry and manly protection of women' as a safeguard against sexual wrongdoing. Both sexes were encouraged 'in these strenuous times' to avoid alcohol altogether.[68]

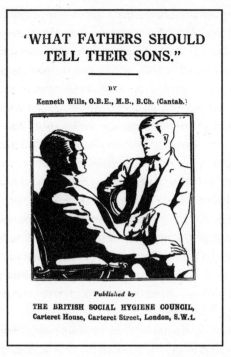

'WHAT FATHERS SHOULD
TELL THEIR SONS."

BY

Kenneth Wills, O.B.E., M.B., B.Ch. (Cantab.)

Published by

THE BRITISH SOCIAL HYGIENE COUNCIL,
Carteret House, Carteret Street, London, S.W.1.

*The front page of a pamphlet produced in 1933 by the British Social Hygiene
Council on sex education for boys. Fathers are told that the best way to talk
to a son 'is to tell him about the way plants are fertilised'.*

The prevailing anxiety about sex was one manifestation of the
impact of psychoanalysis, but the sex drive represented only an
element, though an important one, of the Freudian description of the
mind. Freud himself in an article on psychoanalysis in the *Encyclopae-
dia Britannica* wrote that the future would regard his 'science of the
unconscious' as the most important legacy of psychoanalytic theory.[69]
Much of the discussion during the BMA investigation focused on the
broader issue of just what the unconscious was and its role in shaping
human nature. The doctors were generally sceptical that any useful
division could be made between a conscious, directing mind and an
unconscious mind over which the conscious human had no control.
Wohlgemuth thought the unconscious a 'dangerous term'; another
doctor dismissed it as a 'bag of reptiles', a third as some kind of 'lost-
property office of the mind'.[70] Many psychologists were dismissive

of the idea that an unconscious mind full of repressed matter from the primitive, unmediated impulses of the young child had any real existence, though the concept of an unconscious sphere of activity was not particular to Freud. The collective unconscious was central to Jung's theory of mind, and other psychologists had suggested a 'sub-conscious' to account for non-conscious activities such as dreaming. Most psychologists, however, assumed that the conscious mind was what mattered, and that mental activity was dictated by physiological rather than psychical responses.

This distinction between psychology and psychoanalysis was exemplified in a series of BBC broadcasts in 1935 on 'How the Mind Works' in which Cyril Burt was invited to speak about the conscious mind, and Ernest Jones about the unconscious. The broadcasts were among the first the BBC had made on psychological issues and Jones poked fun at the Corporation in his opening remarks for daring to invite a psychoanalyst, 'an evil ogre', to address the wider public. He used his three talks to try to convey in simple, often anecdotal terms the fact that beneath the conscious, rational mind there lay an active and complex unconscious mind which 'greatly influences us without our ever suspecting it'.[71] He received a large postbag after the first talk from listeners keen to know how to cope with the disharmonies of the unconscious. Jones used the second to explore the idea of the unconscious more fully. The unconscious, he explained, was 'the prime motor of our life, the source of most of our mental energy', but it was for the most part hidden and inaccessible to the individual: 'We are allowed to know only a part of ourselves.' Jones could only have alarmed his listeners by insisting that the imperfect mind of modern man, 'torn by indecisions, doubts and inner dissatisfactions', was only a fraction of the turbulent 'deeper disharmonies' in his nature and that the superficial anxieties of personality concealed inner conflicts over which there was no control. 'What thinking man can be gratified at the picture of the human race,' Jones continued, 'especially at the present moment in the world's history?'[72] He ended by reminding his listeners that the unconscious wielded a great power to do mischief; it existed in a state of permanent and violent conflict, trying to release the primal energies and impulses within into the conscious sphere. Unless the energy could be sublimated in some useful way, its occasional release 'agitates the personality'. The unconscious mind accounted, Jones insisted, for 'the innumerable imperfections and unsatisfactorinesses of human existence', not only in the individual but in national and international life too.[73]

The mature theory of the unconscious took psychoanalysis a long way from its initial therapeutic purposes. In the first place the theory applied to every individual and not only to those who showed symptoms of some form of neurosis; the unconscious is, according to psychoanalysis, one of the defining properties of being human. When Edward Glover was asked during his BMA cross-examination whether he recommended psychoanalysis in a normal person, Jones interjected, 'In a so-called normal person.' Glover thought that everyone would benefit 'enormously'.[74] It was precisely because everyone had an unconscious that Jung first formulated his idea of the collective unconscious to describe the elements that all humans must have in common. In the second place most of the activity of the unconscious mind was concealed, hidden, like genes, from general view. Freud and other psychoanalytic writers saw themselves as explorers of this hidden psychological continent but even by the 1930s the maps were little more than intelligent inference. Barbara Low described the content of the unconscious as 'primitive' – the 'impulses and drives' laid down in early life. Jones suggested that in the first years of life each infant is struggling to compress the experience of 50,000 years of human development into a tiny span.[75] Freud used general non-scientific terms – love, hate, aggression, sadism, masochism, narcissism – to convey a metaphorical image of the unconscious; his idea that these various elements are in a constant state of flux, striving for recognition, perpetually ill-at-ease in their mental prison, meant that every individual was required in the modern age to undertake a successful process of adaptation against forces of exceptional strength, constantly threatening to turn superficial normality into a state of abnormal anxiety.

This view of the human individual directly challenged conventional notions of rationality and free will. The unconscious did not allow its host to make decisions and choices, even to talk freely, as an act of independent will; the principle of association was used by Freud to explain that what might appear to be a rational, conscious choice was linked by association with some deeper psychological drive whose origin and nature could only be guessed at, or extracted in hours of laborious analysis. Psychoanalysis was the science of the irrational. Its challenge to reason seemed in the 1920s a reflection of the wider crisis of civilization and was accordingly mobilized by artists and writers of the avant-garde to justify pushing back the frontiers of art and literature in aggressively modernist forms, though by no means all of them were Freudians. Even though her Hogarth Press published Freud, Virginia Woolf claimed not to have read any of his work until the late 1930s.[76] This was not the case with D. H. Lawrence or James Joyce or a host of other self-consciously modern writers for whom the assault on conventional tastes and moral outlook was as liberating as it was exasperating for conservative opinion. E. M. Forster, reflecting on 'Modern Writing' in 1942, thought Freud had played a part in sowing the idea that 'the individual is not an entity', which ended the liberal view of personality as something in and for itself, durable, stable, comprehensible and rational, and ushered in a literature that saw itself as aggressively 'advanced'.[77]

The celebration of the decline of reason was 'implicit in the thought of the age', claimed the philosopher Cyril Joad, writing in the *Rationalist Annual* in 1935. He blamed D. H. Lawrence and Aldous Huxley in particular for creating an intellectual climate in which reason was unseated in favour of 'man's passional being', a 'stream of impulses and desires', and quoted with disapproval Huxley's assertion that science 'is no truer than common sense or lunacy'.[78] But the same year in a lecture by the German writer René Fülöp-Miller on the 'New Revolt against Reason', translated and published for the first time by the Oxford-based *Hibbert Journal*, it was claimed that modern psychology was 'unanimous in denying that human activities are primarily determined by reason'; other sciences – astronomy, physics, chemistry – had also exposed the 'irrational' character of much of the phenomena of the natural world with which they had to deal. Confronted by the scientific demonstration of the irrational, Fülöp-Miller argued that the modern age would simply have to adjust to creating a different kind of world that could accommodate the irrational in place of the 'logically fashioned system' which modern civilization had constructed hitherto.[79] Gilbert Murray recognized the truth that conventional rationality no longer worked in the sciences, but deplored the idea that the word 'rationalist' had virtually become 'a term of abuse' in the mouths of psychologists who put everything down to complexes, repressions or phobias. Psychoanalysis, he thought, was as responsible as anything for the current moral chaos. It was a doctrine, Murray complained, that was 'very violent and very modern'. The current troubles of the world – Murray was writing in 1932 – sprang, he believed, not from the decline of religion but because modern man had deserted Reason.[80]

The discovery of the apparent source of human irrationality left much room for debate, since individuals were clearly capable of acting unreasonably in ways that appeared entirely conscious or deliberate, just as they were capable of learning by experience the advantage of the rational option. This was the basis on which liberal society was supposedly founded. The poet Stephen Spender later recalled how he could infuriate his Oxford tutor in the late 1920s by mere mention of the word 'unconscious'.[81] In December 1932 the BBC broadcast a face-to-face discussion between Cyril Burt and Ernest Jones on 'Reason and Emotion' which pitted two very different interpretations of human behaviour. Burt was a convinced rationalist and took as his starting point that everyone had the capacity to reason but used it in uneven measure, politicians and statesmen included. Children, he thought, should be taught reasoning at school. Jones hinted at those deeper recesses of the mind (though he hesitated in this case to exploit psychoanalytic language) which were quite capable of overriding the most strenuous effort at reasoning. 'But surely', continued Burt, 'the intellect and reason control the machinery of the mind? How are you to master your emotions if you do not bring reason to bear upon your crude impulses?' Jones tried to explain that even the most rational or fortunate individual could be prompted to melancholia by unconscious psychological forces. Burt made the mistake of assuming that this happened only to the occasional unfortunate neurotic, until Jones put him right: 'My whole point is that every human being is guided in his actions by forces of which he is more or less unconscious.' Burt's rejoinder says much about the challenge that psychoanalysis threw down at the feet of reason: 'Then we are all of us just mechanical puppets – wooden figures jigging about just as the strings are pulled!

Reasoning and will-power count for nothing. Human behaviour is just the inevitable outcome of blind mechanical causes.' Jones took this for assent. 'I shall claim you', he concluded, 'as a convert.'[82]

The idea of the divided self was a difficult concept to accept since it implied like Jekyll and Hyde that civilized man contained within, permanently but usually unobtrusively, the capacity for exotic and primitive behaviour. Much of the popular discussion of psychoanalysis assumed that this dichotomous state suggested a civilized exterior and a savage within, and Freud's own work in *Totem and Taboo*, and the work of contemporary anthropologists, lent weight to the supposition that the infant impulses repressed through childhood were analogous to the gradual restraining effects of civilization on otherwise unmediated violence, or lust or superstition. In his later so-called metapsychology, Freud tried to incorporate this sense of opposites into a definite state of conflict. In *Beyond the Pleasure Principle*, written in 1920 and published in English two years later, he took the radical step of positing two distinct sources of psychological energy, the life drive, or Eros, and the death drive or Thanatos (the term 'death instinct', often used in English, did not, as Jones always reminded translators, properly convey the German word *Todestrieb*). The core idea was the tendency to repetition evident in all clinical studies. Freud adapted earlier scientific speculation that all living organic matter tends back to a previous state in order to argue that human beings seek to return to an earlier condition of immobility and hence death.[83] The death drive, Freud thought, could be used to explain the dynamic urge to aggression and destruction, which he felt his previous work had not explained sufficiently. This was a complex argument, which Freud regarded as conjecture, and not all of Freud's followers accepted it, since the element of hate or destructiveness could also be seen as a secondary response to some other frustration. But the idea of the 'death instinct' was easily popularized and it showed not just a divided self, but a self walking on a tightrope between survival and demolition.[84]

Sooner or later psychoanalysis seemed destined to step beyond its limited sphere of clinical practice into the wider world of non-scientific speculation. The explanatory paradigms mobilized by psychoanalysis seemed appropriate not just for isolated examples of individual anxiety but also for the wider anxieties and fears of the external world, to cure, as one psychologist put it, 'the insanity of nations'.[85] In the summer of 1929 Freud began work on a book that expressed the relationship he had finally come to understand between modernity and human nature. The finished work, written while Freud was in considerable discomfort from a permanent state of illness, was published late in 1929 in Vienna. There was a scramble to publish it in English when news arrived that Freud had written a new 'brochure'. An American agreement was secured immediately, while Leonard Woolf wrote directly to Vienna, instead of going through the London Institute. The book was published in 1930 after much deliberation about an exact rendering of the original German title. Jones thought the German might be conveyed best as the 'Dis-ease of Civilisation', using the word disease in its original sense, but it eventually appeared as *Civilisation and Its Discontents*, a title thought up by the translator, Joan Riviere.[86] The central theme of what Freud himself described as a 'dilettantish' piece was an exploration of the permanent state of conflict between the modern civilizing process and the demands of human instinct. Freud's motive was to try to explain just why modern man was afflicted by a crippling malaise when civilization should have been a source of pleasure rather than pain. It became one of Freud's best-known and best-selling books.

Freud's answers to the questions he set himself were profoundly pessimistic. The opening premise was the impossibility that man could ever be happy in any complete sense since all men were afflicted by three permanent sources of suffering: knowledge that the human body is 'doomed to decay and dissolution'; fear of an external world capable of overwhelming man with 'merciless forces of destruction'; and the demands of living with others, which Freud thought was perhaps the greatest source of human suffering. But this suffering was perennial. It was Nietzsche's eternal recurrence, one of the many debts that *Civilisation and Its Discontents* owed to the German philosopher-poet. The real source of malaise was the particular form that suffering took in the process of becoming civilized, for civilization intensified the repression of an instinctual life and magnified anxiety. In a memorable passage, Freud records his 'astonishing' discovery that 'what we call civilisation is largely responsible for our misery'.[87] In modern life there exists a permanent irreconcilability between individual drives and social demands, between what Freud had earlier called the pleasure principle and the reality principle. The hallmark of modern Western civilization was the excessive repression of the sexual impulses and the tendency to inborn aggression that repression generates in the unconscious mind. The aggressive drive threatens civilization permanently with the prospect of 'disintegration'. The destructive energy, or 'badness', was the expression of Freud's recently elaborated 'death drive'. The conclusion for modern civilization was dangerous in the extreme because the profound dualism at work, 'the struggle between Eros and Death', became more marked and more intense the more 'civilized' a community became. The failure to expend aggression in the external world throws the energy back into the individual and is manifested in a deep sense of guilt. Guilt reflects the ambivalence of the whole project of civilization, and accounts for the loss of happiness, the 'discontents' of the title.[88] Freud ended by suggesting that the 'fateful question' for mankind was simply: could the urge to destruction, the 'death drive', be mastered in an age when humans had the scientific means to exterminate the race? Freud knew he could not supply the answer, but expected that 'Eros' would try to fight back against his 'immortal adversary'. He added a final sentence a year later to the 1931 German edition, which did not appear in the English version until after the Second World War, but is generally regarded as a veiled reference to the growing threat of Hitlerism: 'But who can foresee with what success and with what result?'[89]

Jones read the book in the translated draft late in 1929 and had Freud's German version by December. He told Freud that he had reservations about the use of the 'death drive' as an explanatory tool but was otherwise 'delighted with all the part concerning civilisation' and agreed that human aggression was the greatest threat to its survival. In a letter a few months later he observed that the usual criticism that Freudianism only dealt with the 'pathology of the individual' was now redundant.[90] *Civilisation and Its Discontents* marked the point where psychoanalysis moved from the particular to the general. Freud himself explained that the 'process of human civilisation' and 'the development of the individual', while different objects, observed the same general characteristics.[91] The effect of this conclusion seems to have been liberating for psychoanalysts in Britain, for during the 1930s they chose to write not only about the clinical development of their science but to apply psychoanalysis to current social and international problems by analogy. Over the following decade issues of social order, political behaviour, international crisis and war were subjected to psychoanalytical review. This interest was not indifferent. Freud evidently chose to write about civilization because he thought it was in the throes of crisis. Arnold Toynbee read Freud at just the point when he was formulating his own theories, in 1930. 'When I put the book down,' he wrote to Barbara Hammond, 'my mind was running on the bearing of all this upon the situation now.' Freud prompted in Toynbee the idea of the cycle of tragic end followed by reprieve, which became the later 'rout–rally–rout'.[92] Ernest Jones also saw how pertinent Freud was to the present. In his preface to a book on psychoanalysis and world problems, published in 1933, he observed that at a time when the present state of the world menaced 'the basis of our civilisation' more fundamentally than even the Great War, it was at last being recognized that psychoanalysis might be able to avert the 'threatened danger'. The importance of analogy was evident in Jones's own contribution on the 'Problem of Government', which opened with the blunt assertion that all relationships between the governing and the governed reproduced the relationship of parent and child: 'There is not one single political interaction', Jones continued, 'that is not of this nature.'[93]

Freud's great rival Carl Jung was also affected by the state of apparent crisis in Europe in the late 1920s, though his response was not to despair of civilization but to call for spiritual renewal. He was hostile to Freud's willingness to see the worst in civilization and assumed that Freud was 'under compulsion from the *Zeitgeist* to expose the possible dark sides of the human soul'.[94] In an article published in Britain in 1933 he contrasted his own search for what was 'healthy and sound' in mankind with the 'morbid symptom' of Freud's search for the 'sick man' in the unconscious mind.[95] But it is striking that one of Jung's most important essays, 'The Spiritual Problem of Modern Man', first written in 1928 and published in an English version in a book of essays on *Modern Man in Search of a Soul* in 1932, sets up exactly the same tension as Freud between the anxious despair of the post-war world in the possibilities of civilization and the promise of some future psychic overcoming. Jung argued that modern man had to come to terms with the reality of the war which had shown him up to be 'the disappointment of the hopes and expectations of the ages'. Like Freud, he understood the paradox that modernity promised both apparent progress but also imminent disaster. Every step forward 'steadily increases the threat of a still more stupendous catastrophe'. Recognition of this grim reality, Jung continued, gave modern man 'an almost fatal shock' as a result of which he exhibited a state of 'profound uncertainty'. Jung, too, believed that the discovery of the unconscious had enormous significance for modern man: 'We can no longer deny that the dark stirrings of the unconscious are active powers, that psychic forces exist which . . . cannot be fitted into our rational world order.'[96] In an arresting passage Jung highlights the terrible knowledge that confronts modern man:

If he turns away from the terrifying prospect of a blind world in which building and destroying successively tip the scales, and then gazes into the recesses of his own mind, he will discover a chaos and a darkness there which everyone would gladly ignore. Science has destroyed even this last refuge; what was once a sheltering haven has become a cesspool.[97]

Jung's purpose here was to pave the way, by an exaggerated sense of chaos, for the sublime rediscovery of the spiritual side of man which formed the centrepiece of his analytical psychology, but he leaves the essay, as Freud does his, with an open question whether Western man is actually capable of surviving the contest with 'the dark sway of natural law' (by implication, he is not). Jung's collection of essays was his best-selling book in Britain before 1939, with 9,000 printed and five impressions in a little over thirty months.[98]

The problem for anyone in the 1930s reading the psychological response to crisis, whether in Freud or Jung, was its profoundly ambiguous nature. While psychoanalysts suggested that their science might have the answer to crisis, throw 'light on the darkness' as Jones put it, the explanations for crisis, like Freud's arguments in *Civilisation and Its Discontents*, were essentially pessimistic and made clear that therapeutic intervention was impractical. The root of this ambiguity lay in the dualism posited by Freudian theory, and echoed in Jung's division between light and dark, between the conscious and the unconscious self. During the 1930s much of the work of the Institute of Psycho-Analysis focused on trying to understand the nature of aggression and the mechanisms by which the death drive generated anxiety. The leading advocate of the clinical application of the death drive was the Austrian-born analyst Melanie Klein, who had trained under Karl Abraham in Berlin, and arrived in London in 1926. Encouraged by Jones, she joined the Institute and with the publication of *The Psycho-Analysis of Children* in 1932 became one of the senior figures in the British branch of psychoanalytic theory and practice. Under her influence psychoanalytic theory became increasingly morbid, searching for the roots of violence, conflict and anxiety and positing a profound conflict between the two poles of the infant personality, like the conflict between life and death in civilization itself.[99] She also laid greater emphasis on the early formation of a savagely punitive superego, whose menace induced complex anxieties in both child and adult about 'bad' behaviour. Much of the published work of her colleagues in the Institute in the 1930s accepted the dualistic view of the life/death drive and its pessimistic implication that being human, as Edward Glover suggested in the title of a BBC series he delivered in 1935, was a dangerous thing.

Jones was not immune to the influence of dualistic thinking, despite his reservations about applying the death drive in understanding either contemporary problems or individual psychology. In lecture notes drafted in 1931 he sketched out the argument 'Troubles of the world due to <u>conflict</u> (internal) Good and Evil', and the consequence 'international rivalry and suspicion'.[100] In a letter to *The Times* in 1934 he returned to the argument that psychoanalysis, like religion, posited 'an incessant struggle' between the forces of good and evil, but that, unlike religion, psychoanalysis was more interested in the dark side of human nature, 'the nature of "sinful" impulses and of the sense of sin'.[101] The draft of another lecture on 'Morbid Anxiety' showed the influence of Klein's view that the first source of anxiety in all individuals was 'the working of the death instinct' and the impulse towards death.[102] In 1935 he addressed the Sociology Society at the London School of Economics on 'The Individual and Society'. Although he used the talk as an opportunity to reflect more on the way the psychology of the individual could by analogy be extended to the group, his whole argument hinged around the explanation that human nature could not be understood at all except in terms of a 'constant, profound conflict in the mind' between sexuality and aggression on the one hand and the urge to adapt to social reality on the other, which amounted to much the same as Freud had argued in *Civilisation and Its Discontents*. Jones suggested that modern national and racial hatreds might be understood better by applying the psychoanalytic model; so too the 'mysterious belief in force' which currently caused 'so much trouble in the world'. The threat of war, Jones concluded, emerged not because men were aggressive but because they were fearful. Crisis was the result of an imbalance between the two forces of the personality.[103]

The same concern with the dark side of human nature emerged in the series of lectures on 'The Dangers of Being Human' broadcast by the BBC in October and November 1935. This was the first time the Corporation had devoted an entire series of talks to psychoanalysis and it was hedged about with restrictions. Some of the talks had to be cut because they touched on issues of foreign policy that were currently too sensitive, and in the end Edward Glover, head of research at the Psycho-Analytical Institute, broadcast not under his own name but the bland title 'A Medical Psychologist'. The series was introduced by Dean Inge, to give it the imprimatur of respectability, but he opened with the comment 'I am not myself a Freudian'. He went on to deplore Freud's obsession with 'morbid states' instead of the healthy mind, and echoed Jung's earlier conclusion that the war had provided a nearly 'fatal shock' to modern man, who 'found some very ugly inmates' when he examined his inner mind. Inge concluded that not psychoanalysis but the spirit of God was required to transform the crisis of modern civilization.[104] The six talks that followed were framed by Glover's opening explanation that even the apparently normal individual carried within all the inherited primitive impulses that civilization had sought to restrain. He chose to focus from the outset on the inner drive to death and destruction characteristic of 'savage society'. The impulse to hate, he continued, had abated not a bit in the passage to civilization; everyone under any kind of stress was capable of invoking those primitive impulses that might end in self-destruction. Fear, guilt and anxiety inhabited modern man as they inhabited his ancient ancestor. Civilization, he suggested in his final talk, had reached a dead end from which there was no escape except to hope that in a thousand years' time education might have lifted some of the pressures on moulding little adults. Glover made a point he would have found in *Civilisation and Its Discontents*, that a return to primitive society could scarcely be worse than the dangerous struggle to remain civilized, and he invited listeners to imagine British holidaymakers at the beach to get some idea of just how close to Stone-Age society the modern human really was.[105]

It might well be argued that the pessimistic message was what people either wanted or expected to hear in the 1930s, for it did little to hold back a rising tide of public interest in psychoanalysis and the retreat of the crude hostility and prejudice characteristic of its early years. During the 1930s the number of actively trained analysts increased steadily, and the London Clinic and Institute, thanks to the financial generosity of an American philanthropist, Pryns Hopkins, remained on a sound footing. The Public Lectures Sub-Committee decided in 1932 to shift from lecture series on narrowly theoretical topics to lectures with a more popular appeal, to demonstrate that psychoanalysis 'is the key to the better understanding of psychological and social problems'.[106] The first lectures under the new rubric included 'The Emotional Life of Civilised Men and Women', 'Family Problems' and 'The Psychology of Social Violence', which last included four lectures on the problems of war.[107] The shift to more mundane or accessible topics was reflected in rising attendances. In 1937/8 the Institute mounted five lecture series, ten public lectures and nine lectures for doctors in twelve months.[108] Some of the growing appeal may also have been due to the increasingly democratic nature of Freudian theory, with its emphasis on a shared mental inheritance. The psychologist David Klein described Freudianism in 1933 as 'the first attempt to found a system of psychology on the basis of the common man's story of his life'. Freud's view of man, Klein continued, had about it a 'directness, intimacy and relevance' which distinguished it from conventional scientific psychology.[109] The vulgar dissemination of psychoanalysis also satisfied a public appetite for knowledge about, and a language to describe the anxieties, sexual or otherwise, of modern life. British society, as one anonymous reviewer of a life of Freud explained in 1929, was perceived to have 'an utterly inadequate and defective sex education'.[110]

The public appetite for literature on psychoanalysis or popular psychology also expanded sharply in the 1930s. Some of it was still uncompromisingly old fashioned. In 1929 Alice Raven's *An Introduction to Individual Psychology* was a restatement of the view that the neurotic had to pull himself together and learn the 'discipline of life'. Instead of wallowing in self-pity, the individual should show 'a healthy self-reliance based on personal effort'.[111] But many other popular books reflected the impact of Freud – Jackson and Salisbury's *Outwitting Our Nerves* (first published in 1922 and into its fifth edition by 1937), W. B. Wolfe's *Nervous Breakdown: Its Cause and Cure*, Karen Horney's *The Neurotic Personality of Our Time*, or Joseph Ralph's *How to Psycho-Analyse Yourself*, which suggested that self-analysis among normal people, a 'mental purgation', would prevent them succumbing to the 'unconscious morbid influences' within them.[112] The idea of neurosis became widely accepted as a modern reality and advertisements for all kinds of remedies for everything from stammering to melancholy became the commonplace of every magazine. This development was so marked that Glover used a collage of representative 'neurosis' advertisements to illustrate the published version of his lectures and it clearly reflected the growing popular sense that the anxieties generated by external crisis had some real internal psychological source. Much of this public activity was scientifically worthless but pandered to public concern. The British Institute of Practical Psychology Ltd published a book under the title *I Can . . . and I Will* in 1935 which had by the end of 1937 sold 350,000 (if the figures are to be believed). The book promised to reveal the secrets of 'The Mind behind the Mind', in this case the 'Subconscious' rather than the unconscious mind. The list of conditions apparently susceptible to cure was remarkable: 'Self-consciousness, self-distrust, unsociability, nervous apprehension, bashfulness, depression, worry, sleeplessness, fear, weakness of will, indecision . . . hot hands, trembling limbs, word obsessions' and so on. The selling-line relied on a pseudo-Freudianism – personality defects due to past trauma, early experiences too distant to recall, 'disturbance-centres' in the subconscious mind, negative impulses which 'you cannot control' but which control you.[113] The effect of mass-circulation popular psychology was not to provide effective therapy but to familiarize growing circles of the population with the idea that every individual is the prey of inner demons which could manipulate at will the outer person.

Much of the public discussion of neurotic behaviour was subsumed under the banner of 'fear'. This was a very general term, which described rather than explained a number of different emotional states, but the idea of being afraid, as an emotional condition in its own right, matched much of the popular mood as did the general catch-all category of neurosis or nervous breakdown. Fear meant different things to psychology and psychoanalysis. Cyril Burt, writing in the mid-1920s, argued that 'the instinct' of fear would in the long run prove a much more important source of 'anxiety, worry and even nervous breakdown' than Freud's sex instinct, and it was one wholly conscious.[114] Psychoanalysts, on the other hand, had a special place for fear as a description of the unconscious response to the threat of the superego to punish any attempt to avoid the censor, but they also explained particular fears, such as the fear of death, in terms of specific complexes. Fear of death, according to a paper by Mary Chadwick, read before the Tenth Psycho-Analytical Congress in Innsbruck in 1927, was fear of a terrible giant 'over whom we have no control'. 'It is invisible, intangible, and therefore of a quality so UNKNOWN as to be terrifying in itself . . .' (an insight that scarcely needed psychoanalysis).[115] Another example was the fear that all men were supposed to have of women, which derived, according to Karen Horney, from man's dread of the vagina and fear of its destructive power. Horney suggested that many male dreams enacted this fear – 'a motor-car is rushing along and suddenly falls into a pit and is dashed to pieces; or a boat is sailing in a narrow channel and is suddenly sucked into a whirlpool; there is a cellar with uncanny, blood-stained plants and animals . . .'[116] These discussions of fear as a reflection of unconscious anxieties bore little relation to the public sense of fear generated by real anxieties about war, aerial bombardment, unemployment and so on. This was the sense in which, for example, the all-women's Chalcot Discussion Society in Hampstead approached the issue. In 1930 they listened to a lecture on 'Fear in Modern Life'. In 1938, shortly after the Munich crisis, they returned to the theme of fear in a lecture by a Mrs Liberty, who defined it as an influence for 'uneasiness, distrust or dread' which deeply affected the modern outlook on life, and went on to explore a range of phobias and 'morbid fears' which were an essential part of human nature. In the debate that followed it was generally agreed that fear had been responsible for averting 'catastrophe' during the recent world crisis. When the motion 'Fear Rules the World' was put at the end of the meeting the vote was 14 to 12 in favour of the proposition.[117]

The principal source of fear in the 1930s was the deteriorating international situation and the strong possibility of war. Two months after the Czech crisis, in late November 1938, another Hampstead-based discussion forum, the Federation of Progressive Societies, invited Ernest Jones to lecture to them on what was by then a general fear: 'How Can Civilization be Saved?' Jones was not a surprising choice since the vice-presidents of the federation included Leonard and Virginia Woolf, Cyril Burt and the benefactor of the Institute of Psycho-Analysis, Pryns Hopkins.[118] But the choice of subject was an indication of how far psychoanalysis had come since the early 1920s. Jones was initially asked to reflect on the psychological approach to international problems but the final title of the symposium forced him to think more widely. He did not accept that civilization was about to collapse as far as he could judge; what interested him as a psycho-analyst was the fear that it might do so. Jones took as his starting point the widespread evidence of popular anxiety, 'what we may call a serious dis-ease' (to echo the word he had thought of applying to the title of Freud's book on civilization), for which a psychoanalytical explanation was more appropriate. Fear was the result of unconscious impulses which triggered a strong sense of guilt, as Freud had argued. To cope with the subsequent anxiety people searched for a Messiah figure, as the Germans had done with Hitler; or they projected their 'badness' outwards by expelling the Jews, who were made to carry the rest of the population's guilt and fear. (This example was one of many interesting insights, which historians have generally ignored, in the application of psychoanalytical theory to problems of dictatorship and war.) In general he thought that the century and a half since the

French Revolution had imposed a burden of responsibility on people that was 'greater than they could bear'. For all this he could offer a diagnosis but no prescription. He hoped that psychology might be more widely taught; he even suggested that psychoanalysing the prime minister and the Foreign Secretary would make a crisis like Munich less fearful; but he made it clear to his audience, as Freud had done in *Civilisation and Its Discontents*, that he could offer no 'nostrum or panacea' which could resolve the visible ills that afflicted mankind.[119]

The father of psychoanalysis, Sigmund Freud, after his arrival in England following the German takeover of Austria in 1938. From left to right, Freud's eldest daughter Mathilde, Freud, Ernest Jones and Freud's daughter-in-law, Lucie.

Jones's remarks about National Socialism and the Jews had a particular poignancy, for a few months before, on 4 June 1938, Freud and his family had left Vienna for good following the *Anschluss* with Germany and found refuge in London. The choice was understandable, for after Austria Britain was a second home for psychoanalysis in the 1930s. Jones had intervened with the Home Office to make sure that there would be no problems with Freud's immigration papers and work permit. It was a testimony to his international stature that he was accorded diplomatic status by the British authorities and none of his luggage was searched on arrival at Dover. In September he and his family moved into permanent quarters in Hampstead where Freud, who was now a frail man of 82, continued to receive visitors, write letters and complete the writing and publication of his final book, *Moses and Monotheism*. He lived to see the outbreak of the Second World War and died of cancer on 23 September 1939.[120] The obituary in *The Lancet* observed that Freud, like Galileo and Darwin, was one of those thinkers who had put mankind in its place when he showed that the 'infinitely adaptable and creative' human mind, the crowning of man's achievement, was 'nothing more than the sublimation of the baser instincts'.[121] On 26 September Jones gave the funeral oration to 'a rare spirit'. On the very day of Freud's funeral Leonard Woolf telephoned Ernest Jones to ask if he would write Freud's biography, which he eventually did.[122]

Psychoanalysis in Britain had come a long way from the early, insecure days of Freudian psychotherapy in the early 1920s to the point where it was called upon to explain the wider problems of civilization. Therapy continued to be its principal function, but the shift to a metapsychology in which the individual personality was, by analogy, enlarged into communities, nations or systems that could also be subjected to analysis, gave psychoanalysis an influence far beyond what might be expected with a handful of practitioners and clinical notes on a few hundred patients. The relationship with the external world was a complex one but Jones recognized, when writing about the 'Present State of Psycho-Analysis' in 1930, how important was the influence of 'the social and political milieu' in judging an analytical question, and how resistant a person could be to 'facing his own nature' even when current political conditions cried out for it.[123] The willingness of psychoanalysis and of Jungian thought in the 1930s to engage with the issues of war, peace, racism or national competition reflected a professional interest in the public anxiety and neurosis generated by international and economic crisis. By 1939, as one sociologist put it, there had emerged a wide popular expectation among political and social scientists that only psychoanalysis could properly explain 'many of the causes of our "Modern Discontents"'.[124] Even socialists, argued the journal of the National Labour Colleges, should recognize 'the melancholy truth' that man 'is not at bottom a rational animal' and adapt their tactics accordingly.[125]

The problem posed by psychoanalysis in the wider perception of crisis was its profound ambivalence. Freudianism promised to open up issues of sexuality that had remained deeply repressed, and no doubt it did play an important part in the slow sexual revolution of the inter-war years, but at the same time its central focus on sexuality encouraged popular anxieties about morbidity, decadence and deviancy. The theory of the unconscious, though it was designed at first simply to explain mental illness, was a metaphor of such remarkable explanatory power that it undermined the whole liberal projection of human nature as essentially reasoning and reasonable, or of individuals exercising free will unconditionally. Instead Freudian theory posited a conscious mind that comprised only a small part of the individual's mental makeup; it was unable to make entirely free choices; it was constantly threatened by an invisible conflict between hidden impulses and drives of exceptional power on the one hand and the slender mechanisms of restraint imposed by the civilizing process on the other. The unconscious was represented by psychoanalysts as chaotic, primitive, infantile and arbitrary, and the seething mass of instincts and drives that inhabited it was capable of a terrible aggression and an urge to morbid self-destruction. When this paradigm was applied to society as a whole, as it was regularly throughout the 1930s, it only served to illuminate what many people already suspected, that beneath the thin veneer of civilization there lurked a monstrous other self whose release would spell the end of civilized life and the triumph of barbarism.

To these many ambivalences psychoanalysis had little response. Like genetic theory, it could explain or diagnose, but acting to modify the threats to social order or international peace that the theory implied was, from their nature, impossible. Freud himself offered no solution and his growing pessimism about the impossibility of civilization avoiding the psychological dilemmas prompted by modernity infected much of the psychoanalytic perspective in the 1930s. Jung offered a more hopeful prospect of a final reconciliation of the individual with the collective soul, but as a practical guide to society as a whole this too was a distant hope. Edward Glover, in his remarks on a 'Psychologist's Utopia', concluded that 'the task of civilisation is to make our day-dreams correspond more closely with the capacities of man', but his ideas of a future return to primitivism must have struck his listeners, as they do today, as merely whimsical. In 1938 Pryns Hopkins wrote a book himself on *A Psycho-Analytic View of Society*. In the final chapter on 'The Road to Happiness' he rejected the many scientific criticisms of psychoanalysis and called on psychological education as the key to a future Utopia. Unlike Glover, Hopkins had a practical solution to hand: a government-sponsored nationwide system of psychoanalysis clinics in which the whole population would be both entitled and strongly encouraged to be psychoanalysed. But until, or unless, a national psychotherapy service was available, Hopkins could promise his readers only more of the current 'chaos and tragedy . . . crushing endeavour, blighting hopes, shattering dreams'.[126]

5

Why War?

Fighting is plainly a common, indeed a universal, form of human behaviour. It extends beyond the borders of humanity into the types of mammals most closely related in the evolutionary classification to the common ancestors of man and other apes. War between groups within the nation and between nations are obvious and important examples of this type of behaviour. Edward Durbin and John Bowlby, 1939[1]

Nothing provoked greater public anxiety in Britain in the 1920s and 1930s than fear of war. More than slow economic decline, or the unpredictable workings of genes and instincts, war threatened sudden and certain catastrophe. Though the Great War was popularly described as 'the war to end war', or 'the war for civilization', it was impossible to mask the likelihood that Europe could plunge once again into a terrible conflict even worse than the tragic bloodbath through which it had just passed. Not surprisingly, future war was presented in remorselessly apocalyptic terms, as if it enjoyed an almost independent existence, external to human affairs. Modern mass warfare had shown its exceptional destructive power and war was now given a historical weight quite distinct from the expedient view of war as an arm of foreign policy and imperialism current in the Victorian age. The idea that civilization would not survive another such conflict became a cliché after 1919, but it did so only because the horrors and sacrifices of the recent war fuelled persistent anxiety about its repetition, and an urgent desire to discover its cause and remove its curse. 'The suppression of war', wrote H. G. Wells in 1921, 'is generally regarded as central to the complex of contemporary problems.'[2]

The catastrophic view of war could be found at the highest level of British public life. The Conservative politician Stanley Baldwin, prime minister three times between 1923 and 1937 and a man, as Gilbert Murray once observed, 'by no means . . . given to extravagant fancies', had famously asked in a speech given in January 1927: 'and who in Europe does not know that one more war in the West, and the civilisation of the ages will fall with as great a crash as that of Rome?'[3] Baldwin was no pacifist but he deplored the recent war because it had demonstrated to the whole world, as he put it, 'how thin is the crust of civilisation on which this generation is walking'.[4] In a speech to the International Peace Society in October 1935 he asked his audience to view war not in terms of 'huge cloudy symbols' represented by great-power groupings and their attendant moral and political conflicts, but in acutely personal terms – 'the lives of our children and grandchildren, of our friends and companions'. Modern war, Baldwin continued, risked everything, 'every piece of all the life we and our fathers have made in this land'.[5] During his last premiership, in November 1936, Baldwin gave the speech at the annual banquet of the Lord Mayor of London. It was a despairing survey of the ruined hopes for peace and the looming prospect of a new war so terrible that 'the misery of the last war' would seem like happiness in comparison. War, continued Baldwin, meant degradation, anarchy and world revolution.[6]

Baldwin's prophecies about war, like his famous declaration made in November 1932 that 'the bomber will always get through', became the common currency of public discourse. In a 1934 radio debate between A. A. Milne, a pacifist better known as the author of the children's classic *Winnie the Pooh*, and Anthony Ludovici, who thought pacifism degenerate nonsense, Milne stated his case using the words of Lord Robert Cecil, president of the British League of Nations Union: 'It is no exaggeration to say, with Mr Baldwin, that the next war will mean the destruction of our civilisation.'[7] The anthropologist and pacifist Bronislaw Malinowski, who taught at the London School of Economics in the 1930s, kept a file of press cuttings and pamphlets on war, including reports of Baldwin's speeches. In the margin of an account of the Geneva Disarmament Conference for 1933 he scribbled his own version of Baldwin: 'Next world war would mean the end of human civilisation.'[8] Three years later in a guest lecture to the Phi Beta Kappa Society at Harvard University, Malinowski argued that the last war had so undermined Western civilization that the next one 'may well destroy it' at one blow. At best it would provoke moral and material decay, 'a slow death of humanity'.[9] The pairing of war and civilization lent itself to aphorism. In a book on the causes of war by the Cambridge scholar G. Lowes Dickinson, published in 1923, the argument was summarized in a single sentence: 'If mankind does not end war, war will end mankind.' In *How Shall We Escape?*, published in 1934, the Scottish cleric Norman Maclean wrote that 'if civilisation does not end war, war will put an end to civilisation'.[10] Variations abounded on a constant theme.

Much of this public and private foreboding rested on the clear understanding that the character of war had changed completely and irreversibly as a result of what had happened between 1914 and 1918. Modern weaponry – submarines, chemical warfare, long-range bombers – was evidently capable of inflicting destruction on a hitherto unprecedented scale, not only of the armed forces in the field, but of the distant civilian populations whose labour sustained their combat. The vision of what came to be called 'total war', a term first publicized shortly after the end of the conflict, reinforced the idea that future warfare might result in the total annihilation of all those states who fought it. 'In war,' remarked Baldwin's successor as prime minister in 1937, Neville Chamberlain, 'there are no winners, but all are losers.'[11] In the post-war years there emerged a multitude of imaginative descriptions of what total war might be like, many of which embellished and reinforced the idea that civilization could not possibly survive its impact, but most of which were sheer imagination. They ranged from official publications to fantasy fiction. The most pessimistic anticipated the physical destruction and death of innocent cities and citizens and the onset of an age of moral degradation and cultural extinction. In his debate with Ludovici A. A. Milne also cited the war correspondent Henry Nevinson as an example of the current catastrophist view of war, and the quotation may stand as a model for the genre:

There can be no doubt of the destruction ... all the greatest and most beautiful cities of Europe and of this country will be shattered and burnt; all the treasures of art and literature will be consumed; most of the machinery crushed to ruins; most of the food supply reduced to desert waste; women and children killed by hundreds and thousands; and men, young and old, by millions ...

It was equally certain, Nevinson continued, that 'this is the catastrophe to which we are steadily moving'.[12]

Not everyone accepted that this really was the shape of things to come (and a case can be made that Nevinson, like other catastrophists, exploited alarm to encourage pacifism), but the picture of disaster was repeated so often and endorsed by so many public figures that the paralysing effects of total war became cliché too. The overburdening sense that the civilized world might be capable yet again of plunging into a war of immeasurable destructiveness was taken to be an indication of just how serious the wider crisis of civilization was. Lowes Dickinson, writing in his private notebook of 'Aphorisms', 'watching civilisation crumble about me' in the renewed international tension of the early 1920s, could not decide if he was a sane man in a lunatic asylum or 'a lunatic among sane men'.[13] Arnold Toynbee saw war as the dissolving agent of all past civilizations, the 'malady' that laid low sick societies.[14] Basil Liddell Hart, widely regarded as Britain's foremost military intellectual both at home and abroad, author in 1925 of one of the first and most influential of the alarmist accounts of modern conflict, *Paris, or the Future of War* (named after the Trojan hero, not the French capital city), wrote in 1932 that modern war was the feverish product 'of a diseased state of civilisation'.[15] The same metaphor was used by General J. F. C. Fuller, another of Britain's military thinkers, often regarded as the founding father of the idea of modern armoured warfare, who also assumed that modern war was not itself a disease, but the product of a disease, 'a sickness incubated in peace' within a 'defective society' which, in his view, fully deserved its violent fate.[16]

It is against this background of morbid expectations about the next war that the growing public interest in Britain in the causes of war must be understood. If war really was a disease, what was its origin

One Penny

Who is the Enemy? Not Peoples but Militarism in all Lands
Specially drawn for the *Air Display Special* by the famous Spanish artist, Helios Gomez

20 YEARS AFTER : LEST WE FORGET

The last War cost Britain :—	LOSS OF LIFE IN WARS BETWEEN
812,317 Killed.	1790–1913.
39,000 lost arms or legs, or both.	
2,100 were blinded.	Total number killed, 4,449,300.

A cartoon from the 'Air Display Special', a paper published by the Cambridge Anti-War Council in July 1935 to coincide with the Duxford air display that month, attended by the King. The front-page headline read 'Is There a War Danger? Another 1914?'

and nature? And how could civilization be cured? In the 1920s these questions were seldom addressed very seriously. Explanations for the recent war, or for war in general, scarcely matched the thesis of civilization menaced by obliterating violence. Much of the conventional wisdom on war was supplied by historians or politicians who saw the crisis in terms of day-to-day diplomacy or the role of political personality. The discussion of war stressed the place of historical contingency – the arms race, the ambitions of a few deluded men, a temporary breakdown in the European order, even diplomatic accident. The renewed fears of war in the decade after 1919 were commonly attributed to the political failings of a punitive peace settlement or the more general failure to establish effective international instruments for reducing and regulating economic and national rivalry on rational lines. These arguments suggested that war in 1914 had been accidental rather than systemic, a product of a temporary disequilibrium in the balance of power rather than a consequence of generic reversion to violence in the midst of civilization; by the same token war was something that could be avoided by rational discussion and the reimposition of 'order'. When the former Foreign Secretary Austen Chamberlain, half-brother of Neville, was asked to contribute to a series of BBC talks on the causes of war in 1934, he ridiculed or dismissed the arguments of other contributors, particularly the psychoanalytical explanations for war ('Do you recognise', he asked, 'the motives of yourselves or your neighbours under these strange words?') and insisted that most wars were likely to be caused by frontier disputes.[17] The idea that large wars might have small causes, or scarcely a cause at all, was captured in Lloyd George's famous dictum that the powers had all slithered into the abyss in 1914.

Gilbert Murray, who worked for the League of Nations throughout its twenty-five-year existence, was typical of a generation who lived through an unexpected war and found it difficult to understand its terms or its causes. When he reflected on them himself in the 1920s and 1930s he came back to the liberal belief that war in 1914 was the product of a temporary maladjustment in world affairs, and in particular the failure to restrict the pre-war competition in armaments and to maintain an international commitment to free and open trade. In an article written for a German journal in 1927 on 'The Problems of Tomorrow', Murray argued that the war was the product of a particular point in the recent history of civilized states and not the consequence of primitive and violent emotions. To avoid war again it was simply necessary to regulate 'international competition' and to ensure that access to the world's resources was equitably granted.[18] The failure to regulate, he told an audience at Aberystwyth University in 1934, produced 'economic anarchy' and 'international anarchy', the same disorders of 'maladjustment and chaos' that had provoked war in 1914. Murray was convinced that the rational ordering of world affairs would quell the chaos and make possible the triumph of the Greek 'cosmos', the antithesis of disorder. He identified the League of Nations as the 'Divine Other' to which the Greek Stoics had once given their loyalty.[19] In a letter to Liddell Hart written a few weeks after his address in Wales, Murray returned to the theme that war was best understood as a result of self-evident political causes rather than of any hidden imperative to pugnacity. 'The last war did not start', wrote Murray, 'because Bethmann Hollweg or the Czar, or Asquith, or even the Kaiser, had a lust for killing people.' Political rivalry, he continued, 'made people jumpy or angry', but it was the irrational competition between nations that caused a war that should never have happened.[20]

These explanations were powerfully challenged by the descent into economic and international crisis after 1929. The rational reordering of Europe and the wider world, crowned in triumph it seemed by the signing of the Kellogg–Briand Pact of Paris in 1928, when sixty-five states pledged themselves not to resort to war as an instrument of policy, was exposed as a sham, not only by the failure to collaborate effectively to stem the economic collapse, but also by the failure to prevent Japan from embarking on a programme of military expansion in China with the occupation of Manchuria in September 1931 and the bombing of Shanghai the following year. The rise of aggressive nationalism in Italy and Germany presented more evidence that the liberal ambitions of the League system were scarcely adequate to the apparent crisis of civilization unfolding in the 1930s. 'Why', asked the journalist Hoffman Nickerson, in a book published in London in 1933, 'has our democratic era been the bloodiest in history?' – a question that continues to tax historians to the present day.[21]

Unlike the 1920s, the 1930s generated a wave of popular explanations for the causes of war that threatened to become a flood. The
lead was taken by the League of Nations itself. In 1925 the League had
agreed to establish a permanent Institute of Intellectual Co-operation,
based in Paris, and run by an International Committee. In 1930 the
Institute decided to set up a Permanent Committee on Arts and Letters,
and Gilbert Murray was invited to chair it. One of the Committee's
first recommendations was to initiate an exchange of ideas and letters
in formal 'conversations' and 'correspondences' involving 'the finest
intelligences of the contemporary world'. The brief was to address
issues of fundamental importance to international stability and collaboration. The League Assembly formally approved the scheme in
September 1931 and Murray set about recruiting candidates.[22] He
personally organized the first 'correspondence' under the title 'The
League of Minds'; the second resulted from an invitation to one of
the International Committee members, the German physicist Albert
Einstein, to find a correspondent on a subject of his choice. Einstein
was in Geneva in May 1932 at the invitation of the British No More
War Movement to give a press conference on disarmament, where he
announced that war could not be abolished 'by rules' but only with a
sufficient fund of 'character and will'.[23] Perhaps provoked by this
thought, he arranged a few weeks later for Freud to be his correspondent on the question 'Is there any way of delivering mankind from the
menace of war?'

In Einstein's view this was 'the most insistent of all the problems
civilisation has to face'; like Baldwin, he thought the menace of war
to be 'a matter of life and death for civilisation'.[24] Freud's reply
arrived from Vienna in September. He explained that violence was
characteristic of the whole animal kingdom, 'from which men have
no right to exclude themselves'. Though sensible people might find it
constitutionally impossible not to be pacifists, Freud thought they
were too few. Only fear might be strong enough to inhibit war, but
how a fear of such proportions could be invoked, Freud concluded,
'we cannot guess'.[25] The Committee for Intellectual Co-operation
published the exchange early in 1933 under the title 'Pourquoi la
Guerre?'. The booklet was translated into English and Dutch, and
also published in the German original. The German and British ver-

sions were ordered in a limited edition of 2,000, but they arrived in Germany only after Hitler's appointment as chancellor and their sale or distribution was banned.[26] The Einstein/Freud correspondence was followed up by a conference in Madrid on 'The Future of Civilisation', in which war featured a good deal, and later in 1933 a second conversation on 'Spirit, Ethics and War', which featured a glittering array of intellectuals invited to wrestle with the causes and prevention of modern war. The Committee was disappointed with the results, which generated little more than a great deal of hot air, but at a secret session in December 1933, chaired by Murray, it was agreed in light of the deteriorating international situation that the urgent work of trying to explain how wars happen should continue.[27]

Why War? arrived in Britain at just the point when the public appetite for more profound explanations for war was growing. Einstein and Freud were household names and the pamphlet was rapidly absorbed into the current discussion. It was reprinted in 1934 by New Commonwealth (a movement to promote 'International Law and Order' founded in 1932 by the Liberal peer and pacifist Lord David Davies), and reissued by the Peace Pledge Union in 1939. That same year Freud's reply was published in a selection of his psychoanalytic writings under the title *Civilization, War and Death*.[28] The title *Why War?* was borrowed in 1934 by Edward Conze and Ellen Wilkinson (the MP for Jarrow, known from her bright ginger hair and her radical politics as 'Red Ellen') for a pamphlet published under the auspices of the National Council of Labour Colleges, which argued the socialist line that as long as there was capitalism, there would be war.[29] In the spring of 1939 Cyril Joad published a book also titled *Why War?* as part of a series of popular cheap paperbacks launched two years earlier by Allen Lane's recently founded Penguin Books as Penguin Specials. 'My case', wrote Joad, with unfortunate timing, 'is that war is not something that is inevitable.'[30] 'Why War?' was the title chosen for the opening lecture by Dean Inge in a series of radio broadcasts by the BBC in November and December 1934 under the general title 'The Causes of War'. The eleven talks included contributions from the novelist Aldous Huxley, who wrote about the psychological imperative to inflict pain, and Winston Churchill, who suggested in his talk that the new Germany, raising a generation 'taught from childhood to think of war and conquest as a glorious exercise', might be the most likely cause, not of war in general, but of the next war. The talks generated a lively correspondence in the columns of the BBC journal *The Listener* and a few months later, in response to popular demand, they were published as *The Causes of War*, though without Churchill's undiplomatic essay, which he felt was 'unsuitable for issue in a book'.[31]

A glance at the titles then currently offered by the publisher George Allen & Unwin, who produced the BBC book of talks, conveys the advent of war mania: *The Causes of the World War; Is War Obsolete?; Selling War; War: Its Cause and Cure* (the last promoted under the headline 'World Suicide or War's Abolishment').[32] No doubt publishers played their part in sustaining interest in a subject that had selling power, but the appetite for books on war was a large one that continued unabated throughout the 1930s. Out of thirty-six Penguin Specials published between November 1937 and the outbreak of war no fewer than twenty-one dealt with war or some aspect of the international crisis.[33] Between October 1935 and June 1939 Victor Gollancz, founder of the Left Book Club in 1936, published sixteen out of twenty-four books on issues to do with war, peace and the fascist threat. They enjoyed a total print run of 414,500 copies, including more than 100,000 copies of two books on defence against air raids.[34] One of the biggest sellers of the decade was the wartime autobiography of the novelist Vera Brittain, who had served as a nurse during a conflict that she regarded as a senseless and grotesque abuse of her generation. Her *Testament of Youth* sold 100,000 copies in the first popular edition produced in 1935.[35] The sombre contemplation of what war really meant was reflected in the decision by the Beaverbrook Press to publish in 1934 a book of photographs from the Great War under the title *Covenants with Death*. Published with a black cover, etched with a red skull and scroll on the front, the book contained images that had been thought too shocking for publication while the war was being fought. At the end was a special section secured with a red paper seal of photographs so 'inescapably horrible' that the publisher included a warning that 'highly strung and sensitive persons' should pass them over; the images here included rows of decapitated heads displayed as trophies, and the mutilated and abused bodies of women and children.[36] The purpose of the book, according to the publisher, was to warn the British people of the folly of war and the necessity for peace. When Lord Beaverbrook, editor of the *Express* newspapers, gave one of the BBC lectures in 1934, he confined himself to the single idea that whatever caused war, it could best be avoided by a foreign policy of absolute isolation.[37]

The quality of much that was published on war was, like Beaverbrook's photographs, deliberately sensationalist. Little of it gave hard answers to the questions of what caused war or how it might be set aside. For those like Liddell Hart who despaired of the futility of war, understanding its cause was a scientific ambition of terrible urgency. Liddell Hart was unconvinced by Gilbert Murray's view of war as a result of a civilization temporarily and unnecessarily out of joint. All through the growing international crisis and mounting war hysteria of the 1930s he struggled to make sense of what the root cause of war might be. He had fought in the Great War but was sufficiently disabled by a gas attack in 1916 to avoid further fighting, for which he confessed he had little stomach. Though he hankered for high military office, to be what he called one of the 'masters of war', he was plagued by continuous bad health, a nervous instability that grew more pronounced with the approach of war, and a complete intolerance for stupidity, which he found in unhelpful profusion among Britain's militarists. The novelist Storm Jameson found the tall, bespectacled, fastidious Liddell Hart 'the one rational human being I know'.[38] It was on the basis of that intense rationality that he set out to try to understand the causes of war and through that understanding abolish it. For Liddell Hart the key to unravelling the mystery of persistent conflict lay in the proper application of science to war. In the early 1930s, influenced in his turn by the growing public interest in war, he became obsessed with the current failure to apply the scientific method, as he saw it, to the most dangerous of human activities.

Few people were better qualified than Liddell Hart, whose books on warfare, rather than on war as such, were read across Europe. His interest in mobilizing science was possibly triggered by Julian Huxley, who was asked in November 1933 to give a talk on 'Science and War' in a BBC series on Scientific Research and Social Needs. Huxley sent the draft to Liddell Hart for comment. The second half of the talk was devoted to the prospect that the application of science could somehow make war 'as unlikely as possible', but apart from hoping that the scientific spirit might be applied to curb the urge to nationalism and briefly exploring the 'remote, indeed more utopian' idea that psychoanalysis might unlock the secrets of aggression and the instruments to control it, his conclusion was that without a fundamental alteration in political outlook, war was here to stay. Commenting on the draft, Liddell Hart argued that the only path open to humanity was 'to organise the scientific study of war', but added that after half a lifetime devoted to the endeavour, he found himself 'more uncertain as to the real causes of war than I ever was'.[39] Over the following year he pursued the idea of marrying science to the explanation of conflict. He was attracted to the utopian idea, suggested in Huxley's talk, that the science of the mind might unlock the inner secrets of human nature. In his comments on a book by A. A. Milne, published in autumn 1934 under the title *Peace with Honour* (a quotation from Disraeli made notorious four years later when Neville Chamberlain used it on his return from the Munich Conference), Liddell Hart wrote that beneath the proximate causes of war in economic and political rivalry there lurked a hidden psychological source 'springing from the animal in man'.[40] When he engaged in his correspondence with Gilbert Murray in early November 1934 he insisted that the cause of war could be understood only by combining the study of all past wars with the proper study of psychology.[41]

This ambition thwarted Liddell Hart. He spent much of his career in the years leading up to the outbreak of war and beyond analysing the evolution of methods of warfare and military policy, but on the scientific explanation for the causes of war he failed to do much more than lament its conspicuous absence. Nevertheless, his views on the paramount importance of science were not expressed in isolation, but reflected a growing public awareness of the potential for scientific explanation. This had been the reason behind Einstein's approach to Freud. The sense that science had hitherto abdicated its social responsibility in the case of war featured in another radio conversation in 1933 between Julian Huxley and the mathematician Hyman Levy, who complained that a great many key social problems had been kept in 'scientific darkness', among them the causes of war. Huxley agreed that a change in outlook was necessary – 'that science <u>should</u> be asked to help in tackling such problems'.[42] An editorial in the influential science journal *Nature* in September 1934 on 'Peace and War' noted that the central characteristic of modern civilization was a constant advance towards 'complete scientific understanding' of all areas of human life with the single exception of war, the one element of the human condition with the capacity to 'destroy the civilisation of the western world'.[43] A letter to *The Times* in December 1933 called on the human sciences of anthropology, psychology and physiology to examine the male human being with a view to finally confirming scientifically whether he possessed any innate predisposition to violence or not.[44] It had certainly been the intention of the League of Nations to involve men 'renowned for their scientific work' to answer just such questions in the conversations and correspondences launched in 1931, but no systematic, funded programme of research was ever established. The League was too preoccupied with attempting to contain the real threats to peace to be able to develop a proper science of war.[45]

In the 1930s science, or more precisely the human sciences, tried to rise to this challenge. The widespread sense that science should supply answers fuelled a great deal of popular scientific speculation on the causes of war, some of it driven by career scientists in the natural and social sciences who were willing under the circumstances of the growing crisis to forge links between their academic interests and the wider social and political milieu. Much of this scientific discourse was nourished by the same human sciences – economics, biology and psychology – that contributed in other ways to the wider anxieties of the age. From the core of each of these disciplines could be distilled major theoretical explanations for what were regarded as the fundamental, primary causes of war. Indeed this endeavour proved to be one of the chief meeting points of the human sciences in the 1930s. None of them engaged directly in sustained or systematic programmes of research; in none of them could any meaningful consensus be established on what did or did not explain war; but there existed a self-conscious sense that the question 'Why war?' was one to which the human sciences in particular ought to have an answer. Moreover, the opportunities open to science to enter the public arena were much greater in Britain than in authoritarian Europe; scientists enjoyed a larger freedom to research what they chose and to participate in debates of serious social concern, a position they had already exploited well before 1914. The idea, for example, that war was a product of biological imperatives had a long pedigree, and so too the contention that capitalist economics promoted war, but these earlier claims had in some sense been gratuitous. In the 1930s rising public fears about the possibility of another annihilating war lent a special urgency to the scientific exploration of its roots. As one reviewer put it in *Nature* in 1932, commenting on yet another book with the title *The Causes of War*, published by Commission I of the World Conference for Peace through Religion, 'the calm, serious spirit of science' might emancipate mankind from the shadow of war as it had freed it from religious superstition and disease.[46]

The most widely accepted and keenly publicized of the three scientific approaches to the causes of war was derived from the social sciences and from economics in particular. The argument, simply put, was that modern industrial capitalism causes war. The explanation for war was thus secondary, a consequence, as Allen Hutt put it in 1935 in the portentously titled *This Final Crisis*, 'of the operation of the inherent laws of development of capitalist society'.[47] This meant that not all wars were equally to be condemned. In her pamphlet *Why War?* Ellen Wilkinson explained that 'War is justified if it furthers the interests of the working masses', but not if it promoted imperial expansion and enslavement. In a set of six lessons published by the Marx Memorial Library in London's Clerkenwell Green on 'Marxism and War' it was pointed out that all previous wars were the product of different forms of class society: some had been wars of liberation, but the war of 1914–18 was 'the first imperialist world war'.[48] The argument that capitalist economics necessarily promotes war on the basis of observable economic fact was founded, as the social theorist Morris Ginsberg pointed out in his own analysis of the causes of war published in April 1939, 'on a theory of imperialism rather than war'.[49] This argument was presented in the 1930s as a product of Marxist science, but its origins can be found in the economics of J. A. Hobson whose influential book *Imperialism*, published in 1902, gave a firm intellectual foundation to the connection between capitalism and war. Hobson's argument, already examined in chapter 2, that the domestic economy always tends to over-production and under-consumption could also be used to explain why capitalism was forced to struggle to secure overseas markets and a haven for surplus capital abroad. Hobson assumed that these foreign interests could only be preserved by violence or the threat of violence. Nationalist agitation and militarism were not themselves causes of war, but derived from the impulse for competition in world markets.[50] He continued to believe that modern imperialism, as he expressed it in a lecture on

The Labour MP for Jarrow, Ellen Wilkinson, addressing a sombre crowd on 18 September 1938 at a 'Save Peace' rally in Trafalgar Square, London. She was a popular radical figure, known to her supporters as 'Red Ellen' and in the House of Commons as 'Miss Perky'.

'The Causes of War' in the 1930s, gives an 'increased measure of determination to capitalism' in explaining modern conflict, though he never ignored the role played by nationalism in sharpening those tendencies. His ideas were endlessly repeated in the inter-war discussion of war and economics, and *Imperialism* remained his most important book.[51]

Hobson's views were hijacked in 1917 by Lenin when he published his own pamphlet on 'Imperialism' designed to demonstrate, consistent with Marx's own late thinking on the subject, that the stage of monopoly capitalism characteristic of the pre-war industrial and financial order had resulted in the outbreak of war in 1914. Lenin borrowed freely from what he called Hobson's 'excellent description' in order to demonstrate why capitalism was doomed to build powerful armed blocs of monopolists to protect its interests; no other approach, Lenin argued, could make modern war 'intelligible'.[52] In the preface to the French and German editions, published in 1920, Lenin claimed that his pamphlet proved that the Great War was an imperialist war 'for the partition of the world'. The British left had to wait until 1926 for the first English-language version, published as volume 4 of the Lenin Library by the Communist Party of Great Britain with the wrong sub-title – 'The Last Stage of Capitalism' – and the wrong initial in front of Lenin's name – 'N.' instead of 'V. I.'. A popular edition was published in 1933 in the Little Lenin Library, in a fresh translation with the proper sub-title 'The Highest Stage of Capitalism' and Lenin's correct initials.[53] The pamphlet became the standard Marxist text for understanding the relationship between capitalism and war. The instruction to teachers of the course 'Marxism and War' was to read chapter seven of 'Imperialism' before leading the discussion of the contradictions of capitalism that encourage war – the tendency to 'state monopoly capitalism', in which the state supports its capitalists with naked power, and the tendency to divide the world up between a few powers as colonies.[54]

The idea that imperialist capitalism caused war percolated into the stock of standard ideas in Britain in the 1930s, particularly but certainly not exclusively among those on the left. The policy statement prepared for its 1932 conference by the No More War Movement, the British branch of the War Resisters' International, assumed *a priori* that 'imperialism is the historical cause of modern war'; the Movement's annual report for 1934–5 called for a formal study of the roots of war by focusing on the nature of modern imperialism.[55] The statement of basic policy produced by the Independent Labour Party in 1938 also started out from the assumption that imperialism and capitalism were a permanent threat to peace: '*The price of the continuance of Capitalism is the massacre of millions in war.*'[56] As if to repel all reasonable argument to the contrary a book of 'New Data' for Lenin's *Imperialism* was published in 1938 with updated statistics and an appendix which listed all the cases of armed violence since 1918 occasioned by the capitalist world order: apart from eleven alleged counter-revolutionary wars against the Soviet Union from 1918 to 1938, the authors listed a further sixty-four 'so-called small wars' in all parts of the globe.[57] In *The Coming World War*, published in 1935, Tom Wintringham rejected the 'current chatter about war in the abstract' as a part of human nature, or a psychological necessity. The forces making for war were entirely material: 'markets, rates of profit, monopolies, competition, poverty "caused by plenty", tariffs, class power'. He cited Marx's assertion in the preface to the second edition of *Capital* that the laws of capitalism work 'with iron necessity towards inevitable results' as evidence that war too was inevitable.[58]

The thesis that capitalism equals war was, for all the claims of socialist science, an unsophisticated assertion. Its simplicity perhaps explains its wide appeal well beyond the circles that approved its Marxist nature. To be convincing, however, the thesis had to demonstrate a direct relationship between the two phenomena, and this missing link was supplied in most British accounts by the malign influence of the arms trade. This was the central message in G. D. H. Cole's broadcast in the 1934 BBC series. Under the title 'Hawking War Wares', Cole set out to demonstrate that beyond the standard argument that war was inevitably caused in the modern age by 'rivalries between the great imperialist powers' lay another argument about the power of the arms makers to exploit and manipulate that rivalry in their own interest. Cole had not been the BBC's first choice, which had fallen on the outspoken communist scientist J. B. S. Haldane. He was in Spain when the programme was to be made and Cole was invited in his place.[59] Cole drafted his lecture in some haste, but had a final version ready in time in which he accused armaments firms of 'increasing the dangers of war' by their corrupt pursuit of military orders at all costs.[60] The mid-1930s saw the high point of the campaign against the manufacturers of armaments as the personification of the relationship between capitalism and war. Cole was a member of the New Fabian Research Bureau and in 1936, influenced by the recent Munitions Inquiry in the United States and the nationalization of sections of the armaments industry carried out by the French Popular Front government, the office set up an enquiry into armaments for which Cole drafted an initial memorandum on the 'Socialisation of the Armaments Industry'. Cole's preferred solution, which he announced to the BBC audience, was to nationalize all of the arms industry in Britain regardless and to suspend all shipments of armaments abroad.[61]

Cole was part of a broad assault on the arms trade. A popular indictment, *Merchants of Death*, was published in 1934; Fenner Brockway, a lifelong pacifist and an Independent Labour Party MP, published *The Bloody Traffic* in 1933, whose title spoke for itself; Philip Noel-Baker, a junior minister in the MacDonald Labour government of 1929–31, produced a detailed critical analysis of *The Private Manufacture of Armaments* in October 1936, and a second edition the following April.[62] The message was the same throughout: 'Mankind must either destroy the Bloody Traffic or be destroyed by it,' wrote Brockway, who had once written a play about the arms trade titled *The Devil's Business* but had the misfortune to publish it just after the outbreak of war in 1914: all copies were seized at once by the police and ordered by the court to be destroyed.[63] In order to publicize just who the faceless profiteers of death were, the Labour Party Research Department published in 1935 *Who's Who in Arms*. Inside a blood-red cover sporting a large black skull were to be found page after page of individuals and company shareholders in the arms trade with their worth in sterling. The directory demonstrated, so its authors claimed, that the wire-pullers behind the armaments firms were 'the dominant capitalist groups in British society'.[64] But conservatives could also share these assumptions. Lord Cecil, President of the League of Nations Union, in a letter written in 1934 deplored 'this dangerous trade', run by people who 'do their utmost to stir up suspicions and foment discord between one nation and another'.[65]

So embedded did the image become of the arms trader hand-in-glove with the unscrupulous world of finance that it became the stuff of popular fiction. Leslie Charteris, author of the best-selling 'Saint' books in the 1930s, wrote *Prelude for War* in 1938 in which Simon Templar ('the Saint' of the series) tackles a ruthless financial racketeer by the name of Kane Luker, who to get his way murders a pacifist

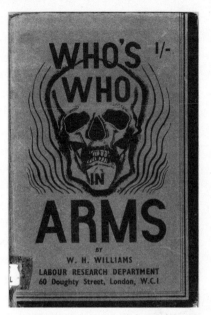

Two pamphlet covers from 1935 and 1936 on the crisis represented by British rearmament and the links between military spending and the arms manufacturers. British Armaments & World Peace *was produced by the Cambridge Anti-War Committee;* Who's Who in Arms *by the Labour Research Department.*

activist ('He used to work so hard and study such a lot and have such impossible ideals,' complains his erstwhile girlfriend) and invests in the armaments business in every rival state, 'the king-pin', Templar explains, 'of what somebody once called the Merchants of Death'. At a critical point in a twisted plot of international fascist conspiracy and illicit trade in arms the Saint explains to the glamorous gold-digger who, predictably enough, has secret documents in a left-luggage office near Paddington station, the true nature of the enemy they both face:

These men are big . . . And I know what kind of bigness they deal in. The only way they can make what they call big money, the only way they can touch the power and glory that their perverted egos crave for, is in helping and schooling nations to slaughter and destroy.[66]

The plots are foiled, but not before the Saint sermonizes again on the evil nature of a world that puts a dividend on killing: 'Some millions of men, women and children will be burned, scalded, blistered, gassed, shot, blown up, and starved to death, and the arms ring will sit back on its foul fat haunches and rake in the profits.'[67]

Charteris reached an audience of tens of thousands of all political hues. He was certainly not drawn from the left like so many of those who wrote about capitalism and war. But there is no doubt that Charteris also gauged what his audience would and would not tolerate and the idea of the arms baron as 'bloodsucker' had a more universal appeal in the 1930s. There were many other non-Marxists who understood the causes of war in economic terms, or who condemned the competition in arms, or who feared that war would produce the final collapse of capitalism. Gilbert Murray laid blame principally on the arms race and competitive tariffs; Norman Angell, whose 1912 book *The Great Illusion* was a pre-war best-seller on the economic futility of war, was a consistent propagandist in the 1930s for the idea that peace would be secured only by putting an end to competitive imperialism and in so doing grant 'economic justice to the "Have-not" states'.[68] Two of the remaining lectures in the BBC series on war were devoted to economic explanations. The first, on 'Is Our Money System to Blame?', added little to the debate, but the talk on 'Economic Factors that May Make for War', despite the caution evident in the title, found the senior economist and government adviser Sir Josiah Stamp prepared to argue that economic factors were one of the 'predisposing causes' of war in all cases where economic grievances and inequalities could not be resolved by politics.[69] The role of economics in promoting or limiting war was central to the world view of the Conservative prime minister Neville Chamberlain, who throughout his premiership hoped that economic concessions might slake the thirst of those states that threatened the existing order: 'Might not a great improvement in Germany's economic situation', he asked, 'result in her being quieter and less interested in political adventures?'[70] The social theorist Morris Ginsberg, one of Malinowski's colleagues at the London School of Economics, though critical of the tendency of Marxism to simplify or exaggerate the relationship between capitalism and war, concluded in 1939 that the thesis as such was not 'fundamentally shaken' by any of the criticisms directed at it, but simply required theoretical clarification.[71] It has been left to historians since 1945 to argue the merits of the case, and they, too, remain divided over the weight to be ascribed to economics and imperialism from the Boer War for gold in 1899 to the Iraq war for oil in 2003.

The argument that capitalist economics from its nature caused war, whether from the laws of economic development or from the desire to redress economic grievance through conquest, was uncomfortably determinist. War was, on this account, unavoidable without the transformation of the economic conditions that gave rise to it. The result was the creation of an almost permanent state of vigilance, what Allen Hutt called an 'eve-of-war age'.[72] The monthly *Communist Review* in June 1934 carried the front-page headline 'On the Eve of a New World War', though the occasion for the article that followed was nothing more menacing than the British decision to impose a quota on the import of Japanese textiles.[73] Conze and Wilkinson's pamphlet *Why War?* was already dedicated in 1934 to those 'who will take part in the Second World War'. As Marxists they argued that the only way to avoid war was to abolish capitalism: 'The argument for revolution is clear and simple.' But when they considered all the possible ways of removing the threat of war, none promised any hope of solution. No 'opiate myths', they continued, could remove the stark reality that war was coming. All that remained was to ensure that the populations of Europe would know how to abolish capitalism after the next war as Lenin and the Bolsheviks had done in Russia after the last.[74] For those like Baldwin who held that civilization was fatally menaced by war, the fear of revolution in its wake was a double catastrophe. Hovering in the wings to exploit the disaster of war, wrote Baldwin in 1934, was international communism, 'an agency, tireless, malevolent, and uncompromisingly destructive of the existing order'.[75]

The second science mobilized to explain the causes of war was biology, a perspective overshadowed by Marx's contemporary, and Britain's greatest nineteenth-century scientist, Charles Darwin. Like the Marxist argument about capitalism and war, Darwin's evolutionary theories, developed first in his 1859 manuscript *On the Origin of Species*, were soon reduced to simplistic formulae. The idea of the struggle for existence lent itself temptingly to the argument that war was simply the human variety of the contest in Nature observed by Darwin and was therefore biologically determined. When to this was added the idea of 'the survival of the fittest', a concept originated by the social philosopher Herbert Spencer, and borrowed by Darwin for his second theoretical statement *The Descent of Man*, published in 1871, war was seen not only as biologically unavoidable but as a positive good in ensuring that those individuals or communities who survived the struggle were, in strictly evolutionary terms, superior to those they vanquished. One of the most notorious statements of this connection was made by the Prussian General Friedrich von Bernhardi in another best-seller from 1912, translated under the title *Germany and the Next War*. Bernhardi asserted that among the 'universal laws which rule all life' war played a central part. 'War is a biological necessity of the first importance,' he continued, 'a regulative element in the life of mankind . . . the basis of all healthy development.' In the 'universal economy of Nature' the weaker go under, the stronger prevail.[76]

Historians usually confine the biological debate on war to the thirty years before 1914, and there is no need here to repeat the arguments for or against that divided the biological community in Britain and Europe over interpretation of Darwin in the lead-up to the Great War.[77] By the early twentieth century a large body of professional scientists rejected the argument that Darwin's thesis demonstrated that war was either natural or biologically useful. In 1919 a book by the German physiologist G. F. Nicolai, a Prussian very different in temper from Bernhardi, was translated into English. A professor at Berlin University before the war, in 1914 his anti-war stance led to his imprisonment in Graudenz fortress where he wrote *The Biology of War*, a densely argued and lengthy indictment of modern war which dismissed the idea that it could serve any useful biological purpose. War, he argued, was not natural but a product of conscious 'human action'; moreover, it represented a 'struggle against existence' by killing off the bravest and best and leaving behind the 'unfit stay-at-home' half of the population.[78] Most eugenist thought in Britain after the war emphasized the dysgenic effects of modern industrialized war, which was more rather than less likely to accelerate evolutionary decline among those states which fought it.[79]

The Darwinist lobby nevertheless survived well into the post-war era. The idea of a link between evolutionary theory and the causes of war may have been scientifically discredited but it was still entertained by a wider public who understood Darwin in simple terms. Scientific argument could do little to set these assumptions aside. In 1938 the Cambridge geneticist Joseph Needham planned a multi-authored volume on 'The Distortions of Science' to address just such a problem. Although the volume never appeared, Needham drafted his own section on 'The "Struggle for Existence" Distortion' in which he deplored the fact that the term had become 'the stock-in-trade of the man-in-the-street'. Darwin's argument that the struggle 'is <u>natural</u>', he continued, was embedded in thought and speech and was still used, eighty years after it was first formulated, as a justification for war. Like Nicolai, Needham could see that victory in war provided practically no biological benefit, but he thought the idea that war was biologically useful had survived 'with the same gusto that it showed in its younger days'.[80]

Needham blamed one scientist in particular for sustaining a crude neo-Darwinist defence of conflict as biologically vital; he cited a lecture by Sir Arthur Keith in 1927 in which the distinguished anatomist and anthropologist had argued that without biological competition the human race would commit suicide.[81] It was true that no other figure played so large a role in keeping alight the flame of popular Darwinism in an age of growing scientific scepticism. Keith wrote regularly for the mass-circulation press, including the London *Evening News* and the *Daily Mail*, and they reciprocated by describing him as Britain's most famous living scientist. Arthur Keith was born in 1866, a few years after *Origin of Species* was published. Though he is sometimes regarded as a product of the nineteenth century, his long and varied career spanned a larger part of the twentieth. He remained actively engaged in writing and broadcasting until his death in 1955 at the age of 89. He was born into a farming household in Aberdeenshire in northern Scotland, one of ten children. Unusually gifted, he studied medicine at Aberdeen University and pursued an early career as a doctor overseas. His interest in anatomy secured him the curatorship of the museum of the Royal College of Surgeons in 1908, where he began his own research on the history of human evolution. By the Great War he had shifted his scientific interests to anthropology but he is best remembered for his work in popularizing the story of

human development from its origins – including his careful reconstruction of the skull of Piltdown Man, hailed in 1914 as the first ancient
hominid remains found in Britain until they were finally exposed as a
fake in 1953. Keith was a distinguished Scotsman, very conscious of
his origins. Hard-working, puritanical in his views on the modern
age, well dressed in wing collar and bow tie long into the age of
greater informality, his severe face with its piercing eyes and narrow
mouth disguised a more humorous and humane personality. He was
dedicated, like so many of his generation, to the idea that the civilization represented by the British Empire and the British people marked,
for the moment, the high point of human evolution.[82]

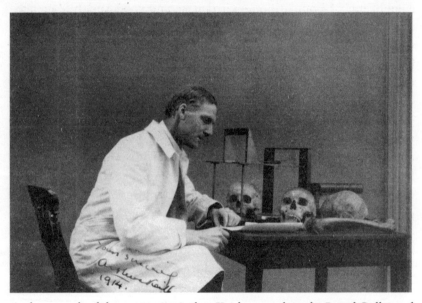

A photograph of the anatomist Arthur Keith at work in the Royal College of
Surgeons in 1914, signed by Keith himself. He used his study of the skulls of
human ancestors to argue the case that it was good for the human race to
struggle to survive.

Arthur Keith is most notorious for a remark he made in his address
to the students of Aberdeen University on 6 June 1931, a few months
after they had elected him rector of the university in succession to
Lord Birkenhead. His chosen title – 'The Place of Prejudice in Modern
Civilization' – was of a piece, according to the report in *Nature*, with

the remainder of a 'boldly provocative' talk.[83] At one point in his discussion of the need to keep humanity divided into different races and nations, he remarked on the function of conflict in human society: 'Nature keeps her human orchard healthy by pruning – war is her pruning hook.'[84] According to the draft of the speech among Keith's papers, he had scribbled this sentence in the margin as an afterthought to the more disturbing assertion, certainly for the youthful audience in front of him, that mankind had to be prepared to sacrifice blood to survive.[85] Yet it was the reference to the 'pruning hook' that caught the public's attention. The account in *Nature* applauded Keith's courage in stating the case for war in Malthusian terms, to preserve the equilibrium of population, environment and food supply, but also observed that his views might seem 'needlessly ruthless'. Keith later wrote that it was 'an ill-chosen simile' which failed to convey his broader conclusion that 'war is the life preserver of nations', but he remained unrepentant about the argument itself, and indeed unrepentant about the simile.[86] In an article written in 1939 for an American journal he suggested that the extermination of the native Americans was a case where the pruning hook was applied so severely that the native population 'wilted and died' under the process. This outcome, he continued, he had observed among the hedgerows in his home county of Kent: 'If they cannot withstand the sacrifice which the pruning hook demands of them, but wither and die, then they are useless for the countryman's purpose . . . It is so with peoples, nations and races.'[87]

Keith's approach to evolutionary development was in reality more sophisticated, and more widely supported, than the reaction to his rectorial address might suggest. He was, partly because of his own intellectual background in anatomy and anthropology, distinct from the school of nineteenth-century Social Darwinists around Thomas Huxley and Herbert Spencer, whose interests were philosophical as much as scientific. Where Spencer emphasized the individual will to compete, and used this as a central feature of his view of a competitive and thus healthy community, the anthropologists were more concerned with the collective will to compete in defence of social or racial unities. This was a theory of social evolution with a strong biological core and it positioned Keith between the Social Darwinists, whose influence had faded a great deal by the 1920s, and the revival of Darwinism in the 1970s in the 'sociobiology' (biology as the root of all social behaviour) pioneered by the American biologist Edward O. Wilson.[88] Keith arrived at his own theory of social evolution during the years just prior to the First World War when he had the opportunity to examine the fossil remains of all known hominids preserved in the museum of the Royal College of Surgeons. He realized, he later wrote, that human development had not been linear, as Darwin suggested, but proceeded 'by a series of zig-zags', progressive groups exterminating their less progressive neighbours and so moving mankind further forward. Keith believed that during the last stages of this process human differentiation arose through the operation of hormones, whose function in determining typical race differences of skin colour and hair type had been discovered only a decade or so before. These differences were then institutionalized by a principle of 'isolation', or 'clannishness', as Keith called it, as humankind divided up not only between different races, but differing tribes within the same race. The principle of isolation was then matched with two complexes, of competition and of enmity, which in the long evolutionary story pitted tribe against tribe and, later, nation against nation. Modern war, Keith believed, 'is just the fierce war of ancient tribal days equipped by science and civilisation'.[89]

The alleged survival of primitive tribal instincts in the mature modern man (and even, Keith thought, the behaviour of distant simian ancestors 'lodged in the most ancient part of the brain') was used as evidence that war must have some kind of evolutionary function. Each self-conscious social unit was an evolutionary unit, primed to maximize its chances of survival. In an article on 'The Crisis of Mankind' in 1934, Keith wrote that as far as he was concerned '*the evidence* is now complete that Nature has brought about the rise of mankind from apedom to its present high estate by the production of competing races'.[90] That competition was expressed sometimes in the search for 'living space', a term made familiar by German geopoliticians in the inter-war years, but the ultimate test was war, provoked by the necessity for the biological survival of particular associations, a view which Keith derived from Darwin himself. Keith believed that modern civilization was doomed if it disregarded 'Nature's scheme' to produce 'a higher type of humanity' through a necessary violence.[91] Consistent perhaps with his own Scottish non-conformist upbringing, Keith thought that the threat facing European civilization proceeded not from war, but from 'luxury and sloth'.[92]

Keith's evolutionary anthropology provoked a divided response, though he was never as isolated as many of his detractors suggested. His views were scarcely scientific in the biologist's sense. Mainstream evolutionary biology had moved a long way by the 1930s; the focus of the science was on the natural, non-human world and the mathematical prediction of variation. The ground of argument over human evolution had shifted to sociologists and anthropologists, some of whom were attracted not to social biological explanations but to theories of culturally induced behaviour. The leading advocate of this argument was the professor of social anthropology at the London School of Economics, Bronislaw Malinowski, who dismissed 'Nature's pruning hook' as the blind instrument of a bygone and uncivilized age.[93] The son of Polish aristocrats from Cracow, Malinowski came to Britain before the First World War. He spent much of his early academic career in the Pacific Ocean region studying the tribal societies of the Trobriand Islands. The fruit of this research, *The Sexual Life of the Trobrianders*, was published in 1929, two years after he took up the chair at LSE (Gilbert Murray, to whom Malinowski sent a complimentary copy, chided him for going out of his way 'to collect obscenities' in the book); one of the purposes of his research was to try to show that, even in contexts where some ritual violence could be observed, there was no anthropological evidence that war was a necessary and permanent state of the human condition.[94] Malinowski was an enthusiastic eugenist and a lifelong pacifist. In a note written for himself in the late 1930s on the principles underlying his own intellectual position he laid out the stall of his beliefs: 'War is not an inherent attribute of human nature'; 'War is not an inevitable, ineluctable part of human destiny'; 'The anthropological argument is this: human development about 600,000 years. About 400[000] of this no war.'[95]

Malinowski could not deny that violence occurred among primitive peoples, though there were anthropologists who tried to make out a persuasive case that early man was by nature as peaceable as the primitive peoples that still inhabited the remoter areas of the globe. The so-called Diffusionist School, supported by the fieldwork of Elliot Smith and W. P. Perry among the native communities of Africa and the Pacific, argued that the behaviour of primitive hunter-gatherers offered little evidence of an innate predisposition to aggression and that the development of warfare was 'an accidental excrescence' of later civilization, above all that of ancient Egypt.[96] Malinowski thought this a nonsense: the archaeological record yielded a wealth of evidence that primitive man had made and used weapons; from his own experience in the field Malinowski was convinced that 'primitive warfare and combativeness are never absent from any savage society'. The reasons were to be found, he believed, 'in some deep layers in human nature' which were now suppressed by a modern web of moral and rational restraints, but the form that primitive violence took was ritualized and culturally determined, not innate.[97] Warfare, Malinowski suggested, went through a number of clear historical stages – primitive fighting, the process of early state-building and the redundant final stage of pointlessly destructive total war. The last of these had no biological or evolutionary function whatsoever; it was driven by an incomprehensible nihilism where earlier forms of warfare had a cultural purpose that could be explained by exploring the ways in which culture harnessed aggression to its social purposes.[98] This left the issue of the causes of war unresolved, for if warfare was indeed a manifestation of some observable cultural function, then the Great War must have represented something equally capable of scientific explanation. The failure to square this logical circle left Malinowski, as it left many of those who regarded modern war as an abomination, with no sensible account of what had happened in the modern age.

Keith had another advantage over Malinowski. As an anatomist with a specialist's knowledge of the development of the brain in hominids he was part of a broader scientific movement trying to demonstrate the relationship between aggression in animals and aggression in man. In the 1920s Keith became particularly interested in gorillas and used the growing body of knowledge on their behaviour and that of the other higher primates to underpin a number of his central conclusions. In the late 1920s he corresponded with a British doctor in West Africa, Neville Dyce Sharp, who was engaged in the scientific observation of gorillas and chimpanzees in the former German colony of Cameroon, an area awarded to British control in 1920 under the League of Nations mandate scheme. Sharp sent Keith detailed accounts of primate behaviour. Some of it was no doubt grist to Keith's evolutionary mill, though much of the information seems to have been based on rumour rather than science. Chimpanzees were shown not to stand and fight when an 'enemy' was sighted, but they were capable of fighting among themselves with sticks. According to Sharp they were also known to catch and tie up antelope which they beat mercilessly, apparently for sadistic pleasure, until the terrified animal was allowed to go free. Gorillas were a better prospect, for not only did they form clearly defined social groups, but the males were fierce defenders against any intrusion or threat. Sharp reported local stories of male gorillas who on being disturbed by hunters would roar horribly and rush at the unfortunate intruders, ripping human flesh with their bare hands.[99] Keith later read accounts of gibbon communities in Siam which displayed a clear territoriality and were capable of sudden spasms of violence in defence of their patch. The field behaviour of howler monkeys, a study published in 1934, demonstrated even more clearly group behaviour in defence of defined feeding areas. The combination of howling, occasional violence and explicit territoriality were identified by Keith, on what was at best a slender foundation, as 'the incipient stage of true war'.[100]

The work on animal aggression that Keith exploited was an increasingly sophisticated branch of experimental psychology and biology. Its purpose was not primarily to prove that animal violence anticipated human violence but to try to understand the nature of animal aggression and the balance between an innate predisposition to aggression and acquired habits. It was commonly understood that 'war' as such was not a characteristic of the animal kingdom, except among certain species of ant; it was also scientifically evident that intraspecies conflicts, including contests for food or a mate, or the special case of the pecking order among hens, were not an analogy for war.[101] Aggression certainly existed and scientists were confident at the time that it was associated with the optic thalamus, a part of the diencephalon or the oldest part of the evolving brain, which developed in early hominids long before the higher brain areas of the cortex reached their full development. This region of the brain produced primitive responses of rage in animals and humans and could be artificially stimulated. One experiment on the brain of a cat reported in 1925 showed that if the cortical material was removed, leaving just the grey matter, the animal remained for hours in a state of simulated rage. The experiments of the Russian behavioural psychologist Ivan Pavlov were well known in Britain and he too could demonstrate that under controlled conditions his dogs could be induced to exhibit enhanced aggression or enhanced submissiveness, or, in special cases, the canine equivalent of a nervous breakdown.[102]

The conclusions to be drawn from these experiments were ambiguous. While some scientists assumed that impulses to aggression were common to animals and man, they did not necessarily assume that this provoked war, though it might explain how individuals could behave violently in situations of combat. In 1939 two psychologists, John Bowlby and Edward Durbin, wrote an account of 'Personal Aggressiveness and War' using material on ape behaviour from the researches of the young zoologist Solly Zuckerman and the work of the child psychologist Susan Isaacs. Zuckerman based much of his account of ape sociology, as he called it, on the community of hamadryas baboons on Monkey Hill in London's Regent's Park Zoo. During the period in which he observed them, eight males and thirty females died from fighting, the females all killed as males disputed for them.[103] Durbin and Bowlby argued that three major factors stimulated fighting – possession, intrusion of a stranger and frustration – and that the naturalistic analogy between ape communities and man was sufficiently marked to justify the assumption that war was a product 'of the most dangerous part of our animal inheritance'. Fighting, they assumed, was so common among animals and humans that it could only be the product of a shared 'basic pattern' of behaviour. This 'powerful or "natural" tendency to resort to force' could be transferred to whole states as a result of what Durbin and Bowlby called the 'transformed aggression' of their citizens. Like tribes of monkeys or groups of children left to their own devices, a human community was capable of both peace and war; as in nature, the choice of war, like the choice of fighting, was a natural and fundamental human tendency.[104]

On these terms zoology was little more helpful than anthropology. Both suggested that primitive impulses to aggression existed in animals or 'savage' societies, but in both cases it was possible to show either that these impulses were provoked by the external environment rather than inner instincts (and therefore capable of some kind of external control) or that they were the product of a remote social and ana-tomical past whose powerful residues still existed in modern man – 'like a savage slightly watered down', as Dean Inge put it – capable of being resurrected at will.[105] The tension between the idea of violence as a cultural construct and violence as a social biological fact has continued to shape debates about the causes of war for the past half century. From both viewpoints war appeared to be as hard to avoid as it did under modern capitalism. Malinowski subsided into a growing despair in the 1930s at the evident contradiction between the idea that war was part of a distant and primitive past and yet also an ever-present reality in the modern age. In a set of 'Personal Opinions' which he drafted in August 1936 he explored the unhappy conse-quences of this paradox: 'It is difficult to fight against pessimism in the present world, especially if one like myself, being a Slav is inclined to take the gloomy view; and being an anthropologist is able to appreciate the savagery of our present-day civilisation in the light of the civilisation of savages . . .'[106] In 1940, after the outbreak of war, he remarked in a lecture to an audience at the American Academy of Medicine that since 'humanity has gone back to savagery', he at least had a job to do as an anthropologist who had spent his life studying primitive societies.[107] Sir Arthur Keith also claimed that he was no more attracted to war as such than was Malinowski. His dream, he wrote on a number of occasions, was for a 'war-less world', but the harsh reality, he warned, was a world in which war was a permanent and necessary condition. 'The mantle of Jeremiah', he complained in the New York Times in 1932, 'has fallen on a modern anthropologist.' Never at a loss for a striking metaphor, Keith wrote in 1934 that the world must 'sleep for ever with its loaded gun by its side'.[108]

Much more was expected in the 1930s from psychology as a means to first understand, then remove, the fundamental causes of war. There were a number of reasons for this. Psychology, and more particularly psychoanalysis, was regarded as a modern science more appropriate

LEFT: *The Professor of Social Anthropology at the London School of Economics, Bronislaw Malinowski, in 1940. He refused to accept that war was biologically necessary.* RIGHT: *The psychoanalyst Edward Glover who popularized the view that understanding the nature of the unconscious might be a way of preventing wars in the future.*

to cope with the problems of the modern world. It was recognized, not least by its practitioners, that its scientific potential was as yet not fully realized, but there existed a wide popular belief, reflected in Einstein's eagerness to involve Freud in his anti-war campaign, that as the workings of the mind were gradually exposed, the psychological roots of violence might be revealed and some appropriate therapy applied. There was also a strong prima facie case for assuming that aggression could be explained more satisfactorily by psychology than by biology or economics because, as Aldous Huxley pointed out in the opening remarks of his contribution to 'The Causes of War' broadcasts in 1934, violence is not produced by systems or environment, but by individuals: 'wherever there are human beings', he continued, 'the question of psychology inevitably arises'.[109] He rejected Arthur Keith's social biology as 'obviously nonsensical'. The causes of war, he wrote in 1937, lie largely in the mind. Economic competition, political rivalry and racial animosity may be the immediate causes of war but all of them were 'ultimately psychological in their nature'.[110]

Huxley was an early convert to the idea that war as a form of collective lunacy might be susceptible to psychotherapy. He was one of the invited contributors to the third 'conversation' organized by the Institute for Intellectual Co-operation in 1933 on 'Spirit, Ethics and War'. He contributed a paper on war and individual psychology. War, he claimed, was an arena of extraordinary emotional intensity which satisfied a psychological yearning in man to destroy and hurt, 'a grand festival of the emotions, a kind of orgy, a saturnalia'. Hatred was a heady wine compared with the 'thin beer' of the general good of mankind. The causes of war he found deep in the emotional life of the individual. Only psychological reform could eliminate war.[111] These same themes resurfaced in his radio broadcast on 'Sadist Satisfactions in War'. So powerful did he consider the impulse to violence that he thought the appeal to religious or ethical restraint would achieve little. 'The psychological causes of war', he pronounced, 'have their root in the unconscious.' Huxley suggested that psychoanalysts should continue to search for the key to unlock the secrets of the unconscious mind and to divert the 'irrepressible primitive impulses' lodged there to some more socially useful outlet.[112]

The obvious starting point for anyone who wanted to unlock the secrets of the unconscious was Freud. He wrote relatively little on war itself but the impact of the war of 1914 helped to shape the development of his theory of the 'death instinct' in the 1920s. His immediate reaction to the Austrian entry into war in 1914 was an unguarded enthusiasm: 'All my libido is given to Austro-Hungary,' he told his brother.[113] But by September 1914 he had abandoned his brief flirtation with patriotism. In December he wrote to a Dutch psychologist, Frederick van Eeden, a letter (which Eeden promptly published abroad and in English) which betrayed a profound despair at what the war had revealed after only a few months:

Psychoanalysis has concluded from a study of the dreams and mental slips of normal people, as well as from the symptoms of neurotics, that the primitive, savage and evil impulses of mankind have not vanished in any individual, but continue their existence, although in a repressed state – in the unconscious, as we call it in our language – and that they wait for opportunities to display their activity.[114]

In the spring of 1915 Freud wrote 'Thoughts for the Time on War and Death', in which he elaborated the idea that man was prey to 'primal impulses' to violence; the fact that the Ten Commandments had to outlaw killing was a sure sign, Freud thought, 'that we spring from an endless series of generations of murderers'.[115] These views had altered little by the time he replied to Einstein in 1932, though in the interval he had developed his general theory of the instincts which shaped the way British Freudians approached the issue of war and aggression when they came to write about it in the 1930s. There is no need to repeat here the principles of Freud's post-war thinking, which have already been explored, but it is necessary to recognize that Freudian views on war were a special instance of the more general psychoanalytic theory.

In *Why War?* Freud took as axiomatic the fact that all conflicts of interest between men 'are settled by the use of violence' until a larger social entity is created that can control that violence and create affective bonds between its members. Each of them carries within an instinct for hatred and destruction as well as the capacity for love, but that aggressive drive cannot be set aside or reduced, and under certain circumstances is projected outwards towards 'extraneous' objects to avoid the excessive and potentially damaging internalization of violence. That act of projecting destruction – Freud seldom talked about war as such – is necessary for the health of the organism. The only prospect of reversing this drive to aggression was to place hope in the power of reason over instinct, but Freud had little confidence that general mankind was remotely capable of such a change in the foreseeable future: 'An unpleasant picture comes to one's mind', he continued, 'of mills that grind so slowly that people starve before they get their flour.'[116] The reception of *Why War?* when it first appeared in English was unenthusiastic. One reviewer thought the asking price of 6/- a lot 'for the slender amount of wisdom and psychology' contained in the letters. Ernest Jones, discussing the pamphlet in the *International Journal of Psycho-Analysis*, recognized that the subject was of 'current and fundamental importance' but shared Freud's pessimistic view that it would take a great deal of time before populations acquired 'a psychical aversion to war'.[117] Jones does not seem to have used Freud's letter in his own work.

The Freudian explanation for the causes of war was developed principally by the psychoanalyst Edward Glover, a colleague of Jones at the British Institute of Psycho-Analysis with a reputation for speaking his mind and a flair for publicity. In 1931 he was invited to give a course of lectures to the summer school of the International Federation of League of Nations Societies on 'Pacifism in the Light of Psycho-Analysis'. The proceedings were later published by the League but Glover wanted a wider audience. The lectures appeared as *War, Sadism and Pacifism* in 1933. In 1936 Glover gave a series of broadcasts on the BBC on psychoanalysis and society, which he later published as *The Dangers of Being Human*. One of the talks included an analysis of the unconscious causes of war. This growing public interest in the relationship between psychoanalysis and war no doubt reflected wider anxieties about the international crisis. Glover succeeded in establishing a popular reputation as the scientist who dared to marry the two things in memorably provocative ways. It was his writing that inspired Aldous Huxley's enthusiasm for psychological interpretations of violence. The son of a Lanarkshire schoolmaster, Glover qualified as a doctor in 1915 but grew dissatisfied with physical medicine and hospital work. He trained in the 1920s as a psychoanalyst in Berlin under the leading German theorist Karl Abraham before returning to London to join the British Freudians at the Institute, where he became director of research. His views on psychoanalysis were described unkindly by the American psychiatrist Karl Menninger as 'cobwebby'. Glover, who played his part in the endless squabbles among the British psychoanalytical community, eventually resigned during the war on grounds that the Institute was no longer authentically Freudian.[118]

Glover's starting point was the idea that deep in the recesses of the unconscious lay impulses which under certain circumstances could be mobilized not just for individual aggression but for the collective 'mass insanity' of war. The source of these impulses reflected the classic Freudian analysis of the early stages of infant life during which the Oedipus complex is laid down. The child has to master the guilt provoked by feelings of hostility towards the mother when the breast (or some other object) is denied it, and the guilt associated with hatred of the intruding father; every individual 'hates the things he loves and must learn to love the things he hates', but as they develop into adulthood, children discover 'the mastery of unconscious guilt' that these emotions provoke.[119] In the child this produces a tension between love and hate, affection and sadism. Glover used the example of a child that has built a tower of bricks 'laboriously and joyfully' and will then destroy it with one blow; as a result of the same psychic processes in adulthood, Glover suggested, soldiers enjoy the destruction they witness or inflict. This argument was developed a few years later by Pryns Hopkins, who funded Glover's Institute, when he claimed that in war the enemy is 'the repressed father-hate of childhood', released by the permissive circumstances of battle. Hopkins thought that there had to be a psychological force even stronger than fear of death to get men to fight; the Oedipus complex, laid down unconsciously in infancy, was just such a force. There exists, he continued, a clear relation between 'cruelty and sex-morbidity' once the urge to destroy is summoned up. Hopkins thought that the violence of the 1930s showed 'the universality and terrifying power' of the deep-seated urge to sadism.[120]

Civilization, as Freud had argued, could scarcely be constructed at all if the primal drives to love and hate were not repressed and sublimated in the growing child. These instincts, Glover noted, were observable in 'infants and primitive savages' but no longer evident in adult life. This meant that an additional trigger had to be supplied among the adult population of a civilized state to provoke the unconscious urge to destroy, but it also meant there existed a permanent potential threat to civilization if for some reason the repression mechanism failed to operate. In most normal adults a rough equilibrium is established between the surviving infantile impulses; the urge to destroy can be compensated, Glover suggested in a later symposium on peace and war, by 'attacks of indigestion or quarrels with bus conductors'.[121] A war psychosis, on the other hand, represents the conscious emergence of an infantile schism: 'Anxiety breeds hate; hate arouses anxiety; both together portend destruction.' The destructive drives are projected outwards and the resulting instinctual crisis creates the prospect of war. Glover recognized that, unless 'the individual psychic situation were not already well-prepared' in the unconscious mind, politicians would be powerless to provoke their peoples to fight.[122] War was a large manifestation of a conflict of sexual human impulses so powerful that, like nuclear fission, it set off a chain reaction of extraordinary destructive power. The predisposition to make war and to destroy civilization, Glover concluded, comes only from within the human mind. 'Man has yet to find out', he told the symposium audience, 'whether it is possible to avoid sowing dragon's teeth in the fertile soil of nursery life.'[123]

Glover was not by any means the first psychologist to talk about instincts or impulses for war. The work of William McDougall, whose book *Introduction to Social Psychology*, first published in 1908, had gone through twenty-five editions by 1943, included a discussion of the 'instinct to pugnacity' among primitive men and the early stages of human civilization, but in his view the 'fighting instinct' was secondary, a response to the inhibition or obstruction of some more primary impulse. The emotional response that this obstruction generates results in a mix of fear, anger and hate, one consequence of which might be warfare.[124] The translation of a book by the director of the Jean-Jacques Rousseau Institute in Geneva, Pierre Boret, appeared in English in 1923 under the title *The Fighting Instinct*. The Institute was dedicated to the study of childhood and child psychology and Boret used this research to suggest that modern war was an analogue of the child's capacity for destructive tantrums: when states 'let themselves go in outbursts of destructive anger' it was an act of regression of 'the collective or group soul' towards an earlier 'infantile mentality'.[125] But by the 1930s the idea of a crude instinctual life was under assault from sociologists and psychologists alike. The impulse to destroy was dismissed by one critic as 'speculative rashness'. McDougall's view that hate sustained modern warfare did not accord with the evidence that among soldiers at the front 'it found little expression'.[126] For social scientists the chief objection to any psychological explanation of war was the failure to recognize that mass violence was socially conditioned and that war was a social institution; psychological causes were regarded as too generalized to be analytically useful. Morris Ginsberg, in his account of the causes of war, urged psychologists to recognize that the mental causes of crisis lay not in the deeply repressed layers of the unconscious, but near the surface in the 'worry, monotony, lack of security' of the modern industrial age. 'Are there not here', he asked, 'enough sources of anxiety and fear to account in large measure for a readiness to seek an escape in war?'[127]

The answer of psychoanalysis in the 1930s was to develop a more sophisticated account of aggression, using some of the same material exploited by social biologists to demonstrate the role of violence in human evolution. The scientific study of early childhood was central to this ambition. Two of Glover's colleagues at the Psycho-Analytical Institute, Melanie Klein and Susan Isaacs, pioneered the psycho-analytical observation of infancy. Though their object was not to demonstrate the roots of warfare, but to find ways of ensuring a psychologically effective environment for the infant human, their clinical results were open to wide interpretation. They argued that the earliest manifestation of the division between aggression and affection in psychoanalytic theory is found in the behaviour of a suckling infant who both sucks and bites the mother's breast. When denied the breast the behaviour is observably aggressive. At the approach of weaning the infant will begin to bite the breast more, as a reaction to the progressive withdrawal of the mother. In these circumstances the infant will both hate the mother for denying what is craved, but love the mother when that craving is satisfied.[128] In some accounts, this link between sex and aggression, nutrition and frustration, was traced to the common secretion in the adrenal gland of the substances that relate to both sexual activity and aggression. Non-Freudian psychologists preferred this idea that aggression was prompted physically by flows of adrenalin.[129] In Klein's psychoanalytical approach, however, this bifurcation is alleged to occur psychically, at a stage where the tendency to both sex and aggression is imprinted by the earliest and most basic of activities. Suckling expresses a cannibalistic desire to eat the mother and a dread of being eaten. The tension generated by these two contrary impulses creates in every infant a manic response, a powerful aggression and a profound fear of the aggressor, which stands as 'the prototype of war psychology' in the adult. The paranoiac response to an external threat is, on this account, the projection of a 'repressed aggression' against the malignant other: the desire to eat the parent has been transformed into a desire to destroy the enemy.[130]

These last arguments were presented to an Oxford audience in March 1936 by the psychologist Roger Money-Kyrle. He was sensible enough, given their radical nature, to offer the caveat that here was 'a sector of the psychoanalytic front line, which is not yet tidied up', but Money-Kyrle was himself no stranger to exotic speculation.[131] In an earlier publication he had insisted that the sexual impulse was paramount in fighting situations, in particular the urge to castrate the male or to bite off the penis, a 'useless female impulse' in women, so he argued, but one whose faint psychological residue in the male took the form of 'the racially useful purpose' of violence towards other men.[132] Two years later, in April 1938, the British Psychological Society hosted a symposium at St Andrews in Scotland to explore the ramifications of a decade of research on human violence by answering the question 'Is Aggression an Irreducible Factor?' The psychologists present represented a cross-section of schools and approaches, but all of the papers presented assumed that aggression was, as the opening speaker asserted, 'always with us'. The subject, he continued, could not have been chosen more appositely for at no point in the history of the world 'have the evidences of aggression been more manifest'.[133] The discussion was dominated by Freudian theory, but not exclusively so. The contrast was brought out between psychoanalytic theory, which suggested that aggression was a projection of internal tensions outwards, and the 'pugnacity instinct' school, where external stimuli provoke inner reaction – a distinction that survived into the post-war debates on aggression generated by the new science of 'ethology' (the psychological study of animal behaviour) developed by Konrad Lorenz.[134] Yet in neither case was the idea of aggression as a central psychological element denied. In an account of infant aggression, Karin Stephen even suggested that aggression was functionally desirable, since it removed a potential deadlock in the expression of infant frustration and fear. Though it was possible for aggression to become 'a dangerous impulse' if the child's struggle to master it created exaggerated anxiety states in later life, there was no prospect of eradicating it, a task, Stephen concluded, that was clearly beyond anything psychology could currently hope to do.[135]

The problem of how to treat the world-as-patient was not lost on psychoanalysis. Glover appended to his lectures on war and sadism a long 'Outline of Research on the Problem of War' for a putative 'War Research Board' which involved three levels of investigation of conscious, pre-conscious and unconscious behaviour, the last to be retrieved by deep hypnosis or analysis, and three kinds of war: adult, adolescent and infantile. Infantile conflict was to be studied in the nursery by close observation of children under the age of eighteen months.[136] Glover was granted the opportunity to give practical effect to the scheme a few years later when he was invited by an independent philanthropist, M. I. David, to draw up a research programme with a view to establishing a high-level international committee, backed by governments, to investigate the 'psychological causes of war'. The proposal was sent to the Foreign Office in September 1936 and then passed on to Gilbert Murray as chairman of the British branch of the Committee for Intellectual Co-operation with Glover's memorandum enclosed. The new proposal drew heavily on what Glover had written three years before, but was modified to allow the participation of sociologists and anthropologists whose expertise was needed to explore group violence more thoroughly. Glover proposed a panel of twelve investigators, four from each discipline, including his own. David added that the proposed Research Board should comprise two psychologists, two psychoanalysts, two sociologists and two anthropologists.[137]

Regrettably for the historian the intriguing prospect of pooling the human sciences on such an issue was never tested, for a few weeks later Murray wrote to David rejecting the proposal on the grounds that no case could be made for believing that the outbreak of war in 1914 had been a result of 'unconscious sadism'.[138] Two years later, however, the British Medical Association, prompted by strongly supported resolutions to its annual congress, proposed to the Council of the League an enquiry into the psychological causes of war to match the League's research on epidemiology, and this was also passed on once again to Gilbert Murray. He invited David and Glover to meet him to discuss what might be done, but David had left for India.[139] The proposal then foundered on the refusal of the British government to provide any further funds for intellectual co-operation, a decision finally reached by Lord Halifax, the Foreign Secretary, in December 1938 on the advice of R. A. Butler, undersecretary of state at the Foreign Office, who thought the whole enterprise too dominated by the French.[140]

The conclusions from psychoanalysis were no more optimistic than

those from economics or biology. Aggression and war were demonstrated to the wider public to be irreducible and permanent features
of the human condition that promised, in the modern age, nothing
less than the destruction of mankind.[141] Glover assumed that war
would always be perceived as a threat to civilization because there
existed 'an unconscious appreciation' of the terrible strength of the
forces that war unleashed. One social psychologist observed that in
many of the explanations for the causes of war were to be found
conditions that seemed 'beyond human control'.[142] John Rickman,
another of Glover's colleagues, responding to the discussion in the
symposium on the psychology of peace and war, suggested that no
effort to change nursery discipline would eliminate the child's propen-
sity to destructive action because in the child's view whatever is
deemed to be a frustration becomes so, irrespective of its objective
character. In this case, Rickman continued, it should at least be considered 'whether any man in the depth of his mind wants a world free
from aggression, or even free from war': modern man might not
regard the abolition of either as desirable.[143] This uncomfortable
assertion fitted much of the theoretical findings of the 1930s. Therapy
was a distant prospect at best. Glover wanted fifty years to complete
the programme of research he outlined in 1933; when Ernest Jones was
asked by Lord Davies how much time would be needed to complete
the psychoanalytical research necessary to prevent future wars, Jones
replied, 'A couple of centuries.'[144] At the end of his radio talk, Aldous
Huxley suggested that the only thing to do in the interval was to
give the patient a sufficiently powerful sedative to stop him 'going
completely out of his mind and committing suicide'.[145]

Science proved a disappointment in the effort to answer the question
'Why war?', or rather the answers were too confused and too many
and the scientific antidotes to war largely unrealizable. Arthur Keith
combed through fifty-eight different authors on the question and listed
twenty-six separate causes: 'Multiplicity of cause', he remarked, 'is
usually a measure of ignorance.'[146] There was nonetheless a wide effort
on the part of the human sciences to engage with an issue that by the
1930s had a clear urgency to it. Confidence in the power of science
to deliver what was appropriate for modern society was widespread;

in turn science enjoyed an exceptional power of suggestion among the wider public, which closely followed the discussion of issues of real contemporary significance. Scientists themselves were not unaffected by the growing international crisis and war anxiety, which explains the willingness of many of them to engage in a scientific dialogue on war that might otherwise have been more muted, or absent altogether, since it was not conventional scientific territory. The letters sent to *The Listener* in response to the broadcasts on the causes of war indicate the extent to which the wider public responded to debates which were more public property than the scientific arguments of the pre-1914 period had been.

There are explanations for the problems scientists faced in confronting war. The nature of war itself, historically disparate, characteristically diverse, made it unlikely that any overarching explanation would make much sense either historically or scientifically without risking a crude reductionism easily open to criticism. Moreover in all three areas of the human sciences war was regarded as a secondary effect of prime movers which it was much more important to understand – the dynamics of capitalism, the complex structure of the unconscious, the social biology of human evolution – but as a consequence all the more difficult to reform or control. At the same time there were profound divisions within the human sciences over almost all the issues of which war was a by-product. They could be reduced in general terms to arguments between essence and environment. The solution to the problem of war looked very different if it was assumed to be a product of environmental or cultural conditions which might be altered by human agency. If, on the other hand, war was the unavoidable consequence of ineluctable economic laws or the unconscious recesses of the mind, human agency was largely powerless. The failure to resolve these issues, which in most cases reflected honest differences in scientific approach, left an ambiguous legacy for a public that wanted hard answers, not open questions. Science represented in this case both promise and threat, the source of truth, but the sponsor of uncertainty and ambivalence. No one reading the accounts of the causes of war in the 1930s could be confident of anything except the certainty of more war.

Scientists were aware that a cure was what the public wanted. It was what Einstein looked for from Freud. A number of practical efforts were made to approach the issue of war through scientific channels. In January 1932, for example, the Netherlands Medical Association wrote to thirty-eight sister organizations worldwide a memorandum on 'The Medical Profession and War Prophylaxis' as part of an initiative to get doctors everywhere involved in eradicating the disease of war. The medical world 'can enlighten mankind, bring it to self-knowledge; warn it', ran the memorandum. The British Association sent polite expressions of support, and two years later was invited to send a delegate to an international conference to be held in Amsterdam in September 1934. The letter that accompanied the invitation ·explained that the current international situation required not 'the slow methods' originally foreseen but 'quick and effective influence of war-prophylaxis'; the Association once again declined to participate.[147] In 1937 the Liverpool social scientist D. Caradog Jones, who had been responsible for the social survey of Merseyside exploited by the eugenics movement in the 1930s, organized a petition to the government to set up an international commission to examine all the facts to do with the world's economic grievances including 'access to raw materials and world markets, colonial development and the problem of surplus population, trade restrictions and international exchange', in the belief that these were direct causes of war. The petition was widely endorsed, particularly in Lancashire, and carried the signatures of H. G. Wells, Virginia Woolf and Somerset Maugham among others; Neville Chamberlain agreed to meet a delegation, which included Caradog Jones, in November 1937, but nothing came of the initiative.[148]

Like the abortive project on the psychology of war, the practical scientific efforts appeared as palliatives quite out of scale with the issue they confronted. Their failure served only to illuminate the reality that war was in some sense preordained and unavoidable, something indeed beyond the means of mankind to avert. 'Ours is a warring civilisation,' wrote the Liverpool psychologist D. W. Harding in 1941.[149] The result was to endow war with an almost metaphysical presence, not something that resulted from the ambitions or miscalculations of a handful of politicians and generals, but something alien and external, endowed with an inexorable force which seemed to obey its own natural laws 'beyond human agency'. Nothing promised to be more destructive, but nothing seemed capable of obstructing its remorseless approach. 'War most impnt. subject,' noted Malinowski for an Oxford lecture, 'example of that vicious whirlpool drags us down'. In war, he concluded, 'we meet the pathogenic and suicidal element in civilisation', for it is the one phenomenon 'likely to kill the civilisation of the Western world'.[150] The approach to war in Britain throughout the 1930s was marked even among non-pacifists by a pronounced fatalism, a consequence in some measure of the ambiguous or pessimistic conclusions of current scientific explanation about its cause.

6

Challenge to Death

What can we do so that it may not be said of us by generations
to follow, that we failed them in this great day ... We are
forced back to the startling truth that the destiny of the human
race lies in our hands.

No More War Movement, annual report, 1932–3[1]

Not everyone in the Britain of the 1930s was convinced that war was
inevitable and the crisis of civilization beyond rescue. If war was a
disease, peace was the cure. This was the conviction at the heart of a
book of essays on peace published in 1934 under the title *Challenge
to Death*. The volume had its origins in a discussion at the Labour
Party Conference in Hastings in October 1933 between the former
MP Philip Noel-Baker and the novelist Storm Jameson. Noel-Baker
was one of the most prominent supporters of the League of Nations
in whose secretariat he had served. Margaret Storm Jameson, whose
books have not survived well as part of the canon of inter-war writing,
was one of the leading novelists and essayists of her generation and a
president of the literary society English PEN. Together they agreed to
invite a number of prominent men and women of letters to a dinner
where they would be asked to contribute in some way to the struggle
against war. Noel-Baker and Lord Robert Cecil, president of the
League of Nations Union, drew up a list of six preferred names: the
novelists Vera Brittain, Winifred Holtby, J. B. Priestley and Rebecca
West, the journalist Beverley Nichols and the poet Charles Morgan.
Storm Jameson was given the task of recruiting the literary guests and
Lord Cecil was to be the host; originally arranged for 7 February, the

dinner had to be postponed to allow Cecil, Noel-Baker and Storm Jameson to attend an international peace congress in Brussels. The company finally assembled at 8 o'clock on 20 February 1934 at the Wellington Club on London's Knightsbridge to be dined, regaled and inveigled into writing a book.[2]

In her memoirs Storm Jameson recalled her scepticism that anything of value would be achieved from the gathering – 'children throwing sand against the wind'. The guests were chosen, according to Vera Brittain, who was among them, on the criterion that they had all at some time betrayed in their writing the wish to combat the 'principle of death' which repeatedly condemned human society 'to its own destruction'.[3] Lord Cecil presided, flanked by the novelists Rebecca West and Rose Macaulay, who had been added to the list. Cecil sat, Jameson recalled, like some giant bird with 'great domed head and forehead, deeply-sunk eyes, superb beak of a nose'. At the end of dinner she invited those present to agree before they left to pen an essay on the current threat to civilization represented by war. Almost all of those present eventually contributed a chapter.[4] Jameson spent months trying to recruit other contributors to fill out the book, and a total of fifteen were eventually found, including Vera Brittain's husband George Catlin, Storm Jameson's own husband Guy Chapman and the well-known political commentator Vernon Bartlett, who was beguiled by Jameson's generous insistence that she had to have the 'glory of his name' in her book.[5] She waived an editorial fee so that her writers could have a more tempting sum from the publisher, but she found her duties as editor beset with difficulties. Her search for what she called a 'Great Name' to write the epilogue proved fruitless. Aldous Huxley refused and Jameson was reluctant, as she told Winifred Holtby, to recruit either H. G. Wells or George Bernard Shaw. 'Wells will talk liberal Fascism,' she wrote, 'and Shaw will make fun of us.' She finally decided that she would do it herself as a mere 'Lesser Name'.[6] The poet Edmund Blunden contributed a ten-stanza poem titled 'War Cemetery' – 'No one can say they are not buried well/ At least as much of them as could be found'. Lord Cecil, after much coaxing from Jameson, and deeply suspicious of the anti-war attitudes of some of his fellow contributors, supplied an introduction in which he deplored the likely return of years of slaughter and waste and pleaded for a 'common civilisation' and a common system of inter-national justice.[7]

Jameson later wrote that the book's publication had just the effect she had expected – 'none' – but at the time she thought it timely and urgent; 'even if we are fighting a lost cause,' she wrote to Vernon Bartlett, 'it is something which has to be done'.[8] *Challenge to Death* received wide coverage in the press when it appeared in November 1934. The *New York Herald Tribune* hailed it as a book by the post-war 'lost generation': 'The world today,' ran the review, 'seen through the disenchanted eyes of these people, is a dangerous, disinte-grating mess.'[9] Jameson spent much of the rest of the decade torn between what she called her only 'immoveable conviction', a hatred of war, and the apparent paradox that aggression could only be halted by the exercise of collective violence, a paradox expressed in Philip Noel-Baker's contribution in the book on an 'International Air Police Force' for world peace. Internationally controlled planes, he argued, could be used, if an aggressor persisted in bombing civilians, 'to bombard *his* cities until he stopped'.[10] This was death challenged not by peace but by more death and it highlighted one of the central issues that divided the broad anti-war movement in the Britain of the 1930s.

The guests at the Wellington Club were each of them against war in their own way. They were representatives of the largest popular mass movement in Britain between the wars. Anti-war sentiment crossed all the conventional lines of party allegiance, social class, gender difference and regional identity. To be anti-war in the 1920s and 1930s was to acquire membership in a broad church, though scarcely a united front. There existed a profusion of anti-war organiza-tions, large and small. Some lasted only a few years, some survived the whole interval between the two world wars. Taken together their active members and supporters certainly numbered millions. If they were united by anything it was the common understanding that peace was the key to the survival of civilization. This relationship was repeated at every opportunity like a piece of established liturgy. 'This meeting', ran a resolution at a League of Nations Union rally in 1933, 'records its unaltered conviction that only through the League of Nations and the collective system can war be averted and civilisation saved.'[11] A resolution of the London Council for the Prevention of

A portrait c. 1930 of the novelist Margaret Chapman, who wrote under the name Storm Jameson, by which she is better known. She was a committed anti-war campaigner in the 1930s until her loathing for fascism persuaded her that 'some things are worth killing for'.

War in 1927 considered it the principal duty of the peace movement 'to arouse the people to the fact that the Western World is heading for disaster'; without a solid peace, it continued, 'a war may occur which will imperil the whole future of civilisation'.[12] Rose Macaulay, one of the guests at the Wellington Club, wrote an 'Open Letter' in 1937 on peace which ended with the following passionate denunciation of the folly of war:

All will be hate, fury, tyranny, dictatorship, brutality, fear – the bestial and stupid aftermath of war. Culture will be gone, barbarism will reign, the clock will have swung back through the centuries to a darker age, because not enough people would reject the conventions of contemporary warfare as too cruel, too horrible, for civilized humanity to accept.[13]

Lord Robert Cecil spent a lifetime arguing that only peace made civilization possible. When he was awarded the Nobel Peace Prize in 1937 this was the principal theme of his address in Oslo. He gave his lecture no title but when it was reproduced in print the Nobel Foundation titled it 'The Future of Civilisation'.[14]

The broad anti-war movement was otherwise divided into numerous sects that approached the issue of peace along different routes, even if the destination was the same. Lord Cecil insisted in his introduction to *Challenge to Death* that he was not responsible for the views of the other contributors and would not endorse them. 'They belong to different schools of thought,' he told Storm Jameson, who had to assure him that the few socialists who had contributed essays were guiltless of saying 'anything very wild'.[15] The most fundamental division was not directly political but practical. Lord Cecil represented what the *Manchester Guardian* called the 'Right-Centre of the peace party', in favour of peace in preference to war but unwilling to renounce violent means to restrain the international law-breaker.[16] Such an attitude was legitimately anti-war but not consistently pacifist. On the other side were the true pacifists who renounced violence of any kind from conscientious conviction that it was morally wrong, unnecessary in practice and, in human terms, an absurd abuse of the legacy of civilization. Pacifism had a strong Christian tradition behind it, but also a long socialist pedigree; in the 1920s and 1930s to be a Christian-socialist pacifist was an unremarkable amalgam. Within the pacifist camp there were also evident sectarian divisions. Rationalist pacifists such as Bertrand Russell found it difficult to endorse Christian pacifism. War resisters advocated radical political solutions as a means to end the threat of war, refusing conscription and promoting direct confrontation with the state; on the other hand, the followers of 'Gandhiism', an idea promoted by the American pacifist Richard Gregg in the 1930s, demanded strict non-violent and non-compliant pacifism, preaching peace by example. What united them all was a conviction of the rightness of their cause, an uncompromising belief that a state of peace in the modern world was rational, natural and just, and the only means of salvation.[17]

The genuinely mass dimension of anti-war sentiment was famously expressed in 1935 in the unofficial plebiscite or 'Peace Ballot' organized by Lord Cecil's League of Nations Union when almost 12 million adult voters expressed support for the League and its work for peace. The idea of a ballot was raised in November 1933 by the secretary of the National Peace Council, set up in 1923 to co-ordinate the activities of the anti-war movement, when he suggested to Walter Layton the idea of 'a national plebiscite or petition' on peace and disarmament.[18] The Council approved the idea in December but it was the League of Nations Union that took up the proposal in earnest in the spring of 1934. In February 1934 Philip Noel-Baker sent a memorandum to the executive committee of the Union also proposing a national plebiscite and the idea was endorsed on 8 March.[19] The campaign, which ran from the autumn of 1934 until the spring of 1935, was dominated by Lord Cecil and Noel-Baker who were throughout the decade the most prominent champions of the idea that the only way to avert war was to secure an effective League of Nations based on the principle of collective security.

Both men had played a part in the early years of the League organization, Cecil as one of its founding fathers, Noel-Baker as a young member of the secretariat. Edgar Algernon Robert Cecil, the third son of the third Marquess of Salisbury, had a long and distinguished career as a barrister, an MP and a minister behind him. He had been Minister of Blockade between 1916 and 1918, and was assistant secretary for foreign affairs in 1918–19. In 1916 he drafted the memorandum that formed the basis of the future Covenant of the League and in 1919 dominated the deliberations of the Paris-based commission that drew up the League of Nations' terms of reference. A tall, spare, patrician figure, with a sharp mind and a lawyer's gift for argument, which he sustained in a thin, reedy but clearly audible voice, an individual of distinctly conservative views, Cecil was an unconventional member of the anti-war constituency. He entered the House of Lords in 1923 as Viscount Cecil of Chelwood and became the country's most prominent spokesman for disarmament and respect for the Covenant of the League in which a commitment to disarmament was enshrined.[20] Throughout the 1930s he complained that he was too old to carry such weighty responsibilities – he was 70 by the time of the ballot – but was persuaded by his own argument that his name and stature were indispensable to the struggle to save peace.

Philip Noel-Baker was a much younger man. He was born plain Philip Baker into a Quaker family; his hatred of war was instilled from childhood by his father, a radical Liberal MP. He was a tall, distinctively good-looking man, a sociable teetotaller well known for his dizzying energy, who sustained a lifelong commitment to sport after he ran the 1,500 metres for Britain in the Olympic Games of 1912 and 1920. During the war he served in the Friends' Ambulance Unit and was decorated for bravery on the Italian Isonzo front. After the war he joined the League of Nations secretariat before becoming professor of international relations in London. In 1922 he added his wife's surname to his own and became Philip Noel-Baker. Unlike Cecil, whose understudy he became in the 1930s, Noel-Baker was a Labour supporter and in 1929–31, and again after 1935, a Labour MP and future Labour minister in the post-1945 Attlee government.[21] The relationship between the two men appears from their correspondence rather as father and son: Noel-Baker anxious to please and dutiful, Cecil more often reproachful, exasperated but indulgent. They were regarded in the 1930s as a League of Nations double act.

Their power base in the anti-war movement was the League of Nations Union. The Union was founded in 1918 and grew rapidly in the 1920s into a countrywide mass movement. In January 1919 there were just 3,841 members, but a year later 10,000 and by 1922 over 150,000. In 1927, after ten years of activity, there were 654,000 members organized in 2,557 branches, 518 junior branches and 2,801

Lord Robert Cecil, the British politician and champion of the League of Nations, addressing a rally of the Women's International League on 20 January 1932 shortly before the opening of the Disarmament Conference at Geneva.

affiliated corporate organizations.[22] From the outset the Union enjoyed a privileged position among the anti-war movements. The senior organizers were also active participants in the League's activities, Cecil as a member of the preparatory commission for disarmament was also the Union's president from 1923; the chairman of the Union, Gilbert Murray, was chair of a number of League committees. David Lloyd George and Stanley Baldwin were honorary presidents. The semi-official character of the Union, with its close links to both Westminster and Geneva and its array of establishment supporters, made it the respectable face of anti-war sentiment. Despite the modest membership fee, a minimum of one shilling in 1920, the sheer scale of membership ensured that there were ample funds for employing a permanent staff and for promoting national campaigns of propaganda and recruitment. As numbers increased, the Union journal *Headway* began to publish guidelines on managing a public meeting, on how to run a branch organization (it must be run, so it was suggested, by people with 'a friendly disposition towards each other') and the organization of prize competitions to link up local members with the national headquarters, which included ideas for a local Union pageant, a design for a Union banner, a Union song or 'League of Nations Union March' or a short story of 3,000 to 5,000 words, 'the plot of which is to centre around the League of Nations'.[23]

Propaganda was deliberately targeted at working-class communities on the assumption that they would be more resistant to Union activity. A plan of propaganda drawn up in the early 1920s began from the obvious proposition that 'Of the people the Manual Working Classes form the Majority' and went on to recommend activity in the Labour Party, the trade union movement, trades councils, working men's clubs (membership 800,000), the Discharged Soldiers' and Sailors' Federation (1.5 million members), the Comrades of the Great War (500,000 members), and a string of other popular associations.[24] The other target was to recruit youth. The League ran its own youth movement with summer camps and communal activities, but the aim was to try to get the principles of the League taught in every school. G. Lowes Dickinson, who wrote one of the Union's first propaganda booklets on 'The Future of the Covenant', mused in his journal on the possibility that in a 'League of Nations world' the habit of keeping the peace might become an acquired and inherited characteristic 'fixed in the offspring'.[25] A Union memorandum recommended that all children, from primary level upwards, should be exposed to the aims and work of the League: 'Teacher shd. have reference books, lantern slides, images Epinal [bright coloured instructional prints], films, reading matter for children . . .' Schools were encouraged to hold 'League Days' and were asked to remove any anti-League literature from the school library.[26] According to one account, teachers could be found organizing a small charade to instil the principles of collective security. One child called 'The Bully' was made to stand at the front of the class. Then all the other pupils were asked to form a circle around their classmate to demonstrate that even if the bully could defeat them one by one, the entire class could keep the bully in place by collective action.[27] In the 1920s the secretary of the Union, the Oxford academic

Maxwell Garnett, succeeded in persuading the Teachers' Association and the local education authorities to accept the teaching of peace and the League as part of the school curriculum.[28] The reward for all these activities was to produce by 1933 a membership on paper of over one million, organized in almost 3,000 local branches.[29]

The Union had nevertheless reached something of a crisis point in the early 1930s, due partly to the fatally slow progress made with the disarmament programme, which took five years before the preparations produced a formal conference in Geneva in February 1932, and partly to the blow struck by Japanese aggression in Manchuria in 1931 which the League failed to prevent or reverse. Efforts to trumpet the achievements of the League after its first ten years, which were published as *Ten Years of World Co-operation* in 1930, could not disguise the facts that what little progress had been made on disarmament had been reached outside the organization and that the League had failed to stem the economic crisis. The disputes submitted to the Assembly amounted to a handful of trivial arguments over frontiers and population transfers, most of which concerned the Balkan States (42 per cent) or the newly created states in central Europe (30 per cent).[30] Cecil confessed to feeling 'profound gloom' over the failure to make progress on disarmament after the high hopes sustained by the Union in the 1920s. When Gilbert Murray suggested a letter signed by British 'writers and savants' in 1932, Cecil was unenthusiastic: 'Aspirations for peace and good-will have been done so much that I feel they have lost their reality.'[31] The most difficult issue was the Union's reaction to the Manchurian crisis in September 1931, which Cecil later admitted had been misjudged. At the time he argued that there was right on both sides and refused openly to condemn Japanese aggression. When Japanese and Chinese representatives briefly established contact in 1932 Cecil hailed it as evidence that 'even in the most distant parts of Asia the League's value is appreciated'.[32] A founder member of the Union wrote to him two years later that he and his fellow members had been puzzled by Cecil's behaviour:

Well, thousands of people like myself have gone to the Albert Hall meetings and drawing room meetings etc. and we all have the feeling that this is all very well but when it came to the bit in September 1931 Viscount Cecil and the League of Nations Union gave the show away.

Cecil jotted down on the letter for his secretary 'no further answer'.[33]

The sense of frustration occasioned by what was in reality a modest international crisis was enough to push Murray to the most pessimistic conclusions when he was asked to write a leaflet for the London Regional Federation of the Union in 1933. His text was a frank admission of failure: in a world of war, economic crisis and failed disarmament, he wrote, 'civilisation itself is in danger, and the League does not seem to be doing much to save it'. Murray emphasized that 'THE LEAGUE IS NOT STRONG ENOUGH' and called for five million members rather than the one million who had already enrolled.[34] Even that figure proved illusory. It was discovered in 1933 that from the one million 'members' only 388,255 subscriptions had been received. The Union journal stopped publishing monthly stat- istics of membership, and the number of fully paid subscriptions, which had actually peaked in 1931, declined steadily.[35] Among the Union leadership and the rank and file there was a sense that the organization stood at a crossroads. Murray wrote to Cecil in March 1933 to complain that the 'enormously important movement' that they led was breaking up by concentrating too much on issues which divided the membership and giving no clear lead on where the Union stood: 'we must not let it collapse', continued Murray, 'either through dissensions that can be avoided or through a merely colourless or timid attitude'.[36] It is against this background of exaggerated gloom that the launch of the Peace Ballot can be understood.

The decision to organize a national plebiscite was taken to try to revive the flagging fortunes of the Union but also to demonstrate to world opinion that Britain, as Murray put it in a memorandum on the ballot, was still 'a champion in the great adventure of ridding the civilised world of war'.[37] The ballot was given the title 'National Declaration' and that was the term used by the Union organizers. It was hoped that other organizations could be persuaded to associate themselves with the declaration, including members of the three main political parties, although the Declaration was intended to be strictly non-partisan. In Manchester and Salford the Union branches from the conurbation's thirteen parliamentary constituencies established an executive committee to oversee the ballot which included representatives from the Labour, Liberal and Conservative parties, the local women's associations and four clerics: an Anglican, a non-conformist, a Catholic priest and a rabbi.[38] There was less success in recruiting other pacifist organizations which distrusted the Union's commitment to the use of force to maintain collective security. In April 1934 Cecil tried to get the prominent pacifist leader and fellow peer Arthur Ponsonby to support a Union memorandum on disarmament and the creation of an international peace-keeping air force, but Ponsonby refused to sanction any discussion 'as to how to wage the next war'. Cecil replied that if the advocates of peace could not agree among themselves 'it is very unlikely that the Government will pay any attention to them' and invited Ponsonby, if he could, 'to remain silent' on the issues that divided them.[39] The main pacifist groups refused to co-operate and the minority of absolute pacifists inside the Union itself expressed growing disquiet about supporting a ballot that apparently committed them to endorsing the international use of force. When Quaker members of the Union organized a debate in the Sussex town of Lewes in November 1934 on the issue of the League's use of armed force the large crowd present voted overwhelmingly and noisily against.[40]

The main issue to be resolved after deciding to launch the National Declaration was the questions to be asked of the voters. Noel-Baker had originally suggested three questions, one on preferring 'pooled security' to an arms race and alliances, one on abolishing weapons of aggression, one on declaring the private manufacture of weapons contrary to the public interest.[41] These were borrowed from a successful independent ballot on the question 'Peace or War?' conducted early in 1934 in the Essex town of Ilford by C. J. Boorman, a Union official and the editor of the local paper, the *Ilford Recorder*. The main question, on whether Britain should remain in the League, was approved overwhelmingly in the Ilford case by 85 per cent of those voting; a further question, on prohibiting the private arms trade, was endorsed by 80 per cent of those voting. The ballot was supported across the town by fifty-one associations and churches, including the Ilford Athletic Club and the Ilford Esperanto Society, and mobilized no fewer than 500 volunteer helpers. The paper expected perhaps 14–15,000 votes, but secured an impressive 26,000.[42] A second local ballot in Luton a few months later produced a further 25,000 votes on the question of League membership, in this case with over 97 per cent in favour; a smaller ballot in Nottingham secured 98 per cent approval.[43]

These experiments augured well for the National Declaration, yet across the summer months of 1934 there were long arguments on the Union executive over the exact wording of the propaganda and the ballot questions. The campaign slogan 'League or War!' adopted in April was altered to 'Peace or War?', the title of the Ilford ballot, but that was in turn withdrawn because of its misleading implication that those who voted negatively were warmongers.[44] Four questions were chosen to start with, but the ballot paper eventually listed six. The first repeated the Ilford and Luton ballots: 'Should Great Britain remain a Member of the League of Nations?' The second asked whether the voter favoured all-round disarmament, the third the abolition of all naval and military aircraft by international agreement. The fourth followed the earlier ballots by asking whether arms manufacture and trade for private profit should be prohibited (but added the rider 'by international agreement', which rendered it all but impossible). The fifth question (eventually divided into two parts) prompted the most heart searching. It asked voters to consider whether they favoured other nations combining to stop an aggressor 'by (a) economic and non-military measures (b) if necessary military measures'.[45] A set of explanatory notes was produced by the Union to spell out in unequivocal terms that a vote for 5(b) was a vote for Britain to use 'in the last resort *military force*' and a vote for collective security 'in the fullest sense of the word'. Perhaps aware that this issue was more divisive than the others, the notes on question 5 did not include, as the other four did, the pre-emptive instruction 'we hope you will answer "yes"'.[46]

The commitment to violence as a last resort had always been explicit in the Covenant of the League. From its birth the League of Nations Union supported the use of force when necessity dictated and refused to follow other anti-war movements into attacks on the armed forces or the principle of military service.[47] Union leaders did not generally approve of complete disarmament and Cecil and Noel-Baker were enthusiastic proselytizers of the idea of an international air force to keep the peace. Both were fond of the analogy of the domestic police force, backed by the whole of society in the task of apprehending and punishing the criminal, as a model for the collective action of the League against an international wrongdoer. The Union was regularly denounced by other anti-war campaigners as an organization of war-mongers and it was difficult, as Gilbert Murray complained during the ballot, to expunge the popular view that the Union regarded the League 'chiefly as an instrument of coercion'.[48] Lord Cecil, for all his rhetoric about the essential need for peace, was not opposed either to armaments or to war as an instrument of international control. In spring 1934, as the National Declaration was being debated, Cecil and Murray joined forces with the Conservative former Foreign Secretary Austen Chamberlain to issue a statement on behalf of the Union in which they not only recognized 'the need for maintaining adequate and efficient naval, military and air forces' and supported the idea of recruiting and training a regular and territorial army of sufficient size, but listed at least three cases in which the use of armed force could be regarded as legitimate – policing the Empire, protecting nationals abroad and enforcing common armed action against an aggressor.[49] A few months later Cecil responded to an idea about regional pacts in place of collective security with unusual candour: 'I should be quite unsatisfied with any arrangement that did not provide for our intervention at an early stage in any war.'[50] The refusal to abjure the use of force led Lord Beaverbrook's *Daily Express* to christen the National Declaration 'The Ballot of Blood'.

The organization of the National Declaration was a task of exceptional magnitude. An executive committee drawn from the different organizations supporting the ballot was set up to oversee the whole project but its success depended on the work of the local branches and their volunteers across the country. Some experience was gained by a separate national canvass on the question 'League or Peace?' which the secretary of the Union had organized in early 1934 before the idea of a National Declaration had been confirmed, and close attention was paid to the way the Ilford and Luton ballots had been organized.[51] The chief administrator was a senior Union official, Dame Adelaide Livingstone, but the progress of the ballot was watched closely by all the senior officers. Each local Union branch was encouraged to set up a National Declaration committee and to recruit and train volunteers from all participating organizations to collect the votes. By August thirty-four national organizations had volunteered support, from the Association of Headmistresses to the National Union of Soroptimist Clubs (though not the pacifist National Peace Council). Between them they recruited 500,000 volunteers to distribute leaflets and posters, to run the local polling offices and to undertake the house-to-house distribution and collection of the ballot papers, a remarkable achievement in itself.[52] The house visit was the most important of the volunteer's activities. Each parliamentary constituency was divided up into council wards where a group would be assigned to secure the votes from their neighbourhood by a personal visit. It was recommended that each worker cover forty houses. A blank refusal by the householder was to be followed up by organizing an appointment with a more senior official. Canvassers were warned that in cases of laziness or ignorance, three or more visits might be necessary. Volunteers were encouraged to digest thoroughly the contents of the Union guide so that they could answer any teasing questions on the spot. For the shy volunteer there were cheery exhortations: 'After the first few houses you will begin to enjoy the fun!'; 'Canvassers do well to hunt in pairs', and so on.[53] Some volunteers left the ballot paper and notes and returned for a second visit to collect it; others chose to stay on the doorstep, or inside, until all the members of the household over the age of 18 had filled in the voting form. Given the complexity of the organization, the number of questions to answer and the general intractability of householders when interrupted by doorstep canvassers, the final achievement of over 30 per cent of the eligible population was testament not only to the conscientious activity of the volunteers but also to the wide publicity that the National Declaration was able to generate.

It was planned to hold the ballot not on any one day but over a number of months, beginning in November 1934 and completing the whole country by Easter 1935. The first results were announced by the BBC on 21 November 1934, by which time almost half the constituencies in the country had a Local National Declaration Committee. The Union hoped for a 60–70 per cent response from the electorate and the first returns were encouraging. The *News Chronicle* and the *Daily Herald* promised to begin regular coverage of the ballot from mid-November 1934, and contacts at the BBC expressed a firm willingness to support the declaration in a spirit of impartiality; among cinema newsreels only Universal was approached because of its pacifist reputation.[54] The final results were gathered in by the late spring of 1935 and showed a surprisingly high turnout. Noel-Baker, convalescent in Greece in May 1935 after an illness, was buoyed by the news – 'a howling success', he wrote to Cecil. 'The foolishness of doubters and pessimists . . .'[55] The tally was formally announced by Lord Cecil at a rally in the Royal Albert Hall on 25 June: a total of 11,627,765 valid votes, 95.9 per cent of them in favour of British membership of the League. Slightly smaller percentages supported questions 2, 3, and 4 but on questions 5(a) and 5(b) there was a sharper division of opinion. Some 10 million people favoured non-military measures against aggression, or 87 per cent of those voting; but only 6.8 million (59 per cent) would accept military action as a last resort. A further 2.36 million gave a straight 'no' answer, and 2.37 million abstained.[56]

The success of the National Declaration in mobilizing around one-third of those eligible to vote was a substantial achievement. A strongly contested and fully funded general election four months later, in November 1935, produced a voting total of 21 million. The outcome can be explained in a number of ways: the wide publicity generated; increased public anxiety about the international situation; a large national organization behind the ballot of equivalent size to a major political party. The National Declaration marked the high-water mark of enthusiasm for the League of Nations. Its impact is harder to assess. The great expectations it raised among the broad anti-war lobby put the eventual failure of the League to contain aggression all the more clearly in focus and sharpened the later disappointment. The direct political impact was largely insignificant. Cecil had asked for the support of his friend Cosmo Lang, Archbishop of Canterbury, who agreed with some reluctance to endorse the Declaration and did so in terms that were clearly equivocal, since he did not want to become embroiled in political argument.[57] Conservative politicians were generally hostile, although they could not afford to say so too openly. Conservative Central Office eventually announced that branches and party members were not forbidden to participate in the ballot, but the party feared that it would be regarded as a vote against the National Government, in which the Conservatives were by far the largest element. Noel-Baker told Cecil that even after the ballot, 'We can't hope to make <u>this</u> Government do anything.'[58] A few months later Cecil observed that the Foreign Office and Stanley Baldwin, who had recently become head of the National Government in place of Ramsay MacDonald, had between them embarked on a strong anti-League line. Even the opposition Labour Party was little more enthusiastic. Arthur Henderson, president of the prorogued Disarmament Conference, told Cecil that there seemed little point in reconvening it.[59] In March 1934, shortly before the Declaration campaign was launched, MacDonald, who was still prime minister, told Cecil that he did not believe in gestures: 'International opinion is not influenced by them and Governments resent them.'[60] When Noel-Baker suggested to Cecil three years later the idea of a second national plebiscite, he dismissed the idea as impractical.

During the months in which the plebiscite was being prepared and carried out a second project was launched to win mass support for a policy of peace. On 16 October 1934 a letter appeared in the *Manchester Guardian* and two other daily newspapers from the popular London clergyman Canon Dick Sheppard. The letter invited men (not women) to write a postcard to him declaring the following pledge: 'I renounce War and never again, directly or indirectly, will I support or sanction another.' Within days the Post Office was delivering replies by the vanload.[61] It is tempting to argue that Sheppard deliberately timed his initiative to spoil the impact of the Peace Ballot by offering an absolute pacifist alternative, but the evidence is not conclusive. The League of Nations Union certainly thought that had been his purpose. Two days after Sheppard's 'Peace Letter' appeared Noel-Baker wrote to him explaining why he and the Union could not renounce violence absolutely as long as dictatorship existed in Europe. Passive resistance, Noel-Baker suggested, meant not only that civilization would be overwhelmed but the end of 'organised Christianity' as well.[62] On 23 October Noel-Baker wrote to Cecil asking him to appeal to Sheppard to invite his correspondents to support the ballot as well as signing the pledge, but Cecil had already written asking for Sheppard's co-operation, and although conciliatory, Sheppard had still made no statement when Cecil wrote to him again five months later.[63] Sheppard, like Ponsonby, was unwilling to compromise on the central issue of violence, but the damage done by the 'Peace Letter' must be judged slight, given the size of the eventual vote.[64]

The attempt to revive the fortunes of absolute pacifism in 1934, like the efforts to reinvigorate support for the League, must be seen in the context of a widespread and popular pacifist movement whose roots lay before 1914 but whose immediate origins lay in the aftermath of the Great War. The many anti-war movements that sprang up were loosely linked in a National Peace Council set up in 1923 whose aim, according to James Hudson, one of the founders, was not to insist 'that ALL must be made quickly into Absolute Pacifists' but to create a framework in which the forces making for peace could be made to move by 'conversion' in that direction.[65] The organization was responsible for annual No More War demonstrations and for an annual National Peace Congress. In 1923 the main rally was held in London's Hyde Park on 28 July, with 300 other demonstrations held countrywide under the slogan 'No More War and Universal Disarmament'. Columns of demonstrators converged on Hyde Park from four different directions carrying, according to a newspaper report, 'gay banners' with homespun pacifist slogans, including the following simple verse: 'Ef you take a sword and dror it/ An' go an' stick a feller thru'/ Guv'ment aint to answer for it/ God will send the bill to you!'[66] In 1926 it was decided to hold the anti-war rallies on the weekend after Armistice Day to give the pacifist message more impact. In 1924 the Council changed its name to the National Council for the Prevention of War and adopted a constitution committing its associated members to work for revision of the peace treaties imposed on Germany and her allies, immediate disarmament and support for the League of Nations, but a large part of the pacifist constituency attached to the Council rejected the moderate League line and called for complete abolition of armaments and an absolute commitment to peace. A special meeting of the Council executive committee convened in November 1928 narrowly defeated a resolution calling on the British government to set an example by immediately adopting total disarmament and abolishing the three armed services.[67]

Although it was constitutionally committed to support the work of the League, the Peace Council was generally supported by organizations and prominent individuals who embraced some form of absolute pacifism and an active hostility to any manifestation of militarism, a simple view encapsulated in the lines of a pacifist song written by a local peace worker in Yorkshire: 'We say "no" to armaments, We say "no" to war!'[68] Anti-militarism separated off the absolute pacifists from the League of Nations Union, which supported limited disarmament but not the abolition of established armed force. The London Council for the Prevention of War, founded in 1924 as an affiliate of the larger National Council, drew together a large number of anti-militarist organizations in the capital. Its constitution was more aggressively anti-militarist and its support for the League very conditional. Out of 272 associated organizations in 1926 there were no League of Nations Union branches, and its rallies were addressed by celebrities who were publicly committed to absolute pacifism, including Bertrand Russell and Arthur Ponsonby, and the veteran Christian socialist George Lansbury.[69]

Arthur Ponsonby was a conscientious pacifist of unusual pedigree. He was the son of Queen Victoria's Principal Private Secretary, General Henry Ponsonby, related through both parents to the British aristocracy. His grandfather had fought at Waterloo. After a conventional upper-class education at Eton and Balliol College, Oxford he joined the diplomatic corps, but grew increasingly critical of the wealthy elite into which he was born. He became a radical Liberal MP for the Scottish seat of Stirling in 1908, but lost it in 1918 after working during the war for the Union of Democratic Control which was hostile to British participation. He converted to the Labour Party in 1921, and became Labour MP for a Sheffield constituency in 1922, and in 1931, after elevation to the peerage a year earlier, Labour leader in the House of Lords. He was a sombre man with a long face, high forehead and lugubrious expression who once wrote that 'when every-thing goes wrong I almost prefer it to a smooth passage'.[70] He was uncompromisingly committed to contest the necessity for war and armaments and after he launched a 'Peace Letter' in 1925 to encourage the public to declare that they would refuse war service if the government resorted to arms he became one of the leading spokesmen for a rational absolute pacifism.[71] In an article for the journal of the No More War Movement in 1932 he summed up the grounds of his conviction:

The Pacifist to-day should be personified by an athletic youth in the prime of life . . . That he should be captured, dressed up and compelled to participate in the wholesale destruction of his fellows with whom he has no quarrel, and be maimed, or blinded or killed, is so monstrous an outrage on the conscience of civilised man and such an insult to the intelligence of an enlightened society, that no argument can be found to justify such an abominable folly.[72]

Throughout the years between the two wars Ponsonby's dignified rejection of war brought him a vast correspondence from a public whose own anxieties he articulated so plainly.

The absolute pacifism represented by Ponsonby was to be found in two distinct constituencies in the 1920s and 1930s, the one more

A delegation of the British No More War Movement youth section at the International Anti-War Youth Conference in September 1924. The movement was part of the War Resisters' International and had branches across the country.

secular and politically radical, the other an expression of Christian commitment to non-violence. Some organizations, such as the Women's International League of Peace and Freedom, founded in 1915 to campaign for peace and social reform, had pacifism as part of a broader programme of social and political emancipation.[73] The No More War Movement, which Ponsonby supported, was committed to only one ambition, to achieve total disarmament worldwide and end war for ever. It was a member organization of the War Resisters' International which advocated refusal to serve in the armed forces. The International was dominated by British pacifists including the radical socialist MP Fenner Brockway, an advocate not only of anti-militarism but of non-violent social revolution, and Hubert Runham Brown, who ran the International from a house in north London.[74] The movement was the leading voice demanding complete disarmament and at the start of the Disarmament Conference in February 1932 it presented a petition to the prime minister signed by 1,450 organizations calling on him 'to disarm Great Britain as an example'.[75] Its support was drawn largely from labour organizations and its language was radical, even revolutionary in tone. In 1932 the national committee drew up plans for a 'Peace Book', suggested by Ponsonby, to rival the government's War Book with its detailed arrangements for national mobilization in case of war. The book called for a pacifist emergency officer in each town and village, enlistment officers to recruit new anti-war volunteers, and a 'street captain' responsible for distributing literature and canvassing for anti-war sentiment. At the point of a war crisis, the officers were to call mass demonstrations, encourage wholesale non-compliance with mobilization orders and draw up local Councils of Action. It had to be clear, it was later stated, that those who took part 'are preparing for unconstitutional and illegal action, pitting moral right against immoral law'.[76] The strategy of non-compliance was consistent with pacifism, but ran the risk of social conflict. Runham Brown thought that if war resistance turned into social revolution 'then armed violence might be and would be condoned' – but added prudently 'we do not admit that'.[77] By the end of 1932 the National Committee was recommending to the annual conference a policy of complete resistance which included a general strike on the outbreak of war, a boycott of 'big capitalist manufacturing', refusal to pay rents, rates or taxes and appeals to soldiers to destroy their weapons. The programme of action was approved at the annual conference in Sheffield a few weeks later. Notes on policy drawn up by the movement's chairman, Wilfred Wellock, early in 1933 were headed 'Revolution'.[78]

Christian absolute pacifism had none of the revolutionary rhetoric of the secular movement. There were Christian pacifists who were also socialists – George Lansbury was the best known among them – but the appeal of most Christians who actively campaigned for peace was to conscience rather than action. The impact of Christianity on the struggle against war was widespread. There was a strong element of religiosity, or religious analogy, running through the language and values of the pacifist cause. The reference to Christian teaching and values as the moral measure of the anti-war campaign was routine; books and pamphlets giving a Christian perspective on contemporary problems with titles such as *Christ and Present World Issues* or *Christianity and the Crisis* jostled on bookshelves alongside their secular companions, but have generally been overlooked in more recent historical narrative. Christian doctrine was nonetheless an important reference point in the 1930s on issues of war or peace, violence or restraint. In a memorandum written in 1933 to challenge the idea of an international police force, the pacifist Ruth Fry argued that 'moral enthusiasm' was more likely to succeed than League coercion: 'Christianity', she continued, 'must obtain between nations as it does between individuals.'[79] Another memorandum on the same subject produced by the Cambridge Scientists' Anti-War Group in 1936, observing that 'Satan can never cast out Satan', argued that only 'good can overcome evil (whole of Christ's teaching and life)'.[80] For some clergymen, though by no means all, a pacifist standpoint was the only one consistent with their role as Christian leaders. In the programme of a Christian Book Club conference in late 1938 to discuss religious freedom under fascism it was declared that war and fascism were not only incompatible with but constituted 'the antithesis of the spirit of Christ'.[81] The Churches Commission of the International Peace Campaign, founded in 1936, declared that clergymen should not be seen simply as passive supporters of peace, but ought to be at 'the centre of peace activity'. The address at the New Year's party of the London

Fellowship of Reconciliation in 1934 was titled 'Christendom's responsibility for World Peace'.[82]

Pacifist enthusiasm was most closely associated with the non-conformist churches, of which the Quakers were the most prominent. Friends House on Euston Road in central London became one of the principal centres for the propagation and dissemination of pacifist literature and activity. The Friends Peace Committee could trace its activities back to 1888 and together with the Northern Friends Peace Board campaigned throughout the inter-war years on a platform of absolute pacifism (though not opposed to sending ambulance units to the Spanish Civil War). The Quaker London Peace Committee called in 1934 for complete national disarmament 'as an effective expression of redemptive and heroic love', and the motion was adopted as policy by the Friends National Peace Committee.[83] The Friends urged voters in the National Declaration to say yes to the League but to write on the ballot paper in answer to questions 2–4 'disarm completely without waiting for others to do so'. To question 5(a) voters were asked to endorse economic means of pressure 'but not including starvation methods', and to reject 5(b) by writing in 'The method of war is in itself wrong'.[84] To coincide with the ballot the Friends sent out over 300,000 leaflets with the title 'Call to Complete Disarmament'.[85] The other main non-conformist denominations were grouped under the Council of Christian Pacifist Groups chaired by Canon Charles Raven, Regius professor of divinity at Cambridge, which acted as a lobby group for the absolute pacifist cause. Anglican clergy were also to be found in the pacifist vanguard, among their number Dick Sheppard. In June 1934 the Bishop of Birmingham, Ernest Barnes, addressed the National Peace Congress assembled in his cathedral with a call for unilateral and complete disarmament and reliance on 'a policy of international righteousness'. He rejected the idea of an armed League and insisted that its authority had to be moral. 'War is of the devil,' he continued, 'not of Christ.'[86]

The official position of the Church of England was more complicated than this because senior church leaders did not want to be seen to be challenging government policy or undermining the League of Nations. The Archbishop of Canterbury, Cosmo Lang, who was appointed in 1928, was a firm supporter of peace and of some aspects

A march for peace organized by the Labour League of Youth on 1 June 1936 on its way through central London. Rallies and demonstrations were held throughout the 1930s reflecting the wide public mood against war.

of the pacifist movement. At the Lambeth Conference of church leaders in 1930 the bishops formally declared that war as a means of settling international arguments was 'incompatible with the teaching and example of our Lord Jesus Christ'.[87] In 1934, at the instigation of the Bishop of Chichester, George Bell, Lang agreed to organize a conference on 'The World's Peace' at Lambeth Palace in London to which he invited the heads of other Christian churches, including the Patriarch of Constantinople, but excluding the Pope or any other Catholic cleric. The congress assembled on 14 May and released a statement on the need for 'an awakened belief in God' as the key to better international understanding.[88] But although Lang, and his future successor William Temple, the Archbishop of York, both preferred peace to war, neither was prepared to abandon the use of force *in extremis*. In a speech to the Anglican Church Congress in October 1935, mindful that the impending crisis in Ethiopia threatened 'a most critical time in the history of the world', Lang announced that he was unable to endorse those, like Sheppard, who insisted 'that in no circumstances can a Christian countenance the use of force'. Without coercion, he concluded, there would be anarchy: 'I cannot believe that Christianity compels me to this conclusion.'[89] When in December 1936 Lang and Temple received a deputation of Anglican pacifist clergy pressing for an Episcopal change of heart, they responded, according to the *Church Times*, with the argument that 'circumstances might arise in which participation in war would not be inconsistent with their duty as Christians'.[90]

The ambivalence of the Christian approach to war reflected the uncertainties and arguments characteristic of the whole anti-war movement. During the early 1930s the growing evidence of world crisis and the apparent inability of the pacifist movement to exert any kind of practical or spiritual influence on the deteriorating course of events provoked an evident despondency among the faithful. The No More War Movement annual report for 1931–2 admitted that the PAX petition presented to the Disarmament Conference bearing more than 8 million signatures gathered from fifty-eight states had had no effect: 'public opinion is not enough', ran the report, '. . . within a short time we shall be swept aside by war'.[91] The annual report three years later concluded that pacifism was now 'a voice crying in the wilderness'. The organization itself went into decline. In 1931 the London offices were closed and smaller premises had to be found; the permanent staff was reduced from nine to three; the movement's journal *New World* ceased publication. Investigations in 1933 found that twenty-eight of the local branches were inactive and they were wound up. A year later, over half of those remaining were found to be poorly supported. Membership declined steadily from almost 3,000 in 1934 to 1,771 by 1936.[92] The London Council for the Prevention of War also found membership and funding in decline by the early 1930s against the background of economic gloom. In 1926, eighty-five participating organizations had sent delegates to the annual council meeting, but in January 1931 only forty-nine and a year later thirty-two.[93] It was into this atmosphere of impending crisis in the peace movement that Dick Sheppard injected the Peace Pledge.

The immediate success of the request for postcards pledging the

The Christian pacifist Canon Dick Sheppard advertising a meeting of the Peace Pledge Union in February 1937. His charismatic personality helped to create a broad absolute pacifist movement in 1936 and 1937 as fear of war deepened in Europe.

writer against any support for war was in large part a result of the peculiar appeal of the man who made it. Hugh Richard Sheppard was by all accounts a man capable of exerting an irresistible charisma – 'one of the most popular human beings', wrote Vera Brittain, 'ever to tread London's crowded pavements'.[94] He was charming, amusing, simplistically attached to the teachings of the Gospels, and unaffected by fame. He was plagued with chronic ill health which left him by 1934 reliant on a rubber oxygen inhaler wherever he went, and in private was prone to severe bouts of depression. His health suffered as a young army chaplain in 1914 and that year he was appointed to St Martin-in-the-Fields in central London, where he became a familiar figure welcoming troops back from France. In the process he turned St Martin's into a vibrant church centre and himself into a clerical celebrity. In 1934, when he launched his Peace Pledge, he was a canon of St Paul's cathedral. His reputation and infectious enthusiasm played their part in sustaining what had been a modest ambition at first. After a year he had 80,000 pledges and eventually secured the support of around 130,000. In July 1935, just two weeks after the triumphal rally of the National Declaration at the Albert Hall, he chose the same venue to launch the Sheppard Peace Movement, which filled the building with 7,000 enthusiastic pacifists – 'the most impressive show I was ever at', Sheppard wrote to Ponsonby a few days later.[95] In early 1936 he decided to give the movement, which had neither organization nor title, a firmer structure. On 22 May the Peace Pledge Union was formally announced and in October 1936 the membership was divided into local branches, 183 to start with but an estimated 1,150 by the outbreak of war. Not all those who had signed the pledge joined the Union, but by September 1937 there were 120,000 paid-up members, most of them men. A Union journal, *Peace News*, was founded and premises acquired in Regent Street, in the heart of London's West End.[96] Though not a mass movement on the scale of the League of Nations Union, Sheppard's movement caught the popular imagination at a moment when absolute pacifism was unfocused and demoralized.

Sheppard succeeded in attracting a cross-section of other celebrities to sponsor the movement, which contributed in turn to its high public profile. They included a number of those who had sat round the table at the Wellington Club to support the League of Nations and, by extrapolation, the use of collective violence to contest aggression. Storm Jameson, who as editor of *Challenge to Death* had played the impresario for the whole project, accepted Sheppard's invitation to become a sponsor with some reluctance, not because she hesitated to overturn her earlier commitment to collective security, but because she regarded herself as a poor public speaker.[97] Rose Macaulay also agreed to adopt the absolute pacifist position (though after a sponsors meeting in July Ponsonby told Sheppard that on pacifist issues neither novelist had thought through her commitment and would 'require education').[98] A more significant convert was Vera Brittain, who in 1934 had been happy to join Cecil and Noel-Baker and to supply a foreword to the book, but two years later, troubled by the reality of international conflict, her views hardened against all forms of violence. In late June 1936 Brittain found herself speaking at a peace rally in Dorchester alongside a largely clerical and pacifist platform. She had not realized in time the nature of the occasion. She abandoned her speech on collective security and made some brief, impromptu and poorly received remarks. In the train back to London she was able to observe Dick Sheppard at close quarters. He later told her that he had not been disposed to like her because of her views, but in fact both overcame their initial reservations.[99] About Vera Brittain's hatred of war there was no doubt. In May 1933 she had written to another of the contributors to *Challenge to Death*, Vernon Bartlett, who had said kind things about her autobiographical *Testament of Youth*, that she had produced her book 'because of the general indictment of a civilisation that goes to war'.[100] Its immediate success on both sides of the Atlantic turned her into a household name and she embarked on a giddy round of talks and lectures on issues of war and peace.

Brittain's passage to absolute pacifism was nevertheless not straight-forward. The Peace Pledge was only opened to women in June 1936 and its previous exaggerated masculinity (Sheppard had called it a 'Peace Appeal to Men') might well have alienated Brittain's strong sense of independent womanhood.[101] On 3 July 1936 she wrote to Sheppard about the effect of the meeting in Dorchester on her own anti-war views. She confessed that for some time she had been moving towards 'the complete pacifist position' and disillusionment with the other peace organizations she worked with for what she called 'their uncomfortable degree of militarism'. But she was torn between loyalty to her established commitments and her conscience. 'I have a strong inclination to join your group,' she continued, and requested a face-to-face discussion.[102] Whatever was said, her indecision lasted almost six months. She embarked on a brief lecture tour for the League of Nations Union, found herself heckled by Peace Pledge Union members with whose views she was largely in accord, and repelled by League supporters calling for violent collective action. Just after Christmas 1936 she finally accepted the invitation to be a sponsor. A few weeks later she wrote to Sheppard about her 'sense of satisfaction and conviction in the complete pacifist cause' which had come only after much argument and soul-searching. 'It is a relief,' she told him, 'to be finished with the doubts and difficulties of "just one more war".'[103] She remained from then onwards a resolute and absolute pacifist and a stern critic of 'all the so-called peace lovers', as she wrote a year later, who 'are back again preferring war to negotiation'.[104]

One of those who inspired her to embrace absolute pacifism was Aldous Huxley, who had been among those who sent a postcard to Sheppard's appeal, and who decided late in 1935 to throw his support behind the Sheppard organization. Huxley had risen to literary prominence in the 1920s as a novelist of the post-war age. Cynical, satirical and mischievous, his novels expressed the prevailing high literary tropes of anxiety and confusion which reflected his own sense of uncertainty and morbid apprehension. His tall, slight, rather fragile appearance and poor eyesight lent him an air of vulnerability that he shared with his equally famous brother, Julian. He was a late convert to complete pacifism. In 1934 he had rejected Storm Jameson's invitation to write an epilogue because, as she told Winifred Holtby, 'his mind isn't clear yet on the whole question'.[105] He was finally led to the movement by his friend Gerald Heard, who had contributed to *Challenge to Death* a futuristic essay on England after a new world war, compelled by the desperate hunt for food to reconquer Ireland. Heard, a journalist, author and broadcaster, attracted to the view that human nature was capable of undergoing a profound spiritual transformation for the better, pioneered a 'New Pacifism' to be sustained by fit young men who trained body and mind for non-violent resistance, an idea that Huxley endorsed with his vision of 'an athletic group' of dedicated peace-lovers.[106] Huxley took the pledge in late October 1935 attracted, according to Heard, by the 'directly spiritual' nature of Sheppard's project and the simple moral outlook of the cause.[107]

Huxley was a difficult recruit. His public stature made him an important sponsor, but he was uncertain about what he could contribute and anxious to keep control of that contribution. 'Thinking, reading, talking and writing', he wrote to Sheppard, 'have been my opium and my alcohol', but 'doing' needed a positive effort.[108] Nevertheless among Huxley's first steps as sponsor was to set up a 'Research and Thinking Committee' with Heard as his deputy and to write a pamphlet on what he called 'constructive' pacifism, which he began to prepare during the early months of 1936. By February he was already anxious about the commitment he had made. Heard wrote to Sheppard that Huxley 'has to take a decision whether to work for peace or to withdraw'; he would only stay if he felt that the 'life change' implied by pacifism was going to lead somewhere. In the end the pamphlet was completed under the title *What Are You Going to Do About It? The Case for Constructive Peace* and published for the Peace Pledge Union by the commercial publisher Chatto & Windus in the summer of 1936.[109] Huxley's contribution to constructive pacifism was to encourage pacifists to lead exemplary and peaceable lives, and to engage in 'group meditation' as an exercise for the soul. 'Constructive Pacifists', he wrote, 'are athletes in training for an event of more than Olympic importance'.[110] In a set of notes on the Peace Pledge Union that he produced in April he elaborated the idea that the perfect pacifist must not only abjure war, but also avoid violence of any kind in 'the economic, social or domestic spheres'. There was, he continued, a 'theology of pacifism' which Christian and non-Christian alike could sign up to, rooted in an 'underlying spiritual reality' in humankind.[111] It is difficult to avoid the view that Huxley used the Sheppard movement not just for its own sake but as a prop to help him elaborate and cement his own increasingly mystical vision of the world. His pamphlet was attacked by the communist poet Cecil Day Lewis in a *Left Review* publication titled 'We're Not Going to Do Nothing' for talking in abstractions and failing to face the threat of fascism.[112]

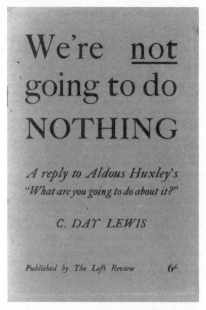

Two pamphlets from 1936 which illustrate the growing divide in the anti-war movement. Aldous Huxley insisted that all violence was wrong and that people should train themselves for a life of peace; C. Day Lewis represented a growing body of opinion that saw violence as necessary in a just cause.

It was the strong religiosity of the Sheppard movement which made it difficult for rationalist pacifists to participate. Arthur Ponsonby, who knew Sheppard well from more than twenty years' acquaintance, hesitated to accept his friend's request that he become a formal sponsor of the movement in May 1936. He admired Sheppard as 'the one really live wire who is <u>doing</u> something', but found it difficult to work with people animated by 'a fervent belief in the teaching of Jesus Christ'. He was not, he told Sheppard, a Christian, nor did he believe in God; he was also unconvinced that most Christians accepted the pacifist argument. Only after Sheppard agreed to make it clear that his movement was ecumenical, open to believers and non-believers as long as they were absolute pacifists, did Ponsonby agree not only to sponsor the movement but to work actively on its behalf.[113] He wrote to Sheppard in July 1936 that after his own experience of 'almost continuous failure' it was a pleasure to find himself working alongside a personality with so much 'drive, tact and persistence', but he remained uncomfortable with his presence at mass meetings that more closely resembled rallies for religious revival.[114] Ponsonby's decision to join Sheppard had more to do with his alienation from the Labour Party as it moved in the autumn of 1936 to endorse the idea of League military action and rearmament against the fascist threat. 'Go Jingo if you like,' he wrote in his diary after reading the speeches at the annual conference in Edinburgh, 'and swallow all you are told, split the party and wave the flag.'[115] Whatever the drawbacks of Sheppard's simple Christian view of war, the initial success of the Peace Pledge Union reflected the realization among the prominent figures and mass supporters of complete pacifism that the gulf separating the two main parties in the anti-war movement had to be made publicly clear as the international crisis deepened.

The peace movement became irretrievably split into two camps in 1936, those for whom violence was always unacceptable, and those for whom violence could be accepted if the threat to peace could not be resolved any other way. The immediate effect of the schism was to weaken the broad anti-war movement inherited from the 1920s and to create among both flocks of the faithful declining confidence in the power of popular opinion to hold back the tide of war and rearmament. The two parties were divided as sharply as Protestant from Catholic had been four centuries earlier. 'Ultimately,' wrote Kingsley Martin in 1938, 'it is a clash between two religions. In a crisis people find out what they are.'[116] Like religious zealots the two sides sniffed out the unorthodox and hunted for witches. The president of a League of Nations Union branch in Sussex complained to Lord Cecil that his members were so divided on partisan lines that it was possible to describe them either as 'warmongers' or as an 'association of conscientious objectors' at one and the same time.[117] A Bradford peace worker, Margery South, complained to Ponsonby about the 'constant "heresy" hunting' among peace groups and the regular denunciations: 'He (or she) is not <u>really</u> a pacifist you know.'[118] The conflict was in large measure a conflict of faiths, which is why the divisions became increasingly bitter. Both sides assumed that the stakes were nothing less than the survival of civilization and their version of the truth was the surer path to salvation. 'The thing is all so big and the period so critical,' wrote Sheppard to Ponsonby over the difficulty of keeping his supporters in step with doctrine.[119] Relations between the League of Nations Union and the Peace Pledge Union reached an open breach by 1937. When Noel-Baker found himself recruited to speak alongside Sheppard at a rally in Trafalgar Square in May 1937 he told Cecil that he could not share the same platform with a man he had come to regard as 'almost actively wicked'. Cecil told him to persevere if he could, 'but to preach sound doctrine with lots of blood and battle'.[120]

The problems confronting the anti-war movement in the mid-1930s were real enough. The failure to prevent Japanese aggression or to influence the abortive disarmament talks was followed by the Italian–Ethiopian war from October 1935, which provoked arguments over sanctions or collective military action to restrain Italian aggression and then, from July 1936, by the divided reaction to the Spanish Civil War. The anti-war and pacifist lobbies achieved almost nothing in the face of the crises and many of the prescriptions for keeping the peace, from the power of prayer to an internationalized military air force, appear today either whimsical or impractical, as they did at the time to many of those who favoured peace. Arguments over means and the lack of any clear achievement in turn provoked demoralization and dismay on all sides. 'We are down in the trough,' complained Gilbert Murray to Cecil in September 1936. 'Pacifists leaving us on the one side, and moderates . . . on the other.'[121] In July that year Norman Angell, a prominent Union supporter and one of the country's best known peace campaigners, wrote that it was now a commonplace 'that disagreement as to the best means of achieving peace was never more profound, nor the confusion of policies and counsels more bewildering'.[122] Kingsley Martin wrote to the social historian J. L. Hammond in August 1936 that as far as he could see the failure of the League had created a hopeless situation: 'There is now no solution of any kind. I can think of no "constructive" policy at the moment which it is not easy to ridicule.'[123]

The demoralization had an infectious effect on the rank and file of the peace movement. The established organizations continued to lose adherents and with them the money necessary to keep the organizations in being. The League of Nations Union declined from a peak of almost 400,000 in 1931 to around 264,000 by 1938. The No More War Movement faced a critical turning point in late 1936 with arguments over help for the Spanish republican cause, though numbers and funds had been in decline for several years. In 1937 it was decided to wind up the affairs of the organization and merge with the Peace Pledge Union, but although the decision was approved by an overwhelming majority of the members (980 to 43 in favour) the merger was delayed and the movement withered. The fraction that insisted on sustaining independence won agreement for a residual group of No More War Movement trustees against the day when there might return 'a rapid growth of Pacifist conviction'.[124] The scale of popular anti-war or pacifist sentiment by the mid-1930s is difficult to gauge with any precision, but there was an evident breach between what the wider public wanted and what the existing leadership of the peace movement could deliver. The fractious doctrinal arguments were alienating for the broad pacifist constituency that wrestled with the same issues as their leaders. Margery South, who kept up a regular correspondence with Arthur Ponsonby from 1936, when she joined the peace movement, confessed to 'some nasty shocks' when she came to confront the divided nature of the cause. 'You must remember that I speak to simple people,' she told Ponsonby, 'whose minds cannot hold much at the same time. If they are to be clear in their pacifism – the pacifism that is preached to them must be simple and unambiguous.'[125] She found the influence of Huxley's contemplative pacifism fine for the 'bourgeois sentimentalist', but the group exercises recommended to build the pacifist personality she found 'absurd' – community singing for eleven minutes, a brief period of manual work (knitting for women, spinning for men), a thirty-minute silence during which 'thoughts relevant to pacifism to be written on a piece of paper', and folk-dancing to encourage 'harmony of mind'. 'I do feel', she concluded, 'it is the gap between the leaders of the movement and the ordinary person that is at the root of much of our lack of progress.'[126]

Increasingly in the mid-1930s pacifists began to develop their own local organizations by creating peace councils made up of delegates from trade unions, local women's groups, the political parties and local societies. Although loosely attached to the National Peace Council, they relied on local initiative and deliberately distanced themselves from the national organizations. Murray complained to Cecil in October 1936 about the burgeoning local movement, which he blamed on communist agitation. 'They cannot really do effectively', he continued, 'the work that we want done.' He cited a report of an Oxford Peace Council meeting – 'a futile crowd of people ... no support, no money, no ideas of how to run the thing, and no treasurer'.[127] Nevertheless the peace council movement grew rapidly during 1936 and 1937. In January 1936 there were five affiliated to the National Peace Council, by June there were seventeen and by the end of the year sixty-five, spread throughout every region of the country.[128] Some were certainly led by communists – one example was the Cambridge Anti-War Council (whose secretary was the Marxist economist Maurice Dobb), which was set up to provide local workers with an alternative anti-war movement to the conventional peace organizations dominated by university progressives.[129] But most local peace councils involved a broad spectrum of enthusiasts for peace who were frustrated by the failure of the peace movement nationally, people such as Margery South, who worked, she claimed, among 'thousands of pacifists who have been left helpless and leaderless'.[130]

The Peace Pledge Union was no more immune from the growing crisis of the peace movement than the other organizations. After a brief honeymoon following the decision to found a formal organization in May 1936, the movement was plagued with difficulties. The Heard–Huxley axis distorted the aims of the Union and exposed it to the accusation that it was run by cranks. 'The complications', Sheppard told Ponsonby in August 1936, 'of keeping Gerald, Aldous and others in step are at times more difficult than I can say!'[131] More problematic was the link between Gerald Heard and the American pacifist and non-resister Richard Gregg, whose ideas on the psychological transformation of the individual through self-disciplined pacifist training matched Heard's own fantastic views about altering human nature by pacifist mind exercises. Gregg wrote to Sheppard in July full of enthusiasm for the Peace Pledge Union ('We are on the winning side!') and faith in the power of love to triumph eventually over militarism and war. Heard persuaded Sheppard to publish a pamphlet by Gregg on 'Training for Peace: A Programme for Peace Workers', with an introduction by Huxley, but the effect was to create a schism almost immediately in the movement.[132] When the pamphlet was distributed 'non-resistance' was stated to be 'definitely' the new policy of the

Union, but other sponsors, Ponsonby among them, strongly disapproved of the attempt to hijack the Sheppard movement and in early January 1937 the organizing secretary of the Union, Margery Rayne, abruptly resigned. Her letter of resignation described a divided and weakly led movement 'in grave danger of betraying the whole cause of pacifism', but a second letter from Sheppard's closest collaborator, General Frank Crozier, explained that 'Greggism' had been the main issue.[133] In February a meeting of the sponsors' committee finally ended the schism, established an executive committee empowered to meet weekly and limited Sheppard's ill-defined and unsupervised authority.[134]

The damage done by the schism was difficult to repair, though it was helped by the sudden defection of Gerald Heard and Aldous Huxley, both of whom left for the United States where they hoped for greater opportunities to find spiritual fulfilment. Heard resigned his sponsorship in November 1936; almost a year later, in October 1937, he wrote to Sheppard from his new home in North Carolina that he had abandoned the peace movement because he had come to realize, together with Huxley, that he could do nothing for peace or for any form of goodness, 'until I am far better myself'. The Peace Pledge Union was hopeless without 'training', he continued, and concluded: 'what is needed is not merely a political protest but another way of living'.[135] He and Huxley sailed to the United States on 7 April 1937. Heard told Julian Huxley a few weeks before that 'old Europe is finished'.[136] Aldous Huxley too had become disillusioned with the peace movement. In September 1936 he had told Sheppard that his union faced 'sterility' unless it could be used as the core of an experiment in pacifist communal life, rather than an ineffective political lobby.[137] His plans to leave for the United States were first made in October 1936, where he intended to stay for perhaps six or nine months to complete 'a philisophico-psychologico-sociological book' on the many ways in which the current problems of the world needed to be tackled, but in the end he stayed as a permanent exile from Europe.[138] The book *Ends and Means* was published in November 1937. In the section on war Huxley explained its appeal as a contrast with the 'apparent pointlessness of modern life in time of peace'. This was due, he thought,

... to the fact that, in the Western world at least, the prevailing cosmology is what Mr Gerald Heard has called the 'mecanomorphic' cosmology of modern science. The universe is regarded as a great machine pointlessly grinding its way towards ultimate stagnation and death; men are tiny off-shoots of the universal machine, running down to their own private death.[139]

Huxley suggested that the key to a pacific world lay in the development of a new cosmology based on an ethic of universal goodness. Margery South wrote to Ponsonby earlier in 1937 that in her view Huxley was 'as mad as anyone'.[140]

The emigration of Heard and Huxley stabilized the movement only briefly. In October General Frank Crozier, one of the founders of the Sheppard movement, died suddenly. Then on the morning of 31 October Dick Sheppard was found dead at his desk in St Paul's, halfway through writing a letter. His body lay in state in St Martin-in-the-Fields and for more than two days people filed past. His funeral procession to St Paul's Cathedral was flanked by huge crowds. Vera Brittain received the news on a visit to the United States. In her autobiography she recalled her immediate feeling that Sheppard represented 'England's only powerful challenge to the impulse of death in society', an echo of the volume she had introduced for Storm Jameson.[141] The Peace Pledge Union continued its work but, unwilling to be involved in politics and uncompromisingly absolute in its pacifism, it became a marginal movement in the run down to war. The union journal *Peace News* sold 20,000 regularly (*Headway* still sold an average of 60,000). Membership did not grow far beyond the initial 120,000 achieved in 1937, though there was a considerable turnover as many people left or joined the movement. As the crisis with Germany worsened, the Peace Pledge Union's commitment to dialogue, even with dictators, brought unwarranted accusations of sympathy for fascism. It remained, nonetheless, the main forum for absolute pacifism through to the wartime years and beyond.[142]

The League of Nations Union failed to stifle the rise of its uncompromising rival. The temporary success of the Peace Ballot also failed to mask the faltering fortunes of a movement whose success relied on the international achievements of the League itself. A set of Union notes for speakers sent out in July 1936 admitted that the League

A 'Peace Bus' organized by the Peace Pledge Union at the end of its long journey from Carlisle to London. The Union had an estimated 1,150 branches countrywide by the outbreak of war in 1939, and is still in existence today.

system had 'suffered a severe defeat', though it blamed not the system but the unwillingness of those who were bound by the Covenant to find the will to maintain it, which was at best a fine distinction.[143] When a BBC producer suggested to Noel-Baker in June 1936 a series of programmes on the League of Nations she thought it should be done sooner rather than later: 'Perhaps it is pessimism too, for I feel that after next summer it may not be possible to discuss a future of the League.'[144] The Union's leaders knew that they faced what Lord Lytton, its vice-chairman, called 'a dark moment' in the League's history, 'when the word peace is on every tongue, but fear of war is in every heart'.[145] During the summer of 1936 Cecil decided on one more major gesture to boost his movement's flagging fortunes and revive the idea that public opinion, expressed with sufficient clarity and vigour, might yet restore faith in collective security and avert war. The gesture he chose was to prove disastrous for the future of the organization. Early in 1936 he was approached by Lt. Commander Edgar Young, a Union officer, on behalf of a group of French pacifists who wanted to create an international peace movement, representing public opinion worldwide, to give popular backing to the League. They had been impressed by the success of the Peace Ballot and hoped to develop a wider international plebiscite on peace. The proposed Rassemblement universel pour la Paix excited Cecil at once and he wrote to Noel-Baker asking him to take on the task of setting it up as 'your first object'.[146] Edgar Young joined Noel-Baker in establishing a loose organization to supervise British participation in a founding Congress at the Brussels Palais du Centenaire across the weekend of 3–6 September 1936.[147]

The Congress was prepared with fanfares of publicity and attracted a large number of delegates. Out of the 4,000 who were present 600 came from Britain, sent by more than 200 British peace societies. Cecil wrote to Sheppard asking him to pool their differences sufficiently to at least make an appearance but Sheppard refused. Cecil sent him a harshly worded rebuke in which he accused him of splitting the peace movement and provoking armaments and war. 'Believe me,' he added, 'there is no chance that your policy will be adopted', but there was every chance of 'a desolating war' and 'centuries of chaos such as followed the downfall of the Roman Empire'.[148] Aldous Huxley was also invited, and was inclined to accept until Sheppard warned him that there would be no platform for true pacifism. Instead Sheppard decided to hold a pacifist public meeting in Brussels the same weekend to rally support for the absolute pacifist case.[149] The Congress was by any standard a success. It was organized almost as a military operation. Delegates were asked to book in advance a hotel in one of four categories, popular, bourgeois, comfortable or de luxe (a sharp reminder of the broad social mix in the anti-war movement). The richer guests ate as they pleased in the hotel restaurant; the others had to present dinner vouchers at a more spartan communal refectory. The newsagent chain W. H. Smith undertook to get the day's newspapers to delegates by 10.30 the same day. Special trains left Liverpool Street station for Harwich where the delegates boarded the SS *Malines* for Zeebrugge, and thence to Brussels, a journey time of over nine hours. Everyone had to display a coloured badge – the Executive

Committee, which included Cecil and Noel-Baker, sported white, the platform guests pink, delegates green, guests lilac, and so on. Delegates who could speak several languages wore distinctive ribbons, French white, English pink, German green.[150] This brightly tagged assembly gathered on 3 September to hear the opening address by the joint presidents of the Congress, Lord Cecil and the French air minister, Pierre Cot.

Cecil argued that the forces making for war were numerous and could act quickly and with vigour; but the forces making for peace 'are badly organised and of practically little effect'. Union was necessary, he continued, to give strength to the forces of peace as it had done for the forces of war. The delegations broke up into separate discussion groups organized according to function – churches, trade unions, psychologists, doctors etc. – and reconvened in the evening to approve a four-point statement of principles: respect for treaties, reduction and limitation of armaments, collective security for mutual assistance against aggression, and remedying international conditions that might lead to war.[151] The Congress broke up the following day after church services, a sports display and a coach tour of Brussels. Cecil returned charged up by the success of the assembly, and determined to get the League of Nations Union to work closely with a British National Committee of what became known in English as the International Peace Campaign. The proposal for close collaboration was put to the Executive Committee of the Union on 15 October, where it was strongly supported. The two organizations were linked not only by the personal participation of Lord Cecil, as president of both, but the work of Noel-Baker and others who acted for the Union on the British National Committee.[152]

The marriage of the two movements immediately provoked protest. The chairman, Gilbert Murray, warned Cecil that the Union was already in financial difficulties and could not afford to pay the £2,000 subsidy promised to the new campaign.[153] Other critics suspected that the whole project was a front for international communism. 'The scheme under discussion', wrote one objector, 'provides for a close if indirect connection between the L.N.U. and the Komintern' (Cecil scribbled '!!!' in the margin).[154] Cecil himself had been alive to this possibility from the start. Early in 1936 he wrote to assure the Archbishop of Canterbury that after searching enquiries he had found no evidence that the proposal was communist inspired, although he never denied that there was some communist participation, as befitted a movement publicly committed to the cause of peace.[155] The anxiety about communist association was fed by the current effort of the Comintern to encourage co-operation with 'bourgeois' elements in popular fronts or peace fronts, but Cecil seems to have been deaf or blind to this development. Why Cecil clung so firmly to the International Peace Campaign in the light of these objections and his own hostility to the extreme left is not easy to explain. The excitement of a genuinely international Congress no doubt recalled the euphoric atmosphere that surrounded the establishment of the League; Cecil was at home on the international stage and perhaps flattered after years of fruitless effort by the idea of becoming briefly again a figure of international standing. His claim that only popular international collaboration, as he put it, could now save 'the peace of the World', though increasingly implausible, was a reminder of the depth of his own fears for the future. His private explanation was simply that the international campaign was the last chance to save the national organization: 'I am quite certain', he wrote to Murray in October 1936, 'that if we are to prevent the Union of [sic] dying of inanition . . . we have got to get a fresh spirit into it.'[156]

Instead, the partnership with the International Campaign, loosely defined as it was, accelerated the Union's decline. The permanent members of staff of the League of Nations Union, led by the movement's general secretary, Maxwell Garnett, were hostile to collaboration with the new organization and resented the sackings and cut in pay they had been forced to take in 1936 while the Union subsidized six new members of staff for the International Campaign.[157] Cecil refused to accept that the staff could dictate policy, and pressed for an even closer marriage of the two bodies. In October 1937 he persuaded the executive to make the National Committee of the International Peace Campaign a sub-section of the Union, with office space and funds provided at Union expense, but free to pursue its own course.[158] Relations between Cecil, Murray and the Union administration deteriorated throughout 1937. In December that year at the annual Christmas party the staff staged a derogatory revue which savagely lampooned Cecil, Murray and the International Peace Campaign. Cecil wanted the culprits dismissed at once and blamed the crisis not on his continued enthusiasm for the international organization, which was its principal cause, but on the negative attitude of the Union: 'the whole tone of the Council, the Executive and most of the meetings which I have attended is in minor key', he told Murray.[159] He succeeded in sending Garnett for six months' 'sick leave' and sacking the author of the lampoon, but the result was to make the staff yet more demoralized and to increase criticism of the cuckoo in the Union nest. 'Unhappily,' concluded Cecil in a letter to Murray setting out conditions for Garnett's leave-of-absence, 'a controversy between the L.N.U. and the I.P.C. has done immense harm in weakening the forces of peace'.[160] He told Adelaide Livingstone, who was now vice-chairman of the National Committee of the new organization, that he would like to emigrate if he could 'to some distant part of the world where neither the I.P.C. nor L.N.U. can get at me!'[161]

The main criticism levelled at Cecil's new campaign was the link with politics, and the lingering suspicion that Cecil had been duped by a communist conspiracy. The effect on support for the League of Nations Union, many of whose members were drawn from a conservative social milieu, was to accelerate the exodus already evident in 1936. 'We are losing members', wrote the secretary of a Surrey branch to Cecil in early 1938, 'and not getting the members we ought to get.' The problem, she suggested, was Cecil and the new campaign. The public was no longer convinced by the argument for collective security highlighted in the principles stated at Brussels; they approved of the League 'but won't have anything to do with the Union'.[162] Noel-Baker attended a Union General Council meeting in October 1937 but found the large hall occupied by a sparse 200 people; 'it was a rather gloomy occasion', he told Walter Layton.[163] Nor was the International Peace Campaign as buoyant as Cecil believed. At the first annual Congress, held at University College, London from 22 to 24 October 1937, the opening address was titled 'Need We Be So Unobtrusive?' The lack of a clear programme of political activity was marked. The delegates were sent away with a new plan of work, but it consisted simply of replicating what the Union had been doing for almost twenty years: 'To issue an immediate call to action, to provide leaflets and posters, to promote national publicity, and to reinforce and encourage activities in the localities'.[164] A few months earlier the chair of the Literature Committee, William Arnold-Forster, had tried to interest Cecil in the idea of making the campaign more populist by recruiting well-known media stars – the singers Paul Robeson and Gracie Fields were on his list – but Cecil refused the idea of 'stunts'.[165] Neither wing of the peace movement loyal to the League was able to survive the crisis in credibility opened up in 1936. The International Peace Campaign for all its high ambitions was no more able to restore belief in the League as an instrument to avert war than the Union had been before it.

The failure of the anti-war movement was perhaps the greatest disappointment of the inter-war years. To great numbers of British people it seemed self-evident that peace and civilization were inextricably entwined and that only peace could keep at a distance the threatened Dark Age. No other movement could count on popular mass support on such a scale. The National Declaration relied on half a million volunteers and secured the votes of almost 12 million people thanks to their enthusiasm and industry. The publications distributed by the peace movement had print runs of hundreds of thousands. The National Declaration produced a total of 14 million documents for distribution, including half a million booklets explaining the purpose of the ballot.[166] The League of Nations Union distributed 2 million leaflets and pamphlets a year. The National Peace Council published or disseminated pamphlets in equally inflated numbers. In 1933 some 70,000 copies of Winifred Holtby's 'The Cloud of Fear' were sent out; four publications in the first months of 1938 had a total print run of 244,000.[167] The sheer scale of the movement seemed to justify the confidence of its leaders that the power of public opinion would be sufficient to force governments to abandon war and rid the world of weapons. In reality the opposite happened. The peak of the peace movement in 1935, with the National Declaration and the Peace Pledge, coincided with universal rearmament in Europe and the collapse of any pretence of collective security.

There are many explanations for this limited achievement. The most obvious was the divided nature of the peace cause. The difference between those who were against war except as an instrument of collective international restraint and those who rejected all forms of violence was not a mere doctrinal squabble. Supporters of the League found themselves by the mid-1930s forced to argue the case for military intervention. An effort was made to mask this by talk of an international police force or a fleet of internationally controlled bombers which would deter all aggression, but League supporters were willy-nilly associated with war as much as with peace. The fact that the League in the end neither made war nor kept the peace made the case all the harder to sustain and created deep fissures both between and within the different peace organizations. Collective security was by 1936 a policy without conviction. When Cecil asked Cosmo Lang to sign yet another letter titled 'Save the League' late in November that year, Lang chided him for trying to put responsibilities on the League 'which it is at present scarcely capable of fulfilling'.[168] For the absolute pacifists, whose numbers grew the greater the threat of war, the problem was to convince any broad constituency that the rejection of violence did not invite an even greater danger. The emphasis among the absolute pacifists on appealing to conscience or hoping for a change in human nature, whatever the virtues of the argument, seemed inappropriate to the age. Vera Brittain's husband, George Catlin, did not agree with her decision to rely on the eventual triumph of moral good sense over practicalities because in his view nothing useful could be achieved in 'measurable time'.[169] Even among those Christians who appealed to the teachings of Christ there was no agreement on the limits of that argument if a sufficient danger made a just war necessary.

A second problem was access to real political influence. The peace movement was in general deliberately non-partisan, and did win support across the social and political spectrum, often in unexpected places. To be anti-war was not to be associated with extremism. Although much of the absolute pacifist movement was politically left of centre, the broader anti-war constituency had a solid middle-class foundation as well. Indeed, most politicians in Britain in the 1920s and 1930s if asked if they were against war would have answered 'yes', whatever their party. The difficulty lay in translating the mass popular opinion against war into anything that might affect government policy, not least because there survived in Britain an extensive militarist culture and a powerful military lobby whose links with government were inevitably both closer and firmer.[170] The limits of the pacifist cause are evident in Cecil's long correspondence with Ramsay MacDonald and Stanley Baldwin, who both largely ignored his recommendations unless they endorsed what the government already knew it wanted. After a peace deputation led by Lord Cecil in May 1936 to see Baldwin and the Foreign Secretary, Anthony Eden, Noel-Baker wrote at the end of his notes on the meeting that their responses were all apologies and alibis: 'If these two men are to save civilisation, Heaven help us!'[171] Baldwin's successor, Neville Chamberlain, was a more obvious enthusiast for peace but when he was invited to become a vice-president of the League of Nations Union in July 1937, shortly after securing the premiership, he agreed to do so only if the Union abandoned its habit of criticizing the government. Cecil's reply was sufficiently reassuring to add Chamberlain's name to the list, but a few months later the prime minister again wrote to the Union asking it to honour its pledge not to interfere in politics.[172] Cecil told Murray that no prime minister was going to dictate Union policy, but the reverse was also true. The many peace movements had a negligible effect on British foreign policy and military preparations.

No doubt part of the reason for the lack of political influence lay with the nature of the anti-war movements themselves. Many of the proposals endlessly debated and elaborated were fanciful or impractical. Resolutions were passed continually, protest letters sent, subcommittees set up, peace delegations organized. It is easy to blame the peace movement for being little more than a talking shop – at times an arcade of shops – but there were clear limits to action. It is more difficult not to judge a great many of the ideas canvassed as wishful thinking, from Richard Gregg's plans for pacifist physical training to the argument of Norman Angell, suggested to the League of Nations Union in 1936, for an 'Alliance for defence' of world states with a 'general staff of the whole' for the collective use of violence or to Cosmo Lang's hopes for the power 'of prayer and thought'.[173] On the fringes were persistent ideas for world government, canvassed most famously by the novelist H. G. Wells, who for more than twenty years tried to sell his idea of a world society to anyone who would listen. Although an early champion of a League of Nations, he was disappointed by the survival of the nation-state system which he blamed for the ever-present danger of war. In the late 1920s he launched what he called 'The Open Conspiracy' to secure converts to his idea of a simple commitment to a common humanity and to resist 'militant and competitive militarism and nationalism'. In August 1939, on the eve of war, he published *The Fate of Homo Sapiens*, in which he finally admitted that his utopian vision of a 'creative world peace' was probably unattainable. His final work, *Mind at the End of its Tether*, reflected Wells's hopeless belief that the battle for a world society was lost and with it any chance of saving the species.[174]

Wells was widely regarded as a maverick, but his vision of a 'world government' appeared in numerous contexts in the 1930s. The future Labour Home Secretary, Herbert Morrison, addressing the Geneva Institute of International Relations in August 1936, told his listeners that it was time to 'build up a World Commonwealth' and a system of 'World Government' or suffer the collapse of civilization.[175] The yearning for some kind of intellectual or practical remedy that would banish the menace of violence is easy to understand. Unrealistic, even utopian, as much of the thinking undoubtedly was, it was difficult for the post-war population to imagine that the Great War had changed nothing either in human nature or in human expectations, even if the scientific evidence, such as it was, suggested otherwise. The effort to 'challenge death' was nevertheless a failure. While millions were invited to identify with the rational pursuit of peace and to understand the futility of war, they did so as an act of faith, not as a political certainty. Failure signalled not a lack of belief but an absence of power. In June 1940 Storm Jameson, who had gathered together the anti-war dinner party at the Wellington Club in 1934, wrote full of pessimism to Liddell Hart about her blighted hopes for peace: 'This moment must have happened again and again in civilisation – the moment when the rigidifying process had advanced so far that the alert minds could not move against it, and the enemy broke in. I suppose we still have a chance to escape, but it must be a very poor one.'[176]

7

Utopian Politics: Cure or Disease?

What you say about creed wars is most suggestive, and I daresay you may be right; but I shall be surprised if it affects the English-speaking world very much. The people of English race and culture never go very far in the direction of fanaticism. They talk as if they are going to, but always draw up at the edge of the precipice.

John Strachey to Beatrice Webb, December 1926[1]

Pacifism, religion and world government were not the only pathways away from the grim realities of crisis in the inter-war years. For millions of Europeans there were new political movements which offered the alluring prospect of escape into the collective energy of the mass and the promise of national or social rebirth that went with it. The ideological forces unleashed by the new movements in the end devoured millions of those who followed them. The orgy of collective political and racial violence set in motion in the 1930s and 1940s accounted for perhaps as many as 20 million European civilian dead from Spain to the eastern Soviet Union. Britain remained largely immune from the political bloodletting beyond a handful of British communist victims in the Soviet terror of the mid-1930s and those who died fighting in the Spanish Civil War. There were no violent 'creed wars' to puncture Britain's continued commitment to a form of parliamentary democracy that flourished almost nowhere in Europe by 1940.

The very term 'creed wars' has an oddly archaic ring to it. The term was commonly understood in the 1920s as an echo of a distant history.

Bertrand Russell lectured on 'The Danger of Creed Wars' to the Fabian Society in 1926; he warned that economic and political 'creed wars' fought over irrational dogma, as the great religious conflicts of the past had been, could become the characteristic feature of the modern age.[2] The political scientist Harold Laski, reviewing Arthur Koestler's *Spanish Testament* in the more dangerous 1930s, painted a lurid picture of 'creed wars' even deadlier than the religious wars of the sixteenth century. The modern ideological conflicts, Laski continued, represented nothing less than 'a struggle between life and death'.[3] This was a contest whose roots were understood to be European rather than British. Soviet communism, Italian fascism and German National Socialism were its principal instigators, and the fear was widespread in Britain in the 1920s and 1930s that British society, in an age of economic crisis and political uncertainty, would find it difficult to remain immune from the seductive and apparently remorseless spread of a violent, authoritarian, ideologically driven politics. These were movements that overflowed national boundaries, observed G. D. H. Cole in an assessment of Mussolini's fascist revolution written in the late 1920s; they preached a gospel, Cole continued, with the power to move any population 'to love and hate, anger and enthusiasm'.[4] An assessment of the current political situation in Britain sent to Cole in 1936 explained the increase in support for British communism and fascism as 'developments and reactions to the futility of (nominally) democratic Governments' and predicted that support was likely to swell with the growing public sense of 'danger and insecurity'.[5] Stanley Baldwin, in a national radio broadcast on 'National Freedom' in March 1934, took the surprising step of admitting that 'a dictator can do much . . . in power he may do everything' – though at the cost of snuffing out conventional freedom and courting civil war. Baldwin, a politician for whom the cloak of dictatorship would have been absurdly ill fitting, urged his listeners to recognize that to adopt dictatorship, fascist or communist, would be 'an act of surrender, of throwing in our hands, a confession that we were unable to govern ourselves'.[6]

Fear of mass extremism turned out to be misplaced, though it was a real enough fear in the context of the collapse of parliamentary government across Europe in the 1930s. There was no mass movement on the right or the left to match the growth of political radicalism in France or Republican Spain, the only other major European democracies left after the Hitler regime came to power in 1933. The British Communist Party never had more than 12,000 members at the peak in the 1920s. By August 1930, when the slump had provoked a mass communist movement in Germany, British membership had dwindled to its lowest point of 2,350. By 1936 this had risen to 11,000, and by 1939 reached around 18,000, against a Labour Party membership of 400,000. The party had a high turnover of members, so that more people had some experience of communist activity than the membership figures on their own would suggest. Most members were concentrated in London and Scotland: some 55 per cent of all members in 1922, 58.7 per cent in 1938. There was only one communist member of parliament in the 1920s, none between 1929 and 1935 and just one again following the election that year in West Fife of Willie Gallacher, one of the founders of the British Communist Party and its future chairman.[7]

The fortunes of British fascism were just as dismal. The only movement of any size was Oswald Mosley's British Union of Fascists, founded in October 1932 following the complete failure of Mosley's 'New Party' in the 1931 elections. The Union of Fascists failed to win a single parliamentary seat, and support peaked as early as 1934, when membership has been estimated at anywhere between 20,000 and 40,000, falling dramatically to less than 5,000 the following year after a violent rally at London's Olympia stadium and slowly recovering to reach 22,500 by the beginning of the war, of whom only an estimated 8,000 were active.[8] In 1939 the movement was proscribed and in 1940 Mosley was interned. For much of its life the Union fought, often literally, against other small fascist or semi-fascist organizations. Public hostility was widespread and often violent. When John Beckett, the former Independent Labour Party MP for Gateshead and a Mosley propagandist, returned to the North East he was faced with an angry crowd of 3,000 in Gateshead and 5,000 in Newcastle.[9] The mass rally of British fascists at Olympia in June 1934 alarmed public opinion because of the disorder it provoked; a fascist march planned through the East End of London on 4 October 1936 prompted a crowd of perhaps as many as 250,000 anti-fascists and forced Mosley's 7,000 blackshirts to abandon the procession. The threat of Mosley's movement led directly to the Public Order Act of 1936 which strengthened the hand of the police in dealing with political extremism, right and left, and outlawed political uniforms, the essential plumage for right-wing extremism. Lord Trenchard, Metropolitan Police Commissioner, had earlier wanted to ban the fascist movement altogether, but the government believed that it posed an insufficiently serious threat. Like British communism, it remained a noisy fringe movement, divided against itself and constantly monitored by a watchful security service and police force.[10]

It is well known that in both cases there were wider circles of sympathizers and potential voters – the 'fellow-travellers' – and a host of smaller, ephemeral groups who mouthed some version of Marxism or fascism, but throughout the 1930s electoral allegiance continued to be given to the three main political parties under the Conservative-dominated National Government set up in 1931 by the Labour prime minister Ramsay MacDonald to cope with the economic crisis. The failure of utopian politics has been attributed to a number of factors, but the absence, even at the height of the slump, of a serious collapse of the economic system together with the sustained rise in real wages in the 1930s for those with jobs, conditions of relative external and internal stability and a powerful and entrenched social elite all clearly played a part in sustaining the conventional parliamentary system.[11] So too, perhaps, did the existence of a nominally National Government which masked the reality of surviving political and class differences and undermined the appeal of extremism. These differences were only exposed clearly when competitive party politics was finally restored in the summer of 1945.

It is possible, nevertheless, to take such arguments too far. The focus on the modest electoral performance of the extremist parties also masks the extent to which 'creed wars' became part of a much broader sphere of public discourse. Indeed, it is striking that for all the political feebleness of communism and fascism as mass political parties, the public arena in Britain was swamped during the 1930s with a remarkable level of engagement with both ideologies. A book on *Soviet Democracy* published in 1937, just after the publication of the new 'Stalin' Constitution, sold 48,000 copies; a Penguin Special

The playwright George Bernard Shaw opening an exhibition of Soviet photography organized by the Society for Cultural Relations with the USSR at the Camera Club in London on 5 December 1930. Shaw had visited the Soviet Union and was an enthusiast for Stalin.

published in January 1939 by Emily Lorimer, an Asian philologist and journalist, on *What Hitler Wants* sold 150,000 copies.[12] By the end of 1938, 89,285 copies of the translated and abridged version of *Mein Kampf* had been sold, and it is difficult to believe that they were only bought by enthusiastic British fascists.[13] The public displayed a sustained appetite for information about the European political extremes and debated the issues surrounding them in a cultural and organizational milieu often quite independent of the party political system or party allegiance.

This wider involvement with political extremism was intimately linked with the debates on the future of civilization. Interest in utopian politics or 'creed wars' can be regarded as a metaphorical appropriation of what was, on mainland Europe, both real and bloody. The development of the Hitler regime and of Stalin's Soviet Union was interpreted in terms of British anxieties about the political and economic future, setting fears of a new barbarism against hopes for a rejuvenated civilization, right or left. Historians have tended to regard this public culture surrounding fascism and communism as manifestations of fellow-travelling, but much of it was not politically committed or partisan, and indeed cannot be properly understood if it is seen through a purely party-political prism. The widespread preoccupation with political radicalism can be understood more readily as an extension of the debates about the dead end of war, slump or demographic crisis into which civilization threatened to run by the 1930s. It was also an expression of uncertainty about the survivability of the parliamentary political system in a Europe rapidly descending into authoritarian politics. It was, in other words, a means of projecting anxieties about the prospects for British society and political institutions onto civil and political conflicts abroad. A minority only of those who interested themselves in fascism, Soviet communism, the Spanish Civil War, pacifism and disarmament were card-carrying Marxists or fascists: the institutional and cultural base of these creed wars by proxy was sustained in the main by individuals who had little sympathy for violent authoritarianism and deeply feared its arrival. There seemed nevertheless a choice to be made. Much of the public debate (and the private fears) surrounding Hitler and National Socialism regarded the movement as barbarous and its ambitions as a profound threat to a British conception of civilization. On the other hand, the Soviet experiment was, for all the reservations expressed about its violence and illiberalism, more generously regarded as a civilization of the future, measured not just against fascism, but against the decayed state of contemporary capitalism.

There has been much debate about the British perception of Hitler and Hitlerism in the 1930s. That he won admirers beyond the fascist faithful is not in dispute. Some were drawn from the same wartime milieu on the Western Front which Hitler had inhabited. Two famous veterans of the Great War, the novelists Henry Williamson and Wyndham Lewis, were attracted by what they saw as Hitler's simple trench truths about the damaged post-war world. Williamson liked to imagine that his unit had fought directly opposite Hitler's on the Western Front. He identified with Hitler's rejection of the self-satisfied bourgeois world he had returned to after the war and admired his capacity to act, his raw élan and his power of seeing. His enthusiasm for Hitler seems to have reflected his own sense of disillusionment and isolation in post-war English society.[14] Wyndham Lewis published the first British biographical study of Hitler in 1931. In an age before cover designers could be certain that the Hitler symbol would sell copies, Chatto & Windus embellished the book's plain cover with a single small swastika (though it was still sufficiently unfamiliar for the arms of the swastika on the spine to point the wrong way). Lewis's Hitler is very similar – a sentimental front-fighter with an almost mystical power over those around him and, above all, 'a man of action' too.[15] Like Williamson, Lewis exhibits an evident desire to identify with Hitler's iconoclasm and to shock conventional opinion. There were also sympathetic conservatives prepared to argue that the horror stories surrounding the new Reich were overdone. Arnold Toynbee, for example, unduly influenced by his German academic correspondents that a decent Germany still survived beneath Hitler's revolution, visited the German leader in February 1936 to discuss issues of foreign policy. Toynbee sent his impressions in a memorandum for Anthony Eden, the recently appointed Foreign Secretary. Aside from recording Hitler's promise to send six divisions and warships to help the British hold on to Singapore ('Singapore would be the eastern frontier of Europe,' Hitler told him), he relayed Hitler's stock argument that he was a man of peace who respected the British Empire and had no designs on the Soviet Union. Toynbee judged him 'sincere'.[16] Toynbee was certainly not alone among a string of distinguished British guests to be seduced by Hitler's apparent reasonableness.[17]

It is important to recognize that these were exceptions. Williamson complained in a letter to a friend that approving comments about Hitler in the preface of his latest book had resulted in sales of less than 1,000 copies and over 100 abusive letters.[18] When Wyndham Lewis's *Hitler* was displayed in Zwemmer's Charing Cross Road bookshop in the weeks after Hitler's appointment as chancellor in January 1933, the shop window had to be cleaned of spittle twice a day.[19] From the very first moments of the Third Reich, Hitler and his movement were pilloried in much of the literature, lectures and public forums in Britain as the new barbarism which threatened the very survival of civilization. National Socialism was widely regarded as a reversion to a bygone age, sometimes pre-Christian, sometimes simply 'medieval'. The programmes of the South Place Ethical Society in 1933 included lectures on 'Barbarism and Progress' (in which Delisle Burns equated German fascism with barbarism) and Hyman Levy on 'The Return to Barbarism', a lecture given shortly after the passing of the Enabling Bill in Germany in March 1933 which gave the Hitler government dictatorial powers. The following year 'Barbarism and Government' returned to the same theme, and in 1935 'The New Paganism' described the anti-Christian credentials of National Socialism.[20] An early discussion of 'Germany in Revolution' in the *Fortnightly Review* invoked the 'invasion of the barbarians'. A review of *Mein Kampf* in 1933 began by describing Germany's reversion 'to the intolerance and barbarism of the Middle Ages'; a review in 1934 of a book titled *Why I Left Germany* found it incredible that 'such barbarities' could be found in a 'so-called civilised country'.[21] These terms were commonplace in public denunciation of Hitler's Reich, echoing the derogatory term 'Hun' used to describe Germans during the Great War, but they were also private judgements and not mere crowd-pleasing rhetoric. Writing to Liddell Hart in 1939 Storm Jameson compared 'this new barbarism' to the crisis that brought the sack of Rome and the end of classical civilization.[22] On listening to a radio broadcast of the wedding in April 1935 of Hermann Göring, the man who had reintroduced beheading as the form of execution in Germany, A. L. Rowse scribbled 'the axe! The barbarians!' in his diary.[23]

The emphasis on 'barbarism' was not just an easy description of the thuggery of young National Socialists as they went on the rampage in 1933 against enemies of the movement, or a reflection of the wide fear of the warlike ambitions of the new Germany, obvious though these explanations are. Many British intellectuals, affected by the new historical language of the Dark Ages, looked expectantly over the parapet of civilization for signs of the barbarian at the gate, and the Hitler movement appeared ideally cast for the part. The language deliberately played with the idea of the fall of the ancient world and it suggested by implication that, just like the Roman Empire, there was something rotten in civilization itself; the arrival of a barbarous Hitler was regarded as not just a temporary anomaly but an unwelcome historical re-enactment. Storm Jameson told Liddell Hart that she could see in Britain no 'visible, hoped for, living signs of a new world', but instead only 'this awful sense of sterility'.[24] A. L. Rowse was also struck by the historical analogy with past crisis. In another diary entry in 1935 he wrote despairingly, 'too, too late to save any liberalism, perhaps too late to save socialism'. The world, he continued, would be handed over to 'the vulpine, the hyena, the jackal' as it had been in the darker Middle Ages.[25] Much of the discussion of Hitlerism assumed that it was a product of failed capitalist society and was therefore something that could happen anywhere in the Western world faced with severe socio-economic crisis and not just in Germany. In one of the earliest biographies of Hitler, published in English in 1932, Emil Lengyel argued that the National Socialist movement was born of the desperate realization among the German people that 'civilisation is no longer a protection but a menace', a trap 'from which there is no escape' except to follow a Messiah into a world of 'insanity'.[26] Another book, *Why Nazi?*, published in 1933 by an anonymous German, argued that supporting Hitler was a conscious attempt to avoid 'the despair, the resignation and inertia, with which the western world is watching its civilisation crumble'.[27] Hitler's triumph, observed Israel Cohen in 1934, was not just a German problem but 'a distressing commentary upon the state of modern civilisation'.[28] In a series of lectures on 'The Meaning of Hitlerism' given at King's College, London in May 1934, the journalist Henry Wickham Steed suggested that 'the problem of free civilisation' could be solved only by reasserting its fading values against the menace of barbarous 'lawless force' which threatened to engulf it.[29]

The preoccupation, even fascination, with Hitler and Hitlerism or National Socialism (or 'Nazism' as it came to be popularly known from the early 1930s onwards) can be seen as an analogue for the widespread fears for the future of civilization. It is otherwise difficult to explain the extraordinary attention paid to Hitler compared with his fellow dictators, Mussolini and Stalin. This preoccupation with the dark threat Hitler posed long predated the overturning of Versailles, the onset of war and the later revelations of the genocide of the Jews. The sales of Mein Kampf reached 50,000 a year by 1938. When the full, 'unexpurgated' translation became available in 1939 it was released in eighteen weekly parts, complete with illustrations and a bright red and yellow cover with the copy lines 'The most widely discussed book of the modern world'.[30] In 1939 the distinguished Oxford historian Robert Ensor lectured at the Royal Institute for International Affairs on 'Mein Kampf and Europe'. He thought it 'a crazy book', but also 'an extremely powerful one'. He concluded, unsurprisingly, that Hitler was 'a world danger', but the remarkable thing about the lecture was the degree of attention given to a book that most critics have rejected as unreadable and that Ensor himself thought few people had read.[31] Hitler became the reference point for so much of the discussion of crisis in the 1930s, a lightning conductor for anxieties or expectations which were as much domestic in origin as they were occasioned by German realities. Not for nothing did What Hitler Wants sell 150,000 copies. When Hermann Rauschning, the former Danzig National Socialist leader before he fled from Germany, published Hitler Speaks in December 1939, another bestseller was born, going through three printings in less than a month.[32]

This process of psychological projection, of using Hitler as the measurement of crisis, was the subject of a book by a medical psychologist, H. G. Baynes, published in 1941 under the title Germany Possessed. It was introduced by Rauschning, who developed the idea that the Hitler phenomenon could be viewed as the precursor of 'the dissolution or self-destruction of civilization'. He continued:

The question arises whether Hitler is not himself the expression of the shadow-side of our whole civilization. Is not National Socialism, with its immediate success, a symptom of the great crisis of civilization ... ? In no sense is Hitler the expression of conscious political and spiritual currents in Europe, neither is he of Germany. He is the symbol of the dark side of our civilizing experiment. He represents the flight from the tormenting tasks of civilization, the grotesque and dæmonic contradiction that runs through our life.[33]

Baynes developed this thesis further by suggesting that Hitler ('He is neither a Christian nor a gentleman,' Baynes lamented) had not only induced a 'mythological madness' into German society, but had 'injected fear into every cranny of our ordered and pacific life' to the extent that he came 'to symbolize the problem of insecurity in everybody's unconscious'.[34] Hitler, Baynes concluded, was a symptom of the disease of modern civilization rather than its cause. People who dreamed of Hitler did so because they had an unresolved psychological issue best represented by a figure universally deemed to be 'the force of evil'. But the key problem, Baynes continued, was the suicidal character of modern civilization which, as Freud had argued, contained within it the capacity for 'wholesale destructiveness'.[35] These were speculations, suggestive rather than proven; yet the fact that people dreamed of Hitler says much in itself about the extent to which the demonic Hitler image had indeed become internalized in the 1930s. It may well help to explain in part the enduring obsession with Hitler in post-war Britain.

The cultural construction of Hitler as the enemy of civilization also relied on other forms of public but non-political activity that underpinned the outpouring of published Hitleriana and dated from the very beginning of the dictatorship. One of the first was the unofficial organization in Britain of a legal commission of enquiry into the circumstances of the burning of the German Reichstag on the night of 27/28 February 1933. The fire was used as the occasion to strengthen emergency powers in Germany and to attack German communism. The Reichstag Fire decree of 28 February was the first internationally understood violation of civil rights by the Hitler government, and it paved the way for the wave of violence and lawlessness directed at enemies of the regime during the spring and summer of that year. Communist activists were arrested, including three Bulgarians, among them Georgi Dimitrov, later secretary of the Moscow-based Comintern. The leader of the parliamentary fraction of the German Communist Party, Ernst Torgler, gave himself up the day after the fire and also stood trial. The four were tried in a Leipzig court alongside the young Dutch communist Marius van der Lubbe, who had been caught at the scene in February.

The arrests caused wide protests outside Germany. They gave foreign opinion a *cause célèbre* (the trial was compared with the ordeal of the French officer Alfred Dreyfus, accused wrongfully of treason and condemned in 1894) with which to challenge the new political system whatever the facts or circumstances of the case. Ellen Wilkinson hosted a cross-party group in her London flat where it was agreed to set up an informal Reichstag Trial Defence Committee, which chose the political scientist George Catlin as their representative at the trial in Germany.[36] The group agreed to organize a 'counter-trial' in London and in September an international commission of ten lawyers and legal experts convened in London to stage it. The chair was taken by the radical British barrister Denis Pritt, who had begun life as a Conservative when a young law student in pre-war London before moving progressively to the left over the wartime period. By the 1930s, though a Labour Party member, he was moving yet further towards orthodox Marxism. He later described the Reichstag fire as 'the most important event between 1917 and 1939', a judgement that has scarcely stood the test of time.[37] The commission began a widely publicized series of four crowded public sittings in the Kingsway Hall, London, where the facts of the case were discussed and elaborated and witness testimony produced as if it were a regular court of law. Legal procedure and protocol were carefully maintained. H. G. Wells came on the opening day and complained that he had 'never attended a duller show in his life'.[38] The final report of the commission was released on 20 September, the day before the start of the Leipzig trial, and received a widely approving press for its modest conclusions and legal scruples. In Leipzig by contrast, George Catlin found little sense of a 'historic trial' comparable to Dreyfus, while inside the courtroom legal decorum vanished in a melee of journalists, flash photographers and noisy, undisciplined witnesses who harangued the judges and flouted procedure.[39]

The commission report based its conclusions partly on the so-called 'Oberfohren Memorandum' smuggled out of Germany by a British journalist in April 1933 and published in extract in the *Manchester Guardian* later that month.[40] The document was said to originate with the former parliamentary leader of the German Nationalist Party, Dr Ernst Oberfohren, who committed suicide on 7 May rather than face a bleak political future. Much was made of the fact that conservative opinion was also outraged by National Socialist lawlessness; more significantly, Oberfohren (or whoever drafted the memorandum) insisted that the new government burnt the Reichstag deliberately to allow them to move against their enemies. Pritt's final report not only asserted that the case against Torgler, Dimitrov and his fellow Bulgarians could not be proved (which was also the judgement of the Leipzig court published on 23 December), but added the cautious legalistic conclusion that there existed 'grave grounds for suspecting that the Reichstag was set on fire by, or on behalf of, leading personalities of the National Socialist Party'.[41] In 1934 Konrad Heiden, an exile German journalist, published the first full history of National Socialism in English, written while the trial was still going on, in which he fuelled the speculation with much additional evidence that in all probability the fire was the work of an unknown 'Nazi incendiary column'.[42] A Cambridge exhibition against fascism and war in 1935 included a photostat document allegedly produced by the SA leader Karl Ernst, murdered on 30 June 1934 in the 'Night of the Long Knives', confirming National Socialist responsibility (alongside whips and cudgels 'actually used by stormtroops').[43] The idea that the Reichstag was burned down deliberately by the Hitler regime became the accepted view in Britain and remained so until long after 1945, when historians finally demonstrated that van der Lubbe, who was convicted and executed in Berlin, really did act alone.

The three Bulgarian defendants, Dimitrov, Blagoi Popov and Vasil Tanev, were eventually released in late February 1934 when the Soviet government offered them sanctuary.[44] Their case had been supported in Britain by a new body, the Dimitroff Committee for the Release of the Reichstag Prisoners, organized by the former Labour MP and campaigner for women's rights Frederick Pethick-Lawrence. The work of the committee was also endorsed by the Union of Democratic Control which sent Dorothy Woodman to Leipzig to look after Dimitrov's wife and daughter while he was in prison. When she visited Dimitrov in his cell she had to masquerade as his lover so that she could talk to him in private. In March the committee decided to send a 'Memorial' to Hitler asking him to release the remaining defendant, Ernst Torgler. It was signed by all fifty-six vice-presidents of the committee which included J. M. Keynes, Julian Huxley, Leonard and Virginia Woolf, Gilbert Murray, H. G. Wells and Siegfried Sassoon.[45] Torgler, though acquitted, was sent to a concentration camp. He was eventually released and ended up working for Joseph Goebbels's Propaganda Ministry as a specialist in anti-Bolshevik propaganda. Public interest in Britain began to die down, but the damage to Germany's reputation remained. In June 1934 *The Reichstag Fire Trial* was published with an introduction from Pritt reminding readers that the issues of law raised by the trial were still as topical as ever. At the end of the book was appended a list of 747 murders of 'defenceless persons' between Hitler's accession and March 1934.[46] The following year Pritt successfully went on to defend the British communists Tom Mann and Harry Pollitt on trial in South Wales for sedition. Although local workers protested in large numbers, the progressive intelligentsia did little. The shadow Reichstag fire trial had not been about support for communists as such but an opportunity to pressure the young Hitler regime into observing normative justice. Many years later Denis Pritt was invited to East Germany to talk to young communists about his fight for justice for Dimitrov in what had become for East Germans the legendary 'Gegen-Prozess', the counter-trial of 1933.[47]

There were greater opportunities to highlight the barbaric nature of Hitler's Germany in the second great cause of 1933, the rescue and rehabilitation of intellectual refugees from Germany. This had an immediate impact because so many of those who fled, including Albert Einstein, the most well known, had close personal ties with scholars and writers in Britain. The campaign for assistance was also genuinely non-partisan and reflected a profound liberal concern with the direct and violent challenge to intellectual freedom represented by the Third Reich. The exodus from Germany was large and continuous, and was not composed only of German professionals and teachers, or exclusively Jewish. Most of the expellees went to destinations other than Britain, where by May 1934 there were only 3,500 registered refugees but around 25,000 in France.[48] But their plight was very public and the individuals concerned were in many cases doctors, scientists, writers or musicians of exceptional talent. In April 1933, following the first expulsions from university and teaching posts in Germany (and the public burning of books in German cities a few weeks later on 10 May), appeals were launched in Britain to help German scholars who were forced into exile. The president of the International Federation of the League of Human Rights in Paris sent a letter to the Foreign Secretary, Sir John Simon, asking Britain both to help the refugees and to give their plight international recognition, but the movement of refugee assistance remained a voluntary one until the League of Nations gave it more formal status in October 1933 with the establishment of a High Commission for German Refugees.[49] Initiative in Britain was taken by a group of prominent British scholars, including among the signatories J. M. Keynes, Gilbert Murray, the historians H. A. L. Fisher and George Trevelyan, and the economist Josiah Stamp. On 22 May an appeal was sent to all British universities announcing that an Academic Assistance Council was to be established – it was formally constituted on 24 May, and held its first meeting on 1 June – and asking them to accommodate refugee scholars in defence of 'learning and science'.[50]

The Council appointed as president the Cambridge physicist Lord Rutherford, famous for his work on 'splitting' the atom. William Beveridge, director of the London School of Economics, and Professor C. S. Gibson were joint secretaries. For the next six years the organization campaigned to raise money and find posts for exile scholars. In October 1933, in collaboration with other refugee organizations and under the general umbrella of the German Refugees Assistance Fund, a gala evening was organized at the Royal Albert Hall with Albert Einstein as the main speaker. The evening was something of a coup, for this was Einstein's first public speech in front of a general audience.[51] Beveridge asked Geoffrey Dawson, editor of The Times, to give the evening and the campaign maximum coverage, and the speeches were broadcast live on the BBC.[52] The speakers included no one obviously from the political left; the Bishop of Exeter, Austen Chamberlain, and the Conservative MP Oliver Locker-Lampson all spoke alongside Rutherford and Beveridge from the Council. Einstein titled his twenty-minute talk 'Science and Civilization'. His was an appeal to the great traditions of European humanism and intellectual freedom, liberty and honour against 'hatred and oppression', civilization against barbarism. These sentiments sat oddly with Austen Chamberlain's vote of thanks in which he observed how easily unaccommodated refugees could become 'an irritant' and Beveridge's announcement that there would only be room in Britain for scholars who could contribute something Britain needed. The meeting raised £2,000.[53]

By October 1933 around 177 refugees had been found academic positions, mostly in Cambridge and London. The Committee of Vice-Chancellors, meeting in June 1933, offered little help unless independent funds could be made available (the vice-chancellor of Sheffield suggested that many 'rich men of the Jewish religion' had more funds than his entire university, and wondered whether they should not be asked for money first).[54] The organization remained sensitive to the charge that it was only designed to help Jews, and advertised its assistance for a tiny number of Russian, Italian, and later Spanish émigrés, but a large proportion of those assisted were German Jewish scholars. By 1938, under the title of the Society for the Protection of Learning and Science adopted in 1936, 251 refugees had been found a post in Britain, and several hundred abroad.[55] The activities of the Society, while modest enough in total, contributed to the widespread sense that National Socialism represented a rejection of the values of the civilized world and a deliberate return to the primitive and irrational values of a past age. In June 1937 *Nature* published a lengthy indictment of the new German order for rejecting 'liberty and reason' and abusing science. 'Our present civilisation', ran the editorial, 'is upheld by the critical and creative efforts of a few.' It was the task of Western scholars to 'resist the dark forces of unreason'.[56] The Archbishop of Canterbury, Cosmo Lang, condemned a German policy which violated the 'basic principles of tolerance and equality' of the civilized world.[57] Following Rutherford's death in 1937, the

Archbishop of York, William Temple, became the Society's president. The campaign for academic freedom helped to sustain a permanent awareness in the minds of Britain's intellectual, cultural and religious elites of the violation done by the Third Reich to a cross-section of its population whom they supposed to be just like them.

The many squalid details of political, cultural, racial and religious repression were widely circulated in Britain from the beginning of the new regime, often supplied by personal friends and colleagues in Germany. The details were not difficult to find since the new government in Germany made little effort to conceal them. The *Times* correspondent in Germany, G. E. R. Gedye, who had sympathized with the German cause up to January 1933, was appalled by the rapid descent into violence and torture that he witnessed and horrified by the wilful blindness to reality among the Germans he knew.[58] The plight of German Jews was also highlighted from the start, often described in the most lurid terms. The British Society of Friends set up a Germany Emergency Committee which published regular accounts of maltreatment and of visits to the concentration camps permitted by the regime. The visits were orchestrated excursions to clean barracks with well-disciplined prisoners, prompted to say how good conditions were, but the reality that mattered to a British audience was the absence of any legal protection for inmates and information on the growing list of cases of torture, debilitation and murder which was supplied by a range of British and international organizations.[59] Among British newspapers *The Times*, despite its reputation as the mouthpiece for appeasement policy, was alive to the reality of the new Germany. The editor, Geoffrey Dawson, agreed to help the campaign to free Dimitrov early in 1934; in January the same year a *Times* correspondent recorded strong National Socialist objections to a British press campaign that presented the German people as 'being fundamentally uncivilised'.[60] On 24 August 1934 the Gestapo confiscated all copies of *The Times* because of a critical article on German camps; an Austrian correspondent on 18 August complained that the German censors had removed two pages of his copy of *The Times* in transit through Germany on account of an article on 'Tension in the Saar'.[61] The first section of the paper's report on the 1934 Nuremberg party rally was devoted to a discussion of 'Anti-Jew Propaganda'. The regular featuring of articles critical of the new Germany prompted one correspondent to ask why *The Times* never said anything good about Hitler.[62]

It has been argued by some historians that the evidence of British appeasement of dictatorship and of fellow-travelling among the political elite and some of the most important newspapers suggests that Hitlerism was neither properly understood nor effectively disapproved of in the Britain of the 1930s. The evidence of just how widespread was public concern with National Socialism, and how persistent was the view that it ultimately represented values that were out of step with modern civilization, suggests that this view is misplaced. A great deal of the public understood long before the final crisis in 1939 what the new German leader stood for and did not approve it. They represented what Noel Annan later described as a majority who were 'vaguely Liberal, faintly Labour, the unpolitical yet opposed to Hitler'.[63] Even fellow-travellers could change their minds. Henry Williamson became disillusioned with Hitler: 'too bright, too unreal, too inhuman, too unbearable', he later wrote.[64] In 1939 Wyndham Lewis published a new book on Hitler, *The Hitler Cult*, in which he declared that his long neutrality towards Hitler was over. To be neutral, he wrote, was to be anti-British. He ended the book with a curious injunction: 'keep hissing! Herr Hitler is a villain who, if he is not sufficiently hissed, becomes really dangerous.'[65] Toynbee soon ended his brief honeymoon with Hitler as a man of peace. In a draft memorandum on 'The World Outlook' after Munich he feared the possibility of a new Europe based upon crude force under the heel of Hitler's 'harsh and brutal dictatorship'.[66]

The Soviet Union suffered without question under a harsh and brutal dictatorship in the 1930s but it was treated quite differently from Hitler's Germany. It is true that in the 1920s there had been a deeply divided response as long as communism looked likely to spread outside Russia's borders. 'Bolshevism' in the 1920s provoked deep anxieties, but also attracted unconditional loyalties. In the 1930s, however, as the regime consolidated and the immediate threat of international communism receded, the public response to the Soviet Union, and to a lesser extent towards Stalin, became increasingly sanguine. There are some obvious reasons for this contrast. The Soviet

Union was for most of its British visitors an exotic destination. Few could speak the language; visits were numerous but for the most part very closely controlled. The milder forced labour colonies were sometimes displayed in carefully staged tours, but the hardcore Gulag concentration camps were not. Many academic and cultural links had been severed during the revolutionary years so that there existed no residue of past association to measure against the present. By the 1930s there was no stream of intellectual refugees to provoke outrage since scholars penalized by the Soviet regime were either sent to camps or killed and the information carefully shielded by the security apparatus. Germany, on the other hand, was a closely integrated part of the West. Many academics and writers could speak and read German and had travelled there freely. They had developed close personal friendships with Germans. They were affronted by what happened to people very like themselves when the new regime came to power. The most significant difference was in perception and expectation. Germany was on probation from 1918. Great hopes had been laid on German democracy after the war; German culture in the 1920s was at the forefront of modernism and German health, welfare and industrial organization were in the civilized vanguard. British critics of Hitler's Reich saw the 1930s as a wilful descent from a peak of decency to a trough of turpitude. Emily Lorimer ended her book on Hitler with a lament for the Germany she had known of 'learning, culture and goodwill, the Germany of scholars and scientists ... of honest merchants and kindly families'.[67] If this was a romantic recollection, it was familiar to many educated Britons who had a yardstick by which to measure Germany's apparent rejection of modern civilization.

The situation for the Soviet Union was precisely the reverse. There was little love lost over the tsarist monarchy, and a general understanding that the Soviet Union was forced to start from scratch under unpropitious conditions. From the ruins of a seismic revolution and civil war, a new society had to be built. The primitive structures of a new administration, welfare system, economy and culture indicated in the 1920s potential for progress from conditions that most British observers could scarcely comprehend. Even those who could be critical of the Soviet regime under Stalin saw this potential. H. G. Wells, for example, writing in 1932 described the system thus: 'Dogmatic, resentful, and struggling sorely, crazy with suspicion and persecution mania, ruled by a permanent Terror, Russia nevertheless upholds the tattered banner of world-collectivity and remains something splendid and hopeful in the spectacle of mankind.'[68] The great advantage held by the Soviet Union from the late 1920s, with the onset of the Five-Year Plans, was the obsession with industrial development, economic planning and city building. Soviet propaganda endlessly evoked the heroic achievements of the Soviet people as they carved out a new modern age in Russia and did so with endless graphs, tables of statistics, and rationalization plans. This appealed to a British public brought up on fears for the capitalist future but frustrated by entrenched resistance to planning. It was also a wholesome contrast with the Nordic racial fantasies of the German new order which to many British critics seemed closer to superstition than science. The language of the Soviet state seemed inherently progressive; the language of the Third Reich did not.

This contrast was evident in the way in which the Soviet Union was portrayed in the literature and public discussions that surrounded it. When the BBC planned a radio series on the new Russia in 1931 it was treated as a curiosity which needed exploring – 'A day in the city' or 'A day on the farm' (though in 1931 a day on a Soviet farm would have discovered it in the throes of violent collectivization).[69] The South Place Ethical Society did not mount weekly discourses on Soviet barbarism. A 1931 talk on 'The Religion of Communism' argued that the Soviet Union had created a more successful sense of community than the Christian West; in 1932 there were talks on 'The Necessity of Communism', 'Marxism and Great Britain' (by the economist Maurice Dobb), and 'The International Significance of the Five Years Plan', whose author tried to demonstrate that public ownership was a practical and moral alternative to private enterprise. Even in 1939, after the signing of the German–Soviet Non-Aggression Treaty and the division of Poland, a lecturer on 'This Russia Business' could argue that even if Hitler and Stalin looked the same, the Soviet Union was nonetheless a force for peace and social progress.[70] G. D. H. Cole, who was not a communist, defended the Soviet record on industrial and social achievement throughout the 1930s in print and on the platform. 'Give men and women a big ideal', he wrote in 1931, 'and they will be ready to make big sacrifices.'[71] On the twentieth anniversary of Lenin's 1917 revolution Cole wrote that the revolution was 'by far the most important historical event' in his lifetime and applauded the fact that the Soviet Union, in the face of 'vast difficulties', had had the strength and tenacity to make such 'tremendous advances'.[72] In 1935 Maurice Dobb, who was a communist, gave a talk on 'Russia' to the Putney Literary Institute in south-west London in which he blinded his audience with statistics on industrial achievement, before going on to insist that the Soviet Union was a real democracy in which the ordinary man had a share in 'executive responsibility' and decision-making and endless opportunities for social advance.[73] Dobb gave a lecture to the Royal Institute of International Affairs in 1933 on 'The Validity of Marxism', during which he explained that the Soviet experiment forced itself into every discussion on current economic and political issues because it pointed the way forward for a world standing uncertainly 'at one of those grand historical crossroads which mark historical epochs'. Very few people, Dobb thought, now challenged the view that Marx was right. The record of the discussion that followed showed a wary response from a socially conservative audience, but no one in the 1930s could have lectured there on 'the validity of Hitlerism'.[74]

Enthusiasm for the Soviet experiment was expressed through a number of cultural organizations and activities that involved social and intellectual circles far beyond the hard core of communist sympathizers. The oldest was the Society for Cultural Relations between the Peoples of the British Commonwealth and the USSR, founded in 1924. By the 1930s it had a wide circle of establishment sponsors from the world of science, politics and culture, including the prominent liberals Keynes and Norman Angell, both the Huxley brothers, H. G. Wells, Virginia Woolf, Bertrand Russell and a dozen peers and knights.[75] The organization had branches around the country. The poet Hubert Nicholson, working in Bristol in the mid-1930s, attended meetings regularly with a membership which embraced 'energetic communists to timid right-wing liberals'. He came away from the meetings convinced that 'a true transformation, a true renaissance' would be possible in a Soviet Britain.[76] The Society's annual report for 1934–5 gives some sense of the range of its activities, some of which were, in the context, a caricature of Englishness. In October 1934 the Society organized its annual 'We-Have-Been-to-Russia Dinner' at the Criterion on London's Piccadilly Circus, attended by a glamorous throng of 235 guests, presided over by Lord Morley, with toasts to the king and the Soviet president Mikhail Kalinin, talks on Russian life and a final address on the buoyant state of the arts in Russia from the novelist Amabel Williams-Ellis, recently returned from the Soviet Writers' Congress (an event that in reality brought artistic independence in the Soviet Union to a shuddering halt).[77] In June the Society organized a summer garden fête chaired by Lord Hastings in a spacious private garden in Wimbledon. Braving torrential rain, more than 300 visitors attended to hear the St Dunstan's Band of War-Blinded Men and the Soviet Singers choir; if they chose they could wander among stalls of produce and games where one supporter could be found giving 'interesting character readings'. Later that year an exhibition of Soviet Art opened at the Bloomsbury Gallery, sponsored by the Society, which eventually toured to major cities throughout England and Scotland.[78]

In 1935 a second organization, the Committee of Peace and Friendship with the USSR, was established in London under the chairmanship of William Hare, Earl of Listowel and a Labour peer. Like the Society, the list of prominent supporters was a who's who of the 1930s, from the composer Ralph Vaughan Williams, the actors Sybil Thorndike and Robert Donat, the artist Eric Gill, to Havelock Ellis, J. A. Hobson, Vera Brittain, Bernard Shaw and the Webbs.[79] The committee arose out of a Congress of Peace and Friendship with the USSR in 1935 and its task was to prepare a second congress for the anniversary year of the revolution. The Congress convened from 13 to 14 March 1937, assembling on the first day at the Friends Meeting House in central London and on the second day in the Cambridge Theatre on Charing Cross Road. There were sessions applauding the new Soviet constitution, Soviet peace policy (addressed by the Duchess of Atholl, Norman Angell and a number of Labour and Conservative MPs), and on cultural development (including a talk intriguingly titled 'A Public Schoolboy and His Impressions'). The second day was devoted to the heavier task of discussing Soviet

S.C.R.
SOCIETY FOR CULTURAL RELATIONS
WITH U.S.S.R.

A

Garden Fete

WILL BE HELD ON

SATURDAY, JUNE 15th

3 to 7 p.m.

AT

42, Marryat Rd., Wimbledon Common, s.w. 19
(Through the kindness of Mr. and Mrs. Geoffrey Reckitt)

The Fete will be opened by Mrs. GEOFFREY RECKITT
Chairman : VISCOUNT HASTINGS

SPEAKERS :
PAUL ROBESON
MRS. CECIL CHESTERTON

H.E. The Soviet Ambassador and Madame Maisky
HAVE KINDLY PROMISED TO BE PRESENT

SOVIET SINGERS AND DANCERS

THE ST. DUNSTAN'S BAND OF WAR-BLINDED MEN
will play in the grounds all the afternoon.

Soviet Embroideries and Curios, Drawings and Paintings.
Palmist. Bookstall. Other Attractions.
A Sandpit and Boating on the Lake for the Children. Deck Tennis.

TEA ON THE TERRACE

TICKETS :

If Bought Before June 8th	...	...	~~1s. 3d.~~ *1/6d*
Afterwards (and at the Gate)	...	...	2s. od.
	Children Half-Price		

Apply for Tickets to S.C.R. 21, Bloomsbury Square, W.C. 1.
S.C.R. Membership Cards Not Available

HOW TO GET THERE—Wimbledon Station (Underground or Southern Railway) bus
to War Memorial.   From Putney, bus No. 93 along Common to War Memorial.
NOTE—Wimbledon Park and Southfields Stations have no buses.

C.P.S.—66164

*A poster advertising the garden fête organized by the Society for Cultural
Relations with the USSR on 15 June 1935. The Society counted among its
patrons a glittering array of literary and political figures.*

planning, led by G. D. H. Cole and John Strachey. Resolutions were passed on establishing closer cultural ties between the two countries.[80] There was no discussion of Soviet repression, though that same month the Central Committee in Moscow approved the launch of what became the 'Great Terror' over the two years that followed, resulting in the judicial murder of over 690,000 people. Later in the year there were celebration dinners to mark the revolutionary birthday. When the publisher Victor Gollancz was asked by the editor of the magazine *Cavalcade* in November 1937 to name his man of the year he chose Stalin: 'the reason being', he wrote, 'that he is safely guiding Russia on the road to a society in which there will be no exploitation'.[81]

The widespread endorsement of the Soviet system has to be explained not in terms of Soviet realities but as a projection of strong impulses for philanthropic relief and social reform in Britain. The Soviet Union was used as a crude measure of what was deemed to be deficient or decadent or unjust about British social realities. Noel Annan later recalled how deep ran the stream of intellectual conviction that society had to change: 'Compassion for the poor and disadvantaged became the most powerful moral principle of Our Age.'[82] That idealism was most marked among two very different constituencies, the hard core of committed communists scattered in the working-class movement and the softer core of educated supporters and fellow-travellers in the older universities ('most of the young men I know are bitten with Communism', wrote E. M. Forster to a friend in October 1937).[83] But many of those who used the Soviet example as a stick with which to beat the National Government were not communists, and did not believe that the Soviet system would necessarily work in Britain. G. D. H. Cole, for example, for all his extolling of Soviet planning, wrote to *The Times* in May 1933 that though he approved of much in the Russian system, 'I do not regard it as applicable without large changes to Great Britain' (though in an idle moment he drafted a play in which he imagined Trotsky as Oxford's vice-chancellor, Stanley Baldwin as a college servant and the undergraduates all working-class – 'The Eclipse, the End of All,' he added).[84] Sidney Webb, during his first visit to the Soviet Union in 1932, confessed to Beatrice after finding a hotel room with 'no bath, <u>no sort of looking glass, no tumblers</u> and no bedside table' that he was 'getting a little tired of

Soviet Russia'.[85] Two years later, after a conversation with the economic historian R. H. Tawney about the prospects of importing the Soviet system into Britain, he told Beatrice, 'I think we cannot do this, and had better not try.'[86]

There are numerous examples of the juxtaposition of an idealized Soviet order with the decadent character of British reality, both private and public. In an unpublished essay in 1931 the Marxist scientist J. D. Bernal, who visited the Soviet Union that year in a group including Julian and Aldous Huxley, wrote how easy the path of the modern intellectual would be if there were 'an ordered reconstruction of society' when everyone shared equally in the labour and the rewards of the collective whole. 'It is so in the Soviet Union,' continued Bernal, 'we know how different it is here.' He drew a familiar contrast between a Russia 'fighting with poor material and mental equipment against the centuries of enforced stupidity and misery' and a Britain where minds and machines lay idle, 'watching the crumbling away of a civilisation of which we were once proud'.[87] A year later another group visit to the Soviet Union was organized by the New Fabian Research Bureau to investigate 'the great Russian experiment'. One of the political tourists was Denis Pritt; he wrote his impressions of the Russian legal system for the book subsequently edited by Cole's wife Margaret, who, 'greatly interested, impressed and excited' by the visit, wanted to rethink British democracy on her return.[88] The contrast with Pritt's later treatment of German legality was stark. He contrasted Britain's harsh penal system and grim prisons with Soviet jails where 'flowers, pictures and photographs' could be seen in the cells and in which warders and prisoners saw themselves as tools of a benign 'co-operative endeavour' in personality reform. His visit to a labour camp showed him 'the quiet encouragement to reform that comes from decent surroundings'. Small wonder, Pritt continued, that a Ministry of Justice official spent three months in one of the prisons 'to see how he liked it'. British prisons and legal procedure had much to learn, Pritt thought, from the Soviet example.[89]

It is easy with hindsight to mock the apparently wilful blindness of the left (and not just the left) in Britain to the realities of the Soviet system. It can be understood only as a measure of the disgust felt about British failings and the apparent absence of other means to express that revulsion. If there was a growing progressive demand in the 1930s for a New Jerusalem, the Soviet Union gave evidence that the Promised Land was a possibility. The rejection of capitalism as a model for social development has already been explored, but the implications were much broader than a preference for industrial planning over the free market. Hugh Dalton, at that time lecturing in economics at the LSE, was on the same Fabians trip to the Soviet Union as Pritt. He became more convinced than ever of the necessity for a transformation of the values of the West: 'I returned home . . . strengthened', he wrote, 'in my belief that, for a community as for an individual, bold and conscious planning of life is better than weak passivity and the tame acceptance of traditional disabilities, that trial and error is better than error without trial.'[90] For better or worse the Soviet Union was exploited to endorse the distant vision of a better Britain; it mattered not so much for itself, but as an instrument of domestic salvation. In 1937 the communist poet Stephen Spender wrote a book for Victor Gollancz called *Forward from Liberalism* in which he argued that the British liberal age was doomed to descend into fascism, and that only communism could ensure the survival of what he called 'the idealist achievements of the liberal state'. Communism was the coming age, Spender argued, alone capable of surviving 'the attacks of barbarism' and creating 'a more extensive civilisation'. When civilization was threatened by war and oppression, he concluded, 'politics become either an affirmation of life or an alliance with death'.[91]

The most famous statement of the link between communism and the crisis of civilization was made by Sidney and Beatrice Webb when they decided, towards the end of their long writing careers, to publish in 1935 a comprehensive study of Soviet conditions under the title *Soviet Communism: A New Civilisation?* It was their last great enterprise and it bore the unmistakable hallmarks of a life spent solely studying the social, administrative and economic institutions of Britain. The decision to research such an exotic system, in a language they could not read, rested partly on their own frustration with the partial and ill-informed accounts of the Soviet Union on which the British public had had to rely throughout the 1920s, partly on a predisposition already formed since the revolution to imagine a Soviet order that had overcome the decaying status of Western capitalism, and partly, it seems, from a desire to educate the Soviet people themselves about the exact nature of the system they inhabited.[92] Beatrice found it daunting to pass judgement on such an upheaval. Writing in her diary in April 1932 as they worked their way through the material, she admitted to moods that swung between 'the wildest hopes and the gloomiest fears' of what they should find. 'All I know', she continued, 'is that I <u>wish</u> Russian Communism to succeed.'[93]

The Webbs set about the task as they would have done studying British municipal councils or the co-operative movement. They hoarded as much detailed official information as they could about every institutional, economic and administrative aspect of the new state. In 1932 they spent almost two months in the Soviet Union. Beatrice stayed in Moscow, too frail for a more vigorous tour, but Sidney travelled to Kharkov, Kiev and the industrial regions of the Ukraine, meeting managers, officials and party leaders, discussing through interpreters any details of the system that he didn't understand. It was a rigorous schedule of long train journeys, poor food, visits to farms and factories. 'I do not think', he wrote to Beatrice, 'that you would have stood the heat, the upsets and the discomfort without internal disorder – which so far I have escaped.'[94] But he was heartened by the ordinary people he saw and met. Watching a parade through Kharkov he found something 'very impressive in the way the proletariat takes itself seriously as being *the* people'.[95] He took his new subject with equal seriousness. He found out how to tune his radio to Soviet stations and in 1934 liquidated his Japanese securities and invested the proceeds in the Moscow Narodny Bank.[96] Beatrice on her return wrote a memoir of her tour in which, though she deplored the mundane absence of chamber pots and a regimen of food 'unsuited to delicate persons', she applauded what she called 'a new civilisation with a new metaphysic and a new rule of conduct'.[97]

Sidney returned to the Soviet Union without Beatrice in September and October 1934, towards the end of the drafting of *Soviet Communism*. His Intourist guide had also been the escort for H. G. Wells, who had visited Stalin shortly beforehand. Wells's 'arrogance and insincerity', he told Sidney, was generally despised. Sidney found it difficult to find any fault on his return visit. Seeing a leather jacket on sale for the equivalent of sixty pounds which would have cost four in London, he concluded that 'clearly people are spending more freely'.[98] He handed out a number of chapters of the book to Soviet officials for checking, but was delighted to find that everything he saw and learned was, he told Beatrice, 'generally confirmatory of what we have written'. He was unimpressed by the Americans and Britons he met who told him of the 6 million famine deaths, or the collapse of the workers' bargaining position in relation to management. 'This seems to me', he wrote to Beatrice, 'a matter of impression. I see no evidence.' What impressed Sidney was the egalitarianism of the system. 'This people is extraordinary,' he wrote after visiting a workers' club, 'free to all comers of either sex or age'.[99] He brought back yet more books and statistics and the conviction that the visit to 'check up' had been indispensable. With the help of a loan from Bernard Shaw of £1,000 the final work of preparing the manuscript could go ahead.[100] In the summer of 1935 two volumes totalling 1,174 pages were published by Longmans priced at 35/-. The publicity leaflet announced that the Webbs would show whether the Soviet Union 'amounts to a New Civilisation' and answer above all the question 'WILL IT SPREAD?'[101]

For all the criticism that the books inspired they were the first and, for many years, the only fully detailed 'scientific' (as it was claimed) account of the structure and behaviour of the Soviet economy, political system and social institutions. The Webbs concentrated their argument around a number of key points: first, that there was genuine equality of opportunity based upon a system of party direction and example, or the Vocation of Leadership as they called it; second, that this was a participatory system with opportunities for popular involvement in running farms and factories on co-operative principles; third, and most controversially, that the Soviet system was not and would not become a dictatorship. On this last point they observed that Stalin had no high executive office in either state or party with the formal power to order people to do things, as Hitler had. Their characteristically narrow empiricism led them to the following conclusion:

We have given particular attention to this point, collecting all the available evidence, and noting carefully the inferences to be drawn from the experience of the last eight years (1926–1934). We do not think that the Party is governed by the will of a single person; or that Stalin is the sort of person to claim or desire such a position. He has himself very explicitly denied any such personal dictatorship in terms . . . which certainly accord with our own impression of the facts.[102]

The cult of personality, whose existence they could hardly have missed, they attributed to Stalin's remarkable successes and the 'traditional reverence' of the Russian people for an autocrat which the 'ruling junta', as they called it, indulged for stability's sake. Stalin was trapped by it, they argued, but not its cause.[103]

A woodcut image of a smiling Stalin, one of a series of woodcuts displayed at the Soviet Graphic Art Exhibition at the Bloomsbury Gallery in central London in December 1938. There were no exhibitions of National Socialist art.

On the question of whether the system they described was a new civilization there remained some equivocation, expressed in the question mark of the title. The Webbs were familiar with Toynbee's first three volumes by the time their book was published and wanted to test whether the Soviet experiment really did qualify as a distinctive civilization. In May 1935 Beatrice asked Toynbee to look at the draft of the book. He agreed, though he warned her that in his view communism was 'both totalitarian and parochial' and was unlikely to last. To rub salt in the wound he added that once communism had collapsed, 'don't you think that the old-fashioned religions may have a second innings?'[104] Toynbee obliged nonetheless with nine pages of detailed comment on four chapters in which he argued that communist success was due to the party's recognition of 'some fundamental spiritual truths'; on reading the final chapters he remarked that communism was as likely as not to turn into a religion 'in the ordinarily accepted sense of the word'.[105] In the end his detailed suggestions came too late to be included, but the Webbs' published conclusions certainly owed something to the correspondence, for they confirmed Toynbee's argument that civilizations are shaped by distinctive spiritual characteristics.[106] The new Soviet morality of 'universalism' and collective obligation, the Webbs argued, was a fundamental contrast with the disunity and disillusionment of Western civilization and they cited approvingly Leonard Woolf's conclusion in his book *Quack Quack!*, published shortly before theirs, that the West was in a final stage of 'decivilisation'.[107] In answering their own question 'Will it spread?' they answered, 'Yes, it will,' but gave no account of how. The answer to whether the Soviet civilization was an advance on the West emerged by implication as a strong affirmative.

The two volumes developed a history of their own. The publishing of the new Soviet constitution in 1936 and the purge trials of 1936–7 had to be accommodated. In October 1937 a second edition was prepared (adding 100 pages to the original) which included the complete text of the constitution, appended to demonstrate beyond argument the justice of the Soviet claim that the Soviet Union possessed the most democratic political system in the world.[108] They had a Russian translation prepared, but the book in English and in Russian was banned from the Soviet Union. A single-volume edition was arranged with Victor Gollancz for the Left Book Club, and over 15,000 sold. The book was regarded as so important it was given a large format and a distinctive grey cover rather than the bright orange used for other Left Book Club publications. Most significant of all, for the second edition the question mark was dropped from the title. Despite the terror, which was now at its height, the book declared that the Soviet Union was, indeed, a new civilization. The Webbs issued a statement about the new edition in which they described the show trials as 'a tragic hangover from the violence of revolution and civil war' but insisted that so much positive good had happened in the three years since they had been in Russia that 'we can take away the question mark'.[109] Throughout, the Webbs were warmly supported by Bernard Shaw, who described the work as their 'masterpiece'. When a revised cheap edition was published in September 1941, Shaw wrote a piece for the popular magazine *Picture Post* in which he explained that the Webbs still 'unhesitatingly' considered the Soviet Union 'a New Civilization', as he did. The preface of the new edition highlighted the conclusions that the Soviet Union was not a dictatorship, but a special variety of political democracy; on the galley proofs of the new introduction Beatrice scribbled in the margin 'Stalin is not a dictator', perhaps to dispel lingering doubts of her own.[110]

The impact of the Webbs' work is difficult to assess. It sold in large numbers – the first edition alone sold 30,000 – and there were numerous approving reviews. Trade union members, students at the Workers' Educational Association classes and Left Book Club subscribers were able to buy the book at a fraction of its published price, 5/- instead of 35/-.[111] The *Left Review* published two short pamphlets at 3d each, distilled by the Webbs from the larger book; 'Soviet Communism – Dictatorship or Democracy?' and 'Is Soviet Communism a New Civilisation?' were both targeted at a much wider working-class audience.[112] The whole idea that the Soviet Union represented a new civilization, which had circulated throughout the 1930s, was now given an imprimatur by the most senior of British social democrats. Even for those daunted by the book's length and detail, the revised title alone made the claim explicit and public.

Yet the book arrived at just the point when the bright view of Soviet prospects under the Five-Year Plans threatened to become tarnished by the Soviet purges and the growing cult of Stalin, and although the Webbs did not ignore either, their explanations for both provoked a good deal of hostility and head-shaking. Sidney had little time for the arguments about the terror, which diverted attention from the real achievements he wanted to display, but Beatrice, while regretting the violence done, even to people she knew, remained an apologist. When her nephew, the journalist Malcolm Muggeridge, wrote from Moscow in 1933 that the system was clearly based 'on the most evil and most cruel elements in human nature' she treated his views with unconcealed hostility.[113] In a memorandum drafted in February 1937 Beatrice tried to explain for herself why the defendants in the purge trials should have embarked on a programme of 'outrageous treason and attempts at murder'; but of the question of their guilt she was in no doubt.[114] To H. G. Wells she wrote in May 1937 that the real question was not the morality of the trials but the question prompted by previous history, 'Will a counter-revolution be avoided?' She thought that on the whole the Soviet government had 'acted with wise restraint' and contrasted the small percentage of victims with the violence of the British during the Irish civil war in 1921–2.[115] In a radio debate in February 1938 on 'Efficiency and Liberty in Russia' she again defended the trials as a justified attempt to avert counter-revolution. 'I am convinced that there was widespread sabotaging of industrial plant,' she continued, 'and some treachery among army officers.' The Soviet government was right, she concluded, 'even from the standpoint of humanity alone'.[116] Kingsley Martin later observed that Beatrice had never shown much concern for the principle of 'individual liberty'.[117]

Other critics on the left were less persuaded that the Soviet Union had not taken a wrong turn. Harold Laski, who wrote a warm personal letter of congratulation to the Webbs after the publication of their book, disliked both the repression and the cult of personality. He told Beatrice directly that they avoided confronting the reality of the dictatorship by 'verbalisms' and refused to share their view that 'Stalin was a "necessary" hero'. The Sovietologist E. H. Carr thought the Webbs' whole enterprise 'inconsistent and muddle-headed', and like Laski chided them for claiming that the Soviet Union was not a dictatorship and for their failure to acknowledge the scope of its repressive apparatus.[118] The experience of communist orthodoxy and violence against socialists and anarchists in Spain during the civil war alienated both communists and non-communists. George Orwell became a committed enemy of Stalinism after his experience as a volunteer in the Spanish Civil War, but so too did the young Hungarian communist writer Arthur Koestler, who lost his faith as a result of Soviet behaviour in Spain and immortalized the show trials for an English audience in *Darkness at Noon*, published in 1940.

There were nevertheless many others on the left who, like the Webbs, were willing to suspend their disbelief because what concerned them was to keep faith with an ideal of the Soviet Union in order to hasten the reform of Britain. Although support for Stalin or the cult of personality was evidently limited in Britain, even among card-carrying communists, it proved possible to distinguish between man and system, even at the cost of a good deal of sophistry.[119] G. D. H. Cole, for example, could write that Stalin's collectivization drive in the Soviet Union was carried out 'with needless cruelty', but nonetheless 'approve of the socialisation of Russian agriculture'.[120] (The historian A. L Rowse observed more candidly in his diary that the Bolsheviks were quite right to be tough on the kulaks: 'Liquidation is the only way!')[121] The Marxist scientist J. B. S. Haldane defended the idea that the Soviet Union, despite the one-party state and one-candidate elections, represented the Greek ideal of democracy because the absence of class conflict had self-evidently made party competition redundant.[122] Victor Gollancz thought the Soviet Union was an embattled system and was 'not only justified but impelled' to use any means to eradicate disloyalty.[123] Even liberals like E. M. Forster could imagine a communist future for all the inadequacies of the Soviet present. Writing to the communist poet Cecil Day Lewis in 1938 he confessed to 'disillusionments' with a Soviet system with 'too much uniformity and too much bloodshed' but added that he had a vision that communism would 'start again and again, always more strongly' until it overcame all the historical catastrophes that confronted it.[124]

Whatever doubts were expressed by the non-communist left about Soviet repression, Stalinist hero-worship and communist violence in Spain, public opinion in the second half of the 1930s was always more favourable towards the Soviet Union and communism than towards Hitler's Germany and fascism. The first opinion polling, which began in 1938 and 1939 in Britain, showed overwhelming majorities in favour of progressive issues. Asked in December 1938 whether they would prefer a Soviet or German victory in a war between the two, only 10 per cent favoured Germany, 59 per cent the Soviet Union. Even more revealing was the question posed in January 1939: 'If you HAD to choose between Fascism and Communism, which would you choose?' To this question 63 per cent opted for communism, 21 per cent for fascism, and this in an electorate which had expressed overwhelming support for Baldwin conservatism at the 1935 general election and almost no mandate for either of the political extremes.[125] All of the poll questions suggested that the only political choice that really mattered was between fascism and communism, even though in the charged ideological atmosphere of 1938 and 1939 support for both British varieties remained tiny. Much of the history of the decade has shared this view that the left–right divide dominated politics and determined popular allegiances. The reality, as many in the centre and centre-left of the political spectrum in Britain understood, was never as stark as this. During the mid-1930s there was growing effort to reassert the centre ground as a real alternative to the extremes, to save civilization not through importing ideologies that were inappropriate or alien to British conditions but by reasserting the core elements of the liberal and social-democratic tradition.[126]

The existence of a broadly 'progressive' but non-communist platform is essential to understanding the political expectations and anxieties of the later 1930s. Those who campaigned for the civilized alternative were drawn from different political backgrounds and parties, or were largely independent of politics entirely. Most would certainly have preferred communism to fascism, if that were the choice, but it was not how they saw British society in the crisis years. In his lecture notes for a talk on 'European Tendencies' to a Conference of Women's Institutes in late 1936, Philip Noel-Baker posed the question whether fascism or communism was the only choice. 'Democracy, Freedom, Co-operation,' he responded, 'still a tremendous force', followed by, 'It can still win – that is real choice.'[127] The defence of existing values was certainly not a fashionable position in the 1930s in the face of growing evidence of international crisis, economic uncertainty and the lure of fanaticism, but it was mounted by a significant array of public figures. In 1934 the writer Storm Jameson, Noel-Baker's collaborator in challenging death, wrote a spirited defence of freedom with the title 'A Faith Worth Dying For' in which she called on all artists and writers to engage with the vital task of saving freedom. 'If we let the barbarians take charge of our city,' she wrote, 'they will light their fires with all our poems.' The heart of liberty, she concluded, was the unconditional right 'to argue, to dissent, to utter freely what is in our minds, to hold what faith we will and to teach it'.[128] This was the same view of freedom championed by E. M. Forster in another radio debate from early 1938 on 'Efficiency and Liberty'. 'Liberty', began Forster, 'is not a goddess, but a condition which occurs in human society'; it permits human beings to say and think what they like. Forster located 'all the great creative actions, all the decent human relations' in the intervals between the assertion of mere force. He continued, 'I call these intervals "civilisation" and I want them to be as frequent and lengthy as possible.'[129]

These were the voices of the progressive community. They were united broadly by their commitment to liberal political freedoms,

A summer school at Stratton Park in 1933 organized by the Federation of Progressive Societies and Individuals. The chief progressive was the philosopher Cyril Joad, seated centre, a philosophy teacher at Birkbeck College, London and the founding father of the Progressive League.

freedom of conscience and thought, some form of economic planning, a concern for social justice, and the pursuit of peace. Some idea of the scale and nature of this progressive centre can be found in two public manifestos on 'Liberty and Democratic Leadership' published in February and May 1934 as a deliberate attempt to rally centre-left opinion. The inspiration behind the appeal was the National Labour politician Clifford Allen and the principal of Ruskin College in Oxford, Alfred Barratt Brown, but Philip Noel-Baker was also involved. The document was conventional enough in its appeal to democratic rule, freedom of expression, international reconciliation and rational politics. It was aimed, so ran the text, at 'an increasing number of men and women of all parties and of none' who reject 'threats of revolutionary action or arbitrary repression' and who seek the democratic path to reconstruction. Although some of those in-volved were members of parliament, the object was to make the progressive movement not obviously partisan.[130] The document was signed by 144 prominent individuals from all walks of life and most shades of opinion – the liberal philosopher Ernest Barker, the trade unionist Ernest Bevin, the anti-war campaigners Vera Brittain and Winifred Holtby, the conditional pacifist Norman Angell, art historian Kenneth Clark, the conservatives Harold Macmillan and John Buchan and the socialists Hugh Dalton, George Lansbury and A. V. Alex-ander, the Huxleys, the Woolfs, the Hammonds, and so on.[131] Though many almost certainly had a deep distrust of communism, and no communist signed the declaration, it was 'anti-fascism' that became one of the principal mobilizing slogans of this otherwise unstable constituency. This was a term which was intended to convey much more than hostility to Hitler or National Socialism. Fascism was increasingly used in a general sense to describe all political and social tendencies which threatened to undermine political liberty and human rights, either abroad or at home. Writing in 1935, Robert Fraser, a leader-writer for the pro-Labour *Daily Herald*, argued that millions of British people could be found in the ranks of anti-fascism across the party spectrum and that above all others this cause would decide the future of the democratic order.[132]

There were evident difficulties in holding so diverse a movement together and of giving it an effective public arena which did not clash directly with the party-political interests of many of its members. It was a straightforward matter to express the pious wish for the survival of democratic civilization, but there were few non-partisan avenues along which the progressive centre could advance so that its voice could be heard and its views clearly explained. Indeed, the lack of neutral public space was testament, paradoxically, to the constricting effects of the parliamentary system and open political competition. A number of initiatives emerged, some prompted by the example of anti-fascist action in France, where the existence of a more serious fascist or quasi-fascist threat prompted a larger and better-organized response than in Britain. In October 1935 the organizers of the Paris-based Comité de Vigilance des Intellectuels Antifascistes, established in March 1934, wrote to a number of prominent British cultural and political figures to encourage them to establish a British branch of the movement by recruiting 'the largest possible number of "big names"' in the anti-fascist cause.[133] Leonard Woolf, Philip Noel-Baker and E. M. Forster agreed to organize a preliminary assembly of appropriately big names and on 5 December 1935, at 50 Gordon Square in London, thirty-two of Britain's leading writers, historians, artists and thinkers assembled. Forster had already attended a Vigilance congress in Paris in the summer, 'to save civilisation', as he put it in a letter to Leonard (though he had been so unfamiliar with using a microphone that no one at the congress could hear what he said). Although Leonard Woolf argued that another organization would simply be supernumerary, he was overruled by the assembled group. A provisional committee was established, and a delegation secured for a large joint congress in Paris in January 1936.[134] In February the British section of the movement was founded under the title For Intellectual Liberty. The executive committee included beside Leonard Woolf, E. M. Forster, and Aldous Huxley (who became the association's president), the scientist J. D. Bernal, the sculptor Henry Moore and the historian R. H. Tawney.[135] The founding pamphlet of the association observed that 'the forces of progress and humanitarianism' had hitherto been largely ineffective, due to the unfortunate tendency of 'liberal-minded people to quarrel among themselves'. The movement pledged itself to defend democracy, freedom of expression and individual liberty, but to do so independent of all party interests.[136]

The organization was no more than a moderate success. The French Vigilance recruited 8,500 'intellectuals' in the first year; by September 1936 For Intellectual Liberty had just 325. At its height in 1938 the membership, distinguished though it undoubtedly was, did not exceed 500, a reflection perhaps of the more pejorative sense in which the term 'intellectual' was understood in Britain.[137] Despite the initial rally of intellectual enthusiasm, the association committee meetings during 1936 were never attended by more than four or five people. The association wrote letters of protest to the press, joined delegations, issued statements. It won some publicity ('Britain's Brainy Men Organise to Fight Dictatorship', ran one newspaper headline in December 1936) and on a number of issues made clear the progressive position on government policy. In the summer of 1936 it was decided to monitor BBC programmes so that protests and recommendations could be sent in where it was felt that the broadcasters had misrepresented controversial issues. E. M. Forster and the writer Rose Macaulay (who was one of many 'Brainy Women' who took part as well) drew up guidelines for listening out for 'positive unfairness', 'omissions' and 'juxtapositions' – the case where 'cricket sometimes precedes an important piece of European news'. Finally, the instructions suggested paying close attention to 'the announcer's tone of voice', because, perhaps under orders, 'he sometimes guys matters that F.I.L. would think important and makes them sound ridiculous ... Whereas he is all respect and concern if a member of the royal family catches a cold'.[138] A few months later Forster resigned from the movement on the grounds that its work was more to do with politics than culture. In January 1938 FIL joined forces with the British section of the International Association of Writers in Defence of Culture organized by the poet Cecil Day Lewis. The new organization, now known as the Association of Writers for Intellectual Liberty, became for the last years of its existence, as Forster had perhaps feared, more clearly associated with the communist intelligentsia.[139]

More was expected from the second import from France, a rallying of progressive political forces in a so-called Popular Front. The electoral alliance of French radicals, communists and socialists, inspired in part by a changed strategy in the Comintern in favour of collaboration with 'bourgeois' political forces, was cemented symbolically on

14 July 1935, Bastille Day, and brought electoral victory the following May. It is worth recalling that the inspiration was not entirely French or communist. The idea of pooling political differences in the face of a common threat to progressive and democratic values had been aired for several years in some Liberal and Labour Party circles, though it had been rejected by the party leaderships. In 1935 the Next Five Years Group, whose initial interest had been in arguing for greater economic planning, began to explore the possibility of a broad non-partisan political alliance as well. One of the leading champions was the liberal editor of the *News Chronicle* and a founder member of the Group, Sir Walter Layton, who came out in favour of a movement 'in which the very forces of civilisation are at stake'. Together with Clifford Allen (Lord Allen of Hurtwood), who was its driving force, the Oxford economist Sir Arthur Salter and the young Conservative MP Harold Macmillan, he hoped to launch in the spring of 1936 a loosely organized cross-party forum designed to create what A. L. Rowse, briefly enthusiastic about the idea, described as 'a Progressive Front'.[140] Little concrete was achieved until, in October 1936, with a Popular Front government not only in France but also in Spain, Harold Macmillan called together a small caucus at the offices of *New Outlook*, the magazine of the Next Five Years Group, to discuss uniting all progressives around a common political programme and an agreed strategy for action – 'A Left Centre rather than a Right Centre', as he put it in a newspaper article in June that year.[141] The Huxley brothers were present again, along with John Strachey, the Labour politician Aneurin Bevan, the Liberal Dingle Foot, the writers Gerald Heard and George Catlin, the Dean of Rochester and a dozen others. A small action committee was set up composed of most of those present, together with G. D. H. Cole who, despite his reservations about what he called a 'false Popular Front' of electoral bargaining and tactical voting, accepted the invitation to join and became briefly a leading spokesman for the idea of democratic unity.[142]

The aim of the group was to rally support for what they termed the 'People's Front', to distinguish it from the French variety ('no slavish imitation of the *Front populaire*', Cole had argued in June 1936) and the high point of the campaign was a congress at the Friends Meeting House on 26 November followed by a mass demonstration on

14 December. A list of 145 was invited to the congress from all walks of public life; speakers were warned that they should bear in mind the weighty responsibility they faced in creating a People's Front 'which affects not only the destinies of all our fellow citizens, but all Europe itself', but the meeting only served to expose the wide political differences between the different leaders.[143] In a letter the following month to Stephen Spender, Cole reminded him that the effort to 'rally all decent people' was for nothing less than 'the defence of civilisation'. Yet for all its portentous credentials and weighty intellectual support the movement faded in the early months of 1937. By March the Labour Party executive began to explore the necessity of expelling from its ranks all those, like Cole, who espoused the idea of a 'People's Front' because of its close association with the Comintern strategy of the same name.[144] At a National Executive meeting it was decided to empower local officials to question members to see if their activities contravened party loyalty and to deny them membership if they judged them unreliable; otherwise, ran the minutes, 'the Communist Party will have captured the leadership of the British Labour Movement'. In reality the popular front was anything but a threat. Most of the leading figures who had flirted with a People's Front movement were far from communist in outlook, including the reform Conservatives around Macmillan, whose interest in a popular front waned once the radical left was involved. During 1937 the project was taken over by Richard Acland, Liberal MP for North Devon, who tried unsuccessfully to persuade Victor Gollancz to accept a book on 'Middle and Left' to publicize his views that the left 'can get nothing on its own'.[145] Shortages of funds brought New Outlook to an end in November, and a conference in a hotel in Ascot in October set up to create the nucleus for a 'National Progressive Council' attracted only sixteen people and led nowhere.[146]

By far the most successful of the efforts to build a broad progressive consensus came not from politics but from publishing. Early in 1936 Victor Gollancz launched the Left Book Club to bring books of topical interest and broadly progressive outlook within the reach of as many subscribers as possible. Gollancz was one of many from the wartime generation who rejected the privileged world in which they had been brought up and embraced the cause of the radical left. After attending

St Paul's School and New College, Oxford, he joined the army in 1914, was court-martialled a year later before he had even seen action for borrowing his colonel's horse without permission and riding it recklessly along the river bank in Newcastle and was fortunate to be seconded to teach in a public school in 1916, thanks to the intervention of influential family friends. He joined Benn Brothers publishers in 1920 and in 1928 founded his own publishing house. In 1936, as his contribution to the effort to unite progressive opinion, he began publishing heavily discounted editions of popular books on politics, economics and social issues originally published by others, as well as commissioning titles on contemporary affairs on his own behalf. He was not a Communist Party member, but was on most issues far to the left of the Labour Party, of which he nevertheless remained a member. But the Left Book Club, according to its membership leaflet, had a simple aim: 'to help in the terribly urgent struggle *for* World Peace & a better social & economic order & *against* Fascism'.[147] Gollancz told G. D. H. Cole that the club was supposed to be 'a sort of reading "Popular Front"'.[148] He did not expect it to be profitable, but, as he told John Strachey, who agreed to serve as an editorial consultant, he wanted to create a large body of informed left-wing readers.[149] There was no membership fee but members were obliged to buy the 'Book of the Month', published in a distinctive soft orange cover, for at least six months. They were also entitled to a free monthly journal, *Left Book News*, which carried articles about current affairs from prominent socialist or communist writers.

The club was an immediate success. In May 1936 there were 6,000 members, two weeks later 12,000, by August over 17,000, by December 35,000.[150] Members immediately formed into local informal discussion groups, where the books were argued over and networks established. There were 147 by October 1936, but by 1938 there were almost 1,000, and membership stood at over 50,000. Gollancz reckoned that around 200,000 people read the key books issued each month.[151] The books themselves had remarkable print-runs, which explained how they could be priced at just 2/6d when most books on current affairs cost anything from four to eight times as much. *The Spirit and Structure of German Fascism*, by the American political scientist Robert Brady, sold 50,000, Spender's *Forward from*

Liberalism 40,000, John Strachey's *What Are We to Do?* 50,000, *The Battle for Peace*, published in June 1938, 60,000; and so on.[152] Though many of those who bought the books were already socialists of one hue or another, it is implausible that they were all, as is sometimes claimed, communist fellow-travellers. The Left Book Club was a home for just that progressive constituency which could not be organized effectively for popular fronts but nonetheless identified with progressive causes. By September 1937 Gollancz was convinced that his offspring had become 'a really powerful political force', even if, as he told Strachey, it had had no real effect on the political situation.[153] Its success prompted a rival Right Book Club, set up in 1937 by the bookshop owner W. A. Foyle and run by his daughter Christina. Founded in February 1937, it claimed 25,000 members by the end of the year. The club was deliberately aimed at reversing what Christina Foyle called 'the murderous embrace of the extremes', and in particular the huge output of books inspired, in her view, by varieties of Marxism. The club was not intended to be reactionary, but an expression of a forward-looking conservatism. Its editorial board was, however, every bit as partisan as that of the Left Book Club, including two members sympathetic to Hitler, and Anthony Ludovici, whose elitist, authoritarian and eugenic prejudices were well known. Book clubs, right and left, contributed to the sharpening of political debate in European terms.[154]

Accusations of communist fellow-travelling could certainly not be lodged against the other great publishing success of the late 1930s, the introduction by Allen Lane of the series of Penguin Specials designed, as Lane wrote in 1938, to reach 'a vast reading public for intelligent books at a low price'.[155] These cheap paperbacks, mostly priced at 6d each, were launched in November 1937 with the publication of an edition of Edgar Mowrer's *Germany Puts the Clock Back*, first published in 1933. A further seventeen were published in 1938, which, apart from a book on ballet and another on literary taste, were all on current affairs and almost all from a centre-left or broadly progressive perspective. They were an immediate success. They sold in numbers even greater than the Left Book Club's titles, in hundreds of thousands, helping to treble Penguin's earnings in three years.[156] An article in the *Democrat* journal in March 1939 applauded

The covers of two top-selling Penguin Specials. Searchlight on Spain *sold 100,000 copies in the first few weeks after it was published in 1938,* What Hitler Wants *sold 150,000 in 1939. The books made current affairs a mass-market concern.*

Allen Lane's initiative in presenting a 'non-partisan' and informative approach to current affairs, in contrast to the Left and Right Book Clubs, and went on to suggest that the result had been 'a notable strengthening of the fundamental democratic principle of the education of public opinion'.[157] Neutrality was nonetheless hard to maintain. The Special *Between Two Wars*, published under the pseudonym 'Vigilantes' in February 1939 by the future Labour MP Konni Zilliacus, was introduced by the liberal Norman Angell as a timely analysis of the barbarism unleashed by Hitler and his imitators which promised 'nothing less than the disintegration of civilisation' and a forlorn world dominated by forces of 'evil, of sadistic cruelty, ruthless terror'.[158] In 1939 and 1940 two Specials by Denis Pritt were published, and *New Ways of War* by the Marxist Tom Wintringham. By the late 1930s it was difficult even for a publisher committed to even-handedness to be anything but left of centre.

One final effort was made to create a progressive front in the last years of peace with the publication on 17 January 1937 of a 'Unity Manifesto' by a number of radical left-wing groups – the Communist Party, the Socialist League (set up by elements on the far left of the Labour Party in 1932), and the Independent Labour Party, the original labour movement founded by Keir Hardie forty years before.[159] The attempt to breathe new life into the idea of the Popular or People's Front was strongly resisted by the Labour Party, whose participation was vital to the success of any united progressive political movement. The shift leftwards also alienated many intellectuals who had thrown their support behind anti-fascism in 1935 and 1936 but began to distance themselves from involvement in any organizations, including For Intellectual Liberty, which wanted to be involved directly in progressive politics or were too overtly Marxist. Leonard Woolf refused to sign a plea from the movement calling for a Popular Front. The letter, he argued, would achieve nothing: 'it is the twitter of sparrows under the shadow of the hawk's wings'.[160] R. H. Tawney also refused to sign and resigned from the organization in December 1936. In February E. M. Forster resigned and withdrew entirely from active political work, though not from sympathy with the cause. When he was invited to a Vigilance meeting in 1938, he refused. 'I feel I have testified enough,' he told the novelist Rosamond Lehmann: 'The only chance is to do something – instead of meeting one another and one another's hangers on.'[161] In June 1937 Aldous Huxley resigned from the presidency, and the same month Kingsley Martin also resigned in order to devote more time to the Union of Democratic Control. Leonard Woolf stayed loyal to the idea of political engagement, but his wife Virginia, who had signed up for many progressive causes in 1935 and 1936, became disillusioned with intellectual commitment. When Rosamond Lehmann asked her to allow her name to be read out as a supporter at a congress in 1937, Virginia replied: 'I wonder if reading names out is any good? – or holding meetings, or writing books, or – ?'[162]

The movement for a United Front or Unity Campaign differed from the Popular Front campaign because it was more clearly a movement with a narrow political agenda. There was little question of involving reform Conservatives or progressive but non-aligned opinion. The

Labour Party and trade union movement remained strongly opposed to any United Front project that compromised their own political programme or undermined their electoral strategy or provided an opportunity for communist 'entryism' into the labour movement, and they did not regard fascism as a serious enough threat to justify a changed outlook. In April 1937 the Labour Party ordered all affiliated associations to refrain from any joint activity with the Communist Party or the ILP.[163] In May the Socialist League, led by the Labour barrister Stafford Cripps, which had been disaffiliated by a National Executive decision in January, agreed to wind itself up rather than risk their members being expelled from the Labour Party.[164] The Labour Party conference was petitioned in September 1937 by the Communist Party and the Marxist Group (Trotskyist) to support the common struggle, but the radical credentials of the movement was betrayed by the Marxist Group's demand for a 'militant United Front' to 'SMASH THE NATIONAL GOVERNMENT NOW'.[165] The shifting political complexion of the unity movement prompted G. D. H. Cole, who was still trying to propagate the original Popular Front ideal, to write in June 1937, when his book *The People's Front* was published by Gollancz, 'I am not, and never have been, a member of the Communist Party.'[166] In a letter to Frederick Pethick-Lawrence, enclosing a copy of the book, he explained that the Front idea had been misunderstood. It was pursued by those who found 'the existing situation of stalemate intolerable' and preferred a progressive unity to the 'appalling muddle of British and world affairs'.[167] Nevertheless, the existence of the radical left United Front fatally undermined the efforts at unity by more moderate sections of opinion.

Despite the profound fear of communism among the party leadership, there was much evidence that among rank-and-file Labour Party supporters and affiliated branches the idea of some form of progressive front was widely canvassed and in some cases actively promoted. A report for the Labour Party Head Office in May 1938 summarized the resolutions received on 'Peace Alliance', 'Popular Front', and attitudes to Spain. Calls for a special party conference on Spain numbered fifty-five, but there were eighty-nine resolutions calling for a 'Popular Front' and eighty-one calling for a United Front or Peace Alliance. Between drafting the report and the National Executive meeting the same month a further forty-one resolutions were received. At least forty-nine constituency parties supported the idea of a common 'front', but only eighteen sent in resolutions supporting the Labour Party ban.[168] Councils of Action had been set up in a number of cities, including Newcastle, Birmingham and Exeter (where a Council of Action for Peace and Democracy was pursuing a Popular Front strategy) and local Labour Party branches were reported to be participating.[169] On 5 May Stafford Cripps, Harold Laski, Denis Pritt and Ellen Wilkinson sent a passionate appeal to the Labour Party executive asking the party to work with Liberals, Communists, the ILP, and the Co-operative Party in a campaign for 'National Unity' by rallying 'the unattached and politically unconscious voters of all shades of progressive opinion and of all classes' and to save democracy from 'capitalist totalitarianism'.[170] Even the Labour Party's own Elections Sub-Committee argued that the electorate was more likely to respond to the idea of 'a new and more real National Unity' than to a traditional party programme.[171]

The Labour Party, with its eye fixed firmly on an impending general election in 1939 or 1940, remained resolute in its resistance to all forms of active political collaboration with either the liberal centre or the Marxist left. In January 1939 Stafford Cripps, who was the leading spokesman of the Labour left on the Unity Front, issued a statement to all party comrades calling on them to abandon narrow party interest, seek electoral alliances and create a broad progressive bloc to oppose the Chamberlain government. After a two-hour meeting of the National Executive called on 13 January to allow Cripps to put his case, the unity programme was rejected by 17 votes to 3.[172] When Cripps persisted in canvassing support among Labour Party members, the Labour Executive reacted by expelling Cripps from the party and drafting its own statement 'Socialism or Surrender: Labour Rejects the "Popular Front"'.[173] More protest letters poured in. Leonard Woolf, the Webbs and J. A. Hobson sent a strongly worded plea for the party to reinstate Cripps and to accept that there was now a widespread popular desire to mobilize all progressive forces, whether Labour voters or not, in a progressive bloc. The letters from the wider public in 1938 and 1939 make it clear that unity was seen as the only answer not just to electoral victory but also to the impending catastrophe facing the democratic world. 'The most important task of the moment is to hold back the onslaught of Fascism and war,' wrote the secretary of the Canterbury branch of the party, 'not after the next election, but now.'[174] 'This is no time for narrow party differences,' wrote a supporter from Liverpool in 1938, 'when the very existence of our liberties and democratic form of government is imperilled.' Another letter in March 1939 demanding a Popular Front deplored Labour's narrow-mindedness while 'civilisation is shaking'.[175] For the progressive public the two years before the coming of war produced a frustrating and ultimately unresolved tension between party interests and the dark vision of fascist triumph. The rallying of the centre proved to be another of the dead ends of the 1930s; on the other hand utopian politics, right or left, were for most Britons disease rather than cure. The political fears this paradox provoked explain much about the growing public acceptance in 1938 and 1939 of a necessary showdown between what were seen as the forces of light and the forces of darkness. But civilization now had to be saved by the most unlikely of champions: Neville Chamberlain and the much-reviled National Government.

There are many explanations for the failure to create a broad progressive alliance in defence of core liberal and democratic values. The Labour Party was, despite the Marxists in its ranks, committed to sustaining those values, as were most Conservatives. The reality of communist political activity in Europe convinced the Labour leadership that any pact with the extreme left would ultimately be destabilizing. The Trojan horse in their own ranks was regarded with deep distrust. Outside the party, among the progressive elements from the reform Conservatives around Harold Macmillan to the Marxist Group on the far left, there was no possibility of real political collaboration. The only base for co-operation remained outside the sphere of formal politics. Indeed, for progressive opinion the only possibility was to rally around causes, not around parties. These causes, from hostility to Hitlerism to support for the Spanish Republic, or the larger cause of pacifism, could attract support from across the political spectrum. But because they were causes rather than political organizations they depended on the willingness and energy of those who supported them in the daily tasks of collecting signatures, writing letters of protest, holding rallies, congresses and meetings and lobbying the politicians. These enthusiasms were difficult to sustain partly because there were so many causes, partly because commitment to the cause did not always mask the political conflicts under the surface. Marxists, liberals and Christians, for example, could appear on the same platform in front of an equally mixed audience, but sustained collaboration was more difficult. The wide intellectual lobby was just as divided and in many cases unaccustomed to the political activities that support for causes inevitably provoked. Asked in 1936 whether he approved affiliation of the Society of Authors to the Trades Union Congress, E. M. Forster replied that as a liberal he was reluctant but added the following: 'I expect my ideas want overhauling and I ought to face the fact that in 1936 every organisation must be political and that it is one's job to affiliate in the right direction.'[176] Forster was one of the many 'big names' who rallied to causes and then as soon abandoned them. In 1939 the Oxford academic Margery Fry, addressing a For Intellectual Liberty rally in Manchester, used the platform for a withering attack on her fellow members: 'We are living with most of our loyalties shattered and feeling utterly ashamed of ourselves for our part in this great tragedy ... I think it is true that intellectuals have not done their bit ...' Intellectuals, she concluded, were 'unorganisable'.[177]

The failure of the rally of 'progressive' forces was not complete. A lack of firm organization, so unlike the rallies and uniforms of the political extremes, arguably reflected one of the strengths of the liberal environment rather than a weakness. Throughout the decade there was a pronounced shift in popular attitudes towards a set of central ideas on the necessity for international peace, social reconstruction and economic reform. This explains why the impact of the European conflict between fascism and communism produced in the end deep fear and hostility towards fascism, and the German variety in particular, and a general sympathy for the ideals of social reform, planning and peace which the new Soviet order, for all the distorting effects of Stalinism, seemed to represent. There can be no doubt that very few Britons wanted to live under either fascist or communist authoritarian regimes. Active political support for the British branch of both movements was always tiny. It is remarkable, given this fact, that so much of the discussion of causes and issues in Britain in the decade before 1939 was dominated by a frame of reference to ideologies and regimes outside Britain. The British public observed the conflict and feared that it might be imported, but they understood the terms of the contest and could easily translate it to the domestic context. This helps to explain the popular demand for a confrontation with Hitler in 1939 and the later public enthusiasm for the Soviet defiance of German armies after 1941.

In these circumstances the traditional dichotomy between left and right makes less historical sense in the Britain of the 1930s. The conflict was perceived to be one between fascism, communism and democracy, either liberal or social-democrat. It was fought out in Britain in a distinct arena, as a kind of submerged 'counter-politics' to the conventional party struggle, fought around causes rather than elections. For most of the decade the conflict was expressed in terms of the survival of civilization as it was popularly understood, sometimes in terms of some promised new civilization. But in every case it was unresolved so that the nature of the political future remained dangerously ambiguous. In this great melodrama Hitler's Germany was the villain; democratic civilization the menaced heroine; the many forces of progressive thinking the simple-minded but courageous hero; Soviet communism the hero's bold but not altogether trustworthy accomplice. By 1939 it was no longer clear how the plot would play out.

8

The Voyage of the 'Death Ship': War and the Fate of the World

'Twice in one generation is pretty stiff!' we said on the morning of September 3rd 1939, when we knew we were at war with Hitler.

Now again, as twenty-five years before, German hands had pulled the levers that had launched the Death Ship.

Hugh Dalton, 1940[1]

It is difficult to date with any precision the point at which war seemed a certainty. Year after year there were discordant voices predicting conflict at any time. Guessing when war would come became a morbid parlour-game of the 1930s. In 1934 the journalist Hubert Knicker-bocker toured Europe's capitals to ask leading political figures when they thought war might break out. At the end of his journey he published *Will War Come to Europe?*, the question, according to the British diplomat John Wheeler-Bennett in his introduction to the book, that 'all thinking men and women in England are putting to themselves today'.[2] The responses Knickerbocker elicited were a mixed bag of gloom and wishful thinking. Admiral Horthy, regent of Hungary, and Thomas Masaryk, president of Czechoslovakia, were the only ones to reply that 'there will be no war'; the Bulgarian premier thought war 'inevitable', and Louis Barthou, the French foreign minister, believed it was about to break out at any moment; Mussolini told Knickerbocker that war would come in several years' time, a prudent response from a leader already planning the invasion of Ethiopia; Edvard Beneš, the Czech foreign minister, came closest when he said the chances were even that war would break out in five years' time.[3] Knickerbocker found throughout his tour the prevalence of what he called 'the catastrophe theory', the view among Europeans of every nationality that when war came it would end civilization.

The guessing game filled almost the whole decade. In *The Shape of Things to Come*, published in 1933, H. G. Wells suggested, with uncanny foresight, that ten years of final world warfare would start around 1940 over the issue of Danzig, a speculative date he shared, among many others, with the economist John Maynard Keynes and with the many distinguished contributors to the volume published by the Inter-Parliamentary Union in 1931, reissued in a popular version in 1933, on *What Would Be the Character of a New War?*, a book so remorselessly certain of war that one reviewer described it as 'the most terrible book that has ever been written'.[4] A millenarian preacher in May 1933 speaking at the Queen's Hall in London told his audience that Hitler was the Anti-Christ and, less plausibly, that the meeting of the World Economic Conference in London a few weeks later was the signal foretold in the Book of Revelation for the onset of Armageddon. He told his acolytes to expect a summons to the righteous on 12 June 1933 and the inauguration of the Millennium in 1940.[5] By the mid-1930s predicting world war at any moment was embedded in popular discussion. The historian Denis Brogan in 'Omens of 1936', published in January that year, observed that the imminence of war, which until recently had been believed only by 'the pessimistic and bitterly acute', was now thought to be true by everyone except 'the most cynical'. At the cusp of the new year, Brogan reflected, 'We all stand in the shadow of a great fear, and if the angel of death is not yet abroad in the land, we can hear the beating of his wings – and see them too, filling our old familiar sky.' Brogan spoke, he said, for the average man who had become aware 'of formidable forces being unchained', a language perhaps more appropriate to the millenarian visionary than the cautious academic.[6]

The mid-1930s seem to have represented a watershed in British perceptions of the inevitable slide to war, encouraged though not entirely caused by the further erosion of the post-war settlement, the Locarno Pact and the covenant of the League by German rearmament and Italian aggression in Ethiopia. Fear of war had deeper roots than these. Brogan's metaphor of 'unchained forces' suggests a more profound concern over the future of civilization rather than reflecting a fear of war alone. The idea of war as the agent of dissolution greatly simplified the web of anxieties about the economy, the demographic future or the nature of modern man because everything was reduced down to an apparently unavoidable choice between death and survival. In June 1936 John Strachey, writing on collective security for the *Left Book News*, insisted that Britain now faced 'the last chance' to try to rescue the civilized order or face a 'Second World War'. The country had less than a year, he estimated, before 'general war is certain'.[7] Louis Fischer, writing to Beatrice Webb in January 1936, explained that in his view the threat of war reflected the fact that 'the whole system is bankrupt'. The question European nations all lived with, Fischer continued, was whether war would come in '1936 or 1937', adding, 'the most people hope for is a postponement to 1938'.[8] By early 1938 the idea of war as a systemic inevitability was widespread. The *New Statesman* editor Kingsley Martin titled his lecture to a University of London weekend school in March 'The Present World War'; a few months before, a Fabian Society lecture presented 'The War Horizon' as if war were now a visible part of the political landscape. The record of a New Fabian Research Bureau two-day symposium in June 1938 on the strategic situation in Europe shows that the assumption of unavoidable war underscored every debate.[9] Even the pacifist National Peace Council, in a statement issued in April 1938 on 'Peace and the Democracies', deplored a world in which 'general war will become inevitable'.[10] From the publication of Knickerbocker's book onwards much of the discussion of war was dominated by the question 'when?' rather than 'whether?'

It is not unreasonable to argue that important sections of the British public were gripped in the last half of the decade by a war psychosis which came to dominate many areas of public discussion, like living, as the pacifist Leslie Paul remarked in 1936, 'in the lunatic asylum of the Universe'.[11] This is not to deny that the international system faced serious difficulties, but the popular view focused not so much on individual points of crisis but on the apparently irremediable nature of a political order doomed to destruction. The view of war as a psychological or physical disease of civilization, or rather of a civilization so pathologically disordered that it could not avoid the self-incurred and self-destructive malady of war, found a ready audience already predisposed to think in morbid terms of the current crisis. There are examples of such fears provoking a physical or psychological reaction among those who suffered them. The historian A. L. Rowse left a revealing account in his diary of the effect prolonged crisis and fear of war had on his own physical disposition. In an entry in August 1937 Rowse found himself 'so disturbed – the papers are full of the world going to pieces', and continued: 'The effect of this endless agony I have been living in since 1931 is curious: I believe the whole of the Left feels it: tiredness, hopelessness. They have us by the balls. There is nothing we can do.' A few lines further on Rowse was tortured by 'the hideous thought' that human society actually needs the disease:

Matter gathers up in the human organism which demands an outlet; they must fire off; they can't stand being at peace . . . Only after a really good 'do' is there an interval of peace, and their spirits are kept down. Then they must break out again, like pus out of a cist, an abscess. The thing is getting such an extension, is growing along all the roots and tendons of society, it is more like a cancer.[12]

The anthropologist Bronislaw Malinowski in correspondence with the pacifist Ruth Fry in 1935 saw his own physical condition – 'over-work, slackness, ill-health' – as a product of the 'universal complaints of our times'. Like Rowse, Malinowski had arrived at a mental dead end: 'I simply cannot see a way out . . . complete lassitude and absolute disenchantment are the key-notes of my present outlook.'[13] A few months later Fry herself, addressing a meeting in Manchester, explained how 'this overshadowing expectation of war' blighted and intimidated every individual effort, 'paralysing them instead of inspiring them'.[14]

This war psychosis was very different from the temporary lust for war that characterized populations in 1914, not only because it was born of a full knowledge of what modern war was capable of inflicting but also because it could operate in a void, independent of a specific crisis. Indeed, the absence of a certain enemy and a sure destination made war more disconcerting and menacing rather than less. Ernest Jones, observing the 'emotional turmoil' lying behind the obsession with war, detected a paralysing ambivalence in the population, 'too anxious about war, too eager for certitude'.[15] The mounting obsession with war was a product of fear, not enthusiasm. It was a fear expressed often enough at the time in terms of the stark physical damage modern warfare could inflict on human minds and bodies: 'Fear of poison gas,' wrote Norman Maclean in 1934, 'fear of bombing planes; fear of bacilli; fear of blight that will blacken the harvest fields; fear of the massacres of whole populations' and, above all, fear as the source of war itself.[16] The phobia about war was fuelled by the constant repetition of this litany of terrible threats at the heart of modern conflict, even though at the time there was no obvious enemy or any state with the capacity to inflict these apocalyptic fantasies on another. Opponents of war painted its reality in such uncompromising terms in the hope that no sane person, once the risks were understood, would contemplate taking part.

The result of this paranoia could be paradoxical. Critics of the anti-war movement saw the public dread of war as in some sense self-defeating, for the more war was discussed and the more lurid the imagery invoked to describe its effects, the more war itself seemed to assume a solid shape in the popular mind and the narrower and more extreme became the options between an unattainable state of peace and an all-too attainable state of catastrophic war. In his book *Peace and War*, translated into English in 1933, the Italian historian Guglielmo Ferrero, recently appointed to a professorship in Geneva, explored the paradox that fear of war might even provoke war: 'people have never thought so much about war and its future horrors, real or imaginary', he wrote. 'It would seem that our age has a foreboding that some day or other it is sure to be wiped out in some nightmare outburst of violence,' and he concluded, 'Pacifism itself is only a form, perhaps the most hopeless form, of the war obsession.'[17] In January 1936 Lawrence Jacks complained in an article on the League that he had just read a book on its future in which the words 'war' and 'aggressor' were used more frequently than any other. He called on the public to 'Stop *talking* about war'; in his view 'If we talk about war much longer we may talk it into existence.'[18] The 1937 *Peace Year Book* was a good example. Leonard Woolf wrote the opening survey, '1936 – A Review', where he chose to describe in gloomy detail every disaster that the international order had faced and failed to solve in 1936, but said almost nothing about peace. The next chapter, devoted to the League, warned that the writing was on the wall 'in glaring capitals': there had to be either manifestation of greater goodwill or the point would soon come 'when war becomes as inevitable as death'.[19]

Pacifism or fear of war did not directly cause the conflict that broke out in 1939, but both sentiments played a central part in preparing the population for its strong possibility and unavoidably linked the expectation of war with the question of the survival or death of contemporary civilization. The discourse on war defined the nature of future conflict not as limited police actions or small-scale inter-vention but always in millennial language. This meant that any crisis faced by the British public in the latter half of the decade would be interpreted in the most acute terms, and bound the idea of war indissolubly with the fate of the world rather than with short-term political or territorial readjustment. The result was a complex and shifting relationship between ideas of peace, war and civilization which eventually locked both politicians and public into an existential dead end in which the civilized world was faced with the real prospect of a destructive war that no one wanted but everyone talked about. It is against this background that the international dramas of the last years of peace were played out.

Of all these crises the most important was the Spanish Civil War. The many ambiguities in the British perception of crisis were suddenly nakedly exposed by the eruption of civil war in Spain following an abortive coup d'état launched on 17/18 July 1936 by a group of nationalist army leaders including General Francisco Franco, who by September had become the dominant figure in the revolt. The impact of the Spanish Civil War on British opinion has seldom had the attention it deserves, but its role as a catalyst in shaping British attitudes towards contemporary crisis was direct and substantial. The Spanish crisis even more than anti-fascism, with which it was closely connected, was appropriated by important areas of British society as prologue to a terrible drama in which they too might be forced to play a leading part. Spain was an issue that compelled attention after years of apparent drift and ambivalence. Noel Annan was an undergraduate in Cambridge when the war broke out. He recalled in his memoirs that the left-wing intelligentsia were obsessed by the outcome of the war and the defeat of 'fascism', but the concern was more universal than that, and not necessarily left wing; Annan himself acknowledged that 'my generation was overwhelmingly on the side of the Republic', and this included many who were, or had been, politically unaligned.[20]

There was support too for Franco's Nationalist cause among British fascists and Catholics repelled by Republican violence towards religion and among the anti-communist elements of the establishment. The journalist Tom Driberg described a pro-Franco meeting at the Queen's Hall in April 1938 where the platform 'bore a rich load of furs, jewels, spats and paunches' and well-modulated voices shouted 'Viva Franco!' as if the words were English.[21] The official government position, decided on in late June 1936 even before the civil war broke out, was to suspend arms shipments for the Republican government for fear of encouraging a move towards a communist Spain. This was followed a few weeks later by a French initiative to establish an international Non-Intervention Committee, which met for the first time in London in September in a vain attempt to prevent the supply of assistance to either side.[22] None of this could reduce the popular response among much of the centre and left of the British political spectrum that the Nationalists represented the forces of fascism while the Republic stood for democracy or, for those further to the left, a communist future. 'Never since the French Revolution', wrote the poet Robert Graves in 1940, 'had there been a foreign question that so divided intelligent British opinion.'[23]

For the broad anti-fascist movement, the Spanish Civil War supplied a real battlefield rather than a metaphorical conflict. 'You will feel you are alive out there,' a friend told the young poet David Gascoyne. 'Here everything is so unreal.'[24] The future film director John Boulting, in correspondence with Marjorie Battcock from the Hampstead Peace Council, complained to her in February 1937 that in London there was only 'dirt, disorder and a terrifying din', which seemed to him 'a fitting accompaniment' for an age that was rushing 'headlong, blindly and almost eagerly towards a gigantic carnival of self-extermination'.[25] But in Spain a few weeks later, a volunteer for the Republican cause, he

A group of workers from the Welsh town of Abertillery display placards in support of the Spanish Republic. The woman pictured in the centre of the photograph is Dolores Ibárruri, known as 'la Pasionaria'; she made famous the slogan 'no pasaran' – 'they shall not pass' – also pictured on the placards.

found a startling contrast, a grandeur, dignity and nobility appropriate to a people marked by exceptional generosity, gallantry and 'grace of action', who made war 'with a vigour and passion' that reflected their instinctive understanding of the seriousness of the conflict.[26] He was one of a brief flood of British literary and artistic visitors and volunteers who also thought they would find in Spain an authenticity and endeavour missing in British society, or who arrived out of curiosity as much as commitment. Though some, like the poet W. H. Auden, stayed very briefly before returning to Britain, the fact that many went at all is remarkable, given the risks they were exposed to, not only from Nationalist fire but from the angry rivalry between communists, social-democrats, anarchists and separatists which cost the lives of thousands supposedly fighting on the same side.

British volunteers numbered around 4,000, with approximately 2,300 enlisted in the International Brigade; they included the novelist

George Orwell, the poets Laurie Lee, John Cornford, Julian Bell, Charles Donnelly, the Marxist critics Christopher Caudwell and Ralph Fox, the writer Hugh Slater alongside scientists and philosophers and ex-soldiers.[27] The majority of the volunteers consisted of British workers, many of them communists, who wanted to fight fascism with guns rather than fighting the British National Government with demonstrations. Tom Wintringham, the soldier who became commander of the British battalion of the International Brigades, thought the men under his command resembled supporters in a football crowd or the stalwarts of a May Day march.[28] They saw their battle, as the commanders of the British battalion explained in a manifesto sent back to Britain in April 1938 to encourage a British popular front, as the front line against fascism in general. 'Why are we here?' ran the manifesto. 'Why did we choose to leave our homes and whatever security and comfort we had to plunge into this hell called war?' The answer given to these questions might now be regarded as propaganda or rhetoric, but these were men exposed to death and injury for their beliefs every day of the fighting. 'We knew that if the aggressors succeeded in Spain,' the manifesto continued, 'not a home in Britain would be safe ... We came here to defend our own homes, the homes of Britain. We came from a peace-loving people prepared to battle for peace.'[29] The News Chronicle journalist Henry Brailsford, who as a young man had volunteered for a Greek foreign legion in 1897 to fight against the Turks over the future of Crete (under the command of the son of the famous Italian guerrilla fighter Giuseppe Garibaldi), encouraged his readers to volunteer for Spain, where they would fight for the 'future of freedom and social justice', and so turn over 'the dismal page that narrates the doings of contemporary Europe'.[30] The men who responded to the call were few of them latter-day Byrons like Brailsford (who failed to point out that the brief war he had been in ended in complete defeat), but they understood the nature of the contest well enough. Writing to his wife from the front in February 1937, the militia commander Bob Edwards talked of bodies that had become 'hard and strong' and minds 'full of love and ideals'.[31]

It is nevertheless the fate of the intellectuals in Spain that has attracted the most attention, just as at the time it alerted the intelligentsia who remained behind in Britain of the stakes their peers were fighting for. George Orwell was the best known of their number. He left London for Barcelona at Christmas 1936. On the train through southern France, crowded with European volunteers for the fight against fascism, Orwell watched peasants in the fields stand upright as they passed, their fists clenched in salute.[32] He arrived in Barcelona around 26 December, rejected the request that he join the propaganda section, volunteered for active service with the independent communist movement (the Partido Obrero de Unificación Marxista or POUM) and after a week was sent to join the POUM militia on the Aragón front near the city of Huesca. He made an immediate impression on his arrival, dressed in a motley assortment of clothes, his head covered by a chocolate-coloured knitted balaclava, two hand grenades dangling at his belt and a small dog at his heels with 'POUM' painted on its side. His commander remembered a man so fastidious about completing his toilet each day that if there was no water to shave in, he would shave in wine.[33] Orwell chafed at the bit on a quiet sector of the front, and thought of transferring to Madrid, but it was outside Huesca on 20 May that he was shot by a Nationalist sniper. The bullet passed through his neck, missing anything anatomically vital. Convalescent, he arrived back in Barcelona just after the local authorities had rounded up, imprisoned or murdered radical anarchists and Marxists (later demonized as Trotskyists) and had to hide for several days until, posing as tourists, Orwell, his wife Eileen (who had come out to nurse him) and several companions succeeded in taking a train out of Spain seated in the restaurant car. Three weeks later the Spanish Tribunal for Espionage and High Treason at the Republican capital in Valencia prepared a document indicting Eric and Eileen Blair ('Orwell' was his pseudonym) as Trotskyite rebels.[34] Orwell returned to England where he wrote Homage to Catalonia, published in April 1938, not by his usual publisher, Victor Gollancz, who thought the book too controversial, but by Secker & Warburg. Orwell blamed orthodox communists for destroying the anarchist experiment in the city, an accusation that distorted the complex political reality in Barcelona. Like many who went to Spain full of enthusiasm for a real united front against the fascist menace, Orwell returned bitterly disillusioned. 'What a show!' he wrote to his fellow POUM fighter

Charles Doran in August 1937. 'To think that we started off as heroic defenders of democracy and only six months later were Trotsky-Fascists sneaking over the border with the police on our heels.'[35]

Orwell was lucky to survive his six months in Spain. Among the other intellectual volunteers there was a high death rate. Christopher Caudwell, the pseudonym for Christopher St John Sprigg, was a committed communist who wrote detective stories under his real name and serious works on philosophy and literary criticism under his *nom de plume*. Caudwell joined the British Battalion of the International Brigade on 11 December 1936, and was killed on 12 February 1937, a member of a machine-gun section who stayed to hold a hill crest against Nationalist forces while his unit retired from the battle. He explained his decision to enlist conventionally enough as the defence of democratic freedom; if the Spanish people failed, he wrote, the struggle 'will certainly be ours tomorrow'. Caudwell was a Communist Party member with a strong commitment to personal freedom. 'Liberty', he wrote in a review of a book of Bertrand Russell's essays, 'does seem to me the most important of the generalised goods – such as justice, beauty, truth – that come so easily to our lips.'[36] But his view of liberty derided the idea of heroic bourgeois individualism in favour of collective efforts at emancipation, which was why he fought in Spain. There were also the poets John Cornford and Julian Bell. Cornford was a young charismatic communist-poet, the son of the Cambridge professor of ancient philosophy Francis Cornford and his poet wife Frances. Noel Annan remembered him working tirelessly fourteen hours a day for the cause, 'his handsome Moorish face, a cigarette hanging from his lips, his shoulders hunched', a personality emitting 'power, energy and conviction'. He joined first the POUM, then the British International Brigade and died at Christmas 1936 the day after his twenty-first birthday on the hills above the Madrid–Córdoba road near the village of Lopera, standing heedlessly in bright sunlight with a white bandage round his head, a magnet for the Moroccan sniper who killed him.[37] His poems were written before the civil war turned sour with internecine strife and his faith could be severely tested. Like Orwell, he seems to have assumed that communists, 'Trotskyists' and anarchists were fighting the same battle.

Nothing brought home the realities of the war as completely as the death of Julian Bell, offspring of the Bloomsbury group. The son of Clive and Vanessa Bell, and Virginia Woolf's nephew, he was a young poet and writer with a simple and direct view of the necessity for violent political engagement. He was in China as a professor of English at Hankow University when the civil war broke out, but returned to London determined to enlist and fight against the fascist threat. The pleas of his mother, and perhaps the pacifist outlook of most of his family circle and friends, persuaded him to go to Spain as a member of the British Medical Unit sponsored by the Spanish Medical Aid Committee and he joined an ambulance crew. His family were surrounded by the campaign to save Spanish democracy and occasionally directly touched by it. Stephen Spender wrote to Virginia Woolf in February that he, too, was going to Spain to give broadcasts, but home again two months later he wrote once more of the disillusioning reality of Spain, where he thought politics distorted everything and trapped the young idealists in its coils: 'The sensitive, the weak, the romantic, the enthusiastic, the truthful live in Hell there and cannot get away.'[38] In June, to mark the fall of the Basque city of Bilbao and the evacuation of 4,000 children to Britain, Virginia Woolf and an array of literary and political figures were invited to sit on the platform at the Albert Hall for a rally to raise funds. By a quirk of fate a number of the children marched through Bloomsbury, where Virginia happened to see them go past in a dishevelled file, 'impelled by machine guns in Spanish fields', she later wrote, 'to trudge through Tavistock Square'.[39]

On 20 July came the news that Julian Bell had died of wounds received from a shell two days before. There are conflicting accounts of the circumstances of his death, but a letter to the *New Statesman* on 28 August 1937 from one of his colleagues in the Medical Unit gave what must be regarded as the fullest account. His ambulance had already been hit and disabled on 15 July by a bomb. He volunteered to do stretcher duty and was driving a lorry early in the morning along a road where the shell holes needed filling in when his vehicle was hit by artillery and he died of shrapnel wounds.[40] For the Bloomsbury families his death proved devastating. 'Lord, why do these things happen?' wrote Virginia Woolf to Vita Sackville-West a few days later, 'I'm not clear enough in my head to feel anything but varieties of dull rage and despair.'[41] Virginia replied in August to Rosamond Lehmann's letter of condolence: 'No, there is nothing to be said. We've been through so much together, but this is the worst . . .'[42] E. M. Forster wrote a few weeks later to Vanessa Bell asking how she had coped with the tragedy. 'Our generation does manage,' he continued. 'I think it is one of the slight advantages we get from being civilised.'[43] The echoes of the grief borne by those who lost sons in the Great War could not have been lost on either the Bell or Woolf households. The deaths of Julian Bell and almost 500 other British volunteers in Spain can be seen as the first casualties in Britain's new world war. Fittingly, after the Brigaders returned home on 8 December 1938, the veterans of the conflict defied government disapproval by marching down Whitehall and laying a wreath at the Cenotaph for their fallen comrades.[44] A National Memorial Fund for the wounded and the dependants of the dead was set up by Charlotte Haldane which aimed to raise £50,000 from public subscription. In July 1939 'Debt of Honour' weeks were organized across Britain to remember the dead and disabled veterans of the conflict.[45]

Those who went to Spain but returned without fighting also played an important part in sustaining a wave of popular interest in the Spanish conflict that took little account of the paradoxes of the war or of the disillusionment of many of those who found combat too hard to stomach or were alienated by the divisive and vicious tensions in the Republican camp. Few people in Britain understood the nature of Spanish politics, even among the more informed sections of the public, and they took the sentimental black-and-white perspective on the war as the reality. W. H. Auden returned from Spain after a two-month spell with a medical unit, unwilling to talk about his experiences, or his doubts after seeing churches burnt to the ground, and in spring 1937 penned one of the best-known of the Spanish Civil War poems, entitled simply 'Spain', with its stark injunction to take sides, 'for I am your choice, your decision. Yes, I am Spain.'[46] There was nothing routinely predictable about how that choice was made. A pamphlet titled 'Spain' published by the British Communist Party in August 1936 was reprinted three times in two weeks, reaching a total of 140,000 copies and read by an audience that was predominantly non-communist.[47] Katherine, Duchess of Atholl, Conservative

MP for the Scottish seat of Perth and Kinross and a woman of strongly progressive views, threw herself into the campaign to save Republican Spain. In early 1937, after a tour of the war-torn areas, she wrote the fourth of the Penguin Specials, *Searchlight on Spain*, which she dedicated to all those Spaniards 'fighting or toiling for democratic government'; published in June 1938, it sold 100,000 copies in a week.[48] George Orwell, remarking on how catalytic the effect of the Spanish Civil War had been on British opinion, found it hard to see how 'patriotic Communists and communistic duchesses' could easily cohabit, but reaction to the war was not determined by partisan considerations.[49] When the Hungarian journalist Arthur Koestler was sent to Spain as a *News Chronicle* reporter and subsequently arrested in Málaga by Franco's forces and sentenced to death, almost half of the fifty-eight members of parliament who petitioned for his release were Conservatives.[50] At the time Koestler was still a Communist Party member and part of the propaganda network set up by the German communist Willi Münzenberg, though he rapidly shed his communism, disillusioned like Orwell by its double-dealing. Koestler wrote an account of his time in Spain, including his spell in a Franco prison, and it was published by the Left Book Club as *Spanish Testament* with an introduction by the Duchess of Atholl. To promote the book, but also to inform the British public about the terms of the war, Koestler was sent on a gruelling publicity tour through England in January 1938, lecturing thirteen times in twelve days, from Plymouth in the south-west to Liverpool, Manchester and Southport in the north.[51]

All writers were encouraged to rally to the cause of Spain, though the unspoken assumption was that they would do so as progressives. Robert Graves, Wyndham Lewis and G. K. Chesterton stood out from the intellectual crowd as partisans for Franco, but their stand was the exception, not the rule. The *Left Review* in June 1937 sent out an appeal under the signature of the writer Nancy Cunard, daughter of the shipping tycoon, asking writers to say in six lines or fewer whether they were for the legal Republican government and whether they were for or against Franco and fascism. The appeal, simply titled 'The Question', said with Auden that it was now time to take sides: 'The equivocal attitude, the Ivory Tower, the paradoxical, the ironic detachment, will no longer do.'[52] Samuel Beckett submitted a single, linguistically progressive word: '¡UPTHEREPUBLIC!' Orwell was infuriated by what he saw as simple posturing and wrote a diatribe which began: 'Will you please stop sending me this bloody rubbish!'[53] The replies, except for Orwell's, were published in December 1937 as 'Authors Take Sides on the Spanish War', though the plural in the title was misleading since support for the Republic was generally taken for granted. Out of 148 entries published there were only five unwilling to endorse the Republic (though most were not actually pro-Franco, except for Evelyn Waugh), 127 for the Republic, and sixteen neutral, including T. S. Eliot, who thought 'a few men of letters should remain isolated'. Vera Brittain expressed her neutrality on the ground that whatever the issues, war was wrong.[54]

Few of those who chose the anti-fascist cause remained or became enthusiastic for communism. The young poet David Gascoyne, tempted by the prospect of a world purer and less decadent, joined the Communist Party in September 1936 as a kind of rite of passage into Spain, went briefly to Barcelona at the end of October to relay propaganda, stayed less than a month and returned to London where, according to his journal, he chose to forget both Spain and communism and immersed himself indulgently once again in London literary life.[55] Another poet, Stephen Spender, again joined the party as an introduction to Spain and went twice in the early spring and again in the summer of 1937, this time as a delegate to the International Writers' Congress held in Madrid, where intellectuals were expected to show their solidarity with the Republican cause. Spender later wrote that the 'circus of intellectuals, treated like princes or ministers, carried for hundreds of miles through beautiful scenery and war-torn towns, to the sound of cheering voices, amid broken hearts, riding in Rolls-Royces, banqueted, fêted ... had something grotesque about it'. The group argued, postured, displayed at times 'hysterical conceitedness'. Spender returned from Spain disillusioned with communism and political engagement and adopted 'an extreme pre-occupation with the problems of self'.[56] For those who bothered to go to Spain and confront its insoluble misery there remained a sense of hopelessness or guilty failure which those who stayed behind could not share.

Yet to understand the profound effect on British society of the

Spanish war it is necessary to recognize that its impact on British opinion was not confined to the intellectual elite. It was difficult for the wider public not to be aware of the conflict and the terms in which it was fought. Popular interest in the civil war was sustained remarkably through almost three years of fighting. From the outset those sympathetic to Spanish democracy, from across a wide political spectrum, organized rallies, demonstrations and fund-raising. Relief committees sprang up all over the country and were centralized under the umbrella of the National Joint Committee for Spanish Relief, which was supported by members of all the major parties and chaired by the Conservative Duchess of Atholl. The Joint Committee had 180 affiliated bodies and links with another 800 organizations of one kind or another. The Committee was so anxious to insist on its non-partisan credentials that at every public meeting a notice was read out announcing that the body served 'no political purpose'.[57] Spain was a cause that called for levels of organization and commitment which had little to do with Spanish realities but much to do with the sudden realization in Britain that Spain provided a rallying point for British arguments over fascism, communism, democracy, war and the future.

The impact on local communities in Britain is worth exploring in some detail because it was the regular day-to-day exposure to the Spanish conflict which explains why Spain became so embedded in British public awareness as a symbol of an age of violent crisis. The surviving records of the campaign in Cambridge provide an interesting if not entirely typical example of this process of public appropriation. The pro-Republican cause was shared between a wide number of institutions from the Trades Council, the trade union movement, the local Labour Party, the university socialist and liberal clubs, the local branch of the Socialist League, the League of Nations Union and the Cambridge peace organizations.[58] The local Catholic Church authorities also organized meetings in support of Franco where stories of communist atrocities against religious communities were read out amid noisy and hostile interruptions from the audience. The local Church network was made a target by those sympathetic to the Republic, who undertook a leaflet campaign using two short pamphlets by the Catholic socialist Monica Whately, issued by Clement

The Spain Shop in Southwark, south London. All over the country Spain shops were opened selling Spanish goods and providing a centre for collecting funds, food and articles of clothing for the victims of the war.

Attlee's constituency in Limehouse, London, under the titles 'Another Catholic looks at Spain' and 'Catholics and their Responsibility for the Spanish Civil War', both published in order to counter accusations of church burnings and the murder of priests. 'If the Fascist rebels win,' she wrote, 'we shall be moved one step nearer, in this country, to the same awful dictatorship to which I believe death to be preferable.'[59] The organizers in Cambridge, among whom the young scientists Joseph and Dorothy Needham were prominent, distributed 1,750 copies of the leaflets to nine volunteers, who then put them through letter boxes or stood outside churches handing them out to congregations. In October the Cambridge Scientists' Anti-War Group produced a local pamphlet on 'Spain: Why Are They Fighting in Spain?' which tackled accusations of the communist nature of the Republic by highlighting the fact that the government was composed of liberals and social-democrats. This was also to be delivered to households, along with a door-to-door collection for Spanish aid and weekend poster parades through the city centre. The city was broken down into areas and streets and a long list of volunteers was recruited to deliver the information material, much as they would be for a general election campaign. In June 1937 a mass rally and demonstration was held on the city-centre common at Parker's Piece inspired by the belief that the German shelling of the port of Almería from the cruiser *Deutschland* meant a German–Spanish war and the onset of a general European conflict.[60]

Cambridge was also one of the cities that volunteered in May 1937 to receive a contingent of thirty evacuated Basque children, part of an exodus of 4,000 to which the British government had finally granted permission for entry in April on condition that they were no burden on public funds, were confined to the age range 5–15 and would be repatriated as soon as it became safe to do so.[61] The campaign to look after the children was formally politically neutral, though few could have been in any doubt about where responsibility lay for driving them to seek asylum in the first place. Their plight brought a nationwide response which was vetted by an emergency Basque Children's Committee, chaired by the Duchess of Atholl with Lord Robert Cecil as honorary treasurer. By the end of May, twenty-three cities had applied to receive the children; 1,200 of them were housed by Catholic institutions and 400 accepted by the Salvation Army. A great deal was made in the publicity about the children's anti-fascist enthusiasm, but they came from a cross-section of Basque society and Spanish politics.[62] The children were placed in children's homes or private households under the supervision of ad hoc committees which mushroomed in response to the crisis, and not only in mining villages and factory towns. In the middle-class suburbs south of London, for example, a whole network of associations developed which linked local communities with the Spanish drama. The Carshalton Basque Children's Association, working with other local Surrey Spanish Aid Committees in Sutton, Wallington and Epsom and with the Basque Children's Committee in Croydon, had regular weekly committee meetings throughout the period 1937–9 with a handful of volunteer officials who supervised the Basque children housed in a local children's home. The committee minutes reveal a succession of educational and cultural initiatives, regular concerts of Basque folk songs and dances performed by the children and, towards the end of the civil war, in January 1939 a gala event at the local cinema which raised £20 for the flood of new refugees from Franco's Spain.[63]

It is not difficult to understand popular support for the Basque children – 'pathetic little orphans of war', as the Duchess of Atholl later described them – but popular local volunteer support ran much deeper than this.[64] All over the country efforts were made to raise money to send food and medical supplies to the victims of war on both sides. In Surrey special stamps were issued in blocks of six with the face value of 1d to help to fund the 'Surrey Spain Foodship'; small milk tokens were sold at 6d each to provide a supply of milk for the children and nursing mothers of Barcelona and other Spanish cities. Collectors with special badges delivered envelopes from house to house to raise funds for Spanish relief (some with 'Entirely Neutral' printed in the corner to demonstrate that this was no communist plot).[65] At national level the National Council of Labour and the Trades Union Congress organized regular contributions from branches and members which reached £130,000 and over 1,000 tons of foodstuffs by the end of 1936; by the end of the civil war over £2 million had been donated, most of it to the Republican cause. Although the Labour Party was cautious about involvement in the Spanish conflict from fear of alien-

Basque children at Watermillock in Lancashire in June 1937 receiving presents of dolls donated by the public. They were part of an exodus of 4,000 child refugees from the civil war in the Basque areas of Spain.

ating some of its working-class Catholic constituency, it sponsored Spain Days and sold flags and leaflets. By the spring of 1938 the International Solidarity Fund, which the National Council of Labour supported, had shipped seventy-six consignments of aid amounting to 5,185 tons of supplies including everything from flour, cigarettes and condensed milk to a ship from Hull loaded with seventeen bales of clothing.[66] Some local organizations were in favour of sending weapons to Spain in defiance of government policy, and plans were made by Trades Councils in Edinburgh and Glasgow to smuggle arms, but the organized labour movement confined its help largely to voluntary humanitarian aid on a quite unprecedented scale. The large national rallies and congresses in favour of saving Spanish democracy held throughout 1937 and 1938 were largely organized through cross-party or non-party efforts and mobilized support from a wide range of institutions. One of the largest, the National Emergency Conference on Spain held at the Queen's Hall in London on 23 April 1938, with an introductory address by Gilbert Murray, attracted 1,806 delegates from 1,205 separate organizations – youth movements, trade unions, co-operatives, Labour Party and Liberal Party branches, Peace Councils, League of Nations Union branches, and so on. In other parts of the country, sixty-eight rallies and demonstrations were staged on the same day.[67] Spain, more than the crisis in central Europe provoked by Hitler, had become for much of British society the touchstone of the future of European civilization.

One issue above most that kept the debate on Spain alive was the bombing of Spanish cities. Bombing touched a raw nerve in Britain, just as it did elsewhere, because of all the elements of modern warfare bombing promised an apparently swift and irrecoverable end to the civilized world. Much has been written on the culture of fear that surrounded the prospect of a bombing apocalypse, a fear that expanded in the 1930s with evidence of what bombing could do in China and Ethiopia. The fear was fed by a stream of scaremongering novels and science-fiction films that traded on the peculiar psychological reaction to death from the air, which was always treated differently from the equally lethal artillery shell and torpedo.[68] The destruction of the Basque city of Guernica on the afternoon of 26 April 1937 became very quickly the symbolic act that stood for bombing atrocity in general, but bombing had begun in 1936 and went on until the end of the civil war. It was joined from the middle of 1937 by the bombing of Chinese cities by the Japanese air force with the onset in July of a second phase of the Sino-Japanese conflict. Bombing was certainly carried out by both sides in Spain, but it was the conspicuous attacks on cities crowded with civilians by the Nationalist forces and the air contingents sent from Italy and Germany that attracted public attention. It was German and Italian planes that attacked Guernica, leaving what is now thought to be around 250 dead and destroying a large part of the central urban area. The Basque city of Durango was also hit several times in the weeks leading up to the Guernica raid and more civilians killed (the headline of one Cambridge leaflet issued in June 1937 read 'Durango! Guernica! Almeria!'), but it is Guernica that became the reference point in popular discussion of bombing in Spain and has remained so ever since.[69]

This was due in part to chance. A *Times* reporter, George Steer, who had already covered the Abyssinian war, was in the northern port of Bilbao together with a group of correspondents on the night Guernica was bombed. Late in the evening they drove out to see the town for themselves and found it a blazing ruin, the squares full of the wounded on tables and mattresses, officials and Basque militiamen dazed and horror-struck. Steer found an incendiary with the name of the German firm that manufactured it stamped on the metal. He returned the following morning to look at the ruins again before filing his story. As a result news broke initially through Reuters, sent by one of Steer's companions, and was published first in Paris. *The Times* published Steer's piece on 30 April and Guernica entered into atrocity's pantheon. The British Consul wrote to the British ambassador, Sir Henry Chilton, the results of his own visit to Guernica, confirming Steer's report. 'Nine houses in ten', he wrote, 'are beyond reconstruction.'[70] At a rally at the Royal Albert Hall on 30 April organized by the League of Nations Union the bombing of Guernica was publicly condemned. A few weeks later, on 6 May, British Gaumont cinemas showed newsreel footage of the ruins while the voiceover talked of 'the most terrible air raid our modern history can yet boast ... This was a city and these were homes, like yours.' Although no mention was made in the newsreel of who was responsible, Guernica had been discussed enough in the press for there to be little doubt. Franco's propaganda office insisted that the town had been burned down by retreating 'Red' forces pursuing a policy of scorched earth, but this was believed only by the most credulous or bigoted. On 29 May, in response to the growing protests against bombing, the League of Nations unanimously called for the withdrawal of foreign forces from Spain and condemned the bombing of open cities by both sides, though without effect.[71]

Bombing continued over the course of the year, with heavy and damaging attacks on Barcelona in particular, and in February 1938 Lord Robert Cecil and Walter Layton organized an appeal to be sent to both sides to suspend bombing attacks against civilians. The brief, pompously worded petition was to be signed by a wide range of public officeholders and famous names: 'The undersigned, representing diverse sections of the British Nation, implore the leaders of

Republican and Nationalist Spain ... to abandon by express agreement the deliberate bombing of civilian populations.' The list of signatories extended to eight typed pages and included fifteen lord mayors of major British cities, the Lord Mayor of London and the Provost of Glasgow (all of whose cities were to experience bombing three years later), the two Protestant archbishops, five bishops, and Inge's successor as Dean of St Paul's. The few who refused to sign almost all applauded the sentiment but felt their official position precluded support.[72] The appeal was drawn up by 7 February and a delegation recruited to present it to the Spanish representatives of the two sides and to Neville Chamberlain. The official Spanish government replied almost at once that it had already ordered air attacks on Nationalist urban targets to be suspended. There was some doubt about how to send the appeal to Franco but it was eventually sent to his headquarters by airmail addressed simply to 'General Franco, Burgos'.[73] His staff took time to reply but rejected the appeal on the grounds that no city was 'open' because the Republican forces deliberately concealed military supplies and installations among residential streets. Renewed bombing finally brought a statement from Chamberlain of his 'horror and disgust'; he told the House of Commons that 'the one definite rule of international law is that the direct and deliberate bombing of non-combatants is in all circumstances illegal', a view that he sustained through to the end of his premiership in May 1940.[74]

As the Spanish war drew to its close the memory of the bombing was kept alive by the decision to exhibit in Britain the large canvas painted in May and June 1937 by Pablo Picasso for the World's Fair in Paris which he titled 'Guernica'. The half-finished painting had been seen by Vanessa Bell and Julian's brother Quentin in Picasso's studio in Paris, where they had gone in May 1937 in an unsuccessful attempt to persuade Picasso to attend the rally in the Albert Hall, though at the time they were not impressed by it.[75] 'Guernica' was displayed in the Spanish pavilion at the fair, where it attracted a mixed response. During 1938 the artist Roland Penrose, supported by the Spanish Relief Committee and the Duchess of Atholl, arranged for the painting to be transferred to the New Burlington Art Gallery in central London for an exhibition in October. Distinguished patrons, including E. M. Forster, Virginia Woolf and Victor Gollancz, subsidized the exhibition.[76] Even here politics intruded, for the art critic Anthony Blunt, much later exposed as a spy for the Soviet Union, took the communist line with Picasso's anarchic style and attacked the painting loudly and publicly. The attendance of 3,000 was disappointing for the organizers, but the preliminary sketches of 'Guernica', which had been sent with the finished painting, toured the country during November and December to wide publicity before they were returned to the Whitechapel Art Gallery in London's East End together with the main painting. This second exhibition in London attracted 15,000 visitors, each presenting as the price of admission a pair of boots for Spanish soldiers, which were lined up each day at the entranceway. The boots and the money raised by the exhibitions were to be sent to what was left of the Republican front in Spain.[77] That same month Barcelona was finally stormed by Nationalist troops and on 28 March Madrid, the last divided Republican bastion, capitulated. At the end of the war British support for the failed Republic reached a peak. Opinion polls taken in October 1938 showed 57 per cent for the Republic, 9 per cent for Franco and 34 per cent undecided; but by January 1939 72 per cent favoured a regime that in practice no longer existed, while for the triumphant Franco there remained the small, hard-core 9 per cent.[78]

By far the most significant effect of the Spanish war was the division it opened up in Britain, in a public where there was overwhelming support for peace, between those who continued to favour non-violence, or some unspecified form of collective pressure, and those who argued that a readiness to use war was now the only way to save the existing world or to build a new one. Here was the central dilemma of the decade and its arduous history coloured every crisis down to the outbreak of war in 1939. Some of the arguments among the anti-war constituency have already been described, but Spain, as Auden realized, forced a decision. Orwell and his commanding officer Bob Edwards had both been absolute pacifists before the war. Fenner Brockway also abandoned his absolute pacifist stand on the understanding that violence was needed to secure the social revolution in Spain, and perhaps elsewhere. Argument over the Spanish conflict, complained Gilbert Murray to Cecil in October 1936, was 'the best way to wreck the peace cause'.[79] The choice between peace and

The Labour Party leader Clement Attlee speaking at a rally in the Whitechapel Art Gallery in December 1938 in front of Picasso's huge painting 'Guernica'. The gallery was visited by more than 15,000 people.

violence was a choice that much of British society found painfully difficult to make because both options, either peace or war, presented imponderable questions for the future of civilization. There was no simple conversion in Britain from a preference for peace to acceptance of war, but a long-drawn-out and often confused debate which took place from Cabinet level down to the branch meetings, lecture evenings and weekend schools of the many public and private organizations whose activities have filled this book. In this debate Spain played a central part.

The Spanish war was the testing ground for this argument not only because it was the first military confrontation in Europe since the close of the Russian Civil War fifteen years before, but because its battle lines, confused as they were in practice, appeared to mirror the existing political fissures in Europe. John Cornford in 'Full Moon at Tierz', written shortly before his death, appealed to anti-fascist sentiment in general with the lines 'O understand before too late/ Freedom was never held without a Fight'.[80] On his way by boat from China to take part in the war, Julian Bell had written a letter to E. M. Forster on the subject 'War and Peace', which Forster received only after Bell's death. In it he argued that the time for saints and enthusiasts was past, and the time of the soldier had arrived. 'At this moment, to be anti-war means to submit to fascism,' he wrote, 'to be anti-fascist means to be prepared for war.'[81] The letter was published early in 1938, alongside Forster's refusal, as he put it, to 'chuck gentleness', but it was circulated before that through the Bloomsbury circles where loathing of war had been a central element in their outlook and its effects were to produce much argument.

Virginia Woolf devoted the months after Julian Bell's death to completing a long and sustained polemic on the close connection evident to her between male vanity and war-making. It was completed in October 1937 and published in June 1938 as *Three Guineas* to mainly half-hearted or hostile reviews.[82] Leonard Woolf did not share Virginia's unconditional pacifism, or that of much of his literary circle, and found it difficult to give his usual support to Virginia's new book. In September 1937 he wrote a harsh review of *Collective Insecurity* by the veteran pacifist Helena Swanwick, who argued much the same as Virginia ('If all men hated war as much as women do, there would be no wars') and insisted that only constructive talking rather than any form of collective violence would save the world. Leonard Woolf had arrived at the view that only collective action, war if necessary, on behalf of victims of aggression would ensure that 'civilisation is to continue'.[83] He first formulated these arguments in a 1934 paper on 'A New Foreign Policy for Labour' in which he recommended a security system in which the collective was obliged to use their combined force to stop aggression while 'under no circumstances to resort to war' – a paradox that nevertheless amounted to making war on war.[84] Helena Swanwick, replying to Woolf's review, pointed out the contradiction: 'As if peace could ever be built', she told him, 'on so rotten a foundation.' Woolf had the last word. In the current state of the world, he insisted, violence could now be overcome only by the simultaneous violence of the virtuous.[85]

These were the terms of many of the arguments that punctuated the years of civil war in Spain. The young poet Hubert Nicholson, who had written about war in 1935 that 'wild horses won't drag me into the lousy game', was transformed by Spain. He shed his pacifism, argued with those who had not, and found among his working-class neighbours in Holborn an exhilarating commitment to the Spanish cause.[86] Just after the outbreak of the war, Aldous Huxley and J. D. Bernal, both central figures in the anti-war movement, engaged in an exchange over Huxley's pamphlet on constructive pacifism which Bernal had criticized for its failure to recognize that in some circumstances force is justified 'in a just cause'. Huxley was sure that even making war to prevent aggression would still 'completely smash the existing order' and leave the victor faced with either 'a chaos or a tyranny' from the physical and moral cost of having to fight. The Spanish Civil War, he argued correctly, would 'become more savage in proportion as it is prolonged'. For Bernal this was the parting of the ways and he became like Woolf committed to the idea that in the end, if peace failed, only violence could prevent a worse fate.[87]

Pacifist organizations paid the price of these arguments. In a stormy meeting of the No More War Movement in November 1936 on the difficulty of reconciling absolute pacifism with the reality of the Spanish crisis, one National Committee member announced that he had decided to abandon pacifism 'in regard to civil war'; over Spain, he continued, 'the cleavage is there'.[88] A few months later the schism provoked in the movement by the Spanish war forced it to consider winding up its activities. The MP Ellen Wilkinson, a sponsor of the Peace Pledge Union, wrote to Dick Sheppard in March 1937 resigning her position: 'I feel in view of the Spanish situation that 100% pacifism is for me impossible,' but added, 'I am sorry to have failed you . . . and I know you are right.'[89] The movement For Intellectual Liberty, to which Bernal and Huxley both belonged, also became sharply divided over the issue of Spain and pacifism. In May 1938 the decision to make a statement against National Service was derided by the MP Eleanor Rathbone, who could no longer see any sense in deploring aggression and at the same time denying the democracies the means to obstruct it. Margaret Gardiner, the secretary of FIL, told Rathbone that the organization was already accused of warmongering for supporting collective security, but would now stand condemned by the other side for opposition to conscription. 'How hard it is', she wrote to Marjorie Fry, a pacifist member of the executive committee, 'to steer a course between this Scylla and Charybdis!'[90]

This was a passage that the government also tried to navigate over the years of international crisis. The position of the National Government was to support the League, deplore war but to embark on limited, step-by-step rearmament. With the breakdown of the Disarmament Conference in October 1933 and the failure to prevent German rearmament the resort to building up national defences was regarded as an unavoidable safeguard. At the same time the National Government sought to avoid any commitments or risks that increased the likelihood of war, while retaining the possibility of having to wage it at some point. This dilemma was captured in Stanley Baldwin's speech in February 1936 at the Conservative training centre at Ashridge: 'I am not one of those who sit down and say that war is inevitable,' he told his audience. 'I only say that it is a ghastly possibility and it is our duty to fight it in every way we can.' This included the resort to war if ever another power imperilled Britain's values and safety: 'then', he continued, 'we have to defend ourselves and defend ourselves to the very end'.[91] This balancing act, like a tightrope walker without a pole, has been harshly judged by posterity but it has to be understood not in terms of what eventually happened in 1939, but in terms of the unknowable risks of placing British civilization once again in the melting-pot of world war. That these risks were regarded as enormous and the possible outcome a catastrophe owed something to the prevalence for seeing many issues, from the survival of the capitalist economy and the parliamentary system to the future development of the race, as potential life-or-death issues. In a memorandum sent to Baldwin by Maurice Hankey, the Cabinet Secretary, in June 1936 Colonel Henry Pownall, who worked with Hankey in the secretariat of the Committee of Imperial Defence observed that Britain had 'everything in the world to lose' from a second conflict and for emphasis added, 'WE SIMPLY CANNOT AFFORD TO LOSE A MAJOR WAR.'[92] Fear of gassing and bombing was only an extreme expression of a wider mood of uncertainty and apprehension that history was pointing to a cul-de-sac, closing one by one the broader avenues that branched off to right or left.

Neville Chamberlain, the man who succeeded Baldwin as prime minister on 28 May 1937, personified this schizophrenic outlook on peace and war. His long struggle between a sincere and passionate longing for peace and the terrible knowledge that war might be unavoidable coloured his whole premiership down to the morning in September 1939 when he found himself declaring it. He discovered that the mental conflict was no easier to endure or to resolve from a position of power than it was for the millions of other Britons who saw war as increasingly inevitable but willed for peace. A great deal has been written about Chamberlain, little of it flattering. Much of the left hated him with a visceral loathing and later took their revenge by shaping the way that history has remembered him as the chief of the 'Guilty Men' who appeased Hitler and failed to prepare adequately for when Hitler's appetite became too large.[93] When he assumed the premiership in 1937 he was already a man in his late sixties born into the secure and apparently progressive high-Victorian age, and shaken by the impact of war and the post-war malaise. He was a successful Conservative statesman, the son of the politician Joseph Chamberlain and half-brother of the former Foreign Secretary Austen. In the 1920s he had been a progressive Minister of Health; in the 1930s he was the National Government's Chancellor of the Exchequer who played a central part in reimposing economic stability and introducing limited elements of what became known as the 'managed economy'. Some critics regarded him as almost a socialist, though he would certainly not have been remembered that way by the millions of unemployed who could not be rescued in the post-depression revival. He was outwardly self-assured, articulate, prejudiced and hard working; among prime ministers, Sir Arthur Salter, a fellow MP, later recalled, he was 'more than usually resolute, authoritarian and strong-willed'.[94] When he was observed at dinner late in 1938 by the *Sunday Times* journalist Virginia Cowles she was surprised to find him vigorous and animated, with a quick sense of humour, but his tall, rather stiff appearance, broad moustache and beak nose made him seem a less imposing figure and the butt of easy caricature.[95] If he had not had to make the choice between peace and war he would almost certainly be remembered now as a successful political modernizer and one of the architects of the mixed economy.

A demonstration in 1937 on its way to Trafalgar Square in support of the Spanish Republic, and against fascism and war. The slogan 'Bullets for Spain, Bullet for Chamberlain' reflects the deep loathing for the new Prime Minister felt by the left long before the Munich crisis.

Chamberlain's natural place was with those who hated war and who thought that constructive discussion would cut through even the most serious obstacle. At the end of a tetchy debate with the Labour leader Clement Attlee on 21 December 1937, Chamberlain insisted that government policy was not drifting but had in front of it 'a definite objective'; this was nothing less, he continued, than 'a general settlement of the grievances of the world without war'.[96] But at the same time Chamberlain had been one of the chief sponsors of the great increase in defence spending between 1934 and 1936 which challenged his peaceable credentials. In February 1938 he told a meeting in Birmingham that he took little pleasure from rearming: 'I must confess that the spectacle of this vast expenditure upon the means of destruction instead of construction has inspired me with a feeling of revolt against the folly of mankind.'[97] He viewed rearmament as a deterrent, by building sufficient strength to discourage other states from aggression. In July he made his most candid speech about his hatred of war in another meeting in the Midland town of Kettering. Taking his cue from the 'horrible barbarities' of the wars in Spain and China, the vast and wasteful expenditure on armaments, and the regular rumours of war, he asked his audience whether the world had ever seen 'such a spectacle of human madness and folly'. The terrible costs of the conflict of 1914–18 compelled him, he claimed, 'to strain every nerve to avoid a repetition of the Great War in Europe'.[98] Although these sentiments were almost certainly shared with a large part of the population, Chamberlain is best remembered as the statesman who could satisfy no one – rearming too much and making war inevitable or rearming too little and forced to appease.

The dilemmas in national policy and public perception alike had to be confronted directly in the crisis that led up to the Munich Conference at the end of September 1938. Recent historical evaluation of the Czech crisis has moved away from the crude anti-appeasement rhetoric that has governed much of the post-war analysis of British policy, and still does among a wider public. There were compelling prudential and political reasons for reaching a settlement short of war but the fact that war was widely expected and feared is testament not so much to the intrinsic nature of the crisis, which could be, and was, resolved at the cost of Czech sovereignty without a European war, but to the long period of war psychosis that had preceded it and the widespread view of Hitler as Europe's demon. There is little evidence that Hitler or the German public viewed the Czech issue as a question of the survival of civilization, but in Britain the crisis was viewed as one in which the highest stakes were gambled. Chamberlain's historic flights to Germany to meet Hitler face to face, which had about them an exceptional sense of drama unlike anything a British prime minister had ever done, show that Chamberlain too had the measure of the stakes involved in saving peace. 'I keep racking my brains', he wrote in early September, 'to try and find some means of averting a catastrophe'; the idea of flying to see Hitler was, he considered, 'unconventional and daring', though a match for the gravity of the hour.[99]

Throughout the summer of 1938, as the crisis over Czechoslovakia began to impose itself on public awareness, there grew a tangible fear of impending disaster. For Intellectual Liberty warned its members a few months before Munich that present government policies 'can only end in universal war'. A public statement issued by the organization in the second week of September described the crisis not in terms of Czech independence but in terms of the survival of European democracy 'and the peace and civilisation of the world'.[100] The crisis prompted the public to brace itself for a war they had been told for years would be a cataclysm of terrible violence. Writing in his diary throughout the crisis Dean Inge was filled with despair: 'We have learned nothing and forgotten nothing. God help us all,' he wrote on 24 September. Four days later, before the agreement was signed, he added: 'Very miserable days; hope of peace almost extinct. The resemblance to August 1914 is terribly close.'[101] Henry Williamson, who like Inge had vivid memories of the last war, wrote from his farm in Norfolk a few weeks before the crisis that 'army lorries, searchlights, etc. thunder past' the local village, while 2,000 soldiers posted nearby engaged in live shell practice and swore and sang until midnight, and added, 'my eyes fill with tears when the thought comes of how things are being let down, down, down everywhere'.[102] The economist J. A. Hobson wrote to Arthur Ponsonby on 26 September that he expected war within a week: 'Twenty years have taught us practically nothing.'[103] Virginia Woolf, writing to Vanessa Bell just after Munich, found everyone in London 'talking loudly about war', while in the streets were piles of sandbags, men digging trenches and loud-speaker vans 'exhorting the citizens of Westminster Go and fit your gas masks'. She found everyone 'perfectly calm; and also without hope. It was quite different from 1914.'[104] In London, 'the feeling of despair and coming death was very genuine'. At home with Leonard Woolf and Kingsley Martin, who were both certain of war (Martin hinted at suicide rather than face a war 'that would last our lifetime'), 'we sat', she continued, 'and discussed the inevitable end of civilisation'.[105]

These reactions can be found repeated across the country. The extent to which dread of war coloured popular perception of the crisis has never been in dispute, just as it genuinely coloured Chamberlain's view of what needed to be done. It is seldom appreciated just how close to the brink Britain came. When the British Cabinet insisted, after Chamberlain's second visit to Hitler on 22 September, that German troops would not be allowed to enter Sudeten territory

Lord Castlerosse confronts a pacifist protester outside a meeting late in 1938. Hostility to war continued to be expressed alongside a growing realization that conflict against fascism was inevitable and necessary.

without international sanction, the course of war seemed unavoidable. Air-raid shelters were hastily dug in Hyde Park, sandbags appeared round London's key buildings and the first evacuees from the cities were collected together and in some cases sent off to the country. The Royal Navy was mobilized, the Royal Air Force put on full alert. On 26 September Chamberlain sent his adviser Sir Horace Wilson to see Hitler to deliver a personal message that if German forces did violate Czech sovereignty France would act and Britain would support her. When Wilson delivered this message in person on the afternoon of 27 September, Hitler asked for the translation to be repeated by the interpreter a second time to be certain that he had understood it. The following day, ill tempered and uncertain, Hitler agreed to the suggestion relayed from Mussolini at British prompting of a four-power meeting in Munich on 29 September.[106] The House of Commons was in session to listen to Chamberlain. 'We came most of us expecting war,' wrote Arthur Salter, 'and war at once.' As Chamberlain prepared his listeners for the worst a note was passed to him with news that Hitler had agreed to a conference; a second message confirmed that there could be a four-power discussion. 'It is difficult', wrote Salter later, 'to recapture, or convey, the mood of the Commons.'[107] Members crossed the chamber to shake him by the hand, some in tears. Over the weeks that followed he received 40,000 letters from the public, desperately hoping that he had saved the peace, and hundreds more from grateful Germans.[108] Dean Inge confessed an overwhelming sense of relief in his diary: 'The general opinion is that the P.M. has saved civilisation . . . No-one either here or on the Continent seems to care which side has got the better of the other. The one thing they care for is that there will be no war . . . Thank God for this great deliverance.'[109]

The hysterical sense of relief that followed the Munich agreement can only be completely explained by the extreme terms in which issues of war and peace were now viewed. In an essay published just after the Munich conference, Arnold Toynbee demanded that something be done 'to remove the uncertainty which has been imported into the daily life of individuals by the constant prospect of "totalitarian war"'.[110] Yet paradoxically the Czech crisis accelerated the current in British opinion that was carrying much of the population towards acceptance that war was in the end unavoidable, not only as a solution to the issues of eastern Europe, for which the public cared not a great deal, but as the only way of resolving the deeper malaise that had overtaken British and European society in the 1930s. This shift in popular opinion has usually been attributed to the reaction to the occupation of Prague on 15 March 1939, in violation of the Munich agreements, when Chamberlain realized that Hitler could no longer be trusted and began to prepare in earnest for a military confrontation and to educate public opinion into accepting it. In reality the process was both less coherent and less chronologically precise than this. A good case can be made for arguing that the final defeat of Republican Spain between January and March 1939 laid bare the harsh reality that fascism would now have to be fought by others. Spain was a defeat for all of those who hated what fascism stood for and it left Britain and France, whose governments had failed in the defence of

Spanish democracy, with no choice but to stand next in line at last against the fascist threat. Only three days separated the fall of Madrid from Chamberlain's guarantee to preserve Polish sovereignty. There is also a good case for arguing that much of the British public arrived at this position with little prompting from the government or the press and that they had begun to do so long before Prague. It is true that a number of major newspapers, most famously *The Times* and the *Manchester Guardian*, shifted editorial ground in 1939 to support the idea of war, but popular views were also shaped by grass-roots discussions and debates and by private reflection, more autonomous than most accounts of the pre-war crisis give them credit for. An early opinion poll in October 1938, just after Munich, in which respondents were asked whether they would rather fight than hand back German colonies – an issue that had hardly featured in the weeks surrounding Munich – found 71 per cent in favour of fighting.[111] This proportion remained broadly constant throughout the year leading to war in September 1939.

No doubt an unquantifiable part of the answer to this shift in the outlook of the British public, which only three years before had cast more than 11 million votes for the Peace Ballot, lies in the straightforward perception that Hitler's Germany constituted an uncontrollable threat to the European order and had to be restrained before it went any further. But it is also necessary to recognize the extent to which by 1938, and even more in 1939, a broad section of opinion had come to accept war in a general sense as unavoidable, even if a large part, perhaps the larger part, would have preferred not to fight – like postponing a life-threatening operation until the point where surgery is preferable to death. This fatalism had much to do with Hitler who was demonized as the agent of destruction, but the sense of certainty that war was coming and the futility of opposing it any longer derived from a popular discourse that saw war for all its arbitrary destructiveness as a possible means to resolve not just narrow issues of foreign policy but other issues to do with the political future and the progress of European civilization, issues which had been central to the debate surrounding Spain. Hitler was in this sense the occasion as much as the cause; British readiness to fight derived from domestic anxieties as much as it did from the merits or otherwise of fighting for Danzig, a National-Socialist-dominated city which could have been negotiated away with much less soul searching than Czechoslovakia. This wider view of war was explored by the historian E. H. Carr in a pamphlet on peace aims published in 1941 in which he claimed that it was unhelpful to regard Hitler as the cause of current problems: 'Economic crisis, unemployment, general disequilibrium were all in existence before Hitler took any part in the world.' It is easy, continued Carr, but untrue 'to father all our troubles onto Hitler'.[112]

The differing reactions to Munich were united in the strong desire to save 'civilization' rather than to save the Czechs or to prevent the city of Danzig from rejoining the German state. The term 'saving civilization' meant different things to different constituencies after Munich, but it defined the terms of a strengthened resolve either to confront Hitler or to redouble efforts for peace. The front cover of the January 1939 edition of the League of Nations Union journal *Headway* carried in bold capitals the headline 'Great Britain, Strong, Resolute, Just, Will Save the World in 1939'.[113] These words symbolized, however crudely, a sense of Britain waking from a doleful slumber, morally armed to assume a responsibility that her place at the imagined heart of Western civilization obliged her to take up, and they were echoed in many other contexts between 1939 and 1945. This did not necessarily mean enthusiasm for war as such, since there remained clear divisions in the way saving civilization was interpreted. On the one hand were those, by far the larger part, who came to believe that civilization could only be saved by waging war. The argument contained an evident logic at the time: war was the greatest and most intractable enemy of civilization; Hitler was the agent of war and barbarism, hence the destruction of Hitler and Hitlerism would save civilization. On the other hand were those who continued to argue that even a victorious war would destroy civilization, and that peace alone, brokered by a collective array of powers, could secure its survival. In between were those who struggled over the year that separated Munich from the outbreak of the Second World War to reconcile their instinctive rejection of war with the realization that it could no longer be avoided and had to be prepared for fully, among whose number could be found Neville Chamberlain. This centre ground feared simultaneously that civilization might be destroyed by war just as it might be sapped by continued peace. Like Chamberlain they 'hoped for the best and prepared for the worst', but would fight, as Chamberlain eventually did, if pressed to do so.[114]

The transformation of opinion can best be illustrated by exploring some of the voyages made by those anti-war campaigners who came to accept the necessity for war after Munich. The novelist Storm Jameson described her move from pacifism to the necessity of war in a long correspondence with Liddell Hart in 1940 and 1941 and it reveals much about the way in which perception of the current state of civilization shaped the pacifist conversion. Jameson described herself as 'a pacifist of the emotional type' who 'loathed and hated the waste and cruelty of war'. From 1933 onwards, she told Liddell Hart, 'my pacifism fought a losing battle with my reason'. She finally abandoned her pacifism after Munich because she had always felt an unresolved contradiction between her hatred of Hitler and war and 'my equal conviction that both were disastrous for civilisation'. Some things, she continued, have to be 'killed for'.[115] At some stage between 1914 and 1939, she wrote in April 1941, 'what we call "our" civilisation passed the point at which it could have been saved to be peaceably adjusted . . . We had fatally weakened aims due, I think, to the inner weaknesses and poverty of our society.' Without war against Hitler over Poland, she wrote, 'our own civilisation would have collapsed'.[116] This was not an easy passage, she recalled; at the time 'a great many knots and twists in my mind remained to be straightened out'.[117] Jameson resigned as a sponsor of the Peace Pledge Union in March 1939 and a little while later broke with her friend and fellow pacifist Vera Brittain. 'I hate war with as much venom as you do,' she wrote, 'but I have come to believe that there are certain values for which it may be necessary to fight . . . I think that pacifists are mentally dishonest.'[118]

The scientists who campaigned against war from the early 1930s also found themselves facing a choice. J. D. Bernal, who began his passage in 1936 with the Spanish Civil War in his arguments with Huxley about 'force', continued to work for anti-war organizations through to 1939 and helped to draft the National Peace Council press release deploring war and calling for an international settlement and disarmament in September 1938.[119] At some point in the intervening year before the outbreak of war he abandoned what remained of his anti-war stance entirely and accepted the necessity of fighting Hitler. He drafted a long memorandum late in 1938 about mobilizing science as fully as possible for the coming war, even to the extent of 'inventing and perfecting new military devices', and he became during the war a prominent contributor to Britain's scientific war effort.[120] In another document drafted in October 1939 setting out 'the ideals of western civilisation for which we are fighting', Bernal explored the reasons for his changed attitude, which closely resembled Jameson's. The conflict was at root an ideological confrontation between 'Nazi barbarism' and 'the principles of European culture', between 'two fundamentally different conceptions of order'. Bernal saw the only prospect of building a better world internationally and domestically in war: 'Western civilisation stands against totalitarianism, belatedly and still only dimly aware of the struggle ahead of it.'[121] His fellow campaigner Joseph Needham found the transition more confusing. In a page of scribbled notes ('shortly after Munich' is written in blue crayon at the top), Needham tried to come to terms with the options he now faced as a lifelong pacifist, Marxist and Christian. He felt that surrender to Hitler at Munich had brought the threat of fascism nearer to home, Czechoslovakia to be followed by Denmark, Holland, Switzerland, Scandinavia, and finally 'us'. 'He'll ask for East Anglia,' Needham added, 'and C[hamberlain] will say we'll localise the conflict.' There was only one thing to do to be saved, Needham concluded, which was 'to make such a demonstration of feeling sweeping the country' that the National Government would be forced to step down, to be replaced by a united front regime under Attlee that would somehow or other 'call a halt to Nazi aggression'. Yet another scribbled note on 30 September found Needham worried that 'Lab Govt would be a cause of war'. Even after the outbreak of war he was still trying to decide for himself whether the war really was anti-fascist and, if so, could be regarded as a just war.[122]

Many of the remaining leading figures in the anti-war movement shed their distaste for war because their distaste for Hitlerism was greater. Gilbert Murray in a letter to Lord Halifax in November 1938 made clear his view that in the last resort force must be used to limit aggression.[123] Norman Angell and Lord Cecil, doyens of the peace movement, both accepted in 1939 the necessity for force, much though they would have preferred peace. Angell chided Liddell Hart for his 'note of hopelessness' about the outbreak of war in September ('But it is here!') and urged him to engage with the conflict, just as he was doing.[124] The Labour Party and much of the non-aligned left hoped that an alliance with the Soviet Union in 1939 would stop Hitler, save peace and provide the platform for a new collective security, but most of the party leadership also came to accept the need for force if all else failed. Victor Gollancz, who before Munich had written to Clement Attlee urging him to do everything for peace or risk the future of civilization, revised his outlook completely by March 1939 with the argument that 'the end of civilisation' could be averted only by preparing to fight war effectively.[125]

The most remarkable convert was the pacifist philosopher Cyril Joad, whose absolute renunciation of war was reiterated publicly right up to its outbreak and beyond. After wrestling with his convictions for some months in 1940 he experienced a dramatic change of heart. Writing in the *Evening Standard* in August 1940 under the headline 'I Was a Life-long Pacifist, but Hitler Changed my Mind', Joad explained that the things he valued about England – 'the free mind and the compassionate heart, the love of truth ... of respect for human personality' – were absolutely endangered by a Hitler victory which would usher in a new Dark Age: 'The Nazi regime fetters the spirit, muzzles the tongue, puts the mind in prison and hands over to the Dictator the keys of the cell ... Future historians will see in it the greatest single setback to humanity that history records.'[126] Only war, Joad thought, could restore civilization. These sentiments, mawkish as they now sound, were essential for many of those who made the passage to war because they could only accept it if the historical justification appeared sufficiently profound to transcend the terrible costs of conflict.

Only the core pacifist movement did not accept after Munich that war was unavoidable. On the contrary, the efforts to find a basis for a collective settlement were pursued with more than ordinary urgency. One reason was the possibility, unrealistic as it now seems, that Munich was the prelude to a return to multilateral discussions which had lapsed in 1934. The National Peace Council, meeting on

18 October 1938, decided to launch a national petition for an international conference. With echoes of the earlier Peace Ballot, the organizers produced 100,000 forms each with room for twenty signatures, 100,000 leaflets explaining the petition and 7,500 posters.[127] The petition was formally launched on 2 November, with the aim of producing one million signatures, to be presented to Neville Chamberlain in March 1939. In a little over three months 1.1 million signatures were collected for a 'New Peace Conference' at which all world issues would be debated between every major and minor power. The petition was presented to Chamberlain on 20 March, just five days after Germany had occupied the rump Czech state, and eleven days before Chamberlain gave his guarantee of Polish sovereignty. The record of the meeting shows a non-committal response from the prime minister.[128] The petition made no difference to policy. Although it gave the National Peace Council something to do, the unrealistic character of its activities consigned it to ineffectual decay. The decline of public support for pacifism had already been evident in 1937, but by the time of Munich and for the year following the process continued apace. At executive committee meetings in May and again in June 1939 there was not even a quorum present.[129] In October 1938 three Peace Councils, in Peterborough, Welwyn Garden City and Barnsley, decided to wind up their activities because of the divisions between pacifists and non-pacifist bodies in their ranks. Only twenty out of fifty-five Peace Councils assisted with the petition and investigations in July 1939 showed that at least eighteen of the organizations were now 'moribund'.[130] It must be assumed that in local branches across the country the same debates over peace versus force, fuelled by the deteriorating international situation, undermined the credibility of continuing pacifist activity.

The absolute pacifists in the Peace Pledge Union also faced growing crisis. After Munich, Arthur Ponsonby tried to reignite enthusiasm for world conferences and conciliation, but he found among the letters from the public growing evidence that the mood had swung away from him. A letter from Leeds claimed there was 'no other way but to fight for peace'; a correspondent from the north London suburb of Willesden, a 21-year-old socialist and anti-war supporter, found it impossible to square the circle of allowing fascism to take over without confronting it with violence ('surely we are chasing ourselves round in circles?').[131] In February Ponsonby drafted a circular letter to send out to all his critics in which he argued that no one should seriously consider fighting to preserve the Versailles order, that dictatorships never lasted, and that 'wrong and evil ideas' could only be overcome by the oppressed population, not by outside intervention.[132] This last idea did not prevent him from writing a letter to Hitler's propaganda minister, Joseph Goebbels, in July 1939 expressing the hope that their two states should talk rather than fight over their differences (there is no record of a reply).[133] Ponsonby was one of the leading pacifist figures arguing for negotiation with Hitler in October 1939 after the defeat of Poland, together with elements in the National Peace Council who urged the government to declare a truce and call an international conference: 'No chance of arriving at an honourable peace', ran the statement issued by the executive committee on 6 October, 'should be neglected.'[134]

The survival of a broader popular pacifism, though much reduced from the peaks of the early 1930s, has been marginalized by historians as it was by politicians at the time. Yet at local level attitudes to the war continued to be sharply divided across the months of phoney war leading up to the German invasion of France in May 1940. A letter sent to Chamberlain from a correspondent in Twickenham claimed that the vast majority of people 'DO NOT WANT THIS WAR' which was 'plunging civilisation in jeopardy'.[135] Bermondsey Borough Council in east London passed a resolution in December 1939 'having regard to the ruin of Western Civilisation' calling on the government to open up negotiations at the first opportunity.[136] The Birmingham branch of the Women's International League of Peace and Freedom organized a demonstration of women in the centre of the city on 16 December to protest against the war and demand peace negotiations with Germany. A further wave of demonstrations was organized for February 1940 countrywide.[137] An opinion poll published after the defeat of Poland by the *News Chronicle* found 11 per cent willing to accept an immediate end to the war on German terms.[138] Peace was a brave option to sustain, but it remained an element of public discussion until well into the war.

Given the very great scale of the anti-war movement in Britain in

A demonstration in Trafalgar Square shortly before the outbreak of war when the public mood had swung in favour of fighting fascism as the International Brigades had done during the Spanish Civil War, a shift represented by the placard visible here: 'All citizens must unite to oppose fascism and save civilisation'.

the 1930s, the survival of a fraction unconditionally dedicated to peace as the surer path to preserve civilization is scarcely surprising. What remains most striking is the movement of opinion the other way, towards a resolute and fatalistic acceptance of war, a mood that grew in strength over the course of the summer as the population adjusted psychologically to the necessity of conflict. Writing to Cyril Joad in 1948 after hearing him claim on the radio that nobody ever wants a war, Liddell Hart insisted that he had not only met people who did, but also recognized the existence of a 'much larger number who tend to get in the mood that war would be better than a continued state of suspense'. He continued: 'I was very much struck by the prevalence of this emotional urge to action – as a relief from tension – in the last few months before the outbreak of war in 1939.'[139] Arnold Toynbee's colleague at the Royal Institute of International Affairs, Geoffrey Gathorne-Hardy, wrote in July 1939 that any surviving talk of peace moves 'plunges me in extreme depression and anxiety' and told Toynbee that if he could be certain that war was inevitable, 'I should breathe a sigh of relief'.[140] Writing just after the outbreak of war in a book on *Europe's Dance of Death*, G. T. Garratt concluded that on the issue of war 'We have felt ourselves being urged along by forces as irresistible as Destiny.' War, he continued, was 'the ultimate catharsis, the process of cleansing and expiation' that would free Europe from a curse that had hung over the continent 'for a generation'.[141] This sense that the war represented something more historically profound and necessary than a patriotic struggle for victory perhaps explains the phenomenon described by Ponsonby in a letter to Lord Stanhope in November 1939 that 'the number of people I meet expressing enthusiasm and orthodox "patriotism" I could count on the fingers of one hand'.[142] A letter to Ponsonby on the day after war broke out from a village in the Midlands also observed that 'people don't seem at all excited or bloodthirsty about this war' but were united by the anti-Hitler argument 'he's got to be stopped' and broad sympathy for the German people who were compelled to follow him.[143] 'In September 1939,' wrote Vera Brittain in the second volume of her autobiography, 'the expected had happened, and was accepted with philosophic pessimism.'[144]

Little of this sentiment was really understood on the German side. A German banker visiting the City of London in May 1939 was mystified by the endless talk of war and the evident preparations for its imminent arrival. George Catlin, Vera Brittain's husband, arrived in Britain from America in April on board the German liner *Bremen*, and found all the German passengers anxious, courteous, 'hoping desperately that war might be averted'.[145] Hitler was reported to have told the British fascist Tom Mitford after Munich that he could not understand any Englishman willing 'to shed his blood for a single Czech'.[146] Throughout the crisis over Poland in 1939 Hitler struggled to grasp why Britain and France would be prepared to fight either for the port of Danzig or for the Polish people. He was fed on a diet of misleading intelligence from London which played on his own belief that Britain was now a decadent state with a ruling class too feeble or debauched to risk war. Despite the evidence of mounting British resolve and direct warnings issued by both Chamberlain and his

Foreign Secretary Lord Halifax, Hitler took the risk that his judgement of Britain was the correct one.[147] Both states were moving on different trajectories in the summer of 1939. Hitler saw each step on its own terms, and neither he nor much of the wider public talked as if the future of civilization were in the scales. In Britain each step was perceived to be a fatal erosion of European stability and a challenge to a Western civilization whose interests would have been best served by peace, but would now have to be saved by war. This is not to ignore Hitler's wider world view or his ill-defined ambitions to build a new European order, but the stakes over Poland were defined on the German side as the overdue rectification of a past injustice. Chamberlain, on the other hand, did have a sense of what was at stake. In the House of Commons on 24 August he told members that if 'we find ourselves forced to embark upon a struggle which is bound to be fraught with suffering and misery for all mankind and the end of which no man can foresee, we shall not be fighting for the political future of a far away city in a foreign land'.[148]

Over the months leading up to war detailed preparations were made for a conflict widely accepted as inevitable. Most of the institutions and organizations featured throughout this book prepared their leave-taking of the crisis years of peace. Arnold Toynbee, who had begun to prepare earlier than most, discussed with government officials turning his Institute into a supplementary branch of the Intelligence Service and by January 1939 his outline plan had been accepted. Toynbee recruited his fellow Oxford historian George Clark who, like the other experts and academics Toynbee invited, had to enrol for National Service, stating their planned wartime occupation.[149] In June 1939 Edward Glover at the British Psycho-Analytical Society sent a circular letter to all medical personnel asking for details by return of post of their preferences for wartime service (hospital work, work with children, work with adults, emergency psycho-therapeutic work etc.). Ernest Jones scribbled at the foot of his form 'Ready for anything. E. J.'[150] Jones decided to shut the society down for the duration of the war, though the government made little use of psychoanalysts when the conflict came.[151] The Population Investigation Committee suspended its activities after Charles Blacker joined the army medical service shortly before the outbreak of war and was posted abroad. A small War Emergency Committee was set up to keep the organization in being.[152] PEP suspended most of its activities to focus on problems of wartime disruption and post-war planning. The London office was kept open pending possible evacuation; in spring 1940 Max Nicholson was seconded to the Ministry of Shipping.[153] The League of Nations Union debated its future and decided to maintain an emergency committee which would work on proposals for peace and a new post-war order, which Lord Cecil began to draft just days after the outbreak of war.[154] The International Peace Campaign, on the other hand, discussed in June 1939 whether it should not now wind up its affairs. The decline in funds made it difficult even to meet the salary costs of the permanent staff while the imminence of war gave a sense of unreality to their remaining activities. By August the leadership of the IPC had come to accept the necessity of a war to stamp out fascism and in October, after three years of energetic campaigning for peace, instructed all its members to accept that war against Hitlerism was essential and should be waged to the end: 'We are resolved of that,' ran the statement. 'We know we have no choice about it: we know we must carry it through.' The decision to embrace war provoked a debilitating argument among the IPC's remaining band of supporters, some of whom refused to accept that the war could be justified, but on 18 January 1940 the decision was taken to discontinue its activities and a year later the National Committee ceased its operations.[155]

The final two weeks of crisis before the declaration of war saw British society brace itself once again for the coming onslaught but this time, unlike the weeks leading up to Munich, few people doubted that war would happen. Indeed, if Hitler had agreed to cease exerting pressure on Poland, Britain would have been left in the autumn of 1939 in a curious limbo with extensive social and psychological mobilization and economic and military commitment for a non-existent conflict. Though so often accused of trying to avoid the logic of the situation, Chamberlain personified the ambivalence – hoping above all that Hitler would back down, fully knowing that a second 'Munich' was no longer acceptable, even to him, and staring the reality of war fully in the face. For a statesman so dedicated to the search for peace the recognition that the future could only be secured by war was an unalloyed tragedy. At 11.15 on the morning of 3 September Chamberlain sat at a desk in Downing Street to broadcast over the radio that Britain was at war with Germany: 'What a bitter blow it is for me that all my long struggle to win peace has failed.'[156] Vera Brittain listened to Chamberlain's broadcast in her cottage in Hampshire sitting on a camp bed between her two children. She wrote in her diary that, though she had fully expected war, 'the tears were running down my cheeks' from realization of failure. She went out into a nearby forest where, 'in the sunny quiet of the gorse and heather, it was impossible to take in the size of the catastrophe'.[157] The lifelong pacifist Helena Swanwick wrote to Ponsonby just after the outbreak of war about the 'lunatic days' just passed. Though 76 years of age, she had volunteered to take evacuees and had two orphaned teenage girls billeted in her house, though after a few weeks they were withdrawn. Her last letters showed a grim awareness of the likely cost of a war directed at women and children; she wished that there were 'Men's towns' and 'Women's towns' that might be treated differently by enemy bombers. In early November she committed suicide with an overdose of Medinal, unable 'to face the sorrow of another war', as a friend wrote after her death.[158]

Hugh Dalton's claim that Germany alone pulled the lever that launched the 'Death Ship' reflected the deep loathing for German fascism that by 1939 permeated much of British society and helps to explain the willingness to engage in a second war in a country where anti-war sentiment had embraced a very large proportion of the population. But Dalton's account largely ignores the contribution made by domestic British circumstances. Willingness to accept not only war but a 'total war', with all the unforeseen consequences involved, was not just the product of a simple response to Hitler and the crises that he provoked but also derived from the widespread public obsession with the stark choice of peace or war as manifestations of a deeper anxiety about the future of civilization. It is possible to argue that the necessity for peace assumed so powerful a claim on the public mind, whether through absolute pacifism, or the League of Nations Union, or the plethora of other anti-war movements, that the failure to maintain peace in the 1930s made total war seem the unavoidable and inevitable antithesis, and thus something to be prepared for whether people liked it or not. The author J. B. Priestley expressed this paradox in 1935, four years before the war:

What with a general atmosphere of fear and suspicion, fighting men itching to be at it, fingers trembling on triggers, war is inevitable. You have all prepared for it. To prepare for something is to start Time bringing it towards you. The war that we expect will surely arrive. It needs only the most trivial excuse . . .[159]

The war psychosis was firmly embedded many years before the Polish crisis in 1939. The scientific evidence that war was economically, biologically or psychologically unavoidable merely predisposed an educated public to a mood of despondent hopelessness about a world where longing for peace was abundantly clear but the certainty of war difficult to challenge. 'I get into a defeatist frame of mind very easily,' wrote the pacifist Rosamond Lehmann shortly after the Munich crisis, 'and feel nothing's any use any more.'[160] This was the sentiment that Orwell also detected among the wider public, expressed in his novel Coming Up for Air, published in 1939: 'I can see that war's coming,' says Orwell's narrator. 'There are millions of others like me. Ordinary chaps that I meet everywhere, chaps I run into in pubs, bus drivers, and travelling salesmen for hardware firms, have got a feeling that the world's gone wrong. They can feel things cracked and collapsing under their feet.'[161]

A mood of despair or helplessness or sober pessimism permeates all the different elements of public discussion examined in this book. Each of the dead ends – the failures of capitalism, the crisis of genetic decline, the psychological distortions of modern life, the naturalness of war, the paradoxes of pacifism, the fruitless search for a progressive consensus – contributed indirectly or directly to the popular reaction to the international situation, which promised a further and more dangerous dead end of universal war. Over the three years between 1936 and 1939, the years of crisis in Spain and central Europe, the balance between saving civilization through peace and saving civilization by war swung decisively in favour of the latter. It is not difficult to show that once war had broken out and the uncertainty and irresolution were for a great many finally over, the war was rationalized as the only way either to save existing civilization or to construct a distant but brighter future. In a debate in March 1940 over whether For Intellectual Liberty should continue its activities the psychologist Barbara Low, author of the first popular book on Freud twenty years before, argued, according to the minutes, that there were fundamentals at stake: the association could prevent 'the death of civilisation' and secure the survival of its cultural values only if its efforts went to the successful prosecution of the anti-fascist war.[162] Victor Gollancz sent the same message to the 50,000 members of the Left Book Club when war broke out despite the communist view, occasioned by the German–Soviet pact signed a week before the German invasion of Poland, that the war was simply a war of capitalist imperialism. 'The purpose of the war, for us,' he wrote in September 1939, 'is more than the defeat of Hitler. It is the establishment of a new international order based on social justice.'[163] Hugh Dalton concluded his book on *Hitler's War* with the view, 'We must first win the war which Hitler made. Then stepping over the foul Nazi carcass, we must choose our road into the future. We must turn aside from the way of Strife and Scarcity, of Massacre and Misery, into the way of Peace and Plenty.'[164]

These were statements easy to make if difficult to fulfil. They reflected the extent to which the discourse between peace and war had shifted ground to the idea of conflict between progress and barbarism, order and chaos. The chiliastic rhetoric matched the current mood and had its roots in the 'either/or' mentality of the inter-war years which permeated much of the public arena and private reflections on the current age. Dread of war and certainty of war cohabited in unnatural union for much of the 1930s but so too did fear and expectation in a great many other fields. In a university sermon preached in Cambridge on 26 October 1941 the Bishop of Chichester, George Bell, took as his theme what he understood to be the most profound either/or: 'the age-long conflict between evil and good'. The current age, he observed, was one of those moments in world history 'when this conflict assumes a special intensity'. Long before the outbreak of the war the struggle had been reduced to a contest between two completely different ways of life, 'order against disorder, charity and freedom against tyranny and brute force'.[165] Sentiments like these reduced a complex historical process to simple categories which were needed for many ordinary people to be able to comprehend or articulate in their own terms what they took to be grand forces of historical change for which a sombre language and morbid assumptions seemed not inappropriate.

9

A Morbid Age

The longer you study modern history, the more evidence you find of Belial's guiding hand.   Aldous Huxley, 1948[1]

When the war for civilization was over, with the destruction of much of Europe and Asia and the deaths of more than 55 million people, the inter-war years assumed their now familiar shape as a gloomy intermission between two catastrophic conflicts. Among those British intellectuals who had inhabited in the second quarter of the twentieth century what Aldous Huxley later called 'a gruesome kind of universe', the inter-war years fell into perspective as years of anxiety, disillusion- ment, sterility, nihilism and danger.[2] In 1947 Huxley decided to write a short science-fiction fantasy about a not-too-distant future, after a Third World War had left a nuclear wasteland inhabited by acolytes of the Devil run by a cynical and vicious Arch-Vicar. Though set in the future, his target was the past. The Arch-Vicar explains to a scientist who has stumbled across the new society on a trip from New Zealand, the only part of the earth to escape atomic destruction, that the thing called Progress was 'too fiendishly ironical' to be anything other than the work of Belial. Mankind wanted peace and tolerance but, he continues, 'at a certain epoch, the overwhelming majority of human beings accepted beliefs and adopted courses of action that could not possibly result in anything but universal suffering, general degradation and wholesale destruction'. From the First World War to the Second they had to do 'what the Belial in them dictated'.[3] Outside the room where the Arch-Vicar is speaking a crowd is baying 'Blood, blood, blood' as deformed babies are speared to death in the name of the Devil. *Ape and Essence* is the most bitter of Huxley's books, a sustained assault on the human failings of his own age. He hoped it might become a stage play or a film, but its savage irony was too much for post-war, baby-booming America, where he was now living.[4]

In the years immediately following the end of the Second World War British society concentrated on building the 'New Jerusalem' around a wide commitment to social and economic modernization and moral reconstruction. Many of the post-war reforms had their roots in the inter-war years and were not post-war inventions. Side by side with the fear of crisis before the war were to be found progressive ideas and policies, partly obscured by the pall of cultural gloom around them, which were able to take root after 1945 as the discourse on 'progress' was reconstructed. It gradually became clear that many of the fears for the future that pervaded pre-war discourses failed to materialize. The population did not decline steeply; ideas of eugenic intervention were modified into positive welfare policies; the capitalist economy was reformed sufficiently to avoid a repeat of the slump but not replaced entirely; the progressive political centre voted overwhelmingly for the Labour Party and ended the political stalemate of the National Government; fascism was utterly discredited but the emergence of Soviet domination in eastern Europe also eroded sympathy for a 'New Civilization' on communist lines; psychotherapy became an accepted branch of medicine and a growing interest in and knowledge of sex did not promote degeneration. Only war remained an apparently intractable issue and fears of the Third World War, the frame for Huxley's diatribe, did not subside until the late 1960s and the era of stand-off deterrence and détente. Confidence in the possibility of progress, despite short-term problems of reconstruction and economic revival, replaced the immanent gloom of pre-1939. If the 1930s had seen a painful slithering to the edge of the precipice, post-1945 could be seen as a brisk uphill walk into the sunlight.

The overwhelmingly morbid character of much of the culture and ideas of the inter-war years is evident from the different strands examined in the book – fear of eugenic disaster, the diseases of capitalism, the dark side of the human mind, the inevitability of conflict, the powerlessness of reason, the fear of political extremism. The language used to address crisis was repeated remorselessly. 'To say, an end to

The novelist Aldous Huxley c. 1935, the year he joined the Peace Pledge Union and opted for absolute pacifism. He came to believe that the key to peace was psychological and that only by understanding man's inner demons could lasting peace be secured.

capitalism, to Western civilisation, is to repeat what has been said so often as to be trite,' wrote the author and future sociologist Tosco Fyvel early in 1940. But, he added, 'in a far deeper sense than most have thought, it is true; we have come to an end, an utter end . . .'[5] Despairing of the future became embedded in inter-war culture in the broadest sense of the term and in a variety of distinct literary, scientific and institutional milieus. The language used was in many cases literally morbid: 'grievously sick' civilization; 'deeply diseased'; 'the sickness of Europe'; and so on.[6] In *Barbarians at the Gate*, written in 1939, Leonard Woolf presented what he called 'the anatomy of civilisation': 'to understand its real nature and plight today we must dissect the rest of the body, its important organs such as the brain and the heart, the whole system of nerves and muscles'.[7] It has already been shown that in many cases despair of a 'sick' civilization was projected backwards to explain an individual's own physical disorder, creating a complete morbid cycle. A. L. Rowse, Beatrice Webb, Bronislaw Malinowski, G. Lowes Dickinson and E. M. Forster were among the sufferers. Henry Williamson was profoundly affected by the problems of the 1930s: 'always thinking of suicide', he wrote shortly before the Munich settlement, 'wondering what was wrong with me, cancer, etc.' In 1945 he wrote to his friend Eric Watkins about his anguish over world events, 'the whole thing is bunged up within this body, personal and impersonal, microcosm and macrocosm'.[8]

The popularization of ideas about human biology and medicine was a central aspect of the culture of the early twentieth century and it supplied a convenient set of metaphors for diagnosing the illnesses of civilization and dissecting its moribund elements. The biological imperative was explored in Aldous Huxley's first fantasy of the future, *Brave New World*, published in 1932, which parodies the idea that biological science will plan society better in the future, but is nonetheless concerned with issues of eugenic selection, sexual liberty and individual freedom which he knew were live contemporary topics. In *Brave New World Revisited*, published a quarter of a century later, Huxley still insisted that to understand the forces in his lifetime that had propelled modern civilization towards a dehumanizing future it was necessary to start 'on the level of biology'.[9] Many of those who helped to shape the discourses on civilization were themselves doctors.

Albert Schweitzer was a doctor-missionary; Sir Arthur Keith wrote about war but was a trained anatomist; Sigmund Freud turned from analysing psychologically disturbed patients to a psychologically disturbed civilization. Ernest Jones and Edward Glover were doctors turned psychiatrists but were happy to diagnose society and explain war as well; Cyril Burt was a doctor with opinions on everything; Charles Blacker a doctor with interests in social biology; and so on. In 1938 a group of doctors published *The Doctor's View of War*, with a foreword by the professor of physic in Cambridge and an introduction which claimed that because the 'elimination of suffering is essentially the doctor's task', and war was the greatest source of suffering, it was quite appropriate for doctors to carry out 'a careful examination of the prophylactic measures that might be taken to minimise the risk of its outbreak'.[10] Throughout the inter-war years there existed what could be called a diagnostic culture, examining the pathology of civilization to isolate its medical conditions and mental defects and to suggest possible cures, palliatives and panaceas.

The concept of civilization as an organism also made it possible to think of the diverse elements of crisis as a unity, distinct maladies attacking the one fragile body. In Joseph McCabe's 1932 book *Can We Save Civilisation?* the contents page listed all the problem areas one after the other – economic crisis, the political problem, war and the international outlook, the problem of population, changes in human nature.[11] In J. A. Hobson's fantasy *The Recording Angel*, also published in 1932, the Messenger returns from Earth with an account of all the issues that oppress contemporary civilization: capitalism, imperialism, population crisis, the failures of parliamentary government, the fear of psychological relapse.[12] Many of those who contributed to popular discussion of these different issues had interests in some or all of them. Aldous Huxley was a pacifist, an enthusiastic eugenist, fearful that Britain's population might dwindle to an unsustainable fraction and fascinated by Freud's exposure of the veiled underside of human nature. Leonard Woolf was anti-war, anti-fascist, interested in eugenics, Freud's publisher, a strong critic of contemporary capitalism and a champion of a 'people's front'. Margaret Storm Jameson was critical of capitalism, hated the political extremes, campaigned against war and violence ('Poverty and war grow in the same soil and have the same smell') and, like Huxley and Woolf, despaired of the tired civilization around her.[13] Those who shared this outlook became part of an informal intellectual network whose views rippled out among the wider population.

For this wider public the many problems of the modern age were the bread and butter of discussion groups and societies. The inter-war programmes of the Newcastle Literary and Philosophical Society, for example, show a regular interest in the fashionable topics of the day from 'The Sub-Conscious Mind' and 'The Recent Development of Mendelism' in 1920, via Sir Arthur Keith on Darwin and early man in 1921, 'Heredity in Man' in 1925, Ernest Jones on 'Psycho-Analysis and the Artist' in 1927, to lecture series in 1931 on 'The Machine Age', in 1934 on 'What's Wrong With ... ?', and, by 1936, 'Nazi Germany Explained', 'The Attack on Democracy' and 'Spain Today'.[14] The lecture programmes and course descriptions of the Workers' Educational Association or of the National Labour Colleges show that arguments and ideas which owed their origin to elite analysis could be passed on, second- or third-hand, to a working-class audience. The leading names in science, literature and politics, who played a role in sustaining these contemporary anxieties, could be found not just in bookshops or on the radio, but in front of audiences from literary and philosophical societies, university clubs, women's guilds, the organizations for workers' education, and church congregations. Anyone who attended them regularly would know that economics, heredity, psychology, pacifism, war, fascism and communism were all part of the collective problem of how to save modern civilization.

How is the whole culture of crisis to be explained? The simple answer might be to look at the circumstances confronting British society from the Great War, through the General Strike, the slump of 1929–32, the international threats of the 1930s and the rise of radical political dictatorship, and the stale politics of the appeasement age. In 1939 Edward Thompson published an account of the twenty years which he called *You Have Lived Through All This*, to remind the British public of all the things they had experienced and might have forgotten. The titles of the first two chapters signalled the main theme of the book – 'Glad, Confident Morning', followed by 'The Beginnings of Sorrows'.[15] It was assumed that there was a direct causal relationship between the chequered history of the inter-war years and the anxieties of the age. No doubt such a relationship existed, but it is too simple an explanation. For one thing the 'crisis of civilization' was at the centre of public debate over the whole period, and though it may have provoked a greater degree of public awareness at acute moments of difficulty, it could be sustained independent of immediate historical reality. 'For the peculiar chaos in the world to-day', wrote the journalist Wickham Steed in 1931, 'there is no precedent. It is ... a chaos of ideas.'[16] The key intellectual and ideological debates of the inter-war years were nourished by the history they confronted, but they were fundamental debates about economic organization, social priorities, or international behaviour that were capable of being sustained as issues of principle as much as questions of political practice. The second problem lies with the nature of the British 'crisis', which was far less dangerous, violent or divisive than the crisis in Europe and beyond. There was violence, but it was exported to the Empire. There was no civil war, declared or undeclared, except for the brief conflict in Ireland in 1920–22. The parliamentary system survived, heavily criticized but unimpaired. The economy suffered less than any of the other developed economies during the slump and real income grew sharply for those in employment, and if Britain had not declared war in 1939, the international crisis would not have threatened Britain directly. Political extremism was contained and social unrest was always more muted than in the other major European states, most of which were transformed into authoritarian dictatorships. It is more difficult to explain why British public culture was so absorbed with crisis than it is for Weimar Germany or late Third Republic France.

One explanation is the special relationship between Britain and Europe which allowed the British public to share Europe's problems as if they were their own and which gave a wide airing to ideas and ideologies that were not British in origin. The view that British society and politics were isolated or detached from European realities in favour of the Empire has always been a distorted image. As a result of intervention in the European war in 1914 and Britain's key role in constructing and trying to sustain the post-war order, the relationship with Europe became yet closer and Britain's sense of responsibility more enhanced. British forces were sent to stem the Bolshevik cause in 1918; they were stationed in Germany until 1930; British statesmen and intellectuals played a prominent part in trying to make the League of Nations, which moved in 1920 from London to Geneva, a going concern. Lord Cecil and Gilbert Murray were international figures in the 1920s and 1930s. In 1933 the World Economic Conference was summoned to London, still the financial hub of Europe. The Disarmament Conference was chaired by the former Labour foreign secretary Arthur Henderson and orchestrated for much of its brief life by British anti-war activists like Philip Noel-Baker. In these circumstances the political complexion and ideological map of Europe mattered a great deal in Britain. Fascism and Soviet communism were closely watched and debated, but in the arts and sciences too European influences were rapidly integrated with the British experience. It still seems remarkable that *All Quiet on the Western Front*, written by a German ex-soldier about the German experience of combat, could sell 300,000 copies in six months when it was published in Britain just ten years after the end of the war.[17]

Very few of the different discourses of crisis did not have reference points back to Europe. Some of the key figures to influence British science, arts and politics were European, many of them German or Austrian – Marx, Nietzsche, Mendel, Freud, Einstein, Schweitzer, Spengler. The greatest influence of all was exerted by an obscure Austrian, Adolf Hitler, whose name sold hundreds of thousands of books in Britain in the 1930s, something that no other German chancellor could have achieved, before or since. In turn British writers or intellectuals were exported to Germany. In 1928 H. G. Wells was invited to address the German parliament (and a year before had lectured at the Sorbonne); Virginia Woolf had a European reputation, and despite her modernism continued to sell books and receive royalties in Hitler's Reich; Arnold Toynbee was well regarded in Germany and lectured there in the Hitler years ('You have a synopsis of World History like no one else,' wrote one approving German professor in 1936).[18] The British intelligentsia brought the experience of Europe to bear in what they wrote and worked with a frame of reference that was anything but parochial, if it could sometimes be misinformed or myopic. For better or worse, the violent tide of European history between the Russian Revolution and the outbreak of the Second World War was appropriated by a British public whose own historical dramas paled by comparison. 'The jealous lover of England', wrote Storm Jameson, 'can no longer separate her in his dreams from the other countries of Europe.'[19] The reaction to the Spanish Civil War, which transcended social class or political allegiance, was only the best example.

Concern for what happened in continental Europe also derived from British perception of global responsibilities. At the heart of a worldwide empire, with an elite that thought in global and cosmopolitan terms and a public with close personal or economic links with the Empire and Commonwealth, Britain had for at least a century and a half assumed a major role in the development of the political geography and economic complexion of large parts of the globe. Those responsibilities expanded with the peace in 1919 when Britain also became a major Middle-Eastern power responsible for territorial mandates from the League of Nations and increasingly concerned with the political evolution of China. It is for this reason, perhaps, that many British politicians and intellectuals saw Britain as the core of 'Western civilization', both shaping it and protecting it through the dissemination of British political and legal traditions. 'It is not too much to say', ran an editorial in the League of Nations Union journal *Headway*, 'that the system of parliamentary government, personal liberty, and equal justice for the private citizen is the great contribution of the British peoples to the common civilisation of mankind.'[20] That special place in the development of a civilization 'whose branches', claimed Toynbee, 'have overshadowed the earth' and 'killed out all its competitors' may lack complete historical credibility, but it was part of the common belief of the age.[21] It also entailed responsibilities which made it seem that the wider world crisis was Britain's crisis and that the British, more than any other people, should set the world to rights. 'It is a measure of her responsibility', wrote Norman Angell in 1936, 'that other nations cannot in fact act without her lead.'[22] At the end of *Challenge to Death*, Storm Jameson summed up the sense of obligation that in her view, and the view of many who despaired of the drift of British politics in the 1930s, rested on British shoulders:

Ours is the largest and most important political unit in the world. Our people occupy territory in every continent; our interests – more penetrating – cross the frontiers of every foreign State. More than any other State, more even than those which exceed us in actual or potential wealth, we can influence world thought. This power we have is recognised by other countries . . . Of the politicians who throng that Hall of Hopes, the Assembly at Geneva, it is the English on whom all wait . . .[23]

By extrapolation the problems of the world became Britain's problems.

In reality Britain faced forces of political and social change over which she could exert almost no effective influence. The Empire was faced with the prospect of growing violence and possible disintegration. Britain's strategic position was compromised by trying to preserve domestic stability and conserve economic strength in the face of multiple areas of potential threat from eastern Asia to the heart of Europe. The capacity to preserve a unitary and stable 'Western civilization' was a fantasy, but it exerted a powerful influence and fed back into domestic anxieties about the failure of contemporary politics or the essential irrationalism of human nature or the survival of a sound 'white race' to keep the British mission going. The manifest failure of Britain to play the role of world leader was blamed on the politicians abroad or at home. Gilbert Murray thought the culprits were foreign extremists suffering from that 'well-known disease of the human mind, fanaticism'.[24] Storm Jameson blamed contemporary British statesmen who 'dodged, shied, put down their heads, stuck in their feet, rolled over', rather than take on responsibility for saving the world.[25] The fruit of the failure was a growing sense of hopelessness in Britain about the possibility of extracting Western civilization from the morass into which it was sliding, and a strong disillusionment with politics and political solutions. In place of politics came popular expectations of the power of science to supply solutions to identifiable problems. The place of science – both social science and natural science – in the unfolding perception of crisis is an important one. Planning was expected to cure economic ills; biological politics would create a healthy population and shed the 'unfit'; psychology could identify the roots of the malaise of modern man and offer therapy; a scientifically ordered world might end the overpopulation, national competition, and economic shortages that caused war.

The search for solutions in science was, as the history of inter-war eugenics or psychoanalysis has shown, essentially ambiguous. This was partly because too much was expected of scientists, partly because some, though by no means all, scientists made claims that could not be realized. In 1931, lecturing at Manchester University, the psychologist William McDougall claimed that only the human sciences, once properly organized, could solve 'the grave disorder and chaos that threatens us' and allow 'civilisation to endure'.[26] Scientific solutions were proposed for a wide range of problems which politicians seemed incapable of solving and enjoyed support from a wide circle of influential thinkers from H. G. Wells to the philosopher Bertrand Russell. The problem was that science was often both solution and problem, both promise and threat. 'Take the scientists, for example,' says Huxley's Arch-Vicar. 'Good, well-meaning men, for the most part. But He got hold of them all the same – got hold of them at the point where they ceased to become human beings and became specialists. Hence, . . . those bombs.'[27] Modern science could supply a stream of helpful inventions but at the same time was responsible for modern weapons of the most sophisticated and deadly kind. Science exposed the reality of inheritance and the apparent dangers of racial degeneration but left the solution to non-scientists whose proposals ranged from lethal chambers to voluntary sterilization. Psychoanalysis, wrote Ernest Jones in a draft lecture, explained the nature of the unconscious but found that the world treated it as 'an attack on the relative security of ignorance it had previously enjoyed'.[28] When applied to the problems of civilization, psychoanalysis was able to identify the apparent source of collective anxiety, but not able to cure it. Discussion of the source of war as a scientific problem suggested a powerful biological or psychological predisposition to violence but no real solution. Science, Bertrand Russell wrote in 1927, 'seems to lessen human power' by suggesting that human nature is predetermined.[29] In a set of notes jotted down after seeing the film of H. G. Wells's *Things to Come* in 1936, the geneticist Joseph Needham reflected on the question 'Can Science Save Civilisation?' only to conclude that its effects were more often than not malign: 'science used for destroying civilisation by air warfare'; 'sci[ence] already used for destroying crops, restricting output – technological unemployment'. He thought science could not save civilization and told himself that the best thing was to join the Labour movement and 'read enormous literature on socialism'.[30]

The relationship between science and society during the inter-war years had a particular character. There was widespread confidence in scientific possibilities and also a conventional acceptance that science represented some form of absolute truth. 'Scientism' – the belief that science rationally applied could solve social and political issues – was at its height and some scientists were happy to collude with these expectations.[31] The result was often an unsophisticated appropriation of scientific developments that were at best provisional or contradictory. Cyril Burt, commenting on J. D. Bernal's *The Social Function of Science*, published in 1939, observed that though his was 'an age of science', it was not an age of 'scientifically minded people'; the public treated serious scientific research with 'indifferent ignorance' and took from it only what they wanted to hear.[32] Lawrence Jacks, writing in *The Listener* in 1938, thought that popular scientific misunderstanding had to be overcome 'if civilisation is to be saved from ruin', and added: 'Misquotations from science are as common as misquotations from scripture.'[33] The gap between popular understanding of science and the reality of scientific research prompted Joseph Needham to organize a book in the late 1930s on 'The Distortion of Science for Politico-Economic Ends', which also covered, in addition to Needham's field of biological sciences, the subjects of sociology, race theory, eugenics, mathematics, physics and technology.[34] But it was also possible for scientists to be quite out of their depth in the world of politics and social policy. Lowes Dickinson thought the scientists he knew were 'rather more than less violent and unreasonable than other men', and all the worse because 'beside being prejudiced, they suppose that the fact that they are men of science gives their prejudices value'.[35]

Of course, most scientists did not become engaged in public life or distort or publicize their research for political ends. They appeared to speak with a forked tongue only because there was real intellectual uncertainty in almost all areas of research, from astronomy to zoology. Vanguard scientific research was unstable and tentative, a work in progress, and its values were in general more narrowly utilitarian. Very little scientific writing could be understood by the layman unless it was presented in a vulgarized form and it was here that science played its part in giving substance to social anxiety by relaying complex arguments in a deceptively simple language. Conversely, the cloak of mystery and uncertainty that surrounded much of the most advanced science had the effect of generating uncertainty among the wider public who snatched at apparent solutions or deplored discoveries that opened up uncongenial conclusions, of which there appeared to be many. By the 1920s the principle of entropy promised a slow end to the universe; it was possible for biologists or psychologists to suggest a process of 'de-evolution' as they examined evidence of genetic defect or declining intelligence; psychoanalysis underscored the unscientific arguments of Spengler or Toynbee that civilization was more vulnerable the more sophisticated it became, prone to unavoidable relapse into barbarism.[36] In this sense science appeared to betray its promise and leave civilization as exposed as ever to the disintegrative effects of the modern age or the threat of extinction.

All of these many explanations for a popular culture of crisis depended on how extensively or easily the core ideas could be communicated. Here too the culture flourished at a particular stage in the development of the modern 'information state', the mass media, and public debate. British society had a thirst for knowledge and a mania for voluntary associations willing to supply it. The state played a part in this process by developing more sophisticated statistical measurement and applying this to areas of policy or by identifying areas of key public concern which the government could review.[37] The government enquiries on the trade in arms, on sterilization policy, mental defect, population development and the depressed areas supplied ammunition for the public debates on social degeneration, economic crisis and war. The mass media expanded dramatically in the inter-war years and through radio and the cinema newsreel or information film brought issues alive in ways that were not possible before 1914. BBC radio licence-holders expanded from 2,178,259 when the BBC became a public corporation in 1927, to 9,082,666 by 1939. It was estimated that by 1935 some 98 per cent of the population could listen to at least one BBC station; there were 73 licences for every 100 households. In addition the BBC published both the *Radio Times* and *The Listener*. By 1935 the first sold 2.4 million weekly, while *The Listener*, which carried articles and debates derived from radio programmes, had sales each week of more than 52,000.[38]

The radio became a popular medium in the inter-war years for communicating new ideas and generating discussion. Here a panel of experts reply to listeners' questions in 'Answering You', a link with the BBC North American service to allow American listeners to ask questions about British opinion.

The range of serious discussion on key issues of social policy, science, international politics, current philosophy, peace and war was very wide and of solid intellectual quality. What would have been arguments confined to a narrow educated elite before the Great War could now be listened to or read by a wide circle. The letters pages of *The Listener* show the extent to which problem subjects were now debated by a wider public. The issues were often controversial, occasionally indelicate. Social mores and sex were talked about more openly than could possibly have been the case in the age of high Victorianism. Here the cinema or the instructional film had a special place. The British Imperial Social Hygiene Council, for example, used film as part of its programme in the 1920s to educate the public about venereal disease. The early titles were sometimes coy – *The Tragedy of Ignorance*, *The Gift of Life* – but often more direct, as in *The Irresponsibles*, *Whatever a Man Soweth*, and by the late 1930s included the film *Sex in Life*. In 1930 the Propaganda Committee agreed that the films should now be 'talkies' to keep the organization up to date.[39] Cinema newsreels were less useful as a source of information or instruction, but in a pre-television age had the effect of bringing audiences regularly face to face with worldwide issues and crises in a more direct and tangible way than the newspaper. By the late 1930s newsreels were watched by an estimated 20 million cinema-goers every week.[40]

Beyond the media lay whole networks of voluntary organizations that channelled academic debate, government information, scientific developments and current crises to society at large. In the days before television and the internet the positive, voluntary pursuit of information was a social phenomenon of great importance. No doubt this practice drew on traditions of voluntarism that were embedded in British public life. In the inter-war years they flourished to a remarkable degree. Every public issue provoked the formation of committees, associations, or societies which in turn established a circle of branches and sub-committees to spread the word countrywide. To assist this process the Labour Colleges ran entire courses on 'The Conduct of Meetings' or 'Chairmanship'; numerous pamphlets and articles explained the secrets of effective public speaking to a less educated or inexperienced audience.[41]

Many of those who organized or participated in voluntary bodies were drawn from more socially advantaged or educated circles, but there were numerous avenues to informed discussion through women's movements, trade unions, Labour Colleges, the Workers' Educational Association or the pacifist and anti-war organizations which brought all sections of society into contact with current issues. In many cases there existed local networks where information was passed from hand to hand, books exchanged, books of the month discussed, reading circles encouraged. The extraordinary expansion of the Left Book Club betrayed a wide public appetite for serious engagement with political and social issues. In 1936 Victor Gollancz responded to public demand for a series of 'short, monthly books dealing simply and authoritatively with various topics' in addition to the regular Book of the Month, and launched a new Educational Section to meet the need.[42] Speakers were recruited to lead the discussion in local Left Book Club groups across the country or to address public meetings, like the one in Mansfield co-operative hall in February 1939 on 'England's Peril – and the Way Out', where the theme of one of the speakers was 'England arise, or the long night will fall'.[43] The publication and circulation of pamphlets, leaflets and short books, often in tens of thousands, was a central concern of all those associations, from birth control to anti-fascism, which wanted to engage public support and sustain public enthusiasm. In the 1920s most major voluntary organizations had a 'propaganda committee' and a 'publications committee' to try to promote public interest and understanding. A memorandum written for the Eugenics Society by its propaganda officials in the early 1930s suggested the publication of simple, widely distributed pamphlets ('How to Give a Eugenic Prognosis' was one example), combined with a vigorous propaganda campaign directed at the medical profession, and lobbying of members of parliament and the trade unions.[44]

The key institution was the public meeting or lecture where experts were brought face to face with the wider public and issues could be argued over by both sides. Most of these were ad hoc meetings or lecture tours which reflected once again a powerful public appetite for direct involvement in causes or issues. During the inter-war years these meetings involved millions of people on a regular basis. The League of Nations Union numbered 400,000 at its peak and held at least twelve meetings of its local branches every day of its existence; the Peace Pledge Union had 130,000 members and preached to a much wider circle of non-members; the Imperial Social Hygiene Council lectured to over 100,000 people in 370 meetings in the second half of 1931 alone.[45] The Labour Colleges between 1922 and 1936 taught a total of 285,000 students in classes and 52,400 through correspondence courses; the Workers' Educational Association had classes of 30,000 a year by the late 1920s.[46] The relentless round of lectures and addresses made heavy demands on the most popular speakers, who had to take audiences as they found them. After talking in Kensington in November 1938 on 'Birth Control and the Population Problem', Charles Blacker complained in a letter that 'the whole of the front row was occupied by very old ladies with walking sticks and ear trumpets', and added, 'I . . . adjusted my remarks to the appearance of the audience.'[47] Vera Brittain was in demand all over the country to talk about pacifism. In early February 1939 she addressed a hall of noisy Welsh students in Aberystwyth; nine days later she gave a talk to 3,000 in Newcastle, where she noted 'no interrupting appeals, no tedious questions', the following day another in Glasgow, two weeks later in London, two weeks after that in Brighton, two days later at the Queen's Hall in London again. In the middle of this schedule she was asked to speak at five other venues, which she refused to do.[48]

There were also regular summer schools, educational weekends, workshops and conferences where big issues were discussed with audiences drawn from many different social constituencies. The residential summer school was another institution that flourished between the wars. They were run by all the major organizations and provided a forum for concentrated debate and the exchange of ideas. The Women's International League for Peace and Freedom, for example, held annual summer schools which covered topics such as 'Psychology' (lectures on the herd mentality, instincts, psychology and peace, domination), 'Internationalism and Civilisation', 'Next Steps in Peace', and so on. The annual summer school in 1928 was held in Selly Oak, Birmingham, on the theme 'New Theories of Government (socialism, Bolshevism, Fascism etc.)' with lectures from John Strachey, Henry Brailsford and Gaetano Salvemini, an intellectual exile from Mussolini's Italy who regularly exposed the excesses of fascism to an English audience. In the evenings there were debates, discussions, Esperanto classes, dancing and games.[49] Weekend or day schools were also a typical forum for workers' education. The Labour Colleges organized a total of 2,520 schools between 1924 and 1939, lecturing to a further 154,500 students.[50] Sometimes longer residential courses were organized for workers who were usually subsidized by local union or co-operative branches. In August 1938, for example, the London Co-operative Societies Education Committee organized a summer school at Bexhill-on-Sea on 'The Position of Post-War

The golden age of the summer school. The picture [top] *shows a summer school of the Society for Cultural Relations with the USSR at Digswell Park Conference Centre, Welwyn Garden City, in June 1938. Below is a summer school of the South Place Ethical Society at the Red House, Ryde, Sussex in the early 1930s.*

Capitalism'. The guest lecturers included Maurice Dobb and Hermann Levy, both stalwarts of the lecture circuit. The cost was £2 12s 6d for a three-week school at a local residential centre (persons from homes with 'infectious diseases' were excluded, and the sexes segregated). The Rising Bell woke students at 7.30 and no one was allowed out past 11 at night. In between there was a rigorous schedule of lectures and discussion groups on the current crisis of the capitalist order. The same year the Committee organized a further five schools in Hove, Kingstown (Eire), Scarborough (twice), a school for adolescents in Ambleside and one for juniors at Southport.[51]

Opportunities for reading, discussion, instruction and information were widespread both geographically and socially. The debates about crisis were not the preserve of the literary, political or scientific elite, though they played an important part in shaping and communicating the key issues of the day. In terms of propaganda, dissemination and persuasion Britain's democratic society was very different from the dictatorships, not only because much of the interest was voluntary, and thus more predisposed to influence, but because there was no control over what could or could not be said. The language and imagery surrounding the crisis of civilization, much of it critical of established authority, or intellectually subversive, or emotionally disturbing, was democratic in its appeal. Gilbert Murray described how this contrast was played out at a discussion on 'The Future of Literature' organized by the Committee for Intellectual Co-operation:

it soon began to range over the future of civilisation in general, and the general outlook was the gloomiest, at any rate among the Europeans. War, impoverishment, civil strife, persecution, the deadening of intellectual and artistic life, tortures in prisons and c[oncentration] camps . . . had made the same impression on every speaker, until we came to the Italian. He was a young Fascist with a pugnacious chin; and he maintained that the outlook was most hopeful and encouraging. A completely new civilisation was being introduced by Italy and Germany over the rotting corpse of Liberalism.[52]

The culture of crisis in Britain was made possible by the freedom to express fears openly and the competition to identify its causes. Anxiety was democratic, certainty totalitarian. These fears fed on aspects of the prevailing reality at home and, more particularly, abroad, but they created an infectious, almost self-indulgent disillusionment with the present. The 'spirit of the age', argued the political scientist Harold Laski, looking back on the inter-war years in 1942, was characteristic of all civilizations in their death throes: lack of faith, insecurity, fear and frustration.[53] This was the prevailing contemporary judgement of the age, to which even Laski, who was impatient of the popular fatalism, was far from immune. The powerful image of a sick civilization with the irrational social anxieties that infected it flourished only because British society at large had unrestricted and extensive exposure to the arguments that sustained it.

It is more difficult to assess the effects of the culture of crisis. Most of those who looked back from the vantage point of post-1945 were aware that there had been something particular about the inter-war years and that the post-war order would generate a different spirit, though in the early post-war period there were still strong echoes of the debate over the future of civilization. Arnold Toynbee planned a conference in 1945 involving all the prominent names who had worked before the war on the destiny of man and the future of Western civilization and could list thirty-six possible participants from across the world.[54] In 1948 he published *Civilization on Trial*, in which he anxiously explored the idea that atomic warfare presented mankind for the first time with the scientific capacity to destroy all human civilization for ever.[55] But after the war Toynbee reflected the public mood less clearly than he had done in the 1930s. The effect of the culture of crisis even before 1939 was not uniform. It influenced important sections of the political, literary and professional elite and played an unquantifiable part in shaping public opinion on a great number of major public issues. The effects were not confined to any one social class or any one political outlook, although the conclusions to be drawn about the crisis of civilization depended on whether it was perceived as something to be restored to health or replaced by a new birth. Much of the development and communication of the culture of crisis was independent of politics in any formal sense, sustained in unofficial or private spheres where discourses could be constructed 'from below' rather than being orchestrated by state propaganda or the press 'from above'. Individual politicians could be found who shared these views, though it did not necessarily shape their political behaviour in more than a general sense. The influence on government policy and the attitude of the state was as a result seldom direct, and where it was exerted did not result in clear initiatives. Sterilization was rejected alongside other positive efforts to improve 'racial hygiene', although the discourse on eugenic reform did encourage the idea of a 'social problem group' and the stigmatized or excluded family.[56] The cult of planning and demands for socialization produced clear effects only after 1945. In each case the failure to secure government action stimulated the very anxieties that policy was supposed to alleviate – fears for the future of the race, or the social dangers of an unplanned capitalism, or the threat to civilization presented by armaments and war.

The inhibiting effects of a cultural malaise are from their very nature difficult to calculate, particularly in circumstances where it has not generated violent social or racial victimization or serious civil strife. Laski thought the motto of every British prime minister from 1919 to 1939 was *'après nous le déluge'* while they muttered 'magic slogans' instead of attempting ruthless diagnosis of the disease.[57] Much of the critical language directed at government during the inter-war years suggested drift or timidity or excessive caution, and a persuasive case can be made to show that the fears for the future of civilization played a part in encouraging excessive prudence and an absence of risk-taking, particularly in the age of appeasing foreign policy, but also in coping with economic crisis and its social outcomes. The poet Hubert Nicholson, writing in 1941, could already see the recent era as one of 'frittering energy and social decay', smothered over with a 'miasma' that filtered into everyday life, provoking 'irresponsibility, destructiveness, the road to disintegration'.[58] The most important consequence of this mood was the effect on popular opinion in the 1930s as it became apparent that peace was unlikely to be preserved. The public, despite widespread support for anti-war causes, slowly came to believe that civilization could be saved only by war. During the process Hitler and 'fascism' became defined as the enemies of civilization while much of the population prepared to expect a war of world-historical significance, possibly a war of total destructiveness. The deeper domestic malaise was linked to the idea of a war to save civilization because the reform of social institutions or the transformation of capitalism came to be regarded by the late 1930s as something that would only be achieved, like a proper system of world government or collective peace, once the major threat to civilization had been overcome. The domestic malaise was thus projected outwards rather than feeding on itself and war was presented as something ineluctably linked to the wider salvation of civilized values. The 'escape into war' was the most profound consequence of the growing fear of the debilitating effects of a permanent state of unresolved tension and frustrating inactivity. It also explains the disillusionment with the months of phoney war between September 1939 and the opening of the land war in Scandinavia in April 1940, when British society had been braced for some kind of apocalypse from the first day. The later Blitz ended the period of uncertainty, ushered in the kind of war British society had been led to expect and confirmed the belief that Hitler's Germany was the one real enemy of civilization.

The constant theme of civilization in crisis, if repeated often enough and in different contexts, develops an explanatory power that does not have to take account of any existing disjuncture between historical reality and the language of threat. British society did not enter the last stages of the end of civilization in the 1920s and 1930s but the constant repetition of the language and cultural tropes of crisis made it seem as if that possibility was real. The fears were underpinned by historical theories of cyclical change and uncertainties about the biological survival of the race or of a sound economic system or of a political order free of extremes, and above all by the idea that war was an endemic feature of all human evolution. Many of these fears of a future dystopia, of the disastrous consequences if the democratic utopianism of pacifism or race improvement or world government or planned economics should fail, were just as irrational in their turn as the utopian dreams promoted by the European dictatorships Britain confronted. Democracies are no more immune from the distortion of reality or from the dangerous power of popular fear that provokes it, either then or now.

Notes

Introduction: Cassandras and Jeremiahs

1. J. A. Hobson, *The Recording Angel: A Report from Earth* (London, 1932), p. 104.
2. P. Buchanan, *The Death of the West* (New York, 2002); R. Koch and C. Smith, *Suicide of the West* (London, 2006); J. Jacobs, *Dark Age Ahead* (New York, 2004); F. Fukuyama *The End of Order* (London, 1997).
3. H. Nicholson, *Half My Days and Nights* (London, 1941), p. 100.
4. M. Pugh, *'We Danced All Night': A Social History of Britain between the Wars* (London, 2008).
5. London School of Economics (LSE), Political and Economic Planning papers, PEP I, A/7/3, memorandum from the chairman, 'Freedom and Planning: Collapsing Civilisation', 3 March 1932, p. 1.
6. A. Huxley, *Brave New World* (London, 1994), p. 205.
7. 'To-Day and Tomorrow', series catalogue, p. 3, in F. C. S. Schiller, *Cassandra or The Future of the British Empire* (London, 1927).
8. A. Koestler, *Darkness at Noon* (London, 1940), p. 52.
9. LSE, Malinowski papers, 22/7, 'Oxf. Lect.' (n.d.), p. 1.

Chapter 1: Decline and Fall

1. G. N. Clark, 'The Instability of Civilization', *Hibbert Journal*, 31 (1932/3), p. 645.
2. Mansfield College archives, Oxford, minutes of College Council meeting, 14 Oct. 1921.
3. C. T. Campion (ed.), *Albert Schweitzer: Philosopher, Theologian, Musician, Doctor. Some Biographical Notes* (London, 1928), p. 3.
4. E. Micklem, 'Dr Albert Schweitzer and Mansfield', *Mansfield College Magazine*, 146 (Jan. 1955), p. 255.

5. Schweitzer to Anna Schäffer, 25 March 1922, in *Albert Schweitzer: Leben, Werk und Denken 1905–1965, mitgeteilt in seinen Briefen* (Heidelberg, 1987), pp. 65–6.

6. *Oxford University Gazette*, 19 Jan. 1922, p. 301.

7. Mansfield College archives, minutes of College Council meeting, 11 May 1922, 23 June 1922; E. Kaye, *Mansfield College Oxford: Its Origin, History and Significance* (Oxford, 1996), p. 179; Schweitzer to Werner Reinhart, 1 Jan. 1924, in *Albert Schweitzer: Leben, Werk und Denken*, p. 371.

8. A. Schweitzer, *The Decay and the Restoration of Civilization* (2 vols., London, 1923), vol. I, pp. vii, 1, 3.

9. H. G. Wells, 'Introduction' to J. M. Kenworthy, *Will Civilisation Crash?* (London, 1927), p. iv.

10. H. G. Wells, *The Salvaging of Civilization* (London, 1921), p. 1.

11. A. J. Toynbee, *Experiences* (London, 1969), pp. 199–200.

12. L. Woolf, *Barbarians at the Gate* (London, 1939), pp. 16–18; Toynbee, *Experiences*, p. 187.

13. Woolf, *Barbarians at the Gate*, pp. 162–3.

14. R. Hart-Davis (ed.), *Siegfried Sassoon Diaries, 1915–1918* (London, 1983), p. 282.

15. University Library, Cambridge, Geoffrey Keynes papers, ADD 8633, Box 9A, Sassoon to Geoffrey Keynes, 2 June 1938.

16. W. Lewis, *Hitler* (London, 1931), pp. 128–9.

17. See, for example, J. Lawrence, 'Forging a Peaceable Kingdom: War, Violence, and Fear of Brutalization in Post-First World War Britain', *Journal of Modern History*, 75 (2003), pp. 557–89; J. Bourke, *An Intimate History of Killing: Face to Face Killing in Twentieth-Century Warfare* (London, 1999), chs. 5, 11. See too B. Davis, 'Experience, Identity, and Memory: The Legacy of World War I', *Journal of Modern History*, 75 (2003), pp. 111–31 for an introduction to recent literature.

18. University of Exeter, Special Collections, Williamson papers, MS 43/1359, draft, 'Reality in War Literature', 1928, p. 4.

19. Ibid., MS 43/1359, 'Reality in War Literature', p. 33.

20. Ibid., MS 43/A45, proofs of 'After Ten Years', 1928/9 (published as *The Wet Flanders Plain*), p. 2.

21. H. Barbusse, *Under Fire: The Story of a Squad* (London, 1926); University of Exeter, Special Collections, Williamson papers, MS 43/1359, 'Reality in War Literature', pp. 7–8.

22. King's College, Cambridge, Lowes Dickinson papers, GLD 1/18, draft review of *All Quiet on the Western Front* for *Cambridge Review*, 3 May 1929, p. 412; E. M. Remarque, *All Quiet on the Western Front* (London, 1929), p. 288.

23. C. E. M. Joad, review of *World Without Faith* in the *Fortnightly Review*, 138 (July–Dec. 1935), pp. 751–2.

24. G. Murray, *The Ordeal of this Generation: The War, the League and the Future* (London, 1929), pp. 173–5, 190.

25. University of Exeter, Special Collections, Williamson papers, MS 43/B60, drafts of 'Soldier's Diary of the Great War', Introduction, p. 10.

26. University of Sussex Library, Leonard Woolf papers, MS 13, part I, Q.3c, Woolf to Daniel Woodward (Univ. of Virginia) (n.d. but Dec. 1962); Woolf, letter, 23 March 1966. See too L. Woolf, *Downhill all the Way: An Autobiography of the Years 1919–1939* (London, 1967), pp. 64–5, 75.

27. University of Sussex Library, Leonard Woolf papers, MS 13, part I, L.2, letter signed 'A Social Animal' to Woolf, 27 Nov. 1940. See too L. Woolf, *After the Deluge* (London, 1931). A Pelican paperback edition followed in 1937.

28. There is now a very large literature on this. See especially D. Todman, *The Great War: Myth and Memory* (London, 2005), which is among the very best recent accounts; J. Winter, *Sites of Memory, Sites of Mourning: The Great War in European Cultural History* (Cambridge, 1998); A. Gregory, *Silence of Memory: Armistice Day 1919–1946* (Oxford, 1994); and the classic P. Fussell, *The Great War and Modern Memory* (London, 1975). On the pre-1914 background see P. Blom, *The Vertigo Years: Change and Culture in the West, 1900–1914* (London, 2008).

29. Clark, 'Instability of Civilization', p. 646.

30. King's College, Cambridge, Forster papers, EMF 18/608, Forster to Leonard Woolf, 27 March 1936; EMF 18/553, Forster to Elizabeth Trevelyan, 10 Oct. 1937.

31. King's College, Cambridge, Lowes Dickinson papers, GLD 1/5, Journal, 1916–1932, entries for 9 May 1922, 17 June 1932. The last entry was dated 11 July 1932.

32. Magdalene College, Cambridge, Old Library, Inge diaries and papers, 33/diary 1931–3, entry for 18/26 Sept.; 35/diary 1936–7, entry for 22 Nov.; 36/diary 1938–9, 1939 summary.

33. Camden Local History Archives Centre, London, Hampstead Ethical Institute, ST2/5B/12, Minute Book 1900–March 1922.

34. London School of Economics Archive Centre, Fabian Society papers, C17, Executive Committee Minute Book, 1928–1933, (t) lecture list 1921–32; C18, Minute Book 1933–1937; C19, Executive Committee Minute Book, 1938.

35. H. G. Wells, *The Fate of Homo Sapiens* (London, 1939), p. 312.

36. L. Stoddard, *The Revolt against Civilization: The Menace of the Under-Man* (London, 1922), pp. 1, 27.

37. F. C. Schiller, *Tantalus or The Future of Man* (London, 1924). Schiller

also wrote *Cassandra or The Future of the British Empire* (London, 1925). For details on the series see University College, London, Routledge & Kegan Paul collection, 23h, Publishing Journal, vol. VIII, 1921–39. *Tantalus* sold 6,500 copies, *Cassandra* 3,000.

38. Schiller, *Tantalus or The Future of Man*, pp. 39, 42.

39. Ibid., pp. 52–3.

40. C. Dawson, 'Man and Civilisation', *The Listener*, 10 (July–Dec. 1933), p. 280.

41. Camden Local History Archives Centre, Chalcot Discussion Society papers, Annual Report for 1927–1928; Clark 'Instability of Civilization', p. 655.

42. G. K. Bowes, '"The Decline of the West" in Actual Progress', *Hibbert Journal*, 33 (1934/5), p. 194.

43. R. F. Rattray, 'Will Our Civilisation Survive?', *Hibbert Journal*, 34 (1935/6), pp. 57–8.

44. P. Chalmers Mitchell, 'The Twilight of Civilization', in *The Rationalist Annual*, 1940, pp. 32–3.

45. Ibid., p. 36. As a zoologist he based his argument on the idea that all things in nature have a natural life cycle, human societies included.

46. H. G. Wells, *The Shape of Things to Come* (London, 1933), pp. 89, 104. See too I. Patterson, *Guernica and Total War* (London, 2007), p. 79; N. Royden-Smith review of Wells, *The Shape of Things to Come* in the *Fortnightly Review*, 134 (July–Dec. 1933), pp. 506–7.

47. G. West, 'Decline and Fall', *Fortnightly Review*, 139 (Jan.–June 1936), p. 245.

48. L. Jacks, 'The Saving Forces of Civilisation', *Hibbert Journal*, 30 (1931/2), pp. 1, 4. Jacks's comments brought a strong protest from one correspondent that Jeremiah was always regarded simply as the bearer of gloom, when the Bible shows that he offered hope as well as warning to those who 'would have courage'. See Harris Manchester College, Oxford, Lawrence Jacks papers, D. J. Stephen to Lawrence Jacks, 22 Oct. 1931.

49. South Place Ethical Society Library, London, list of lectures 1930–1939; Monthly Record, May 1936, pp. 3–5.

50. University of Sussex Library, Leonard Woolf papers, MS 13, part I, L.2, Donald Brace to Leonard Woolf, 28 Dec. 1934; Woolf to Brace, 10 Jan. 1935.

51. Ibid., Victor Gollancz to Woolf, 19 Oct. 1938; Woolf to Gollancz, 27 Oct. 1938 and 9 May 1939.

52. Ibid., Donald Brace to Woolf, 14 June 1939 and 23 June 1939; telegram Woolf to Harcourt, Brace, 29 June 1939.

53. C. Bell, *Civilization: An Essay* (London, 1928), pp. vi–vii; part of the wartime draft, in which the quotation can be found, is in Trinity College, Cambridge, Bell papers, BELL 2/10, draft manuscript, 'Civilization'. It is clear from the writing that this dates from 1918 and not 1928, the date given in the papers.

54. Bell, *Civilization*, pp. 163–4.

55. Ibid., pp. 167, 181.

56. University of Exeter, Special Collections, Rowse papers, MS 113, 2/1/10b, diary manuscript, March 1935–Aug. 1939, entry for 29 April 1936.

57. Schiller, *Tantalus or The Future of Man*, p. 34.

58. Toynbee, *Experiences*, pp. 200–201. See the discussion in P. Brendon, *The Decline and Fall of the British Empire* (London, 2007), pp. xiii–xviii, 7–8.

59. Earl of Cromer, *Ancient and Modern Imperialism* (London, 1910), pp. 33, 127.

60. King's College, London, Liddell Hart Archive Centre, Liddell Hart papers, LH1/538, file of obituaries of Gilbert Murray; 'Birthday People: Gilbert Murray', *Observer*, 1 Jan. 1956. In a private letter to the historian J. L. Hammond, Lord Robert Cecil observed that Murray 'really is an angelic person'. See Bodleian Library, Hammond papers, vol. XXV, Cecil to Hammond, 17 Feb. 1936.

61. Bodleian Library, Murray papers, file 499, draft lecture, 'European Civilisation' ('Christian' and 'Western' both deleted) (n.d. but 1945/6), pp. 2–3, 392; G. Murray, 'Die Probleme von morgen', *Nord und Süd*, 50 (1927), pp. 354–6.

62. Bodleian Library, Murray papers, file 499, draft, 'Address to the Conference of European Universities' (n.d. but 1950?), pp. 1, 4.

63. J. Nelson, 'The Dark Ages', *History Workshop Journal*, 63 (2007), pp. 194–6, 200.

64. Ibid., p. 200; C. Oman, *The Dark Ages, 476–918* (London, 6th edn, 1923).

65. W. P. Ker, *The Dark Ages* (Edinburgh, 1904). See the discussion in R. Osborne, *Civilization: A New History of the Western World* (London, 2006), pp. 134ff., and B. Ward-Perkins, *The Fall of Rome and the End of Civilization* (Oxford, 2005), chs. 1 and 7.

66. C. Caudwell, *Further Studies in a Dying Culture* (London, 1949), p. 126.

67. L. Woolf, *Imperialism and Civilization* (London, 1928), pp. 9, 16.

68. Woolf, *Barbarians at the Gate*, p. 163.

69. E. Kanter, 'Away with Civilisation!', *The Plebs*, 23 (1931), pp. 103–4; T. David, 'Does History Justify a Belief in Progress?', *The Plebs*, 28 (1936), pp. 214–15.

70. University of Sussex Library, Leonard Woolf papers, MS 13, part I, L.3, Victor Gollancz to Woolf, 21 July 1939, encl. memorandum by John Strachey, pp. 1–5, 25–7.

71. Woolf, *After the Deluge*, vol. I, p. 53.

72. A. M. Ludovici, *Nietzsche: His Life and Works* (London, 1912), and *Who Is to Be Master of the World? An Introduction to the Philosophy of Friedrich Nietzsche* (London, 1909); O. Levy (ed.), *The Will to Power: An Attempted Transvaluation of all Values* (trs. A. M. Ludovici, London, 1913). On Nietzsche's reception in Britain see D. Stone, 'An "Entirely Tactless Nietzschean Jew": Oscar Levy's Critique of Western Civilisation', *Journal of Contemporary History*, 36 (2001), pp. 271–92.

73. F. Nietzsche, *Ecce Homo* (London, 1992), p. 97.

74. H. Kessler, *The Diary of a Cosmopolitan, 1918–1937* (London, 1971), p. 333, entry for 15 Oct. 1927.

75. O. Spengler, *Der Untergang des Abendlandes: Umrisse einer Morphologie der Weltgeschichte* (2 vols., Munich, 1922–3). On Spengler see J. Farrenkopf, *Prophet of Decline: Spengler on World Politics and History* (Baton Rouge, La., 2001), esp. pp. 12–13, 27–41; J. O'Hagan, *Conceptualizing the West in International Relations: From Spengler to Said* (London, 2000), ch. 3.

76. J. Shotwell, 'Spengler', in Shotwell (ed.), *Essays in Intellectual History* (New York, 1929), p. 57; H. S. Hughes, *Oswald Spengler: A Critical Estimate* (New York, 1952), p. 89. By 1931 sales of Spengler's title had reached a reputed 170,000 copies. See Jacks, 'The Saving Forces of Civilisation', p. 1.

77. Spengler, *Untergang*, p. 1; A. Helps (ed.), *Spengler Letters, 1913–1936* (London, 1966), p. 72, Spengler to Georg Misch, 5 Jan. 1919.

78. Shotwell, 'Spengler', pp. 62–6; W. J. Dannhauser, 'Nietzsche and Spengler on Progress and Decline', in A. M. Melzer, J. Weinberger and M. R. Zinman (eds.), *History and the Idea of Progress* (Ithaca, N.Y., 1995), pp. 124–7.

79. Cited in Hughes, *Oswald Spengler*, p. 86.

80. Shotwell, 'Spengler', p. 62.

81. *Spengler Letters*, p. 264, Edwin Payr to Spengler, 21 Oct. 1931; see too Bowes, ' "The Decline of the West" in Actual Progress', pp. 179–95.

82. C. Dawson, 'Herr Spengler and the Life of Civilisations', *Sociological Review*, 14 (1922), pp. 104, 108; see too Dawson's own account of the issues: 'The Life of Civilisations', *Sociological Review*, 14 (1922), pp. 51–68.

83. S. Unwin, *The Truth about a Publisher: An Autobiographical Record* (London, 1960), p. 199.

84. O. Spengler, *The Decline of the West* (2 vols., London, 1926–8), p. ix.

85. G. P. Gooch, *Germany* (London, 1925), p. 329; R. W. S. Merrell, review of *Decline of the West* in the *Quarterly Journal*, 250 (Jan.–April 1928), p. 71.

86. Hughes, *Oswald Spengler*, p. 89; Unwin, *Truth about a Publisher*, p. 199. Sales figures from Reading University, Special Collections, George Allen & Unwin archive, Spengler files.

87. L. Mumford, 'Spengler: Dithyramb of Doom', in Mumford, *Interpretations and Forecasts 1922–1972* (London, 1973), p. 221.

88. E. H. Goddard and P. A. Gibbons, *Civilisation or Civilisations: An Essay in the Spenglerian Philosophy of History* (London, 1926), p. xiv.

89. Ibid., pp. 2, 7.

90. W. M. Flinders Petrie, *The Revolutions of Civilisation* (London, 1911), pp. 2–5.

91. Ibid., pp. 9–10, 123–4, 126.

92. Rattray, 'Will Our Civilisation Survive?', pp. 57–8.

93. University of Sussex Library, Monk's House collection, MS 18/B16 (f) 2, 'As I See It', radio broadcast by G. B. Shaw, 2 Nov. 1937.

94. A. J. Toynbee, *World Order or Downfall* (BBC pamphlet, 1931), p. 43.

95. Bodleian Library, Toynbee papers, Box 6, BBC script, 'The Study of History', 4 Jan. 1948, pp. 1, 9; transcript of discussion between Professor Toynbee and Professor Geyl, 4 Jan. 1948, p. 3. The Spengler comparison was developed in F. Neilson, 'Toynbee's "A Study of History"', *American Journal of Economics and Sociology*, 6 (1947), pp. 452–65. On Toynbee see O'Hagan, *Conceptualizing the West*, ch. 4.

96. A. J. Toynbee, *Civilization on Trial* (New York, 1948), p. 10: 'Where the German *a priori* method drew a blank, let us see what could be done by English empiricism.'

97. Toynbee, *Experiences*, pp. 81–99. On the remarkable amount of published material see M. Popper, *A Bibliography of the Works of Arnold Toynbee, 1910–1954*, Royal Institute of International Affairs, 1955.

98. Toynbee, *Experiences*, p. 101; Bodleian Library, Toynbee papers, Box 122, Caroline Hill (Oxford University Press) to Toynbee, 7 Feb. 1949, encl., 'Toynbee, draft for the record', p. 3.

99. Oxford University Press archive, Toynbee files, PB/ED/019415, Box 2777, Arnold Toynbee to Joseph Willits, 17 Oct. 1944, p. 2.

100. Bodleian Library, Toynbee papers, Box 3, draft lecture, 'The Downfall of Civilisation', 1939, pp. 2–3.

101. Ibid., Box 3, draft BBC talk, 'Whither Mankind?', 26 March 1931, p. 6.

102. Ibid., Box 63, Toynbee to Arnold Wilson, 16 Nov. 1931, p. 2.

103. Ibid., Box 39, note, 'Subjects for Individual Research' (n.d. but Feb. 1932), p. 8; Box 128, George Panichas to Toynbee, 18 Oct. 1969, encl., typescript draft, 'Toynbee', p. 7.

104. R. Stromberg, 'A Study of History and a World at War: Toynbee's

Two Great Enterprises', in C. T. McIntire and M. Perry (eds.), *Toynbee Reappraisals* (Toronto, 1989), pp. 166–7.

105. Bodleian Library, Toynbee papers, Box 39, note, 'Subjects for Individual Research', pp. 9–10.

106. Oxford University Press (OUP), Toynbee files, PB/ED/019415, Box 2777, Toynbee to Willits, 17 Oct. 1944, p. 1; Margaret Cleeve (RIIA) to Sir Humphrey Milford (OUP), 20 Oct. 1944.

107. Bodleian Library, Toynbee papers, Box 19, A. J. P. Taylor, 'History and Politics', *Manchester Guardian*, 1 Dec. 1939; Box 122, Toynbee to Sir Humphrey Milford, 3 Feb. 1940 and Box 83, Toynbee to David Morgan, 25 April 1940, which give figures of 40 and 41 days before the war, respectively.

108. A. J. Toynbee, *A Study of History: Abridgement of Volumes I–VI* by D. C. Somervell (Oxford, 1946), passim (on Nyasaland, pp. 85–6).

109. Ibid., chs. 18–19, 21. See too W. W. Wagar, 'Toynbee as a Prophet of World Civilization', in McIntire and Perry, *Toynbee Reappraisals*, pp. 127–38. See too Bodleian Library, G. N. Clark papers, file 213, Toynbee to Clark, 3 Oct. 1936: 'I have long had a notion that the key to our own present plight – a painful one, as you say – might be found in something that happened towards the end of the 17th century . . .'

110. Toynbee, *Study of History*, pp. 588–9.

111. R. H. Tawney, 'Dr Toynbee's Study of History', *International Affairs*, 18 (1939), pp. 799–801.

112. University of Sussex Library, Leonard Woolf papers, MS 13, part I, M.5, Toynbee to Leonard Woolf, 29 Aug. 1934; Bodleian Library, Toynbee papers, Box 19, L. Woolf, 'Civilisation', *New Statesman*, 18 Aug. 1934, p. 213.

113. OUP, Toynbee files, PB/ED/019415, Box 2777, minute dated 26 July 1934 (initialled A.P.N.).

114. Ibid., minute for Geoffrey Cumberledge, 30 Oct. 1939; minute initialled G.W.S.H. for Cumberledge (n.d. but Oct. 1939).

115. Bodleian Library, Toynbee papers, Box 122, Humphrey Milford to Toynbee, 1 Feb. 1940; J. Joll, 'Two Prophets of the Twentieth Century: Spengler and Toynbee', *Review of International Studies*, 11 (1985), p. 91. Seven thousand complete sets of the *Study* were sold after the final volumes appeared.

116. OUP, Toynbee files, Box 2777, Humphrey Milford to Margaret Cleeve, 23 Oct. 1944; D. C. Somervell to Toynbee, 31 Oct. 1944; OUP to OUP New York, 9 Jan. 1946; note, biography of D. C. Somervell (n.d.). J. G. Frazer, *The Golden Bough* (12 vols., London, 1906–15), an expansion of the original published in two vols. in 1890.

117. OUP, Toynbee files, Box 2777, Gerard Hopkins (Political Intelligence division, Foreign Office) to Toynbee, 19 Sept. 1945; minute for Geoffrey Cumberledge, 19 Sept. 1945; OUP to Toynbee, 6 Dec. 1945. Review in Bodleian Library, Toynbee papers, Box 19, German transcript of radio review by Thilo Koch, 23 March 1953.

118. Bodleian Library, Toynbee papers, Box 6, draft BBC broadcast, 'The Abolition of War', 1 Dec. 1930, p. 11.

119. Toynbee papers, Box 3, draft lecture for Williamstown University, 'A British View of the World Economic Order', 1932, p. 14.

120. Stromberg, 'A Study of History', pp. 152–3; Bodleian Library, Toynbee papers, Box 3, Institute of Politics, 'Round Table on the Disintegration of the Modern World Order', First Meeting, 29 July 1932, p. 1.

121. King's College, London, Liddell Hart Archive Centre, Liddell Hart papers, LH1/698, Toynbee to Liddell Hart, 26 May 1938, encl. letter from Toynbee to Lord Allen, 11 May 1938; Liddell Hart to Toynbee, 27 May 1938.

122. Bodleian Library, Toynbee papers, Box 39, C. Mair (LSE) to Toynbee, 23 Oct. 1936; Mair to Toynbee, 28 Oct. 1936; covering letter, RIIA to Toynbee, 4 Nov. 1936 asking him to turn down the invitation for 1937; Box 3, draft, 'The Downfall of Civilisations', 1939 (delivered 23 May 1939), pp. 1, 3–8.

123. Ibid., Box 63, Toynbee to Arnold Wilson, 16 Nov. 1931, p. 2.

124. University of Sussex Library, Leonard Woolf papers, MS 13, part I, M.5, Toynbee to Woolf, 29 Aug. 1934, p. 2.

125. University Library, Cambridge, Joseph Needham papers, L/32, Arnold Toynbee, 'Religion and Race', Universal Christian Council for Life and Work, July 1935, pp. 5, 11.

126. Bodleian Library, Toynbee papers, Box 3, draft, 'Sermon in University Church, Oxford', 1940, pp. 18–19.

127. A. J. Toynbee, *Christianity and Civilisation* (London, 1940) (Burge memorial lecture, Oxford, 23 May 1940), p. 27.

128. Bodleian Library, Toynbee papers, Box 122, draft for record, p. 4 (see n. 98).

129. Bodleian Library, Clark papers, file 213, Toynbee to Clark, 3 Oct. 1936; Toynbee to Clark, 9 Dec. 1936. Toynbee papers, Box 81, Clark to Toynbee, 30 Sept. 1936; Clark to Toynbee, 18 Dec. 1936.

130. Bodleian Library, Toynbee papers, Box 39, draft letter from Toynbee to the Abbot of Ampleforth, 16 Jan. 1937.

131. Bodleian Library, Hammond papers, vol. XXV, Lord Robert Cecil to Hammond, 25 April 1937. Cecil added, 'but is he "converted"?' On

Toynbee's later religious interests see C. T. McIntire, 'Toynbee's Philosophy of History: His Christian Period', in McIntire and Perry, *Toynbee Reappraisals*, pp. 73–80.

132. Bodleian Library, Hammond papers, vol. XXX, Murray to Barbara Hammond, 6 July 1940.

133. Review of *Christianity and Civilisation* by E. F. Carritt in the *Hibbert Journal*, 38 (1940), p. 434.

134. R. Lloyd, 'Christian Opinion in England To-Day', *Quarterly Review*, 274 (1940), pp. 303–4.

135. C. Dawson, *The Dynamics of World History* (ed. J. J. Mulloy, London, 1957), pp. 392–7; A. J. Toynbee, *A Study of History*, vol. XII: *Reconsiderations* (Oxford, 1961), p. 534.

136. L. Jacks, 'Mr Wells on the Fate of Homo Sapiens', *Hibbert Journal*, 38 (1939/40), p. 173.

137. J. McCabe, *The End of the World* (London, 1920), pp. 244–5, 263.

138. E. Guest, *At the End of the World: A Vision* (London, 1929), pp. 10, 38, 67.

139. Magdalene College, Cambridge, Old Library, Inge diaries and papers, 33/diary 1931–3, entries for 21 Oct. and 22 Nov. 1931. See too W. R. Inge, *The Fall of the Idols* (London, 1940), pp. 39–44.

140. Magdalene College, Cambridge, Old Library, Inge diaries and papers, 33/diary 1931–3, entry for 22 Nov. 1931.

141. Bodleian Library, Toynbee papers, draft BBC talk, 'Whither Mankind?', no. 6, 26 March 1931, p. 2.

142. F. C. Palmer, 'The Death Instinct and Western Man', *Hibbert Journal*, 51 (1953), p. 333.

143. South Place Ethical Society, Monthly Record, June 1924, p. 7.

144. R. B. Perry, 'The Meaning of Death', *Hibbert Journal*, 33 (1934/5), pp. 161–78; J. Buckham, 'Death', *Hibbert Journal*, 36 (1937/8), pp. 93–9.

Chapter 2: The Death of Capitalism

1. E. Mendelson (ed.), *The English Auden: Poems, Essays and Dramatic Writings, 1927–1939* (London, 1977), p. 480.

2. London School of Economics (LSE), Fabian Society papers, A4/12, R. R. Clark Ltd to Sidney Webb, 21 Sept. 1922; Sidney Webb to F. Galton (secretary of the Fabian Society), 28 Sept. 1922, who wrote about *The Reign of Capitalism*, 'or some such title'; Stanley Unwin to Galton, 10 Oct. 1922 and Galton to Unwin, 13 Oct. 1922, confirming the new title as *The Decay of Capitalist Civilisation*.

3. LSE, Fabian Society papers, A4/12, Galton to R. R. Clark Ltd, 25 Sept., 14 Dec. 1922.

4. Ibid., R. R. Clark Ltd to Galton, 14 Dec. 1922; LSE, Passfield papers, 5/2/3, publicity leaflet for *The Decay of Capitalist Civilisation*, 3rd impression, 1923.

5. LSE, Passfield papers, 2/4/6, George Bernard Shaw to Beatrice Webb, 11 Oct. 1922.

6. Ibid., 7/2/9, draft introduction, 'The Decay of Capitalist Civilisation', pp. 1, 3. Full version in B. Webb and S. Webb, *The Decay of Capitalist Civilisation* (London, 1923), pp. 4–6.

7. G. B. Shaw to Eric Bentley, 11 June 1948, in D. H. Laurence (ed.), *Bernard Shaw: Collected Letters, 1926–1950* (London, 1988), p. 823.

8. LSE, Passfield papers, 1/1/36, Beatrice Webb diary, 17 Sept. 1920–10 Feb. 1923, entry for 11 Jan. 1923.

9. Ibid., entry for 9 Feb. 1923.

10. Ibid., 6/84, draft of BBC talk by Beatrice Webb, 21 Jan. 1932, 'Diseases of Organised Society III', pp. 2, 4.

11. Webb and Webb, *Decay of Capitalist Civilisation*, pp. 165, 166–7.

12. Ibid., pp. 163, 165, 174.

13. LSE, Passfield papers, 5/2/3, cover proof of *Soviet Communism*, 1941 edn, quotations from *Picture Post*, 13 Sept. 1941; Laurence, *Bernard Shaw: Collected Letters*, p. 823, also p. 669.

14. B. Webb, *Our Partnership* (London, 1948), pp. 3–5; G. B. Shaw to Eric Bentley, 11 June 1948 in Laurence, *Bernard Shaw: Collected Letters*, p. 822; Shaw to J. M. Keynes, 7 May 1943, ibid., p. 669, 'She was, to her great credit, a self-made ethical socialist . . .'

15. A. J. Toynbee, *Acquaintances* (London, 1967), p. 108.

16. K. Martin, *Editor: A Volume of Autobiography, 1931–1945* (London, 1968), p. 79.

17. B. Webb, *Our Partnership*, p. 11; Martin, *Editor*, pp. 76–7, 79.

18. Martin, *Editor*, p. 68. See too G. D. H. Cole, *Persons and Periods* (London, 1938), pp. 327–8, 329–30 on the dominant role that the Webbs' view of socialism came to play in Britain after 1919.

19. LSE, Passfield papers, 2/4/H, file 1, Henry Massingham to Beatrice Webb, 27 Jan. 1923.

20. Ibid., 6/82, draft of BBC talk by Beatrice Webb, 24 July 1930, 'Can we make our Parliamentary institutions equal to their task?', p. 22.

21. LSE, Fabian Society papers, A5/3, Beatrice Webb to Galton, 23 Jan. 1931.

22. Ibid., Beatrice Webb to Galton, 30 Jan. 1931; Galton to Beatrice Webb,

20 Dec. 1938; C17, agenda for meeting of Executive Committee, Fabian Society, 22 Feb. 1933, 'Kingsway Hall lectures 1921–1932'.

23. Bristol University, Special Collections, Allen Lane archive, DM 1819/26/1, Sidney Webb to Allen Lane, 14 Nov. 1937, 1 Jan. 1938. 'But I must observe', Sidney wrote, not altogether truthfully, 'that none of our books is "dead". They all yield a small but steady annual income.'

24. LSE, Passfield papers, 2/5/7, Beatrice Webb to Ruth Cavendish-Bentinck, 28 Sept. 1939, 19 Sept. 1940.

25. Nuffield College Oxford, Cole papers, A1/40/2, Fabian Society lecture, 'Can Capitalism Survive?', 22 Oct. 1936, pp. 26–7

26. J. A. Hobson, *From Capitalism to Socialism* (London, 1932), p. 29.

27. South Place Ethical Society library, Report of Committee 1920–1921, pp. 3–4.

28. King's College, Cambridge, J. M. Keynes papers, RV/1, lecture notes, 'The Economic Position in England', Moscow, 14 Sept. 1925, p. 5: 'I emphasise that the economic problem of England is essentially a problem of social and economic disequilibrium and not primarily a problem of poverty or a lack of technical capacity to produce wealth.' Ibid., Hogarth Essays, *A Short View of Russia* (London, 1925), p. 25; draft lecture, 'The Economic Transition in England', Moscow, 15 Sept. 1925, p. 3.

29. Marshall Library, Cambridge, A. C. Pigou papers, 1/7/1, 'An Analytical Account of the General Economic Movement in the United Kingdom between the Armistice and the Restoration of the Gold Standard' (n.d. but late 1941), pp. 2, 61–3.

30. For an excellent discussion of the issues surrounding the popular culture of Free Trade see F. Trentmann, *Free Trade Nation: Commerce, Consumption and Civil Society in Modern Britain* (Oxford, 2008), pp. 328–30, 348–61.

31. LSE, L/D702, 'Education and World Crisis: The Presidential Address of W. A. Strawbridge of the Tenth Annual Meeting of the National Council of Labour Colleges', 3 July 1931, pp. 3–5, 8–9. See too L/107, 'Education for Emancipation', NCLC, Feb. 1937. By 1936 there were 2.2 million affiliated.

32. LSE, L/D659, WEA Western District, 'Fifty Years in the Life of a Voluntary Movement 1911–1961' (n.d. but 1961), pp. 4–6; M. Stocks, *The Workers' Educational Association: The First Fifty Years* (London, 1953), pp. 101, 116–17.

33. Marshall Library, Cambridge, A. C. Pigou papers, 1/7/1, review of *The Theory of Unemployment*, 'Professional Economics' (n.d. but 1931).

34. King's College, Cambridge, Joan Robinson papers, xv/2, cited in review by C. Clark of *The Economics of Imperfect Competition* in the *Cambridge Review*, 10 Nov. 1933, p. 91. On these dilemmas see too L. H. Fraser,

'How Do We Want Economists to Behave?', *Economic Journal*, 42 (1932), pp. 555–70. 'Economists', Fraser wrote, 'cannot remain in the secluded contemplation of pure truth' (p. 569).

35. Cited in Bertil Ohlin's review of Keynes's *Essays in Persuasion* in the *Economic Journal*, 42 (1932), p. 260.

36. K. Marx, *Capital: A Critical Analysis of Capitalist Production* (London, 1903), pp. ix–xiv.

37. K. Marx, *Capital* (intro. by G. D. H. Cole, 2 vols., London, 1930). The quotation is on the dust jacket.

38. G. D. H. Cole, *Persons and Periods* (London, 1938), p. 261. For a discussion of the role of Marx's thinking on the British labour movement see R. Toye, *The Labour Party and the Planned Economy, 1931–51* (London, 2003), pp. 11–12.

39. University of Hull, Special Collections, Hobson papers, DHN/24, draft lecture, 'Remaking the World', July 1932, p. 13; H. N. Brailsford, *The Life-Work of J. A. Hobson: L. T. Hobhouse Memorial Lecture* (Oxford, 1948), pp. 6–7; M. Schneider, *J. A. Hobson* (London, 1996), p. 8.

40. University of Hull, Special Collections, Hobson papers, DHN/24, draft lecture, p. 13; Brailsford, *J. A. Hobson*, p. 6; J. A. Hobson, *Confessions of an Economic Heretic* (London, 1938), pp. 35–6; J. Townshend, *J. A. Hobson* (Manchester, 1990), pp. 67–9.

41. J. A. Hobson and A. F. Mummery, *The Physiology of Industry, Being an Exposure of Certain Fallacies in Existing Theories of Economics* (London, 1889); Brailsford, *J. A. Hobson*, pp. 5–9; Hobson, *Confessions*, p. 30.

42. University of Hull, Special Collections, Hobson papers, DHN/24, 'Dr C. E. M. Joad on J. A. Hobson', South Place Ethical Society, Monthly Record, May 1940, pp. 5–6; Martin, *Editor*, pp. 158–9; South Place Ethical Society, Monthly Record, Nov. 1921, p. 5, 'John A. Hobson'.

43. University of Hull, Special Collections, Hobson papers, DHN/24, 'Remaking the World', pp. 11–12; see too DHN/19, 'Underconsumption: An Exposition and a Reply', *Economica*, Nov. 1933, pp. 403–27. South Place Ethical Society, *Monthly Record*, March 1922, 'Mr Hobson on Unemployment', pp. 5–6.

44. See the analysis in *Plan*, 2 (April 1935), p. 9; and University of Hull, Special Collections, Hobson papers, DHN/24, 'Remaking the World', pp. 15–16. These arguments were also developed in J. A. Hobson, 'A Rejoinder to E. F. M. Durbin', *Economica*, 13 (1933), p. 426: 'In an equalitarian society a larger *amount* of saving would occur', Hobson claimed, but the rate, or proportion would be different. See also Schneider, *Hobson*, pp. 63–4.

45. G. D. H. Cole, *An Intelligent Man's Guide Through World Chaos* (London, 1932), p. 337.

46. Review of Hobson's *Rationalisation and Unemployment* in the *Economic Journal*, 41 (1931), p. 79.

47. J. A. Hobson, *Wealth and Life: A Study of Values* (London, 1929), p. 447.

48. Brailsford, *J. A. Hobson*, p. 13; see too H. Thomas, *John Strachey* (London, 1973), pp. 56–7.

49. University of Hull, Special Collections, Hobson papers, DHN/24, 'Remaking the World', p. 16. See the discussion of Hobson's thinking in N. Thompson, 'Hobson and the Fabians: Two Roads to Socialism in the 1920s', *History of Political Economy*, 26 (1994), pp. 203–20.

50. Brailsford, *J. A. Hobson*, p. 18.

51. University of Hull, Special Collections, Hobson papers, DHN/24, draft lecture, 'The Popular Mind' (n.d.), p. 19; draft lecture, 'The Social Sense of Responsibility' (n.d.), p. 112.

52. J. A. Hobson, *The Recording Angel: A Report from Earth* (London, 1932), pp. 53, 56.

53. Cole, *Guide Through World Chaos*, p. 338.

54. L. P. Carpenter, *G. D. H. Cole: An Intellectual Biography* (Cambridge, 1973), pp. 46–70.

55. Cole, *Persons and Periods*, pp. 282–3. See too N. Riddell, '"The Age of Cole"? G. D. H. Cole and the British Labour Movement, 1929–1933', *Historical Journal*, 38 (1995), pp. 933–57.

56. Nuffield College, Oxford, Cole papers, A1/40/8, draft article, 'Changing Economic Order' (1935–6), p. 5.

57. Ibid., pp. 6, 23.

58. Trinity College, Cambridge, Dobb archive, DB 3, 'Paper on the Social Distress Attending the Industrial Revolution and Its Connection with Power Machinery', essay for C. R. Fay, 1919/20 session, Pembroke College, Cambridge, p. 22.

59. Ibid., DA 117, 'Maurice Dobb: Random Biographical Notes', *Cambridge Journal of Economics*, 2 (1978), pp. 115–18.

60. Ibid., DD 11, notes, 'Decline of Capitalism' (n.d. but 1923?); DD 54, lecture notes, 'Imperialism' (n.d. but 1935/6?), p. 1.

61. Ibid., notes for a talk, 'Features of Final Stage', 1923/4.

62. Ibid., DD 3, draft notes for a talk, 'Modern Imperialism' (n.d. but 1923?), p. 16.

63. Ibid., DD 53, 'The Position of British Capitalism', Marx House lecture, 14 Oct. 1934, p. 5.

64. University of Hull, Special Collections, Hobson papers, DHN/24, draft lecture, 'Thoughts on our Present Discontents' (n.d. but 1937?), pp. 5–6.

65. Marshall Library, Cambridge, A. C. Pigou papers, 1/7/1, 'An Analytical Account . . .', p. 81.

66. King's College, Cambridge, J. M. Keynes papers, A/30, draft article, 16 May 1929.

67. Ibid., draft article, 'A British View of the Wall Street Slump', Nov. 1929, pp. 2–3.

68. Ibid., notes for 'The Great Slump of 1930', p. 1.

69. King's College, Cambridge, Lowes Dickinson papers, GLD 1/5, Journal 1916–1932, entry for 17 June 1932.

70. Strachey papers (in private possession), Box 4, C. Moxon, 'Buchmanism and Psychotherapy: A Study in Bourgeois Escapism' (n.d.), p. 2.

71. Nuffield College, Oxford, Cole papers, A1/40/8, 'Changing Economic Order', p. 10. 'Others', Cole added, 'take to mass-religion, and find in "house-parties" of 20,000 Buchmanites a spiritual "uplift" . . .'

72. Details in I. Thomas, *The Buchman Groups* (London, n.d.), pp. 1–7; W. H. Clark, *The Oxford Group: Its History and Significance* (New York, 1951), pp. 31, 76.

73. P. Howard, *That Man Frank Buchman* (London, 1946), pp. 34–5.

74. Strachey papers, Box 4, 'Buchmanism', p. 2. See too W. H. Auden, *The Dance of Death* (London, 1933), pp. 9, 12.

75. Nuffield College, Oxford, Cole papers, A1/39/1, 'The Present Confusion', 26 Aug. 1933; A1/39/4, 'The Case for Socialism'; A1/39/8, draft, 'The Present Position of World Capitalism', pp. 6–7.

76. King's College, Cambridge, J. M. Keynes papers, A/32/1, draft, 'The Dilemma of Socialism', p. 2; A/31, draft, 'Proposal for Revenue Tariff', March 1931. The first essay appeared in the *Political Quarterly*, April–June 1932. See too D. Moggridge (ed.), *The Collected Writings of John Maynard Keynes*, vol. XXI, *Activities, 1931–1939* (London, 1982), pp. 33–48.

77. King's College, Cambridge, J. M. Keynes papers, A/32/1, draft, 'The World Economic Outlook', submitted to the *Atlantic Monthly*, 10 Feb. 1932, p. 10.

78. LSE, Passfield papers, 6/84, draft of BBC talk, 21 Jan. 1932, 'The Diseases of the Capitalist System', p. 5.

79. Salford University, Special Collections, Greenwood papers, WGP 1/2/1, manuscript copy, 'Love on the Dole'. The title page has 'The Lovers. A Tale of Two Cities' and over the top in pencil in capital letters 'LOVE ON THE DOLE'. It is not clear if this was Greenwood's decision or that of the publisher, but it was an inspired alteration. Details of his early life in WGP 3/5/1, 'Shakespeare on the Dole', *The People* (n.d. but Feb. 1935).

80. Reading University, Special Collections, Jonathan Cape archive, Ms 2446. See too S. Constantine, ' "Love on the Dole" and its Reception in the 1930s', *Literature and History*, 8 (1982), p. 233, who gives different dates; price details in WPG 3/1.

81. Reading University, Jonathan Cape archive, Ms 2446.

82. Salford University, Greenwood papers, WPG 3/1, review, *Manchester Evening News* (n.d. but June 1933); quotations in W. Greenwood, *Love on the Dole* (London, 1933), title page, pp. 9–10.

83. Salford University, Greenwood papers, WPG 2/1/1, Edith Sitwell to Walter Greenwood, 25 March 1935; 3/1, review of *Love on the Dole* (n.d.); review in the *Daily Despatch*, 15 June 1933.

84. Ibid., WPG 3/1, review in *John O'London*, 16 Feb. 1935.

85. Greenwood, *Love on the Dole*, p. 262.

86. Salford University, Greenwood papers, WPG 3/1, review by William Rollins in *New Republic*, 2 Jan. 1935.

87. Ibid., WPG 3/1, review in the *Saturday Review of Literature New York*, 25 Aug. 1934.

88. Ibid., WPG 3/35/1, W. Greenwood, 'Poverty or Freedom', *Spectator*, 22 Nov. 1935, p. 860.

89. Ibid., WPG 3/1, review in the *Daily Telegraph*, 20 June 1933; review in the *Daily Express*, 19 June 1933; review in the *News Chronicle*, 19 June 1933; review in the *Times Literary Supplement*, 29 June 1933.

90. Ibid., WPG 3/5/4, review in the *Sketch*, 13 Feb. 1935 ('causes us to look within, and especially below us'); review in the *Stage*, 9 Feb. 1935; reviews in the *Daily Herald*, 31 Jan. 1935, 1 Feb. 1935 and *Cavalcade*, 25 Sept. 1937.

91. On the ambiguous nature of the message of book and film see C. Levine, 'Propaganda for Democracy: The Curious Case of *Love on the Dole*', *Journal of British Studies*, 45 (2006), pp. 846–74; R. Webster, '*Love on the Dole* and the Aesthetic of Contradiction', in J. Hawthorn (ed.), *The British Working Class Novel in the Twentieth Century* (London, 1984), pp. 49–61.

92. Salford University, Greenwood papers, WPG 3/5/1, review in the *People*.

93. Ibid., WPG 3/1, review in the *New Clarion*, 8 July 1933.

94. Ibid., review in the *Evening Chronicle*, 21 June 1933.

95. Marshall Library, Cambridge, A. C. Pigou papers, 2/3/3, review of *The Theory of Unemployment* (n.d.).

96. Nuffield College, Oxford, Cole papers, A1/40/8, 'Changing Economic Order', pp. 20, 22.

97. King's College, Cambridge, J. M. Keynes papers, BR/1, draft mss. for CBS, 12 April 1931, pp. 1–2.

98. Ibid., A/30, draft notes for 'The Great Slump of 1930', p. 2.

99. O. Mosley, *My Life* (London, 1968), pp. 344–6; W. M. Thomas, *Out on a Wing* (London, 1964), p. 176: 'Nuffield openly admitted that he believed in government by benevolent dictator.' On Morris see R. J. Overy, *William Morris, Viscount Nuffield* (London, 1976), ch. 5.

100. Martin, *Editor*, pp. 45–6; Thomas, *John Strachey*, p. 96.

101. King's College, Cambridge, J. M. Keynes papers, L/31, Mosley to Keynes, 23 Jan. 1931; Keynes to Mosley, 2 Feb. 1931. Mosley had tried to secure Keynes's advice in early 1930 on work-creation investment. See M/2, Mosley to Keynes (n.d. but Jan. 1930); Mosley to Keynes, 6 Feb. 1930. See too D. Moggridge (ed.), *Collected Writings of John Maynard Keynes*, vol. XX, *Activities, 1929–1931* (London, 1981), pp. 473–6, 'Sir Oswald Mosley's Manifesto'.

102. Thomas, *John Strachey*, pp. 103–5.

103. The best account is the excellent book by D. Ritschel, *The Politics of Planning: The Debate on Economic Planning in Britain in the 1930s* (Oxford, 1997). See too R. Toye, *The Labour Party and the Planned Economy, 1931–1951* (London, 2003), esp. chs. 1–2.

104. LSE, Passfield papers, 6/84, 'The Diseases of the Capitalist System', 21 Jan. 1932, pp. 10–11, 14.

105. B. Wootton, *Plan or No Plan* (London, 1934), p. 271.

106. Details from Thomas, *John Strachey*, chs. 3–7. See Toye, *Labour Party and Planned Economy*, pp. 35–40.

107. Strachey papers, Box 2, Strachey to *International Literature*, 19 Jan. 1934.

108. Ibid., Victor Gollancz to Strachey, 2 May 1935; Warwick University Modern Records Centre, Gollancz papers, MSS 318/2/1/9, Production Book, 1934–5; 318/2/1/12, Production Book, 1937–9. Rather different figures are given for the first book in Thomas, *John Strachey*, p. 139, a total of 6,136.

109. Strachey papers, Box 4, draft lecture, 'Class Society – Its Origin and Development', 6 March 1937, pp. 44–6.

110. Warwick University Modern Records Centre, Gollancz papers, MSS 318/2/1/10, Production Book, 1935–6.

111. Trinity College, Cambridge, Dobb archive, DD 43, paper for Centenary Meeting of British Association, 1932, 'Current Economic Theory in Relation to the Five Year Plan', pp. 2–3; DD 63, lecture to Marx House summer school, Aug. 1936, 'The General Crisis of Capitalism'.

112. Ibid., DD 65, draft lecture to Leeds Economic Society, 12 Jan. 1937, 'Britain Without Capitalists', pp. 2–5.

113. LSE, HF/B1, M. Dobb, 'Planning and Capitalism', Workers' Educational Trade Union Committee, 1937, p. 8.

114. *Britain Without Capitalists: A Study of What Industry in a Soviet Britain Could Achieve* (London, 1936).

115. Ibid., pp. 1, 15.

116. Ibid., pp. 350–51.

117. Nuffield College, Oxford, Cole papers, A1/75/4/12, draft lecture for Second Congress of Peace and Friendship with the USSR, p. 12.

118. LSE, HF (42)/D154, G. D. H. Cole, *A Plan for Britain* (London, 1933), pp. 15, 30.

119. Nuffield College, Oxford, Cole papers, A1/60/1/4, *Fabian News*, 46 (Nov. 1935), p. 42. See too G. D. H. Cole, *The Machinery of Socialist Planning* (London, 1938), and *A Plan for Britain* (London, 1933).

120. Edinburgh University, Special Collections, Koestler archive, MS 2363/3, Ivor Lewis (secretary Federation of Progressive Societies) to Koestler, 25 June 1942, encl. leaflet 'Progressive League', pp. 2–4. See too R. A. Wilford, 'The Federation of Progressive Societies and Individuals', *Journal of Contemporary History*, 11 (1976), pp. 49–82.

121. *Plan*, 5 (Jan. 1938), p. 2; list of vice-presidents, *Plan*, 2 (Oct. 1935), p. i; Edinburgh University, Special Collections, Koestler archive, MS 2363.3, 'Progressive League', p. 1.

122. *Plan*, 2 (April 1935), p. 2; Wilford, 'Federation', p. 51.

123. LSE, Political and Economic Planning, First Series, PEP I A/5/1, 'A National Plan for Great Britain', *Week-End Review*, supplement, 14 Feb. 1931; PEP I UP/10, 'Key Dates 1930–1940' (n.d.); Kenneth Lindsay, 'The Early Days of PEP', 24 Oct. 1947. See too Ritschel, *Politics of Planning*, pp. 145–6.

124. LSE, PEP I UP/10, 'The Early Days of PEP'; 'Key Dates 1930–1940'; National Plan, circulation list (n.d. but late 1930), which lists sixty-nine people from the political, academic and business worlds, including Montagu Norman, governor of the Bank of England.

125. Ibid., 'Key Dates 1930–1940'; 'A History of PEP' (n.d. but July 1947?), pp. 1–3.

126. LSE, PEP I A/5/2, reprint from *Week-End Review*, 21 March 1931, 'The National Plan: A Society'.

127. Ritschel, *Politics of Planning*, pp. 171–4.

128. LSE, PEP I A/5/2, 'A View on Planning', spring 1933, pp. 3–4 (Nicholson drafted the argument with the help of an informal committee).

129. LSE, PEP I A/7/3, memorandum by the chairman, 'Freedom and Planning. Collapsing Civilisation', 3 March 1932, pp. 1, 3; A/7/5, Provisional Agenda for Cookham weekend (n.d. but spring 1932?). See Ritschel, *Politics of Planning*, pp. 155–6, who rightly argues that in the context of the slump these were not unexpected responses.

130. LSE, PEP I A/6/1, Annex to Bulletin no. 4, 30 Dec. 1933, p. 2.

131. LSE, PEP I A/5/1, 'A National Plan for Great Britain', pp. i, iii–iv, vi.

132. LSE, PEP I A/1/1, note, 'Alphabetical list of PEP Members', 9 Sept. 1931; 'Working members and contacts, Sept. 1938'; A/1/3, Bulletin List, 30 Jan. 1934; Chairmen of Groups list, 27 Feb. 1934 (Huxley later resigned from pressure of work); Report for the Year 1935–6 and Programme for 1936–7, 27 Feb. 1936, pp. 1–2; on *Planning*, A/9/2, Report of the Executive to Working Members, 29 March 1935; on the Club, A/6/1, Bulletin no. 2, 1 Nov. 1933.

133. LSE, PEP I A/5/2, 'A View of Planning', pp. 15–26 for details of the groups; A/7/4 TEC PLAN, answers to Directorate, 18 March 1932; UP/10, 'PEP. A History of PEP', July 1947, pp. 2–3; Ritschel, *Politics of Planning*, p. 174.

134. LSE, PEP I UP/10, 'PEP. A History of PEP', p. 3; A/7/2, Max Nicholson to Basil Blackett, 20 June 1932: PEP was, he thought, 'incompatible with the elementary principles of planning'.

135. LSE, PEP I UP/10, 'PEP. A History of PEP, p. 5.

136. LSE, PEP I A/1/1, note, 'Broadsheet Govt. List' (n.d.).

137. LSE, PEP I A/9/3, PEP report for the year 1935–6, p. 2; A/9/2, PEP Report of the Executive, 29 March 1935, p. 9.

138. LSE, PEP I A/7/3, 'Some Notes on Conversations heard at the PEP Dinner', 29 March 1933, pp. 2–3.

139. LSE, PEP I A/7/1, note, 'Absentees at General Meeting', 16 Jan. 1933.

140. LSE, PEP I A/9/2, Executive note, 'Preliminary Notes for a Redefined Aim of PEP', 19 March 1935.

141. LSE, PEP I A/5/3, *Free Press*, Oct. 1935, 'Amazing Plan Threatens Freedom'; UP/10, 'PEP. A History of PEP', p. 6; *Britain Without Capitalists*, p. 350.

142. LSE, PEP I UP/10, 'History', p. 5.

143. LSE, PEP I A/9/2, Michael Zvegintzov to Nicholson, 10 April 1935, p. 1.

144. LSE, PEP I A/9/2, note on conversation between Lord Allen of Hurtwood, Sir Arthur Salter and Max Nicholson, 12 Dec. 1935; see too Ritschel, *Politics of Planning*, pp. 259 ff. for the development of the Next Five Years Group.

145. LSE, PEP I A/9/4, PEP Slump Control and Public Works, 22 June 1937, pp. 1–2.

146. Martin, *Editor*, p. 42.

147. A. Salter, *Personality in Politics: Studies of Contemporary Statesmen* (London, 1947), p. 139.

148. LSE, Lionel Robbins papers, 1/1, Robbins's notes on the Council committee (n.d.).

149. Martin, *Editor*, pp. 41–3. King's College, Cambridge, J. M. Keynes papers, PS/5, notes for a lecture to the House of Commons, p. 10: 'During the last 12 years I have had very little influence, if any, on policy. But in the role of Cassandra I have had a considerable success . . .'

150. Strachey papers, Box 1, Keynes to Strachey, 5 Jan. 1926; see the account in Thomas, *John Strachey*, pp. 51–3.

151. Martin, *Editor*, p. 159; Schneider, *Hobson*, pp. 13–14.

152. P. Clarke, 'Hobson and Keynes as Economic Heretics', in M. Freeden (ed.), *Reappraising J. A. Hobson* (London, 1990), pp. 105–6.

153. King's College, Cambridge, J. M. Keynes papers, BR/1, draft broadcast for CBS, 12 April 1931, pp. 4–5. See too Moggridge, *Collected Writings*, vol. XX, pp. 515–20.

154. King's College, Cambridge, J. M. Keynes papers, A/32/1, draft article, 'The Dilemma of Socialism', Jan. 1932, pp. 1–3; on his criticism of the MacDonald government see L/31, draft letter from Keynes to MacDonald, 5 Aug. 1931, in which he told the prime minister that his views were 'not fit for publication'. Government wage policy was 'a most gross perversion of social justice', while deflation was 'both futile and disastrous'.

155. Ibid., GTE/8, Macmillan & Co. pamphlet, 'The General Theory of Employment, Interest and Money' (n.d.).

156. D. Moggridge (ed.), *The Collected Writings of John Maynard Keynes*, vol. IX, *Essays in Persuasion* (London, 1972), p. 288 on the failure of enlightened self-interest.

157. King's College, Cambridge, J. M. Keynes papers, GTE/8, reviews of the *General Theory* in the *British Weekly*, 5 March 1936, and the *Daily Worker*, 8 April 1936.

158. King's College, Cambridge, Robinson papers, vii/240, Keynes to Robinson, 2 Dec. 1936.

159. See Ritschel, *Politics of Planning*, pp. 329–30, 335–8.

160. King's College, Cambridge, J. M. Keynes papers, A/34, draft, 'An Open Letter to President Roosevelt' (Dec. 1933), p. 1. See too J. R. Hicks, 'Mr Keynes' Theory of Employment', *Economic Journal*, 46 (1936), pp. 239, 252–3.

161. Warwick University Modern Records Centre, Gollancz papers, MSS 157/4/LB/1, review by Strachey of *Can Capitalism Last?* in the *Left News*, Jan. 1938, p. 652.

162. A. Forbath (ed.), *Europe into the Abyss: Behind the Scenes of Secret Politics* (London, 1938), pp. 49–50, 52. See too Nuffield College, Oxford,

Cole papers, A1/77, draft chapter for 'Europe into the Abyss'; Alex Forbath to Cole, 26 Aug. 1937. The book, Forbath wrote, anticipating his contributors' agenda, 'should be a perfectly clear review of the actual situation, outlining the fatal consequences it has for the prosperity of Europe'.

163. Nuffield College, Oxford, Cole papers, A1/40/2, Fabian Society lecture, 'Can Capitalism Survive', p. 27. See too G. D. H. Cole, *Economic Prospects: 1938 and After* (London, 1938), esp. pp. 77–86.

164. Trinity College, Cambridge, Dobb archive, DD 74, lecture to London Co-operative Societies' Summer School, Aug. 1938, 'Position of Post-War Capitalism', p. 3.

165. University of Sussex Library, Kingsley Martin papers, MS 11/24/1, draft, 'The War Generation in England', p. 13 (published in *Revue des sciences politiques*, 48 (1925)).

166. J. Huxley, *On Living in a Revolution* (New York, 1942), p. 23.

167. King's College, Cambridge, J. M. Keynes papers, PS/5, draft, 'Economic Possibilities for Our Grandchildren' (n.d.), p. 2. The talk was given in Madrid in June 1930.

168. Ibid., A/32/1, draft, 'Some Consequences of the Collapse of Money Values', Oct. 1931, p. 10: 'Perhaps, indeed, it is an attractive alternative, this committing of suicide by the capitalists. For under the pressure of hardship and excitement, we might find out some much better way of managing our affairs.'

169. P. V. Mini, *Keynes, Bloomsbury and 'The General Theory'* (London, 1991), p. 211.

170. Levine, 'Propaganda for Democracy', p. 846.

171. G. B. Shaw, *The Political Madhouse in America and Nearer Home* (London, 1933), pp. 8–9.

Chapter 3: A Sickness in the Racial Body

1. Wellcome Institute, London, Contemporary Medical Archives Centre (CMAC), SA/EUG/C.185, Huxley correspondence, draft article, 'What Are We to Do with Our Mental Defectives?' (n.d. but Dec. 1930), p. 3.

2. CMAC, SA/FPA/A.23/54, notice from Dr Edith Summerskill for International Birth Control Movement (n.d.); announcement of the Malthusian Ball; *Sketch*, 15 March 1933, p. 461, 'The Malthusian Ball Discussed'.

3. CMAC, SA/FPA/A.23/54, 'The Malthusian Ball' programme, 22 March 1933.

4. Ibid., Elaine Laski to R. G. Morton, 19 April 1933.

5. London School of Economics (LSE), Coll. Misc. 0435/12, Birth Control

ephemera, Malthusian League, 'What Can We Do?' (n.d.). See too M. Sanger, *My Fight for Birth Control* (London, 1932), pp. 83, 92–7. On the League and the Bradlaugh–Besant trial see R. A. Soloway, *Demography and Degeneration: Eugenics and the Declining Birthrate in Twentieth-Century Britain* (Chapel Hill, 1995), pp. 86–7, and *Birth Control and the Population Question in England, 1877–1930* (Chapel Hill, 1982), pp. 52–6.

6. LSE, Coll. Misc. 0435/12, The Malthusian League, Rules and Principles, 1915, p. 3.

7. Sanger, *My Fight*, pp. 101–2; M. Stopes, 'Some New Concepts and Laws in Human Biology', Mothers' Clinic pamphlet, London, Aug. 1934, p. 2.

8. CMAC, Marie Stopes papers, PP/MCS/B.6, Marie Stopes to the Malthusian League, 6 Dec. 1921. On Stopes's early career see R. A. Soloway, 'The Galton Lecture 1996: Marie Stopes, Eugenics and the Birth Control Movement', in R. A. Peel (ed.), *Marie Stopes and the English Birth Control Movement* (London, 1997), pp. 49–54.

9. M. Stopes, *Contraception: Its Theory, History and Practice* (London, 1928), pp. 146–7, 150, and 'Preliminary Notes on Various Technical Aspects of the Control of Conception', Mothers' Clinic pamphlet, March 1930, p. 43. See too Soloway, 'Galton Lecture 1996', pp. 64–5.

10. CMAC, SA/EUG/K.1, correspondence with Marie Stopes, 'The Mothers' Clinic For Birth Control', 1921, pp. 1–11.

11. LSE, Coll. Misc. 0435/6, *Queen's Hall Meeting on Constructive Birth Control: Speeches and Impressions* (London, 1921), p. 37: J. H. Clynes, 'Impressions'.

12. Ibid., pp. 8, 29–32, 39, 43.

13. LSE, Coll. Misc. 0435/6, George Whitehead, *Birth Control and Race Culture: The Social Aspects of Sex* (London, 1925), p. 9.

14. Stopes, *Contraception*, Introductory Note by Sir James Barr, p. xix.

15. LSE, Coll. Misc. 0435/6, Whitehead, *Birth Control*, pp. 5–7.

16. Ibid., 0435/1, 'Points for Propagandists on the Problem of Population and Its Solution', May 1925, pp. 1–5; M. Sanger, *The Pivot of Civilization* (London, 1923), esp. pp. 39–40.

17. CMAC, PP/MCS/D.19, 'Ideals and Practice of Constructive Birth Control', address given at Cambridge, 29 April 1930, pp. 4–5.

18. Details on her son's marriage in J. Rose, *Marie Stopes and the Sexual Revolution* (London, 1992), pp. 234–5; on race suicide, CMAC, PP/MCS/E.3, Marie Stopes to the *Daily Telegraph*, 5 Dec. 1922.

19. E. W. McBride, 'Birth Control and Human Biology', *Nature*, 127 (1931), p. 511; LSE, Coll. Misc. 0435/1, 'Points for Propagandists', p. 6.

20. LSE, Coll. Misc. 0435/1 'Points for Propagandists', p. 4.

21. C. J. Bond, *Some Causes of Racial Decay: An Inquiry into the Distribution of Natural Capacity in the Population* (London, 1928), pp. 4–5. On the role of language in linking the human sciences and social theory see the papers in parts I and II of S. Maasen, E. Mendelsohn and P. Weingart (eds.), *Biology as Society, Society as Biology: Metaphors* (Dordrecht, 1995).

22. F. H. Hankins, 'Civilization and Fertility: Has the Reproductive Power of Western Peoples Declined?', *Eugenics Review*, 23 (1931/2), pp. 145–6, paper read to the General Assembly of the International Population Union, June 1931. See too C. Gini, *Nascità, Evoluzione e Morte delle Nazioni* (Rome, 1930), esp. pp. 49–61.

23. Bond, *Racial Decay*, p. 4.

24. C. Ward Crampton, 'Aristogenics', in *A Decade of Progress in Eugenics: Scientific Papers of the Third International Congress of Eugenics* (Baltimore, 1934), p. 381.

25. L. Darwin, 'Message to the International Congress of Eugenics', ibid., p. 24.

26. L. Darwin, *The Need for Eugenic Reform* (London, 1926), pp. 315–17.

27. G. R. Searle, *Eugenics and Politics in Britain, 1900–1914* (Leyden, 1976), p. 1; R. A. Fisher, 'Eugenics: Can It Solve the Problem of Decay of Civilizations?', *Eugenics Review*, 18 (1926/7), pp. 129, 136.

28. See for the early history of eugenics Searle, *Eugenics and Politics*, pp. 4–10; Soloway, *Demography and Degeneration*, pp. 18–30.

29. W. E. Castle, *Genetics and Eugenics* (Cambridge, Mass., 1925), pp. 55–8.

30. S. Mawer, *Gregor Mendel: Planting the Seeds of Genetics* (New York, 2006), pp. 91–103; Castle, *Genetics*, pp. 120–25.

31. Searle, *Eugenics and Politics*, pp. 10–15; F. Schenk and A. S. Parkes, 'The Activities of the Eugenics Society', *Eugenics Review*, 60 (1968), pp. 142–61.

32. C. B. Davenport, 'The Development of Eugenics', in *A Decade of Progress in Eugenics*, p. 22.

33. *Nature*, 6 June 1931, p. 865, reporting Inge's speech to the Royal Institution, 29 May 1931. On the evolution of Keynes's views see J. Toye, *Keynes on Population* (Oxford, 2000).

34. J. A. Thomson, 'Biology and Education', *Quarterly Review*, 258 (1932), p. 327. See too J. A. Thomson, 'Biology and Social Hygiene', *Health and Empire*, 2 (1927), pp. 198–207.

35. A. Carr-Saunders, *Eugenics* (London, 1926); University College, London, Routledge & Kegan Paul collection, 23h, Publishing Journal, vol. VIII, 1921–39; H. G. Wells, G. P. Wells and J. Huxley, *The Science of Life* (London, 1938), p. xxii. See too J. Huxley, *Memories* (2 vols., London,

1970), vol. I, pp. 155–9; H. G. Wells, *Experiment in Autobiography, being the Autobiography of H. G. Wells* (2 vols., London, 1934), vol. II, pp. 722–4.

36. C. E. M. Joad, 'The Progress of Science', *Fortnightly Review*, 130 (1931), p. 602. Russell thought that at least 75 per cent of women would have to share the same fate.

37. LSE, Carr-Saunders papers, A/2/12, draft of Eugenics Society Annual Report 1936/7, p. 2.

38. Ibid., pp. 4–5.

39. CMAC, Blacker papers, PP/CPB/ J.3/29–40, ff. 296–7, letter from Blacker (n.d. but March 1937); PP/CPB/B.6, draft, 'The Aims and Objects of the Eugenics Society', pp. 6–7.

40. Lord G. Riddell, 'Sterilisation of the Unfit', paper read before the Medico-Legal Society, 25 April 1929 (London, 1929), pp. 20–21; see too British Medical Association archive, London (BMA), B/239/1/1, Mental Deficiency Committee, memorandum, R. G. Gordon, 'The Limits of Mental Deficiency', pp. 1–3.

41. University College, London, Galton collection, 138/8, notes on the feeble-minded and draft 'family history' card, 26 May 1905; 138/1, abstract of a paper by W. McDougall to the School of Economic and Political Science (n.d.).

42. 'Disease and Defect: Some New Pedigrees from Rural England', *Eugenics Review*, 22 (1930), p. 35, pedigrees attached after p. 84.

43. University of Liverpool, Special Collections, Cyril Burt papers, D191/ 57/2, 'Inheritance in Man: Traits Alleged to Conform to Mendelian Principles' (n.d. but early 1930s), pp. 1–3; see too R. Ruggles Gate, 'The Inheritance of Mental Defect', *British Journal of Medical Psychology*, 13 (1933), pp. 254–66: 'There is no reason for doubting that all forms of mental defect and aberration will be found to follow definite Mendelian rules of inheritance . . .' (p. 266).

44. University of Liverpool, Special Collections, Cyril Burt papers, D191/ 49/3–4, part I, 'The Inherent Difference in Mental Quality in Children', 10 March 1916, pp. 1–2.

45. Ibid., D191/57/3, Heath Clark lectures, 1934, lecture II, 'The Mentally Deficient', pp. 1–2. The lectures were enlarged and published later. See C. Burt, *The Subnormal Mind* (Oxford, 1937).

46. Eliot Slater, 'The Inheritance of Mental Disorder', *Eugenics Review*, 28 (1936/7), pp. 277–83; Ruggles Gate, 'Inheritance of Mental Defect', pp. 155–6.

47. R. Austin Freeman, *Social Decay and Regeneration* (London, 1921), p. 243.

48. Whitehead, *Birth Control and Race Culture*, pp. 13, 15, 23.

49. Freeman, *Social Decay*, p. 263.

50. University of Liverpool, Special Collections, Cyril Burt papers, D191/58/2, draft response on prostitution to Board of Control, Nov. 1932, p. 1; note, 'Analysis of Histories of 101 typical certified feebleminded adults (women)'. See too C. Burt, 'The Causes of Sex Delinquency in Girls', *Health and Empire*, 1 (1926), pp. 251–71.

51. B. Mallett, 'The Social Problem Group', *Eugenics Review*, 23 (1931/32), pp. 204–5; CMAC, SA/EUG/D.196, D. Caradog Jones, 'Mental Deficiency on Merseyside: Its Connection with the Social Problem Group', pp. 1–2. For a general discussion see E. A. Carlson, *The Unfit: A History of a Bad Idea* (New York, 2001), and J. Welshman, *Underclass: A History of the Excluded, 1880–2000* (London, 2006).

52. CMAC, PP/CPB/B.1/2, Leonard Darwin to Blacker, 10 Sept. 1933, p. 2; Darwin to Blacker, 3 Feb. 1935, pp. 2, 8; draft by Darwin, 'The Social Problem Group', Oct. 1933, pp. 1–6.

53. University of Liverpool, Special Collections, Cyril Burt papers, D191/57/3, Heath Clark lectures, 1934, lecture III, 'The Dull and Backward', p. 1.

54. CMAC, SA/EUG/D.196, Caradog Jones, 'Mental Deficiency on Merseyside', p. 1.

55. CMAC, SA/EUG/C.185, Huxley correspondence, draft article, 'What Are We to Do with Our Mental Defectives?', p. 2 for 'carriers'; 'grave disasters' from L. Darwin, 'The Eugenics Policy of the Society', *Eugenics Review*, 18 (1926/7), p. 94.

56. 'Summary Report of the Mental Deficiency Committee, 1929', *Health and Empire*, 6 (1931), pp. 54–5; Mallett, 'Social Problem Group', p. 204; K. B. Aikman, 'The Multiplication of the Less Fit', *Edinburgh Review*, 250 (1929), p. 85.

57. Aikman, 'Multiplication of the Less Fit', p. 82 (note); Mallett, 'Social Problem Group', p. 204; E. Moore, 'Our National Burden: A Survey of the Report on Mental Deficiency', *Eugenics Review*, 21 (1929/30), p. 125.

58. Cited in Riddell, 'Sterilization of the Unfit', p. 25.

59. University of Liverpool, Special Collections, Cyril Burt papers, D191/57/3, Heath Clark lectures, 1934, lecture II, pp. 10–12.

60. CMAC, SA/EUG/D.196, Caradog Jones, 'Mental Deficiency on Merseyside', pp. 6–7. The report was published as *The Social Survey of Merseyside* (Liverpool, 1934).

61. See, for example, C. B. Hodson, *Human Sterilization To-day: A Survey of the Present Position* (London, 1934), pp. 11–12; Austin Freeman, *Social Decay*, pp. 366–7. There are many more.

62. C. B. Hodson, 'Contra-selection in England', in *A Decade of Progress in Eugenics*, p. 376 (Hodson was Blacker's predecessor as secretary of the Eugenics Society); see too C. P. Blacker, *Voluntary Sterilization* (Oxford, 1934), p. 66, note 1, who recommended the English edition of a book on human heredity by Baur, Fischer and Lenz. This was the book alleged to have shaped Hitler's attitude to hereditarian issues in the early 1920s. On German genetics and politics see R. Weikart, *From Darwin to Hitler: Evolutionary Ethics, Eugenics, and Racism in Germany* (London, 2004).

63. A. White, *Efficiency and Empire* (London, 1901), pp. 116–17, and *The Views of Vanoc: An Englishman's Outlook* (London, 1911), p. 288. On the origins of the idea see D. Stone, *Breeding Superman: Nietzsche, Race and Eugenics in Edwardian and Interwar Britain* (Liverpool, 2002), pp. 125–30.

64. Whitehead, *Birth Control and Race Culture*, p. 25; see too White, *Efficiency and Empire*, pp. 116–17.

65. J. F. C. Fuller, *The Dragon's Teeth: A Study of War and Peace* (London, 1932), pp. 14–15.

66. A. Ludovici, *The Night Hoers* (London, 1928), pp. 250–51.

67. Darwin, *Need for Eugenic Reform*, pp. 171, 184; CMAC, PP/CPB/B.1/2, Blacker to Darwin, 28 Aug. 1933; Darwin to Blacker, 10 Sept. 1933; Blacker to Darwin, 21 Aug. 1933. On Ludovici's views after the Second World War see Stone, *Breeding Supermen*, pp. 132–3.

68. CMAC, SA/EUG/D.196, Caradog Jones, 'Mental Deficiency on Merseyside', p. 8; L. Fearn, 'A Eugenist Runs Amok', *Plan*, 3 (1936), p. 15.

69. E. Faulks, *The Sterilisation of the Insane* (London, 1911), pp. 12–13, 15; A. W. Daniel, *Some Statistics about Sterilisation of the Insane* (London, 1912), pp. 12–13 (reprint from *Journal of Mental Science*, Jan. 1912).

70. R. Reid Rentoul, *Proposed Sterilization of Certain Mental and Physical Degenerates* (London, 1903), pp. 7, 9–10; Searle, *Eugenics and Politics*, pp. 92–3.

71. CMAC, SA/EUG/E.1, Birthright Inc., 'Sterilization officially reported from States Having a Sterilization Law up to 1 January 1944', publication 5, 1944. See too Searle, *Eugenics and Politics*, pp. 91–3.

72. CMAC, PP/CPB/B.1/7, Darwin to Blacker, 24 Jan. 1938. See too Darwin, *Need for Eugenic Reform*, pp. 184–5.

73. Riddell, 'Sterilization of the Unfit', pp. 14–16.

74. CMAC, EUG/C.185, 'An Outline of a Practical Eugenic Policy', p. 2. For a discussion of the ethical issues see Austin Freeman, *Social Decay*, pp. 379 ff.

75. University of Liverpool, Special Collections, Cyril Burt papers, D191/11/3, transcript, BBC debate, 16 Nov. 1935, p. 11. See too 'Who Should Bring Up

Our Children?', *The Listener*, 14 (1935), pp. 951–3. The published version did not include Burt's intervention.

76. CMAC, PP/CPB/B.5/1, memorandum from Havelock Ellis, 'The Proposal for Legalizing Sterilization' (n.d. but Dec. 1930), p. 2.

77. CMAC, PP/MCS/D.19, 'Ideals and Practice of Constructive Birth Control', address given by Marie Stopes at Cambridge, 29 April 1930, pp. 10, 21–2. On the reverse of an invitation card to a lecture at the Eugenics Society in 1922 Stopes scribbled 'feeble-minded – sterilisation': British Library, Stopes papers, ADD MSS 58644, ticket for lecture by Harold Cox, 14 March 1922.

78. J. Huxley, *On Living in a Revolution* (New York, 1942), p. 106.

79. J. Huxley, 'Eugenics and Society', *Eugenics Review*, 28 (1936/7), pp. 30–31. See too CMAC, SA/EUG/C.185, Huxley to Blacker, 6 Feb. 1931. See too his earlier 'The Case for Eugenics', *Sociological Review*, 18 (1926), esp. pp. 289–90 on the threat to civilization.

80. CMAC, SA/EUG/C.185, Huxley correspondence, draft article, 'What Are We to Do with Our Mental Defectives?', p. 6.

81. CMAC, Family Planning Association papers, SA/FPA/A.14/47.1, 'Julian Huxley's Plan to Raise Britain from C3 Nation', *Scottish Daily Express*, 19 Nov. 1934.

82. Cited in Soloway, *Demography and Degeneration*, p. 186.

83. CMAC, PP/CPB/H.1/1–6, C. P. Blacker, 'The Modern Conception of the World', paper delivered to the Cinquième Congrès Annuel de la Fédération Internationale des Unions Intellectuelles, Prague, 1–3 October 1928, pp. 10, 13–14, 17–18, 22.

84. Blacker, *Voluntary Sterilization*, p. 74 for reference to 'social hygiene'. See too Welshman, *Underclass*, pp. 53–6 for the origins of the 'social problem group'.

85. BMA, B/239/1/1, Committee for Legalizing Eugenic Sterilization, 'Eugenic Sterilization', 2nd edn, 1931, preface; CMAC, SA/FPA/SR24a/17, Committee for Legalizing Eugenic Sterilization, 'Better Unborn', p. 1.

86. CMAC, SA/EUG/E.6, Blacker to H. S. A. Gerson (Cambridge Eugenics Society), 1 Feb. 1932; Cambridge Eugenics Society programme, 1930; Cambridge Eugenics Society, programme for 1931; E. J. Lidbitter to C. B. Hodson (Eugenics Society), 12 March 1930. On the support of working-class audiences see the *Eugenics Review*, 23 (1931/2), p. 291.

87. CMAC, SA/FPA/SR24a/17, 'Better Unborn', p. 16.

88. Birmingham City archives, National Women's Council papers, MS 841/B/43, minutes of committee meeting of Birmingham branch, 27 Feb. 1931.

89. BMA, B/239/1/2, Mental Deficiency Committee, agenda and minutes, 20 Nov. 1931, p. 22.

90. CMAC, SA/FPA/SR14/15, Report of the Committee for Legalizing Eugenic Sterilization (n.d. but early 1931), pp. 28-9.

91. CMAC, Sir Bernard Mallett papers, SA/EUG/I.2, minute on sterilization bill; memorandum, 'Proposed Activities for Eugenics Society' (n.d. but July 1930?), pp. 1-2; Committee for Legalizing Eugenic Sterilization, Report of the Voluntary Eugenic Sterilization Conference, 23 May 1932 (London, 1932), pp. 21-2.

92. Hansard, Parliamentary Debates, 5th ser., vol. 255, 1930-31, cols. 1250-58, 21 July 1931.

93. CMAC, PP/CPB/B.5/1, Havelock Ellis to Blacker, 22 July 1931; Blacker to Ellis, 23 July 1931.

94. BMA, B/239/1/2, draft report of the Mental Deficiency Committee, 8 Jan. 1932, pp. 40-43; Dr H. B. Brackenbury's redraft, 'Suggested Substitution for Part III' (approved by the committee on 23 Feb. 1932); on 'public school' comparison see Mental Deficiency Committee, agenda and minutes, 25 Sept. 1931, 'An Ideal Colony', p. 5.

95. Hodson, *Human Sterilization*, pp. 45-7.

96. CMAC, SA/EUG/D.150, memorandum on the formation of a Workers' Committee for Legalizing Sterilization of the Unfit (n.d. but Jan. 1935?); Caroline Maude to Ernest Thurtle, 8 Feb. 1935; Maude to Blacker, 8 June 1935.

97. CMAC, PP/CPB/B.1/6, Blacker to Leonard Darwin, 24 March 1937. On the attitude of the left towards eugenics see M. Freeden, 'Eugenical Progressive Thought: A Study in Ideological Affinity', *Historical Journal*, 22 (1979), pp. 645-71; G. Jones, 'Eugenics and Social Policy between the Wars', *Historical Journal*, 25 (1982), pp. 722-4.

98. L. Hogben, *Nature and Nurture: The 1933 William Withering Memorial Lectures* (London, 2nd edn, 1939), p. 32.

99. University Library, Cambridge, J. D. Bernal papers, ADD MS 8287, Box 83, Hogben to Bernal, 21 Jan. 1936; C. P. Blacker, *Eugenics in Prospect and Retrospect*, 1945 Galton lecture (London, 1945), p. 21. See too L. Hogben, *Genetic Principles in Medicine and Social Science* (London, 1931), pp. 209-14.

100. J. B. S. Haldane, *Keeping Cool and Other Essays* (London, 1940), p. 159; on Needham see University Library, Cambridge, Joseph Needham papers, G/59, notes for a lecture, 'Heredity and Social Problems', pp. 15-17. Needham argued that certain groups might have to be forced not to procreate.

101. CMAC, PP/CPB/B.1/3, Darwin to Blacker, 7 Jan. 1934; Darwin to Byrom Bramwell, 19 July 1934.

102. LSE, Carr-Saunders papers, A/2/12, Joint Committee on Voluntary Sterilization, Third Annual Report, 1936-7, pp. 1-2.

103. CMAC, PP/CPB/B.5/1, Blacker to Havelock Ellis, 19 July 1932; University College, London, Galton collection, 138/8, draft 'Family history' card; 138/9b, draft 'Register of able families' form; 138/1 draft 'Hereditary diploma'.

104. CMAC, PP/CPB/B.1/4, Darwin to Blacker, 27 Nov. 1935; on sperm bank, Blacker to Darwin, 21 Nov. 1935.

105. F. C. S. Schiller, 'Eugenics as a Moral Ideal', *Eugenics Review*, 22 (1930/1), pp. 108–9.

106. CMAC, PP/CPB/B.1/3, Blacker to Darwin, 11 Oct. 1934; Darwin to Blacker, Oct. 1934; SA/EUG/C.185, 'An Outline of a Practical Eugenic Policy' (n.d.), p. 3 ('to connive at such marriage [of those with 'defects'] being made a penal offence').

107. CMAC, PP/CPB/J.3/350, 'Health Examinations before Marriage: For Those About to Get Married: Also, to Their Parents', Eugenics Society, pp. 3–5; Blacker, *Eugenics in Prospect and Retrospect*, p. 19.

108. Birmingham City archives, MS 841/B/296, Birmingham Advisory Council on the Marriage Relationship, 'To Those Thinking of Marriage' (n.d.), pp. 2–5.

109. LSE, Coll. Misc. 0435/6, T. H. Reynolds, *Birth Control: Its Use and Abuse* (2nd edn, London, 1937), pp. 7–8.

110. G. Leybourne, 'The Future Population of Great Britain', *Sociological Review*, 26 (1934), pp. 131, 134. See too Toye, *Keynes on Population*, pp. 200–205.

111. CMAC, SA/FPA/A.14/47.1, A. Huxley, 'Turning Point', *Everyman*, 7 Dec. 1934.

112. LSE, Carr-Saunders papers, B/3/4, London and Cambridge Economic Service, Special memorandum no. 40, Enid Charles, 'The Effect of Present Trends in Fertility and Mortality upon the Future Population of England and Wales and Upon Its Age of Composition', Aug. 1935, pp. 9–13; see also Royal Economic Society, Special memorandum no. 55, 1935.

113. LSE, Carr-Saunders papers, B/3/4, 'Bachelor MPs Discuss Population Problems in Parliament', *Birth Control News*, 15 (1937), pp. 105–9.

114. CMAC, PP/CPB/J.3/ff. 299–300, 'People heading for Disappearance', cutting from *The Times*, 11 Feb. 1937. The meeting was held at the Sheffield Luncheon Club on 10 February.

115. R. F. Harrod, 'Modern Population Trends', *Manchester School*, 10 (1939), p. 5; King's College, Cambridge, Joan Robinson papers, vii/191, Harrod to Robinson, 12 Jan. 1938. See too Harrod to Robinson, 18 and 27 Jan. 1938: 'I shudder to think what will come of Nature being allowed to make an adjustment of colossal importance by Natural Selection . . .'

116. G. Chapman, *Culture and Survival* (London, 1940), pp. 210–11.

117. C. P. Blacker, 'The Future of Our Population', *Eugenics Review*, 28 (1936/7), pp. 210–11; 'Population Investigation Committee: Second Annual Report', *Eugenics Review*, 30 (1938/9), pp. 269–74.

118. LSE, Carr-Saunders papers, A/2/12, Eugenics Society Council meeting, 15 March 1938; memorandum, 'Population Policies Committee, Scope of Investigation', 25 May 1938; Blacker, *Eugenics in Prospect and Retrospect*, pp. 21, 23; PEP, *Planning*, 166, 23 April 1940, pp. 2, 6.

119. Birmingham City archives, MS 841/B/44, National Women's Council papers, Birmingham Branch Committee Meeting, 25 Nov. 1937, encl., 'The Case for Voluntary Sterilisation', *Birmingham Post*.

120. Magdalene College, Cambridge, Old Library, Inge diaries and papers, 35/diary 1936–7, entries for 6 and 24 Oct. 1936.

121. LSE, Carr-Saunders papers, A/2/12, memorandum, 'Population Policies Committee', 25 May 1938; PEP, 'General Principles of Population Policy', 1 May 1939, p. 3.

122. C. P. Blacker, 'Problems of Population and Birth Control in Great Britain', *Journal of Contraception*, 3 (1938), p. 28.

123. LSE, Carr-Saunders papers, B/3/4, Cambridge University Democratic Front, 'Report of the Discussion Group on Population' (n.d. but 1937), pp. 1–5.

124. On neurasthenia see Hankins, 'Civilization and Fertility', p. 149; on 'cannon fodder' see Blacker, 'Problems of Population', p. 27; LSE, Carr-Saunders papers, B/3/4, Cambridge University Democratic Front report, p. 3.

125. CMAC, PP/CPB/B.1/7, Darwin to Blacker, 12 June 1938.

126. Birmingham City archives, MS 841/B/44, National Women's Council papers, 'The Case for Voluntary Sterilisation'; CMAC, PP/CPB/B.1/5, Blacker to Darwin, 27 July 1936: 'While I admire the thoroughness with which the Germans are tackling the problem, I dislike the methods they employ and I am quite certain that their experiment has done the cause of eugenics and the cause of voluntary sterilization much harm in this country.' See too C. P. Blacker, *Eugenics: Galton and After* (London, 1952), p. 141.

127. Chapman, *Culture and Survival*, pp. 242–3.

Chapter 4: Medicine and Poison: Psychoanalysis and Social Dismay

1. T. Reik, *From Thirty Years with Freud* (London, 1942), p. 99.

2. University of Liverpool, Special Collections, Cyril Burt papers, D191/11/3, Nesta Pain to Burt, 23 Feb. 1946, encl., draft script, 'The Human Mind', p. 3.

3. B. Low, *Psycho-Analysis: A Brief Account of the Freudian Theory* (London, 1920), pp. 34–5.

4. Low, *Psycho-Analysis*, pp. 35–6, 160–63.

5. E. Jones, *What Is Psycho-Analysis?* (London, 1949), p. 120. The book was published some twenty years after Jones wrote it, almost certainly as a booklet for the BMA Psycho-Analysis Committee which he joined as a member in 1927. See British Medical Association archive, London (BMA), B/286/1/3, Report of the Psycho-Analysis Committee, 29 June 1929, p. 1, documents prepared for the Committee.

6. Low, *Psycho-Analysis*, pp. 160–61.

7. Jones, *What Is Psycho-Analysis?*, pp. 8, 15.

8. British Psycho-Analytical Society archive, London (BP-AS), Ernest Jones collection, G13/BD/010, draft review of J. P. Hodi, *The Dilemma of Being Modern* (n.d.).

9. BP-AS, Ernest Jones collection, GB1404/PE/JON, draft lecture, 'The Present State of Psycho-Analysis', 1930, p. 5.

10. For a very clear discussion of Freud see J. E. Nicole, *Psychopathology: A Survey of Modern Approaches* (London, 1942), pp. 10–26. See too A. Strachey, *The Unconscious Motives for War: A Psycho-Analytical Contribution* (London, 1958), part I, chs. 2–11.

11. Nicole, *Psychopathology*, pp. 27–33.

12. Ibid., pp. 34–46; BP-AS, Ernest Jones collection, notes for a lecture to the Oxford Psychoanalytical Society, 'History of P-a', 26 Feb. 1936, p. 2; 'filth' reference in Clara Thompson, review of Jung's *Modern Man in Search of a Soul* in the *International Journal of Psycho-Analysis*, 15 (1934), pp. 349–50. On Jung's biography see G. Wehr, *Jung: A Biography* (Boston, 2001), esp. chs. 9–10; D. Bair, *Jung: A Biography* (Boston, 2003), chs. 15–17.

13. P. Grosskurth, *Melanie Klein: Her World and Her Work* (London, 1985), pp. 154–7.

14. Freud to Jones, 31 Oct. 1909, in R. A. Paskauskas (ed.), *The Complete Correspondence of Sigmund Freud and Ernest Jones, 1908–1939* (Cambridge, Mass., 1993), p. 32.

15. Jones to Freud, 22 July 1913, in Paskauskas, *Complete Correspondence*, p. 213.

16. Freud to Jones, 10 Aug. 1913, ibid., p. 217.

17. BP-AS, Ernest Jones collection, J/A CFC/F05, circular letter from Ernest Jones, 31 Dec. 1920; M1, minutes of committees files, minutes of meeting, 20 Feb. 1919; meeting of members and associate members, 17 Oct. 1923. See too B. Maddox, *Freud's Wizard: The Enigma of Ernest Jones* (London, 2006), pp. 110–11, 147–8.

18. BP-AS, M1, 'The London Clinic of Psycho-Analysis – Decennial Report May 1926–May 1936', pp. 4–12; Institute of Psycho-Analysis, report for the year ending 30 June 1936, pp. 5, 7–9.

19. *The Listener*, 25 Sept. 1935, p. 508.

20. B. Shephard, *A War of Nerves: Soldiers and Psychiatrists 1914–1994* (London, 2000), pp. 83–9.

21. Ibid., pp. 144, 158.

22. University College, London, Routledge & Kegan Paul collection, 23h, Publishing Journal, vol. VIII, 1921–39; 23i, Publishing Journal, vol. IX, 1928–38; 23j, Production Book, 1930–48.

23. BP-AS, M1, Publications papers, GO4/BA/F01, Stanley Unwin to Jones, 14 Dec. 1923 and 23 Feb. 1924; Jones to Unwin, 26 Feb. 1924; agreement between Hogarth Press and International Psycho-Analytical Press, 3 July 1924. On the role of the Woolfs see J. H. Willis, *Leonard and Virginia Woolf as Publishers: The Hogarth Press 1917–1941* (Charlottesville, Va., 1992), pp. 297–300.

24. BP-AS, Strachey papers, James Strachey to Jones, 18 July 1945. On Strachey's role see 'Bloomsbury and Psychoanalysis: James and Alix Strachey', *Charleston Magazine*, 16 (1997), pp. 53–5.

25. BP-AS, M1, GO4/BA/F01, Note on publications (n.d. but July 1924); GO4/BA/F05, Hogarth Press royalty statement 1930; 'Statistics of Book Sales', 31 Dec. 1927; GO4/BA/F06, Hogarth Press royalty statements 1935, 1936, 1937, 1938, 1939 (all dated 31 March); Leonard Woolf to Sylvia Payne, 20 July 1938.

26. T. W. Mitchell, 'Psychology and the Unconscious', *British Journal of Psychology: Medical Section*, 1 (1920/21), p. 340.

27. BP-AS, Bowlby papers, CBB/F11, John Bowlby to Jones, 2 Sept. 1943.

28. Wellcome Institute, London, Contemporary Medical Archives Centre (CMAC), Blacker papers, PP/CPB/H.1, C. P. Blacker, 'The Modern Conception of the World', Oct. 1928, pp. 17–18; University of Sussex Library, Kingsley Martin papers, MS 11/24/1, draft, 'The War Generation in England', p. 13 (published in *Revue des Sciences Politiques*, 48 (1925), pp. 211–30).

29. BMA, B/286/1/3, minutes of Psycho-Analysis Committee meeting, 21 Feb. 1929, p. 1; 20 Dec. 1928, p. 11.

30. BMA, B/286/1/1, minutes of Psycho-Analysis Committee meeting, 28 June 1927; B/286/1/3, Report of the Psycho-Analysis Committee, 29 June 1929, p. 1.

31. BMA, B/256/1/1, minutes of Psycho-Analysis Committee meeting, 3 May 1927, 'Questionnaire on Psychological Analysis', prepared by Isabel Hutton,

pp. 1–4; 16 Jan. 1928, appendix, 'Analysis of the Replies to the Questionnaire on Psychological Analysis', prepared by R. Gordon, pp. 1–2, 4–6.

32. BMA, B/286/1/2, memorandum prepared by Dr A. Wohlgemuth for the Psycho-Analysis Committee, 5 July 1928, p. 2.

33. BMA, B/286/1/3, memorandum by W. Brown, 'Mental Analysis and Psychotherapy', 26 Oct. 1928, p. 5.

34. BMA, B/286/1/2, Wohlgemuth memorandum (see n. 32), pp. 3–4.

35. BMA, B/286/1/1, memorandum by Dr J. S. Manson, 'Observations of Dr Gordon's Memorandum on the Methods of Psychotherapy', 31 May 1927, p. 1.

36. BMA, B/286/1/2, memorandum by J. R. Rees, 'Observations on the Minor Neuroses', 26 Sept. 1927, p. 1.

37. Ibid., minutes of Psycho-Analysis Committee, 7 June 1928, encl., 'Memorandum on Psycho-Analysis by P. McBride'; 5 July 1928, McBride cross-examination, pp. 3–8.

38. BMA, B/286/1/3, minutes of Psycho-Analysis Committee, 22 Nov. 1928, Glover cross-examination, p. 9.

39. Ibid., minutes of Psycho-Analysis Committee, 21 Feb. 1929, appendix, 'Continuation of Report of Committee', pp. 3–4; 22 May 1929, 'Suggested Additions by Dr Parry', pp. 1–2; report of the Psycho-Analysis Committee, 29 June 1929, § 47.

40. B. Russell, *The Scientific Outlook* (London, 1931), pp. 184–5; A. Lynch, 'The Depths of Freudianism', *English Review*, 57 (1933), p. 623. See too E. Glover, *The Social and Legal Aspects of Sexual Abnormality* (London, 1947), p. 2 on the early reaction to Freud's emphasis on sex. The British, Glover suggested, treated it typically as 'bad form'.

41. N. Haire (ed.), *The Sexual Reform Congress: London 8–14. ix. 1929* (London, 1930), p. xvi.

42. Haire, *Sexual Reform Congress*, Dora Russell, welcome address, p. xx; letter from Julian Huxley to conference organizers, 15 Aug. 1929, p. xxiii; M. Stopes, 'Birth Control', pp. 105–8; B. Russell, 'The Taboo on Sex Knowledge', pp. 395–404. Freud sent a warm letter of support.

43. See, for example, the excellent study by C. J. Dean, *The Frail Social Body: Pornography, Homosexuality and other Fantasies in Interwar France* (Berkeley, 2000).

44. BP-AS, M1 minutes and reports, minutes of meeting of 13 May 1920; minutes of meeting, 18 Oct. 1922; minutes of meeting, 5 Nov. 1924, encl., J. Rickman, 'Photography as a Pseudo-Perversion'.

45. BMA, B/286/1/2, minutes of Psycho-Analysis Committee, 7 June 1928, pp. 2–3.

46. BMA, B/286/1/3, minutes of Psycho-Analysis Committee meeting, 6 Dec. 1928, p. 8. Dr Manson was representing the views of the psychologist William Rivers, who assumed that most psychoanalysts showed 'perverse tendencies and prurient ideas' at every opportunity. Manson concluded that Rivers considered it 'natural that the laity with a less scientific mind might have a similar or worse view'.

47. Ibid., minutes of Psycho-Analysis Committee, 22 May 1929, p. 1.

48. BP-AS, Rickman collection, Box 1, CRR/F09, *The Lancet* (assistant editor) to Rickman, 16 Feb. 1929.

49. Ibid., draft, 'The Treatment of Inversion'; *The Lancet* to Rickman, 30 April and 13 May 1929.

50. BMA, B/286/1/3, minutes of Psycho-Analysis Committee, 20 Dec. 1928, pp. 4–5, 7–8.

51. University of Liverpool, Special Collections (ULSC), Cyril Burt papers, D191/58/2, lecture draft, 'The Contribution of Psycho-Analysis to Social Hygiene', 15 Oct. 1925, p. 15. This was reproduced in *Health and Empire*, 1 (1926), pp. 13–37. See the discussion in R. F. Rattray, 'The Nature and History of Sex', *Quarterly Review*, 266 (Jan.–Apr. 1936), pp. 266–71.

52. ULSC, Burt papers, D191/58/2, draft paper on prostitution (n.d. but 1925), pp. 1–4. Part of this draft was subsequently used in Burt's article in *Health and Empire* (see n. 51).

53. ULSC, Burt papers, draft, 'What's Wrong with the New Psychology?', 5 Nov. 1934, pp. 16–17; see too Newcastle Literary and Philosophical Society archives, report for the year ending 31 Dec. 1934, appendix C, 'Films and Lectures'.

54. ULSC, Burt papers, D191/11/3, draft radio broadcast, 'Sigmund Freud', 16 Dec. 1938; E. H. Wall (BBC programme division) to Burt, 14 Dec. 1938.

55. ULSC, Burt papers, D191/20/4, draft paper, 'The Cinema', for Cinema Commission of Enquiry (n.d. but c. 1921), pp. 5–7. See too notes for a lecture, 'The Effect of the Cinema on the Mind of the Child', 5 April 1922. Cinema, Burt argued, appealed only to the 'primitive emotions and instincts'. He continued: 'owing to the enormous power and universality of sex, the love interest is even more inevitable in the photo play [sic] than in the cheap novel or the popular melodrama'.

56. ULSC, Burt papers, D191/20/4, draft final report, Psychological Research Sub-Committee, Cinema Commission of Enquiry.

57. Birmingham City archives, National Women's Council papers, Birming-ham branch, MS 841/B/43, minutes of Social and Moral Welfare Sectional Committee meetings, 23 Nov. 1928, 23 May 1930 and 23 Oct. 1931.

58. CMAC, SA/EUG/D.177, Public Morality Council, Howard Tyres (Secretary, PMC) to Eugenics Society, 26 Aug. 1931.

59. CMAC, British Social Hygiene Council papers, SA/ BSH/C.1/7, minutes of Propaganda Committee meeting, 29 Nov. 1928, p. 4. Figures from *Health and Empire*, 6 (1931), pp. 40–42. The total of 2.6 million was a 75 per cent increase on the figure for 1920.

60. CMAC, SA/BSH/C.1/7, report of the Work of the District Representatives, Dec. 1929; minutes of Propaganda Committee meeting, 15 Feb. 1931.

61. CMAC, SA/BSH/F.6, minutes of the Sub-Committee on Preparation for Marriage, 1 July 1931, pp. 4–6.

62. Ibid., minutes of meeting, 6 Nov. 1931, p. 1.

63. C. Burt, 'The Contribution of Psychology to Social Hygiene', *Health and Empire*, 1 (1926), pp. 24–6. See too his 'The Causes of Sex Delinquency in Girls' in the same issue, pp. 251–71.

64. CMAC, Marie Stopes collection, PP/MCS/E.2, draft, 'The Secret Enemy', c. July 1940, p. 6.

65. Rattray, 'Nature of Sex', p. 271; 'Sex Instruction – When It Should Be Given', the results of a questionnaire in *Plan*, 2 (April 1935), pp. 3–7.

66. CMAC, Medical Women's Federation papers, SA/MWF/N.2, *Lady's Companion*, 'What Every Mother Should Tell Her Children', by 'A Workaday Mother' (n.d.), pp. 18–20.

67. CMAC, SA/MWF/N.2, Beatrice Webb, 'The Teaching of Young Children and Girls as to Reproduction', 12th edn, 1937, pp. 12–15.

68. CMAC, SA/MWF/N.2, Kenneth Wills, 'What Fathers Should Tell Their Sons' (British Social Hygiene Council, 1933).

69. D. B. Klein, 'Psychology and Freud: An Historico-Critical Appraisal', *Psychological Review*, 40 (1933), p. 440.

70. BMA, B/286/1/1–2, memorandum by Dr A. Wohlgemuth (see n. 32), p. 2; minutes of Psycho-Analytical Committee, 5 July 1928, pp. 6–7; 31 May 1927, memorandum by Dr J. S. Manson (see n. 35), pp. 1–2.

71. E. Jones, 'What Is Psycho-Analysis?', in C. Burt (ed.), *How the Mind Works* (London, 1935), pp. 73–4.

72. E. Jones, 'The Power of the Unconscious', ibid., pp. 81–2.

73. Ibid., pp. 87–8.

74. BMA, B/286/1/3, minutes of Psycho-Analysis Committee meeting, 22 Nov. 1928, pp. 8–9.

75. Low, *Psycho-Analysis*, p. 42; E. Jones, 'The Individual and Society', *Sociological Review*, 27 (1935), p. 247.

76. D. Cohen, 'Fry, Freud and Formalism', *Charleston Magazine*, 17 (1998), p. 34.

77. King's College, Cambridge, Forster papers, EMF 6/11, draft of a talk, 'Modern Writing' (1942).

78. C. E. M. Joad, 'The Challenge to Reason', in *The Rationalist Annual, 1935*, pp. 56–7.

79. R. Fülöp-Miller, 'The New Revolt Against Reason', *Hibbert Journal*, 34 (1935), pp. 187–91.

80. G. Murray, 'A Plea for Reason', in *The Rationalist Annual, 1932*, pp. 4–6, and *The Ordeal of this Generation* (London, 1929), p. 188.

81. S. Spender, *World Within World* (London, 1951), p. 42.

82. ULSC, Burt papers, D191/11/2, transcript, BBC discussion, 'Reason and Emotion', 13 Dec. 1932, pp. 1–6, 8.

83. These arguments were summed up in Freud's lecture on 'Anxiety and Instinctual Life', reproduced in S. Freud, *New Introductory Lectures on Psycho-Analysis* (London, 1933), pp. 135–42.

84. On the 'death instinct' see F. C. Palmer, 'The Death Instinct and Western Man', *Hibbert Journal*, 51 (1953), pp. 329–37; S. Bernfeld and S. Feitelberg, 'The Principle of Entropy and the Death Instinct', *International Journal of Psycho-Analysis*, 12 (1931), pp. 61–81; D. C. Abel, *Freud on Instinct and Morality* (Albany, N.Y., 1989), pp. 41–55; T. Johnston, *Freud and Political Thought* (New York, 1965), pp. 56–60. On the origins of Freud's ideas on aggression, P. Roazen, *Freud: Political and Social Thought* (New York, 1968), pp. 195–9, 213.

85. R. Money-Kyrle, 'A Psychological Analysis', *The Listener*, 7 Nov. 1934, p. 773.

86. BP-AS, CRA/F14, John Rickman to Ernest Jones, 18 Sept. 1929; Jones to Rickman, 23 Sept. 1929 ('I saw Freud in June and he told me he was not writing anything. About three weeks ago, however, he wrote saying he was publishing this brochure'). See too Freud to Jones, 25 Aug. 1929; Jones to Freud, 27 Aug. 1929 and 1 Jan. 1930, in Paskauskas, *Complete Correspondence*, pp. 663, 666–7; E. Jones, *Sigmund Freud: Life and Work*, vol. III (London, 1957), pp. 157–8; Willis, *Leonard and Virginia Woolf as Publishers*, pp. 407–9. The translation sold 5,157 copies in the years 1930–34.

87. S. Freud, 'Civilisation and Its Discontents', in *The Complete Psychological Works of Sigmund Freud*, vol. XXI, *1927–1931* (London, 1961), pp. 77, 86.

88. Ibid., pp. 119–22.

89. Ibid., p. 145. On the impact of the book see P. Gay, 'Introduction', in S. Freud, *Civilization and its Discontents* (New York, 1989), pp. xxi–xxiii; J. Laffey, *Civilization and its Discontented* (Montreal, 1993), pp. 130–46; M. von Unwerth, *Freud's Requiem: Mourning, Memory and the Invisible History of a Summer Walk* (London, 2006), pp. 36–7, 128–33.

90. Jones to Freud, 1 Jan. and 5 April 1930, in Paskauskas, *Complete Correspondence*, pp. 667, 669.

91. Freud, 'Civilisation and its Discontents', pp. 139–40. See too P. Rieff, 'The Authority of the Past – Sickness and Society in Freud's Thought', *Social Research*, 21 (1954), pp. 428–30, 443–9.

92. Bodleian Library, Hammond papers, vol. XXIII, Toynbee to Barbara Hammond, 15 Oct. 1930.

93. BP-AS, Ernest Jones collection, G13/BB/004, draft preface, 'Psycho-Analysis and World Problems'. The phrase 'state of the world' was substituted for the original wording 'The present World Depression', whose double meaning perhaps struck Jones as too obvious. See too typescript draft, 'The Problem of Government' (n.d.).

94. C. Jung, 'Sigmund Freud in His Historical Setting', *Character and Personality*, 1 (1932), p. 53.

95. C. Jung, 'Freud and Jung', in *Modern Man in Search of a Soul* (London, 1932), p. 135.

96. C. Jung, 'The Spiritual Problem of Modern Man', in *Collected Works*, vol. X, *Civilization in Transition* (London, 1964), p. 80.

97. Ibid., p. 82. This translation differs from the one in 1933. The last line reads 'Science has destroyed even the refuge of the inner life. What was once a sheltering haven has become a place of terror' (*Modern Man in Search of a Soul*, p. 236).

98. University College, London, Routledge & Kegan Paul collection, 23j, Production Book, 1930–48. The production book shows an original publication date of June 1932, though the final publication date was postponed until September 1933. The next impressions were printed in Oct. 1933, Dec. 1933, March 1934, 1936 and 1940.

99. See particularly M. Klein and J. Riviere, *Love, Hate and Reparation* (London, 1938). On Klein's entry to the Institute see Grosskurth, *Melanie Klein*, 159–65; on Klein and the death drive see E. Sánchez-Pardo, *Cultures of the Death Drive: Melanie Klein and Modernist Melancholia* (Durham, N.C., 2003), pp. 137–54.

100. BP-AS, Ernest Jones collection, GO9/BC/O27, Ernest Jones lecture notes, 'Psycho-Analysis and Mental Hygiene', 10 Dec. 1931. His notes refer to Klein's work: 'Fear. Guilt. Punishment esp. moral'.

101. Ibid., G13/BD/009, draft letter to *The Times*, 18 Dec. 1934.

102. Ibid., G13/BB, draft for lecture, 'Morbid Anxiety', pp. 12–13; Klein quotation in Sánchez-Pardo, *Cultures of the Death Drive*, p. 386.

103. Jones, 'The Individual and Society', pp. 249, 253–4.

104. W. Inge, 'The Dangers of Being Human', *The Listener*, 2 Oct. 1935, p. 547.

105. E. Glover, 'The Cost of Becoming Civilised', *The Listener*, 9 Oct. 1935, pp. 599–600. One reviewer observed that no reader would be left in doubt 'that the peril of being human which comes from unconscious mental forces far exceeds in urgency and importance all other dangers put together' (*International Journal of Psycho-Analysis*, 17 (1936), p. 521).

106. BP-AS, M1, GO9/BA/F03, Interim Report, Public Lectures Sub-Committee, 30 Nov. 1932.

107. Ibid., Institute of Psycho-Analysis, Prospectus of Public Activities, spring 1934; agenda, Public Lectures Sub-Committee, 13 April 1934.

108. BP-AS, M1, committee minutes, Institute for Psycho-Analysis, report for the year ending 30 June 1938.

109. Klein, 'Psychology and Freud', pp. 441–2.

110. Review of Fritz Wittels, *Sigmund Freud: His Personality, His Teaching, and His School* (London, 1929) in the *Sociological Review*, 21 (1929), p. 166.

111. Review of Alice Raven, *An Introduction to Individual Psychology* (Cambridge, 1929) in the *Sociological Review*, 21 (1929), pp. 360–61.

112. University College, London, Routledge & Kegan Paul collection, 23h, Publishing Journal, vol. VIII, 1921–39, for details of J. A. Jackson and H. M. Salisbury. W. B. Wolfe, *Nervous Breakdown: Its Cause and Cure* (London, 1933); K. Horney, *The Neurotic Personality of Our Time* (London, 1937); J. Ralph, *How to Psycho-Analyse Yourself: Theory and Practice of Remoulding the Personality by the Analytic Method* (London, 1937), pp. vii, 240.

113. London School of Economics, Malinowski papers, 28/7, advertisement for *I Can . . . and I Will* in the *Radio Times*, 5 Nov. 1937, p. 39.

114. ULSC, Burt papers, D191/58/2, draft paper on prostitution, p. 4. On the history of fear see J. Bourke, *Fear: A Cultural History* (London, 2005), esp. parts 3 and 4.

115. M. Chadwick, 'Notes Upon Fear of Death', *International Journal of Psycho-Analysis*, 10 (1929), p. 322.

116. K. Horney, 'Observations on a Specific Difference in the Dread Felt by Men and by Women Respectively for the Opposite Sex', *International Journal of Psycho-Analysis*, 13 (1932), pp. 350, 351–2.

117. Camden Archive Centre, London, Chalcot Discussion Society papers, annual reports for the years 1929 and 1930; minute book 1929–38, minutes of meeting 31 Oct. 1938.

118. Edinburgh University, Special Collections, Koestler archive, MS 2363/3, Ivor Lewis (secretary Federation of Progressive Societies) to Koestler, 25 June 1942, encl. pamphlet, 'The Progressive League', p. 1.

119. E. Jones, 'How Can Civilisation be Saved?' in *Essays in Applied Psycho-*

Analysis, vol. I, *Miscellaneous Essays* (London, 1951), pp. 236, 239–40, 242–6, 250.

120. Jones, *Sigmund Freud*, vol. III, pp. 237–8, 243, 247–50, 262–3; Maddox, *Freud's Wizard*, pp. 230–36.

121. BP-AS, Rickman collection, Box 1, CRR/F10/002, Sigmund Freud obituary, *The Lancet*, 30 Sept. 1939, p. 764.

122. Jones, *Sigmund Freud*, vol. III, p. 264; BP-AS, Strachey papers, Jones to James Strachey, 28 Sept. 1939: 'Leonard Woolf rang me up on the day of the funeral with the request for a prompt biography'.

123. BP-AS, Ernest Jones collection, G13/BD/004, draft lecture, 'The Present State of Psycho-Analysis', 1930, p. 5.

124. T. Maling, 'Psycho-Analysis and the Study of Politics', *Sociological Review*, 31 (1939), p. 215.

125. L. Hutchinson, 'The Weapon of Psychology', *The Plebs*, 30 (1938), pp. 115–17.

126. P. Hopkins, *The Psychology of Social Movements: A Psycho-Analytic View of Society* (London, 1938), pp. 277–80.

Chapter 5: Why War?

1. E. F. Durbin and J. Bowlby, *Personal Aggressiveness and War* (London, 1939), p. 3.

2. H. G. Wells, *The Salvaging of Civilisation* (London, 1921), p. 3.

3. Bodleian Library, Murray papers, file 393, 'The Cult of Violence: Being an Address Given at the Opening of the Session 1933–4 at Aberystwyth', p. 6; see too J. F. C. Fuller, *The Dragon's Teeth: A Study of War and Peace* (London, 1932), p. 6.

4. S. Baldwin, *On England and Other Addresses* (London, 1927), p. 229, speech in the House of Commons, 23 July 1923. Baldwin's book was reprinted five times between April 1926 and the first cheap edition in April 1927.

5. University Library, Cambridge, Baldwin papers, S.1/212, International Peace Society, speech delivered by Stanley Baldwin for the 19th annual meeting, 31 Oct. 1935, pp. 3–4.

6. Ibid., Lord Mayor's Banquet Speech, 9 Nov. 1936, press cutting from *The Times*, 10 Nov. 1936.

7. 'Should We Disarm?', *The Listener*, 14 Nov. 1934, pp. 834–5.

8. London School of Economics (LSE), Malinowski papers, 22/10, notes on a leaflet, 'Disarmament – February 1932 – February 1933 – ?'

9. Ibid., 22/11, rough notes for Phi Beta Kappa exercises at Harvard (n.d.; talk given on 17 Sept. 1936).

10. G. Lowes Dickinson, *War: Its Nature, Cause and Cure* (London, 1923), p. 7; N. Maclean, *How Shall We Escape? Learn or Perish* (London, 1934), p. xix.

11. L. Fuchser, *Neville Chamberlain and Appeasement* (New York, 1982), p. 34.

12. 'Should We Disarm?', *The Listener*, 14 Nov. 1934, p. 835.

13. King's College, Cambridge, Lowes Dickinson papers, GLD 1/5, Journal 1916–1932, entry for 9 May 1922.

14. A. J. Toynbee, *Civilization on Trial* (New York, 1948), p. 23.

15. B. Liddell Hart, *Thoughts on War* (London, 1944), p. 10 (entry from March 1932).

16. Fuller, *Dragon's Teeth*, pp. 116–19.

17. A. Chamberlain, 'Analysis of Divers Descriptions', *The Listener*, 19 Dec. 1934, p. 1043.

18. Bodleian Library, Murray papers, file 392, G. Murray, 'Die Probleme von morgen', *Nord und Süd*, 50 (1927), pp. 348–9; see too, ibid., *Das Problem der auswärtigen Politik* (Stuttgart, 1922), pp. 96, 100.

19. Ibid., file 393, 'The Cult of Violence . . .', pp. 17–23.

20. King's College, London, Liddell Hart Archive Centre, Liddell Hart papers, LH1/538, Gilbert Murray to Liddell Hart, 2 Nov. 1934.

21. H. Nickerson, *Can We Limit War?* (London, 1933), p. 5. This question is explored interestingly in M. Geyer, ' "There is a Land Where Everything is Pure: Its Name is the Land of Death": Some Observations on Catastrophic Nationalism', in G. Eghigian and M. P. Berg (eds.), *Sacrifice and National Belonging in Twentieth-Century Germany* (College Station, Tex., 2002), pp. 118–47. For general accounts see W. Sofsky, *Violence* (London, 2003) and N. Ferguson, *War of the World: History's Age of Hatred* (London, 2007).

22. Bodleian Library, Murray papers, file 347, Committee on Intellectual Co-operation, Minutes of the Thirteenth Session, 20–25 July 1931, pp. 13–23; Report of the Thirteenth Plenary Session, 5 Aug. 1931, pp. 8, 17–18; Report of the Sixth Committee Meeting, 21 Sept. 1931, p. 5.

23. Bodleian Library, Ponsonby papers, MS Eng. Hist. C673, No More War Movement, statement on Einstein/Ponsonby visit (n.d. but May 1932); War Resisters' International memorandum, 'Professor Einstein and Lord Ponsonby, Meeting with International Journalists, 23 May 1932', p. 2. On Einstein's involvement see G. Pflug, *Albert Einstein als Publizist, 1919–1933* (Frankfurt am Main, 1981), pp. 46–7.

24. A. Einstein and S. Freud, *Why War?* (London, 1933), pp. 2–3.

25. On the invitation to Freud see O. Nathan and H. Norden, *Einstein on Peace* (New York, 1960), pp. 185, 191. On Einstein's links with Freud,

A. Fölsing, *Albert Einstein: A Biography* (New York, 1997), pp. 609, 651; E. Jones, *Sigmund Freud: Life and Work*, vol. III, *The Last Phase, 1919–39* (London, 1980), pp. 186–7.

26. Pflug, *Einstein als Publizist*, pp. 49–50.

27. Bodleian Library, Murray papers, file 348, International Committee for Intellectual Co-operation, Report of the Committee on the Fifteenth Plenary Session, 10 Aug. 1933, p. 4; reel 349, Report of the Sixteenth Plenary Session, 11 Aug. 1934, p. 4; reel 310, Murray's notes on a secret session of the ICIC, December 1933.

28. New Commonwealth, *Why War?* (London, 1934); J. Rickman (ed.), *Civilization, War and Death: Selections from Three Works by Sigmund Freud* (London, 1939), pp. 82–97. On New Commonwealth see Maclean, *How Shall We Escape?*, pp. 223–32, Appendix by Lord Davies, 'The Way to Peace as Proposed by the New Commonwealth'.

29. E. Conze and E. Wilkinson, *Why War? A Handbook for Those Who Will Take Part in the Second World War* (London, 1934).

30. C. E. M. Joad, *Why War?* (Harmondsworth, 1939), cover and p. 247; Bristol University Library, Allen Lane archive, DM 1819/10/8, notebook (n.d.), list of publications 1935–1940, specials S1 to S60. Joad's book was published on 28 March 1939.

31. A. Huxley, 'Sadist Satisfactions in War', *The Listener*, 14 Nov. 1934, pp. 799–802; W. S. Churchill, 'Causes of War', *The Listener*, 21 Nov. 1934, pp. 841–2, 872. On the decision not to publish Churchill's essay, H. J. Stenning (ed.), *The Causes of War* (London, 1935), p. 8.

32. Stenning, *Causes of War*, endpapers.

33. Bristol University Library, Allen Lane archive, DM 1819/10/8, Notebook (n.d.), list of publications 1935–40, specials. By 1939 'specials' made up almost one-quarter of the year's published titles.

34. Warwick University Modern Records Centre, Gollancz papers, MSS 318/2/1/9–12, Production Books, 1934–5, 1935–6, 1936–7, 1937–9. J. B. S. Haldane's two books on *A.R.P.* and *How to Be Safe from Air Raids* sold 54,000 and 52,000 respectively.

35. Warwick University Modern Records Centre, Gollancz papers, MSS 318/2/1/9, Production Book, 1934–5. The first cheap edition sold 35,783 between 1935 and 1937.

36. Daily Express, *Covenants with Death* (London, 1934). A similar book was published in 1932 by the National Council of Labour Colleges titled *War Against War*. It was advertised as 'A Collection of War Photographs that will make the blood of the most bigoted war-monger run cold.' See *The Plebs*, 24 (1932), p. 51.

37. Lord Beaverbrook, 'Peace Through Imperial Isolation?', *The Listener*, 31 Oct. 1934, pp. 719–20.

38. S. Jameson, *Journey from the North: Autobiography of Storm Jameson* (2 vols., London, 1969), p. 413. On Liddell Hart see A. Danchev, *Alchemist of War: The Life of Basil Liddell Hart* (London, 1998), esp. pp. 69–70.

39. King's College, London, Liddell Hart Archive Centre, Liddell Hart papers, LH1/394, Julian Huxley to Liddell Hart, 21 Nov. 1933; Liddell Hart to Huxley, 22 Nov. 1933, p. 2; J. Huxley, 'Science and War', *The Listener*, 29 Nov. 1933, p. 848.

40. Liddell Hart, *Thoughts on War*, p. 16. See too review of Milne, *Peace with Honour* in the *Fortnightly Review*, 136 (July–Dec. 1934), p. 750, which summarized Milne's thesis as 'war is silly; war is wrong; war is unnecessary; war can be prevented'.

41. King's College, London, Liddell Hart Archive Centre, Liddell Hart papers, LH1/538, Liddell Hart to Murray, 1 Nov. 1934.

42. J. Huxley and H. Levy, 'What Is the Use of Science to Society?', *The Listener*, 10 (July–Dec. 1933), p. 545.

43. 'Peace and War', *Nature*, 17 Feb. 1934, pp. 229, 230–31.

44. LSE, Malinowski papers, 22/7, letter to *The Times* from Gregory Bateson, 12 Dec. 1933, 'Psychology and War'.

45. Bodleian Library, Murray papers, file 347, International Committee on Intellectual Co-operation, Minutes of the Thirteenth Session, 20–25 July 1931, p. 21. On the general efforts to cope with the threat of war see A. Webster, 'The Transnational Dream: Politicians, Diplomats and Soldiers in the League of Nations' Pursuit of International Disarmament, 1920–1938', *Contemporary European History*, 14 (2005), pp. 493–518.

46. *Nature*, 2 July 1932, p. 4; see too A. Porritt (ed.), *The Causes of War: Economic, Industrial, Racial, Religious, Scientific and Political* (London, 1932).

47. A. Hutt, *This Final Crisis* (London, 1935), p. 177.

48. Conze and Wilkinson, *Why War?*, p. 7; D. Torr, 'Marxism and War', Marx House Syllabus no. 7, Marx Memorial Library, 1941.

49. M. Ginsberg, 'The Causes of War', *Sociological Review*, 31 (1939), p. 122.

50. J. A. Hobson, *Imperialism* (London, 1902), passim. The arguments were clearly set out in Hobson's *The Recording Angel: A Report from Earth* (London, 1932), pp. 122–3: 'With the collapse of profiteering Capitalism, militant Nationalism and Imperialism would be deprived of their main incentive, and the cause of pacific Internationalism would then pass from its phase of sentimental idealism into actuality.'

51. University of Hull, Special Collections, Hobson papers, DHN 24, draft lecture, 'The Causes of War' (n.d. but 1937?), pp. 9–10. See too DN 27, H. N. Brailsford, *The Life-Work of J. A. Hobson: The Hobhouse Memorial Lecture* (Oxford, 1948), pp. 26–7 on the 'Hobson school' on imperialism.

52. N. Lenin [sic], *Imperialism: The Last Stage of Capitalism* (London, 1926), pp. ii, 1. Subsequent English editions had a different translation. For example 'excellent description' in the 1933 edition was translated as 'very good and detailed'. A clear example of the impact that Lenin's writing had can be found in the chapter on 'roots of war' in T. Wintringham, *The Coming World War* (London, 1935), pp. 181–4.

53. V. I. Lenin, *Imperialism: The Highest Stage of Capitalism* (London, 1933). Lenin's general writings on war were published in English in volume 2 of the Little Lenin Library as *The War and the Second International* (London, 1931). A more developed analysis of imperialism was then published as *Lenin on Britain* (London, 1934). All were published by Martin Lawrence (later Lawrence & Wishart).

54. Torr, 'Marxism and War', p. 8.

55. Friends House, London, TEMP MSS 579/2, 'Recommendations on Policy' for annual conference of No More War Movement, Nov. 1932, p. 1; 579/1, No More War Movement, Annual Report, 1934–5, p. 1.

56. Independent Labour Party, *The Socialist Challenge to Poverty, Fascism, Imperialism, War: Basic Policy of the I.L.P.* (London, 1938), pp. 2–3.

57. E. Varga and L. Mendelsohn (eds.), *New Data for V. I. Lenin's 'Imperialism, the Highest Stage of Capitalism'* (London, 1938), pp. 264–6.

58. Wintringham, *Coming World War*, pp. 12, 14.

59. G. D. H. Cole, 'Hawking War Wares', *The Listener*, 28 Nov. 1934, pp. 888–91; on Haldane see Stenning, *Causes of War*, p. 9.

60. Nuffield College, Oxford, Cole papers, A1/68/1–5, three drafts for 'Causes of War' (n.d.). The quotation was added in pencil to the first draft, p. 8. Cole ended his draft with conventional catastrophism: '. . . the next war, if it is allowed to come, will be devastating beyond all precedent . . .' (draft 1, p. 10).

61. Nuffield College, Oxford, Cole papers, D1/58/2, New Fabian Research Bureau (NFRB), memorandum 'Socialisation of the Armaments Industry: Draft Heads for an Inquiry' (n.d. but Aug. 1936); NFRB, 'Nationalisation of Armaments in France', translation of legislation, 11 Aug. 1936; Cole, 'Hawking War Wares', p. 890.

62. H. C. Engelbrecht and J. C. Hanighen, *Merchants of Death* (London, 1934); F. Brockway, *The Bloody Traffic* (London, 1933); P. Noel-Baker, *The Private Manufacture of Armaments* (London, 1937). See University College,

London, Routledge & Kegan Paul collection, 23i, Publishing Journal, vol. IX, 1928–38, for details on *Merchants of Death*, which had a print run of 5,000 in the first two editions.

63. Brockway, *Bloody Traffic*, pp. 11–12.

64. W. H. Williams, Labour Research Department, *Who's Who in Arms* (London, 1935), p. 47; see too Cambridge University Anti-War Committee, *British Armaments and World Peace* (Cambridge, 1936), esp. pp. 26–30.

65. British Library, Cecil papers, ADD MSS 51169, Cecil to A. Murphy, 20 Nov. 1934.

66. L. Charteris, *Prelude for War* (London, 1938), pp. 39, 168.

67. Ibid., p. 285.

68. N. Angell, *Must it Be War?* (London, 1938), p. 225.

69. J. Stamp, 'Economic Factors that May Make for War', *The Listener*, 12 Dec. 1934, pp. 973–4; C. R. Douglas, 'Is Our Money System to Blame?', *The Listener*, 5 Dec. 1934, pp. 929–30.

70. Cited in S. Newman, *March 1939: The British Guarantee to Poland* (Oxford, 1976), p. 41.

71. Ginsberg, 'Causes of War', p. 130.

72. Hutt, *Final Crisis*, p. 161.

73. L. Magyar, 'On the Eve of a New World War', *Communist Review*, 7 June 1934, pp. 81–4.

74. Conze and Wilkinson, *Why War?*, pp. 40, 54–5; Wintringham, *Coming World War*, pp. 12–14.

75. University Library, Cambridge, Baldwin papers, S.1/201, notes for a speech (n.d. but 1934), p. 2.

76. F. von Bernhardi, *Germany and the Next War* (London, 1914), pp. 18–19.

77. See in particular P. Crook, *Darwinism, War and History* (Cambridge, 1994) and M. Hawkins, *Social Darwinism in European and American Thought, 1860–1945: Nature as Model and Nature as Threat* (Cambridge, 1997).

78. G. F. Nicolai, *The Biology of War* (London, 1919), pp. 13, 38; see too the discussion in D. Pick, *War Machine: The Rationalization of Slaughter in the Modern Age* (New Haven, 1993), pp. 82–3.

79. See, for example, J. A. Thomson, *What is Man?* (London, 1923), pp. 201–3: 'Biologically regarded [war] is a reversion to the earliest mode of the struggle for existence ... In many ways it is dysgenic: selecting in the wrong direction, reversion dragging evolution in the mud.'

80. University Library, Cambridge, Joseph Needham papers, K/34, rough notes, 'The Distortion of Science for Political and Economic Ends' (n.d. but

1938); K/35, typescript draft, 'The "Struggle for Existence" Distortion' (n.d.), pp. 1–2.

81. Ibid., typescript draft, pp. 7–8.

82. Details from A. Keith, *An Autobiography* (London, 1950); see too Crook, *Darwinism*, pp. 166–7. On Keith's views on the British people see Royal College of Surgeons, Keith papers, MS 0018/2/10, A. Keith, 'The Last Chapter of Life: Humanity's Grand National and the Kind of Man who Will Win It', *Evening Standard*, 14 Oct. 1927 ('I back the Caucasians, and in particular the "British breed"').

83. *Nature*, 15 Nov. 1930, pp. 779–80; 20 June 1931, pp. 901, 917.

84. *Nature*, 20 June 1931, p. 917.

85. Royal College of Surgeons, Keith papers, MS 0018/2/10–11, draft, 'The Place of Prejudice in Modern Civilization. Rectorial Address. Aberdeen University, 5 June 1931', p. 47.

86. A. Keith, *Essays on Human Evolution* (London, 1946), p. 133.

87. LSE, Malinowski papers, 22/8, A. Keith, 'Must a Rationalist be a Pacifist?', *The Truth Seeker*, 66 (1939), p. 34. See too the reply by Jack Benjamin, 'Rationalism as a Pruning Hook', *The Truth Seeker*, 66 (April 1939), pp. 49–51; A. Keith, 'A History of Some of My Heresies', in *The Rationalist Annual, 1939*, pp. 3–13. This was a debate with a wide currency. See J. S. Clarke, 'The Fallacies of Sir Arthur Keith', *The Plebs*, 23 (1931), p. 159. Clarke, writing for the Labour Colleges, regarded the arguments as 'pure drivel'.

88. On sociobiology see Hawkins, *Social Darwinism*, pp. 294–304. Wilson's approach to ethnocentrism and conflict bears a striking resemblance to Keith's views.

89. Keith, *Human Evolution*, pp. 130, 134, 144–6.

90. Royal College of Surgeons, Keith papers, MS 0018/2/9, A. Keith, 'The Crisis of Mankind', *Evening Standard*, 24 Oct. 1934.

91. Ibid., MS 0018/1/9–10, A. Keith, 'What Is Wrong with the World?', draft for *New York Times*, 12 July 1932, pp. 13–15.

92. Ibid., MS 0018/2/9, draft review of Gerald Heard, *The Source of Civilisation*, 'Civilisation Doomed?', for the *Sunday Times*, 17 Nov. 1935.

93. LSE, Malinowski papers, 22/2, draft, 'Oxf. Lect.' (1936), pp. 1–2: 'The biologist in his leisure moments often talks nonsense about war as "nature's pruning hook".'

94. Ibid., 29/11, Gilbert Murray to Malinowski, 30 Aug. 1929.

95. Ibid., 22/23, draft notes, 'The Background of Principles' (n.d.), p. 1.

96. J. Cohen, *Human Nature, War and Society* (London, 1946), pp. 125–7; W. J. Perry, *The Growth of Civilisation* (Harmondsworth, 1937). Perry's

book, first published in 1924, was designed to show that civilization had grown from a common Egyptian, or Nilotic, root, 'diffused' throughout areas of human habitation.

97. LSE, Malinowski papers, 22/1, draft manuscript, 'Man's Primeval Pacifism and the Modern Militarist Argument', pp. 3–4 (later published in an abridged version in *New Leader*, 2 May 1924).

98. Ibid., 22/4, notes for a lecture, 21 Dec. 1932; war lecture IX, 'Disarmament', 17 Feb. 1933, esp. p. 18: 'you cannot fail to see that as a piece of Social Engineering [war] is at present completely unfeasible and impossible and self-destructive'.

99. Royal College of Surgeons, Keith papers, MS 0018/2/4, N. Dyer Sharpe to Keith, 20 Feb. 1929, memorandum, 'Gorilla and Chimpanzees'.

100. Keith, *Human Evolution*, pp. 149–52.

101. Cohen, *Human Nature*, pp. 94–5, 96–8. The lack of analogy in nature was well understood in the 1930s. See, for example, A. Huxley, *What Are You Going to Do About It? The Case for Constructive Peace* (Peace Pledge Union, 1936), pp. 4–5: '"War" in the sense of conflict between armies exists only among certain species of social insects'; University Library, Cambridge, J. D. Bernal papers, ADD MS 8287, Box 83, Gerald Heard to J. Bernal, 13 Aug. 1936: 'You agree that warfare in the accurate sense of the word does not exist in nature except perhaps among deranged bees and among termites and ants . . .' On ants see M. Maeterlinck, 'The Life of the Ant', *Fortnightly Review*, 128 (July–Dec. 1930), pp. 455–8: 'The ants, alone among the insects, have organised armies, and undertake offensive wars.'

102. Cohen, *Human Nature*, p. 111. Pavlov's work was published in a popular English edition by Y. P. Frolov, *Pavlov and His School: The Theory of Conditioned Reflexes* (London, 1937). On the 'experimental neuroses' see ch. 7.

103. S. Zuckerman, *The Social Life of Monkeys and Apes* (London, 1933), pp. 217–21.

104. Durbin and Bowlby, *Personal Aggressiveness*, pp. 8–11, 25–9.

105. E. Glover, *The Dangers of Being Human* (London, 1936), introduction by Dean Inge, p. 22.

106. LSE, Malinowski papers, 22/9, draft notes, 'Personal Opinions', 21 Aug. 1936, p. 1.

107. Ibid., 22/18, lecture to the American Academy of Medicine, 11 Jan. 1940, p. 1.

108. Royal College of Surgeons, Keith papers, MS 0018/2/9, draft, 'What Is Wrong with the World', p. 17; A. Keith, draft foreword to A. Machin, *Darwin's Theory Applied to Mankind*, p. viii. See too A. Machin, *Darwin's*

Theory Applied to Mankind (London, 1937). Machin was a keen supporter of Keith. 'Man is, in short,' Machin argued, 'just a bundle of survival values' (p. 276).

109. Huxley, 'Sadist Satisfactions', p. 793.

110. A. Huxley, *Ends and Means: An Enquiry into the Nature of Ideals and into the Methods Employed for Their Realization* (London, 1938), pp. 90, 99.

111. A. Huxley, 'Lettre sur la guerre et la psychologie de "individu"', in Institut international de coopération intellectuelle, *L'Ésprit, l'éthique et la guerre* (Paris, 1934), pp. 58, 67–8.

112. Huxley, 'Sadist Satisfactions', p. 803.

113. P. E. Stepansky, *A History of Aggression in Freud* (New York, 1977), p. 153.

114. Stepansky, *Aggression in Freud*, pp. 160–61. Something along the same lines was argued by Freud's British disciple Ernest Jones in 1915 in his essay 'War and Individual Psychology'. See E. Jones, *Essays in Applied Psycho-Analysis*, vol. I, *Miscellaneous Essays* (London, 1951), pp. 64–5.

115. S. Freud, 'Thoughts for the Times on War and Death', in Freud, *Collected Works*, vol. IV (London, 1956), pp. 295–6, 312. This was first published in England in 1926.

116. A. Einstein and S. Freud, 'Why War?', in Freud, *Collected Works*, vol. V (London, 1956), p. 213. See the discussion in Pick, *War Machine*, pp. 214–20; J. Rose, *Why War?* (London, 1993), pp. 16–18.

117. Review of Einstein and Freud, *Why War?* in the *British Journal of Psychology* (General Section), 24 (1933), p. 242; E. Jones, review of Einstein and Freud, *Why War?*, *International Journal of Psycho-Analysis*, 14 (1933), pp. 418–19.

118. On Glover's resignation, British Psycho-Analytical Society archive, Jones/Glover correspondence, CGA/F30, Glover to Ernest Jones, 11 Dec. 1944. On 'cobwebby' see H. J. Faulkner and V. D. Pruitt (eds.), *The Selected Correspondence of Karl A. Menninger* (New Haven, 1988), p. 141, letter to Smith Jelliffe, 8 March 1933. See also E. Sánchez-Pardo, *Cultures of the Death Drive: Melanie Klein and Modernist Melancholia* (Durham, N.C., 2003), pp. 3–4.

119. E. Glover, *War, Sadism and Pacifism: Further Essays on Group Psychology and War* (2nd edn, London, 1947), pp. 31, 48–9.

120. Glover, *War, Sadism*, p. 11; P. Hopkins, *The Psychology of Social Movements: A Psycho-Analytic View of Society* (London, 1938), pp. 107–11, 117–18.

121. E. Glover and M. Ginsberg, 'A Symposium on the Psychology of Peace and War', *British Journal of Medical Psychology*, 14 (1934), p. 277. On

survival of the primitive instincts see also Glover, *Dangers of Being Human*, pp. 92–3, 96.

122. Glover, *War, Sadism*, pp. 18–21, 26–9.

123. Glover and Ginsberg, 'Symposium', p. 280; Glover, *War, Sadism*, p. 49.

124. Cohen, *Human Nature*, pp. 36–7; H. Goldhamer, 'The Psychological Analysis of War', *Sociological Review*, 26 (1934), pp. 250–57, 260.

125. P. Boret, *The Fighting Instinct* (London, 1923), p. 7.

126. Goldhamer, 'Psychological Analysis', pp. 257, 260–61.

127. Ginsberg, 'Causes of War', p. 140.

128. Cohen, *Human Nature*, pp. 47–8; R. E. Money-Kyrle, 'The Development of War: A Psychological Approach', *British Journal of Medical Psychology*, 16 (1937), p. 222. On the work of Susan Isaacs see D. W. Harding, *The Impulse to Dominate* (London, 1941), pp. 96–9. On Klein's psychology see Sánchez-Pardo, *Cultures of the Death Drive*, pp. 139–47.

129. Cohen, *Human Nature*, p, 46. 'As one might expect,' wrote Cohen, 'fighting animals own a strikingly large and wide adrenal cortex, whereas a timid creature like the rabbit has only a narrow strip of this gland.'

130. Money-Kyrle, 'Development of War', pp. 222–3.

131. Ibid., p. 223–4.

132. R. Money-Kyrle, *The Development of the Sexual Impulses* (London, 1932), pp. 75–6. Money-Kyrle did not accept the death instinct/life instinct dichotomy in Freud, but related aggression to adrenalin release and frustrated sexual impulse.

133. W. R. D. Fairbairn, 'Is Aggression an Irreducible Factor?', *British Journal of Medical Psychology*, 18 (1939/40), p. 163.

134. See particularly the contribution to the symposium by A. W. Wolters, 'Aggression', *British Journal of Medical Psychology*, 18 (1939/40), pp. 171–7. On post-war theory, K. Lorenz, *On Aggression* (London, 1966), which was first published in Vienna in 1963.

135. K. Stephen, 'Aggression in Early Childhood', *British Journal of Medical Psychology*, 18 (1939/40), pp. 184, 189.

136. Glover, *War, Sadism*, pp. 76–9.

137. Bodleian Library, Murray papers, file 364, Walter Roberts (Foreign Office) to Gilbert Murray, 3 Oct. 1936, encl. 1, E. Glover, 'Memorandum on War Research'; encl. 2, 'Mr M. I. David's Observations on Dr Glover's Memorandum'.

138. Bodleian Library, Murray papers, file 364, Murray to David, 28 Oct. 1936: 'the psycho-analytical approach is not the most promising'.

139. Bodleian Library, Murray papers, file 365, Murray to David, 4 June 1938; Edward Glover to Alexander Farquharson (British National Committee

on Intellectual Co-operation), 27 June 1938. BMA initiative in British Medical Association archive, London (BMA), A/1/1/35, Annual Representative Meeting, 20 July 1937, p. 32; supplement, 'Psychology of War', *British Medical Journal*, 31 July 1937, p. 91.

140. Bodleian Library, Murray papers, file 365, Murray to R. A. Butler, 20 April 1938; Murray to Lord Halifax, 22 Oct. and 8 Nov. 1938 ('Are we not to check war at all?'); Halifax to Murray, 21 Dec. 1938.

141. Hopkins, *Psychology of Social Movements*, p. 131.

142. Glover, *War, Sadism*, p. 49; M. A. May, *A Social Psychology of War and Peace* (New Haven, 1943), pp. 1, 13.

143. Glover and Ginsberg, 'Symposium', p. 289.

144. Jones, *Essays in Applied Psycho-Analysis*, p. 76.

145. Huxley, 'Sadist Satisfactions', p. 803.

146. Keith, *Human Evolution*, p. 142.

147. BMA, B/55/1/13, BMA Council Agenda, 27 Jan. 1932, memorandum, 'Medical Profession and War Prophylaxis', pp. 222–3; B/55/1/15, BMA Council Agenda, 6 June 1934, p. 622; Minutes of Council, 6 June 1934, p. 710. See too H. Joules (ed.), *The Doctors' View of War* (London, 1938), which promised 'a careful examination of the prophylactic measures that might minimize the risk of [war's] outbreak or spread' (p. 19).

148. University of Liverpool, Special Collections, D. Caradog Jones papers, D48/5, 'Petition to His Majesty's Government', 6 June 1937; note, 'Attempt to Avert the Last Great War by the Mobilisation of Public Opinion' (n.d.); list of 'Signatories of Letters asking support for the Petition' (n.d. but autumn 1937); Caradog Jones to Graham White MP, 12 Oct. 1937.

149. Harding, *Impulse to Dominate*, p. 243.

150. LSE, Malinowski papers, 22/7, rough notes for 'Oxf. Lect.' (1936).

Chapter 6: Challenge to Death

1. Friends House, London, TEMP MSS 579/1, No More War Movement, annual report, 1932–3, p. 11.

2. Hull Central Library, Winifred Holtby collection, WH 5/5.26, diary 1934; WH 6/6.2, Vera Brittain to Winifred Holtby, 29 Jan. 1934 ('most exciting dinner' was Vera Brittain's description); S. Jameson (ed.), *Challenge to Death* (New York, 1935), pp. vii–ix (foreword by Vera Brittain). Visit to Brussels in Churchill College, Cambridge, Archive Centre (CCAC), Noel-Baker papers, 4X/104, Report of the International Congress in Defence of Peace, 15–17 Feb. 1934.

3. S. Jameson, *Journey from the North: Autobiography of Storm Jameson*

(2 vols., London, 1969), vol. I, p. 326; Jameson, *Challenge to Death*, p. viii.

4. Jameson, *Journey from the North*, vol. I, p. 327.

5. British Library, London, Vernon Bartlett correspondence, ADD MSS 59500, Storm Jameson to Bartlett, 29 March and 13 June 1934, the latter thanking him for his chapter: 'much the best of the 10 chapters I have had'.

6. Hull Central Library, Winifred Holtby collection, WH 5/5.20, Jameson to Holtby, 29 March and 1 April 1934. On Jameson's problems as editor see Harry Ransom Humanities Research Center, Austin, Texas, Storm Jameson papers, Jameson to Mr Macdonald, 21 Oct. 1934 and 8 Jan. 1935.

7. British Library, Cecil papers, ADD MSS 51132, Storm Jameson to Gilbert Murray, 28 April 1934; 51193, Cecil to Jameson, 1 May 1934; Jameson to Cecil, 3 May 1934; Jameson to Cecil, 16 Aug. 1934, asking him at the publisher's behest to delete the sentence in the introduction in which he claimed that he had not read the book.

8. Jameson, *Journey from the North*, vol. I, p. 327; British Library, Bartlett correspondence, 59500, Jameson to Bartlett, 29 March 1934.

9. Hull Central Library, Winifred Holtby collection, WH 3/3.19, folder 2, *New York Herald Tribune*, books review, 19 May 1935.

10. P. Noel-Baker, 'The International Air Police Force', in *Challenge to Death*, pp. 231–3.

11. CCAC, Noel-Baker papers, 4/497, draft resolutions for Albert Hall meeting, 13 Nov. 1933.

12. London School of Economics (LSE), National Peace Council papers, NPC 6/1, London Council for the Prevention of War, minutes of executive meeting, 7 March 1927, resolution (3).

13. National Museum of Labour History, Manchester, pamphlet collection, 327.362, R. Macaulay, *An Open Letter* (Peace Pledge Union, 1937), p. 8.

14. Viscount Cecil, 'The Future of Civilization', in F. W. Haberman (ed.), *Peace: Nobel Lectures, 1926–1950* (3 vols., Amsterdam, 1972), vol. II, p. 246.

15. British Library, Cecil papers, ADD MSS 51193, Lord Cecil, proofs of Foreword, Oct. 1934; Storm Jameson to Cecil, 21 Aug. 1934.

16. Hull Central Library, Winifred Holtby collection, WH 3/3.19, *Manchester Guardian*, 'Books of the Day', 19 Nov. 1934.

17. On the history of British pacifism in the early part of the century see the standard work by M. Ceadel, *Pacifism in Britain, 1914–1945: The Defining of a Faith* (Oxford, 1980). See too P. Brock, *Freedom from War: Nonsectarian Pacifism 1814–1914* (Toronto, 1991), ch. 20.

18. Trinity College, Cambridge, Layton papers, Box 6, Gerald Bailey (NPC) to Layton, 30 Nov. 1933.

19. CCAC, Noel-Baker papers, 2/22, LNU (League of Nations Union),

minutes of special meeting of the Executive Committee, 8 March 1934; 2/27, Noel-Baker to Maxwell Garnett, 21 Feb. 1934.

20. See Viscount Cecil, *A Great Experiment: An Autobiography* (London, 1941), chs. 1–2.

21. See D. J. Whittaker, *Fighter for Peace: Philip Noel-Baker, 1889–1982* (York, 1989), chs. 1–4.

22. *Headway*, 10 (1928), monthly LNU news.

23. *Headway*, 2 (1919/20), 'How to Arrange a Public Meeting', pp. 111–15; 3 (1920), 'Competition Scheme', pp. 61–4.

24. Bodleian Library, Murray papers, file 244, memorandum by Stewart Murray, 'Propaganda Programme for Covering all the Various Sections of the Working Class' (n.d. but 1920/1).

25. King's College, Cambridge, Lowes Dickinson papers, GLD 1/5, Journal, 1916–1932, entry for 2 Nov. 1922, 'Biological Inheritance'. He added, 'the change in conditions (e.g. to a League of Nations world) might produce great change in conduct by encouraging expression of one kind of instinct and discouraging that of another'.

26. Bodleian Library, Murray papers, file 244, note, 'Instruction of Youth in Aims and Work of League' (n.d.).

27. Bodleian Library, Ponsonby papers, MS Eng. Hist. C679, Margery South to Ponsonby, 12 March 1937.

28. British Library, Cecil papers, ADD MSS 51081, Cecil and Gilbert Murray to Ramsay MacDonald, 15 Nov. 1929; J. Bell, 'The Schools and the League: What They are Doing in Great Britain', *Headway*, 14 (1932). See too D. S. Birn, *The League of Nations Union, 1918–1945* (Oxford, 1981), pp. 138–43.

29. 'The Million', *Headway*, 15 (1933), April supplement.

30. League of Nations, *Ten Years of World Co-Operation* (Geneva, 1930), pp. 25–6.

31. British Library, Cecil papers, ADD MSS 51101, Cecil to H. StGeorge Saunders, 18 July 1932; 51132, Murray to Cecil, 12 June 1932; Cecil to Murray, 13 June 1932.

32. British Library, Cecil papers, ADD MSS 51197, draft of 'Manchuria', for *Quarterly News*, Jan. 1932, p. 11.

33. Ibid., ADD MSS 51169, W. J. Johnston to Cecil, 12 Feb. 1934.'I hate to have to listen to speeches,' Cecil's correspondent continued, 'and then say "Very fine, but where was he in September 1931?"'

34. Ibid., LNU London Regional Federation to Cecil, 20 March 1934, encl., 'A Personal Message from Professor Gilbert Murray', pp. 2–3.

35. Birn, *League of Nations Union*, pp. 129–30; 'The Million', *Headway*, 15 (1933), April supplement.

36. Ibid., ADD MSS 51132, Murray to Cecil, 31 March 1933, encl. memorandum by Murray to Hills (LNU), pp. 1, 3.

37. Bodleian Library, Murray papers, file 243, draft statement, 'The Declaration' (n.d. but 1934).

38. C. E. Clift, 'Manchester Sums Up', *Headway*, 17 (1935), p. 132; CCAC, Noel-Baker papers, 2/22, 'Memorandum for the Executive Committee of the L.N.U.' (n.d. but Feb. 1934).

39. British Library, Cecil papers, ADD MSS 51169, Ponsonby to Cecil, 5 April 1934; Cecil to Ponsonby, 10 April 1934.

40. Ibid., Lord Gage to Cecil, 27 Nov. 1934, encl. newspaper cutting, 'League of Nations: Armament Debate at Lewes'.

41. CCAC, Noel-Baker papers, 2/22, 'Memorandum for the Executive Committee of the L.N.U.'

42. British Library, Cecil papers, ADD MSS 51169, note for Lord Cecil on the Ilford ballot, 8 Feb. 1934; Ilford LNU to Cecil, 2 Feb. 1934; ballot paper, 'Peace or War? It is for YOU to decide'. See too A. Livingstone, *The Peace Ballot: The Official History* (London, June 1935), pp. 7–8; Birn, *League of Nations Union*, pp. 143–4.

43. *Headway*, 16 (1934), pp. 162, 168–9.

44. Livingstone, *Peace Ballot*, p. 14; Lambeth Palace Library, Cosmo Lang papers, vol. LIV, Cecil to Cosmo Lang, encl. memorandum, 'League or War!'

45. CCAC, Noel-Baker papers, 2/22, leaflet, 'Peace or War? Plan of a National Declaration' (n.d.), p. 1.

46. Ibid., leaflet draft, 'Peace or War? Commentary on the Five Questions in the Ballot Paper' (n.d.), pp. 3–4.

47. See for example 'The League of Nations Union Summer School 1920', *Headway*, 3 (1920), p. 21, report of inaugural address: 'The safe way of progress does not seem to me by way of attack upon the army and navy, or upon military training . . .'. For a general account of the tension in the movement generated by absolute pacifism see J. A. Thompson, 'Lord Cecil and the Pacifists in the League of Nations Union', *Historical Journal*, 20 (1977), pp. 949–55.

48. British Library, Cecil papers, ADD MSS 51132, Murray to Cecil, 16 Nov. 1934. See too C. Moorehead, *Troublesome People: Enemies of War, 1916–1986* (London, 1987), pp. 120–21.

49. CCAC, Noel-Baker papers, 4/497, proof of 'A Statement on the League of Nations Union' by Austen Chamberlain, Lord Cecil and Gilbert Murray (n.d. but March 1934).

50. British Library, Cecil papers, ADD MSS 51169, Cecil to Lord Philip Lothian, 5 July 1934. It is not clear from this remark whether Cecil meant

intervention between the combatants, or British involvement in keeping the peace militarily through collective action, but the context suggests the latter.

51. CCAC, Noel-Baker papers, 4/497, leaflet, 'League or War?', Feb. 1934, encl. ballot paper for LNU canvass; 'The Lesson of Luton', *Headway*, 16 (1934), pp. 168–9.

52. Ibid., 2/22, file note, 'National Organisations Co-Operating in the National Declaration', 16 Aug. 1934; Livingstone, *The Peace Ballot*, pp. 26–8; Birn, *League of Nations Union*, pp. 146–7.

53. CCAC, Noel-Baker papers, 2/22, National Declaration Committee, 'Hints at Organisation', 7 Nov. 1934; Lambeth Palace Library, Cosmo Lang papers, vol. LIV, memorandum, 'League or War!', p. 4.

54. Trinity College, Cambridge, Layton papers, Box 6, internal memorandum, A. J. Cummings (*News Chronicle*) for Layton, 9 Oct. 1934; CCAC, Noel-Baker papers, 2/27, Noel-Baker to Cecil, 28 Sept. 1934; 2/22, Cecil to Noel-Baker, 23 Nov. 1934.

55. British Library, Cecil papers, ADD MSS 51108, Noel-Baker to Cecil, 15 May 1935.

56. CCAC, Noel-Baker papers, 4/484, LNU speakers' notes, June 1935, p. 30. The final tally was almost 12 million when the last results were returned. See 'How Nearly 12,000,000 Voted', *Headway*, 17 (1935), p. 131 and p. 122, which confirmed the final total of 11,627,765.

57. British Library, Cecil papers, ADD MSS 51154A, Cosmo Lang to Cecil, 28 July 1934; Cecil to Lang, 31 July 1934; Lambeth Palace Library, Cosmo Lang papers, vol. LIV, Cecil to Cosmo Lang, 23 July 1934; Cosmo Lang to Cecil, 28 July 1934, encl. draft letter endorsing the National Declaration.

58. Lambeth Palace Library, Cosmo Lang papers, vol. LIV, Cecil to Cosmo Lang, 23 July 1934; British Library, Cecil papers, Add MSS 51108, Noel-Baker to Cecil, 15 May 1935. See too Birn, *League of Nations Union*, pp. 147–8 on Conservative Party opposition.

59. British Library, Cecil papers, ADD MSS 51108, Noel-Baker to Cecil, 30 Oct. 1934; Cecil to Noel-Baker, 8 Nov. 1935.

60. British Library, Cecil papers, ADD MSS 51081, Ramsay MacDonald to Cecil, 5 March 1934.

61. Lambeth Palace Library, Sheppard papers, MSS 3744, Douglas Goldring to Sheppard, 6 Sept. 1934. Goldring read Sheppard's draft and commented, 'It should bring in a number of honest-to-God plain men who can't bear the sight of "pacifists" – professional pacifists that is . . .' See too D. C. Lukowitz, 'British Pacifists and Appeasement: The Peace Pledge Union', *Journal of Contemporary History*, 9 (1974), pp. 116–17; Moorehead, *Troublesome People*, pp. 122–4.

62. Lambeth Palace Library, Sheppard papers, MSS 3744, Noel-Baker to Sheppard, 18 Oct. 1934 and 23 Oct. 1934; CCAC, Noel-Baker papers, 2/27, Noel-Baker to Dorothy Eltingen, 26 Oct. 1934: 'The pacifists have been trying to use it [the Sheppard Pledge] to discredit the Declaration.'

63. Lambeth Palace Library, Sheppard papers, MSS 3744, Cecil to Sheppard, 16 Oct. 1934 and 14 Feb. 1935.

64. See, for example, CCAC, Noel-Baker papers, 2/27, Noel-Baker to Maude Royden (one of Sheppard's collaborators), 20 Oct. 1934, on the issue of violence.

65. LSE, National Peace Council papers, NPC 1/3, 'Special Prefatory Note' to 'The NPC and the Prevention of the Next War', 23 Oct. 1923.

66. Friends House, London, No More War Movement papers, TEMP MSS 579/1, programme for demonstration, 28 July 1923; 'No More War', *Observer*, 29 July 1923 for details of the banners.

67. LSE, National Peace Council papers, NPC 1/3, constitution of the National Council for Prevention of War, 8 May 1924; annual report of the National Council for the Prevention of War, 1925/6, p. 1; minutes of special meeting, 15 Nov. 1928, pp. 2–3.

68. Bodleian Library, Ponsonby papers, MS Eng. Hist. C678, Margery South to Ponsonby, 14 July 1936.

69. LSE, National Peace Council papers, NPC 6/1, Executive Committee report, London Council for the Prevention of War, 23 Oct. 1926; Minutes of Executive Committee, 21 July 1926.

70. Lambeth Palace Library, Sheppard papers, MSS 3744, Ponsonby to Sheppard (n.d. but late 1936). On Ponsonby's early life see R. A. Jones, *Arthur Ponsonby: The Politics of Life* (Bromley, 1989), chs. 1–4.

71. Jones, *Arthur Ponsonby*, pp. 165–6.

72. Lord Ponsonby, 'Message for 1932', *The New World: Journal of the No More War Movement*, 2 (Jan. 1932), p. 1.

73. LSE, Women's International League papers 5/11, lecture and summer school programmes, 1921–8.

74. *The War Resister*, 21 (Oct. 1928), pp. 3–5. See too Ceadel, *Pacifism*, pp. 70–77.

75. Friends House, No More War Movement (NMWM) papers, TEMP MSS 579/1, No More War Movement annual report, 1931–2, p. 1.

76. Ibid., memorandum, 'A Peace Strategy', 20 July 1932, pp. 2–6; 579/2, memorandum by Reginald Reynolds, 'Implementing the Peace Strategy' (n.d. but Sept. 1932). See too Peace Pledge Union archives, London, Sponsors' Minute-Book, meeting of sponsors, 5 May 1937. Ponsonby tried to persuade the Union to adopt his idea of a 'Peace Book' as well.

77. Friends House, NMWM papers, TEMP MSS 579/2, minutes of National Committee meeting, 10/11 Sept. 1932, p. 6.

78. Ibid., 'Recommendations on Policy', National Committee report for the annual conference, Nov. 1932, pp. 3–4; 'Notes on Policy', by Wilfred Wellock (n.d. but early 1933).

79. LSE, National Peace Council papers, NPC 11/1, memorandum by Ruth Fry, 'An International Force?', 20 Nov. 1933, p. 3. On the development of Christian pacifism see Ceadel, *Pacifism*, pp. 63–70.

80. University Library, Cambridge, Joseph Needham papers, K/29, memorandum, Cambridge Scientists' Anti-War Group, June 1936, p. 1.

81. University of Hull, Special Collections, Rev. Stanley Evans papers, DEV 1/11, programme for conference on 'Religious Freedom in Germany', 10 Dec. 1938.

82. Ibid., DEV 1/5, papers for IPC First National Congress, memorandum on the Churches Commission, 23 Oct. 1937; LSE, Fellowship of Reconciliation papers, Box 4(1), programme for New Year party, London Union of Fellowship, 13 Jan. 1934; newsletter, Beatrice Brown to London Union members, 27 Dec. 1933.

83. Friends House, Friends Peace Committee papers, Minute-Book, Feb. 1934 –Sept. 1938, minutes of Peace Committee meeting, 3 May 1934.

84. Ibid., minutes of special Peace Committee meeting, 2 Aug. 1934, pp. 1–2.

85. Ibid., general report on 'Call to Complete Disarmament', Sept.–Oct. 1934. Many letters were sent in about the appeal, including one in Latin which said the idea was lunacy.

86. LSE, National Peace Council papers, NPC 16/7, 'Abhor That Which Is Evil', NPC address by Bishop E. W. Barnes, 24 June 1934, in Birmingham Cathedral. Barnes was president of the National Peace Council in 1937.

87. E. N. Porter Goff, 'A Christian Peace Policy', in P. Dearmer (ed.), *Christianity and the Crisis* (London, 1933), p. 507.

88. Lambeth Palace Library, Cosmo Lang papers, vol. LIV, Cosmo Lang to Archbishop of Uppsala, 5 March 1934; 'World Peace', press statement from Peace Conference, 15 May 1934.

89. Ibid., 'The Present Crisis', address by the Archbishop of Canterbury at the Church Congress, Bournemouth, 8 Oct. 1935. See too C. Lang, 'Disarmament', in Dearmer, *Christianity and the Crisis*, pp. 501–5.

90. Lambeth Palace Library, Sheppard papers, MSS 3744, cutting from the *Church Times*, 4 Dec. 1936.

91. Friends House, NMWM papers, TEMP MSS 579/1, No More War Movement annual report, 1931–2, p. 1.

92. Ibid., No More War Movement annual report, 1932–3, p. 1; No More

War Movement annual report, 1935–6, p. 1; Mabel Eyles, 'Memo on Reorganisation' (n.d. but April 1933), pp. 1–2; 579/2, minutes of National Committee meeting, 1 Dec. 1934, pp. 2–3.

93. LSE, NPC London Council for the Prevention of War, minutes of Executive Committee, 7 April 1930; annual Council meetings, 26 June 1931 and June 1932.

94. V. Brittain, *Testament of Experience* (London, 1979), p. 165. For a sympathetic portrait of Sheppard see C. Scott, *Dick Sheppard: A Biography* (London, 1977), esp. pp. 186–91 on Sheppard's turn to pacifism in 1929–30.

95. Bodleian Library, Ponsonby papers, MSS Eng. Hist. C676, Sheppard to Ponsonby, 24 July 1935. On the Sheppard movement see Lukowitz, 'British Pacifists', pp. 116–18; Moorehead, *Troublesome People*, pp. 122–5.

96. Lukowitz, 'British Pacifists', p. 117; Peace Pledge Union, Sponsors' Minute-Book, meeting of sponsors, 22 May 1936.

97. Lambeth Palace Library, Sheppard papers, MSS 3744, Storm Jameson to Sheppard, 1 May 1936. She tried to withdraw on grounds of ill-health in October but was persuaded to stay on: Storm Jameson to Sheppard, 6 Oct. 1936.

98. Ibid., MSS 3746, Ponsonby to Sheppard, 10 July 1936. Ponsonby added, 'But the splendid thing is that you have roped in these sort of people who haven't thought the thing out but would paint their faces black if you told them to do it.'

99. Brittain, *Testament of Experience*, pp. 164–7. See too P. Berry and M. Bostridge, *Vera Brittain: A Life* (London, 1995), pp. 354–5. On the context of Brittain's pacifism see C. Baldoli (ed.), *Marie Louise Berneri e Vera Brittain: Il seme del chaos: Scritti sui bombardamenti di massa* (Santa Maria Capua Vetere, 2004), pp. 10–22.

100. British Library, Vernon Bartlett correspondence, ADD MSS 59500, Vera Brittain to Bartlett, 17 and 23 May 1933. It seemed odd, Brittain wrote, that anyone who had contact with the war 'retained any sanity at all'. 'Our nerves, of course,' she continued, 'are not what they should be but we do . . . retain an appearance of surface normality.'

101. Ceadel, *Pacifism*, p. 233. Men made up two-thirds of all members. Only in September was it finally agreed that the wording of the pledge should be the same for women as for men: Peace Pledge Union, Sponsors' Minute-Book, meeting of sponsors, 3 Sept. 1936.

102. Lambeth Palace Library, Sheppard papers, MSS 3744, Vera Brittain to Sheppard, 3 July 1936. See too Berry and Bostridge, *Vera Brittain*, p. 356.

103. Brittain, *Testament of Experience*, pp. 172–3; Lambeth Palace Library, Sheppard papers, MSS 3744, Vera Brittain to Sheppard, 26 Jan. 1937.

104. Somerville College, Oxford, Vera Brittain archive, VB D, typescript diary, 1932–9, entry for 14 March 1938: 'L.N.U., Labour Party & all the so-called peace lovers (except the P.P.U.) are shouting war!'

105. Hull Central Library, Winifred Holtby collection, WH 5/5.20, Storm Jameson to Winifred Holtby, 29 March 1934.

106. G. Heard, 'And Suppose We Fail? After the Next War', in Jameson, *Challenge to Death*, pp. 154–70; Lambeth Palace Library, Sheppard papers, MSS 3745, Gerald Heard to Sheppard, 31 Oct. and 7 Nov. 1935. See too S. Bedford, *Aldous Huxley: A Biography*, vol. I, *1894–1939* (London, 1973), pp. 310–11 and the profile of Huxley in Ceadel, *Pacifism*, pp. 183–7. On the so-called 'New Pacifism' see G. K. Hibbert (ed.), *The New Pacifism* (London, 1936).

107. Lambeth Palace Library, Sheppard papers, MSS 3745, Heard to Sheppard, 31 Oct. 1935.

108. Ibid., MSS 3746, Aldous Huxley to Sheppard, 9 Nov. 1935.

109. Ibid., MSS 3745, Heard to Sheppard, 1 Jan., 9 Feb. and 24 Feb. 1936. A. Huxley, *What Are You Going to Do About It? The Case for Constructive Peace* (London, 1936). On the Research and Thinking Committee see Bodleian Library, Ponsonby papers, MS Eng. Hist. C678, Sheppard to Ponsonby, 7 May 1936.

110. Huxley, *What Are You Going to Do About It?*, p. 34.

111. Lambeth Palace Library, Sheppard papers, MSS 3746, Huxley to Sheppard, 15 April 1936, encl., 'suggested answers to Mealand's [?] questions', pp. 1–2.

112. G. Smith (ed.), *Letters of Aldous Huxley* (London, 1969), p. 411, Huxley to C. Day Lewis (c. 6 Jan. 1937); D. K. Dunaway, *Huxley in Hollywood* (London, 1989), pp. 24–6 for details of the arguments with Day Lewis, and the *Left Review*; C. Day Lewis, *We're Not Going to Do Nothing* (Left Review, London, 1936). See too S. Spender, 'An Open Letter to Aldous Huxley', *Left Review*, 2 (1936), pp. 539–41, attacking the pamphlet on the grounds that it misunderstood the pacifist credentials of the USSR.

113. Lambeth Palace Library, Sheppard papers, MSS 3746, Ponsonby to Sheppard, 11 May 1936; Jones, *Arthur Ponsonby*, pp. 202, 207–8.

114. Lambeth Palace Library, Sheppard papers, MSS 3746, Ponsonby to Sheppard, 10 July 1936. See too Peace Pledge Union, Sponsors' Minute-Book, meeting of sponsors, 7 July 1936, when Ponsonby among others got Sheppard to accept that the organization 'is not on a definitely Christian basis'.

115. Jones, *Arthur Ponsonby*, p. 209.

116. Cited in Brittain, *Testament of Experience*, p. 169.

117. British Library, Cecil papers, ADD MSS 51169, Lord Gage to Cecil, 2 Dec. 1934.

118. Bodleian Library, Ponsonby papers, MS Eng. Hist. C681, Margery South to Ponsonby, 8 Jan. 1939.

119. Ibid., MS Eng. Hist. C678, Sheppard to Ponsonby, 3 Aug. 1936.

120. CCAC, Noel-Baker papers, 9/89, Noel-Baker to Cecil, 11 May 1937 (note from Lord Cecil written at foot of the letter).

121. British Library, Cecil papers, ADD MSS 51132, Murray to Cecil, 25 Sept. 1936.

122. Ibid., ADD MSS 51146, LNU memorandum by Norman Angell, 'Collective Security', 14 July 1936, p. 1. See the discussion in Thompson, 'Pacifists', pp. 958–9.

123. Bodleian Library, Hammond papers, vol. XXV, Kingsley Martin to Lawrence Hammond, 13 Aug. 1936.

124. League Union figures in Birn, *League of Nations Union*, p. 130; Friends House, NMWM papers, TEMP MSS 579/2, minutes of National Committee meeting, 21 Nov. 1936; 'Statement to Movement by the Chairman' (n.d. but Jan. 1937?); minutes of National Committee meeting, 6 Feb. 1937; 'Statement in Favour of the Independent Continuation of the NMWM' (n.d. but Jan. 1937).

125. Bodleian Library, Ponsonby papers, MSS Eng. Hist. C678, Margery South to Ponsonby, 6 July 1936.

126. Ibid., MS Eng. Hist. C679, Margery South to Ponsonby, 10 Jan. 1937.

127. British Library, Cecil papers, ADD MSS 51132, Murray to Cecil, 12 Oct. 1936.

128. LSE, National Peace Council papers, NPC1 1/4, minutes of Council meetings, 16 Jan., 5 June and 19 Nov. 1936.

129. Trinity College, Cambridge, Dobb archive, DA117, Maurice Dobb Memorial Issue, *Cambridge Journal of Economics*, 2 (1978), p. 118; H4, Cambridge Anti-War Council notices.

130. Bodleian Library, Ponsonby papers, MS Eng. Hist. C679, Margery South to Ponsonby, 12 March 1937.

131. Ibid., MS Eng. Hist. C678, Sheppard to Ponsonby, 3 Aug. 1936.

132. Lambeth Palace Library, Sheppard papers, MSS 3744, Richard Gregg to Sheppard, 26 July 1936; National Museum of Labour History, pamphlet collection, 328.641, Richard Gregg, 'Training for Peace: A Programme for Peace Workers' (Peace Pledge Union, 1936). On 'Greggism' see the brief history in Ceadel, *Pacifism*, pp. 250–54.

133. Bodleian Library, Ponsonby papers, MS Eng. Hist. C679, Margery Rayne to all PPU sponsors, 5 Jan. 1937; General Crozier to all sponsors, 7 Jan. 1937.

134. Ibid., minutes of meeting of Sponsors' Committee, PPU, 1 Feb. 1937; Sheppard to Ponsonby, 2 Feb. 1937; Jones, *Arthur Ponsonby*, pp. 210–11.

135. Lambeth Palace Library, Sheppard papers, MSS 3745, Gerald Heard to Sheppard, 29 Oct. 1937.

136. Bedford, *Aldous Huxley*, p. 336.

137. Lambeth Palace Library, Sheppard papers, MSS 3746, Huxley to Sheppard, 23 Sept. 1936.

138. Smith, *Letters of Aldous Huxley*, pp. 410, 416–17: Huxley to Harold Raymond, 30 March 1937. See too Dunaway, *Huxley in Hollywood*, pp. 31–53 for the first months of Huxley's life in the United States.

139. A. Huxley, *Ends and Means: An Enquiry into the Nature of Ideals and into the Methods Employed for their Realization* (London, 1938), pp. 123, 303.

140. Bodleian Library, Ponsonby papers, MS Eng. Hist. C679, Margery South to Ponsonby, 12 Jan. 1937.

141. Brittain, *Testament of Experience*, pp. 185–6; Scott, *Dick Sheppard*, pp. 244–6.

142. Birn, *League of Nations Union*, p. 133; Lukowitz, 'British Pacifists', pp. 121–6.

143. CCAC, Noel-Baker papers, 4/484, LNU Speakers' Notes, July–Aug. 1936, 31 July 1936, p. 1.

144. Ibid., 8/3/3, memorandum from BBC, 'Broadcasts on War and Peace', 11 May 1936; Mary Adams (BBC) to Noel-Baker, 1 June 1936. Noel-Baker then drew up a brief synopsis of the subjects for a series on the League which included a programme on the Corfu incident of 1923 and on 'The Demir Kapon Dispute' between Bulgaria and Greece as examples of League success.

145. University of Hull, Special Collections, Edgar Young papers, DYO 10/27, Speech by Lord Lytton, Congress of Peace, 3–6 Sept. 1936.

146. British Library, Cecil papers, ADD MSS 51108, Cecil to Noel-Baker, 28 Feb. 1936; 51154A, Cosmo Lang to Cecil, 25 Feb. 1936; Cecil to Cosmo Lang, 26 Feb. 1936. See too Whittaker, *Fighter for Peace*, pp. 155–6.

147. University of Hull, Special Collections, Edgar Young papers, DYO 10/3, Rassemblement universel pour la Paix, journal of the Congress, 4–6 Sept. 1936.

148. Lambeth Palace Library, Sheppard papers, MSS 3744, Cecil to Sheppard, 29 Aug. 1936; delegates from CCAC, Noel-Baker papers, 5/132, *Rassemblement*, 2 (4 Sept. 1936); University of Hull, Special Collections, Edgar Young papers, DYO 10/19, Liste des Délégués Britanniques qui assisteront au Congrès'.

149. Lambeth Palace Library, Sheppard papers, MSS 3746, Huxley to

Sheppard, 9, 28 and 31 Aug. 1936. See too Peace Pledge Union, Sponsors' Minute-Book, meeting of sponsors, 3 Sept. 1936.

150. University of Hull, Special Collections, Edgar Young papers, DYO 10/4, programme of First Congress, 3–6 Sept. 1936, p. 17; 10/13, administrative details, Congrès de Bruxelles; 10/17, International Peace Campaign, British Committee, travel arrangements (n.d.); 10/18, British National Delegation, administrative details (n.d.).

151. Ibid., DYO 10/3, Rassemblement universel pour la Paix, 'Résumé des exposés de Lord Cecil et de M. Pierre Cot', p. 1 (author's translation); CCAC, Noel-Baker papers, 5/132, *Rassemblement*, 4 (6 Sept. 1936).

152. British Library, Cecil papers, ADD MSS 51146, minute for Executive Committee, 21 Oct. 1937; Cecil to Murray, 15 Oct. 1936.

153. Ibid., ADD MSS 51132, Murray to Cecil, 25 Sept. 1936, encl. memorandum, 'The L.N.U. and the I.P.C.'.

154. Ibid., ADD MSS 51146, papers for the Executive Committee, 17 Nov. 1936, encl., 'The Union and the International Peace Campaign', pp. 1–2.

155. Ibid., ADD MSS 51154A, Cecil to Lang, 26 Feb. 1936; 51146, 'Note by Lord Cecil' for Executive Committee meeting, 17 Nov. 1936.

156. Ibid., ADD MSS 51132, Cecil to Murray, 15 Oct. 1936.

157. Ibid., memorandum by Murray for Cecil, 25 Sept. 1936; Cecil to Murray, 26 Sept. 1936: 'Are you not a little over anxious? . . . the staff must not dictate our policy . . .'

158. Ibid., ADD MSS 51146, minutes of Executive Committee, LNU, 21 Oct. 1937.

159. Ibid., ADD MSS 51132, Cecil to Murray, 30 and 17 Dec. 1937; Murray to Cecil, 3 Jan. 1938; 51142, Adelaide Livingstone to Cecil, 28 Dec. 1937. See too Whittaker, *Fighter for Peace*, pp. 158–60.

160. Ibid., ADD MSS 51132, Cecil to Murray, 19 Jan. 1938, encl. draft document for Garnett and Adelaide Livingstone to take six months' leave.

161. Ibid., ADD MSS 51142, Cecil to Adelaide Livingstone, 30 Dec. 1937.

162. Ibid., ADD MSS 51133, Mary Belton to Murray, 16 Feb. 1938 (from St John's Wood branch of the LNU, London).

163. Trinity College, Cambridge, Layton papers, Box 7, Noel-Baker to Layton, 13 Oct. 1937.

164. University of Hull, Special Collections, Edgar Young papers, DYO 10/51, IPC Monthly Bulletin, Nov.–Dec. 1937, reports on First British National Congress, pp. 3–4, 6–7.

165. British Library, Cecil papers, ADD MSS 51140, William Arnold-Forster to Cecil, 4 Aug. 1937; Cecil to Arnold-Forster, 6 Aug. 1937.

166. Trinity College, Cambridge, Layton papers, Box 6, National Declaration Committee to Mr Wills, 18 Feb. 1935, encl. budget of the Peace Ballot.

167. Birn, *League of Nations Union*, p. 133; LSE, National Peace Council papers, NPC 2/5, NPC Finance Committee meeting, 6 May 1938; NPC 1/4, minutes of Council meeting, 16 Nov. 1933.

168. British Library, Cecil papers, ADD MSS 51154A, Cosmo Lang to Cecil, 30 Nov. 1936.

169. Brittain, *Testament of Experience*, p. 171.

170. See the discussion in M. Paris, *Warrior Nation: Images of War in British Popular Culture, 1850–2000* (London, 2000), ch. 5.

171. CCAC, Noel-Baker papers, 4/497, memorandum for the Executive Committee of the LNU (n.d. but April 1936), 'Note of a Conversation with the Prime Minister', 4 May 1936.

172. Ibid., 4/506, correspondence of Cecil and Neville Chamberlain, reproduced in *The Times*, 7 July 1937; British Library, Cecil papers, ADD MSS 51133, Neville Chamberlain to Cecil, 9 Feb. 1938; Cecil to Murray, 11 Feb. 1938.

173. British Library, Cecil papers, ADD MSS 51146, memorandum by Norman Angell, 'Collective Security', 14 July 1936, pp. 6–8; Lambeth Palace Library, Cosmo Lang papers, vol. LIV, Lang to Archbishop of Uppsala, 5 March 1934, p. 1.

174. A. Salter, *Personality and Politics* (London, 1947), pp. 129–30; H. G. Wells, *The Fate of Homo Sapiens* (London, 1939), pp. 293–5, and *The Open Conspiracy* (2nd edn, London, 1930), p. 182.

175. CCAC, Noel-Baker papers, 4/484, draft speech by Herbert Morrison, delivered at Geneva Institute of International Relations, 21 Aug. 1936, pp. 16–17.

176. King's College, London, Liddell Hart Archive Centre, Liddell Hart papers, LH1/408, Storm Jameson to Liddell Hart, 26 June 1940, p. 2.

Chapter 7: Utopian Politics: Cure or Disease?

1. London School of Economics (LSE), Passfield papers, 2/4/11, file 3, John Strachey to Beatrice Webb, 12 Dec. 1926.

2. Bodleian Library, Toynbee papers, Box 39, Fabian Society lecture programme, 'The Shrinking World: Dangers and Possibilities', synopsis iii, 'The Danger of Creed Wars', 3 Nov. 1926.

3. Warwick University Modern Records Centre, Gollancz papers, MSS 157/4/LB/1, review by Harold Laski in the *Left News*, Dec. 1937, p. 608.

4. Nuffield College, Oxford, Cole papers, A1/75/13, draft of 'Mussolini's Revolution' (n.d. but 1929), p. 1.

5. Ibid., D5/2/1, Allan Young (editor *New Outlook*) to Cole, 19 June 1936, encl., 'The Popular Front', p. 1.

6. University Library, Cambridge, Baldwin papers, S.1/212, 'Political Freedom', broadcast 6 March 1934.

7. A. J. Thorpe, 'Stalinism and British Politics', *History*, 83 (1998), pp. 609–10, 613–14; '"The Only Effective Bulwark against Reaction and Revolution": Labour and the Frustration of the Extreme Left', in A. J. Thorpe (ed.), *The Failure of Political Extremism in Inter-War Britain* (Exeter, 1989), pp. 11–27; and 'The Membership of the Communist Party of Great Britain, 1920–1945', *Historical Journal*, 43 (2000), pp. 781, 790, 795–6.

8. R. Thurlow, *Fascism in Britain: From Oswald Mosley's Blackshirts to the National Front* (London, 1998), pp. 91–3; T. Linehan, *British Fascism, 1918–1939: Parties, Ideology and Culture* (Manchester, 2000), pp. 160–61. For a recent general history see M. Pugh, *Hurrah for the Blackshirts! Fascists and Fascism in Britain between the Wars* (London, 2005).

9. Thurlow, *Fascism in Britain*, p. 70.

10. Ibid., pp. 82–3; G. D. Anderson, *Fascists, Communists and the National Government: Civil Liberties in Great Britain, 1931–1937* (Columbia, Miss., 1983), pp. 175–88.

11. See the discussions in Thorpe, *The Failure of Political Extremism*, esp. pp. 6–9 for a summary of the arguments.

12. Warwick University Modern Records Centre, Gollancz papers, MSS 318/2/1/11, Production Book, 1936–7.

13. J. J. Barnes and P. P. Barnes, *Hitler's 'Mein Kampf' in Britain and America: A Publishing History, 1930–1939* (Cambridge, 1980), pp. 16–17.

14. University of Exeter, Special Collections, Williamson letters, MS106, Box 1, Henry Williamson to Eric Watkins, 4 May 1945.

15. P. W. Lewis, *Hitler* (London, 1931), esp. pp. 129–31.

16. Bodleian Library, Toynbee collection, Box 76, Thomas Jones to Anthony Eden, 9 March 1936, encl., memorandum from Toynbee. The meeting took place on 28 February 1936 in the presence of Joachim von Ribbentrop (German foreign minister from 1938). Toynbee concluded that if Hitler could get what he wanted 'in a way that might lead to peace instead of war, I believe he would be vastly relieved'.

17. See, for example, I. Kershaw, *Making Friends with Hitler: Lord Londonderry, the Nazis and the Road to World War II* (London, 2004).

18. University of Exeter, Special Collections, Williamson letters, MS106, Henry Williamson to Eric Watkins, 18 Aug. 1936.

19. P. O'Keeffe, *Some Sort of Genius: A Life of Wyndham Lewis* (London, 2000), p. 399.

20. South Place Ethical Society Library, Society lecture lists, 1930–39.

21. H. Brown, 'Germany in Revolution', *Fortnightly Review*, 133 (Jan.–June 1933), p. 443; I. Cohen, 'The Jews in Germany', *Quarterly Review*, 261 (July–Oct. 1933), p. 2; review of *Why I Left Germany*, in *Quarterly Review*, 263 (July–Dec. 1934), p. 175.

22. King's College, London, Liddell Hart Archive Centre, Liddell Hart papers, LH1/408, Storm Jameson to Liddell Hart, 14 Sept. 1939, p. 1.

23. University of Exeter, Special Collections, Rowse papers, MS 113, 2/1/10b, diary Manuscript March 1935–Aug. 1939, entry for 10 April 1935.

24. King's College, London, Liddell Hart Archive Centre, Liddell Hart papers, LH1/408, Jameson to Liddell Hart, 14 Sept. 1939, p. 2.

25. University of Exeter, Special Collections, Rowse papers, MS 113, 2/1/10b, diary manuscript March 1935–Aug. 1939, entry for 29 April 1935.

26. E. Lengyel, *Hitler* (London, 1932), pp. 239–40. On Hitler as the consequence of failed capitalism see particularly R. Pascal, *The Nazi Dictatorship* (London, 1934); R. Olden, *Hitler the Pawn* (London, 1936).

27. Anon., *Why Nazi?* (London, 1933), pp. 11–12.

28. I. Cohen, 'The Jewish Tragedy', *Quarterly Review*, 263 (July–Oct. 1934), p. 252.

29. W. Steed, *The Meaning of Hitlerism* (London, 1934), pp. ix–x, 206.

30. *Hitler's Mein Kampf* (18 parts, London, 1939–40). Hutchinson advertised an elegant binder to hold the weekly parts with the caption 'When this work is complete you will say "What a fine edition!"'

31. R. C. K. Ensor, '*Mein Kampf* and Europe', *International Affairs*, 18 (1939), pp. 479, 487–8.

32. H. Rauschning, *Hitler Speaks* (London, 1939). The book was prepared with the help of the American journalist Emory Reves and was almost certainly a fabrication or elaboration based on recollections of Hitler's remarks together with quotations from other accounts of his conversations. The validity of the book as a historical source has invited continuous debate. See T. Schieder, *Rauschnings 'Gespräche mit Hitler' als Geschichtsquelle* (Opladen, 1972); P. Nordblom, 'Wider die These von der bewussten Fälschung. Bemerkungen zu den "Gesprächen mit Hitler"', in J. Heusel and P. Nordblom (eds.), *Hermann Rauschning. Materialen und Beiträge zu einer politischen Biographie* (Warsaw, 2002).

33. Hermann Rauschning, 'Introduction', in H. Baynes, *Germany Possessed* (London, 1941), pp. 12–13.

34. Baynes, *Germany Possessed*, pp. 16–19.

35. Ibid., p. 243.

36. V. Brittain, *Testament of Experience* (London, 1957), p. 98.

37. D. N. Pritt, *The Autobiography of D. N. Pritt: Part I, From Right to Left* (London, 1965), pp. 41, 53–5.

38. Ibid., p. 57; Brittain, *Testament of Experience*, p. 98.

39. Relief Committee for the Victims of German Fascism, *The Burning of the Reichstag: Official Findings of the Legal Commission of Inquiry, London, Sept. 1933* (London, 1933), pp. 2–3, 15–16; Brittain, *Testament of Experience*, pp. 99–100.

40. German Information Bureau, *The Oberfohren Memorandum: What German Conservatives Thought about the Reichstag Fire* (London, 1933), pp. 5–6.

41. Relief Committee, *Burning of the Reichstag*, p. 24.

42. K. Heiden, *A History of National Socialism* (London, 1934), p. 228.

43. University Library, Cambridge, Joseph Needham papers, K/40, exhibition programme 'Fascism & War', 4–9 Nov. 1935, p. 4. The terror following the fire was described as 'a new Bartholomew's Eve, a night of arrests, pogrom-killings and mediaeval tortures in the Brown House [NSDAP headquarters]'.

44. A. Dallin and F. I. Firsov (eds.), *Dimitrov & Stalin, 1934–1943: Letters from the Soviet Archives* (New Haven, 2000), pp. 5–6.

45. Churchill College, Cambridge, Archive Centre (CCAC), Noel-Baker papers, 9/94, F. W. Pethick-Lawrence to Philip Noel-Baker, 16 Feb. and 1 March 1934; Pethick-Lawrence to Noel-Baker, 9 March 1934, encl. 'Memorial: Draft' and list of signatures. On Dorothy Martin see K. Martin, *Editor: A Second Volume of Autobiography, 1931–1945* (London, 1968), pp. 157–8. Torgler's release was announced in Britain in summer 1935. See *Evening News*, 14 June 1935, 'Torgler May Have to Stay'.

46. *The Reichstag Fire Trial: The Second Brown Book of the Hitler Terror* (London, 1934), pp. vii–ix, appendix pp. 338–62. The book was compiled by exiled German communists. See D. Cesarani, *Arthur Koestler: The Homeless Mind* (London, 1998), pp. 105–6.

47. LSE, Pritt papers, 2/12, Dr Wolf, Deutsche Akademie, Berlin, to Pritt, 11 July 1969; Director, George-Dimitroff Museum to Pritt, 30 Dec. 1970. Pritt replied on 9 Jan. 1971 that the trial seemed to him 'of yesterday'. On the Mann/Pollitt trial see J. Mahon, *Harry Pollitt: A Biography* (London, 1976), pp. 186–7.

48. N. Bentwich, *The Refugees from Germany: April 1933 to December 1935* (Report of the High Commission for Refugees) (London, 1936), pp. 107–13.

49. Ibid., p. 63; CCAC, Noel-Baker papers, 4/269, President, Ligue des Droits de l'Homme to Sir John Simon, 12 April 1933.

50. Bodleian Library, Society for the Protection of Science and Learning

(SPSL) papers, 1/8, Academic Assistance Council circular letter, 22 May 1933; Academic Assistance Council letter to all vice-chancellors, 16 June 1933. See too D. Snowman, *The Hitler Emigrés: The Cultural Impact on Britain of Refugees from Nazism* (London, 2003), pp. 101–5; J. Medawar and D. Pyke, *Hitler's Gift* (London, 2000), pp. 52–8.

51. Bodleian Library, SPSL papers, 1/9, C. Cooley (Refugee Assistance Fund) to William Beveridge, 21 Sept. and 23 Sept. 1933.

52. Ibid., Beveridge to Geoffrey Dawson, 27 Sept. 1933; BBC payment slip, 3 Oct. 1933. Einstein was paid 10 guineas (£10 10s) for the broadcast.

53. Ibid., programme, Royal Albert Hall meeting, 3 Oct. 1933; Walter Adams (General Secretary of the AAC) to Beveridge, 1 Oct. 1933, encl., 'Draft Notes of Platform Speeches, Einstein Meeting', pp. 8, 9; Bentwich, *Refugees*, p. 47.

54. Bodleian Library, SPSL papers, 51/1, digest of replies from vice-chancellors (n.d. but June 1933); A. W. Pickard-Cambridge (vice-chancellor, University of Sheffield) to Beveridge, 21 June 1933; W. B. Brander (secretary of the Universities Bureau of the British Empire) to Beveridge, 3 July 1933, reporting the meeting of the Committee of Vice-Chancellors and Principals where 'there were strong objections to utilizing free money for other than their own students and staff'.

55. Ibid., 1/1–6, Academic Assistance Council, annual report, 1 May 1934, pp. 4–6, 12–13; SPSL, fourth annual report, Nov. 1938; 59/1, notes for a talk, 'Displaced University Teachers', 13 Nov. 1937, esp. p. 5 on Italian victims of fascism: 'They have received less organised assistance than any other class of scholar exile'; 3/2, SPSL Executive Committee meeting, 12 May 1938, appendix, 'Refugee Scholars from Spain'.

56. Ibid., 59/1, reprint of 'Freedom of the Mind', *Nature*, 139 (1937), pp. 2–4.

57. Bentwich, *Refugees*, pp. 199–200.

58. G. E. R. Gedye, 'Impressions of Hitler's Germany', *Contemporary Review*, 143 (Jan.–June 1933), pp. 669–73.

59. CCAC, Noel-Baker papers, 4/270 (file 2), memorandum, Germany Emergency Committee, notes on cases (n.d.); Germany Emergency Committee, 'Internment Camps', 24 July 1934; Germany Emergency Committee, 'Report of W. R. Hughes on a Visit to Lichtenburg Concentration Camp', 1 June 1934; (file 3) Commission of Enquiry, Labour and Socialist International, Zürich, 'Communications on the Conditions of Political Prisoners', 30 Dec. 1933. See too Strachey papers (in private possession), Box 2, 'The Other Germany: Bulletin of the Ernst Eckstein Fund', Jan.–Feb. 1935, with appended list of workers killed or beheaded.

60. Churchill College, Cambridge, Noel-Baker papers, 4/270 (file 3), Wickham Steed to *The Times*, 23 Jan. 1934.

61. Ibid. (file 1), extract from *The Times*, 25 Aug. 1934.

62. Ibid., letter to *The Times*, 16 Aug. 1934 signed 'W'; 'Herr Hitler's Call', *The Times*, 8 Sept. 1934.

63. N. Annan, *Our Age: The Generation that Made Post-War Britain* (London, 1990), p. 234. For the view that the British press and sections of the elite were seduced by Hitlerism see B. Granzow, *A Mirror of Nazism: British Opinion and the Emergence of Hitler, 1929–1933* (London, 1964). For a more balanced view see D. Stone, *Responses to Nazism in Britain, 1933–1939* (London, 2003), esp. pp. 1–13.

64. University of Exeter, Special Collections, Williamson letters, MS 106, Box 1, Williamson to Eric Watkins, 4 May 1945.

65. W. Lewis, *The Hitler Cult* (London, 1939), pp. vii, 132. See too O'Keeffe, *Some Sort of Genius*, p. 399. The book was originally titled 'The Jingo God'.

66. Bodleian Library, Toynbee papers, Box 76, memorandum, 'After Munich: The World Outlook', 1 Nov. 1938, p. 28.

67. E. O. Lorimer, *What Hitler Wants* (London, 1939), p. 185.

68. D. B. Lloyd, 'The World and Mr Wells', *Quarterly Review*, 259 (July–Oct. 1932), pp. 56–7. On Wells's view of Stalin and the Soviet experiment see too 'Stalin and Wells: A Comment by Bernard Shaw', *New Statesman*, 8 (July–Dec. 1934), pp. 613–14, and H. G. Wells, 'A Reply to Mr Shaw', ibid., pp. 654–5.

69. CCAC, Noel-Baker papers, 8/3/3, Lionel Fielden (BBC) to Noel-Baker, 6 March 1931, pp. 1–2.

70. South Place Ethical Society Library, list of lectures 1930–39.

71. Nuffield College, Oxford, Cole papers, A1/75/3, draft article, 'Eyes on Russia', for the *Clarion* (n.d. but 1931), p. 43. It was vital, wrote Cole, 'that the Russian adventure should succeed'.

72. Ibid., A1/60/3, draft note for *Labour Monthly*, 17 Sept. 1937.

73. Trinity College, Cambridge, Dobb archive, DD 57, notes for a lecture to Putney Literary Institute, 30 Jan. 1935, pp. 4–6.

74. Ibid., CA32, Margaret Cleeve (RIIA) to Dobb, 4 Feb. 1933, encl. draft, 'Validity of Marxism To-Day'; original draft of lecture in DD46, draft, 'The Validity of Marxism', p. 1.

75. Warwick University Modern Records Centre, Gollancz papers, MSS 157/3/RU/14, M. E. Pheysey to Gollancz, 22 Jan. 1936.

76. H. Nicholson, *Half My Days and Nights: A Memoir of the 1920s and 1930s* (London, 1941), pp. 137–8.

77. Warwick University Modern Records Centre, Gollancz papers, MSS 157/3/RU/15, SCR eleventh annual report, 1934–5, p. 4; Society for Co-operation in Russian and Soviet Studies archive, London (SCRSS), Box 1, Events SCR 1924–42, dinner invitations, menus and programmes.

78. Warwick University Modern Records Centre, Gollancz papers, SCR eleventh annual report, pp. 3–4; SCRSS, Box 1, Events SCR 1924–42, programme of summer fête, 15 June 1935.

79. Warwick University Modern Records Centre, Gollancz papers, MSS 157/3/RU/9, Josephine Smith (secretary of Committee) to Gollancz, 4 Oct. 1936; MSS 157/3/RU/10, Josephine Smith to Gollancz, 13 Jan. 1936.

80. Nuffield College, Oxford, Cole papers, A1/75/5, A. S. Hooper to Cole, 8 March 1937; A1/75/7, official programme, second congress, 13–14 March 1937; A1/75/8, *Manchester Guardian*, 15 March 1937 'Russia's Loyalty to the League'.

81. Warwick University Modern Records Centre, Gollancz papers, MSS 157/3/RU/1–41, Gollancz to William Brittain, 5 Nov. 1937. Gollancz was invited to a dinner in Holborn for the twentieth anniversary, where the Labour leader Clement Attlee and the Soviet ambassador Ivan Maisky were both due to speak (MSS 157/3/POL/1–106).

82. Annan, *Our Age*, p. 240.

83. King's College, Cambridge, Forster papers, EMF 18/553, Forster to Elizabeth Trevelyan, 10 Oct. 1937.

84. Nuffield College, Oxford, Cole papers, A1/75/15, Cole letter to *The Times*, 2 May 1933; A3/3/3/4, fragment of a play (n.d.). The idea that Soviet success would nonetheless create the conditions that would force reform in Britain was developed by Cole in his 1931 article for the *Clarion* (see n. 71): 'I believe success in Russia would speedily alter the entire face of British politics ... It would mean the formulation of a plan for the complete reorganization of the British economic system ...'

85. LSE, Passfield papers, 2/3/1, Sidney Webb to Beatrice Webb, 24 June 1932.

86. Ibid., Sidney Webb to Beatrice Webb, 5 Feb. 1934.

87. University Library, Cambridge, J. D. Bernal papers, ADD MS 8287, Box 90, L.4, 'Programme of the Party of English Scientists', 13 Aug. 1931; SCR tour of scientists, list of visits in USSR, 18 July 1931; list of members of party of scientists, 18 July 1931; Box 51, B.4.13, draft essay, 'What Is an intellectual?' (n.d. but 1931), pp. 2, 14.

88. LSE, Passfield papers, 2/4/J, Margaret Cole to Beatrice Webb, 11 Sept. 1932.

89. D. N. Pritt, 'The Russian Legal System', in M. I. Cole (ed.), *Twelve Studies in Soviet Russia* (London, 1933), pp. 161–4, 168, 175; Pritt, *Autobiography: Part I*, pp. 36–9, who added the disingenuous claim that his was 'the most left-wing of the studies'.

90. H. Dalton, 'A General View of the Soviet Economy with Special Reference to Planning', in Cole, *Twelve Studies*, pp. 32–4.

91. S. Spender, *Forward from Liberalism* (London, 1937), pp. 24–5. The original title was to have been 'Approach to Communism', Warwick University Modern Records Centre, Gollancz papers, MSS 318/2/1/10, Production Book, 1936–7.

92. For an excellent introduction to the story of the book see K. Morgan, *The Webbs and Soviet Communism* (London, 2006), pp. 208–13.

93. M. Cole (ed.), *Beatrice Webb's Diaries, 1924–1932* (London, 1956), p. 305, entry for 5 April 1932.

94. LSE, Passfield papers, 2/3/1, Sidney Webb to Beatrice Webb, 20, 21, 22, 23 June 1932; quotation in letter of 24 June 1932.

95. Ibid., Sidney Webb to Beatrice Webb, 25 June 1932.

96. Ibid., Sidney Webb to Beatrice Webb, 22 and 29 Jan. 1934.

97. Ibid., 7/1/58, Beatrice Webb, 'Russian Trip' (n.d. but July 1932), pp. 11, 20.

98. Ibid., 2/3/1, Sidney Webb to Beatrice Webb, 7 and 9 Sept. 1934.

99. Ibid., Sidney Webb to Beatrice Webb, 10, 13 and 30 Sept. 1934.

100. Ibid., Sidney Webb to Beatrice Webb, 29 Jan. 1934.

101. S. Webb and B. Webb, *Soviet Communism: A New Civilisation?* (2 vols., London, 1935). Advertisement in LSE, Passfield papers, 5/2/1, Longman & Co. publicity leaflet, 1935.

102. Webb and Webb, *Soviet Communism*, pp. 431–2; Morgan, *Webbs and Soviet Communism*, pp. 218–20; Thorpe, 'Stalinism and British Politics', pp. 620–21.

103. Webb and Webb, *Soviet Communism*, pp. 438–9.

104. LSE, Passfield papers, 2/4/J, Toynbee to Beatrice Webb, 15 May 1935, pp. 2–4.

105. Ibid., Toynbee to Beatrice Webb, 19 May and 1 Oct. 1935, p. 4.

106. Bodleian Library, Toynbee papers, Box 86, Beatrice Webb to Toynbee, 23 Aug., 3 Sept. and 4 Oct. 1935. In the last letter she assured Toynbee that atheism was not necessarily a part of Soviet dogma. Christianity, she continued, 'seems far more in harmony with Soviet economics than with capitalist economics'.

107. Webb and Webb, *Soviet Communism*, pp. 1119–41.

108. LSE, Passfield papers, 5/2/1, Longman & Co., 'Postscript Notice', 1937; Fabian Society papers, A/4/14, Sidney Webb to F. Galton, 2 Sept. 1937.

109. Warwick University Modern Records Centre, Gollancz papers, MSS 318/2/1/11, Production Book, 1936–7 (total sales were 15,372); MSS 157/4/LB/1, 'Soviet Communism: What the Authors Say about the New Edition', *Left News*, Aug. 1937, p. 468.

110. Ibid., MSS 157/4/LB/1, G. B. Shaw, 'The Webbs' Masterpiece', *Left*

News, Aug. 1937, p. 467; LSE, Passfield papers, 5/2/3, G. B. Shaw's corrections to cover draft of popular edition of *Soviet Communism*, Sept. 1941; *Picture Post*, 13 Sept. 1941, pp. 20–23; 7/2/13, galley proofs of introduction '1941'.

111. Warwick University Modern Records Centre, Gollancz papers, MSS 157/4/LB/2/1, Left Book Club membership leaflet, 1937, p. 3; LSE, Fabian Society papers, Sidney Webb to Galton, 2 Sept. 1937. Figure of 30,000 from preface to second edition of *Soviet Communism*. On the WEA National Museum of Labour History, Manchester (NMLH), Brailsford papers, HNB/2, Harold Shearman (WEA) to Brailsford, 10 March 1937.

112. *Left Review*, 2 (1936), p. 698, and back cover, Dec. 1936.

113. LSE, Passfield papers, 2/4/J, Malcolm Muggeridge to Beatrice Webb, 8 Feb. 1933, p. 2.

114. Ibid., 7/1/86, Beatrice Webb, 'A Memo on the Meaning of the Moscow Trials', p. 1. Beatrice blamed the conspiracy on the failure of leading Bolsheviks to shed the habits of underworld politics absorbed before 1917.

115. Ibid., 2/5/6, Beatrice Webb to H. G. Wells, May 1937.

116. Ibid., 6/90, draft transcript of broadcast, 4 Feb. 1938, 'Efficiency and Liberty in Russia', p. 9.

117. Martin, *Editor*, p. 75.

118. E. H. Carr, 'Russia through Fabian Eyes', *Fortnightly Review*, 139 (Jan.–June 1936), pp. 243–4; review by H. Laski of *Stalin* by Henri Barbusse, in the *New Statesman and Nation*, 10 (July–Dec. 1935), pp. 646–8. Laski regarded it as nothing but hagiography, 'a pamphlet that will edify the faithful'. On his views of the Webbs' book: LSE, Passfield papers, 2/4/J, Harold Laski to Beatrice Webb, 9 March 1935.

119. See on this Thorpe, 'Stalinism and British Politics', pp. 622–6; P. Corthorn, 'Labour, the Left, and the Stalinist Purges of the Late 1930s', *Historical Journal*, 48 (2005), pp. 179–207.

120. Nuffield College, Oxford, Cole papers, A1/75/15, letter to *The Times*, 2 May 1933.

121. University of Exeter, Special Collections, Rowse papers, MS113, 2/1/10b, diary manuscript March 1935–Aug. 1939, entry for 29 April 1936. See too Maurice Dobb's comment in his lecture on 'The Validity of Marxism' in which he argued that the kulaks must have been capitalists because otherwise there would have been no conflict with them! (Trinity College, Cambridge, Dobb archive, CA32, 'The Validity of Marxism To-Day', p. 23).

122. University College, London, Haldane papers, Box 7, draft, 'Democracy' (n.d.), pp. 3–4.

123. NMLH, Brailsford papers, HNB/2, Victor Gollancz to Brailsford, 10 Dec. 1937, p. 3.

124. King's College, Cambridge, Forster papers, EMF 18/148, Forster to Cecil Day Lewis, 30 Oct. 1938.

125. LSE, Carr-Saunders papers, B/3/4, British Institute of Public Opinion, 'What Britain Thinks', 1939, pp. 19–20.

126. On the reconstruction of the centre see J. Stapleton, 'Resisting the Centre at the Extremes: "English" Liberalism in the Political Thought of Inter-war Britain', *British Journal of Politics and International Relations*, 1 (1999), pp. 270–92, who argues that only planning really separated British liberals from the progressive left. On the appeal of Baldwin's world view see P. Williamson, 'The Doctrinal Politics of Stanley Baldwin', in M. Bentley (ed.), *Public and Private Doctrine: Essays in British History Presented to Maurice Cowling* (Cambridge, 1993), pp. 181–208. The best accounts of the rise of a progressive centre are to be found in D. Blaazer, *The Popular Front and the Progressive Tradition: Socialists, Liberals and the Quest for Unity, 1884–1939* (Cambridge, 1992), chs. 6, 7, and D. Ritschel, *The Politics of Planning: The Debate of Economic Planning in Britain in the 1930s* (Oxford, 1997), esp. pp. 280–315.

127. CCAC, Noel-Baker papers, 8/16 (4), notes for a lecture on 'European Tendencies' to the Women's Institutes' Conference, 19 Nov. 1936, pp. 9–10.

128. S. Jameson, 'A Faith Worth Dying For', *Fortnightly Review*, 135 (Jan.–June 1934), p. 418.

129. King's College, Cambridge, Forster papers, EMF 6/7, transcript of BBC broadcast 'Efficiency and Liberty: A Discussion between Capt. A. M. Ludovici and E. M. Forster', 4 March 1938, pp. 1, 3. See too P. N. Furbank, *E. M. Forster: A Life* (London, 1977), pp. 224–9 on Forster's pessimism in 1938.

130. CCAC, Noel-Baker papers, 4/249, manifesto, 'Liberty and Democratic Leadership' (n.d. but Feb. 1934), p. 2; 'Liberty and Democratic Leadership: A Further Statement' (n.d. but May 1934) had a set of proposed policy areas for lobbying the government and educating public opinion. The manifestos were reproduced in *The Next Five Years: An Essay in Political Agreement* (London, 1935), pp. 312–15. See too Ritschel, *Politics of Planning*, pp. 246–7.

131. Churchill College, Cambridge, Noel-Baker papers, 4/249, 'Liberty and Democratic Leadership', pp. 3–4.

132. R. Fraser, 'The Front Against Fascism', in G. Catlin (ed.), *New Trends in Socialism* (London, 1935), pp. 77–8. See too Martin, *Editor*, p. 149, who described fascism in the 1930s as 'a loosely used word' to describe fears that 'capitalists would become increasingly afraid for their property and find a way of destroying our civil liberties'.

133. University of Sussex Library, Leonard Woolf papers, MS 13, part I, G.6, Charles Mauron to Leonard Woolf, 20 Oct. 1935 ('Ensuite mobiliser le plus grand nombre possible de "big names" dans nos deux pays pour exercer une influence morale'); University Library, Cambridge, Joseph Needham papers, K/321, Leonard Woolf, Philip Noel-Baker and E. M. Forster to Joseph Needham, 22 Nov. 1935.

134. University Library, Cambridge, Joseph Needham papers, K/321, memorandum by Margaret Gardiner (n.d. but Dec. 1935); University Library, Cambridge, For Intellectual Liberty (FIL) papers, ADD 9369/A1, minutes of meeting of Provisional Committee of the Paris Conference, 5 Dec. 1935. Forster comment in King's College, Cambridge, Forster papers, EMF 18/608, Forster to Leonard Woolf, 21 March 1935.

135. University Library, Cambridge, FIL papers, ADD 9369/A1, minutes of meetings, 5 Dec. 1935, 9 Feb. 1936.

136. Ibid. (Bernal collection), ADD 9369/B3, founding pamphlet, 'For Intellectual Liberty', May 1936, p. 2; King's College, Cambridge, Rosamond Lehmann papers, Misc. 42B/9, programme, 'Writers Against Fascism', 8 June 1938, pp. 1, 9: 'Fascism is the political embodiment of all those forces, of ignorance, intolerance, violence, militarism and contempt for the individual . . .'

137. University Library, Cambridge, FIL papers, ADD 9369/A1, minutes of meeting, 21 Sept. 1936; University of Sussex Library, Leonard Woolf papers, MS 13, part I, G.6, circular letter from Comité de Vigilance to Leonard Woolf, 15 Oct. 1935. See the discussion on the term 'intellectual' in S. Collini, *Absent Minds: Intellectuals in Britain* (Oxford, 2006), pp. 1–3.

138. University Library, Cambridge, FIL papers, ADD 9369/A3/1, minute, 'For Intellectual Liberty: Report on the BBC', June 1936; memorandum by E. M. Forster and Rose Macaulay, 'For Intellectual Liberty: Note on the BBC' (n.d. but June 1936), p. 1. On 'Brainy Men' ADD 9369/A2, *Star*, Dec. 1936.

139. Ibid., ADD 9369/B1, Forster to Miss Pritchett, 24 Feb. 1937; ADD 9369/A4, FIL to all members, 31 Jan. 1938, pp. 1–2.

140. A. L. Rowse, 'A British Popular Front?', *Quarterly Review*, 266 (Jan.–April 1936), pp. 328–35; Blaazer, *Popular Front*, pp. 174–7; *The 'Next Five Years' Group* (London, 1935), pp. 2–4. The Group included among its sponsors Lord Robert Cecil, the Archbishop of York, the Marquess of Lothian, Norman Angell, Julian Huxley and A. Barratt Brown, who acted as the general secretary and who had also helped to organize the 1934 manifestos on liberty and democratic leadership. See too B. Pimlott, *Hugh Dalton* (London, 1985), pp. 219–21.

141. A. Horne, *Macmillan, 1894–1956* (London, 1988), p. 105.

142. Nuffield College, Oxford, Cole papers, D5/1/10, minutes of New Out-look meeting, 15 Oct. 1936; D5/2/2, Cole to Allan Young, 22 June 1936; D5/2/16, J. Murphy (secretary of Popular Front Propaganda Committee) to Cole (n.d. but 25 Nov. 1936?).

143. Ibid., D5/2/1, Allan Young to Cole, 19 June 1936, encl., 'The Popular Front', p. 1; D5/2/16, 'List of people invited to the meeting of November 26 1936'; D5/2/16 (2), circular letter from Allan Young, 'Notes to the Speakers at Friends House December 14', 2 Dec. 1936.

144. Ibid., D5/2/24, Cole to Stephen Spender, 8 Jan. 1937, p. 4. See too Blaazer, *Popular Front*, pp. 175–6; Ritschel, *Politics of Planning*, pp. 308–10; NMLH, Labour Party papers, NEC minutes, 17 and 24 March 1937.

145. Strachey papers, Box 4, Richard Acland to Gollancz, 6 Feb. 1937.

146. Trinity College, Cambridge, Layton papers, Box 8, Allan Young to Layton, 7 April 1937; Programme, weekend conference at Berystede Hotel, Ascot, 23–24 Oct. 1937; report of conference at Ascot, Oct. 1937.

147. R. D. Edwards, *Victor Gollancz: A Biography* (London, 1987) for details of his early life, pp. 93–4 for his court-martial. Warwick University Modern Records Centre, Gollancz papers, MSS 157/4/LB/2, Left Book Club leaflet, p. 1.

148. Edwards, *Gollancz*, p. 238.

149. Strachey papers, Box 3, Gollancz to Strachey, 26 Feb. 1936.

150. Warwick University Modern Records Centre, Gollancz papers, MSS 157/4/LB/2, *Left Book News*, June 1936; MSS 157/4/LB/1, *Left Book News*, Aug., Sept. and Dec. 1936.

151. Ibid., *Left Book News*, Oct. 1936; MSS 157/4/LB/2, Left Book Club leaflet, Sept. 1938.

152. Gollancz papers, MSS 318/2/1/11, Production Book, 1936–7.

153. Strachey papers, Box 4, Gollancz to Strachey, 29 Sept. 1937.

154. T. Rodgers, 'The Right Book Club: Text Wars, Modernity and Cultural Politics in the Late Thirties', *Literature and History*, 12 (2003), pp. 1–4. On the role of the right in general see R. Griffiths, *Fellow-Travellers of the Right: British Enthusiasts for Nazi Germany, 1933–1939* (Oxford, 1983).

155. A. Lane, 'Books for the Millions', *Left Review*, 4 (1938), p. 969. See too Stone, *Responses to Nazism*, p. 5.

156. Bristol University, Special Collections, Allen Lane archive, DM 1819/10/8, notebook, list of publications, 1935–40, Specials S1–S60; statistics on earnings. The raw figures show earnings of £55,724 in 1936 and £156,227 in 1939. See too J. E. Morpurgo, *Allen Lane: King Penguin* (London, 1979), pp. 130–32. When some hostile critics suggested that Lane was in fact a

communist because of some of the books he published he reacted, according to Morpurgo, with 'bewilderment' and 'spluttering protests'. Also W. E. Williams, *Allen Lane: A Personal Portrait* (London, 1973), pp. 54–6. Some Specials sold up to 250,000.

157. Bristol University, Special Collections, Allen Lane archive, DM 1294, scrapbook (ii), cutting from the *Democrat*, March 1939.

158. Ibid., *Manchester Evening News*, review, 27 Feb. 1939; 'Vigilantes', *Between Two Wars* (London, 1939), p. 8.

159. G. D. H. Cole, *The People's Front* (London, 1937), pp. 357–9 reproduced the manifesto.

160. University Library, Cambridge, FIL papers, ADD 9369/B1, Leonard Woolf to Margaret Gardiner, 1 Aug. 1936.

161. FIL papers, ADD 9369/B1, R. H. Tawney to Margaret Gardiner, 26 Sept. and 14 Dec. 1936; King's College, Cambridge, Rosamond Lehmann papers, Misc. 42/37, Forster to Lehmann, 27 April 1938.

162. King's College, Cambridge, Rosamond Lehmann papers, Misc. 42/35, Virginia Woolf to Rosamond Lehmann (n.d. but early 1937); University Library, Cambridge, FIL papers, ADD 9369/B1, Aldous Huxley to Margaret Gardiner (n.d. but June 1937); Kingsley Martin to P. S. Blackett, 3 June 1937.

163. CCAC, Noel-Baker papers, 2/34, circular letter, Labour Party to all affiliated organizations, 26 May 1937.

164. Ibid., Margaret McCarthy (Socialist League) to all members, 19 May 1937.

165. Ibid., Marxist Group to J. Middleton (Labour Party general secretary) (n.d. but Aug. 1937?); manifesto of the CPGB for Labour Party annual conference 1937, 'We stand for Democracy. We stand for Peace'.

166. Cole, *People's Front*, p. 35.

167. Trinity College, Cambridge, Pethick-Lawrence papers, 1/164, Cole to Pethick-Lawrence, 2 July 1937.

168. CCAC, Noel-Baker papers, 2/40, Labour Party Head Office, report re resolutions on 'Peace Alliance', 'Popular Front', 'Spain' etc. up to 4 May 1938, Table II, Table III. NMLH, Labour Party papers, NEC minutes, minutes of meeting, 5 May 1938.

169. Ibid., report re resolutions, pp. 7–9.

170. Ibid., memorandum for members of the National Executive Committee, 5 May 1938, p. 3.

171. NMLH, Labour Party papers, NEC minutes, minutes of Elections Sub-Committee, 2 May 1938, attached to NEC meeting, 26 May 1938, pp. 8–10.

172. Ibid., NEC minutes, 13 Jan. 1939.

173. CCAC, Noel-Baker papers, 2/40, Labour Party leaflet no. 85; Blaazer, *Popular Front*, pp. 187–9; Trinity College, Cambridge, Pethick-Lawrence papers, 5/51, Stafford Cripps to Pethick-Lawrence, Jan. 1939; Trinity College, Cambridge, Layton papers, Box 8, Cripps to Layton, 27 March 1939, encl., 'The Petition of the British People to the Labour, Liberal and Co-Operative Parties'.

174. Churchill College, Cambridge, Noel-Baker papers, 2/40, R. H. Tawney, Leonard Woolf, Sidney and Beatrice Webb, J. A. Hobson to Middleton (n.d. but March 1939); Canterbury Divisional Labour Party to NEC, 1 May 1938. Noel-Baker considered Cripps 'lamentable' and 'destructive': see Trinity College, Cambridge, Layton papers, Box 7, Noel-Baker to Layton, 14 Feb. 1939.

175. Churchill College, Cambridge, Noel-Baker papers, 2/41, William Jones to Noel-Baker, 28 April 1938; Charles King to Noel-Baker, 9 March 1939. There are many more letters in the files from 1938 and 1939 with identical sentiments.

176. King's College, Cambridge, Forster papers, EMF 18/148, Forster to Cecil Day Lewis, 6 June 1936.

177. University Library, Cambridge, FIL papers, ADD 9369/A2, 'The Task of the Intellectual', *Manchester Evening News*, 27 Jan. 1939.

Chapter 8: The Voyage of the 'Death Ship': War and the Fate of the World

1. H. Dalton, *Hitler's War: Before and After* (London, 1940), p. 9.

2. John Wheeler-Bennet, 'Introduction', in H. R. Knickerbocker, *Will War Come to Europe?* (London, 1934), p. v.

3. Knickerbocker, *Will War Come?*, pp. 51, 54, 92, 127, 177, 269–71.

4. Inter-Parliamentary Union, *What Would Be the Character of a New War?* (2nd edn, London, 1933), p. iii; N. Royde-Smith, review of H. G. Wells, *The Shape of Things to Come*, in the *Fortnightly Review*, 134 (July–Dec. 1933), p. 506.

5. Ibid., pp. 506–7.

6. D. W. Brogan, 'Omens of 1936', *Fortnightly Review*, 139 (Jan.–June 1936), pp. 1–2, 6.

7. Warwick University Modern Records Centre, Gollancz papers, MSS 157/4/LB/2, *Left Book News*, June 1936, pp. 23–4.

8. London School of Economics (LSE), Passfield papers, 2/4/K, Louis Fischer to Beatrice Webb, 14 Jan. 1936.

9. LSE, Fabian Society papers, J16/10, New Fabian Research Bureau, 'The

Strategic Situation in Europe', 18–19 June 1938; C18, Fabian Society Executive Committee Meeting, 22 July 1937, list of lectures; University Library, Cambridge, J. D. Bernal papers, ADD MS 8287, Box 90, University of London, Saturday School programme, March 1938. See too K. Martin, 'Present World War', *Plan*, 5 (1938), pp. 4–10.

10. LSE, National Peace Council papers, 2/5, NPC statement, 'Peace and the Democracies', 12 April 1938.

11. L. Paul, 'The European Peril', *Plan*, 3 (1936), p. 2.

12. University of Exeter, Special Collections, Rowse papers, MS 113, 2/1/10b, diary manuscript March 1935–Aug. 1939, entry for 17 Aug. 1937. The quotations are taken from the handwritten original, much of which was later altered by Rowse.

13. LSE, Malinowski papers, 29/5, Malinowski to Ruth Fry, 13 Jan. 1936.

14. Bodleian Library, Ponsonby papers, MS Eng. Hist. C679, A. Ruth Fry, 'Asses, Fools and Prating Coxcombs', speech given at Manchester, 7 Feb. 1937, reprinted March 1937, p. 4.

15. E. Jones, 'The Individual and Society', *Sociological Review*, 27 (1935), p. 262.

16. N. Maclean, *How Shall We Escape? Learn or Perish* (London, 1934), pp. 174–5.

17. Guglielmo Ferrero, 'Ferrero on War', *Quarterly Review*, 261 (July–Oct. 1933), p. 337.

18. L. P. Jacks, 'The Future of the League', *Fortnightly Review*, 140 (July–Dec. 1936), pp. 397, 402.

19. LSE, National Peace Council papers, 13/17, *Peace Year Book, 1937* (London, 1937), pp. 9–21.

20. N. Annan, *Our Age: The Generation That Made Post-War Britain* (London, 1990), pp. 247, 252.

21. Warwick University Modern Records Centre, Gollancz papers, MSS 157/3/102/1, Driberg to Gollancz, 4 April 1938, encl., 'Their Other Anthem'. During the rally Dean Inge claimed 50,000 had been butchered in Madrid and Barcelona by the Reds; Sir Henry Page Croft claimed that 80–100,000 'foreigners' were fighting with the Reds, at which point someone in the audience shouted out, 'Jews!'

22. E. Moradiellos, 'The Origins of British Non-Intervention in the Spanish Civil War: Anglo-Spanish Relations in Early 1936', *European History Quarterly*, 21 (1991), p. 359; G. Howson, *Arms for Spain: The Untold Story of the Spanish Civil War* (London, 1998), pp. 53, 114, 115–18.

23. R. Graves and A. Hodge, *The Long Week-End: A Social History of Great Britain, 1918–1939* (London, 1940), p. 337.

24. D. Gascoyne, *David Gascoyne: Collected Journals, 1936–42* (London, 1991), p. 26.

25. Bodleian Library, MS Autogr. d.39, John Boulting to Marjorie Battcock, 24 Feb. 1937.

26. Ibid., Boulting to Battcock, 16 May 1937 ('not so very far from Madrid').

27. J. Symons, *The Thirties: A Dream Revolved* (London, 1960), pp. 109–11. The figure of 2,300 from R. Baxell, *British Volunteers in the Spanish Civil War: The British Battalion in the International Brigades, 1936–1939* (London, 2004), pp. 8–9. This figure includes those who volunteered for the Brigade, but does not include the other irregulars and volunteers, or the contingent from the Independent Labour Party which fought with the POUM (see p. 323). See too T. Buchanan, *Britain and the Spanish Civil War* (Cambridge, 1997), pp. 122–45.

28. Symons, *The Thirties*, p. 109.

29. Trinity College, Cambridge, Layton papers, Box 11, appeal from the International Brigade, 25 April 1938. On motivation see the useful examples in Baxell, *British Volunteers*, pp. 26–30. An interesting account of the tensions between expectation and reality and memory can be found in J. McLellan, 'The Politics of Communist Biography: Alfred Kantorowitz and the Spanish Civil War', *German History*, 22 (2004), esp. pp. 545–50.

30. National Museum of Labour History (NMLH), Manchester, Brailsford papers, HNB/3, 'International Brigade', *News Chronicle*, 30 Dec. 1936.

31. NMLH, Edwards papers, Box 5, Bob Edwards to May Edwards, 3 Feb. 1937.

32. P. Davison (ed.), *Orwell in Spain* (London, 2001), p. 4: Orwell radio broadcast 'As I Please', 42, 15 Sept. 1944.

33. NMLH, Edwards papers, Box 5, *Birmingham Post*, 6 Aug. 1966, Midland magazine section.

34. Davison, *Orwell in Spain*, pp. 24–7; see too G. Orwell, *The Collected Essays, Journalism and Letters*, vol. I (London, 1968), pp. 311–12, Orwell to Rayner Heppenstall, 31 July 1937. Orwell collected all the newspaper reports of the alleged POUM uprising so that he could demonstrate their mendacity. See University College, London, Orwell archive, C/3b, C/3d. Only the *Manchester Guardian* printed Orwell's protests. The *News Chronicle* and the *Daily Herald*, both left-wing newspapers, declined or refused to acknowledge Orwell's correspondence.

35. Davison, *Orwell in Spain*, pp. 245–7, Orwell to Charles Doran, 2 Aug. 1937.

36. C. Caudwell, *Studies and Further Studies in a Dying Culture* (New York, 1949), pp. v, xi, introduction by John Strachey. See too J. K. Hopkins, *Into* *the Heart of the Fire: The British in the Spanish Civil War* (Stanford, Calif., 1998), pp. 60–66.

37. Annan, *Our Age,* p. 250; Baxell, *British Volunteers*, pp. 64–5. *Left Review*, 3 (1937), pp. 67–8 for Cornford's obituary; also pp. 2–4 for obituary of Ralph Fox, who died on the same front a few days after Cornford.

38. University of Sussex Library, Leonard Woolf papers, MS 13, part II, D.5a, Spender to Virginia Woolf, 15 Feb. and 2 April 1937. See too J. Sutherland, *Stephen Spender: The Authorized Biography* (London, 2004), pp. 221–2.

39. J. Mepham, *Virginia Woolf: A Literary Life* (London, 1991), p. 166.

40. King's College, Cambridge, Julian Bell papers, 4/14, obituary of Julian Bell, *The Leightonian*, 15 (Dec. 1937), pp. 164–5; Spanish Medical Aid Committee, bulletin, Aug. 1937, p. 3.

41. J. T. Banks (ed.), *Congenial Spirits: The Selected Letters of Virginia Woolf* (London, 2003), p. 388, Virginia Woolf to Vita Sackville-West, 26(?) July 1937.

42. King's College, Cambridge, Rosamond Lehmann papers, Misc. 42/35, Virginia Woolf to Rosamond Lehmann, Aug.(?) 1937.

43. King's College, Cambridge, Charleston papers, CHA 1/207, E. M. Forster to Vanessa Bell, 9 Aug. 1937.

44. On the return of the brigade see NMLH, Spanish Civil War collection, Misc. 1/20, *The Voice of East London*, Jan. 1939, pp. 1–4.

45. NMLH, Labour Party International Department papers, LP/SCW/1–19, Charlotte Haldane to James Middleton, Labour Party, 30 June 1939.

46. R. Skelton (ed.), *Poetry of the Thirties* (London, 1964), p. 135.

47. University Library, Cambridge, Joseph Needham papers, K/102, Emile Burns, 'Spain', 11 Aug. 1936.

48. Duchess of Atholl, *Searchlight on Spain* (Harmondsworth, 1937), p. vii, and *Working Partnership* (London, 1958), pp. 209–10, 215.

49. Orwell, *The Collected Essays*, pp. 383–4, from *New English Weekly*, 21 July 1938.

50. Symons, *The Thirties*, p. 117.

51. Warwick University Modern Records Centre, Gollancz papers, MSS 157/4/LB/1, *Left News*, Dec. 1937, p. 607. On Koestler and Münzenberg see D. Cesarani, *Arthur Koestler: The Homeless Mind* (London, 1998), pp. 103–6, 146–50.

52. University College, London, Orwell archive, C/4b, manifesto, 'Spain: The Question', June 1937.

53. Davison, *Orwell in Spain*, pp. 248–9, Orwell to Nancy Cunard, 3–6(?) Aug. 1937. This reply was discovered only in 1994, scribbled by Orwell on the back of the appeal, although a separate copy of the appeal can be found in the Orwell archive.

54. N. Cunard (ed.), *Authors Take Sides on the Spanish War* (Left Review, London, 1937), passim.

55. Gascoyne, *Collected Journals*, pp. 30–41. The length of his stay is uncertain. He left London on 22 Oct. 1936, stayed in Paris, went to Barcelona and was back in London in December.

56. S. Spender, *World within World* (London, 1951), pp. 241–3, 255; Sutherland, *Stephen Spender*, pp. 208–28 for a full account of Spender's time in Spain.

57. British Library, Cecil papers, ADD MSS 51142, Duchess of Atholl to Lord Cecil, 15 Dec. 1937. Details on the Committee in B. Shelmerdine, *British Representations of the Spanish Civil War* (Manchester, 2006), p. 149.

58. University Library, Cambridge, Joseph Needham papers, K/103, demonstration leaflet, 6 June 1937, 'Durango! Guernica! Almeria!'

59. Ibid., K/74, H. C. Roeder (Limehouse Labour Party) to Needham, 9 Sept. 1936; Limehouse Labour Party leaflet, 'Catholics and Their Responsibility for the Spanish Civil War' (n.d.), p. 4; G. Spicer (Castle ward LP) to Dorothy Needham, 15 Sept. 1936.

60. Ibid., Cambridge Scientists' Anti-War Group, 'Spain: Why Are They Fighting in Spain?', Oct. 1936; George Thomson to Joseph Needham, 4 Oct. 1936.

61. NMLH, Labour Party International Dept., LP/SWC/1–19, note, 31 May 1937, 'Approved Centres'; Basque Children's Committee, minutes of Executive Committee, 31 May 1937, p. 2; National Joint Committee for Spanish Relief, 'Note on the Question of the Evacuation of Basque Children to this Country', 23(?) April 1937.

62. See, for example, R. Ellis, 'Bilbao and Back', in Y. Cloud (ed.), *The Basque Children in England* (London, 1937), pp. 60–61: 'By every small means in their power they declare themselves anti-Fascist.'

63. NMLH, Carshalton and District Basque Children's Association, Misc. 1/01–23, programme, 'Concert: Spanish Songs and Dances', 19 May 1938; minutes of committee meetings, 26 Jan. 1938 to 18 Jan. 1939; letter from Carshalton Committee to Reigate and Redhill Basque Children's Committee, Jan. 1938.

64. Ibid., Duchess of Atholl to Committee, 11 Oct. 1943. See too Atholl, *Working Partnership*, pp. 213–15.

65. NMLH, Spanish Civil War collection, Misc. 1/23, leaflet, 'Spain' (n.d.), milk token, foodship stamps, collector's official card, collectors' envelopes: 'Food for Spain!' and 'Don't Let Babies Starve'.

66. NMLH, Labour Party International Department, LP/SCW/06, National Council of Labour, 'Statement on the Labour Relief Work for Spain' (n.d.

but late 1936; a note was added asking for the statistics to be kept within the organization and not given wide publicity); circular letter, James Middleton to all LP branch secretaries, May 1938; National Council of Labour, 'Summarized Report of Relief Work in Spain undertaken by the International Solidarity Fund, 1938', pp. 4–5; Shelmerdine, *British Representations*, pp. 149–50. See the debate about the role of the Labour Party in the Spanish aid programme in T. Buchanan, *The Spanish Civil War and the British Labour Movement* (Cambridge, 1991) and J. Fyrth, 'The Aid Spain Movement in Britain, 1936–39', *History Workshop Journal*, 35 (1993), pp. 153–64.

67. Ibid., Henry Brailsford to LP executive, 11 April 1938 on arms smuggling; National Emergency Conference on Spain, 23 April 1938, 'Report of Delegates from London Trades Council'; National Conference on Spain Committee, conference programme.

68. See, for example, the excellent account in I. Patterson, *Guernica and Total War* (London, 2007). Also U. Bialer, *The Shadow of the Bomber: The Fear of Air Attack and British Politics, 1932–1939* (London, 1980); M. Paris, *From the Wright Brothers to Top Gun: Aviation, Nationalism and Popular Cinema* (Manchester, 1995); C. Frayling, *Mad, Bad and Dangerous? The Scientist and the Cinema* (London, 2005), ch. 3.

69. On the bombing in Spain see G. Thomas and M. W. Witts, *Guernica: The Crucible of World War II* (New York, 1975); K. Maier, *Guernica: 26.iv.1937: Die deutsche Intervention in Spanien und der 'Fall Guernica'* (Freiburg im Breisgau, 1975). The figure of 250 comes from Gernika Museum of Peace, *Gernika Exhibition* (Gernika, n.d.), pp. 18, 24. The dead in Durango totalled 248. Current estimates for Guernica range from 200 to 250.

70. N. Rankin, *Telegram from Guernica: The Extraordinary Life of George Steer, War Correspondent* (London, 2003), pp. 119–24. See too Steer's own account in G. Steer, *The Tree of Gernika: A Field Study of Modern War* (London, 1938), pp. 236–45.

71. Details in Patterson, *Guernica and Total War*, p. 69; Rankin, *Telegram from Guernica*, pp. 128–9.

72. Trinity College, Cambridge, Layton papers, Box 11, circular letter from Walter Layton and Lord Cecil, 3 Feb. 1938, encl., 'The Appeal'; list of signatories to appeal (n.d. but Febr. 1938). The list included 115 names.

73. Ibid., *News Chronicle* memorandum, 7 Feb. 1938; Ambassador Azcarate to Layton and Cecil, 10 Feb. 1938.

74. Ibid., Box 11, memorandum from Cliff (*News Chronicle*) to Layton, 7 March 1938; see too University Library, Cambridge, Joseph Needham papers, K/104, Spanish Press Services London, 'The Bombardment of Open Towns'. This was a Nationalist leaflet published in spring 1938 explaining

that the Republican forces had undertaken 2,091 air raids and inflicted 18,985 casualties in Nationalist-held areas. Chamberlain's comments in University Library, Cambridge, FIL papers, A4, FIL Statement, 31 March 1938, p. 2.

75. Mepham, *Virginia Woolf*, p. 166.

76. G. van Hensbergen, *Guernica: The Biography of a Twentieth-Century Icon* (London, 2004), pp. 83–90; see too Warwick University Modern Records Centre, Gollancz papers, MSS 157/3/POL/1, Sybil Stephenson (secretary, National Joint Committee for Spanish Relief) to Gollancz, 12 Sept. 1938.

77. Van Hensbergen, *Guernica*, pp. 91–2, 94–6.

78. University Library, Cambridge, Joseph Needham papers, K/102, Parliamentary Committee for Spain, 'British and American Views of Spain' (n.d. but Feb. 1939?); LSE, Carr-Saunders papers, B/3/4, British Institute of Public Opinion, 'What Britain Thinks', p. 19.

79. British Library, Cecil papers, ADD MSS 51132, Gilbert Murray to Lord Cecil, 12 Oct. 1936. On Brockway see NMLH, pamphlet collection, 328.641, A. Fenner Brockway, 'Pacifism and the Left Wing', Pacifist Publicity Unit, 1938, p. 18: 'The practical question which we have to answer, therefore, is whether we would rather have the social revolution with violence or not have the social revolution at all. The answer of the ILP is that it would rather have the social revolution.'

80. John Cornford, 'Full Moon at Tierz', *Left Review*, 3 (1937), pp. 69–70.

81. P. N. Furbank, *E. M. Forster: A Life* (London, 1977), pp. 223–4; Mepham, *Virginia Woolf*, pp. 168–9.

82. M. Barrett, 'Introduction', in Virginia Woolf, *Three Guineas* (London, 1993), pp. xxviii–xxix, xxxv–xl; Mepham, *Virginia Woolf*, pp. 169–72. *Three Guineas* was published in June 1938 and sold 8,000 copies by the end of the year.

83. University of Sussex Library, Leonard Woolf papers, MS 13, part I, M.5, Helena Swanwick to Leonard Woolf, 25 Sept. 1937; Woolf review of Swanwick, *Collective Insecurity*, in the *New Statesman and Nation*, 8 Sept. 1937; H. Swanwick, *Collective Insecurity* (London, 1937), pp. 284–5.

84. LSE, Fabian Society papers, J35/3, Leonard Woolf, 'A New Foreign Policy for Labour', New Fabian Research Bureau, 5 June 1934, pp. 7–8, 12.

85. University of Sussex Library, Leonard Woolf papers, MS 13, part I, M.5, Swanwick to Woolf, 25 and 30 Sept. 1937; Woolf to Swanwick, 1 Oct. 1937: 'The only conceivable way of dealing with the force problem seems to me to be some sort of system of "collective security", a system of collective resistance to any state resorting to war.'

86. H. Nicholson, *Half My Days and Nights: A Memoir of the 1920s and 1930s* (London, 1941), pp. 145, 177–8.
87. University Library, Cambridge, J. D. Bernal papers, ADD MS 8287, Box 83, file C, Aldous Huxley to Bernal, 8 Aug. 1936. Bernal received a similar letter from Gerald Heard: file A, Heard to Bernal, 13 Aug. 1936: 'To use the wrong means is to operate with septic instruments, the end of the operation to save the patient's life is defeated.'
88. Friends House, London, No More War Movement papers, TEMP MSS 579/2, minutes of National Committee meeting, 21 Nov. 1936; see too minutes of NMWM Trustees, 3 July 1937, p. 4, discussion of 'resistance to an anti-fascist war'.
89. Lambeth Palace Library, Sheppard papers, MSS 3744, Ellen Wilkinson to Dick Sheppard, 30 March 1937.
90. University Library, Cambridge, FIL papers, ADD 9369/B1, Eleanor Rathbone to Margaret Gardiner, 4 May 1938; Gardiner to Rathbone, 5 May 1938; Gardiner to Marjorie Fry, 5 May 1938.
91. University Library, Cambridge, Baldwin papers, vol. CCIII, report of an address at Ashridge, 14 Feb. 1936, p. 11.
92. Ibid., D.1, Maurice Hankey to Stanley Baldwin, 16 June 1936, encl., Col. H. Pownall, 'The Role of the Army in a Major Continental War', p. 9.
93. There is a huge literature on Chamberlain starting with 'Cato', *Guilty Men* (London, 1940), written by Michael Foot and others. See in particular D. Dutton, *Neville Chamberlain* (London, 2001); R. A. C. Parker, *Chamberlain and Appeasement: British Policy and the Coming of the Second World War* (London, 1993); W. Wark, 'Appeasement Revisited', *International History Review*, 17 (1995), pp. 545–62. The standard life is K. Feiling, *The Life of Neville Chamberlain* (London, 1946).
94. A. Salter, *Personality in Politics: Studies of Contemporary Statesmen* (London, 1947), p. 67.
95. V. Cowles, *Looking for Trouble* (London, 1941), pp. 188–9.
96. N. Chamberlain, *The Struggle for Peace* (London, 1939), p. 61.
97. Chamberlain, *Struggle for Peace*, p. 67, speech to Midland Union of Conservative Associations, Birmingham, 4 Feb. 1938. See too Harris Manchester College, Oxford, Lawrence Jacks papers, MS Jacks/1, L. P. Jacks, 'Relation of Morals to Scientific Progress', *The Listener*, 16 Feb. 1938, p. 374, in which Jacks quoted Chamberlain on armaments: 'Nothing so impresses me with the incredible folly of our civilisation.'
98. Chamberlain, *Struggle for Peace*, p. 238, speech at National Government rally, Kettering, 2 July 1938.
99. Lord Simon, *Retrospect* (London, 1952), p. 244. On Chamberlain's

dramatic confrontations with Hitler see the fine account in D. Reynolds, *Summits: Six Meetings that Shaped the Twentieth Century* (London, 2007), pp. 37–95.

100. University Library, Cambridge, FIL papers, ADD 9369/A4, FIL statement, 31 March 1938, p. 1; ADD 9369/A6, declaration by the Association of Writers for Intellectual Liberty, Sept. 1938. See too ADD 9369/A10, FIL pamphlet, 'For Intellectual Liberty' (n.d. but late 1938), p. 1: 'we are faced with the prospect of the destruction of western civilization'.

101. Magdalene College, Cambridge, Old Library, Inge diaries and papers, 36/diary 1938–9, entries for 24, 25–29 Sept. 1938.

102. University of Exeter, Special Collections, Williamson letters, MS239, Henry Williamson to Stuart Mais, 16 Aug. 1938.

103. Bodleian Library, Ponsonby papers, MS Eng. Hist. C680, J. A. Hobson to Arthur Ponsonby, 26 Sept. 1938.

104. Banks, *Congenial Spirits*, pp. 407–8, Virginia Woolf to Vanessa Bell, 1 Oct. 1938.

105. Ibid., pp. 407, 412, Virginia Woolf to Vanessa Bell, 1 and 3 Oct. 1938.

106. *Akten der Deutschen auswärtigen Politik*, Series D, vol. II, p. 772, minutes of meeting between Hitler and Horace Wilson, 27 Sept. 1938.

107. Salter, *Personality in Politics*, pp. 76–7.

108. Cowles, *Looking for Trouble*, p. 190.

109. Magdalene College, Cambridge, Old Library, Inge diaries and papers, 36/diary 1938–9, entry for 30 Sept. 1938.

110. Bodleian Library, Toynbee papers, Box 39, Toynbee to Geoffrey Gathorne-Hardy, 31 March 1938; Box 76, draft, 'After Munich: The World Outlook', 1 Nov. 1938, p. 27.

111. LSE, Carr-Saunders papers, B/3/4, British Institute of Public Opinion, 'What Britain Thinks', p. 19. The result was 71 per cent for fighting, 20 per cent against and 9 per cent with no opinion.

112. LSE, National Peace Council papers, 14/12, E. H. Carr and S. de Madariaga, 'The Future of International Government', Peace Aims Pamphlet no. 4, p. 1.

113. *Headway*, Jan. 1939, front cover.

114. Feiling, *Neville Chamberlain*, p. 385.

115. King's College, London, Liddell Hart Archive Centre, Liddell Hart papers, LH1/408, Storm Jameson to Basil Liddell Hart, 21 Dec. 1941.

116. Ibid., Storm Jameson to Liddell Hart, 19 April 1941, p. 2. See too letter from Jameson to Liddell Hart, 3 April 1941, p. 2.

117. Ibid., Storm Jameson to Liddell Hart, 21 Dec. 1941, p. 1.

118. Somerville College, Oxford, Vera Brittain archive, VB C2, file 2, letter

from Storm Jameson to Vera Brittain, 4 Sept. 1941; VB D, diary file 1939, entry for 3 March 1939.

119. LSE, National Peace Council papers, 2/5, special meeting of Executive Committee, 5 Sept. 1938; minutes of Executive Committee, 19 Sept. 1938.

120. King's College, London, Liddell Hart Archive Centre, Liddell Hart papers, LH1/65/3, J. D. Bernal to Liddell Hart, 13 Nov. 1938, encl., 'Science and National Defence', pp. 1–3. Bernal discussed the idea of mobilizing science for war preparations with Julian Huxley and Solly Zuckerman. See too A. Brown, *J. D. Bernal: The Sage of Science* (Oxford, 2005), pp. 134–5.

121. LSE, Bernal papers, 1, 'European Order and World Order: What We Are Fighting For', 10 Oct. 1939, pp. i, 1–3.

122. University Library, Cambridge, Joseph Needham papers, K/108, notes, 'shortly after Munich' (n.d.); notes on back of draft letter to the *Manchester Guardian*, 30 Sept. 1938; rough notes, October 1939, on Hitler peace offer; rough notes of a conference (n.d.), Maurice (Dobb) paper.

123. Bodleian Library, Murray papers, file 365, Murray to Lord Halifax, 8 Nov. 1938.

124. King's College, London, Liddell Hart Archive Centre, Liddell Hart papers, LH1/16, Norman Angell to Liddell Hart, 24 Sept. 1939.

125. Warwick University Modern Records Centre, Gollancz papers, MSS 157/3/POL/1, Gollancz to Clement Attlee, 25 Sept. 1938; V. Gollancz, *Is Mr Chamberlain Saving Peace?* (London, 1939), p. 7.

126. King's College, London, Liddell Hart Archive Centre, Liddell Hart papers, LH1/412, 'I Was a Life-Long Pacifist', *Evening Standard*, 13 Aug. 1940.

127. LSE, National Peace Council papers, 1/4, minutes of Council meeting, 18 Oct. 1938.

128. Ibid., 2/5, minutes of Executive Committee, 13 Feb., 13 March and 17 April 1939; 16/10, 'National Petition for a New Peace Conference', 2 Nov. 1938.

129. Ibid., minutes of Executive Committee, 8 May and 12 June 1939.

130. Ibid., 1/4, minutes of Council meeting, 18 Oct. 1938 and 7 July 1939.

131. Bodleian Library, Ponsonby papers, MS Eng. Hist. C681, J. Craig Walker to Ponsonby, 20 Jan. 1939; C. J. Hills to Ponsonby, 23 Jan. 1939.

132. Ibid., draft circular letter by Ponsonby, Feb. 1939.

133. Ibid., draft letter Ponsonby to Joseph Goebbels, 3 July 1939 (sent 12 July).

134. LSE, National Peace Council papers, 2/5, 'Hitler's Peace Proposals: Statement Adopted by the Executive Committee of the NPC', 6 Oct. 1939.

135. Bodleian Library, Ponsonby papers, MS Eng. Hist. C681, F. G. Wilden to Neville Chamberlain (copy), 7 Oct. 1939.

136. LSE, Peace Pledge Union papers, Coll. Misc. 0825, file 3, PPU Information Service, no. 5, 5 Jan. 1940, p. 5.

137. Birmingham City archives, MS ZZ/71A, Women's International League of Peace and Freedom, minutes of committee meeting, Nov. 1939 and 6 Feb. 1940.

138. LSE, Peace Pledge Union papers, Coll. Misc. 0825, file 3, PPU Information Service, no. 5, 5 Jan. 1940.

139. King's College, London, Liddell Hart Archive Centre, Liddell Hart papers, LH1/412, Liddell Hart to Cyril Joad, 13 Apr. 1948; he continued, 'But such an urge to get relief from tension is a matter of emotion that is quite regardless of reason.'

140. Bodleian Library, Toynbee papers, Box 81, Gathorne-Hardy to Toynbee, 24 July 1939.

141. G. T. Garratt, *Europe's Dance of Death* (London, 1940), p. 292.

142. Bodleian Library, Ponsonby papers, MS Eng. Hist. C681, Ponsonby to Lord Stanhope, 19 Nov. 1939.

143. Ibid., Sheila (?) to Ponsonby, 4 Sept. 1939. The village was Arnold in Nottinghamshire.

144. Brittain, *Testament of Experience*, p. 215.

145. Bank of England archive, OV 34/87, memorandum from the deputy governor, 11 May 1939, reporting on the visit of Karl Blessing: 'he professed to be most surprised at the fact that everywhere in this country the prevailing topic of conversation was the imminence of war with Germany'; Brittain, *Testament of Experience*, pp. 198–9.

146. Cowles, *Looking for Trouble*, p. 193. Hitler had also asked Tom Mitford why there were trenches dug in Hyde Park, and when he was told they were air-raid shelters 'threw back his head and laughed loudly'.

147. See R. J. Overy, 'Strategic Intelligence and the Outbreak of the Second World War', *War in History*, 5 (1998), pp. 456–64.

148. Hansard vol. 351, session 1938–9, 24 Aug 1939, col. 10.

149. Bodleian Library, Clark papers, file 213, Toynbee to Clark, 30 Sept. 1938 and 30 Jan. 1939.

150. British Psycho-Analytical Society, Jones/Glover correspondence, CGA/F30, circular letter from Glover to all members of the Society, 8 June 1939.

151. Ibid., Glover to Jones, 28 Jan. 1944; B. Shephard, *A War of Nerves: Soldiers and Psychiatrists 1914–1994* (London, 2000), pp. 167–8.

152. Wellcome Institute, London, Contemporary Medical Archives Centre, SA/EUG/D.110, draft memorandum, War Emergency Committee, Population Investigation Committee (n.d. but 1943), p. 1.

153. LSE, PEP I, A/6/6, PEP Bulletin no. 123, 14 Nov. 1939 and 9 April 1940.

154. British Library, Cecil papers, ADD MSS 51146, draft memorandum, 'Action in the Event of War', 28 Aug. 1939.

155. Churchill College, Cambridge, Archive Centre, Noel-Baker papers, 5/132, minutes of IPC Executive Committee meeting, 20 June 1939; IPC British Committee, Monthly Letter no. 1, Oct. 1939, p. 1; minutes of British National Committee (IPC), 18 Jan. 1940; 4/506, League of Nations Union, recommendations of Emergency committee, 16 Sept. 1940. See too University of Hull, Special Collections, Edgar Young papers, DYO 10/44, National Committee circular to all members of IPC, 24 Feb. 1940; A. D. Lindsay to British National Committee, 9 Jan. 1941.

156. Feiling, *Neville Chamberlain*, pp. 415–16.

157. Somerville College, Oxford, Vera Brittain archive, VB D, diary file 1939, entry for 3 Sept. 1939.

158. Bodleian Library, Ponsonby papers, MS Eng. Hist. C681, Helena Swanwick to Ponsonby, 7 and 19 Sept., 11 Oct. 1939; Molly Trevelyan to Ponsonby, 20 Nov. 1939. See too Brittain, *Testament of Experience*, p. 226.

159. University Library, Cambridge, Joseph Needham papers, K/33, 'Behind the Gas Mask' (n.d. but 1935), p. 1.

160. Bodleian Library, MS Autogr. d.39, Rosamond Lehmann to Marjorie Battcock, 19 Oct. 1938.

161. G. Orwell, *Coming Up for Air* (London, 1939), p. 158.

162. University Library, Cambridge, FIL papers, ADD 9369/A6, minutes of General Meeting, 14 March 1940, p. 1.

163. Warwick University Modern Records Centre, Gollancz papers, MSS 157/4/LB/2, 'Appeal to Members by Victor Gollancz', insert in *Left Book News*, May 1940.

164. Dalton, *Hitler's War*, p. 181.

165. University Library, Cambridge, Joseph Needham papers, L/31, Bishop George Bell, 'University Sermon, 26 October 1941', *Cambridge Review*, 1 Nov. 1941, p. 62.

Chapter 9: A Morbid Age

1. A. Huxley, *Ape and Essence* (London, 1948), p. 94.

2. A. Huxley, *Brave New World Revisited* (London, 1958), p. 3.

3. Huxley, *Ape and Essence*, pp. 93, 95–6; G. Smith (ed.), *Letters of Aldous Huxley* (London, 1969), p. 569, Huxley to Anita Loos, 26 March 1947. Huxley developed the idea of the 'devil within' in a letter to Dick Sheppard in 1937 about Anglican attitudes to just war: 'It is as if they were possessed by devils . . . doing things they know are fatal, that they know are wrong; doing them in spite of that knowledge or perhaps actually because of it, in some queer way.' See Lambeth Palace Library, Sheppard papers, MSS 3746, Huxley to Sheppard, 7 Feb. 1937.

4. Smith, *Letters of Aldous Huxley*, p. 589, Huxley to Victoria Ocampo, 9 Jan. 1949; p. 600, Huxley to Philip Wylie, 9 June 1949.

5. T. R. Fyvel, *The Malady and the Vision: An Analysis of Political Faith* (London, 1940), p. 11.

6. Quotations from G. T. Garratt, *Europe's Dance of Death* (London, 1940), p. 29; London School of Economics (LSE), Malinowski papers, Box 2, notes for Oxford lecture (n.d. but 1936?); Bodleian Library, Toynbee papers, Box 3, 'An Unfinished Tale', *The Listener*, 25 March 1931, p. 489.

7. L. Woolf, *Barbarians at the Gate* (London, 1939), p. 93.

8. University of Exeter, Special Collections, Williamson letters, MS239, Williamson to Stuart Mais, 19 Aug. 1938; MS106, Williamson to Eric Watkins, 4 May 1945.

9. Huxley, *Brave New World Revisited*, p. 7.

10. H. Joules (ed.), *The Doctor's View of War* (London, 1938), p. 19.

11. J. McCabe, *Can We Save Civilisation?* (London, 1932), p. 5. The chapter titles were as follows: 'The Special Malady of Great Britain'; 'The Economic Problem'; 'The Political Problem'; 'The Population Problem'; 'The International Problem'; 'The Problem of War'; 'Can We Change Human Nature?'; 'The Problem of Education'; 'The Question of Ideals'.

12. J. A. Hobson, *The Recording Angel: A Report from Earth* (London, 1932), esp. pp. 59–75.

13. S. Jameson (ed.), *Challenge to Death* (London, 1934), p. 323.

14. Newcastle Literary and Philosophical Society, annual reports 1921–40; Committee Book, 1933–8.

15. E. Thompson, *You Have Lived Through All This* (London, 1939), p. 9.

16. W. Steed, 'Where Do We Stand?', *Fortnightly Review*, 130 (July–Dec. 1931), p. 1.

17. E. M. Remarque, *All Quiet on the Western Front* (London, 1929). The book was reprinted twenty times in six months.

18. H. G. Wells, *Experiment in Autobiography, being the Autobiography of H. G. Wells* (2 vols., London, 1934), vol. II, pp. 745–6. On Virginia Woolf see University of Sussex Library, Leonard Woolf papers, MS 13, part I, D.1, letter and royalty statement from Curtis Brown to Hogarth Press, 17 June 1936 (the royalty in 1936 only amounted to 88 marks). On Toynbee, Bodleian Library, Toynbee papers, Box 76, Ernst Curtius to Arnold Toynbee, 3 Feb. 1936.

19. Jameson, *Challenge to Death*, p. 328.

20. Churchill College, Cambridge, Archive Centre, Noel-Baker papers, 2/26, draft article for *Headway* (n.d. but Oct. 1934), p. 1.

21. Bodleian Library, Toynbee papers, Box 3, 'An Unfinished Tale', *The Listener*, 25 March 1931, p. 489.

22. British Library, Cecil papers, ADD MSS 51146, memorandum by Norman Angell for LNU members, 'Collective Security', 14 July 1936, p. 10.

23. Jameson, *Challenge to Death*, p. 329.

24. Bodleian Library, Gilbert Murray papers, file 499, draft lecture, 'The Deeper Issue' (n.d. but 1941?), p. 12.

25. Jameson, *Challenge to Death*, p. 329.

26. *Nature*, 6 June 1931, p. 866. Lecture of 19 May.

27. Huxley, *Ape and Essence*, p. 97.

28. British Psycho-Analytical Society, Ernest Jones papers, GB1404/PE/JON, draft lecture, 'The Present State of Psycho-Analysis', 1930, p. 5.

29. B. Russell, 'Is Science Superstitious?', in *The Rationalist Annual*, 1927, p. 34.

30. University Library, Cambridge, Joseph Needham papers, G/57, rough notes, 'Can Sci[ence] Save Civilisation?' (n.d. but 1936), pp. 1–3.

31. There were numerous articles published on this theme between the wars. A good example is J. Gillespie, 'How Much Can We Expect from Science', *The Plebs*, 30 (1938), pp. 66–8, who argued that since Thomas Huxley science had been 'cursed with the idea of regarding itself as the discoverer and upholder of universal truth'.

32. University of Liverpool, Special Collections, Cyril Burt papers, D191/55/3, draft review, 'Science and Society' (n.d. but 1940), p. 1. Burt thought scientists were to blame as well for not understanding 'the social consequences of their work'.

33. Harris Manchester College, Oxford, Lawrence Jacks papers, MS Jacks/1, 'Relation of Morals to Scientific Progress', *The Listener*, 16 Feb. 1938, p. 336.

34. University Library, Cambridge, Joseph Needham papers, K/34, draft synopsis, 'The Distortion of Science for Politico-Economic Ends' (n.d. but 1938); contents page, 'The Distortion of Science'. The epilogue of the book was provisionally titled 'War and causes. Eradication'.

35. King's College, Cambridge, Lowes Dickinson papers, GLD 1/5, Journal, 1916–1932, entry for 8 March 1929, 'the perils of science'.

36. On intelligence see, for example, G. K. Bowes, 'Declining Intelligence in Western Civilisation', *Hibbert Journal*, 36 (1937), pp. 187–92; on physical decline see E. Moore, 'Social Progress and Racial Decline', *Eugenics Review*, 18 (1926/7), pp. 124–7.

37. On the development of statistical measurement and the state see the introduction to A. Tooze, *Statistics and the German State, 1900–1945: The Making of Modern Economic Knowledge* (Cambridge, 2001); E. Higgs, *The Information State in England: The Central Collection of Information on Citizens since 1500* (London, 2004), chs. 5–6.

38. A. Briggs, *The Golden Age of Wireless* (Oxford, 1965), pp. 253, 281.

39. Wellcome Institute Library, London, Contemporary Medical Archives Centre (CMAC), papers of the Imperial Social Hygiene Council, SA/BSH/C.1/7, 'Report of the Work of the District Representatives', Dec. 1928, passim; minutes of the Propaganda Committee, 23 July 1930, p. 8 on 'talkies'; report of the Propaganda Committee, 21 Feb. 1938, p. 4.

40. N. Pronay, 'British Newsreels in the 1930s: Audience and Producers', in British Universities Film Video Council, *Yesterday's News: The British Cinema Newsreel Reader* (London, 2002), p. 140.

41. LSE, L/107, NCLC, 'Education for Emancipation', Feb. 1937, p. 21.

42. National Museum of Labour History, Manchester, Brailsford papers, HNB/2, Left Book Club, memorandum, 'Left Book Club: Educational Section', Oct. 1936; Victor Gollancz to Brailsford, 18 March 1937: 'and I simply must get going on that "educational series" for the club is clamouring for it'.

43. University of Hull, Special Collections, Rev. Stanley Evans papers, DEV 1/11, draft lecture for Mansfield LBC by Evans; ticket for Mansfield LBC meeting, 14 Feb. 1939.

44. CMAC, Mallet papers, SA/EUG/I.2, memorandum, 'Proposed Activities for Eugenics Society' (n.d. but 1930), pp. 1–2.

45. CMAC, Social Hygiene Council, SA/BSH/C.1/7, minutes of Propaganda Committee, 15 Feb. 1932, report of activity, 1 July 1931–31 Jan. 1932, p. 3.

46. Calculated from LSE, L/107, NCLC, 'Education for Emancipation', pp. 8–9. WEA figure from M. Stocks, *The Workers' Educational Association: The First Fifty Years* (London, 1953), p. 116.

47. CMAC, Blacker papers, PP/CPB/H.4, notes of a speech at North Kensington Birth Control Clinic, 29 Nov. 1938.

48. Somerville College, Oxford, Vera Brittain archive, VB D, typescript diary 1932–9, entries from 3 Feb. to 18 March 1939.

49. LSE, Women's International League for Peace and Freedom papers, 5/11, final programme, international summer school, Westhill Training College, 27 July–10 Aug. 1928.

50. Calculated from LSE, L/107, NCLC, 'Education for Emancipation', p. 9 and J. P. M. Millar, *The Labour College Movement* (n.d. but 1964), pp. 252, 267.

51. Trinity College, Cambridge, Dobb archive, DD 74, summer school programme, Bexhill-on-Sea, 6–27 Aug. 1938.

52. Bodleian Library, Murray papers, file 499, 'The Deeper Issue', 1940, p. 1.

53. H. Laski, *Reflections on the Revolution of our Time* (London, 1943), pp. 17–18.

54. Bodleian Library, Toynbee papers, Box 39, Toynbee to John Marshall, The Rockefeller Foundation, 14 Feb. 1945, encl., 'Possible Participants in a Post-War Conference on the Study of the Nature and Destiny of Man'.

55. A. J. Toynbee, *Civilization on Trial* (New York, 1948), p. 25.

56. J. Welshman, *Underclass: A History of the Excluded* (London, 2006), pp. 53–7.

57. Laski, *Reflections on the Revolution of our Time*, p. 7.

58. H. Nicholson, *Half My Days and Nights: A Memoir of the 1920s and 1930s* (London, 1941), pp. 190, 203.

Bibliography and Sources

The section is arranged as follows: Archive sources; Contemporary newspapers and periodicals (p. 479); Published documents, memoirs and diaries (p. 480); Contemporary sources (pre-1950) (p. 482; Secondary sources (post-1950) (p. 492).

Archive sources

London School of Economics, London
Passfield papers (Beatrice and Sidney Webb)
Dalton papers
Malinowski papers
Fabian Society papers
J. D. Bernal papers
League of Nations Union papers
Coll. Misc. 0420 Laski/Huebsch correspondence
William Beveridge papers
R. H. Tawney papers
National Peace Council papers
Peace Pledge Union
Coll. Misc. 0435/1 Birth control ephemera
Carr-Saunders papers
D. N. Pritt papers
Political and Economic Planning (PEP) papers (I and II)
Women's International League for Peace and Freedom papers
Lionel Robbins papers
Fellowship of Reconciliation papers

University Library, Cambridge
Geoffrey Keynes papers

Baldwin papers
For Intellectual Liberty collection (Margaret Gardiner, J. D. Bernal)
C. C. Hurst papers
J. D. Bernal papers
Joseph Needham papers

Bodleian Library, Oxford
　Gilbert Murray papers
　Arnold Toynbee papers
　Society for the Protection of Science and Learning
　MS Eng. Lett. c 300, Sir James Marchant correspondence
　MS Autogr. d.39, letters of Marjorie Battcock
　Arthur Ponsonby papers
　G. N. Clark papers
　J. L. Hammond papers
　Sidgwick & Jackson production books

University of Exeter, Special Collections
　MS43 Henry Williamson collection
　MS106 Henry Williamson letters to Eric and Kathleen Watkins
　MS113 A. L. Rowse papers
　MS239 Henry Williamson letters to Stuart Petre Mais

King's College, London
　Liddell Hart papers
　Tom Wintringham collection

Wellcome Institute for the History of Medicine
　Eugenics Society papers
　C. P. Blacker collection
　Family Planning Association (Spring Rice collection)
　British Social Hygiene Council papers
　Marie Stopes collection
　Sir Bernard Mallett papers
　C. J. Singer papers
　Medical Women's Federation papers

University of Sussex Library
　Monk's House collection (Virginia and Leonard Woolf)
　Leonard Woolf papers
　Kingsley Martin papers

Imperial War Museum, London
  Siegfried Sassoon collection

University College, London
  George Orwell archive
  Haldane papers
  Francis Galton collection
  Routledge & Kegan Paul collection

Mansfield College, Oxford
  College Council minutes
  Dale lectures collection

British Psycho-Analytical Society
  M1 Committees of the British Psycho-Analytical Society
  Ernest Jones papers
  Edward Glover collection
  James Strachey papers
  Sigmund Freud correspondence
  John Rickman collection
  Lecture series collection

Camden Local Studies Centre, London
  Chalcot Discussion Society papers
  Hampstead Ethical Institute

Somerville College, Oxford
  Vera Brittain (Paul Berry) archive

Friends House, London
  National Peace Council
  No More War Movement papers
  Friends Peace Committee minutes
  Friends Anti-War Group
  Northern Friends Peace Board collection

Warwick University Modern Records Centre
  MSS 157 Victor Gollancz private papers
  MSS 318 Victor Gollancz business papers

Magdalene College, Cambridge, Old Library
  Dean Inge diaries and papers

British Medical Association, London
Psycho-Analysis Committee
Mental Deficiency Committee
Council minute books
Annual representative meetings

Lambeth Palace Library
Richard Sheppard papers and correspondence
Bishop Bell papers
Cosmo Lang papers

Royal Anthropological Institute
Sir Arthur Keith papers
Council minute books

Birmingham City Archives
Birmingham branch, Women's International League of Peace and Freedom
National Women's Council papers

Newcastle Literary and Philosophical Society
Annual reports and papers, 1917–40
Committee books

Edinburgh University Library, Special Collections
Arthur Koestler archive

King's College, Cambridge, Archive Centre
E. M. Forster papers
G. Lowes Dickinson papers
George Rylands papers
W. J. H. Sprott papers
Rosamond Lehmann papers
Charleston papers (Clive Bell)
Julian Bell papers
Joan Robinson papers
J. M. Keynes papers

Bristol University Library, Special Collections
Penguin archive
Allen Lane archive
Eunice Frost papers
Hamish Hamilton archive

University of Liverpool Library, Special Collections
Cyril Burt papers
D. Caradog Jones papers

Nuffield College, Oxford
G. D. H. Cole papers

Royal College of Surgeons
Sir Arthur Keith papers
C. J. Bond papers

Oxford University Press, Oxford
Toynbee files

South Place Ethical Society, Holborn, London
Monthly and annual reports, lecture series

Harris Manchester College, Oxford
Lawrence Jacks papers
George Hicks papers

Trinity College Library, Cambridge
Maurice Dobb archive
Clive Bell papers
Rose Macaulay papers
Walter Layton papers
Frederick Pethick-Lawrence papers

Churchill College, Cambridge, Archive Centre
Philip Noel-Baker papers
Fenner Brockway papers
Paul Einzig papers

Birmingham University Library
Neville Chamberlain papers

National Museum of Labour History, Manchester
Brailsford papers
Bob Edwards papers
Walter Gregory collection
Spanish Civil War collection, Misc. 1/1–23
Labour Party archive

University of Hull, Special Collections
J. A. Hobson papers

Stanley Evans papers
Edgar Young papers

Hull Central Library
Winifred Holtby collection

Marshall Library, Cambridge
A. C. Pigou papers

University of Salford, Special Collections
Walter Greenwood papers

John Strachey papers (in private possession)

Harry Ransom Humanities Research Center, Austin, Texas
Storm Jameson papers

British Library, London
Lord Cecil of Chelwood papers
Marie Stopes papers
Macmillan publishers
Vernon Bartlett correspondence
H. G. Wells papers

Peace Pledge Union, London
PPU Sponsors' minute-book

Society for Co-operation in Russian and Soviet Studies archive, London
SCR Papers, 1924–42

Contemporary newspapers and periodicals

Annals of Eugenics: A Journal for the Scientific Study of Racial Problems
L'année politique: française et étrangère
British Medical Journal
Character and Personality
Communist Review
Contemporary Review
The Economist
Edinburgh Review
English Review
Eugenics Review
Foreign Affairs
Fortnightly Review

Headway
Health and Empire
Hibbert Journal
The Human
International Journal of Psycho-Analysis
Left News (formerly *Left Book News*)
Left Review
The Listener
Man
Manchester Guardian
Nation
Nature
Plan
The Plebs
Quarterly Review
The Rationalist Annual
Revue des deux mondes
The Shield
Social Research
Spectator
The Times

Published documents, memoirs and diaries

Annan, N. *Our Age: The Generation that Made Post-War Britain* (London, 1990)

Baldwin, S. *On England and Other Addresses* (London, 1927)

Banks, J. T. (ed.). *Congenial Spirits: The Selected Letters of Virginia Woolf* (London, 2003)

Bartlett, V. *And Now, Tomorrow* (London, 1960)

Brittain, V. *Testament of Experience* (London, 1957)

Cecil, Lord Robert. *A Great Experiment: An Autobiography* (London, 1941)

Chamberlain, N. *The Struggle for Peace* (London, 1939)

Chesterton, G. K. *Autobiography* (London, 1936)

Committee for Legalizing Eugenic Sterilisation. 'Report of the Voluntary Eugenic Sterilization Conference', 23 May 1932 (London, 1932)

Cowles, V. *Looking for Trouble* (London, 1941)

Dallin, A. and Firsov, F. I. (eds.). *Dimitrov & Stalin, 1934–1943: Letters from the Soviet Archives* (New Haven, 2000)

Davison, P. (ed.). *Orwell in Spain* (London, 2001)

A Decade of Progress in Eugenics: Scientific Papers of the Third International Congress of Eugenics (Baltimore, Md., 1934)

DeSalvo, L. and Leaska, M. A. (eds.). *The Letters of Vita Sackville-West to Virginia Woolf* (New York, 1985)

Drake, B. and Cole. M. I. (eds.). *Our Partnership by Beatrice Webb* (London, 1948)

Freud, S. *Briefe: 1873–1939* (Frankfurt am Main, 1968)

Grimm, H. *Englische Rede: wie ich den Engländer sehe* (Gütersloh, 1938)

Haberman, F. W. (ed.). *Peace: Nobel Lectures, 1926–1950* (Amsterdam, 1972)

Haire, N. (ed.). *The Sexual Reform Congress: Proceedings, London 8–14. IX. 1929* (London, 1930)

Hart-Davis, R. (ed.). *Siegfried Sassoon Diaries, 1915–1918* (London, 1983)

Huxley, J. *Memories* (2 vols., London, 1970)

Inter-Parliamentary Union. *What Would Be the Character of a New War?* (London, 1932)

Jameson, S. *Journey from the North: Autobiography of Storm Jameson* (2 vols., London, 1970)

Kessler, H. *The Diaries of a Cosmopolitan, 1918–1937* (London, 1971)

Laurence, D. H. (ed.). *Bernard Shaw: Collected Letters, 1926–1950* (London, 1988)

Low, D. *Low's Autobiography* (London, 1956)

Mackenzie, N. and Mackenzie, J. (eds.). *The Diary of Beatrice Webb*, vol. III, *1905–1924: 'The Power to Alter Things'* (London, 1984)

—— *The Diary of Beatrice Webb*, vol. IV, *1924–1943: 'The Wheel of Life'* (London, 1985)

Marquardt, V. H. (ed.). *Survivor from a Dead Age: The Memoirs of Louis Lozowick* (Washington, DC, 1997)

Martin, K. *Editor: A Second Volume of Autobiography, 1931–1945* (London, 1968)

Moggridge, D. (ed.). *The Collected Writings of John Maynard Keynes*, vol. XXI, *Activities, 1931–1939* (London, 1982); vol. XX, *Activities, 1929–1931* (London, 1981)

Mosley, O. *My Life* (London, 1968)

Nathan, O. and Norden, H. (eds.). *Einstein on Peace* (London, 1963)

Nicholson, H. *Half My Days and Nights: A Memoir of the 1920s and 30s* (London, 1941)

Ollard, R. (ed.). *The Diaries of A. L. Rowse* (London, 2003)

Paskauskas, R. A. (ed.). *The Complete Correspondence of Sigmund Freud and Ernest Jones, 1908–1939* (Cambridge, Mass., 1993)

Pritt, D. N. *The Autobiography of D. N. Pritt: Part I, From Right to Left* (London, 1965)

The Reichstag Fire Trial: The Second Brown Book of the Hitler Terror (London, 1934)

Report of the Mental Deficiency Committee (London, 1929)

Albert Schweitzer: Leben, Werk und Denken, 1905–1965: mitgeteilt in seinen Briefen (Heidelberg, 1987)

Self, R. (ed.). *The Neville Chamberlain Diary Letters* (4 vols., Aldershot, 2000)

Simon, Lord John. *Retrospect* (London, 1952)

Skelton, R. (ed.). *Poetry of the Thirties* (London, 1964)

Smith, G. (ed.). *Letters of Aldous Huxley* (London, 1969)

Spender, S. *World within World* (London, 1951)

Thomas, W. M. *Out on a Wing* (London, 1964)

Toynbee, A. J. *Acquaintances* (London, 1967)

—— *Experiences* (London, 1969)

Unwin, S. *The Truth about a Publisher: An Autobiographical Record* (London, 1960)

Wells, H. G. *Experiment in Autobiography, being the Autobiography of H. G. Wells* (2 vols., London, 1934)

Woolf, L. *Downhill All the Way: An Autobiography of the Years 1919–1939* (London, 1967)

Contemporary sources (pre-1950)

Adams, M. (ed.). *The Modern State* (London, 1933)

Angell, N. *Must It Be War?* (London, 1938)

Atholl, Duchess of. *Searchlight on Spain* (London, 1937)

Auden, W. H. *The Dance of Death* (London, 1933)

Barbusse, H. *L'Enfer* (Paris, 1937)

Bartlett, F. C. *Psychology and the Soldier* (Cambridge, 1927)

Baynes, H. G. *Germany Possessed* (London, 1941)

Bell, C. *Civilization: An Essay* (London, 1928)

Benjamin, W. *Selected Writings*, vol. I, *1913–1926* (Cambridge, Mass., 2002)

—— *Zur Kritik der Gewalt und andere Aufsätze* (Frankfurt am Main, 1966)

Bentwich, N. *The Refugees from Germany: April 1933 to December 1935* (London, 1936)

Bernays, R. 'The Nazis and the Jews', *Contemporary Review*, 144 (July–Dec. 1933), pp. 523–31

Bernfeld, S. and Feitelberg, S. 'The Principle of Entropy and the Death Instinct', *International Journal of Psycho-Analysis*, 12 (1931), pp. 67–81

Beveridge, W. *The Price of Peace* (London, 1945)

Birkenhead, Earl of. *The World in 2030* (London, 1937)

Blacker, C. P. *Eugenics: Galton and After* (London, 1952)

—— *Eugenics in Prospect and Retrospect* (London, 1945)

—— *Voluntary Sterilization* (Oxford, 1934)

Bloch, E. *Geist der Utopie* (Berlin, 1923)

Bond, C. J. *Racial Decay: The Galton Lecture, Feb. 1928* (London, 1928)

Bowes, G. K. ' "The Decline of the West" in Actual Progress', *Hibbert Journal*, 33 (1934/5), pp. 187–92

Brailsford, H. N. *The Life-Work of J. A. Hobson: L. T. Hobhouse Memorial Lecture* (Oxford, 1948)

Bratt, K. A. *That Next War?* (London, 1930)

Britain without Capitalists: A Study of what Industry in a Soviet Britain Could Achieve (London, 1936)

Brockway, F. *This Bloody Traffic* (London, 1933)

Brown, H. 'Germany in Revolution', *Fortnightly Review*, 133 (Jan.–June 1933), pp. 441–52

Buckham, J. 'Death', *Hibbert Journal*, 36 (1937/8), pp. 93–9

Burns, C. D. *Modern Civilization on Trial* (London, 1931)

—— 'War and Peace', *Contemporary Review*, 144 (July–Dec. 1933), pp. 673–81

Burns, E. *What is Marxism?* (London, 1939)

Burt, C. 'The Causal Factors of Juvenile Crime', *British Journal of Psychology (Medical Section)*, 3 (1923), pp. 1–33

—— 'The Causes of Sex Delinquency in Girls', *Health and Empire*, 1 (1926), pp. 251–71

—— 'The Contribution of Psychology to Social Hygiene', *Health and Empire*, 1 (1926), pp. 13–37

—— 'Delinquency and Mental Defect', *British Journal of Psychology (Medical Section)*, 3 (1923), pp. 168–78

Burt, C. (ed.). *How the Mind Works* (London, 1935)

Cambridge Scientists' Anti-War Group. *The Protection of the Public from Aerial Attack* (London, 1937)

Campion, C. T. (ed.). *Albert Schweitzer: Philosopher, Theologian, Musician, Doctor: Some Biographical Notes* (London, 1928)

Carr-Saunders, A. M. *Eugenics* (London, 1926)

Catlin. G. (ed.). *New Trends in Socialism* (London, 1935)

Caudwell, C. (pseudo. Sprigg, C. St J.). *Studies in a Dying Culture* (London, 1938)

Chadwick, M. 'Notes upon the Fear of Death', *International Journal of Psycho-Analysis*, 10 (1929), pp. 321–34

Chalmers-Mitchell, P. 'The Twilight of Civilization', *The Rationalist Annual*, 1940, pp. 31–6

Chapman, G. *Culture and Survival* (London, 1940)

Charlton, L. E. O. *War from the Air: Past, Present and Future* (London, 1935)

Charteris, L. *Prelude for War* (London, 1938)

Childe, V. G. *What Happened in History* (London, 1942)

Clark, G. N. 'The Instability of Civilisation', *Hibbert Journal*, 31 (1932/3), pp. 645–53

Cloud, V. (ed.). *The Basque Children in England* (London, 1937)

Cochrane, A. L. 'Elie Metschnikoff and his Theory of an "Instinct de la Mort"', *International Journal of Psycho-Analysis*, 15 (1934), pp. 265–70

Cohen, I. 'The Jews in Germany', *Quarterly Review*, 261 (July–Oct. 1933)

Cohen, J. *Human Nature, War and Society* (London, 1946)

Cole, G. D. H. *Economic Prospects: 1938 and After* (London, 1938)

—— *An Intelligent Man's Guide Through World Chaos* (London, 1932)

—— *The Machinery of Socialist Planning* (London, 1938)

—— *The People's Front* (London, 1937)

—— *Persons and Periods* (London, 1938)

—— *A Plan for Britain* (London, 1933)

Cole, M. I. (ed.). *Twelve Studies in Soviet Russia* (London, 1933)

Cowles, V. *Looking for Trouble* (London, 1941)

Cromer, Earl of. *Ancient and Modern Imperialism* (London, 1910)

Czernin, Count F. *Europe: Going, Going, Gone!* (London, 1939)

Daniel, A. W. *Some Statistics about Sterilisation of the Insane* (London, 1912)

Darwin, L. *Eugenics during and after the War* (London, 1915)

—— *The Need for Eugenic Reforms* (London, 1926)

Dawson, C. 'Herr Spengler and the Life of Civilisations', *Sociological Review*, 14 (1922), pp. 194–201

—— 'The Life of Civilisations', *Sociological Review*, 14 (1922), pp. 51–68

Dawson, S. 'Intelligence and Fertility', *British Journal of Psychology (General Section)*, 23 (1932), pp. 42–51

Dearmer, P. (ed.). *Christianity and the Crisis* (London, 1933)

Decugis, H. *Le Destin des races blanches* (2nd edn, Paris, 1936)

Delafield, E. M. *Straw without Bricks: I Visit Soviet Russia* (London, 1937)

Drascher, W. *Die Vorherrschaft der weissen Rasse* (Stuttgart, 1936)

Duhamel, G. *The White War of 1938* (London, 1939)

Durbin, E. F. M. and Bowlby, J. *Personal Aggressiveness and War* (London, 1939)

Dyrenforth, J. and Kester, M. *Adolf in Blunderland* (London, 1939)

Einstein, A. *The World as I See It* (London, 1935)

Einzig, P. *Hitler's 'New Order' in Europe* (London, 1940)

Ellis, H. (ed.). *Sex in Civilisation* (London, 1929)

Engelbrecht, H. *Revolt against War* (London, 1938)

Engelbrecht, H. and Hanighen, J. *Merchants of Death* (London, 1934)

Ensor, R. C. K. '"Mein Kampf" and Europe', *International Affairs*, 18 (1939)

Faulks, E. *The Sterilisation of the Insane* (London, 1911)

Flewelling, R. T. *The Survival of Western Culture: An Inquiry into the Problem of Decline and Resurgence* (New York, 1943)

Forbath, A. *Europe into the Abyss: Behind the Scenes of Secret Politics* (London, n.d. but 1938/9)

Fraser, L. H. 'How Do We Want Economists to Behave?' *Economic Journal*, 42 (1932), pp. 555–70

Frazer, J. G. *The Golden Bough* (12 vols., London, 1906–15)

Freeman, R. A. *Social Decay and Degeneration* (London, 1921)

Freud, S. *New Introductory Lectures on Psycho-Analysis* (London, 1933)

Frolov, Y. P. *Pavlov and His School: The Theory of Conditioned Reflexes* (London, 1937)

Fuller, J. F. C. *The Dragon's Teeth: A Study of War and Peace* (London, 1932)

Fyvel, T. R. *The Malady and the Vision: An Analysis of Political Faith* (London, 1940)

Gibbs, P. *The Day After To-Morrow: What Is Going to Happen to the World?* (London, 1928)

Gini, C. *Nascità, evoluzione e morte delle nazioni* (Rome, 1930)

Glover, E. *The Dangers of Being Human* (London, 1936)

—— *The Social and Legal Aspects of Sexual Abnormality* (London, 1947)

Goddard, E. H. and Gibbons, P. A. *Civilisation or Civilisations: An Essay in the Spenglerian Philosophy of History* (London, 1926)

Goldhamer, H. 'The Psychological Analysis of War', *Sociological Review*, 26 (1934), pp. 249–67

Gollancz, V. *Is Mr Chamberlain Saving the Peace?* (London, 1939)

—— *Russia and Ourselves* (London, 1941)

Gooch, G. P. *Germany* (London, 1925)

Graves, R. and Hodge, A. *The Long Week-End: A Social History of Great Britain, 1918–1939* (London, 1940)

Guest, E. *At the End of the World* (London, 1929)

Haldane, J. B. S. *The Causes of Evolution* (London, 1932)

—— *Keeping Cool and Other Essays* (London, 1940)

—— *Possible Worlds and Other Essays* (London, 1927)

Harding, D. W. *The Impulse to Dominate* (London, 1941)

Harris, H. W. *The Future of Europe* (London, 1932)

Haycraft, J. B. *Darwinism and Race Progress* (London, 1895)

Heard, G. *These Hurrying Years: An Historical Outline, 1900–1933* (London, 1934)

Heiden, K. *A History of National Socialism* (London, 1934)

Hobson, J. A. *Confessions of an Economic Heretic* (London, 1938)

—— *From Capitalism to Socialism* (London, 1932)

—— *Imperialism* (London, 1902)

—— *The Recording Angel: A Report from Earth* (London, 1932)

—— 'Underconsumption: An Exposition and a Reply', *Economica*, 13 (1933), pp. 403–27

—— *Wealth and Life: A Study of Values* (London, 1929)

Hobson, J. A. and Mummery, A. F. *The Physiology of Industry, Being an Exposure of Certain Fallacies in Existing Theories of Economics* (London, 1889)

Hodson, C. B. *Human Sterilization To-day: A Survey of the Present Position* (London, 1934)

Hogben, L. *Nature and Nurture* (London, 1933, 2nd edn, 1939)

Hopkins, P. *The Psychology of Social Movements: A Psycho-Analytic View of Society* (London, 1938)

Horney, K. *The Neurotic Personality of Our Time* (London, 1937)

—— 'Observations on a Specific Difference in the Dread Felt by Men and by Women Respectively for the Opposite Sex', *International Journal of Psycho-Analysis*, 13 (1932), pp. 348–60

Howard, P. *That Man Frank Buchman* (London, 1946)

Howe, E. Graham. *War Dance: A Study of the Psychology of War* (London, 1937)

Huxley, A. *Ape and Essence* (London, 1948)

—— *Brave New World* (London, 1932)

—— *Brave New World Revisited* (London, 1958)

—— *Ends and Means: An Enquiry into the Nature of Ideals and into the Methods Employed for their Realization* (London, 1938)

—— *What Are You Going to Do About It? The Case for Constructive Peace* (London, 1936)

Huxley, J. 'The Case for Eugenics', *Sociological Review*, 18 (1926), pp. 279–90

—— *If I Were Dictator* (London, 1934)

Inge, W. R. *The Fall of the Idols* (London, 1940)

Is it a New World? (London, 1920)

Jacks, L. 'Mr Wells on the Fate of Homo Sapiens', *Hibbert Journal*, 38 (1939/40), pp. 161–73

—— 'The Saving Forces of Civilisation', *Hibbert Journal*, 30 (1931/2), pp. 1–6

Jackson, J. A., Salisbury, H. M. and Wolfe, W. B. *Nervous Breakdown: Its Cause and Cure* (London, 1933)

Jameson, S. 'A Faith Worth Dying For', *Fortnightly Review*, 135 (Jan.–June 1934)

Jones, D. Caradog. *The Social Survey of Merseyside* (Liverpool, 1934)

Jones, E. *Essays in Applied Psycho-Analysis*, vol. I, *Miscellaneous Essays* (London, 1951)

—— 'The Future of Psychoanalysis', *International Journal of Psycho-Analysis*, 17 (1936), pp. 269–77

—— 'The Individual and Society', *Sociological Review*, 27 (1935), pp. 245–63

—— 'Recent Advances in Psycho-Analysis', *British Journal of Psychology (Medical Section)*, 1 (1920/1), pp. 49–71

—— *What Is Psychoanalysis?* (London, 1949)

Joules, H. (ed.). *The Doctor's View of War* (London, 1938)

Jung, C. *Modern Man in Search of a Soul* (London, 1936)

Keith, A. *Darwinism and What It Implies* (London, 1928)

Kenworthy, J. M. *Will Civilisation Crash?* (London, 1927)

Klein, D. B. 'Psychology and Freud: An Historico-Critical Approach', *Psychological Review*, 40 (1933), pp. 440–56

Klein, M. and Riviere, J. *Love, Hate and Reparation* (London, 1938)

Knibbs, G. H. *The Shadow of the World's Future: Or the Earth's Population Possibilities and the Consequences of the Present Rate of Increase of the Earth's Inhabitants* (London, 1928)

Knickerbocker, H. R. *Can Europe Recover?* (London, 1932)

—— *Germany – Fascist or Soviet?* (London, 1932)

—— *Will War Come to Europe?* (London, 1934)

Koestler, A. *Darkness at Noon* (London, 1940)

Langdon-Davies, J. *Air Raid: The Technique of Silent Approach, High Explosive, Panic* (London, 1938)

Lasswell, H. D. *World Politics and Personal Insecurity* (New York, 1935)

Lee, I. *USSR: A World Enigma* (London, 1927)

Lengyel, E. *Hitler* (London, 1932)

Levy, O. (ed.). *The Will to Power: An Attempted Transvaluation of all Values* (London, 1913)

Lewis, C. Day. *The Complete Poems* (London, 1992)

—— *Selected Poems* (London, 1940)

Lewis, C. Day (ed.). *The Mind in Chains: Socialism and the Cultural Revolution* (London, 1937)

Lewis, P. W. *Hitler* (London, 1930)

—— *The Hitler Cult* (London, 1939)

Leybourne, G. 'The Future Population of Great Britain', *Sociological Review*, 26 (1934), pp. 130–38

Liddell Hart, B. *Thoughts on War* (London, 1944)

Liepmann, H. *Death from the Skies: A Study of Gas and Microbial Warfare* (London, 1937)

Lorimer, E. O. *What Hitler Wants* (London, 1939)

Low, B. *Psycho-Analysis: A Brief Account of Freudian Theory* (London, 1920)

Ludovici, A. M. *Nietzsche: His Life and Works* (London, 1912)

—— *The Night-Hoers* (London, 1933)

—— *The Specious Origins of Liberalism* (London, 1967)

—— *Who Is to Be Master of the World? An Introduction to the Philosophy of Friedrich Nietzsche* (London, 1909)

Lynch, A. 'The Depth of Freudism', *English Review*, 57 (1933), pp. 622–9

Machin, A. *Darwin's Theory Applied to Mankind* (London, 1937)

MacNeice, L. *Poems* (London, 1935)

Mannheim, K. *Man and Society in an Age of Reconstruction: Studies in Modern Social Structure* (London, 1940)

Marchin, M. G. *Britain's Jewish Problem* (London, 1939)

Maroi, L. *I fattori demografici del conflitto europeo* (Rome, 1919)

May, M. A. *A Social Psychology of War and Peace* (New Haven, 1943)

McCabe, J. *Can We Save Civilisation?* (London, 1932)

—— *The End of the World* (London, 1920)

Milner, G. *The Problems of Decadence* (London, 1931)

Mitchell, T. W. 'Psychology and the Unconscious', *British Journal of Psychology (Medical Section)*, 1 (1920/1), pp. 327–40

Money-Kyrle, R. E. *The Development of the Sexual Impulses* (London, 1932)

Montagu, M. F. Ashley, *Man's Most Dangerous Myth: The Fallacy of Race* (2nd edn, New York, 1945)

Muirhead, J. T. *Air Attack on Cities: The Broader Aspect of the Problem* (London, 1938)

Mumford, P. S. *Humanity, Air Power and War* (London, 1936)

Muret, M. *The Twilight of the White Races* (London, 1926)

Murphy, J. *Adolf Hitler* (London, 1934)

Murray, G. *The Ordeal of this Generation: The War, the League and the Future* (London, 1929)

—— 'Die Probleme von morgen', *Nord und Süd*, 50 (1927), pp. 344–57

Needham, J. *Man a Machine* (London, 1927)

Neilson, F. 'Toynbee's "A Study of History"', *American Journal of Economics and Sociology*, 6 (1947), pp. 452–65

The Next Five Years: An Essay in Political Agreement (London, 1935)

Nickerson, H. *Can We Limit War?* (London, 1933)

Nicolai, G. F. *The Biology of War* (London, 1919)

Nicole, J. E. *Psychopathology: A Survey of Modern Approaches* (London, 1942)

Nordau, M. *Degeneration* (London, 1895)

Olgin, M. J. *Why Communism? Plain Talks on Vital Problems* (Workers' Library, New York, December 1933)

Orwell, G. *Coming Up for Air* (London, 1939)

Palmer, F. C. 'The Death Instinct and Western Man', *Hibbert Journal*, 51 (1953), pp. 329–37

Pascal, R. *The Nazi Dictatorship* (London, 1934)

Paul, L. *The Annihilation of Man: A Study of the Crisis in the West* (London, 1944)

Pearson, K. 'On Our Present Knowledge of the Relationship of Mind and Body', *Annals of Eugenics*, 1 (1925/6), pp. 382–406

Perry, R. B. 'The Meaning of Death', *Hibbert Journal*, 33 (1934/5), pp. 161–78

Perry, W. J. *The Growth of Civilisation* (London, 1924)

Petrie, W. M. Flinders. *The Revolutions of Civilisations* (London, 1911)

Porritt, A. (ed.). *The Causes of War: Economic, Industrial, Racial, Religious, Scientific and Political* (London, 1932)

Ralph, J. *How to Psycho-Analyse Yourself: Theory and Practice of Remoulding the Personality by the Analytic Method* (London, 1937)

Rather, A. W. *Is Britain Decadent?* (London, 1931)

Rattray, R. F. 'Will Our Civilisation Survive?', *Hibbert Journal*, 34 (1935/6), pp. 57–64

Rauschning, H. *Hitler Speaks* (London, 1939)

Remarque, E. M. *All Quiet on the Western Front* (London, 1928)

Rentoul, R. R. *Proposed Sterilization of Certain Mental and Physical Degenerates* (London, 1903)

Riddell, G. *Sterilization of the Unfit* (London, 1929)

Rowse, A. L. 'A British Popular Front', *Quarterly Review*, 266 (Jan.–April 1936)

—— *Poems of a Decade, 1931–1941* (London, 1941)

Rüdin, E. *Psychiatric Indications for Sterilization* (London, 1929)

Ruggles Gate, R. 'The Inheritance of Mental Defect', *British Journal of Medical Psychology*, 13 (1933)

Russell, B. *Sceptical Essays* (London, 1935)

—— *The Scientific Outlook* (London, 1931)

Salmon, D. *Jungle Doctor: The Story of Albert Schweitzer* (London, 1948)

Salomon, S. *The Jews of Britain* (London, 1938)

Sanger, M. *The Pivot of Civilization* (London, 1923)

Schiller, F. C. *Cassandra or The Future of the British Empire* (London, 1926)

—— *Tantalus or The Future of Man* (London, 1924)

Schweitzer, A. *The Decay and the Restoration of Civilization: The Philosophy of Civilization, Part I* (London, 1923)

Sforza, C. *Europe and Europeans: A Study in Historical Psychology and International Politics* (New York, 1936)

Shaw, G. B. *Everybody's Political What's What?* (London, 1944)

—— *The Political Madhouse in America and Nearer Home* (London, 1933)

Shotwell, J. *On the Rim of the Abyss* (New York, 1936)

—— 'Spengler', in Shotwell, J. (ed.), *Essays in Intellectual History* (New York, 1929)

Shrubsall, F. C. 'Delinquency and Mental Defect', *British Journal of Psychology (Medical Section)*, 3 (1923), pp. 179–87

Siegfried, A. *Europe's Crisis* (London, 1935)

Smith, N. C. and Garnett, J. C. Maxwell. *The Dawn of World-Order: An Introductory to the Study of the League of Nations* (Oxford, 1932)

Spaight, J. M. *Air Power and the Cities* (London, 1930)

Spaulding, O. L. *Ahriman: A Study of Air Bombardment* (Boston, Mass., 1939)

Spender, S. *Forward from Liberalism* (London, 1937)

Spengler, O. *The Decline of the West* (2 vols., 1926–8)

—— *Pessimismus?* (Munich, 1922)

—— *Der Untergang des Abendlandes* (2 vols., Munich, 1922–3)

Spiller, G. 'Francis Galton and Hereditary Genius', *Sociological Review*, 24 (1932), pp. 47–56, 155–64

Stansfield, T. E. *Heredity and Insanity* (London, 1911)

Steed, W. *The Meaning of Hitlerism* (London, 1934)

Stoddard, L. *Clashing Tides of Colour* (London, 1935)

—— *The Revolt against Civilization: The Menace of the Under-Man* (London, 1922)

Stopes, M. C. *The Human Body* (London, 1926)

Storck, J. *Man and Civilization: An Inquiry into the Bases of Contemporary Life* (London, 1929)

Swanwick, H. *Collective Insecurity* (London, 1937)

Tansley, A. G. *The New Psychology* (London, 1920)

Tenenbaum, J. *The Riddle of Sex* (London, 1930)

Thompson, E. *You Have Lived Through All This* (London, 1939)

Thomson, J. A. 'The Biological Control of Life', *Health and Empire*, 2 (1927), pp. 198–207

—— 'Outline of Bio-Sociology', *Health and Empire*, 3 (1928), pp. 107–19

—— 'The Trajectory of Life: Its Sequence of Risks and Rewards', *Health and Empire*, 3 (1928), pp. 6–27

—— *What Is Man?* (London, 1923)

Thuillier, H. F. *Gas in the Next War* (London, 1939)

Toynbee, A. J. *Christianity and Civilisation* (London, 1940)

—— *Civilization on Trial* (New York, 1948)

—— *A Study of History* (10 vols., Oxford, 1934–56)

—— *A Study of History: Abridgement of Volumes I–VI* (Oxford, 1946)

Wallas, G. *The Great Society: A Psychological Analysis* (London, 1936)

—— *Human Nature in Politics* (London, 1924)

Watts, C. *The Meaning of Rationalism and Other Essays* (London, 1905)

Weatherhead, L. D. *Psychology and Life* (London, 1934)

Webb, B. and Webb, S. *The Decay of Capitalist Civilization* (London, 1923)

—— *Soviet Communism: A New Civilisation?* (2 vols., London, 1935)

—— *Soviet Communism: A New Civilisation* (London, 1937)

Webb, S. 'Freedom and Soviet Russia', *Contemporary Review*, 143 (Jan.–June 1933), pp. 11–21

Wells, H. G. *After Democracy: Addresses and Papers on the Present World Situation* (London, 1932)

—— *The Common Sense of War and Peace: World Revolution or War Unending* (London, 1940)

—— *Experiment in Autobiography: Being the Autobiography of H. G. Wells* (2 vols., London, 1934)

—— *The Fate of Homo Sapiens: An Unemotional Statement of the Things that Are Happening to Him Now and of the Immediate Possibilities Confronting Him* (London, 1939)

—— *The New World Order* (London, 1940)

—— *The Open Conspiracy* (2nd edn, London, 1930)

—— *The Salvaging of Civilization* (London, 1921)

—— *The Shape of Things to Come* (London, 1933)

Wells, H. G., Wells, G. P. and Huxley, J. *The Science of Life* (London, 1938)

White, A. *Efficiency and Empire* (London, 1901)

—— *The Views of Vanoc: An Englishman's Outlook* (London, 1911)

Why Nazi? (London, 1933)

Wilkinson, E. and Conze, E. *Why War?* (London, 1934)

Williams, L. 'The Constituents of the Unconscious', *British Journal of Psychology (Medical Section)*, 2 (1921/2), pp. 259–72

Williams, W. H. *Who's Who in Arms* (Labour Research Dept, London, 1935)

Wintringham, T. *The Coming World War* (London, 1935)

Woolf, L. *Barbarians at the Gate* (London, 1939)

—— *Imperialism and Civilization* (London, 1928)

—— *The War for Peace* (London, 1940)

The Yellow Spot: The Outlawing of Half a Million Human Beings (London, 1936)

Zuckerman, S. *Functional Affinities of Man, Monkeys and Apes* (London, 1933)

—— *The Social Life of Monkeys and Apes* (London, 1933)

Secondary sources (post-1950)

Abel, D. C. *Freud on Instinct and Morality* (Albany, N.Y., 1989)

Anderson, G. D. *Fascists, Communists and the National Government: Civil Liberties in Great Britain, 1931–1937* (Columbia, Miss., 1983)

Atholl, Duchess of. *Working Partnership* (London, 1958)

Audoin-Rouzeau, S., Becker, A., Ingrao, C. and Rousso, H. (eds.). *La Violence de guerre 1914–1945* (Paris, 2002)

Bair, D. *Jung: A Biography* (Boston, 2003)

Baldoli, C. (ed.). *Marie Louise Berneri e Vera Brittain: Il seme del Caos: Scritti sui bombardamenti di massa* (Santa Maria Capua Vetere, 2004)

Barnes, J. J. and Barnes, P. P. *Hitler's 'Mein Kampf' in Britain and America: A Publishing History, 1930–1939* (Cambridge, 1980)

Baxell, R. *British Volunteers in the Spanish Civil War: The British Battalion in the International Brigades, 1936–1939* (London, 2004)

Becker, A. 'The Avant-Garde, Madness and the Great War', *Journal of Contemporary History*, 35 (2000), pp. 71–84

Bedford, S. *Aldous Huxley: A Biography*, vol. I, *1894–1939* (London, 1973)

Berry, P. and Bostridge, M. *Vera Brittain: A Life* (London, 1995)

Birn, D. S. *The League of Nations Union 1918–1945* (Oxford, 1981)

Bialer, U. *The Shadow of the Bomber: The Fear of Air Attack and British Politics 1932–1939* (London, 1980)

Blaazer, D. *The Popular Front and the Progressive Tradition: Socialists, Liberals and the Quest for Unity, 1884–1939* (Cambridge, 1992)

Blom, P. *The Vertigo Years: Change and Culture in the West, 1900–1914* (London, 2008)

Bogacz, T. 'War Neurosis and Cultural Change in England, 1914–1922: The Work of the War Office Committee of Enquiry into "Shell-Shock"', *Journal of Contemporary History*, 24 (1989), pp. 227–56

Bourke, J. *Fear: A Cultural History* (London, 2005)

—— *An Intimate History of Killing: Face-to-Face Killing in Twentieth-Century Warfare* (London, 1999)

Brendon, P. *The Dark Valley: A Panorama of the 1930s* (London, 2000)

—— *The Decline and Fall of the British Empire* (London, 2007)

Briggs, A. *The Golden Age of Wireless* (Oxford, 1965)

Brock, P. *Freedom from War: Nonsectarian Pacifism, 1814–1914* (Toronto, 1991)

Brooks, P. and Woloch, A. (eds.). *Whose Freud: The Place of Psychoanalysis in Contemporary Culture* (New Haven, 2000)

Brown, A. *J. D. Bernal: The Sage of Science* (Oxford, 2005)

Buchanan, P. J. *The Death of the West* (New York, 2002)

Buchanan, T. *Britain and the Spanish Civil War* (Cambridge, 1997)

—— *The Spanish Civil War and the British Labour Movement* (Cambridge, 1991)

Caedel, M. *Pacifism in Britain, 1914–1945: The Defining of a Faith* (Oxford, 1980)

Carlson, E. A. *The Unfit: A History of a Bad Idea* (New York, 2001)

Carpenter, L. P. *G. D. H. Cole: An Intellectual Biography* (Cambridge, 1973)

Clark, W. H. *The Oxford Group: Its History and Significance* (New York, 1951)

Clarke, P. *The Cripps Version: The Life of Sir Stafford Cripps, 1889–1952* (London, 2002)

—— 'Hobson and Keynes as Economic Heretics', in Freeden, M. (ed.). *Reappraising J. A. Hobson* (London, 1990)

Collini, S. *Absent Minds: Intellectuals in Britain* (Oxford, 2006)

Constantine, S. ' "Love on the Dole" and its Reception in the 1930s', *Literature and History*, 8 (1982), pp. 232–47

Copsey, N. *Anti-Fascism in Britain* (London, 2000)

Corthorn, P. 'Labour, the Left, and the Stalinist Purges of the late 1930s', *Historical Journal*, 48 (2005), pp. 179–207

Crook, P. *Darwinism, War and History* (Cambridge, 1994)

493

Danchev, A. *Alchemist of War: The Life of Basil Liddell Hart* (London, 1998)

Dannhauser, W. J. 'Nietzsche and Spengler on Progress and Decline', in Melzer, A. M., Weinberger, J. and Zinman, M. R. (eds.), *History and the Idea of Progress* (Ithaca, N.Y., 1995)

Davis, B. 'Experience, Identity, and Memory: The Legacy of World War I', *Journal of Modern History*, 75 (2003), pp. 111–31

Dawson, C. *The Dynamics of World History* (London, 1957)

Dean, C. J. *The Frail Social Body: Pornography, Homosexuality and Other Fantasies in Interwar France* (Berkeley, 2000)

Dunaway, D. K. *Huxley in Hollywood* (London, 1989)

Dutton, D. *Neville Chamberlain* (London, 2001)

Edwards, R. D. *Victor Gollancz: A Biography* (London, 1987)

Eksteins, M. *Rites of Spring: The Great War and the Birth of the Modern Age* (New York, 1989)

Farrenkopf, J. *Prophet of Decline: Spengler on World Politics and History* (Baton Rouge, La., 2001)

Ferguson, N. *War of the World: History's Age of Hatred* (London, 2007)

Field, F. *Three French Writers and the Great War: Barbusse, Drieu La Rochelle, Bernanos* (Cambridge, 1975)

Fisher, K. *Birth Control, Sex and Marriage in Britain, 1918–1960* (Oxford, 2006)

Fordham, F. *An Introduction to Jung's Psychology* (London, 2nd edn, 1959)

Frayling, C. *Mad, Bad and Dangerous? The Scientist and the Cinema* (London, 2005)

Freeden, M. 'Eugenics and Progressive Thought: A Study in Ideological Affinity', *Historical Journal*, 22 (1979), pp. 645–71

Fromm, E. *The Anatomy of Human Destructiveness* (London, 1974)

Fuchser, L. *Neville Chamberlain and Appeasement* (New York, 1982)

Fukuyama, F. *The End of Order* (London, 1997)

Furbank, P. N. *E. M. Forster: A Life* (London, 1977)

Fyrth, J. 'The Aid Spain Movement in Britain, 1936–39', *History Workshop Journal*, 35 (1993), pp. 153–64

Geyer, M. ' "There is a Land Where Everything is Pure: Its Name is the Land of Death": Some Observations on Catastrophic Nationalism', in Eghigian, G. and Berg, M. P. (eds.), *Sacrifice and National Belonging in Twentieth-Century Germany* (College Station, Tex., 2002), pp. 118–47

Gilman, S. L. *The Case of Sigmund Freud: Medicine and Identity at the Fin de Siècle* (Baltimore, Md., 1993)

Ginsberg, M. *On the Diversity of Morals* (2 vols., London, 1956)

Grant, M. *Propaganda and the Role of the State in Inter-war Britain* (Oxford, 1994)

Granzow, B. *A Mirror of Nazism: British Opinion and the Emergence of Hitler, 1929–1933* (London, 1964)

Gregory, A. *The Silence of Memory: Armistice Day, 1919–1946* (Oxford, 1994)

Griffiths, R. *Fellow-Travellers of the Right: British Enthusiasts for Nazi Germany, 1933–1939* (Oxford, 1983)

—— 'The Reception of Bryant's *Unfinished Victory*: Insights into British Public Opinion in Early 1940', *Patterns of Prejudice*, 38 (2004), pp. 18–36

Grosskurth, P. *Melanie Klein: Her World and Her Work* (London, 1985)

Hawkins, M. *Social Darwinism in European and American Thought, 1860–1945: Nature as Model and Nature as Threat* (Cambridge, 1997)

Hensbergen, G. van. *Guernica: The Biography of a Twentieth-Century Icon* (London, 2004)

Herman, A. *The Idea of Decline in Western History* (New York, 1997)

Higgs, E. *The Information State in England: The Central Collection of Information on Citizens since 1500* (London, 2004)

Horne, A. *Macmillan, 1894–1956* (London, 1988)

Howson, G. *Arms for Spain: The Untold Story of the Spanish Civil War* (London, 1998)

Hughes, H. S. *Oswald Spengler: A Critical Estimate* (New York, 1952)

Ipsen, C. *Dictating Demography: The Problem of Population in Fascist Italy* (Cambridge, 1996)

Jacobi, J. *The Psychology of C. G. Jung* (3rd edn, London, 1973)

Johnston, T. *Freud and Political Thought* (New York, 1965)

Joll, J. 'Two Prophets of the Twentieth Century: Spengler and Toynbee', *Review of International Studies*, 11 (1985), pp. 91–104

Jones, E. *Sigmund Freud: Life and Work*, vol. III (London, 1957)

Jones, G. 'Eugenics and Social Policy between the Wars', *Historical Journal*, 25 (1982), pp. 717–28

Jones, R. A. *Arthur Ponsonby: The Politics of Life* (Bromley, 1989)

Kaye, E. *Mansfield College: Its Origin, History and Significance* (Oxford, 1996)

Kershaw, I. *Making Friends with Hitler: Lord Londonderry, the Nazis and World War II* (London, 2004)

Koch, R. and Smith, C. *Suicide of the West* (London, 2006)

Köhler, J. *Nietzsche's Secret: The Interior Life of Friedrich Nietzsche* (New Haven, 2002)

Laffey, J. *Civilisation and its Discontented* (Montreal, 1993)

Lawrence, J. 'Forging a Peaceable Kingdom: War, Violence and Fear of Brutalization in Post-First World War Britain', *Journal of Modern History*, 75 (2003), pp. 557–89

Leed, E. 'Fateful Memories: Industrialized Warfare and Traumatic Neuroses', *Journal of Contemporary History*, 35 (2000), pp. 85–100

Leventhal, F. M. 'H. N. Brailsford and the *New Leader*', *Journal of Contemporary History*, 9 (1974), pp. 91–114

Levine, C. 'Propaganda for Democracy: The Curious Case of *Love on the Dole*', *Journal of British Studies*, 45 (2006)

Linehan, T. *British Fascism 1918–1939: Parties, Ideology and Culture* (Manchester, 2000)

Long, D. and Wilson, P. (eds.). *Thinkers of the Twenty Years' Crisis: Inter-War Idealism Reassessed* (Oxford, 1995)

Lorenz, K. *On Aggression* (London, 1966)

Lukowitz, D. C. 'British Pacifists and Appeasement: The Peace Pledge Union', *Journal of Contemporary History*, 9 (1974), pp. 115–28

Maasen, S., Mendelsohn, E. and Weingart, P. (eds.). *Biology as Society, Society as Biology: Metaphors* (Dordrecht, 1995)

Maddox, B. *Freud's Wizard: The Enigma of Ernest Jones* (London, 2006)

Mahon, J. *Harry Pollitt: A Biography* (London, 1976)

Maier, K. *Guernica: 26.iv.1937: Die deutsche Intervention in Spanien und der 'Fall Guernica'* (Freiburg im Breisgau, 1975)

Mantovani, C. *Rigenerare la società: L'eugenetica in Italia dalle origine ottocentesche agli anni trenta* (Rubbentino, 2004)

McIntire, C. T. and Perry, M. (eds.). *Toynbee Reappraisals* (Toronto, 1989)

Medewar, J. and Pyke, D. *Hitler's Gift* (London, 2000)

Mepham, J. *Virginia Woolf: A Literary Life* (London, 1991)

Millar, J. P. M. *The Labour College Movement* (London, n.d. but 1964)

Miller, T. *Late Modernism: Politics, Fiction, and the Arts Between the World Wars* (Berkeley, 1999)

Mini, P. V. *Keynes, Bloomsbury and 'The General Theory'* (London, 1991)

Moorehead, C. *Troublesome People: Enemies of War, 1916–1986* (London, 1987)

Moradiellos, E. 'The Origins of British Non-Intervention in the Spanish Civil War: Anglo-Spanish Relations in Early 1936', *European History Quarterly*, 21 (1991), pp. 339–64

Morgan, K. *The Webbs and Soviet Communism* (London, 2006)

Morpurgo, J. E. *Allen Lane, King Penguin: A Biography* (London, 1979)

Mumford, L. *Interpretations and Forecasts, 1922–1972* (London, 1973)

O'Hagan, J. *Conceptualizing the West in International Relations* (London, 2002)

O'Keefe, P. *Some Sort of Genius: A Life of Wyndham Lewis* (London, 2000)

O'Leary, S. D. *Arguing the Apocalypse: A Theory of Millennial Rhetoric* (New York, 1994)

Ollard, R. *A Man of Contradictions: A Life of A. L. Rowse* (London, 2000)

Overy, R. J. 'Air Power and the Origins of Deterrence Theory before 1939', *Journal of Strategic Studies*, 15 (1992), pp. 73–101

Paris, M. *From the Wright Brothers to Top Gun: Aviation, Nationalism and Popular Cinema* (Manchester, 1995)

—— *Warrior Nation: Images of War in British Popular Culture, 1850–2000* (London, 2000)

Parker, R. A. C. *Chamberlain and Appeasement: British Policy and the Coming of the Second World War* (London, 1993)

Patterson, I. *Guernica and Total War* (London, 2007)

Peel, R. A. (ed.). *Essays in the History of Eugenics* (London, 1998)

—— *Marie Stopes, Eugenics and the English Birth Control Movement* (London, 1997)

Pflug, G. *Albert Einstein als Publizist, 1919–1933* (Frankfurt am Main, 1981)

Pick, D. *War Machine: The Rationalization of Slaughter in the Modern Age* (New Haven, 1993)

Pogliano, C. 'Scienze e stirpe: eugenica in Italia (1912–1939)', *Passato e presente*, 5 (1984)

Pugh, M. *Hurrah for the Blackshirts! Fascists and Fascism in Britain between the Wars* (London, 2005)

—— *'We Danced All Night': A Social History of Britain between the Wars* (London, 2008)

Rankin, N. *Telegram from Guernica: The Extraordinary Life of George Steer, War Correspondent* (London, 2003)

Reynolds, D. *Summits: Six Meetings that Shaped the Twentieth Century* (London, 2007)

Riddell, N. ' " The Age of Cole"? G. D. H. Cole and the British Labour Movement, 1929–1933', *Historical Journal*, 38 (1995), pp. 933–57

Ritschel, D. *The Politics of Planning: The Debate on Economic Planning in Britain in the 1930s* (Oxford, 1997)

Roazen, P. *Freud: Political and Social Thought* (New York, 1968)

Robitscher, J. (ed.). *Eugenic Sterilization* (Springfield, Ill., 1973)

Rodgers, T. 'The Right Book Club: Text Wars, Modernity and Cultural Politics in the Late Thirties', *Literature and History*, 12 (2003), pp. 1–15

Rose, J. *Why War?* (London, 1993)

Sánchez-Pardo, E. *Cultures of the Death Drive: Melanie Klein and Modernist Melancholia* (Durham, N.C., 2003)

Schmölders, C. *Hitler's Face: The Biography of an Image* (Philadelphia, 2006)

Schneider, M. *J. A. Hobson* (London, 1996)

Scott, C. *Dick Sheppard: A Biography* (London, 1977)

Searle, G. R. (ed.). *Eugenics and Politics in Britain, 1900–1914* (Leyden, 1976)

Self, R. *Neville Chamberlain: A Biography* (Aldershot, 2006)

Shelmerdine, B. *British Representations of the Spanish Civil War* (Manchester, 2006)

Shephard, B. *A War of Nerves: Soldiers and Psychiatrists, 1914–1994* (London, 2000)

Skidelsky, R. *John Maynard Keynes: Fighting for Britain, 1937–1946* (London, 2000)

Snowman, D. *The Hitler Emigrés: The Cultural Impact on Britain of Refugees from Nazism* (London, 2003)

Sofsky, W. *Violence* (London, 2003)

Soloway, R. *Birth Control and the Population Question in England, 1877–1930* (Chapel Hill, 1982)

Soros, G. *The Age of Fallibility: The Consequences of the War on Terror* (London, 2006)

Stapleton, J. 'Resisting the Centre at the extremes: "English" Liberalism in the Political Thought of Inter-War Britain', *British Journal of Politics and International Relations*, 1 (1999), pp. 270–92

Steiner, Z. *The Lights that Failed: European International History, 1919–1933* (Oxford, 2005)

Stepansky, P. E. *A History of Aggression in Freud* (New York, 1977)

Stevenson, J. *British Society, 1914–1945* (London, 1984)

Stocks, M. *The Workers' Educational Association: The First Fifty Years* (London, 1953)

Stone, D. *Breeding Superman: Nietzsche, Race and Eugenics in Edwardian and Interwar Britain* (Liverpool, 2002)

—— 'An "Entirely Tactless Nietzschean Jew": Oscar Levy's Critique of Western Civilisation', *Journal of Contemporary History*, 36 (2001), pp. 271–92

—— 'Race in British Eugenics', *European History Quarterly*, 31 (2001), pp. 397–426

Strachey, A. *The Unconscious Motives for War: A Psycho-Analytical Contribution* (London, 1958)

Symons, J. *The Thirties: A Dream Revolved* (London, 1960)

Thomas, G. and Witts, M. W. *Guernica: The Crucible of World War II* (New York, 1975)

Thomas, H. *John Strachey* (London, 1973)

Thompson, K. W. *Toynbee's Philosophy of World History and Politics* (Baton Rouge, La., 1985)

Thompson, N. 'Hobson and the Fabians: Two Roads to Socialism in the 1920s', *History of Political Economy*, 26 (1994), pp. 203–20

Thorpe, A. J. (ed.). *The Failure of Political Extremism in Inter-War Britain* (Exeter, 1989)

—— 'The Membership of the Communist Party of Great Britain, 1920–1945', *Historical Journal*, 43 (2000), pp. 777–800

—— 'Stalinism and British Politics', *History*, 83 (1998), pp. 608–27

Thurlow, R. *Fascism in Britain: From Oswald Mosley's Blackshirts to the National Front* (London, 1998)

Todman, D. *The Great War: Myth and Memory* (London, 2005)

Tooze, A. *Statistics and the German State, 1900–1945: The Making of Modern Economic Knowledge* (Cambridge, 2001)

Townshend, J. *J. A. Hobson* (Manchester, 1990)

Toye, J. *Keynes on Population* (Oxford, 2000)

Toye, R. *The Labour Party and the Planned Economy, 1931–1951* (London, 2003)

Toynbee, A. J. et al. (eds.). *Man's Concern with Death* (London, 1968)

Trentmann, F. *Free Trade Nation: Commerce, Consumption and Civil Society in Modern Britain* (Oxford, 2008)

Unwerth, M. von. *Freud's Requiem: Mourning, Memory and the Invisible History of a Summer Walk* (London, 2006)

Vickers, R. *The Labour Party and the World*, vol. I, *The Evolution of Labour's Foreign Policy, 1900–1951* (Manchester, 2003)

Vovelle, M. 'Rediscovery of Death since 1960', *Annals of the American Academy of Political and Social Science*, 447 (1980), pp. 89–99

Waelder, R. *Progress and Revolution: A Study of the Issues of Our Age* (New York, 1967)

Wager, W. W. *Good Tidings: The Belief in Progress from Darwin to Marcuse* (Bloomington, Ind., 1972)

Webster, A. 'The Transnational Dream: Politicians, Diplomats and Soldiers in the League of Nations' Pursuit of International Disarmament, 1920–1938', *Contemporary European History*, 14 (2005), pp. 495–518

Webster, R. '*Love on the Dole* and the Aesthetic of Contradiction', in Hawthorn, J. (ed.). *The British Working-Class Novel in the Twentieth Century* (London, 1984), pp. 49–61

Wehr, G. *Jung: A Biography* (Boston, 2001)

Welshman, J. *Underclass: A History of the Excluded* (London, 2006)

Whittaker, D. J. *Fighter for Peace: Philip Noel-Baker, 1889–1982* (York, 1989)

Whitworth, M. *Virginia Woolf* (Oxford, 2005)

Wilford, R. A. 'The Federation of Progressive Societies and Individuals', *Journal of Contemporary History*, 11 (1976), pp. 49–82

Williams, W. E. *Allen Lane: A Personal Portrait* (London, 1973)

Williamson, P. 'The Doctrinal Politics of Stanley Baldwin', in Bentley, M. (ed.). *Public and Private Doctrine: Essays in British History Presented to Maurice Cowling* (Cambridge, 1993), pp. 181–208

Willis, J. H. *Leonard and Virginia Woolf as Publishers: The Hogarth Press, 1917–1941* (Charlottesville, Va., 1982)

Winter, J. *Sites of Memory, Sites of Mourning: The Great War in European Cultural History* (Cambridge, 1995)

Winter, J. and Prost, A. *The Great War in History: Debates and Controversies 1914 to the Present* (Cambridge, 2005)

Wistrich, R. 'The Last Testament of Sigmund Freud', *Leo Baeck Institute Yearbook*, 49 (2003), pp. 87–104

Wohl, R. 'Heart of Darkness: Modernism and Its Historians', *Journal of Modern History*, 74 (2002), pp. 573–621

Index